mocritus (460–370 B.C.)
Plato (c. 427–347 B.C.)
Aristotle (384–322 B.C.)

99 B.C.)

Sextus Empiricus (second–third centuries A.D.)
St. Augustine (354–430)

(c. 485–c. 380 B.C.)

Plato (c. 427–347 B.C.)
Diogenes Laertius (third century B.C.)
Pyrrho (c. 360–270 B.C.)

Plato (c. 427–347 B.C.)   Epictetus (A.D. 60–117)   St. Augustine (354–430)
399 B.C.)
Aristotle (384–322 B.C.)
Aristippus (435–350 B.C.)
century B.C.)
Zeno of Citium (334–262 B.C.)
Epicurus (341–270 B.C.)

Plato (c. 427–347 B.C.)   Cicero (106–43 B.C.)   St. Augustine (354–430)
Aristotle (384–322 B.C.)

Mencius (371–289 B.C.)
ourth century B.C.)

(Continued on back endpaper)

Philosophy

THE POWER OF IDEAS

Philosophy

THE POWER OF IDEAS

Brooke Noel Moore / Kenneth Bruder

California State University, Chico

MAYFIELD PUBLISHING COMPANY

Mountain View, California
London • Toronto

Library of Congress Cataloging-in-Publication Data

Moore, Brooke Noel.
   Philosophy: the power of ideas / Brooke Moore, Kenneth Bruder.
   p.   cm.
   Includes bibliographical references.
   ISBN 0-87484-769-9
   1. Philosophy—Introductions.   2. Philosophy—History.
I. Bruder, Kenneth. II. Title.
BD21.M62   1990   89-35928
100—dc20   CIP

Manufactured in the United States of America

10 9 8 7 6 5 4

Mayfield Publishing Company
1240 Villa Street
Mountain View, California 94041

Sponsoring editor, James Bull; managing editor, Linda Toy; production editor, Sondra Glider; manuscript editor, Victoria Nelson; text and cover designer, Gary Head; illustrator, Kevin Opstedal.

The text was set in 10/12 Melior by Graphic Typesetting Service and printed on 50# Mead Pub Matte by R. R. Donnelley & Sons Co.

Cover photograph: The Image Bank West/Garry Gay

Text and illustration credits appear on a continuation of the copyright page, p. 619.

To Linda Moore, Kathryn Dupier Bruder, and Albert Bruder

Contents

4 *The Rejection of Absolute Idealism* 97

PART 2 *EPISTEMOLOGY: THEORY OF KNOWLEDGE* 125

---

5 *Skepticism and Philosophy* 127

PART 4 *POLITICAL PHILOSOPHY* 283

---

10   *Contemporary Theory*   341

12 *God in the Age of Science*   410

Preface

This is a straightforward, ungimmicky historical introduction to philosophy.

Unlike other historical texts, this one is topically subdivided. In it you will find separate historical overviews of major branches of philosophy, of important philosophies-of-discipline and philosophies-of-subject, and of the analytic and continental traditions.

We arranged the book this way to make it easier for beginning philosophy students to follow themes. Philosophy is not just a parade—Socrates, Plato, Aristotle, and the rest. It is a progression of ideas about being, about knowledge, about goodness, about justice, about the state, and so forth. The approach we take here is intended to help students perceive philosophy in its thematic development.

Consider, for example, political theory as it evolved from Hobbes to Rawls. It is not easy to follow this development even if one shines the light directly on it. But beginners seem to find it especially difficult to follow if, having learned about Hobbes's views on the state, they are then asked to take up various other subjects emphasized by Spinoza and Leibniz before returning to political theory with Locke—and then to abandon the subject once again with Berkeley. We fear that individual threads may too easily be lost when they are overlaid with those from several other philosophical inquiries, creating the impression that philosophy is a tangle of unconnected speculations.

Still, we think that students, from their first exposure to philosophy, should acquire some sense of the history of the field, which the non-historical "problems" approach of many introductory texts may fail to provide. This text represents something of a middle road between the two traditional approaches to philosophy.

Coverage

The discipline of philosophy can be divided according to several different principles. In this text we examine four of the main *branches* of philosophy (metaphysics, epistemology, ethics, and political philosophy) and two *philosophies-of-subject* (philosophy of mind and philosophy of religion).

We also cover the two main *traditions* of twentieth-century philosophy, analytic philosophy and continental philosophy.

In addition, we have devoted a chapter to Eastern philosophy.

We might mention that one of the authors was trained in the analytic tradition and the other in the continental European tradition. Whether this fact contributes appreciably to a balanced perspective we leave to you to decide.

Readings

Should beginning philosophy students be given original readings? Well, probably. But there are problems. For example, although Hobbes's stark conception of human nature is easy enough to grasp when it is stated straight up, and the dark novels and movies that portray it are often deeply engrossing, Hobbes's own prose presents insurmountable difficulties for many students. Yet Hobbes is one of the *easiest* of the great philosophers to read.

We are sensitive to these considerations. This text contains readings from most major philosophers. But we try not to overwhelm beginning students with difficult selections, whether from Hobbes or anyone else. So the readings we include usually are fairly nontechnical and rather brief, though not so brief as to be unmemorable or so nontechnical as to be meaningless.

Boxes

In most introductory texts, boxes tend to be reserved for secondary or incidental material—historical asides, anecdotes, whatnot. That's not the case here. The plain truth is that material found in boxes is often more likely to be noticed and remembered than the same stuff would be if it were buried within the text proper. So in this book students will find a variety of materials in the boxes—not just anecdotes and historical marginalia but also *important* concepts and principles and distinctions. The boxes in this text carry their own fair share of the burden of instruction.

Most people would prefer to read about the lives of the great philosophers than about their philosophies. That's because philosophy takes more effort to understand than biography. Nevertheless, it's most important for beginning students to master the philosophy.

At the same time, no introductory text should be completely lacking in biographical information on the great philosophers. We have found that our students are much more apt to remember an idea if they connect it with an actual person who had it than if it just seems to float in from outer space. In this text students will find short biographical profiles on most of the major philosophers.

Checklists

At the end of each chapter—except the first, which is introductory—we have included a checklist of the key philosophers and concepts discussed. For each philosopher on the list we provide a *very* short summary of his leading theories.

Granted, these summaries are simplifications of complex ideas, but they should serve to remind a reader of the full set of details given in the chapter itself.

Questions and Readings

Also at the end of each chapter after the first are a bank of questions and a list of suggested further readings. Some of the questions are straightforward, intended mainly for review; others are more subtle and call for careful reflection. The reading lists are lightly annotated to help students choose what will most interest them.

Glossary

Terms in bold print in the text are defined in a glossary at the end of the book. The glossary contains around 175 entries and is, we hope, a reasonably complete brief compendium of philosophical concepts, distinctions, and theories. We think readers will benefit if they refer to it frequently.

Additional Features

- The text contains three appendices: on logic, truth, and knowledge. The appendix on logic is a practical guide to some common types of arguments.

- Chapter 3, on modern metaphysics, is structured around the mind-body problem, a simple organizational principle that we think makes this important period in philosophy as easy as possible to understand.
- Part 2, on epistemology, is focused on skepticism, which, in our experience, is more accessible to introductory students than other topics in epistemology.
- Part 4, on political philosophy, contains a short subsection on American Constitutional theory.

Flexibility

Instructors who favor an introductory course that is a history of philosophical figures will find this book adaptable to their needs if they focus their lectures on the branch of philosophy that seems to them to be central to the history of philosophy—for example, metaphysics. Then, if the sections of the book on the other branches and aspects of philosophy are assigned as supplementary material to be read along with the "main" material, the evolution of major philosophical themes will still be more visible than it might be in a text devoted solely to historical figures.

Powerful Stuff

We concluded many years ago that most people like philosophy if they understand it, and most understand it if it isn't presented to them in an idiom that is exhausting to read. In this text we strive above all else to make philosophy understandable while not oversimplifying it (dumbing it down).

But we also concluded many years ago that some people just aren't moved by philosophy. Worse, we learned that among those who aren't are a few who are sane, intelligent, well informed, and reasonable; and who have generally sound ideas about the world, vote for all the right people, and are even worth having as friends. Philosophy, we learned, just isn't for everyone and no text and no instructor can make it so.

So we don't expect that every student, or even every bright student, who comes in contact with philosophy will necessarily love the field.

But we do think it reasonable to expect every student who has had an introductory course in philosophy to appreciate the fact that philosophy is more than so much inconsequential mental flexing. Philosophy contains powerful ideas, and it affects the lives of real people. Consequently, it must be handled with due care. The text, we think, makes this point clear.

Acknowledgments

We certainly did not write this book without help from others. In particular, we would like to thank our friends and colleagues at California State University, Chico, both within philosophy and without, whose assistance came in many forms. Dan Barnett, Maryanne Bertram, Cathy Brooks, Judy Collins, Frank Ficarra, Esther Gallagher, Ron Hirschbein, Alexandra Kiriakis, Scott Mahood, Greg Maxwell, Clifford Minor, Adrian Mirvish, Anne Morrissey, Richard Parker, Michael Rich, Dennis Rothermel, Robert Stewart, Greg Tropea, Alan Walworth all contributed mightily to the completion of this text.

Also, for their wise and helpful comments on the manuscript we wish to thank Sue Armstrong-Buck, Humboldt State University; Edward Bloomfield, Cerritos College; Raymond Herbenick, University of Dayton; Jacqueline Kegley, California State University, Bakersfield; Clysta Kinstler, American River College; Thomas Nenon, Memphis State University; Don Porter, College of San Mateo; Joan Price, Mesa Community College; Dennis Rohatyn, University of San Diego; and Mark Williamson, Southwest Texas State University.

Without the help of the talented staff at Mayfield Publishing Company, this book would never have come to be. So we wish to express our gratitude to this outstanding group of people, especially Jim Bull, Kirstan Price, Sondra Glider, Vicki Nelson, Tom Broadbent, and Pam Trainer.

Very special thanks are due to Ralph J. Moore, the father of Brooke Moore, for his detailed and painstaking commentary on several chapters of the manuscript, and for his contribution of the section on American Constitutional theory.

Special thanks are due also to Betty Ames for her kind permission to use Van Meter Ames's metaphor of philosophy as explosive and dangerous material, a metaphor that was an inspiration for this book.

Finally, Brooke Moore thanks his family: his ever-supportive and caring wife, Linda Moore, and his patient and semi-neglected children, Sherry and Bill.

Dangerous Stuff

Beware when the great God lets loose a thinker on this planet. Then all things are at risk. The very hopes of man, the thoughts of his heart, the religion of nations, the manners and morals of mankind are all at the mercy of a new generalization.

—EMERSON

I do not know how to teach philosophy without becoming a disturber of the peace.

—BARUCH SPINOZA

There are two powers in the world, the sword and the mind. In the long run, the sword is always beaten by the mind.

—NAPOLEON

For a revolution you need more than economic problems and guns. You need a philosophy. Wars are founded on a philosophy, or on efforts to destroy one. Communism, capitalism, fascism, atheism, humanism, Marxism—philosophies all of them. Philosophies give birth to civilizations. They also end them.

The philosophy department works with high explosives, Van Meter Ames liked to say. It handles dangerous stuff. This book is an introduction to philosophy. From it you will learn, among other things, why philosophy, as Ames said, is dynamite.

You will also see that philosophy is foundational to many other disciplines. What yesterday was called philosophy today is often called psychology or government or physics or some other subject, or even just plain common sense. Many of the *basic* concepts you have come from philosophy, maybe more so than from physics or psychology or biology or sociology or any other field. Whether it's a concept about the way the world is, or about the way people are or should be, or about what is and can be known, or about what's right and wrong and beautiful and ugly—at bottom, it's in large part philosophy. Other fields fill in the details, but the basic conceptual framework is mostly pure philosophy. Even the Judaeo-Christian concept of God we are familiar with today owes much to philosophy—as you will see.

So the questions philosophers raise can strike right at the foundations of what we think and do and claim to know—and can send tremors through our entire edifice of beliefs.

The power of the subject is surprising when you consider that philosophy has spent most of its history shrinking. Philosophy once encompassed nearly everything that counted as human knowledge. Among the ancient Greeks nearly every subject that is currently listed in college catalogues was or would have been considered philosophy. One by one, these intellectual enterprises gained sufficient maturity and stature to stand alone as separate subjects. Mathematics, rhetoric, physics, biology, government, politics, law—all once fell under the general heading of philosophy.

The word *philosophy*, as every introductory book on the subject tells us, comes from the two Greek words *philein*, which means "to love," and *sophia*, which means "knowledge" or "wisdom." Because knowledge can be discovered in many fields, the Greeks thought of any person who sought knowledge in any area as a philosopher.

Consider physics for a moment. One of the first known Greek philosophers, Thales, was actually doing what we might call "speculative physics" (in contrast to experimental physics) when he claimed that everything in the natural world was made of water. Two other ancient Greeks, Leucippus and Democritus, arrived at the conclusion that all matter was made from tiny particles—atoms—that were similar except for their size and shape, but that accounted for differences in larger bodies by means of their different arrangements.

Should we think of these early thinkers as physicists or philosophers? The Greeks had no difficulty answering this question, because they thought of physics as a part of philosophy. And this view of physics persisted for over two thousand years. The full title of Isaac Newton's *Principles*, in which Newton set forth his famous theories of mechanics, mathematics, and astronomy, is *Mathematical Principles of Natural Philosophy*. Physics, even by the seventeenth century, was still thought of as a variety of philosophy. By the twentieth century, however, physics had outgrown the nest and, though it still has important points of contact, is no longer considered a part of philosophy. Similar stories can be told for each of the disciplines listed a couple of paragraphs back.

If philosophy can no longer claim those subject areas that have grown up and moved out, what's left for it to claim? As you'll see by the end of this book, the current list of philosophical subjects is by no means short and discloses the deep and wide concern of philosophy for some very important questions about the universe, the earth, humankind and all life, and each of us. Just what is this concern? What is philosophy today?

Mathematics, the physical and biological sciences, economics and political science, and the full array of existing intellectual disciplines, including theology, leave unanswered in part some of the most important and fundamental questions a person can ask.

Philosophical Questions

- Is it possible to know anything with absolute certainty?
- Do people really have free will?
- Are some actions really right and others wrong?
- Does life have a purpose?
- Is a person anything more than a physical body?
- Does the world have to be just the way it is, or could it have been different?
- What is art?
- Is there a God?
- What difference does it make if there is or isn't a God?

Perhaps it's possible to go through life and never spend a minute wondering about such questions. But most of us have at least occasional moments of reflection about one or another of them. In fact, it's really pretty difficult *not* to think philosophically from time to time. For one thing, it's just plain *boring* always to be thinking and talking about everyday affairs and objects—say, shopping, for instance. And what's more, any time we think or talk about a topic long enough, if our thinking or discussion is the least bit organized we may well become engaged in philosophy.

As an example, let's just take shopping. If, while shopping, you have ever taken a break for a soft drink or a cup of coffee, some conscientious person may have observed that the styrofoam cup you are drinking from is manufactured by a process that contributes to the breakdown of the ozone layer and unnecessarily contributes to a rise in skin cancer. You, in return, may have said, or at least have thought, that what *you* as an individual do is not going to have much of an effect on the styrofoam industry or the fastfood business or the ozone layer. But by this time you're no longer thinking or talking about a cup of Diet Pepsi, you're pondering a matter of moral obligation, one of ethical philosophy.

Unfortunately, when people get to this point in their thinking or conversation, they often just stop. They don't know what to think or say next in the matter.

Or, to take another example of philosophy lurking in a situation, if you've seen any of the *Star Wars* movies it may have occurred to you to wonder whether a robot really could feel emotions, as the sweet little guys in the movies seem to do. Could a robot feel an emotion as we do? It's just a machine—is there anything about feelings that says they couldn't be experienced by the right kind of machine? But how could we ever know for sure that a machine was having feelings? For that matter, how do we ever know that any of us really has them?

Now, each of the four questions posed in this last paragraph is a philosophical question, and each is the kind of question a thoughtful person might be inclined to ask after seeing *Star Wars*—or after listening to some enthusiast make predictions for computers. In later chapters we'll consider just such questions, for this process of analyzing and trying to answer such questions is the task of philosophers.

You're wondering, maybe, just what makes these questions—or any other philosophical question—*philosophical*? Unfortunately, no very precise definition of "philosophical question," or of philosophy itself, that is satisfactory to many philosophy teachers has ever been formulated. True, the definition of philosophy as the love or pursuit of wisdom is widely circulated, but this is altogether too vague and general to be particularly helpful. Do you know of any discipline that doesn't pursue wisdom in one way or another?

The problem is that what philosophy *is* is itself a philosophical issue, and the issue hasn't yet been settled. It's like asking, What is art?—another philosophical question that has not been answered to the satisfaction of very many philosophers.

One important feature of philosophical questions is that they can't be answered just by looking around—that is, by the discovery of some fact or collection of facts. Philosophy, in other words, is not an empirical science. That part of the wisdom business has now been turned over to physics, chemistry, and the rest of the sciences. Of course, facts are often *relevant* to a philosophical question, but they cannot by themselves provide us with an answer. What observable "fact" would settle whether or not a robot could feel pain? Clearly, no fact by itself will do: the problem must be approached in some other way.

Many philosophical questions concern norms. **Normative** questions ask about the value of something. The sciences are interested in finding out how things *are*, but they cannot tell us how things *ought* to be. When we decide that this or that is good or bad, right or wrong, beautiful or ugly, we are applying ethical or aesthetic norms, which are standards of one kind or another. How can we establish that doing one thing is morally acceptable whereas doing something else is morally wrong? Does it just *strike* us that way? Is it what the majority of people in one's society thinks that determines the issue? Is some *feature* of the action right or wrong, or is it the *consequences* of the action? What *is* morally right, anyway? All these are philosophical questions, and nearly any answer to each is based on a commitment to some kind of ethical theory or principle. To

Philosophical Questions

Although philosophical questions crop up in even commonplace discussions, they arise from the human need to understand the deepest mysteries of existence. The following important questions are all philosophical.

What am I?

                           Is there a single, first cause of all things?

What is the human mind?

                           Is the first cause equivalent to God?
                           Or nature? Or the laws of the universe?

What is life?   What is being?

Does life have meaning?   Does the universe have purpose?

Would life have meaning without death?

Why is there death?

                       Is there order in the cosmos independent of what is put there by the mind?

Is death an evil?

                       Could reality be different from what we can conceive it to be?

Is there life after death?

                   Is anything certain?

What is good and what is evil?

---

many people, indeed, philosophy *is* ethics, and even though that's not correct—many philosophical questions have nothing to do with ethics—there's no denying that ethics is important stuff. People may *kill* you if they think it's morally right to do so.

Often, too, philosophers ask questions about things that seem so obvious we might not wonder about them—for example, *the nature of change,* an issue within that branch of philosophy known as metaphysics. What is change? Perhaps that seems a strange thing to ask because in a way we all know what change is. If something changes, it becomes different. But then—and here's the problem—if we have a different thing after the change, then we are considering *two* things, the original thing and the new and different thing. If something changes, then it is different from the way it was, and if it is different, then is it the same thing?

Further, if after the change we have a new thing, then were we wrong to speak of the original thing as *changing?* Wasn't the original thing in fact *replaced* rather than changed? Isn't there only replacement of, rather than change in, things, and so only continuous replacements, rather than changes, of the universe, of the earth, and of each of us?

Two "Philosophical" Questions

What comes to mind for many people, when they think of philosophy and of philosophical questions, is either or both of these inquiries: "Which came first, the chicken or the egg?" And: "If there's nobody around, does a tree falling in a forest make a sound?"

The first question is not particularly philosophical and, in the light of evolution, is not even especially difficult: The egg came first.

The second question is often supposedly resolved by distinguishing between sound viewed as the mental experience of certain waves contacting certain sensory organs and sound as the waves themselves. If sensory organs are absent, it is said, there can be no sound-as-experience but there can still be sound-as-waves. Philosophy, however, asks not simply whether a tree falling in the forest makes a sound if no one is there, but rather, *If nobody is there, is there even a forest?* Is there even a universe? In other words, the question, for philosophers, is whether things depend for their existence on being perceived, and if so, how we know that. A somewhat similar question (equally philosophical) is debated by contemporary astrophysicists, who wonder whether the universe and its laws require the presence of intelligent observers for their existence.

Here you may suspect that an easy solution is at hand. When something changes, it need not become *entirely* different. It may change only in this or that respect. Or it may retain many of its original constituents or features. Suppose a thing retains a lot of its original features or constituents. Then, if only a few other of its features or constituents change, it will still be the same thing. It will now have some different features or constituents, true, but it won't be a different thing.

Unfortunately, this solution is not wholly satisfactory, and, in addition, it leads to further mystery. It is not satisfactory, because some things do change entirely, that is, in all respects. An old oak, for example, and the tiny seedling from which it grew are the same tree, yet the old oak is in no respect like the seedling, and none of the molecules that existed in the seedling needs to be present in the old oak. When he was a child, one of the authors found an ugly green sluglike little thing that, after a while, became a beautiful butterfly that in no way resembled the thing it had been originally.

Granted, the oak and the seedling (and the butterfly and the larva) are thought to be unfoldings of the same *genetic pattern*: the oak, as Aristotle would say, is the actualization of the potential in the seedling. But does this thought help us understand how it can be said of *two* things that are entirely different, both in features and even in constituents, that they are *one*?

That easy solution mentioned here also leads to a further mystery, for even if it explains how a thing can change, it leaves us puzzling about how a thing's *features* may change. If a thing's changing is to be under-

Are Philosophical Questions Unanswerable?

Philosophical questions are unanswerable and philosophy never makes any progress. If you haven't heard someone say that already, you will sooner or later.

Therefore you should know this: though many philosophical questions have not been *answered*, that a question is truly *unanswerable* would be considered by many philosophers a reason for abandoning the question.

As for progress, you should remember that it is not easily defined. It is probably not true in any case that progress occurs only when questions are answered. Questions can also be clarified. They can be subdivided or abandoned. They can be discovered to rest on confusions or to be unanswerable. All this is progress, according to most conceptions of progress. For that matter, if earlier answers to a question are seen to be inadequate, that constitutes progress even if the question has not been finally answered.

Finally, notice that it isn't entirely clear in the first place just what counts as progress or as an answer to a question. As a matter of fact, the question of what does count is itself a question of philosophy.

Another idea some people have is that as soon as any headway is made in a philosophical inquiry, the matter is abandoned to (or becomes) another field of learning. True, as mentioned at the beginning of the chapter, many disciplines that are relatively independent of philosophy today had their origin within philosophy. But philosophy does not always relegate to some other discipline subjects in which clear progress is made.

To take the most obvious example, *logic*—despite an enormous expansion in scope, complexity, and explanatory power, especially during the last hundred years—is still a branch of philosophy.

stood in terms of some of its features becoming different, then how is a feature's changing to be understood?

The problem of change leads to other difficult philosophical questions. For example, is the man who committed a heinous deed, perhaps as a child, the same person as an adult and as such still to be looked upon with horror or censure? Of course, we think of him as still John Doe, or whatever his name is. But is this philosophically correct, since the chemical and physical constituents of the child's body and brain may have been completely replaced by new material and his mind by new mental elements, whatever the "elements" of the mind really are? Has the child not indeed been replaced? And if so, can his guilt possibly pertain to his replacement?

These considerations suggest also that the problem of change, of whether what we call change is really replacement, is not merely an unimportant question of semantics. For what is at stake is whether the man did indeed do the awful deed. It's pretty hard to see how whether he did or did not is a simple matter of semantics.

Here again you can see why it might be said that philosophy lies right at the foundation of thought. Practically everything we think—and do—depends on our understanding of what it is for things to change.

Sometimes philosophical questions come to light when our beliefs seem to conflict with one another. Let's take a look at a question of this sort, this time considering the matter in a bit more detail.

We would be willing to wager a rather large sum of money that you believe that people should be held accountable for what they do voluntarily. If you choose to drink and then you choose to drive and you end up killing someone, well, you are to blame, because your actions were voluntary.

We'd bet you would also say that when someone chooses to do something, he or she chooses it because he or she wants to do it, or at least wants to do it more than he or she wants not to do it. True, we often choose to do what we think is right even though sometimes it isn't pleasant to do what is right. But still, when we do this it is because we want to do what is right.

We'd bet on something else, too. We'd bet that, after considering the matter, you will concede that a person is not responsible for having the wants he or she has. You do not yourself cause or create your wants. You do not yourself determine what you like or desire. We, for example, Moore and Bruder, wanted to write this book, but we didn't *cause* ourselves to want to write it. And you—do you like reading this book? If you do, would you say that you *caused* yourself to like to read it? Or, if you hate it, would you say that you *made* yourself hate it? We'd bet your answer to both questions is "no." Our wants, desires, preferences, likes, and so on all seem to be something *we just have*. They are not things we *made* ourselves have.

So it seems, then, that our wants are not our doing. And it also seems that we shouldn't be held responsible for what is not our doing. But it also seems that our wants determine what we choose to do. So how can we be held responsible for what we choose to do? Does this make sense? If, in other words, our voluntary acts are the result of what we want to do, but we can't be held responsible for what we want to do, how can we be held responsible for our voluntary acts?

"Interesting," you may be thinking, "but unconvincing, because we *are* responsible for what we want." After all, we can determine our wants, if we feel like it. Consider, for instance, someone who doesn't like vegetables. He may decide that it would be nice to like vegetables, and he may then set about acquiring this new want by telling himself how good vegetables are, by forcing himself to eat them, or by mixing them with something he does like, say, jelly. Ultimately he may succeed in acquiring a taste for the straight goods.

Notice, though, when you examine a case like this carefully, it seems that what the person has done is only this: he has talked to himself about how good vegetables are and has made himself eat them. But whether or not these actions had the effect he hoped for—namely, instilling a fondness for vegetables—is something beyond his control. These actions might have made him positively detest vegetables, too, and if they had, that wouldn't have been his doing, either.

Or, to take a different example, let's say that Harold likes wine a bit too much and goes to a psychiatrist hoping that she can rid him of this problem. Suppose, then, that Harold does what his psychiatrist prescribes, and the therapy is successful: he no longer craves wine quite as much as he did earlier. But is this *Harold's* doing? He followed his psychiatrist's advice, yes, but whether or not her advice *would actually work* is not something *Harold* can control.

So, when you look closely at cases in which we appear to cause ourselves to change our wants or desires, what happens is that we do certain things, perhaps hoping that the result will be an alteration of our likes and preferences. Whether or not the hoped-for alteration takes place, however, is arguably not our doing.

Let's apply these considerations to a concrete case. Do you smoke? If you do, you may well regret ever having started. And if you are like most of us, you may be inclined to suppose that it was *your fault* that you took up smoking. You may say, "I have only myself to blame, after all. No one forced me to keep lighting up those first times, and I knew very well I might get hooked."

But is this correct? Is it really *your fault*? Consider. You kept lighting up those first times because you wanted to, certainly. It's unlikely that it was the flavor or effect of cigarette smoke that made you keep smoking at first. More likely it was that you wanted to be like your friends or wanted to have a challenge. In any case, you wanted to smoke more than you wanted not to smoke, and it was because of this that you kept lighting up. And it was because you kept lighting up that you are now an addicted smoker, both physically and mentally.

Now since, apparently, it was because of your wants that ultimately you became a smoker, then, if you aren't responsible for having those wants, it doesn't seem that *you* are to blame for having gotten hooked. Are you responsible for having had those wants? Assuming that you kept smoking because you wanted to be like your friends, did you *cause* yourself to have this want? Did you *make* yourself have a desire to be like your friends? Did you *create* within yourself this fondness for being like them?

When the question is posed this way, it doesn't seem completely plausible to suppose that you did create your wants. *You* didn't make yourself desire to be like your friends, just as we, the authors, didn't make ourselves like to write philosophy texts. Having these wants just happened to us, and wanting to be like your friends just happened to you.

Still, it may occur to you that, when you kept lighting up there at first, you were *giving in* to your wants and *allowing* yourself to be governed by your desire to be like your friends (or whatever). And therefore you *are* to blame for having been hooked because it was you who gave in to your wants.

But notice that even if you did give in to your wants, then you did so because you wanted to more than you wanted not to. So again we trace your actions back to a set of wants that it seems implausible to suppose you created.

Perhaps by now it's clear that what's really at stake here is a profoundly important and basic question: *Are we ever really to blame for what we do?* This is a philosophical question, one that comes to light because some of our beliefs seem not to get along so well together. On one hand, it seems that we are to blame for what we choose to do, but on the other, if what we choose to do is the result of our wants, and if we aren't to blame for our wants, then how *can* we be to blame for what we choose to do?

Let's conclude this discussion by turning to something a bit more important than cigarettes or wine. Let's talk about one Ted Bundy, who was executed in 1989 in Florida for having committed several brutal rape-murders. Bundy was not found insane: presumably he knew the difference between right and wrong, and knew that what he was doing was wrong. Why did he do what he did? Ultimately because he wanted to do it more than he wanted not to: his actions resulted from what he wanted to do.

But now, *if* this wanting to do it more than wanting not to do it is not something Bundy could be blamed for, then can he really be blamed for what he did? And can he be blamed for wanting to do it more than wanting not to do it, if we do not create our wants?

The basic issues here—whether we are accountable for what we want and, if we are not, whether we are accountable for what we do—are not going to be resolved through scientific research. These are philosophical issues, and they are issues of considerable importance. Whether we should execute people like Ted Bundy depends on their outcome.

Perhaps these few examples of philosophical questions will convince you that studying philosophy might be both interesting and worthwhile. We understand that these few examples are not going to make the nature of philosophical questions as clear as window glass. But that's what the rest of the book is for, to give you a reasonable understanding of some of the central philosophical questions and issues and how they have been treated over the years.

Philosophy Pies

Now, just how do the various philosophical questions and issues relate to one another? First, philosophy as an entire subject consists of seven interrelated branches or fields or main areas. These are:

- **Metaphysics,** which studies the nature of being. What *is* being? What are its fundamental features and properties? These are two basic questions of metaphysics.

    Metaphysics, by the way, as a branch of philosophy, has precious little to do with the occult, but we'll get to that later.

- **Epistemology,** the theory of knowledge. What is knowledge? Is knowledge possible? These are the basic questions of epistemology.
- **Ethics**, the philosophical study of moral judgments, which includes, most importantly, the question: Which moral judgments are correct?
- **Social philosophy**, the philosophical study of society and its institutions. This branch of philosophy is concerned especially with determining the features of the ideal or best society.
- **Political philosophy**, which focuses on one social institution, the state, and seeks to determine its justification and ethically proper organization. Political philosophy is so closely related to social philosophy that it is common to treat them as a single area, *social-political philosophy*.
- **Aesthetics**, the philosophical study of art and of value judgments about art, and of beauty in general.
- **Logic**, the theory of correct reasoning, which seeks to investigate and establish the criteria of valid inference and demonstration.

So philosophy as a big pie can be cut up in terms of its seven major fields. Needless to say, this is not a quantitative division of the pie. The pie slices in the diagram are equal in size, but we are not suggesting that each of the branches of philosophy contains an equal number of theories or concepts or words. Your library probably has more holdings under political philosophy than under any of the other areas, and fewest under epistemology or aesthetics.

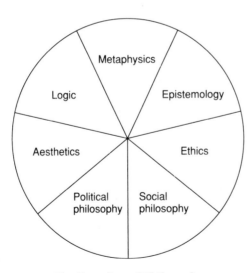

The Branches of Philosophy

In terms of historical periods, the same philosophy pie is subdivided into four pieces:

- **Ancient philosophy** (sixth century B.C. through, approximately, the third century A.D.)
- **Medieval philosophy** (fourth through sixteenth centuries, approximately)
- **Modern** (fifteenth through nineteenth centuries, approximately)
- **Contemporary** (twentieth century)

Thus:

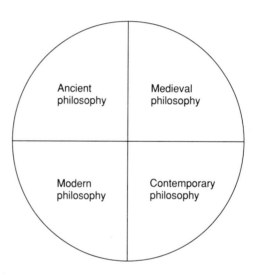

Historical Periods of Philosophy

There are other ways of dividing the philosophy pie. The fundamental assumptions and methods of many disciplines and areas of intellectual inquiry have been examined philosophically (which perhaps isn't too surprising because at one time or other nearly every intellectual endeavor counted as a part of philosophy). Thus, the philosophical pie can also be cut up in slices such as philosophy of science and philosophy of mathematics. Some of the most important of these "philosophy-of-discipline" areas are—in addition to those just listed, and in no particular order—philosophy of law, philosophy of education, philosophy of biology, and philosophy of psychology. So here's another way of dividing the pie:

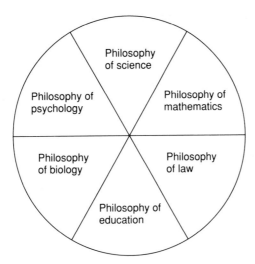

Philosophies-of-Discipline

Then the philosophy pie can be divided according to the philosophies-of-subject. To name a few, there are philosophy of mind, philosophy of religion, philosophy of history (sometimes classified as a philosophy-of-discipline), philosophy of sport, philosophy of love, philosophy of culture, and (very important of late) philosophy of feminism—feminist philosophy. Philosophies-of-subject and philosophies-of-discipline cut across the branches of philosophy and involve issues from more than one branch. For example, philosophy of religion and philosophy of sci-

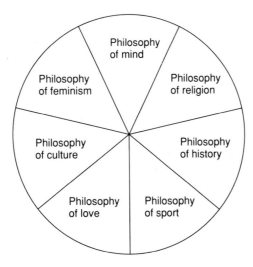

Philosophies-of-Subject

ence involve both metaphysical and epistemological issues, and philosophy of law involves questions of ethics, metaphysics, and epistemology.

The pie can also be divided geographically, Eastern philosophy and Western philosophy being the main division, with further subdivisions of the obvious sort—American philosophy, Indian philosophy, Scandinavian philosophy, Continental philosophy (referring to the European continent), etc., etc.

In this century, the predominant interests and methods of philosophers in the West have tended to separate them into three fairly distinct "traditions."

- **Analytic philosophers** believe (or are the intellectual descendents of those who did believe) that the proper method of philosophy is what is called analysis. They focus on problems that can be resolved through analysis, which is something we'll explain in a separate section on analytic philosophy.

- **Existentialists** focus their attention on the problems that arise from our living in a world that in many ways is unreasonable and absurd.

- **Phenomenologists,** while suspending assumptions and presuppositions, investigate and describe phenomena as they are apprehended. What exactly this means we'll explain in the appropriate section.

In the twentieth century, as it so happens, generally (and with important exceptions) the predominant tradition in English-speaking countries is analytic philosophy, and you sometimes hear the expression *Anglo-*

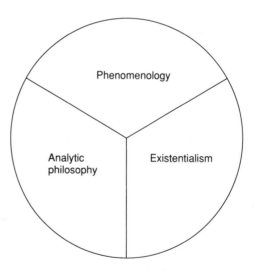

Contemporary Philosophical Traditions

American philosophy used as a virtual synonym for analytic philosophy. And generally (and again with important exceptions) the predominant traditions in continental Europe are phenomenology and existentialism, and often the expression *Continental philosophy* is used to refer to philosophy that is focused in either existentialist or phenomenological traditions. So, as odd as it sounds, if an American or British philosopher happens to be an existentialist or phenomenologist, as many are, it is acceptable to refer to him or her as a Continental philosopher even if he or she never set foot on the European continent.

And by the way, many philosophers would list *Marxism* along with analytic philosophy, existentialism, and phenomenology as a fourth "tradition," but we'll treat Marxism as a species of political philosophy.

As is quite evident, a whole range of classification schemes applies to philosophy. As you read this book, you should refer back to these various diagrams when you need to get your bearings.

Preview

In this book we want to give some exposure to most of these divisions. So we'll present material on some of the main branches of philosophy, on two important philosophies-of-subject, on the traditions of contemporary philosophy, and on Eastern philosophy. To be more specific:

The first through fourth parts of the book deal with metaphysics, epistemology, ethics, and political philosophy, four of the main fields of philosophy.

The fifth part is an introduction to the philosophy of religion, one of the most important philosophies-of-subject.

You ought also to know something about analytic philosophy, existentialism, and phenomenology, the three great traditions of contemporary philosophy. This material is located in Parts 6 and 7.

Part 6 on analytic philosophy, incidentally, does double duty. In that part we concentrate on the philosophy of mind, an area of philosophy that has received much attention by analytic philosophers. So the part not only will give you some understanding of the methods and concerns of analytic philosophy but also will introduce you to a second important philosophy-of-subject.

In the final part, you'll learn something about Eastern philosophy, which, in many ways, is as different from Western philosophy as acupuncture is from Western medicine.

In all the parts the subjects we've selected for discussion are introduced in their original historical context. What you will be getting is a historical overview of these various major subjects of philosophy.

Remember, if you forget how the various sections and topics relate to one another and to philosophy as a whole, refer back to the diagrams.

Philosophy and a Philosophy

There's a difference between *philosophy* and *a philosophy*. Philosophy is the discipline that comprises logic, metaphysics, ethics, epistemology, and so on, as explained in the text. A philosophy is a system of beliefs, concepts, or attitudes of an individual or group, or a theory about or underlying a sphere of activity or thought. Everybody, without ever having read a book in philosophy, has a philosophy of some sort or other—several of them, in fact.

Often, someone's or some group's philosophy becomes a subject for examination and discussion within the discipline of philosophy. In this way those philosophies listed at the beginning of the chapter as explosive forces in the world, such as atheism, communism, and so forth, are a part of the subject matter of philosophy, the discipline. Many such philosophies were originally expounded by individuals who were *philosophers*, that is, students of the discipline, philosophy.

Studying philosophy, the discipline, will inevitably affect your own philosophy (or philosophies), we certainly hope for the better.

The Benefits of Philosophy

The importance of some philosophical questions—like, "Is there a God who is attentive, caring, and responsive to us?" and "Is abortion morally wrong?"—is obvious and great. A justification would have to be given for *not* contemplating them. But, quite honestly, some philosophical questions are of more or less obscure, and seemingly only academic or theoretical, consequence. Not everything philosophers consider is dynamite. The questions posed earlier about robots having feelings would be perceived by many as pretty academic and theoretical.

But then, every field has its theoretical and nonpractical questions. Why do astronomers wonder about the distance and recessional velocity of quasars? Why are paleontologists interested in 135-million-year-old mammalian fossil remains in northern Malawi? Why do musicologists care whether Bach used parallel fifths? The answer is that some questions are *inherently* interesting to those who pose them. An astronomer wonders about a quasar *just because it is there*. And some philosophical questions are like that, too: the philosopher wants to know the answer just simply to know the answer.

But there are side benefits in seeking answers to philosophical questions, even those that are difficult, abstruse, or seemingly remote from practical concerns. Seeing philosophical answers usually entails making careful distinctions in thought, words, and argument, and recognizing subtle distinctions among things and among facts. Philosophical solutions require logical and critical thinking, discussion, and exposition. So students of philosophy learn to look carefully for similarities and differences among things. They also develop an ability to spot logical diffi-culties in what others write or say, and to avoid these pitfalls in their own thinking. In addition, they learn to recognize and critically assess the important unstated assumptions people make about the world and them-selves and other people and life in general. These assumptions affect how people perceive the world and what they say and do, yet for the most part people are not aware of them and are disinclined to consider them at all critically. These abilities are of great value in any field that requires clear thinking.

It is not surprising, therefore, that according to *The Economist* (April 26, 1986), "philosophy students do better in examinations for business and management schools than anybody except mathematicians—better even than those who study economics, business or other vocational sub-jects." It's possible, of course, that philosophy attracts unusually capable students to begin with and that this accounts for results like these. But there is at least some reason to believe that the kind of training philosophy provides helps students to think, read and write, and possibly speak more critically, carefully, and cogently.

Finally, students who have learned their philosophical lessons well are not as likely as those who haven't to become trapped by dogmatism. Such students have learned the value of keeping an open mind and seek-ing solutions to problems that meet standards of coherence and reason-ableness. These general attitudes, along with the critical skills that come with practice of philosophical argumentation, can stand a person in good stead when he or she is faced with many of the problems life generously provides for us.

These days the idea is that someone who lists his or her profession as philoso-phy either doesn't do anything at all or is a teacher. True, not too many indi-viduals outside teaching get paid to philosophize. Yet philosophical skills, like basic verbal and mathematical skills, are useful in many fields, as the text explains. And see the next box.

Two Myths About Philosophy

We'll close this chapter by mentioning two misconceptions some people have about philosophy.

1. First, there's the notion that in philosophy one person's opinion is as valid as the next person's and that therefore anything you write or say goes and probably should get a good grade. Some people who have this idea may sign up for a philosophy course thinking that it's maybe an easy way to bolster the GPA.

We will jump all over this line of thought, but there is something in it that's not completely false. As you will see in Chapter 5, according to an old and respectable tradition in philosophy known as **skepticism**, there is no certain criterion for judging the truth of anything and therefore all arguments are equally valid. Now, a good bit of hard and disciplined thinking has been done in support of these and other skeptical contentions. And, though some philosophers may well be skeptics of sorts, not many of them are likely to be much impressed with some half-baked form of skepticism that someone assumes *unthinkingly*.

Most philosophers make a distinction between philosophy and mere opinion, the difference being that philosophy at the very least involves opinion supported by good reasoning. Someone who expresses his or her own views without providing the supporting reasoning may be commended by a philosopher for having interesting *opinions*, but he or she is probably not going to receive high marks for having produced good *philosophy*.

Philosophy requires you to support your claims with careful application of argument, and that is *hard work*. You should be aware of this.

2. Another wrong idea some people have is that philosophy is *light reading*, something you relax with in the evening, after all the serious work of the day is done.

In reality, philosophical writing is often complex and technical and almost always takes time and effort to understand. Philosophical prose

Some Comments on Philosophy

Wonder is a feeling of a philosopher, and philosophy begins in wonder.—Plato

All *definite* knowledge—so I should contend—belongs to science; all *dogma* as to what surpasses definite knowledge belongs to theology. But between theology and science there is a No Man's Land, exposed to attack from both sides; this No Man's Land is philosophy.—Bertrand Russell

Without it [philosophy] no one can lead a life free of fear or worry.—Seneca

Uncertainty, in the presence of vivid hopes and fears, is painful, but must be endured if we wish to live without the support of comforting fairy tales. . . . To teach how to live without certainty, and yet without being paralyzed by hesitation, is perhaps the chief thing that philosophy, in our age, can still do for those who study it.—Bertrand Russell

The most important and interesting thing which philosophers have tried to do is no less than this; namely: To give a general description of the whole Universe, mentioning all of the most important kinds of things which we *know* to be in it, considering how far it is likely that there are in it important kinds of things which we do not absolutely *know* to be in it, and also considering the most important ways in which these various kinds of things are related to one another.
—G. E. Moore

The philosopher has to take into account the least philosophical things in the world.
—C. Chincholle

Life involves passions, faiths, doubts, and courage. The critical inquiry into what these things mean and imply is philosophy.
—Josiah Royce

PHILOSOPHY, n. A route of many roads leading from nowhere to nothing.
—Ambrose Bierce

What is philosophy but a continual battle against custom; an ever-renewed effort to transcend the sphere of blind custom?
—Thomas Carlyle

[Philosophy] consoles us for the small achievements in life, and the decline of strength and beauty; it arms us against poverty, old age, sickness and death, against fools and evil sneerers.—Jean de la Bruyère

Not to care for philosophy is to be a true philosopher.—Blaise Pascal

All philosophies, if you ride them home, are nonsense; but some are greater nonsense than others.—Samuel Butler

There is no statement so absurd that no philosopher will make it.—Cicero

The most tragic problem of philosophy is to reconcile intellectual necessities with the necessities of the heart and the will.
—Miguel de Unamuno

Without philosophy we would be little above animals.—Voltaire

Philosophy asks the simple question, What is it all about?—Alfred North Whitehead

Philosophy limits the thinkable and therefore the unthinkable.—Ludwig Wittgenstein

Philosophers rule the world—five hundred years after they are dead.
—Archbishop Temple

often does not *seem* particularly complex or technical, because often it is written in familiar, everyday language. But that wrapping of familiar, everyday language is deceiving. Really, it is best to approach a work in philosophy with the kind of mental preparedness and alertness appropriate for a textbook in mathematics or science. As a general rule of thumb, you might expect to be able to read an *entire novel* in the time it takes you to get through just a chapter or two of good philosophy. To understand philosophy, you usually have to reread a passage several times and think about it a lot.

Of course, you don't have to read a philosophy book slowly and carefully. But if you don't, you may well find it dull and uninteresting, sort of like baseball is to someone who doesn't understand the game and doesn't get involved in what's going on.

Having been forewarned, you can turn your attention to Part 1, on metaphysics.

Suggested Further Readings

Five of the best reference books on philosophy in the English language are these:

F. C. Copleston, *History of Philosophy* (New York: Doubleday, 1965); nine volumes. The most complete history of philosophy available to English-only readers.

Paul Edwards, ed., *The Encyclopedia of Philosophy* (New York: Macmillan, 1967); also in eight volumes. If you need to find out something about a philosopher or philosophical topic, begin here.

W. T. Jones, *History of Western Philosophy*, 2nd ed. (New York: Harper & Row, 1976), in five volumes. Shorter than Copleston but a little more difficult to read, in our view.

Bertrand Russell, *A History of Western Philosophy* (New York: Simon & Schuster, 1945). As readable as a novel, though some critics find Russell brash and opinionated.

Albert Hakim, *Historical Introduction to Philosophy* (New York: Macmillan, 1987). An extensive collection of short original readings.

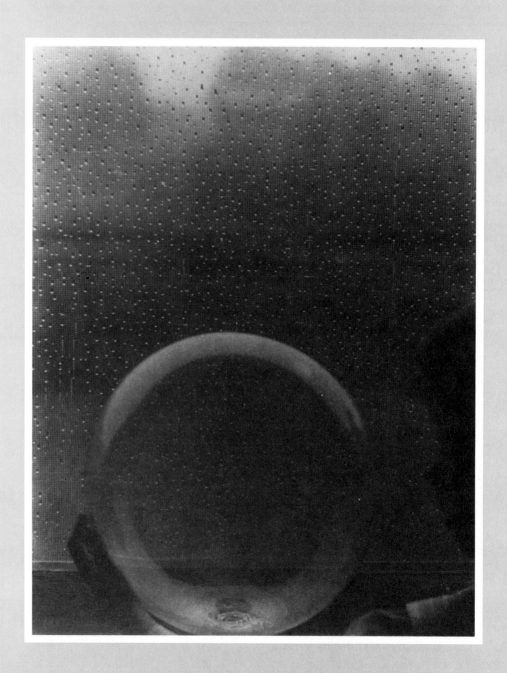

Metaphysics

The First Metaphysicians

It is wise to agree that all things are one.

—HERACLITUS

Everything should be as simple as it is, but not simpler.

—EINSTEIN

The word *metaphysics* has strange and forbidding associations in its popular usage. "Metaphysical bookstores," for example, specialize in all sorts of occult subjects from channeling, harmonic convergence, and pyramid power to past-life hypnotic regression, psychic surgery, and spirit photography. If you know something about the history of metaphysics, you tend to be amused by this association with the occult, especially given the way in which the term was originally coined. Here is the true story.

Aristotle (384–322 B.C.) produced a series of works on a wide variety of subjects, from biology to poetry. One set of his writings is known as the *Physics*, from the Greek word *physika*, which means "the things of nature." Another set, to which Aristotle never gave an official title but which he referred to occasionally as "first philosophy" or as "wisdom," was called simply "the books after the books on nature" (*ta meta ta physika biblia*) by later writers and particularly by Andronicus of Rhodes, who was the cataloger of Aristotle's works in the first century B.C. The word *metaphysics*, then, translates loosely as "after the *Physics*."

The subjects Aristotle discussed in these works are more abstract and difficult to understand than those he examined in the *Physics*. Hence later authorities determined that their proper place was indeed "after the *Physics*," and thus "*Metaphysics*" has stuck as the official title of Aristotle's originally untitled work and, by extension, as the general name for the study of the topics treated there—and related subjects. As you will see, philosophers before Aristotle had also discussed some of these things.

What Is the Nature of Being?

When a philosopher asks, "What is the nature of being?"—and who besides philosophers would ask?—he or she may have in mind any number of things, including one or more of the following:

- Is being a *property* of things, or is it *some kind of thing* itself? Or is there some third alternative?

- Is being basically *one*, or are there *many* beings?

- Is being *fixed* and *changeless* or is it constantly changing? What is the relationship between *being* and *becoming*?

- Does everything have the *same kind* of being?

- What are the fundamental *categories* into which all existing things may be divided?

- What are the fundamental *features* of reality?

- Is there a fundamental *substance* out of which all else is composed? If so, does it have any properties? Must it have properties?

- What is the world like *in itself*, independently of our perception of it?

- What manner of existence do *particular things* have, as distinct from *properties*, *relations*, and *classes*? What manner of existence do *events* have? What manner do *numbers*, *minds*, *matter*, *space*, and *time* have? What manner do *facts* have?

- That a particular thing has a certain characteristic—is that a fact about the *thing*? Or is it a fact about the *characteristic*?

Several narrower questions may also properly be regarded as questions of metaphysics, such as: Does God exist? Is what happens determined? Is there life after death? and Must events occur in space and time?

We'll admit that some of these questions are none too clear, but they indicate some of the directions a person might take in coming to answer the question, "What is the nature of being?" or in studying metaphysics. Because they are so numerous, they also indicate that we'll have to make some choices about what topics to cover in the pages that follow. We cannot go on forever.

This means that, though Aristotle's works are the source of the term *metaphysics*, Aristotle was not the first metaphysician.

The fundamental question treated in Aristotle's *Metaphysics*, and thus the fundamental metaphysical question, can be put this way: *What is the nature of being?* But a number of different subjects might qualify as "related" to this question. So you should not be surprised that in contemporary philosophical usage metaphysics is rather a broad and inclusive field, though for most philosophers it doesn't include such subjects as astral projection, psychic surgery, or UFOs.

What is the nature of being? One of the authors used to ask his introductory classes to answer that question in a brief essay. The most common response, along with "Huh?" "What?" "Are you serious?" and "How do you drop this class?" is "What do you *mean*, 'What is the nature of being?'" People are troubled by what the question means and are uncertain what sort of thing is expected for an answer. It's this way, incidentally, with a lot of philosophical questions—you don't know exactly what is being asked or what an answer might look like.

27

The First Metaphysicians

In this chapter we'll see several different approaches that have been taken to this question through the history of philosophy.

Early Metaphysics: The Pre-Socratics

We'll begin with a discussion of the earliest metaphysicians—Greeks living in Ionia, on the coast of Asia Minor, during the sixth century B.C. These philosophers are known collectively as the **pre-Socratics,** a loose chronological term applied to all the Greek philosophers who lived before **Socrates** (c. 470–399 B.C.). Most left little or nothing of their own writings, so scholars have had to reconstruct their views from what contemporaneous and later writers said about them.

Before we start, let's just say one thing. Experience indicates that it is sometimes difficult to relate to people who lived so long ago. If you have this problem with what follows, then it may help if you remember this:

It was during this period in Western history—ancient Greece before Socrates—that the decisive change in perspective came about that ultimately made possible a deep understanding of the natural world. It wasn't *inevitable* that this change would occur, and there are societies that exist today whose members, for lack of this perspective, do not so much as understand why their seasons change. We are not arguing for the virtues of advanced technological civilization over primitive life in a state of nature, for advanced civilization is in some ways a mixed blessing. But advanced civilization is a fact, and that it is a fact is a direct consequence of two developments in thought. One of these, which we will not discuss, is the discovery by the Greeks of mathematics. The other, which we are about to discuss immediately, is the invention by the Greeks of philosophy, specifically metaphysics.

The Milesians

Philosophy began with metaphysics. And metaphysics began when it occurred to **Thales** (c. 640–546 B.C.), a citizen of the wealthy Greek seaport town of Miletus, to consider whether there might be some *fundamental kind of stuff* out of which everything else is made. Today we are so accustomed to thinking of the complex world we experience as made up of a few basic substances (like hydrogen, oxygen, carbon, and the other elements) that we are surprised there ever was a time when people did not think this. But before Thales people did not think this. So Thales deserves credit for introducing a new and rather important idea into Western thought.

What is this basic substance, according to Thales? Unfortunately, his answer was that *all is water,* and this turns out to be wrong. But it was *not* an especially silly answer for him to have come up with. You can imagine him looking about at the complicated world of nature and reasoning: Well, if there is some underlying, more fundamental level than that of appearances, and some kind of substance exists at that level out of which everything else is made, then this basic substance would have to be something very flexible, something that could appear in many forms. And of the candidates Thales saw around him, the most flexible would have been water—something that can appear in three very different states. So we can imagine Thales thinking that if water can appear in these three very different forms that we know about, it may be that water can also appear in many others that we do not understand. For example, when a piece of wood burns, it goes up in smoke, which looks like a form of steam. Therefore, perhaps—Thales might have speculated—the original piece of wood was actually water in one of its more exotic forms.

We're guessing about Thales's reasoning, of course. And in any case Thales did come to the wrong conclusion with the water idea. But let's just be really clear that it wasn't Thales's *conclusion* that was important: it was what Thales was *up to.* Thales attempted to explain the complex world that we see in terms of a simpler underlying reality. This attempt marks the beginning of metaphysics and, for that matter, of science. Science is largely just an effort to finish off what Thales started.

Two other Milesians at about this time advanced alternatives to Thales's theory that the basic stuff is water. One, **Anaximenes** (c. 585–528 B.C.), pronounced the basic substance to be air and said that air becomes different things through the processes of condensation and rarefaction. The other, **Anaximander** (c. 611–547 B.C.), a pupil of Thales, argued that the basic substance out of which everything comes must be even more elementary than water and air and indeed every other substance of which we have knowledge. The basic substance, he thought, must be ageless, boundless, and indeterminate. Anaximander, by the way, made a map of the "world" and a model of the "universe." He also believed that humans developed from fish.

Pythagoras

Quite a different alternative was proposed by the followers of **Pythagoras** (c. 582–c. 507 B.C.), who lived in the Greek city of Croton in southern Italy at the beginning of the sixth century B.C. The Pythagoreans maintained that *all things are numbers.* Numbers, of course, are not exactly a kind of "stuff." But the Pythagoreans had discovered that the relationships between musical notes can be expressed numerically, so they believed that all relationships can likewise be expressed numerically. This bold theory may be considered something of a leap, but fresh ideas are often a leap.

Thales and the Corner on Olives

Thales (c. 640–546 B.C.) was considered by many to be the wisest of the seven wise men of the ancient Greek world. But not by everyone. Once, when Thales was studying the stars, he stumbled into a well and was found by a Thracian maiden, who was inclined to think that Thales might know much about the heavens but was a bit dull when it came to what was right before his eyes.

But Thales was not dull. Aristotle called him the first philosopher, and he was also a valued political advisor. His prediction of an eclipse of the sun probably impressed even the Thracian maiden. Once, according to Bertrand Russell, when an Egyptian king asked Thales to determine the height of a pyramid, Thales simply measured the height of the pyramid's shadow at the time of day when his own shadow equaled his own height.

When Thales took time away from his higher pursuits, he could be extremely practical. To counter the criticism of his fellow Milesians concerning his poverty, he used his knowledge of the heavens to foresee a bumper crop of olives. Then he hired all the olive presses in Miletus and Chios. When the crop came and the olives were harvested, Thales could rent the presses at his own price.

Philosophers, naturally, have said that this was Thales's way of showing that a philosopher could easily be wealthy, if he had any interest in money.

The Pythagoreans also had noted the connection between number, on one hand, and size and shape on the other (one is a point, two points make a line, three points a triangle, etc.). Thus they concluded, not unreasonably, that numbers are the ultimate building blocks of everything.

Today we don't really think of things as *being* numbers. Still, most of us tend to believe that many (and perhaps all) physical laws, characteristics, and relationships can be expressed numerically, so the Pythagorean view should not seem totally alien.

It is important to notice, too, that the Pythagoreans in effect combined mathematics and philosophy. This combination gave birth to a very important concept in metaphysics, one that we will encounter frequently. This is the idea that the fundamental reality, like the truths of mathematics, is ideal, perfect, eternal, unchanging, and accessible only to reason. Often this notion about fundamental reality is said to come from Plato, but it originated with the Pythagoreans.

Heraclitus and Parmenides

Another important pre-Socratic was **Heraclitus** (c. 535–c. 475 B.C.), a Greek nobleman from Ephesus, who proposed yet another candidate as the basic element. According to Heraclitus, *all is fire*. In fixing fire as the basic element, Heraclitus wasn't just listing an alternative to Thales's water and Anaximenes's air. For Heraclitus wished to call attention to what he thought was the essential feature of reality, namely, that it is

Pythagoras and the Pythagoreans

Pythagoras (c. 582–c. 507 B.C.) was born on the Greek island of Samos. You may safely disregard the reports that he descended from the god Apollo because he was really the son of a prominent citizen named Mnesarchus.

Not much is known for certain about the life of Pythagoras, though it is known that eventually he traveled to southern Italy, where he founded a mystical-scientific school in the Greek-speaking city of Croton. The Pythagoreans believed in the transmigration of the soul, shared their property, and followed a strict set of moral maxims that, among other things, forbade eating beans.

Unfortunately for the Pythagorean community, it denied membership to a rich and powerful citizen of Croton named Cylon. After Pythagoras retired to Metapontium to die, Cylon had his fellow Cronians attack the Pythagoreans and burn their buildings to the ground. Worse still, from the Pythagorean point of view, he had all the Pythagoreans killed, except for two.

The Pythagorean school was eventually restarted at Rhegium, where it developed mathematical theorems, a theory of the structure of sound, and a geometrical way of understanding astronomy and physics. To what degree these ideas actually stem from Pythagoras is a matter of conjecture.

---

ceaselessly changing. There is no reality, he maintained, save the reality of change: permanence is an illusion. Thus fire, whose nature it is to ceaselessly change, is the root substance of the universe, he said.

Heraclitus didn't believe that the process of change is random or haphazard. Instead, he saw all change as determined by a cosmic order that he called the *logos*, which is Greek for "word." He taught that each thing contains its opposite, just as, for example, we are simultaneously young and old, and coming into and going out of existence. Through the *logos* there is a harmonious union of opposites, he thought.

Change does seem to be an important feature of reality, as Heraclitus said. Or does it? A younger contemporary of Heraclitus, **Parmenides**, thought otherwise. Parmenides's exact dates are unknown, but he lived during the first quarter of the fifth century B.C.

Parmenides wasn't interested in discovering the fundamental *substance* or *things* that underlie or constitute everything, or in determining what the most important *feature* of reality is, and his whole method of inquiry was really quite unlike that of his predecessors. In all probability the Milesians, Heraclitus, and the Pythagoreans reached their conclusions by looking around at the world and considering possible candidates for its primary substance or fundamental constituents. Parmenides, by contrast, mainly simply assumed some very basic principles and attempted to *deduce* from these what he thought *must* be the true nature of being. For Parmenides it would have been a complete waste of time to look to the world for information about how things really are.

Principles like those Parmenides assumed are said in contemporary jargon to be "principles of reason" or *a priori* principles, which just means that they are known "prior" to experience. It's not that we learn these principles first chronologically, but rather that our knowledge of them does not depend on our senses.

For example, consider the principle: "You can't make something out of nothing." If you wished to defend this principle, would you proceed by conducting an experiment in which you tried to make something out of nothing? In fact, you would not. You would base your defense on our inability to *conceive* of ever making something out of nothing.

Parmenides based his philosophy on principles like that. One of these principles was that if something changes, it becomes something different. Thus, he reasoned, if Being itself were to change, then it would become something different. But what is different from Being is Non-Being, and Non-Being just plain *isn't*. Thus, he concluded, Being *does not change*.

What is more, Being is *unitary*—it is a single thing. For if there were anything else, it would not be Being; hence it would not be. (The principle assumed in this argument is something like: a second thing is different from a first thing.)

Further, Being is an *undifferentiated whole*: it does not have any parts. For parts are different from the whole. And if something is different from Being, it would not be Being; hence, it would not be.

Further, Being is *eternal*: it cannot come into existence because, first, something cannot come from nothing (remember?) and, second, even if it could, there would be no explanation why it came from nothing at one time and not at another. And because change is impossible, as already demonstrated, Being cannot go out of existence.

By similar arguments Parmenides attempted to show that motion, generation, and degrees of being are all equally impossible.

So, whereas for Heraclitus being is ceaselessly changing, according to Parmenides being is absolutely unchanging. Being is One, Parmenides maintained: it is permanent, unchanging, indivisible, and undifferentiated. Appearances to the contrary are just gross illusion.

Empedocles and Anaxagoras

The philosophies of Parmenides (Being is unchanging) and Heraclitus (Being is ceaselessly changing) seem to be irreconcilably opposed. The next major Greek philosopher, **Empedocles** (c. 495 –c. 435 B.C.), however, thought that true reality is permanent and unchangeable; yet he *also* thought it absurd to dismiss the change we experience as mere illusion. Empedocles quite diplomatically sided in part with Parmenides and in part with Heraclitus. He was in fact the first philosopher to attempt to reconcile and combine the apparently conflicting metaphysics of those who came earlier.

Additionally, Empedocles's attempt at reconciliation resulted in an understanding of reality that in many ways is very much like our own.

According to Empedocles, the objects of experience *do* change, but these objects are composed of basic particles of matter that do *not* change. These basic material particles themselves, Empedocles held, are of four kinds: earth, air, fire, and water. These basic elements mingle together in different combinations to form the objects of experience as well as the apparent changes among these objects.

The idea that the objects of experience, and the apparent changes in their qualities, quantities, and relationships, are in reality changes in the positions of basic particles is very familiar to us and is a central idea of modern physics. Empedocles was the first to have this idea.

Empedocles also recognized that an account of reality must explain not merely *how* changes in the objects of experience occur, but *why* they occur. That is, he attempted to provide an explanation of the *forces* that cause change. Specifically, he taught that the basic elements enter new combinations under two forces, Love and Strife, which are essentially forces of attraction and decomposition.

Empedocles's portrayal of the universe as constituted by basic material particles moving under the action of impersonal forces seems very up to date and "scientific" to us today, and, yes, Empedocles was a competent scientist. He understood the mechanism of solar eclipses, for example, and determined experimentally that air and water are separate substances. He understood so much, in fact, that he proclaimed himself a god. Empedocles was not displeased when others said that he could foresee the future, control the winds, and perform other miracles.

A contemporary of Empedocles was **Anaxagoras** (c. 500–428 B.C.). Anaxagoras was not as convinced of his own importance as Empedocles was of his, but Anaxagoras was just as important historically. For one thing, it was Anaxagoras who introduced philosophy to Athens, where the discipline truly flourished. For another, he introduced into metaphysics an important distinction, that between *matter* and *mind*.

Anaxagoras accepted the principle that all changes in the objects of experience are in reality changes in the arrangements of underlying particles. But unlike Empedocles, he believed that everything is *infinitely* divisible. He also held that each different kind of substance has its own corresponding kind of particle, and that each substance contains particles of every other kind. What distinguishes one substance from another is a preponderance of one kind of particle. Thus fire, for example, contains more "fire particles" than, say, water, which presumably contains very few.

Whereas Empedocles believed that motion is caused by the action of two forces, Anaxagoras postulated that the source of all motion is something called **nous.** The Greek word *nous* is sometimes translated as "reason," sometimes as "mind," and what Anaxagoras meant by *nous* is apparently pretty much an equation between mind and reason. Mind, according to Anaxagoras, is separate and distinct from matter in that it alone is unmixed. It is everywhere and animates all things but contains nothing material within it. It is "the finest of all things, and the purest, and it has all knowledge about everything, as well as the greatest power."

Before mind acted on matter, Anaxagoras believed, the universe was an infinite, undifferentiated mass. The formation of the world as we know it was the result of a rotary motion produced in this mass by mind. In this process gradually the sun and stars and moon and air were separated off, and then gradually too the configurations of particles that we recognize in the other objects of experience.

Notice that according to Anaxagoras, mind did not *create* matter but only acted on it. Notice also that Anaxagoras's mind did not act on matter for some *purpose* or *objective*. These are strong differences between Anaxagoras's mind and the Judaeo-Christian God, though in other respects the concepts are not dissimilar. And, although Anaxagoras was the first to find a place for mind in the universe, Aristotle and Plato both criticized him for conceiving of it, mind, as merely a mechanical cause of the existing order.

Notice finally that Anaxagoras's particles are not physical particles like modern-day atoms. This is because, if every particle is made of smaller particles, as Anaxagoras held, then there are no smallest particles, except as abstractions, as infinitesimals, as idealized "limits" on an infinite process. For the idea that the world is composed of actual physical atoms, we must turn to the last of the pre-Socratics we shall mention here, the Atomists.

The Atomists

The Atomists were **Leucippus** and **Democritus.** Not too much is known of Leucippus, although he is said to have lived in Miletus during the mid-fifth century B.C., and the basic idea of atomism is attributed to him. Democritus (460–370 B.C.) is better known today, and the detailed working out of atomism is considered to be the result of his efforts. Democritus is yet another philosopher who was also a brilliant mathematician.

The Atomists held that all things are composed of physical atoms—tiny imperceptible, indestructible, indivisible, eternal, and uncreated particles composed of exactly the same matter but different in size, shape, and (though there is controversy about this) weight. Atoms, they believed, are infinitely numerous and eternally in motion. By combining with one another in various ways they comprise the objects of experience. They are continuously in motion, and thus the various combinations come and go. We, of course, experience their combining and disassembling and recombining as the generation, decay, erosion, or burning of everyday objects.

Some qualities of everyday objects, such as their color and taste, are not really "in" the objects, said the Atomists, though other qualities, like their weight and hardness, are. This is a distinction that to this day remains embodied in common sense—and yet, as you will see in Part 2, it is totally beset with philosophical difficulties.

Anyway, the Atomists, unlike Anaxagoras, believed that there is a smallest physical unit beyond which further division is impossible. And also unlike Anaxagoras, they saw no reason to suppose that the original motion of atoms resulted from the activity of mind; indeed, they did not believe it necessary in the first place to explain the origin of their motion. As far as we can tell, they said in effect that the atoms have been around forever and they've been moving for as long as they've been around.

Democritus

Democritus was the most widely traveled of the early philosophers. On the death of his father, he took his inheritance and left his home in Abdera, Thrace, to learn from the Chaldean Magi of Persia, the priest-geometers of Egypt, and the Gymnosophists of India. He may also have gone to Ethiopea. But he came to Athens as an unknown, for Democritus despised fame and glory.

Democritus thought that most humans waste their lives pursuing foolish desires and pleasures. He himself was far more interested in pursuing wisdom and truth than riches, and he spent his life in relative poverty. He found the cemetery a congenial place in which to cogitate.

This Atomist depiction of the world is quite modern. It is not such an extravagant exaggeration to say that, until the convertibility of matter and energy was understood in our own century, the common scientific view of the universe was basically a version of atomism. But the Atomist theory did run up against one problem that is worth looking at briefly.

The Greek philosophers generally believed this: for motion of any sort to occur, there must be a void, or empty space, in which a moving thing may change position. But Parmenides had argued pretty convincingly that a void is not possible. For empty space would be nothingness, that is, nonbeing, and therefore does not exist.

The Atomists' way of circumventing this problem was essentially to ignore it (though this point, too, is controversial). That things move is apparent to sense perception and is just indisputable, they maintained. And because things move, they held, empty space must be real—for otherwise motion would be impossible.

One final point about the Atomist philosophy must be mentioned. The Atomists are sometimes accused of maintaining that chance collisions of atoms cause them to come together to form this or that set of objects and not some other. But even though the Atomists believed that the motion of the atoms fulfilled no purpose, they also believed the atoms operate in strict accordance with physical laws. Future motions would

Free Will vs. Determinism

Here are two beliefs that are both dear to common sense. Note that we hold the first belief thanks (in part) to the Atomists.

1. The behavior of atoms is governed entirely by physical law.
2. Humans have free will.

Do you accept both (1) and (2)? We are willing to wager a very large sum of money that you do.

Unfortunately, (1) and (2) do not get along comfortably with each other. Here's why. It seems to follow from (1) that, whatever an atom does, it had to do, given the existing circumstances. For physical laws determine what each atom does in the existing circumstances. Thus, if the laws determine that an atom does X in circumstance C, then, given circumstance C, the atom has to do X.

But anything that happened as a result of free will presumably did not have to happen. For example, suppose that I, of my own free will, move my arm. Whatever the circumstances were in which I chose to move my arm, I could always have chosen otherwise and not moved my arm. Therefore, when I moved my arm of my own free will, my arm, and thus the atoms in my arm, did not have to move, even given the existing circumstances. Thus, if (2) holds, it is *not* true that an atom must have done what it did, given the existing circumstances. But if (1) holds, then it *is* true.

Now, (1) and (2) are equally basic postulates of common sense. But it seems difficult logically to accept them both. One or the other, therefore, has to be rejected, if they are logically incompatible.

Philosophy has a way of showing that basic beliefs are sometimes incompatible. It can be a troublemaker.

be completely predictable, they said, for anyone with sufficient infor-mation about their shapes, sizes, locations, direction, and velocities. In this sense, then, the Atomists left nothing to chance; according to them, purely random events, in the sense of just "happening," did not occur.

The view that future states and events are completely determined by preceding states and events is called **determinism.**

Let's sum up to this point. Despite the alternative theories the pre-Socratics advanced, an important common thread runs through their speculation, and it is this:

All believed that *the world we experience is merely a manifestation of a more fundamental, underlying reality.*

That this thought occurred to people represents a turning point in the history of the species and may have been more important than the invention of the wheel. Had it not occurred, then any scientific under-standing of the natural world would have proved to be quite impossible.

The desire to comprehend the reality that underlies appearances did not, however, lead the various pre-Socratic philosophers in the same direction. It led the Milesians to consider possible basic substances and the Pythagoreans to try to determine the fundamental principle on which all else depends. It led Heraclitus to try to determine the essential feature of reality, Parmenides to consider the true nature of being, and Empe-docles to try to understand the basic principles of causation. Finally, it led Anaxagoras to consider the original source of motion and the Atom-ists to consider the construction of the natural world. Broadly speaking, these various paths of inquiry eventually came to define the scope of scientific inquiry. But that was not until science and metaphysics parted ways about two thousand years later.

Plato and Aristotle

Two very important philosophers of ancient Greece, and of all time, were **Plato** (c. 427–347 B.C.) and **Aristotle** (384–322 B.C.). Plato was the pupil of Socrates and the teacher of Aristotle. Plato and Aristotle were both interested in practically every subject, and both said something worth listening to about the great majority of philosophical topics and prob-lems. But their metaphysical ideas were especially important for poster-ity. Platonic metaphysics, for example, formed the model for Christian theology for around fifteen centuries, and this model was superseded only because the translations of Aristotle's works were rediscovered by European philosophers and theologians in the thirteenth century A.D. Then, after the rediscovery of Aristotle, *his* metaphysics came to pre-dominate in Christian thinking, though Christianity remained and is still Platonic in many, many ways.

What we shall do now is examine Plato's conception of reality, which is encapsulated in what is known as the Theory of Forms.

What About Socrates?

If you have heard of only one philosopher, it is **Socrates** (470–399 B.C.). Despite having written nothing, Socrates was one of the most influential thinkers in the history of Western civilization, primarily because he gave the discipline its preeminent method. But we won't focus on Socrates in the main text in this chapter because he advanced no metaphysical theory.

To this day, over twenty centuries after his death, most philosophers equate proficiency within their own field with skill in the Socratic method. So let us take a brief look at it.

The Socratic method is intended to unlock the true nature of an abstract thing such as justice or beauty or knowledge through a search for its proper definition, a definition that won't permit refutation under Socratic questioning. Here's an example.

Suppose Bruder and Moore wish to find out what knowledge is. Bruder proposes, tentatively, that knowledge is strong belief. Moore asks if that means that people who believe strongly that fairies exist automatically know that fairies exist. Bruder, seeing that he has made a mistake, reconsiders and offers a revised thesis: Knowledge, he says, is not belief that is strong, but belief that is true.

Moore then says, "Well, suppose my true belief is just based on a guess. This is true belief, but is it knowledge?" Bruder then sees that knowledge isn't just true belief and so he proposes a further revision or an alternative analysis. Eventually, Bruder and Moore may find a definition of knowledge that neither one can refute.

This method does not imply that the questioner knows the essential nature of the thing under consideration, but only that he or she be adept at detecting misconceptions of it and at revealing these misconceptions through appropriate questioning. Though in many cases the process may not actually disclose the essence of the thing (if Plato's dialogues are an indication, Socrates himself did not have at hand many final, satisfactory definitions) it will, presumably, bring those who practice it closer to this terminal understanding.

We can therefore understand why, when the Delphic oracle pronounced Socrates the wisest man alive, Socrates thought the pronouncement must have been a reference to the fact that he, unlike most men, was aware of his ignorance. For as one applies the Socratic method, one becomes skilled at discerning misconceptions of things, that is, one learns to recognize ignorance, including one's own.

The most detailed source of information about Socrates's philosophy is Plato's dialogues, especially the early dialogues, in which Socrates is the star. There is controversy about how accurately these dialogues represent Socrates; the later dialogues almost certainly reflect Plato's own view, even though "Socrates" is doing the speaking in them.

Socrates was famous among his contemporaries not only for his philosophical ability but also for his virtue, courage, and stamina. His trial and subsequent death by drinking hemlock after conviction for religious heresy and "corrupting the young" is reported by Plato in the powerful and gripping dialogue, the *Apology*.

Plato and the Theory of Forms

The Theory of Forms is discussed in several of the some two dozen compositions that are known as Plato's dialogues. The best known account is given in Plato's most famous dialogue, the *Republic*. The *Republic* comes from the so-called middle period of Plato's writings, during which Plato is thought to have reached the peak of genius.

According to Plato's Theory of Forms, what is truly real is not the objects we encounter in sensory experience but rather **Forms,** and these can only be grasped intellectually. Therefore, once you know what Plato's Forms are, you will understand the Theory of Forms and the essentials of Platonic metaphysics.

An example or two will help to make it clear what a Form is. The Greeks were excellent geometers, which isn't too surprising, since they invented the subject. Now, when a Greek geometer demonstrated some property of, say, *circularity,* he was not demonstrating the property of something that could actually be found in the physical world. After all, you don't really find circularity in the physical world: what you find are *things*—various round objects—that approach perfect circularity but are not *perfectly* circular. Even if you are drawing circles with an excellent compass and are paying close attention to what you are drawing, your "circle" is not really perfectly circular. Thus, when a geometer discovered a property of circularity, for example, he was discovering something about an *ideal* thing. Circularity doesn't really exist in the physical world. Circularity, then, is an example of a Form.

Let's take another example. Consider the horse. Notice we did not say, consider *a* horse, like the one grandmother owns. What we said was, consider *the* horse. Grandmother never owned *the* horse, and neither did anyone else. *The* horse is not located on any farm or in any zoo. No matter how long you live or how hard you look, you will never meet up with *the* horse. This is because *the* horse, like *the* circle or circularity itself (and these are exactly the same), is a Form. It is an ideal thing, not a concrete thing.

You may be tempted to suppose that the Form *horse* and the Form *circle* are just ideas or concepts in someone's mind. But this might be a mistake. Before any people were around there were round things, logs and sand dollars and so on—that is, things that came close in varying degrees to being perfectly circular. What they came close, in varying degrees, to being therefore existed at the time. So it seems that circularity existed even when there were no people around or people-heads to have people-ideas in. Or, to take a different line of argument: You have an idea or concept of the horse, correct? Therefore, your idea and what it is an idea *of*—the Form *horse* itself—are not the same thing. The same argument holds true for the ideas of every person; therefore the Forms are not just ideas in people's heads.

Unfortunately, sometimes Plato's Forms are referred to as **Ideas,** and the Theory of Forms is also said to be the Theory of Ideas. But *Idea* is misleading because, as you can see, Plato's Forms are not the sort of ideas that exist in people. So we will stick with the word *Forms.*

At this point let's consider two important features of the two Forms we have been using as examples. We'll begin by asking: How *old* is the Form *horse?* Immediately on hearing the question you should realize that *the* horse is not any age. Grandmother's horse is some age or other, and so is every other flesh-and-blood horse. But *the* horse is not the same age

Profile: Aristocles, a.k.a. "Plato" (c. 427–347 B.C.)

"Plato" was the nickname of an Athenian whose true name was Aristocles. The nickname, which means "broad shoulders," stuck, and so did this man's philosophy. Few individuals, if any, have had more influence on Western thought than Plato.

Plato initially studied with Cratylus, who was a follower of Heraclitus, and then with Socrates. He was also influenced by the Pythagoreans, from whom he may have derived his great respect for mathematics. Plato thought that the study of mathematics was a necessary introduction to philosophy, and it is said that he expelled students from his Academy who had difficulty with mathematical concepts.

Plato founded his Academy in 387, and it was the first multisubject, multiteacher institution of higher learning in Western civilization. The Academy survived for nine centuries until the emperor Justinian closed it to protect Christian truth.

Plato's dialogues are divided into three groups. The earliest include most importantly the *Apology*, which depicts and philosophically examines Socrates's trial and execution, the *Meno*, which is concerned with whether virtue can be taught, and the *Gorgias*, which concerns the nature of right and wrong. The dialogues from the middle period include the *Republic*, *Phaedo*, *Symposium*, *Phaedrus*, *Timaeus*, and *Philebus*. In the most famous of these, the *Republic*, Plato explains and interrelates his conceptions of justice, the ideal state, and the theory of Forms. Plato's later dialogues include most notably the *Theaetetus*, which concerns the nature of knowledge, the *Parmenides*, which treats the relations between the one and the many, the *Sophist*, which examines the nature of nonbeing, and most of the *Laws*, which is concerned with what laws there should be in a good constitution. The *Laws* is Plato's longest dialogue, and the only dialogue in which Socrates is not present.

as grandmother's horse or as any other horse, either. *The* horse has *no* age. And the same thing is true of circularity, the Form. So we can see that the Forms are ageless, that is, *eternal*.

They are also *unchanging*. Your grandmother's horse may grow from a small colt to a large horse and eventually get grey and arthritic, but the same won't happen to *the* horse, the Form. And you, having learned that the circumference of the circle is equal to π times twice the radius distance, aren't apt to worry that someday the circle may change and that when it does the circumference will no longer equal $2\pi r$. Mathematics teachers didn't have to revise what they knew about circularity when New Math came in.

Finally, the Forms are *unmoving* and *indivisible*. Indeed, what sense would it make even to suppose that they might move or be physically divided?

When you think of these various characteristics of Forms and remember as well that Plato equated the Forms with true reality, you may begin to see why we stated that Plato's metaphysics formed the model for Christian theology. You may also be reminded, we hope, of what Parmenides said about true being (i.e., that it is eternal, unmoving, unchanging, and indivisible). Of course, you should also remember that for Parmenides there is only one Being, but for Plato there are many Forms.

But why did Plato say that only the Forms are truly real? Stop and think: An animal is a horse only if it sufficiently resembles *the* horse, just as a figure is a circle only if it is sufficiently possessed of circularity. If a figure doesn't resemble the Form *circle*, then it just isn't a circle; and if an animal doesn't resemble the Form *horse*, then it isn't a horse. It's the same with all things. If a thing doesn't resemble the Form *cat*, then it isn't a cat. If it doesn't resemble the Form *bed*, then it isn't a bed. Sensible objects—that is, the things we encounter in experience—are what they are only if they sufficiently resemble their corresponding Form. So the *true* reality belongs to the Forms.

Many people tend to scold philosophers, mathematicians, and other thinkers for being concerned with abstractions and concepts. "That's all very interesting," they say about some philosophical or mathematical theory, "but I'm more interested in the *real* world." By "real world" they mean the world you experience with your senses. On the face of it, at least, Plato makes out a convincing case that that world is *not* the real world at all.

Of course, Plato was aware that there is a sense in which the objects we see and touch are real. Even appearances are *real* appearances. But Plato's position is that the objects we see and touch have a *lesser* reality. They have a lesser reality because they can only approximate their Form and thus are always to some extent flawed. Any particular horse will always be a flawed horse as compared with the Form *horse*. And, as any particular horse owes whatever degree of flawed reality it has to the Form *horse*, the Form is the source of what limited reality the individual horse possesses.

Thus, Plato introduced into Western thought a *two-realms* concept. On one hand, there is the realm of particular, changing, sense-perceptible or "sensible" things. This realm Plato likened to a cave. It is the realm of flawed and lesser entities. Consequently it is also, for those who concern themselves with sensible things, a source of error, illusion, and ignorance. On the other hand there is the realm of Forms, eternal, fixed, and perfect, the source of all reality and of all true knowledge. This Platonic dualism, you shall see, was incorporated into Christianity and transmitted through the ages to our thought today, where it lingers still and affects our views on virtually every subject.

Now Plato believed that some forms, especially the Forms *truth*, *beauty*, and *goodness*, are of a higher order than other Forms. For example,

Plato's Cave

In the *Republic* Plato uses a vivid allegory to explain his two-realms philosophy. He invites us to imagine a cave in which some prisoners are bound so that they can only look at the wall in front of them. Behind them is a fire whose light casts shadows of various objects on the wall in front of the prisoners. Because the prisoners cannot see the objects themselves, they regard the shadows they see as the true reality. One of the prisoners eventually escapes from the cave and, in the light of the sun, sees real objects for the first time, becoming aware of the big difference between them and the shadow images he had always taken for reality.

The cave, obviously, represents the world we see and experience with our senses, and the world of sunlight represents the realm of Forms. The prisoners represent ordinary people, who, in taking the sensible world to be the real world, are condemned to darkness, error, ignorance, and illusion. The escaped prisoner represents the philosopher, who has seen light, truth, beauty, knowledge, and true reality.

Of course, if the philosopher returns to the cave to tell the prisoners how things really are, they will think his brain has been addled. This difficulty is sometimes faced by those who have seen the truth and decide to tell others about it.

you can say of the Form *circularity* that it is beautiful, but you cannot say of the Form *beauty* that it is circular. So the Form *beauty* is higher than the Form *circularity*. This fact will turn out to be very important when we consider Plato's ethics in the third part of this book.

Also, as we shall see in Part 4, Plato connected his Theory of Forms with a theory of the ideal state.

In Selection 2.1, from the dialogue *Parmenides*, Plato criticizes his own Theory of Forms. Plato puts the criticisms in the mouth of a wise old "Parmenides" who is conversing with a young "Socrates." Parmenides is the first to speak.

Parmenides makes two criticisms of the Theory of Forms. The second, known as the "Third Man" criticism, is stated twice. Try to figure out why this criticism is called the "Third Man."

Why did Plato raise objections to his own theory? He realized that his theory was not beyond criticism and evidently wished to state these criticisms as fairly as he could. Many philosophers think the Third Man criticism is fatal to Plato's theory.

▶ S E L E C T I O N 2.1

From Plato, PARMENIDES

However that may be, tell me this. You say you hold that there exist certain forms, of which these other things come to partake and so to be called after their names; by coming to partake of likeness or largeness or beauty or justice, they become like or large or beautiful or just?

Certainly, said Socrates.

Then each thing that partakes receives as its share either the form as a whole or a part of it? Or can there be any other way of partaking besides this?

No, how could there be?

Do you hold, then, that the form as a whole, a single thing, is in each of the many, or how?

Why should it not be in each, Parmenides?

If so, a form which is one and the same will be at the same time as a whole, in a number of things which are separate, and consequently will be separate from itself.

No, it would not, replied Socrates, if it were like one and the same day, which is in many places at the same time and nevertheless is not separate from itself. Suppose any given form is in them all at the same time as one and the same thing in that way.

I like the way you make out that one and the same thing is in many places at once, Socrates. You might as well spread a sail over a number of people and then say that the one sail as a whole was over them all. Don't you think that is a fair analogy?

Perhaps it is.

Then would the sail as a whole be over each man, or only a part over one, another part over another?

Only a part.

In that case, Socrates, the forms themselves must be divisible into parts, and the things which have a share in them will have a part for their share. Only a part of any given form, and no longer the whole of it, will be in each thing.

Evidently, on that showing.

Are you, then, prepared to assert that we shall find the single form actually being divided? Will it still be one?

Certainly not.

No, for consider this. Suppose it is largeness itself that you are going to divide into parts, and that each of the many large things is to be large by virtue of a part of largeness which is smaller than largeness itself. Will not that seem unreasonable?

It will indeed.

And again, if it is equality that a thing receives some small part of, will that part, which is less than equality itself, make its possessor equal to something else?

No, that is impossible.

Well, take smallness. Is one of us to have a portion of smallness, and is smallness to be larger than that portion, which is a part of it? On this supposition again smallness itself will be larger, and anything to which the portion taken is added will be smaller, and not larger, than it was before.

That cannot be so.

Well then, Socrates, how are the other things going to partake of your forms, if they can partake of them neither in part nor as wholes?

Really, said Socrates, it seems no easy matter to determine in any way.

Again, there is another question.

What is that?

How do you feel about this? I imagine your ground for believing in a single form in each case is this. When it seems to you that a number of things are large, there seems, I suppose, to be a certain single character which is the same when you look at them all; hence you think that largeness is a single thing.

True, he replied.

But now take largeness itself and the other things which are large. Suppose you look at all these in the same way in your mind's eye, will not yet another unity make its appearance—a largeness by virtue of which they all appear large?

So it would seem.

If so, a second form of largeness will present itself, over and above largeness itself and the things that share in it, and again, covering all these, yet another, which will make all of them large. So each of your forms will no longer be one, but an indefinite number. . . .

But, Parmenides, the best I can make of the matter is this—that these forms are as it were patterns fixed in the nature of things. The other things are made in their image and are likenesses, and this participation they come to have in the forms is nothing but their being made in their image.

Well, if a thing is made in the image of the form, can that form fail to be like the image of it, in so far as the image was made in its likeness? If a thing is like, must it not be like something that is like it?

It must.

And must not the thing which is like share with the thing that is like it in one and the same thing [character]?

Yes.

And will not that in which the like things share, so as to be alike be just the form itself that you spoke of?

Certainly.

If so, nothing can be like the form, nor can the form be like anything. Otherwise a second form will always make its appearance over and above the first form, and if that second form is like anything yet a third. And there will be no end to this emergence of fresh forms if the form is to be like the thing that partakes of it.

Quite true.

It follows that the other things do not partake of forms by being like them; we must look for some other means by which they partake.

So it seems.

You see then, Socrates, said Parmenides, what great difficulties there are in asserting their existence as forms just by themselves?

I do indeed.

Aristotle

Plato's most distinguished pupil was Aristotle (384–322 B.C.), on whom Plato had a tremendous influence. Aristotle was eventually hired to be a teacher of Alexander the Great, but if Aristotle in turn had a tremendous influence on Alexander, there is little evidence of it. It's a good bet that Alexander, who conquered the world, had other things on his mind besides philosophy.

We noted earlier that we owe the term *metaphysics* to Aristotle, or at least to those who catalogued his works. But metaphysics formed just a part of Aristotle's interests. Aristotle was interested in every subject that came along, and he had something reasonably intelligent to say about all of them, from poetry to physics, from biology to friendship.

Aristotle's books are more systematic than Plato's, providing evidence of his more painstaking attention to nature. It should tell you something, however, that although Plato is a main staple of any decent literature program, Aristotle is not. Cicero did praise Aristotle for his "copious and golden eloquence," but many find Aristotle a bit tedious. Maybe that's because what we have from Aristotle is mainly lecture notes edited by some of his students.

Nevertheless, Aristotle was a careful observer and a brilliant theorizer, and his thought influenced philosophy in the future. Some fifteen centuries after his death, he was considered the definitive authority on all subjects outside religion, a fact that may have impeded scientific progress more than it helped. This is because science, to get anywhere, cannot assume that something is so just solely because some authority says that it is so, even if that authority is Aristotle.

What we call metaphysics Aristotle called "first philosophy." First philosophy, in Aristotle's view, is in some sense more abstract and general than the specific sciences, and it considers the most basic questions of existence. Therefore, since the most basic question of existence is, What is it to be? we'll begin there.

In Aristotle's opinion, to be is to be a particular thing. And each thing, he maintained, is a combination of *matter* and *form*. A statue, for example, is a chunk of marble with a certain form. It is the same with other things, too. There is some stuff out of which each thing is made, and there is the particular form this bit of stuff takes. Without the stuff the thing wouldn't exist, because you can't have a thing made out of nothing. And without the form the thing wouldn't exist, either. Without form, the stuff would not be some *particular kind of thing*, it would just be *stuff*. So the form is what determines what the thing is. It is the essential nature of the thing.

To illustrate this, the marble of the statue is the same marble as it was when it was cut into a block at the quarry. But now it has a new form, and that form is what distinguishes the marble now from the marble in the block in the quarry. Yes, the marble has always had *some* form or other, but its transformation to this particular form is what makes it a

Profile: Aristotle (384–322 B.C.)

Aristotle wasn't correct about everything. He thought that the brain was a minor organ compared with the heart and that eels are spontaneously generated from mud. He also thought that parsnips cause erections and that women are an inferior product.

But he did know a great deal. In fact, Aristotle systematized all that was then known and, as if that weren't sufficient, he extended the limits of knowledge in virtually every existing subject, including biology, psychology, zoology, physics, and astronomy as well as in those areas that today are deemed the province of philosophy, including ethics, politics, aesthetics, metaphysics, and logic. His work was of enormous and lasting significance.

Aristotle was born in Stagira, a Greek colony along the Macedonia coast. His father, Nicomachus, was the physician of the king of Macedonia, Amyntas II. When he was eighteen, Aristotle went to Athens, where he studied under Plato at Plato's Academy for some twenty years. Plato may ultimately have come to resent Aristotle, and Aristotle eventually discovered that he disagreed with important Platonic doctrines, but Aristotle always retained a great respect for his teacher.

In 342, Aristotle was hired by Philip of Macedonia to tutor his son, Alexander, who was thirteen at the time. Alexander, of course, went on to conquer most of the then civilized world, but we suspect that none of this was the result of anything Aristotle taught him. Whatever Alexander learned from Aristotle he repaid by sending Aristotle zoological specimens from his many travels and by funding his studies.

In 335, Aristotle formed his own school at the Lyceum, in Athens, and some of the sharper members of the Academy joined up with Aristotle. Because of his practice of lecturing in the Lyceum's walking place or *peripatos*, Aristotle's followers became known as the peripatetics, the "walkers."

Aristotle emphasized the importance of direct observation of nature and believed that you must obtain factual data before you can begin to theorize. He also maintained that knowledge of things requires description, classification, and causal explanation. This is, of course, the modern scientific view, though (as we explain in the text) Aristotle emphasized a different aspect of causation from that stressed in modern science.

Aristotle's works are often classified under five headings: the *Organum*, which consisted of six treatises on logic; the *Rhetoric* and the *Poetics*; his works on natural science, including most importantly the *Physics* and *De Anima* (on the soul); *Metaphysics*; and the works on ethics and politics, which include the *Nicomachean Ethics*, *Eudemian Ethics*, and *Politics*.

statue. Thus, the form is what determines what a thing is, and for this reason Aristotle equated a thing's form with its essence.

So you need both form and matter to have a thing, and, with the exception of god, discussed later, neither form nor matter is ever found in isolation from the other, according to Aristotle.

Things do change, of course: they become something new. Thus another basic question is: What produces a change? Now because in Aristotle's opinion each change must be directed toward some end, we get the result that there are really just *four* ultimately basic questions that can be asked of anything:

1. *What is the thing?* In other words, what is its form? Aristotle called this the **formal cause** of the thing. We don't use the word *cause* that way, but Aristotle did, and we just have to accept that.

2. *What is it made of?* Aristotle called this the **material cause.**

3. *What made it?* This was called the **efficient cause**—and this is what today we often mean by "cause."

4. *What purpose does it serve?* That is, for what end was it made? This was called the **final cause.**

Consider again a statue, Michelangelo's David, for example. What it is, (1), is a statue. What it is made of, (2), is marble. What made it, (3), is Michelangelo (or Michelangelo's chisel on the marble). And (4), it was made for the purpose of creating a beautiful object. Of course, natural objects were not made by humans for their purposes, but they still do have "ends." The end of an acorn, for instance, is to be a tree.

But consider the acorn example more closely. The acorn is not actually a tree, only potentially so, correct? Change can therefore be viewed, according to Aristotle, as movement from potentiality to actuality. Therefore, because actuality is the source of change, *pure actuality* is the *ultimate* source of change. Pure actuality is thus the unchanged changer or unmoved mover or, in short, god. It should be noted that the pure actuality that Aristotle equated with god is not God, the personal deity of the Jewish or Christian religions.

It is an important fact that Aristotle took great issue with Plato's Theory of Forms. For Plato, two or more animals can both be said to be horses if they approximate—or, as Plato said, "participate"—in a third thing, the Form *horse*. According to Plato, the Form *horse* exists apart or separately from individual horses and they are dependent on it for their existence, as explained earlier. But according to Aristotle, this talk of approximating and participating is metaphorical and meaningless. Further, he thought that Plato was mistaken in holding that, although individual horses depend for their existence on the Form *horse*, the reverse does not hold true. For in fact (believed Aristotle), the reverse does hold true: if there weren't individual horses, there would be no such thing as the Form *horse*.

Most important, the Form *horse*, in Aristotle's opinion, is a *universal*—something that more than one thing can be. Many different things can be green, or human, or circular, or horses; so greenness, humanness, circularity, and "horseness" are universals. But only one thing can be you, and only one thing can be Aristotle, so you and Aristotle are not universals, but particulars. Universals, Aristotle insisted, do not exist separately or apart from particulars. Circularity and greenness, for example, have no independent existence apart from particular round things and particular green things.

Aristotle is fairly convincing when he tells us what is wrong with Plato's Theory of Forms, but he is less helpful in explaining just what universals are. The apparent failure of Aristotle (or Plato, or their contemporaries) to produce a satisfactory theory of universals and their relationship to particulars resulted in an obsession with the problem through many centuries, and we will elaborate on the problem in a later box.

Now, a summary statement of the differences between Plato's and Aristotle's metaphysics in a few sentences is bound to be a grotesque oversimplification, unless the sentences were to be very complicated. Nevertheless, the overly simplified difference comes to this: according to Plato, there are two realms. One is the realm of particular, changing, sensible things, and the other is a separate and superior realm of eternal, fixed, and unchanging Forms to which the particular things owe their reality. According to Aristotle, forms are found only within particular things, which are an embodiment of both form and matter. Aristotle did not disdain having knowledge of particular, sensible things, and, therefore, because these things are always changing, Aristotle was much concerned with change itself. This concern led him to his theory of the four causes that underlie change.

In Selection 2.2, Aristotle subjects the Theory of Forms to some heavy criticism.

▶ S E L E C T I O N   2.2

From Aristotle, METAPHYSICS

As for those who posit the Ideas as causes, firstly, in seeking to grasp the causes of the things around us, they introduced others equal in number to these, as if a man who wanted to count things thought he would not be able to do it while they were few, but tried to count them when he had added to their number. For the Forms are practically equal to—or not fewer than—the things, in trying to explain which these thinkers proceeded from them to the Forms. For to each thing there answers an entity which has the same name and exists apart from the substances, and so also in the case of all other groups there is a one over many, whether the many are in this world or are eternal.

Further, of the ways in which we prove that the Forms exist, none is convincing; for from some no inference necessarily follows, and from some arise Forms even of things of which we think there are no Forms. For according to the arguments from the existence of the sciences there will be Forms of all things of which there are sciences and according to the "one over many" argument there will be Forms even of negations, and according to the argument that there is an object for thought even when the thing has perished, there will be Forms of perishable things; for we have an image of these. Further, of the more accurate arguments, some lead to Ideas of relations, of which we say there is no independent class, and others introduce the "third man."

Further . . . if the Ideas and the particulars that share in them have the same form, there will be something common to these . . . If they have not the same form, they must have only the name in common, and it is as if one were to call both Callias and a wooden image a "man," without observing any community between them.

Above all one might discuss the question what on earth the Forms contribute to sensible things, either to those that are eternal or to those that come into being and cease to be. For they cause neither movement nor any change in them. But again they help in no wise either towards the knowledge of the other things (for they are not even the substance of these, else they would have been in them), or towards their being, if they are not *in* the particulars which share in them . . .

But, further, all other things cannot come from the Forms in any of the usual senses of "from." And to say that they are patterns and the other things share in them is to use empty words and poetical metaphors. For what is it that works, looking to the Ideas? And anything can either be, or become, like another without being copied from it, so that whether Socrates exists or not a man like Socrates might come to be; and evidently this might be so even if Socrates were eternal. And there will be several patterns of the same thing, and therefore several Forms; e.g. "animal" and "two-footed" and also "man himself" will be Forms of man. Again, the Forms are patterns not only of sensible things, but of Forms themselves also . . .

Again, it would seem impossible that the substance and that of which it is the substance should exist apart; how, therefore, could the Ideas, being the substances of things, exist apart? In the *Phaedo* the case is stated in this way—that the Forms are causes both of being and of becoming; yet when the Forms exist, still the things that share in them do not come into being, unless there is something to originate movement; and many other things come into being (e.g. a house or a ring) of which we say there are no Forms. Clearly, therefore, even the other things can both be and come into being owing to such causes as produce the things just mentioned.

Before he died in 323 B.C. at age thirty-two, Aristotle's student, Alexander the Great, son of the Macedonian king Philip II, had conquered the entire civilized Western world, pulverizing all opposition and naming a score of cities after himself to ensure that everyone got the message. This period of Macedonian domination of the Greek-speaking world, known as the **Hellenistic age** (*Hellene* means "Greek"), was a period of major achievements in mathematics and science.

Having started with Alexander around 335 B.C., Macedonian hegemony was carried forth by the families of three of Alexander's generals and lasted about a century and a half, until Philip V of Macedon and Antiochus III of Syria were each defeated (around 190 B.C.) by a new ascending power: Rome. From that time on for approximately the next seven hundred years, the Western world *was* the Roman Empire, built on plunder and the power of the sword.

For two centuries, beginning in 27 B.C. with the reign of Julius Caesar's grandnephew Octavian, who was known as "Augustus, the first Roman emperor and savior of the world," the Roman Empire enjoyed peace, security, and political stability. But eventually, after the reign of Marcus Aurelius (A.D. 161–180), conditions deteriorated into chaos. Nevertheless, the ultimate fall of the empire was postponed by Diocletian, who divided the empire into eastern (Byzantine) and western (Roman) halves, and by Constantine I, who granted universal religious tolerance, thus in effect recognizing Christianity. Finally, however, internal anarchy opened the Roman frontiers to the barbarians. Although the Eastern empire survived until the fifteenth century, in 476 the last emperor of the West was deposed by the Goths. The Dark Ages followed.

If the Romans were anything, they were practical. They built aqueducts and underground sewers and had glass windows. Wealthy Romans lived in lavish townhouses equipped with central heating and running water. Roman highways were built on roadbase 4 feet thick and were paved with concrete and squared stone. Roman roads and bridges are still used today and some may outlive the Interstates.

But although they were masters of the applied arts and of practical disciplines such as military science and law (Roman law provided the basis for modern civil law), the Romans had little use for art for art's sake, or for literature or science. From the Roman perspective, no form of entertainment was quite so satisfying as watching men fight other men to the death, although seeing humans fight animals came in a close second. Witnessing public torture was a popular amusement.

In philosophy the contributions of the Romans were minimal and almost entirely unoriginal. During Hellenistic and Roman periods there were four main traditions or "schools" of philosophy; three of these arose around the time of Alexander and were in fact products of Greek culture, not Roman. Two of these—known as **Stoicism** and **Epicureanism**—were concerned mainly with the question of how the individual should best conduct his affairs. If there had been supermarkets at the time, then Stoic and Epicurean advice would have been available in paperbacks for sale at the checkout counters. But these schools of philosophy are a subject for our section on ethics. The third school—**Skepticism**—was concerned with the possibility of knowledge, and so it is covered in Part 2.

The remaining school, unlike these other three, did arise during Roman times, but this school was for all intents and purposes a revision of Plato's philosophy. It is known as **Neoplatonism.** Because it had considerable influence on the metaphysics of Christianity, we should say something about Neoplatonism now.

Plotinus

The great philosopher of Neoplatonism was **Plotinus** (c. 204–270). During Plotinus's lifetime the Roman Empire was in a most dismal state, suffering plague, marauding barbarian hordes, and an army incompetent to do anything but assassinate its own leaders. Civilization was in fact tottering dangerously near the abyss. Plotinus, however, was inclined to ignore these earthly trifles, for he had discovered that by turning his attention inward he could achieve union with god.

Now think back for a moment to Plato. According to Plato's metaphysics, there are two worlds. On one hand, there is the cave, that is, the world of changing appearances: the world of sensation, ignorance, error, illusion, and darkness. On the other hand there is the light, that is, the world of forms: the world of intellect, knowledge, truth, reality, and brightness. With Plotinus this Platonic separation of realms is acknowledged, but *smoothed out*, so that all things are part of a single and continuous system.

What is real, according to Plotinus, is rooted in unity and permanence, for what *is* is single and unchanging. For Plato, the source of reality is the Forms, particularly the Form of the Good. Plotinus further specified this ultimate source as god or the One. For Plotinus, god is above and beyond everything else—utterly transcendent.

But Plotinus's god, like Plato's Good, and unlike the Christian God, is not a *personal* god. God, according to Plotinus, is indefinable and indescribable, because to define or describe god would be to place limitations on what has no limits. About god it can only be said that god is. And god can be apprehended only through a coming together of the soul and god in a mystical experience. This mystical "touching" of god, this moment in which we have the "vision," is the highest moment of life.

Nor is god, according to Plotinus, a creator. To create is to be active, and god, which is single and unchanging, cannot be active. Reality, according to Plotinus, *emanates* from the One, much as light emanates from the sun or ripples on a pond emanate from a central source. It emanates first to the realm of the spirit or intellect, then to the realm of the soul, then to the physical realm, and as it does so its light becomes fainter and fainter. Thus matter, the final emanation, stands on the edge

Plotinus

Plotinus's interest in philosophy began when he was twenty-eight in Alexandria (the most famous Alexandria, the one in Egypt). His first teacher was Ammonius, the "Sack Carrier," who was so called because he earned his living as a gardener.

About 244, Plotinus traveled to Rome and founded what came to be a renowned school of Neoplatonic philosophy. Even the Emperor Gallienus and his wife Salonina patronized the school. Plotinus tried to get his students to ask questions for themselves; consequently the discussions were lively and sometimes almost violent. On one occasion Plotinus had to stop a particularly ugly confrontation between a senator and a rich man; he urged both parties to calm themselves and think rather only of the One (about which see the text).

Plotinus himself was a quiet, modest, and selfless human being. He was thought to possess an uncanny ability to penetrate into the human character and its motives, and for this reason he was sought out for all manner of practical advice.

He would not, however, acknowledge his birthday. This is because, at least according to Porphyry, who wrote a biography of Plotinus, Plotinus was ashamed that his immortal soul was contained in a mortal body, and the event of his soul entering his body was therefore something to be regretted. He also would not allow his face to be painted or his body to be sculpted. In fact, his long disregard of his body eventually caused him to lose his voice, and his hands and feet festered with abscesses and pus. Because Plotinus greeted his students with an embrace, the net result was a falling off in enrollment.

Plotinus's philosophy had a great influence on St. Augustine and others doctors and fathers of the Church. Christian theology is unthinkable without the mystical depth that comes from him.

of utter darkness or total nonbeing. As matter is furthest from the light, it is accordingly the most imperfect of things and is thus the closest to being "evil."

Plotinus was the last of the ancient philosophers, and after him for several centuries the task of philosophizing was undertaken by Catholic thinkers, at least in the western part of the Roman Empire. Or what remained of the western part. The influence of the ancient philosophers, especially Plato and Plotinus, on one of these earlier churchmen, who also happens to be one of the two or three most important Christian theologians of all time, was considerable. We are talking about **St. Augustine** (354–430), who came from the town of Tagaste, near what is today the Algerian city of Annaba. Through Augustine, Platonic and Neoplatonic themes were transferred to Christianity and transported down through the ages to us today, where they affect the thought of both Christian and non-Christian.

St. Augustine

"Whenever Augustine," Thomas Aquinas later wrote, "who was saturated with the teachings of the Platonists, found in their writings anything consistent with the faith, he adopted it; and whatever he found contrary to the faith, he amended." Through Augustine, Christianity became so

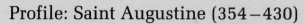

Profile: Saint Augustine (354–430)

Augustine grew up in northern Africa. His father was a successful man of the world, and Augustine was expected to follow a similar path. Accordingly, he studied rhetoric in Carthage. While there, however, he fell in with a group of students known as the "rebels," who found amusement in such pasttimes as attacking innocent passersby at night. Augustine, to his credit, did not participate in these episodes, though he did steal fruit from a neighbor's tree for the sheer perversity of doing so.

As a young man Augustine also indulged in many love affairs. He took a concubine and the union produced a son. He came to have doubts about his lifestyle, however, and eventually these doubts began to take the upper hand. With the encouragement of his family, he became engaged to a young woman of a prominent family. But Augustine grew impatient and took a new lover.

In the meanwhile, Augustine's studies had taken him to Rome and to Milan, where he became a professor of rhetoric. His mother, Monica, had already become a Christian. Through her encouragement and through Augustine's exposure to St. Ambrose, the celebrated preacher, Augustine was baptized into Christianity at the age of thirty-three. He returned to northern Africa and soon thereafter was called on to serve as Bishop of Hippo.

As bishop, Augustine used his rhetorical abilities to the full in fiercely attacking what he perceived to be the many heresies of the time. His thinking was dominated by two themes, the sinfulness of human beings and the inscrutability of God. At the age of seventy-two, he withdrew from the world and died in self-chosen solitude.

permanently interwoven with elements of Platonic thought that today, as William Inge said, it is impossible to remove Platonism from Christianity "without tearing Christianity to pieces."

St. Augustine regarded Plotinus and Plato as having *prepared* him for Christianity by exposing him to important Christian principles before he encountered them in Scripture. (Neither Plato nor Plotinus was Christian, it should be clear.) Augustine had a very strong inclination toward skepticism and was tempted to believe that "nothing can be known." Plato and Plotinus enabled Augustine to overcome this inclination.

We should be more specific, however. Today we take for granted the concept of a separate, immaterial reality known as the transcendent God. Even those who do not believe in God are familiar with this concept of an immateriality and are not inclined to dismiss it as blatant nonsense (though some, of course, do). But careful reflection reveals that there isn't much within experience that gives rise to this concept, for we seem to experience only concrete, physical things. Through the influence of Plato and Plotinus, St. Augustine perceived that belief in a distinct immaterial reality was not the blindly superstitious thing that it might seem. And

Augustine, God, and Time

The ex nihilo theory (God created it all out of nothing) invites a troublesome question for Christian theology: Why did God choose to create the world at the time he did and not at some other? Thanks to Plato and Plotinus, Augustine was able to provide a potentially reasonable answer to this question.

According to Augustine, the question rests on a false assumption, that God (and his actions) exist *within* time. On the contrary, Augustine maintained, God does not exist in time; instead, time began with the creation by God of the world. God is *beyond* time. In this way the timeless attribute of Plato's Good and Plotinus's One was transferred by Augustine to the Christian God.

But what exactly, Augustine wondered, is time? Here Augustine broke new philosophical ground by coming forth with a very tempting answer to this question.

"What, then, is time?" he asked. "If no one asks of me, I know; if I wish to explain to him who asks, I know not." On one hand only the present exists, for the past is no more, and the future is not yet. But on the other hand certain things did happen in the past and other things will happen in the future, and thus past and future are quite real. How can the past and the future be both real and nonexistent?

Augustine's answer to this almost hopelessly baffling question is that past and future exist only in the human mind. "The present of things past is memory; the present of things present is sight; and the present of things future is expectation."

Thus, Augustine's analysis of time is that it is a subjective phenomenon. It exists "only in the mind." (Thus, before God created us, there was no time.) The idea that time is subjective was later developed by Kant into the theory that time, space, causation, and other basic "categories" of being are all subjective impositions of the mind on the world. The same idea was then carried to its ultimate conclusion by the "Absolute Idealists," who said that the world *is* mind. We will turn to all this in due course.

through Augustine's thought the Christian belief in a nonmaterial God received a philosophical justification, a justification without which (it is arguable) this religion would not have sustained the belief of thoughtful people through the ages. (Other explanations of the durability of the Christian belief in God are, of course, possible.)

Augustine accepted the Platonic view that "there are two realms, an intelligible realm where truth itself dwells, and this sensible world which we perceive by sight and touch." Like Plato before him, St. Augustine thought that the capacity of the human mind to grasp eternal truths implies the existence of something infinite and eternal apart from the world of sensible objects, an essence that in some sense represents the source or ground of all reality and of all truth. This ultimate ground and highest being Augustine identified with God, rather than Platonic Forms.

Augustine, however, accepted the Old Testament idea that God created the world out of nothing. This idea of creation **ex nihilo,** creation out of nothing, is really quite a startling concept when you think about it, and Greek thinkers had had trouble with it. Their view had been that getting something from nothing is impossible.

Augustine also accepted, of course, the Gospel story of the life, death, and resurrection of Jesus Christ and believed that God took on human form in the person of Jesus. Thus the Augustinian theology gives God a human aspect that would have been unthinkable for Neoplatonists, who thought that the immaterial realm could not be tainted with the imperfection of mere gross matter.

It is sometimes said that St. Augustine is the founder of Christian *theology*. Certainly his influence on Christian thought was second to none, with the exception of St. Paul. One very important aspect of his thought was his concept of evil, in which the influence of Plato and Plotinus is again evident. We will say something about this in Part 3 on ethics.

In Selection 2.3 you can see the influence of Platonic philosophy on Augustine. Notice that for Augustine, as for Plotinus and Plato, what truly *is* is totally unchanging. Also notice, however, that for Augustine, in contrast with Plato, what truly is is *single*.

▶ S E L E C T I O N   2.3

From St. Augustine, AN AUGUSTINE SYNTHESIS arranged by Erich Przywara

Anything whatsoever, no matter how excellent, if it be mutable has not true *being*; for true being is not to be found where there is also *non-being*. Whatever hath in it the possibility of change, being changed is not what it was. If that which was is not, a kind of death hath taken place there; something that was there, and is not, has been destroyed. . . . Something is changed and is that which was not. I see there a kind of life in that which is, and death in that which has been. . . . Examine the mutations of things and thou wilt everywhere find "has been" and "will be." Think on God and thou wilt find "is" where "has been" and "will be" cannot be. . . .
—*In Joannis Evangelium tractatus*

The more thou lovest *being*, the more wilt thou yearn for eternal life, and wilt long to be so formed that thy affections be not temporal, burnt in and stamped by the love of temporal things; which temporal things before they are, are not; and when they are, pass away; and when they are passed away, will not be. And so when they are future, they not yet are; and when past, they no longer are. How then shall they be held so that they remain, when their beginning, that they may be, is their passing on, that they not be? But he who loves being, approves these things in so far as they are, and loves that which ever is. And if he was inconstant in his love of the former, he will be strengthened in his love of the latter; and if he wasted himself in the love of transitory

things, he will be confirmed in the love of what endures; and he will stand fast and attain to that very being, which was the object of his will when he feared the not-being, and, entangled as he was in the love of fugitive things, could not stand firm. . . .
—De libero arbitrio

Being is a term for immutability. For all things that are changed cease to be what they were, and begin to be what they were not. True being, pure being, real being has no one save Him who does not change. . . .What does "I AM WHO AM" (Exod. iii, 14) mean but "I am Eternal"? What does "I AM WHO AM" mean but "I cannot be changed"? . . .
—Sermones

As wisdom is so called from that quality which is being wise, and knowledge from knowing, so from being (esse) comes that which is called essence. . . . Hence the only immutable substance or essence is He who is God, to whom certainly Being itself (whence comes the term essence) most especially and truly belongs. For that which is changed does not retain its own being, and that which can be changed, though it be not actually changed, is able not to be that which it had been. And therefore that which not only is not change, but also is even incapable of being changed at all, alone falls most truly and indubitably under the category of Being. . . .
—De Trinitate libri quindecim

For being in the highest sense of the word is that which ever continues the same, which is throughout like itself, which cannot in any part be corrupted or changed, which is not subject to time, which admits of no variation in its present as compared with its condition at any other time. This is being in its truest sense. For in this significance of the word being there is implied a nature which is self-contained and which endures immutably. This can be said only of God, to whom there is nothing contrary, strictly speaking. For the contrary of being is non-being. . . .
—De moribus Ecclesiae catholicae

All that is body is certainly composed of parts. . . . For heaven and earth are parts of the whole bulk of the universe; and the earth by itself, and the heaven by itself is composed of innumerable parts. . . . And in each several body size is one thing, colour another, shape another; for the same colour and the same shape may remain with the magnitude diminished; and the same shape and the same size may remain with the colour changed; and the shape may not remain the same, yet the body may be just as large and coloured in the same way. . . . The spiritual creature also, that is, the soul, is indeed if compared with the body the more simple of the two, but if we omit the comparison with the body, it is manifold, and even it is not simple. For it is on this account more simple than the body, that it is not diffused in bulk through extensions in space, but in each body it is both whole in the whole, and whole in each several part of it; and therefore, when anything takes place in any small particle whatever of the body such as the soul can feel, although it does not take place in the whole body, yet the whole soul feels it, since the whole soul is conscious of it. Nevertheless, since in the soul also it is one thing to be skilful, another to be indolent, another to be intelligent, another to be of retentive memory; and since cupidity is one thing, fear another, joy another, sadness another; and since things innumerable and in innumerable ways are to be found in the nature of the soul, some without others, and some more, some less, it is manifest that its nature is not simple but manifold. For nothing simple is mutable; but every creature is mutable.

Now God is truly called in manifold ways great, good, wise, blessed, true, and whatsoever thing seems to be not unworthy to be said of Him; yet his greatness is the same as His wisdom, for He is not great by bulk but by power; and His goodness is the same as His wisdom and greatness, and His truth is the same as all those things; and in Him it is not one thing to be blessed, and another to be great, or wise, or true, or good, or to be wholly Himself. . . .

—De Trinitate libri quindecim

The Middle Ages

Augustine died in 430, some forty-six years before the date usually assigned as the end of the (Western) Roman Empire. The final centuries of the empire had witnessed the spread of Christianity through all classes of society and eventually an alliance between the Church and the state. They also had seen a growing belief in demons, black magic, astrology, and other dark superstitions. After the abdication of the last Roman emperor in 476, the light of reason was all but extinguished in Europe and only a few candles flickered in the night. These Dark Ages lasted to about 1000. Compared with the shining cultures of the East at the same time, Europe barely qualified as a civilization.

Precipitating the fall of the empire were the barbarian incursions, and after the fall the invading hordes arrived in waves. In the first wave a group of Germanic kingdoms replaced the empire. In the next century (i.e., the sixth), Justinian, the Byzantine emperor, partially reconquered the Western empire, but shortly after his death Italy was invaded by the ferocious Lombards, and Syria, Egypt, and Spain were conquered by the Muslims. The Carolingian Franks under Charlemagne restored stability for a brief time, bringing into existence (on Christmas Day, 800) what later was called the Holy Roman Empire, though subsequent invasions by the Vikings and Muslims again spread chaos and destruction. During this period Slavic conquests of the Balkans separated Greek and Latin cultures, and the Greek and Latin churches also gradually drew apart.

Original philosophy was virtually nonexistent during the Dark Ages, though the two most capable and learned thinkers of this grim and lightless period, **Boethius** in the sixth century (who was executed for treason) and **John Scotus** in the ninth (whose work was posthumously condemned), were both philosophers of remarkable ability. The thought of both men, though basically Neoplatonic, was original and profound.

By about 1000, the age of invasions was substantially over. The assorted northern invaders had been Christianized, a series of comparatively stable states was spread over Europe, and a relationship of rough interdependence and equality existed between the Pope and the various secular authorities.

Then, during the high Middle Ages, as the next few centuries are called, the Pope became essentially the most powerful leader in Europe. This was to be expected, for the Church controlled royal marriage and divorce, not to mention the pathway to heaven. The Church was the unifying institution of European civilization, and no monarch could act in total defiance of it.

In the growing security and prosperity that followed the Dark Ages urban centers grew, and intellectual life, centered in the great universities that arose under the auspices of the Church, was stimulated through commercial and military contact with Greek, Arabian, Jewish, and (more indirectly) Indian cultures.

Still, independent or unorthodox thinking was not without its hazards, especially if it laid any foundation for what Church authorities perceived to be an heretical viewpoint. During the medieval *Inquisition* those accused of heresy were brought to trial. The trials, however, were secret, and there was no such thing as the right to counsel. One's accusers were not named, and torture was used in service of the truth. An interesting practice was that of torturing not only the accused but those speaking on behalf of the accused. As might be imagined, one was apt to find few witnesses on one's behalf. So it was not unusual for heretics to recant their sins.

Nevertheless, despite all this, the high Middle Ages was a period of growing personal liberty, spreading literacy, and increasing intellectual vigor. In a nearby box we explain the philosophical problem that was most important to thinkers of the time.

Contact with the Arabian world during the high Middle Ages led to a rekindling of interest among European churchmen in the philosophy of Aristotle. Through the centuries the Muslim world had enjoyed greater access to ancient Greek philosophy than had the Christian, and many Christian thinkers first encountered Aristotle's philosophy through Arabian commentaries on Aristotle and through Latin translations of Arab translations of Greek texts. Because Aristotle's repudiation of Plato's realm of Forms seemed at odds with Christian philosophy, which was Augustinian and Platonic in outlook, some Church thinkers (notably Bona-

The Problem of Universals

The three main philosophical problems from around 1000 to 1200 were these: (1) rationally proving the existence of God, (2) understanding the relationship between reason and faith, (3) solving the "problem of universals." Herewith, more about (3).

Some words name a single thing—for example, *George Bush, Aristotle, Billy the Kid.* Other words are general or "universal" words that apply to several things—for example, *tree, philosopher, horse.* The so-called problem of universals concerns general words.

Pretty clearly, individual things—this tree, that philosopher, this horse—exist out there in the world. Do general things such as tree, philosopher, horse—and let's just call these **universals**—also exist out there in the world, or do they just exist in the mind? The theory that universals exist outside the mind is known as **realism,** and the theory that they don't is called **conceptualism.**

Before you say, "Why would anyone care?" think of this. According to Christianity, the Father, the Son, and the Holy Spirit, three individual things, are the selfsame thing, God. The word *God,* therefore, like the word *horse,* applies to separate individuals and in this respect seems to denote a general thing, a universal.

Or take another example: According to Christianity, when Adam and Eve ate the apple, thereby committing "original sin," the sin tainted *humankind,* and that is why all people need baptism. Humankind, of course, is a general thing, a universal.

Thus the question as to the status of general things is most important from a Christian standpoint. If only individual things exist, as conceptualists maintain, then the three persons of the Trinity apparently are three separate individuals, and in that case there are three Gods rather than one. If only individual things exist, then only the *individuals* Adam and Eve sinned, and there is no such thing as a general or universal humankind or human nature to be tainted.

Questions about the nature and status of universals are important not merely for their connection with theological issues. Experience itself requires universals, because experience involves *categorizing* particular things, that is, recognizing particular things as this or that *kind* of thing. "Kinds," of course, are universals. A complete theory of experience would therefore require a satisfactory accounting of universals. To date, an entirely satisfactory account has not yet been found, despite the fact that philosophers of all periods have attempted to discover one.

ventura, 1221–1274) thought it necessary to reject Aristotle. Others (notably Albert the Great, 1193–1280), came to regard Aristotle as the greatest of all philosophers and concluded that there must be an underlying accord between Christian principles and Aristotle's philosophy.

The most important of those who belonged to the second group was **St. Thomas Aquinas** (1225–1274), whose philosophy was deemed by Pope Leo XIII in 1879 to be the official Catholic philosophy. To this day Aquinas's system is taught in Catholic schools as the correct philosophy, and so Aquinas's thought continues to affect living people directly.

Aquinas

Aquinas had access to translations of Aristotle that were directly from the Greek (and not Latin translations of Arab translations), and his knowledge of Aristotle was considerable and profound. In a manner similar to that in which Augustine had mixed Platonic philosophy with Christianity, Aquinas blended Christianity with the philosophy of Aristotle, in effect grafting the principles and distinctions of the Greek philosopher to Christian revealed truth. The result was a complete Christian philosophy, with a theory of knowledge, a metaphysics, ethical and political philosophies, and a philosophy of law. You should expect to encounter Aquinas again in this book.

Another way in which Aquinas is important is this. At Aquinas's time a distinction was finally beginning to be made between *philosophy* and *theology*. No person was more concerned with tracing the boundaries of the two fields than Aquinas. His main idea was that philosophy is based on precepts of reason and theology on truths of revelation held on faith. We shall return to the subject in a later chapter.

As for Aquinas's metaphysics, some of the main points may be summarized as follows. *Change*, Aquinas thought, can be explained using the Aristotelian four-cause theory: the efficient cause is that which produces the change; the material cause is the stuff that changes; the formal cause is the form the stuff takes; and the final cause is what explains why there was a change.

All physical things are composed of matter and form, he said, following Aristotle. Matter, which remains constant throughout a change, is that which a thing is made out of, and form is that which determines what sort of thing it is. By virtue of being separate glumps of matter these two rocks are different, and by virtue of having the same form these two rocks are both rocks and thus are the same. Contrary to the Platonic-Augustinian tradition, Aquinas held that the form of a thing cannot exist apart from matter.

The universe, he wrote, is a series of things ascending from potentiality to actuality, from the four elements (earth, air, fire, and water), through plants, animals, humans, and immaterial intelligences (angels) to God, who is pure act. Because God is pure act, He is changeless; and thus He is without beginning or end (you can't have beginning and end without change).

All living things have a soul, which is indeed the life of a living thing. The human soul, however, can exist apart from the body, and it is the direct creation of God and not of the individual's parents. Further, it is indivisible (and hence immortal). Finally, it stands in a relationship of mutual interdependency relative to the body. A human being is a *unity* of body and soul, Aquinas taught, for without the soul the body would be formless, and without a body the soul would have no access to knowledge derived from sensation.

That God exists, Aquinas said, is a fact evident to reason unaided by faith (Aquinas's famous Five Ways of proving God's existence will be explained in the section on philosophy of religion). Our knowledge of God's *nature*, however, is in terms of what God is *not*. For example, because God is unmoved and unchangeable, God is eternal. Because He is not material and without parts, He is utterly simple. And because He is not

Teleological Explanations

Why do human beings stand upright? Aquinas gives four reasons: (1) Animals use their sense organs for seeking food. Thus, because the sense organs are located chiefly in the face, their faces are turned to the ground. We humans, by contrast, use the senses in the pursuit of truth as well as food, and for this purpose it is better to have the sense organs looking up and about. (2) The brain functions better when it is lifted up above the other parts of the body. (3) If we walked on all fours, our hands would not be available for other purposes. Further, (4) we would have to take hold of food with our mouths, which would require our mouths to protrude and our tongue and lips to be thick and hard, and this would hinder speech.

Now, we mention this not just to amuse you. We want you to note the *kind* of explanation that Aquinas has advanced. Aquinas explains our walking erect in terms of the function of purpose that is served by our doing so—doing so enables us to speak and look out at the world. An explanation of something in terms of its ends, goals, purposes, or functions is known as a **teleological explanation.**

Compare Aquinas's explanation with a modern biological explanation of a human characteristic. According to the latter, chance genetic mutations result in new characteristics in organisms, and those that are not detrimental to the survival of the organisms will be the most influential in the continuing survival of that species of organism and will tend to become characteristics of the species.

In this way the characteristics of all species are to be explained as the result of the "natural selection," over the millennia, of comparatively advantageous changes in the gene pool.

Notice that in the modern biological explanation no mention is made of the "purpose" of a characteristic. The explanation looks entirely backward in time and points to those antecedent conditions and events that *produced* or *caused* the characteristic in question (e.g., changes in genes). For this reason it is sometimes called a **causal explanation.** The teleological explanation, by contrast, looks forward in time to the purpose that is served by the characteristic (e.g., by having this characteristic, that type of organisms will be able to do such and such).

Is this important? You bet. A teleological explanation implicitly points to an *agency* that determines the purpose served by the characteristics of a species: it points to a designing intelligence, a god. A causal explanation doesn't, although some think that it points toward some original episode of causation.

Further, a switch in emphasis from teleological explanations to causal explanations is a major factor that accompanied and helped make possible the scientific revolution.

Of course, for Aquinas as for Aristotle, a teleological explanation *is* a type of causal explanation. It is an explanation in terms of what Aristotle and Aquinas called a "final" cause.

---

a composite, He is not a composite of essence and existence: His essence is His existence, which means that His nature is to be.

In Selection 2.4, Aquinas maintains that man is not only a soul, but something composed of soul and body.

St. Thomas Aquinas lived during the zenith hour in the power of the Church and Pope. After 1300 there began a long decline (that continues still) in the importance of the Church as a political institution and of religion as a governing factor in daily life.

From St. Thomas Aquinas, SUMMA THEOLOGICA

Fourth Article: Whether the Soul Is Man?

We proceed thus to the Fourth Article:—Objection 1. It would seem that the soul is man. For it is written (2 Cor. iv. 16): *Though our outward man is corrupted, yet the inward man is renewed day by day.* But that which is within man is the soul. Therefore the soul is the inward man.

Obj. 2. Further, the human soul is a substance. But it is not a universal substance. Therefore it is a particular substance. Therefore it is a *hypostasis* or a person; and it can be only a human person. Therefore the soul is a man, for a human person is a man.

On the contrary, Augustine commends Varro as holding *that man is not the soul alone, nor the body alone, but both soul and body.*

I answer that, The assertion, *the soul is a man,* can be taken in two senses. First, that man is a soul, though this particular man (Socrates, for instance) is not a soul, but composed of soul and body. I say this, because some held that the form alone belongs to the species, while matter is part of the individual, and not of the species. This cannot be true, for to the nature of the species belongs what the definition signifies, and in natural things the definition does not signify the form only, but the form and the matter. Hence, in natural things the matter is part of the species; not, indeed, signate matter, which is the principle of individuation, but common matter. For just as it belongs to the nature of this particular man to be composed of this soul, of this flesh, and of these bones, so it belongs to the nature of man to be composed of soul, flesh, and bones; for whatever belongs in common to the substance of all the individuals contained under a given species must belong also to the substance of the species.

That *the soul is a man* may also be understood in this sense, namely, that this soul is this man. Now this could be held if it were supposed that the operation of the sensitive soul were proper to it without the body; because in that case all the operations which are attributed to man would belong only to the soul. But each thing is that which performs its own operations, and consequently that is man which performs the operations of a man. But it has been shown above that sensation is not the operation of the soul alone. Since, then, sensation is an operation of man, but not proper to the soul, it is clear that man is not only a soul, but something composed of soul and body.—Plato, through supposing that sensation was proper to the soul, could maintain man to be *a soul making use of a body.*

Reply Obj. 1. According to the Philosopher [Aristotle], each thing seems to be chiefly what is most important in it. Thus, what the governor of a state does, the state is said to do. In this way sometimes what

is most important in man is said to be man: sometimes it is the intellectual part which, in accordance with truth, is called the *inward* man;
and sometimes the sensitive part with the body is called man in the
opinion of those who remain the slaves of sensible things. And this is
called the *outward* man.

Reply Obj. 2. Not every particular substance is a hypostasis or a
person, but that which has the complete nature of its species. Hence
a hand, or a foot, is not called a hypostasis, or a person; nor, likewise,
is the soul alone so called, since it is a part of the human species.

The decline was the result of many factors, but the immediate causes
were probably these four:

1. Corruption and internal discord within the Church, which led
    to dissident movements. During the Great Schism in the late four-
    teenth century, two and even three simultaneously ruling "Popes"
    spent their time excommunicating each other.

2. The emergence of strong, central monarchies in place of the feu-
    dal political structures on which the older social order depended.

3. A terrific resurgence of interest during the fifteenth and sixteenth
    centuries in classical literature, art, and philosophy.

4. Increased literacy, which was aided by Johann Gutenberg's inven-
    tion of movable type in the fifteenth century.

By the sixteenth century, dissident movements within the Church
had turned to open revolt in the Protestant Reformation. The questioning
of accepted truths and traditional authorities that accompanied the theological turmoil of the sixteenth century then helped make possible the
Scientific Revolution in the next century. With the rise of science, the
modern period in philosophy and history begins, and to it we turn.

Checklist

To help you review, here is a checklist of the key philosophers and concepts of
this chapter. The brief descriptive sentences that appear with each philosopher
summarize one of his leading ideas. Keep in mind that some of these summary
statements represent terrific oversimplifications of complex positions.

Philosophers

- **Thales** Held that the basic stuff out of which all else is composed is water.
- **Anaximander** Held that the original source of all things is a boundless, indeterminate element.

- **Anaximenes**   Said that the underlying principle of all things is air.
- **The Pythagoreans**   Maintained that numbers constitute the true nature of things.
- **Heraclitus**   Held that the only reality is ceaseless change and that the underlying substance of the universe is fire.
- **Parmenides**   Said that the only reality is permanent, unchanging, indivisible, and undifferentiated Being and that change and motion are illusions of the senses.
- **Zeno**   Devised clever paradoxes seeming to show that motion is impossible.
- **Empedocles**   Held that apparent changes in things are in fact changes in the positions of basic particles, of which there are four types: earth, air, fire, and water. Said that two forces cause the basic changes: Love and Strife.
- **Anaxagoras**   Maintained that all things are comprised of infinitely divisible particles; said that the universe was caused by mind (*nous*) acting on matter.
- **The Atomists** (especially Democritus and Leucippus)   Said that all things are composed of imperceptible, indestructible, indivisible, eternal, and uncreated atoms. Held that motion needs no explanation.
- **Socrates**   Not primarily a metaphysician. Practitioner of the Socratic method.
- **Plato**   Most influential in metaphysics for his doctrine of two separate worlds and his Theory of Forms.
- **Aristotle**   Held that particular things embody both form and matter (no separate realms); proposed a four-cause explanation of change.
- **Plotinus**   Held that reality emanates from the One.
- **St. Augustine**   Provided Platonic philosophical justification for the Christian belief in a nonmaterial God.
- **St. Thomas Aquinas**   Blended Christianity with the philosophy of Aristotle; delineated boundary between philosophy and theology.

Concepts

metaphysics

the question, "What is the nature of Being?" in all its aspects

basic substance/element/stuff

a priori principle

illusion/reality

nous

determinism

free will vs. determinism

Theory of Forms (Ideas)

allegory of the cave

peripatetic

formal, efficient, material, and final causes

Neoplatonism

creation *ex nihilo*

universal
conceptualism
realism
teleological explanation
causal explanation

Questions for Discussion and Review

1. Explain the derivation of the word *metaphysics*.

2. Provide some possible interpretations of the question, "What is the nature of Being?"

3. Compare and contrast the metaphysics of the three Milesians. Whose metaphysics seems most plausible to you, and why?

4. The Pythagoreans theorized that all things are numbers. Interpret this theory; that is, what does it mean? Why would anyone hold it?

5. Compare and contrast the metaphysics of Heraclitus and Parmenides.

6. Explain and critically evaluate Parmenides's arguments that Being is unitary, undifferentiated, and eternal.

7. Compare and contrast the metaphysics of Empedocles, Anaxagoras, and the Atomists. Whose views are the most plausible, and why?

8. Plato's metaphysics incorporates ideas from some of the other, earlier philosophers mentioned in this chapter. Identify as many of those philosophers and ideas as possible.

9. "The behavior of atoms is governed entirely by physical law." "Humans have free will." Are these statements incompatible? Explain.

10. Give an example of a Platonic Form other than one mentioned in the text. Now explain whether or not it really exists, and why.

11. What are some reasons for believing that a world of Forms exists separately from the world of concrete, individual things?

12. Are appearances real for Plato? Are they real in fact?

13. What are the four Aristotelian causes of a baseball?

14. What does it mean to say that change is a movement from potentiality to actuality? Is this a reasonable way of viewing change?

15. Aristotle believed that if individual horses didn't exist, then there would be no such things as the Form *horse*. Is this correct?

16. What is creation *ex nihilo*? What are some reasons for thinking that creation *ex nihilo* is impossible?

17. Compare and contrast Plato's the Good, Plotinus's One, and Augustine's God.

18. Explain the difference between realism and conceptualism. What theory is more plausible, and why?

19. Can we only say what God is not?

20. Give a teleological explanation of why polar bears have white fur.

Aristotle, *Metaphysics*, in J. Barnes, ed., *The Complete Works of Aristotle*, vol. 2 (Princeton: Princeton University Press, 1984). Aristotle's *Metaphysics* is pretty easy to read and understand (for the most part), and entertaining, too. Don't hesitate to have a look. It contains useful information on Aristotle's predecessors, too.

Augustine, *Confessions*, John K. Ryan, trans. (Garden City, N.Y.: Image Books, 1962). Much in this isn't purely philosophical, but most of it is interesting.

John Burnet, *Early Greek Philosophy*, 4th ed. (London: Macmillan, originally published in 1930). This is something like the standard work on the subject.

M. T. Clark, ed., *An Aquinas Reader* (New York: Image Books, 1955). Aquinas wrote too much to read it all; a reader may prove more useful.

E. Gilson, *History of Christian Philosophy in the Middle Ages* (New York: Random House, 1955). A work by one of the foremost medieval authorities. See also Gilson's *The Christian Philosophy of Saint Augustine*, L. Lynch, trans. (New York: Random House, 1960), and *The Christian Philosophy of St. Thomas Aquinas*, L. Shook, trans. (New York: Random House, 1956).

E. Hamilton and H. Cairns, eds., *The Collected Dialogues of Plato* (New York: Bollingen Foundation, 1961). This is what you need to acquaint yourself firsthand with Plato's dialogues. Be sure to read the *Republic*, if you haven't already.

G. S. Kirk, J. E. Raven, and M. Schofield, *The Presocratic Philosophers: A Critical History with a Selection of Texts*, 2nd ed. (Cambridge: Cambridge University Press, 1983). This is a comprehensive recent treatment of the pre-Socratics.

A. E. Taylor, *Plato: The Man and His Works* (New York: Methuen, 1960). A standard introduction to Plato's philosophy.

Suggested Further Readings

Modern Metaphysics

Every part of the universe is body, and that which is not body is no part of the universe.

   —Thomas Hobbes

Wood, stone, fire, water, flesh . . . are things perceived by my senses; and things perceived by the senses are immediately perceived; and things immediately perceived are ideas; and ideas cannot exist outside the mind.

   —George Berkeley

The substance of anything that exists is its self-identity; for its want of self-identity or oneness with itself would be its dissolution. But self-identity is pure abstraction; and this is just thinking. . . . Here we find contained the principle that Being is Thought.

   —Hegel

So much, then, for metaphysics in the early Greek, Hellenistic, and medieval periods in Western history.

The transitional period between medieval and modern times was the Renaissance (fourteenth through sixteenth centuries). Through its emphasis on worldly experience and reverence for classical culture, the Renaissance helped emancipate Europe from the intellectual authority of the Church. The modern period in history (and philosophy) that followed lasted through the nineteenth century. Its interesting cultural and social developments include, among other things, the rise of nation states, the spread of capitalism and industrialization, the exploration and settlement of the New World, the decline of religion, and the eventual domination of science as the most revered source of knowledge. The last development is the most important to a history of metaphysics.

To most educated Westerners today, it is a matter of plain fact that there exists a universe of physical objects related to one another spatio-temporally. These objects are composed, we are inclined to believe, of minute atoms and subatomic particles that interact with one another in mathematically describable ways.

We are also accustomed to think that in addition to the spatio-temporal *physical* universe there exist human (and perhaps other) observers who are able to perceive their corner of the universe and, within certain limits, to understand it. The *understanding*, we are inclined to suppose, and the *minds* in which this understanding exists, are not themselves physical entities, though we also tend to think that understanding and minds depend in some sense on the functioning of physical entities such as the brain and central nervous system. They, the understanding itself and the minds that have it, unlike physical things, exist in time but not space. They, unlike physical things, are not bound by the laws of physics and are not made up of parts.

Thus, today it is a matter of plain common sense that reality has a dual nature. The world or the universe, we believe, consists of physical objects on one hand, and minds on the other. In a normal living person mind and matter are intertwined in such a way that what happens to the body can affect the mind and what happens in the mind can affect the body. The clearest examples of mind-body interaction occur when the mind, through an act of will, causes the body to perform some action or when something that happens to the body triggers a new thought in the mind.

So this *common-sense metaphysics*, as we have been describing it, is dualistic: it supposes that two different kinds of things or phenomena, physical and mental, exist. This is essentially the "two worlds view" invented by Plato, incorporated with changes into Christianity by Augustine and others, and transmitted to us in its contemporary form by early modern philosophers.

But, though our common-sense metaphysics is dualistic, it did not have to be that way. In particular, we might have adopted three other metaphysical perspectives:

- **Materialism.** This is the view that holds *only* the physical exists. According to this view, so-called mental things are in some sense or other manifestations of an underlying physical reality. (Don't confuse metaphysical materialism with the doctrine that the most important thing is to live comfortably and acquire wealth.)

- **Idealism.** This is the view that holds only the mental exists. According to this view, so-called physical things are in some sense or other manifestations of the mind or of thought. (And don't confuse this type of idealism with the views of the dreamer who places ideals above practical considerations.)

From a common-sense point of view, brains are made out of matter. But notice that the second student didn't think that the first student lacked a *mind.* That's because, from a common-sense point of view, we make a distinction of some sort between the mind and the brain. The brain, we think, is a physical (material) thing. The mind, we think, is not a physical thing. Common sense subscribes to the theory of **dualism,** according to which there are two kinds of things, material things (like brains and shoes and quarks) and nonmaterial things (like minds and thoughts and, maybe, God).

- **Neutralism.** This is the view that holds that what exists is *neither* mental nor physical or, alternatively, is *both* mental and physical. According to this view, the mental and the physical are just different ways of looking at the same things, which in themselves are "neutral."

Thanks to the legacy of Greek and Christian influences on Western civilization, dualism continued (and continues) to command the assent of common sense. (Read through the alternative positions again. *You* believe in dualism, don't you?) Increasingly, however, the march of science seemed (and seems) philosophically to undermine metaphysical dualism. Thus, given the preeminence of science, the alternatives to dualism have to be considered. *Modern metaphysics is largely an attempt to ascertain the validity of each of the four metaphysical perspectives listed here: dualism, materialism, idealism, and neutralism.*

In what follows we will consider each of these metaphysical theories as it arose during the modern period of philosophy.

Descartes and Dualism

The Renaissance and the Protestant Reformation and Catholic Counter-Reformation had led many European thinkers of the late sixteenth century to question established precepts, and above all to question the accepted authorities as the spokesmen for the truth, at least in questions of fact. In other words, that so-and-so said that *P* is true was no longer automatically accepted as proof that *P* is true, no matter who or what so-and-so is. This tendency to question authority effectively set the stage for the Scientific Revolution and modern philosophy, both of which are products of the seventeenth century.

Modern philosophy began with **René Descartes** (1596–1650), philosopher, mathematician, and scientist. Descartes's importance to Western intellectual history absolutely cannot be overestimated. Others we have mentioned may have equaled him in significance, but none surpassed him.

Descartes was a Catholic, but he also believed that there are important truths that cannot be ascertained through the authority of the Church. These include those truths that pertain to the ultimate nature of existing things.

But what, then, he wondered, is to be the *criterion* of truth and knowledge in such matters? What is to be the criterion by which one might separate *certain knowledge* about matters of fact from inferior products such as *mere belief?*

To find an answer, to find a criterion of truth, Descartes considered whether among his various beliefs there were any that could not possibly

Profile: René Descartes (1596–1650)

Descartes had the great fortune to be able to transform his inheritance into a comfortable annual income from which he lived. And he did not waste his time. Before he died he had made important advances in science, mathematics, and philosophy. His work in optics was significant. He originated the Cartesian coordinates and Cartesian curves. Descartes founded analytic geometry and contributed to the understanding of negative roots. He wrote a text in physiology and did work in psychology. His contributions in philosophy, explained in this chapter and in Part 2 on epistemology, are of enormous importance.

As a youth, Descartes attended the Jesuit College at La Fleche and the University of Poitiers. When he was twenty-one, he joined the Dutch army and, two years later, the Bavarian army. His military experience allowed him to be a spectator of the human drama at first hand and granted him free time to think. In 1628, he retired to Holland, where he lived for twenty years in a tolerant country where he was free from religious persecution.

Descartes was a careful philosopher and a cautious person. Although he took great issue with the medievalist thinking of his teachers, he did not make them aware of his reactions. Later, when he heard that the Church had condemned Galileo for his writings, he decided that he would have his works published only 100 years after his death. He subsequently changed his mind, though he came to wish that he hadn't. For when he did publish some of his ideas, they were bitterly attacked by Protestant theologians; Catholic denunciations came later. This caused Descartes to say that if he had been smarter, he would not have written anything so that he would have had more peace and quiet to think.

Two incidents in Descartes's life are always mentioned in philosophy texts. One is that the insights that underlay his philosophy came to him in dreams after spending a winter day relaxing in an oven in the army in Bavaria. The other is that he accepted an invitation, with some reluctance, to tutor Queen Christina of Sweden in 1649. This was a big mistake, for the cold weather and early hour of his duties literally killed him. It is not known what the queen learned from the episode.

Descartes's principal philosophical works: *Discourse on Method* (1637), *Meditations on First Philosophy* (1641), and *Principles of Philosophy* (1644).

be doubted. For if any such absolutely certain truths could be found among his beliefs, he reasoned, he could examine them to see what it was about them that made them so certain. In this way he thought he could extract from an examination of his certain beliefs an absolutely reliable criterion of truth. Then, armed with this criterion, he would be able to determine which other propositions are absolutely true and certain. And then he would know which of his metaphysical beliefs were true.

The details of Descartes's search for a criterion of truth are a story for our next section. What must be noted here is Descartes's approach to metaphysical issues. Instead of asking "What is the basic stuff?" or "Of what does reality consist?" Descartes took an indirect approach and asked, in effect, "What do I know is the basic stuff?" and "Of what can I be certain about the nature of reality?" What we are saying is that Descartes tried to discover *metaphysical* truth about what *is* through *epistemological* inquiry about *what can be known.* Epistemology, you may recall from Chapter 1, is the theory of knowledge.

We'll call this approach to metaphysical truth the **epistemological detour.** After Descartes and because of him, modern philosophy has attached considerable importance to epistemology, and metaphysical inquiry is often conducted via the epistemological detour.

That Descartes was greatly concerned with finding a criterion of knowledge is not too surprising, for (as already explained) during the times in which he lived determining just who or what should be regarded as the proper or final authority regarding the truth had become a somewhat problematic task. Descartes simply hoped to find the ultimate authority within his own thoughts.

Two Separate and Distinct Substances

But to get to the point that concerns us in this chapter, Descartes ultimately discovered that he knew for certain, and therefore it was the case, that, beyond God, there are two separate and distinct substances, and that reality thus has a dual nature. On one hand is *material* substance, whose essential attribute is *extension* (occupancy of space), and on the other hand is *mind*, whose essential attribute is *thought.* Because a substance, according to Descartes, "requires nothing other than itself to exist," it follows that mind and matter are totally independent of each other. Still, he thought that in a living person the mind and the material body interact, the motion of the body being sometimes affected by the mind and the thoughts of the mind being influenced by physical sensations.

This is, of course, familiar stuff, since our common-sense metaphysics is pretty much the dualistic metaphysics of Descartes. Unfortunately, there are unpleasant difficulties in the Cartesian dualistic metaphysics. These difficulties vexed Descartes and haven't yet been plausibly resolved. In Part 6 on analytic philosophy, we explain these difficulties in some detail.

To anticipate what is said there, Descartes thought that

1. *Material things, including one's own body, are completely subject to physical laws.*

But he also thought that

2. *The immaterial mind can move one's body.*

Parallelism

Some of Descartes's followers proposed a solution to the problem of how the immaterial mind interacts with the material body, given that the body is supposed to be subject to physical laws. The solution is called **parallelism.**

The mind, they argued, doesn't *really* cause the body to move. When I will that my hand should move, my act of willing only *appears* to cause my hand to move.

What actually happens is two parallel and coordinated series of events, one a series of mental happenings and the other a series that involves happenings to material things. Thus my act of willing my hand to move doesn't cause my hand to move, but the act of willing and the movement of the hand *coincide.* Hence it *appears* that the willing causes the moving.

Why do these events just happen to coincide? To account for the coinciding of the mental happenings with the physical happenings, Descartes's followers invoked God. God, they said, is the divine coordinator between mental and material happenings.

This theory of parallelism seems far fetched, true. But perhaps that only illustrates how serious a difficulty it is to suppose both that material things, including one's body, are completely subject to physical laws and that the immaterial mind can move one's body.

The difficulty is that if the immaterial mind can do this, then one's body evidently is *not* completely subject to physical laws after all. It seems contradictory to hold both (a) and (b). Do *you* hold both (a) and (b)?

Descartes also found it difficult to understand just how something immaterial *could* affect the movement of something material. He said that the mind interacts with the body through "vital spirits" in the brain, but he recognized that this explanation was quite obscure and almost wholly metaphorical. It was, in short, a dodge.

To date, a satisfactory explanation of this difficulty still has not been found.

Despite these problems, Descartes thought he had succeeded in establishing metaphysical dualism as absolutely certain. He also thought that he had shown that the mind, because it is not in space and hence does not move, is not in any sense subject to physical laws and therefore is "free." The metaphysical dualism that survives today as mere "common sense," though it originated with Plato and was incorporated into Christianity by Augustine, survives in the form developed by Descartes. Yesterday's philosophy became today's common sense.

In Selection 3.1 Descartes explains his view that he is a thinking thing—a mind—a thing that is one and indivisible but "intermingled" at the same time with something entirely different, a body—a thing that is divisible and has parts.

After the selection, we turn to materialism.

*From René Descartes, MEDITATIONS ON FIRST PHILOSOPHY**

[B]ecause I know that all things which I apprehend clearly and distinctly can be created by God as I apprehend them, it suffices that I am able to apprehend one thing apart from another clearly and distinctly in order to be certain that the one is different from the other, since they may be made to exist in separation at least by the omnipotence of God . . . and therefore, just because I know certainly that I exist, and that meanwhile I do not remark that any other thing necessarily pertains to my nature or essence, excepting that I am a thinking thing, I rightly conclude that my essence consists solely in the fact that I am a thinking thing . . . [and as] I possess a distinct idea of body, inasmuch as it is only an extended and unthinking thing, it is certain that this I is entirely and absolutely distinct from my body, and can exist without it. . . .

There is certainly further in me a certain passive faculty of perception, that is, of receiving and recognising the ideas of sensible things, but this would be useless to me, if there were not either in me or in some other thing another active faculty capable of forming and producing these ideas. . . . [A]nd since God is no deceiver, [and since] He has given me . . . a very great inclination to believe that [these ideas] are conveyed to me by corporeal objects, I do not see how He could be defended from the accusation of deceit if these ideas were produced by causes other than corporeal objects. Hence we must allow that corporeal things exist. . . . [And] we must at least admit that all things which I conceive in them clearly and distinctly, that is to say, all things which, speaking generally, are comprehended in the object of pure mathematics, are truly to be recognised as external objects. . . .

[O]n the sole Ground that God is not a deceiver . . . there is no doubt that in all things which nature teaches me there is some truth contained. . . . But there is nothing which this nature teaches me more expressly than that I have a body which is adversely affected when I feel pain, which has need of food or drink when I experience the feelings of hunger and thirst, and so on; nor can I doubt there being some truth in all this.

Nature also teaches me by these sensations of pain, hunger, thirst, etc., that I am not only lodged in my body as a pilot in a vessel, but that I am very closely united to it, and so to speak so intermingled with it that I seem to compose with it one whole. For if that were not the case, when my body is hurt, I, who am merely a thinking thing, would not feel pain, for I should perceive this wound by the understanding only, just as the sailor perceives by sight when something is damaged in his vessel. . . .

[T]here is a great difference between mind and body, inasmuch as body is by nature always divisible, and the mind is entirely indivisible. For, as a matter of fact, when I consider the mind, that is to say, myself inasmuch as I am only a thinking thing, I cannot distinguish in myself any parts, but apprehend myself to be clearly one and entire; and although the whole mind seems to be united to the whole body, yet if a foot, or an arm, or some other part, is separated from my body, I am aware that nothing has been taken away from my mind. And the faculties of willing, feeling, conceiving, etc. cannot be properly speaking said to be its parts, for it is one and the same mind which employs itself in willing and in feeling and understanding. But it is quite otherwise with corporeal or extended objects, for there is not one of these imaginable by me which my mind cannot easily divide into parts, and which consequently I do not recognise as being divisible. [T]his would be sufficient to teach me that the mind or soul of man is entirely different from the body, if I had not already learned it from other sources.

I further notice that the mind does not receive the impressions from all parts of the body immediately, but only from the brain, or perhaps even from one of its smallest parts, to wit, from that in which the common sense is said to reside.

---

*Edited slightly for the modern reader.

Hobbes and Materialism

Thomas Hobbes (1588–1679), read Descartes's *Meditations* before their publication, and his objections to this work were published by Descartes along with what Descartes took to be a rebuttal. About ten years later, in 1651, Hobbes published his own major work, *Leviathan*.

Hobbes was on close terms with many of the best scientists and mathematicians of the period, including most significantly Galileo, and their discoveries seemed to him to imply clearly that all things are made of material particles and that all change reduces to motion. Accordingly, the basic premise of Hobbes's metaphysics is that *all that exists is bodies in motion*, motion being a continual relinquishing of one place and acquiring of another. Because, according to Hobbes, there are two main types of bodies, physical bodies and political bodies, there are two divisions of philosophy, natural and civil. Here we are concerned with Hobbes's natural philosophy. Later we will examine his "civil" or political philosophy, which was enormously important.

Now, this business that all that exists is bodies in motion *might* sound plausible, until you consider such things as thoughts or acts of volition or emotion. Can it really be held that *thought* is just matter in motion? That *emotions* are? That *hatred* is? "Yes," said Hobbes.

75

Modern Metaphysics

Perception

Hobbes's strategy was to show that there is a basic mental activity, *perception*, or, as he called it, "sense," from which all other mental phenomena are derived, and that perception itself reduces to matter in motion.

Perception, he maintained, occurs as follows: Motion in the external world causes motion within us. This motion within (which Hobbes called a "phantasm") is experienced by us as an external object (or group of objects) having certain properties. The properties do not *really* exist in the objects, Hobbes said: they are just the way the objects *seem* to us: *"The things that really are in the world outside us are those motions by which these seemings are caused."*

So motion outside us causes motion within us, which is a perception. If the internal motion remains for a while even after the external object is no longer present, it is then *imagination* or *memory*. And *thinking*, he said, is merely a sequence of these perceptions. (There are subtleties in his account of thinking which we won't now bother with.)

Now humans, unlike animals (Hobbes said), are able to form signs or names (words) to designate perceptions, and it is this ability that allows humans to reason. *Reasoning*, in Hobbes's view, is nothing but "adding and subtracting of the consequences of general names." Reasoning occurs, for example, when you see that the consequences of the name "circle" are, among other things, that if a straight line is drawn through the center of a circle, the circle has been divided into two equal parts.

As for *decisions* and other voluntary actions such as walking or speaking or moving our arms, these are all movements of the body that begin internally as "endeavors," caused by perceptions. When the endeavor is toward something that causes it, this is *desire*; when away from it, it is *aversion*. *Love* is merely desire, and *hate* merely aversion. We call a thing "good" when it is an object of desire, and "bad" when it is an object of aversion. *Deliberation* is simply an alternation of appetites and aversions, and *will* is nothing but the last desire or aversion remaining in a deliberation.

We've left out the finer details of Hobbes's account, but this should show you how Hobbes tried to establish that every aspect of human psychology is a derivative of perception, and that perception itself reduces to matter in motion.

This theory that all is matter in motion may well strike you as implausible, maybe even ridiculous. Nevertheless, as you will see in Part 6, it expresses in a rudimentary form a view that is quite attractive to many contemporary philosophers and brain scientists, namely, that every mental activity is a brain process of one sort or another. So let us try to focus on the difficulties in this theory that make it seem somewhat implausible.

God, Free Will, Immortality

Modern metaphysics is to a large extent a competition among the four metaphysical perspectives mentioned in the text, dualism, materialism, idealism, and neutralism. Three important questions are at stake in this competition:

1. Does an immaterial God exist?
2. Do humans have free will?
3. Is there life after death?

These questions are at stake because materialism, the theory that all that exists is physical, suggests that the answer to each of these questions is "no." Unfortunately for those who would prefer the answer to one or another of these questions to be "yes," materialism seems to be the metaphysics implied by modern science. This is because a scientific understanding of the world does not seem to require a belief in the existence of anything other than matter, broadly construed.

So that is one major reason why modern metaphysics is explosive stuff. Riding on the outcome of the competition among dualism, idealism, neutralism, and materialism is the rationality of believing in an immaterial God, human free will, and existence in the hereafter.

Difficulties

The most serious difficulty in Hobbes's theory is probably this. All psychological states, according to Hobbes, are derivatives of perception. So if there is anything wrong with his account of perception, there is something wrong with his entire account of mental states.

According to Hobbes, perception is merely a movement of particles within the person, a movement of particles within that is caused by a movement of particles without.

Thus, when I perceive a lawn (for instance), a movement of particles takes place within me, according to Hobbes, that is the perception of a soft, green lawn, and this internal motion of particles is caused by the motion of particles outside me. But here is the difficulty: when I look at the lawn, the internal movement (i.e., the perception) is not *itself* green and soft. Neither, according to Hobbes, is the lawn. So how is it that the internal movement of particles is experienced *as* a soft, green lawn? And, further, *what is it* that *experiences* the internal movement? The internal movement is, after all, just movement. In other words, *how* do the qualities of softness and greenness become apparent, and *to what* do they become apparent?

Later, in Part 6, we will go into this difficulty in more detail and we will see that it is still a problem even for the most up-to-date versions of materialism.

Let's just say in conclusion that Hobbes's philosophy aroused considerable antagonism—the charge was that Hobbes was an atheist—and in his later years his work had to be printed outside his own country, in Amsterdam. Still, in the long run, and despite the entrenchment of Cartesian dualism in common sense, variations of Hobbes's materialist philosophy were and are accepted by some of the keenest intellects of philosophy and science.

In Selection 3.2, taken from Hobbes's *Leviathan,* remember that by "sense" Hobbes meant what we have been calling "perception."

▶ S E L E C T I O N   3.2

*From Thomas Hobbes, LEVIATHAN**

Part I. Of Man

Chapter I. Of Sense

Concerning the thoughts of man, I will consider them first singly, and afterwards in sequence, or dependance upon one another. Singly, they are every one a representation or appearance of some quality or other accident of a body without us; which is commonly called an *object.* Which object works on the eyes, ears, and other parts of man's body; and by diversity of working, produces diversity of appearances.

The original of them all is that which we call *sense* (for there is no conception in a man's mind, which has not at first, totally, or by parts, impressed upon the organs of sense.) The rest are derived from that original. . . .

The cause of sense is the external body or object, which presses the organ proper to each sense, either directly, as in the taste and touch; or indirectly, as in seeing, hearing, and smelling: which pressure, by the intervention of nerves and other strings and membranes of the body, continues inward to the brain and heart, causing there a resistance or counter-pressure or endeavor of the heart to deliver itself: which endeavor because outward seems to be some matter without. And this seeming or fancy is that which men call *sense;* and consists, to the eye in a light or color figured; to the ear, in a sound; to the nostril, in an odor; to the tongue and palate, in a savor; and to the rest of the body in heat, cold, hardness, softness, and such other qualities as we discern by feeling. All which qualities, called sensible, are in the object that causes them but so many several motions of the matter, by which it presses our organs diversely. Neither in us that are pressed, are they anything else but diverse motions; (for motion produces nothing but motion). . . .

Chapter II. Of Imagination

After the object is removed or the eye shut, we still retain an image of the thing seen, though more obscure than when we see it. And this is what the Latins call *imagination*. . . . Imagination therefore is nothing but decaying sense; and is found in men, and many other living creatures, sleeping as well as waking. . . .

Any object being removed from our eyes, though the impression it made in us remain; yet other objects more present succeeding, and working on us, the imagination of the past is obscured and made weak; as the voice of a man is in the noise of the day. From whence it follows that the longer the time is after the sight or sense of any object, the weaker is the imagination. For the continual change of man's body destroys in time the parts which in sense were moved: So that distance of time and of place have one and the same effect in us. For as at a great distance of place, that which we look at appears dim and without distinction of the smaller parts; and as voices grow weak and inarticulate: so also after great distance of time, our imagination of the past is weak; and we lose (for example) of cities we have seen, many particular streets; and of actions, many particular circumstances. This decaying sense, when we would express the thing itself . . . we call *imagination*, as I said before: But when we would express the decay, and signify that the sense is fading, old, and past, it is called *memory*. So that imagination and memory are but one thing, which for diverse considerations has diverse names.

Much memory, or memory of many things, is called *experience*. Again, imagination being only of those things which have been formerly perceived by sense, either all at once or by parts at several times; the former (which is the imagining the whole object as it was presented to the sense) is simple imagination; as when one imagines a man, or horse which he has seen before. The other is compounded; as when from the sight of a man at one time and of a horse at another, we conceive in our mind a Centaur. . . .

Chapter VI. Of the Interior Beginnings of Voluntary Motions; Commonly Called the Passions. And the Speeches by Which They Are Expressed

There are in animals two sorts of motions peculiar to them: Once called *vital;* begun in generation, and continued without interruption through their whole life; such as are the course of the blood, the pulse, the breathing, the concoction, nutrition, excretion, etc.; to which motions there needs no help of imagination. The other is animal motion, otherwise called *voluntary motion;* as to go, to speak, to move any of our limbs, in such manner as is first fancied in our minds. . . . Imagination is the first internal beginning of all voluntary motion. These small beginnings of motion within the body of man, before they appear in walking, speaking, striking, and other visible actions, are commonly called *endeavor.*

This endeavor, when it is toward something which causes it, is called *appetite* or *desire;* the latter, being the general name; and the other, often restrained to signify the desire of food, namely hunger and thirst. And when the endeavor is from something, it generally is called *aversion*. . . .

That which men desire they are all said to *love*: and to *hate* those things for which they have aversion. So that desire and love are the same thing; except that by desire we always signify the absence of the object; love, most commonly the presence of the same. So also by aversion we signify absence; and by hate, the presence of the object.

----

*Edited slightly for the modern reader.

Spinoza and Neutralism

About the time Hobbes was having to send his work to Amsterdam for publication, **Benedictus de Spinoza** (1632–1677) was completing his major work, *Ethics*. The reason Hobbes was able to print his work in Amsterdam rather than England was that Holland, during this period of history, was the most intellectually permissive of all European countries, sort of a seventeenth-century Berkeley, California. It was probably also the only country in which the government would have tolerated Spinoza's opinions, which were considered, like Hobbes's, to be atheistic and repulsive.

Spinoza's *Ethics* consists of some 250 "theorems," each of which he attempted to derive by rigorous deductive logic from a set of eight basic definitions and seven self-evident axioms (see the box on Spinoza's geometric method). Given his axioms and definition of substance (that which depends on nothing else for its conception; i.e., that which is self-subsistent), Spinoza is able to prove that there are no multiple substances, as Descartes thought, but only one infinite substance. Spinoza equated this substance with God, but we must not be misled by his proof of God. Spinoza's "God" is just simply *basic substance*: it is not the personal Judaeo-Christian God; rather it is simply the sum total of everything that is. It is reality, nature. Spinoza was not an atheist; on the contrary, he was a pantheist: God is all.

Because there is only one substance, according to Spinoza, thought and extension are not the attributes of two separate and distinct substances, mind and matter, as Descartes had thought. What they are, in Spinoza's system, are different attributes of the one basic substance— they are alternative ways of conceiving of it.

So a living person, from Spinoza's point of view, is not a composite of two different things. The living person is a single unit or "modification" of substance that can be conceived either as extension or as thought. Your "body" is a unit of substance conceived as extension; your "mind" is the selfsame unit of substance conceived as thought.

Because, according to Spinoza, the infinite substance is infinite in all respects, it necessarily has infinite attributes. Therefore thought and

Profile: Benedictus de Spinoza (1632–1677)

The gentle Spinoza was among the most ethical men ever to have lived. "As a natural consequence," Bertrand Russell observed, "he was considered, during his lifetime and for a century after his death, a man of appalling wickedness."

Spinoza's family was one of many Jewish families that fled Portugal for Holland to escape the terrors of the Inquisition. His serious nature and love of learning were appreciated by all until he pointed out that the Old Testament and Biblical tradition were full of inconsistencies. This produced a venomous wrath in the Jewish community. At first Spinoza was offered an annual pension for concealing his doubts, and when this failed the logical next step was taken and an attempt was made to murder him. He was finally, of course, excommunicated from the synagogue.

For a time, Spinoza lived in the house of his Latin teacher, though he later rented a room in a tiny house in Rhynsburg, now a suburb of Leyden, where he earned a sparse living by grinding glass lenses. He lived a modest and frugal existence and preferred to work on his philosophy than to do anything else.

Spinoza became known despite his quiet and retiring existence, and at one point he was offered a professorship at Heidelberg. He declined the appointment, realizing that there would be restrictions on his academic freedom and fearing that his philosophy might draw sharp reactions in German society. In the latter suspicion he was probably correct, if the fact that many German professors referred to him as "that wretched monster" is any indication.

Still, after his death eventually some of the greatest thinkers came to appreciate his depth, including Goethe, Lessing, and Schleiermacher. Hegel went so far as to say that all subsequent philosophy would be a kind of Spinozism.

Spinoza died when he was forty-four, from tuberculosis. His condition was aggravated by the glass dust that he was forced to breathe in his profession. Today, the society for out-of-work American philosophers is called "The Lensgrinders."

extension are not the only attributes of substance; they are just the only attributes we know—they are the only ways of characterizing or conceiving substance available to us. They are, so to speak, the only "languages" in terms of which we can speak and think about reality or substance.

Accordingly, for Spinoza there is no problem in explaining how the mind interacts with the body, for they are one and the same thing. Wondering how the mind and the body interact is like wondering how your last glass of *wine* and your last glass of *vino* could mix with each other.

Spinoza's Geometric Method

Spinoza's philosophy is interesting not merely for its content but for its form. He attempted to geometrize philosophy to an extent unequaled by any other major philosopher.

You may recall that in his *Elements*, Euclid began with a set of basic definitions and unproved postulates and from them logically derived a set of theorems. Likewise, Spinoza began with definitions and (seemingly) self-evident axioms and then proceeded to derive theorems or "propositions" from them.

For example, Proposition III states, "Things which have nothing in common cannot be one the cause of the other." And under the proposition is given a "Proof": If they have nothing in common, it follows that one cannot be apprehended by means of the other (Axiom v), and, therefore, one cannot be the cause of the other (Axiom iv). Q.E.D. Thus, Proposition III is derived logically from Axioms iv and v (which we won't state, since we are only trying to give you an idea of Spinoza's method). Thus, assuming the axioms are beyond doubt and assuming no mistakes in logic have been made, Spinoza's entire philosophy is beyond doubt. In this sense Spinoza geometrized philosophy and attempted to provide an absolutely certain metaphysical system.

The mind and the body are the same thing, conceptualized from different viewpoints.

In Spinoza's system, there is no personal immortality after death. Further, free will is an illusion; whatever happens is caused by the nature of substance. Material bodies are governed by the laws of physics, and what happens to them is completely determined by what happened before. Because the mental and the material are one and the same, what happens in minds is as inevitable as what happens in bodies. Everything was, is, and will be exactly as it must be.

There is certainly more to Spinoza's philosophy than this, but this is enough for our purposes here. Where Descartes had postulated two separate substances, both Hobbes and Spinoza postulated only one. For Hobbes, however, what exists is only material; a nonmaterial mental realm does not exist. For Spinoza, what exists is both material and mental, depending on how it is conceptualized. Thus, although neither Hobbes nor Spinoza is faced with Descartes's problem of explaining how two realms, the mental and the material, interact, Hobbes is faced with a different problem, that of *explaining away* the mental realm. We are inclined to ask Hobbes just how and why does this illusory mental realm seem so clearly to be real when in fact it is not? For Spinoza, the mental realm is real and there is nothing that he needs to explain away.

Selection 3.3 will give you a good example of Spinoza's geometric method, discussed in the nearby box.

From Benedictus de Spinoza, ETHICS

Readings

Definitions and Axioms

DEFINITIONS

I. By that which is *self-caused*, I mean that of which the essence involves existence, or that of which the nature is only conceivable as existent.

II. A thing is called *finite after its kind*, when it can be limited by another thing of the same nature; for instance, a body is called finite because we always conceive another greater body. So, also, a thought is limited by another thought, but a body is not limited by thought, nor a thought by body.

III. By *substance*, I mean that which is in itself, and is conceived through itself: in other words, that of which a conception can be formed independently of any other conception.

IV. By *attribute*, I mean that which the intellect perceives as constituting the essence of substance.

V. By *mode*, I mean the modifications of substance, or that which exists in, and is conceived through, something other than itself.

VI. By *God*, I mean a being absolutely infinite—that is, a substance consisting in infinite attributes, of which each expresses eternal and infinite essentiality.

Explanation.—I say absolutely infinite, not infinite after its kind: for, of a thing infinite only after its kind, infinite attributes may be denied; but that which is absolutely infinite, contains in its essence whatever expresses reality, and involves no negation.

VII. That thing is called free, which exists solely by the necessity of its own nature, and of which the action is determined by itself alone. On the other hand, that thing is necessary, or rather constrained, which is determined by something external to itself to a fixed and definite method of existence or action.

VIII. By *eternity*, I mean existence itself, in so far as it is conceived necessarily to follow solely from the definition of that which is eternal.

Explanation.—Existence of this kind is conceived as an eternal truth, like the essence of a thing, and, therefore, cannot be explained by means of continuance or time, though continuance may be conceived without a beginning or end.

AXIOMS

I. Everything which exists, exists either in itself or in something else.

II. That which cannot be conceived through anything else must be conceived through itself.

III. From a given definite cause an effect necessarily follows; and, on the other hand, if no definite cause be granted, it is impossible that an effect can follow.

IV. The knowledge of an effect depends on and involves the knowledge of a cause.

V. Things which have nothing in common cannot be understood, the one by means of the other; the conception of one does not involve the conception of the other.

VI. A true idea must correspond with its ideate or object.

VII. If a thing can be conceived as non-existing, its essence does not involve existence.

Seven Propositions on Substance

PROPOSITIONS

PROP. I. *Substance is by nature prior to its modifications.*

Proof.—This is clear from Deff. iii. and v.

PROP. II. *Two substances, whose attributes are different, have nothing in common.*

Proof.—Also evident from Def. iii. For each must exist in itself, and be conceived through itself; in other words, the conception of one does not imply the conception of the other.

PROP. III. *Things which have nothing in common cannot be one the cause of the other.*

Proof.—If they have nothing in common, it follows that one cannot be apprehended by means of the other (Ax. v.), and, therefore, one cannot be the cause of the other (Ax. iv.). Q.E.D.

PROP. IV. *Two or more distinct things are distinguished one from the other, either by the difference of the attributes of the substances or by the difference of their modifications.*

Proof.—Everything which exists, exists either in itself or in something else (Ax. i.),—that is (by Defs. iii. and v.), nothing is granted in addition to the understanding, except substance and its modifications. Nothing is, therefore, given besides the understanding, by which several things may be distinguished one from the other, except the substances, or, in other words (see Ax. iv.), their attributes and modifications. Q.E.D.

PROP. V. *There cannot exist in the universe two or more substances having the same nature or attribute.*

Proof.—If several distinct substances be granted, they must be distinguished one from the other, either by the difference of their attributes, or by the difference of their modifications (Prop. iv.). If only by the difference of their attributes, it will be granted that there cannot be more than one with an identical attribute. If by the difference of their modifications—as substance is naturally prior to its modifications (Prop. i.),—it follows that setting the modifications aside, and considering substance in itself, that is truly, (Defs. iii. and vi.), there cannot be conceived one substance different from another,—that is (by Prop. iv.), there cannot be granted several substances, but one substance only. Q.E.D.

PROP. VI. *One substance cannot be produced by another substance.*

Proof.—It is impossible that there should be in the universe two substances with an identical attribute, i.e. which have anything common to them both (Prop. ii.), and, therefore (Prop. iii.), one cannot be the cause of another, neither can one be produced by the other. Q.E.D.

Corollary.—Hence it follows that a substance cannot be produced by anything external to itself. For in the universe nothing is granted, save substances and their modifications (as appears from Ax. i. and Defs. iii. and v.). Now (by the last Prop.) substance cannot be produced by another substance, therefore it cannot be produced by anything external to itself. Q.E.D. This is shown still more readily by the absurdity of the contradictory. For, if substance be produced by an external cause, the knowledge of it would depend on the knowledge of its cause (Ax. iv.), and (by Def. iii.) it would itself not be substance.

PROP. VII. *Existence belongs to the nature of substance.*

Proof.—Substance cannot be produced by anything external (Corollary, Prop. vi.), it must, therefore, be its own cause—that is, its essence necessarily involves existence, or existence belongs to its nature.

Berkeley and Idealism

Descartes, Hobbes, and Spinoza all belonged to the lively seventeenth century, the century that produced not only great philosophy but also some of the most important scientific discoveries of all time. The seventeenth century, you may recall from your history books, was also the century of the Thirty Years' War (1618–1648), which was the most brutal European war before this century, and the English Civil War. It also witnessed the Sun King (Louis XIV of France), the opening of Harvard, the founding of Pennsylvania, and the popularization of smoking.

For an example of idealism, which is the last of the four metaphysical philosophies, idealism, we turn to the early eighteenth century and **George Berkeley** (1685–1753).

The eighteenth century, remember, was the Enlightenment. Despite the American and French revolutions, it was marked by comparative peace and stability, an improved standard of living, and an increase in personal freedom. Fewer witches were prosecuted in this century, and the burning of heretics became rare. Religion continued to decline in importance politically, socially, and intellectually. The growth of money through commerce laid the foundations for the Industrial Revolution. In short, all was well. Handel composed *The Messiah*.

Profile: George Berkeley (1685–1753)

Berkeley was born in Ireland and studied at Trinity College, Dublin. He was made a Fellow of the College in 1707. His *Treatise Concerning the Principles of Human Knowledge* (1709) was a great success and gave Berkeley a lasting reputation, though few accepted his theory that nothing exists outside the mind.

Berkeley eventually became Dean of Derry, a post that included a lucrative stipend. But Berkeley gave up the post in what proved to be a futile attempt to establish a college in the Bermudas to convert the Indians in North America. He was made Bishop of Cloyne in 1734.

Berkeley was known for his generosity of heart and mind, and also for his enthusiasm for tar water. He especially liked the fact that tar water did not have the same effects as alcohol. His writings about the healthy benefits of drinking tar water actually caused it to become a fad in English society for a time.

Berkeley's main works, in addition to the one mentioned above, are *Essay Towards a New Theory of Vision* (1709) and *Three Dialogues Between Hylas and Philonous* (1713).

Berkeley, California, was named after Berkeley because of his line of poetry: "Westward the course of empire takes its way."

It should be very easy to remember Berkeley, whose most important work was done early in the century. Berkeley denied that matter exists. This theory, naturally, convinced many that he was a crackpot. It did not help matters that, in his later years, he came to be rather overly focused on the healthful benefits of tar water. Nevertheless, Berkeley's youthful work contained some very powerful arguments.

Berkeley too (like Descartes) took the epistemological detour to metaphysical issues, and this means that we will have a closer look at Berkeley's philosophy in the next chapter. But we will say enough here to show that Berkeley's denial of matter was not sheer lunacy.

Self-Contradictory to Believe in Matter

First of all, Berkeley fully recognized that, at first glance, nothing "can be more fantastical or more repugnant to Common Sense" than to believe there is no such thing as matter. But he maintained that, if you consider the subject very closely, it is the belief in matter that is fantastical.

What is wrong with the belief in matter? Berkeley's answer is that the very concept of matter is self-contradictory. How so? Let's back up just a bit.

When you experience a sensible object—a table, chair, tree, or any other thing that you perceive by sense—what you experience (said Berkeley) is always a combination of certain qualities. For example, when you pick up and examine a coin, you see a certain color and shape, feel a certain texture, and so forth. These qualities, Berkeley argued, are only ideas, and exist only in your mind.

Why did he say this? Why on earth call the qualities I perceive "ideas" and say they exist *only in the mind?*

Berkeley had a couple of arguments to establish his thesis, but the simplest is that the qualities perceived are always relative to the observer. For instance, from one angle the shape you perceive when you look at the coin will be round, from another it will be elliptical; as you move away from the coin, the size you perceive will grow smaller; and all the other qualities you perceive (color, texture, taste, odor—if you like to taste and smell coins) are also relative to you. Because the coin cannot be both round and elliptical, because it cannot be both large and small, the size and shape you perceive must be ideas in your mind rather than the qualities of something outside your mind; similar reasoning leads to the same conclusion for any of the other qualities.

Of course, our inclination is to distinguish the perceived size from an unperceived size "that is the object's true size." But Berkeley argued that size, shape, color, and so on are *perceived* qualities. Talking about an unperceived size is nonsense. It's like talking about unfelt pain. And thus sensible objects, because they are nothing more than their qualities, are themselves only ideas and exist only in the mind.

But isn't there really matter "out there"? Aren't there really material bodies that have their own size, shape, texture, and the like? Berkeley's answer is that it is contradictory to suppose that size, shape, texture, and so on could exist in unthinking stuff, for size, shape, texture, and so on are ideas, and it is contradictory to suppose that ideas could exist in unthinking stuff. If, therefore, the concept of matter is the concept of unthinking stuff that nevertheless can have size, shape, texture, and so on, then the concept of matter is contradictory.

Simplified to its basics, this line of reasoning involves just two steps. First, Berkeley used the "relative to the observer" argument to show that size, shape, color, and all other qualities, just like pain and sweetness, exist only in the mind. Then he argued that sensible objects are nothing more than these various qualities. This line of reasoning enabled him to conclude that sensible objects exist only in the mind.

Refutations

Berkeley does not mean, however, that the physical world is a mere dream, or that it is imaginary or intangible or ephemeral. Dr. Samuel Johnson believed that he had refuted Berkeley by kicking a stone, evidently thinking that the solidity of the stone was solid disproof of Berkeley. In fact, Johnson succeeded only in hurting his foot and demonstrating that he

Berkeley and Atheism

In Berkeley's opinion, the great virtue of his idealist system was that it alone did not invite skepticism about God.

Dualism, he thought, by postulating the existence of objects outside the mind, made these objects unknowable and was just an open invitation to skepticism about their existence. And skepticism about the existence of sensible objects, he thought, would inevitably extend itself to skepticism about their creator, God.

Materialism, he believed, made sensible objects independent of God and thus it, too, led to skepticism about God.

He thought that his own system, by contrast, made the existence of sensible objects undeniable (they are as undeniably real as are your own ideas). This meant for Berkeley that the existence of the divine mind, in which sensible objects are sustained, was equally undeniable.

did not understand Berkeley. A stone is just as hard an object in Berkeley's philosophy as it is to common sense, for the fact that a stone exists only in the mind does not make its hardness disappear.

As for the stones found in dreams, Berkeley distinguished unreal dream stones from real stones just the way you and we do. Stones found in dreams behave in an irregular and chaotic manner—they can float around or change into birds or whatever—compared with those found in waking life. And stones that we conjure up in our imagination Berkeley distinguishes from real stones by their lack of vividness and also by the fact that they, unlike real stones, can be brought into existence by an act of our will.

Thus, according to Berkeley, sensible objects exist, but these are not material objects. Because sensible objects are just ideas, only ideas and the minds that have them exist. The most important of these other minds, Berkeley went on to say, is God. God, according to Berkeley, is the source of the sensible objects that make up the world around us. The objects, and the world itself, are thus ideas in the mind of God.

Selection 3.4 is from Berkeley's *Three Dialogues Between Hylas and Philonous* (1713). Philonous, who represents Berkeley, has just convinced Hylas ("Mr. Matter") that pain and pleasure, heat and cold, and tastes and odors do not exist outside the mind. Now he argues that sounds also have no being except in the mind. Eventually Philonous maintains that *none* of the qualities attributed to bodies can exist outside the mind, though we don't have the space here to reproduce the entire dialogue.

With Berkeley, Hobbes, Descartes, and Spinoza the four basic metaphysical positions of modern philosophy were set out, and these four positions do seem to exhaust the possibilities. Either reality is entirely physical (Hobbes), or it is entirely nonphysical or "mental" (Berkeley), or it is an even split (Descartes), or "matter" and "mind" are just alternative ways of looking at one and the same stuff (Spinoza). You may take your choice.

Obviously Descartes's view won out in common sense, though among twentieth-century professional philosophers in the English-speaking world materialism in various forms has had more adherents. Interestingly enough, however, it was idealism—which from a common-sense point of view is the most bizarre of the four possibilities—that was advocated by the most important philosophers of the nineteenth century. But the nineteenth-century version of idealism was rather different from Berkeley's idealism, as we will now see.

▶ S E L E C T I O N 3.4

From George Berkeley, "FIRST DIALOGUE BETWEEN HYLAS AND PHILONOUS"

Sounds

PHIL. Then as to *sounds*, what must we think of them: are they accidents really inherent in external bodies, or not?

HYL. That they inhere not in the sonorous bodies is plain from hence: because a bell struck in the exhausted receiver of an air-pump sends forth no sound. The air, therefore, must be thought the subject of sound.

PHIL. What reason is there for that, Hylas?

HYL. Because, when any motion is raised in the air, we perceive a sound greater or lesser, according to the air's motion; but without some motion in the air, we never hear any sound at all.

PHIL. And granting that we never hear a sound but when some motion is produced in the air, yet I do not see how you can infer from thence, that the sound itself is in the air.

HYL. It is this very motion in the external air that produces in the mind the sensation of *sound*. For, striking on the drum of the ear, it causeth a vibration, which by the auditory nerves being communicated to the brain, the soul is thereupon affected with the sensation called *sound*.

PHIL. What! is sound then a sensation?

HYL. I tell you, as perceived by us, it is a particular sensation in the mind.

PHIL. And can any sensation exist without the mind?

HYL. No, certainly.

PHIL. How then can sound, being a sensation, exist in the air, if by the *air* you mean a senseless substance existing without the mind?

HYL. You must distinguish, Philonous, between sound as it is perceived by us, and as it is in itself; or (which is the same thing) between the sound we immediately perceive, and that which exists without us.

The former, indeed, is a particular kind of sensation, but the latter is merely a vibrative or undulatory motion in the air.

PHIL. I thought I had already obviated that distinction, by the answer I gave when you were applying it in a like case before. But, to say no more of that, are you sure then that sound is really nothing but motion?

HYL. I am.

PHIL. Whatever therefore agrees to real sound, may with truth be attributed to motion?

HYL. It may.

PHIL. It is then good sense to speak of *motion* as of a thing that is *loud, sweet, acute, or grave.*

HYL. I see you are resolved not to understand me. Is it not evident those accidents or modes belong only to sensible sound, or *sound* in the common acceptation of the word, but not to *sound* in the real and philosophic sense; which, as I just now told you, is nothing but a certain motion of the air?

PHIL. It seems then there are two sorts of sound—the one vulgar, or that which is heard, the other philosophical and real?

HYL. Even so.

PHIL. And the latter consists in motion?

HYL. I told you so before.

PHIL. Tell me, Hylas, to which of the senses, think you, the idea of motion belongs? to the hearing?

HYL. No, certainly; but to the sight and touch.

PHIL. It should follow then, that, according to you, real sounds may possibly be *seen* or *felt*, but never *heard*.

HYL. Look you, Philonous, you may, if you please, make a jest of my opinion, but that will not alter the truth of things. I own, indeed, the inferences you draw me into sound something oddly; but common language, you know, is framed by, and for the use of the vulgar: we must not therefore wonder if expressions adapted to exact philosophic notions seem uncouth and out of the way.

PHIL. Is it come to that? I assure you, I imagine myself to have gained no small point, since you make so light of departing from common phrases and opinions; it being a main part of our inquiry, to examine whose notions are widest of the common road, and most repugnant to the general sense of the world. But, can you think it no more than a philosophical paradox, to say that *real sounds are never heard*, and that the idea of them is obtained by some other sense? And is there nothing in this contrary to nature and the truth of things?

HYL. To deal ingenuously, I do not like it. And, after the concessions already made, I had as well grant that sounds too have no real being without the mind.

Absolute Idealism After Berkeley, the two most important philosophers of the eighteenth century were **David Hume** (1711–1776), and **Immanuel Kant** (1724–1804). We have much to say about Hume and Kant in Part 2 because both spent more time on questions of epistemology. Still, it is important to note the following here.

Hume and Kant were both very dubious about allowing even the possibility of metaphysical knowledge. Hume, on one hand, believed that all our knowledge is limited to what we experience, namely, sensory impressions. (Although he wasn't willing to go with Berkeley and say that sensible objects just are clusters of sensory impressions.)

Kant, on the other hand, was slightly more generous about what we can know. We do have knowledge of objects that exist outside the mind, Kant said, but our knowledge is of these objects only *insofar* as they are *experienceable*. About external objects *as they are in themselves* we can have no knowledge, he said.

To be more specific, according to Kant human reason can discover categories and principles that apply *absolutely and without exception* to experienceable objects. These categories and principles apply absolutely and without exception to experienceable objects because, according to Kant, the mind arranges or orders raw sensation in accordance with them. It is only by being so arranged, he said, that *raw sensation* can qualify as *experience*. If the data of raw sensation were not so organized, it would be mere stimulation and not experience.

In short, according to Kant, the mind *imposes* a certain form and order on experienceable objects. For example, the mind imposes spatio-

Ding-an-sich

Kant drew a distinction between **phenomena,** things as they are as experienced, and **noumena,** things as they are apart from and independent of our experience of them, things as they are "in themselves." **Das Ding-an-sich** is German for "the thing as it is in itself."

Kant maintained that our minds process the raw data of sensation according to certain principles and categories (and philosophers should make it their business to understand and analyze these principles and categories, he thought). For example, according to Kant our minds process the data

of sensation in such a way that we perceive a world of *objects* that are related to one another *spatio-temporally* and by *cause* and *effect*. But how the world is in itself—that is, independently of the principles and categories that our minds impose on it as we experience it—is something we cannot know. We cannot know anything about noumena, about *das Ding-an-sich.*

The Absolute Idealists had no truck with the notion that we can have no knowledge of "the thing in itself." What could there possibly be that the mind could not know as it really is, Hegel asked.

temporal relations on the things we experience. But it is beyond our capacities, he said, to know anything about **things-in-themselves,** things as they are apart from and independent of experience; and whenever we attempt to apply the concepts that pertain to experienceable objects to things-in-themselves, paradoxes and errors result.

Now the German idealists, the most important philosophers of the first part of the nineteenth century, among whom **Georg Wilhelm Friedrich Hegel** (1770–1831) was the most prominent, vastly extended Kant's theory that the mind imposes concepts upon experienceable objects and took it to its ultimate conclusion. The mind, or thought, or reason, they said (and they equated these three things), does not merely impose categories on things. No. The categories of thought, they said, *are* the categories of being. All reality—**the Absolute**—they held, is the unfolding or expression of thought or reason. Thus, in one fell swoop they removed the troublesome problem of unknowable things-in-themselves. If it is

Profile: Georg Hegel (1770–1831)

There was a sort of incredible solemnness about Hegel that earned him the nickname "the old man" even while he was still a university student at Tübingen, Germany. He was serious about everything he did and was even somber when he drank. In high school he devoted his time to collecting copious notes concerning what he thought were the ultimate questions of life, a sure sign that he would wind up as a philosopher.

Hegel's fellow university student, Friedrich Schelling, gained a fabulous reputation in philosophy early in life. But for Hegel it was a struggle. After having served as a private tutor, newspaper editor, and as a director of a high school, he was given a professorship at Heidelberg and then at Berlin, where, finally, he became famous. His lectures, despite his tendency to stop and start and break off in mid-sentence to page furiously through his notes, drew large audiences, for his listeners could sense that something deep and important was happening. Hegel was quite handsome and became popular with the society women of Berlin. All this satisfied him enormously.

Not everyone admired Hegel, however. Schopenhauer, another famous philosopher we will mention in a bit, described Hegel as an unimaginative, unintelligent, disgusting, revolting charlatan who ruined the entire generation of intellectuals who followed him. You should bear in mind, though, that poor Schopenhauer attempted to schedule his lectures at Berlin at the same hour as Hegel and found himself lecturing to an empty hall.

Hegel's main works are *Phenomenology of Mind* (1807), in which he first presented his metaphysical system, *Science of Logic* (1812–1816), *Encyclopedia of the Philosophical Sciences* (1817), and *Philosophy of Right* (1821).

Some Main Themes of Hegel

1. Hegel wrote: "Everything depends on grasping the truth not merely as Substance but as Subject as well." This means that what is true, what is real, is not merely that which is thought *of*, but that which *thinks*. Thus what is most real—the Absolute—is thought thinking of itself.

2. Hegel's idealism is different from Berkeley's. For Berkeley, the objective world in fact exists in the minds of individuals. For Hegel, the objective world is an unfolding or expression of infinite thought, and the individual mind is the vehicle of infinite thought reflecting on itself.

3. Reality, the Absolute, for Hegel, is not a group of independent particulars or states of affairs but rather, like a coherent thought system such as mathematics, it is an integrated whole in which each proposition (each state of affairs) is logically connected with all the rest. Thus an *isolated* state of affairs is not wholly real; likewise, a proposition about this or that aspect or feature of reality is only partially true. The only thing that is totally true (or totally real, because these amount to the same thing) is the complete system.

4. According to Hegel, the Absolute, the sum total of reality, is a system of conceptual triads. To formalize Hegel's system somewhat artificially, for proposition or concept A there is a negation, *not-A*, and within the two there is a synthetic unity, or synthesis, B. B, however, has a negation, *not-B*, and within B and *not-B* there is a synthesis, C. And so on. Thus, the higher levels of the system are implicit in the lower levels—for example, C and B are both implicit in A. In this way the entire system of thought and reality that is the Absolute is an integrated whole in which each proposition is logically interconnected with the rest.

Note that for Hegel this triadic structure is not a *method* by means of which we discover truth but is instead the way things are: it is the actual structure of thought. Thus, for example, the most basic or fundamental category or concept is *being*. But being is nothing without *not-being*, which is its opposite. And the synthesis of these opposites is *becoming*; hence the Absolute is becoming. In similar fashion, at each stage of his exposition Hegel posits a *thesis*, to which there belongs an *antithesis*, and the thesis and antithesis are a unity in a higher *synthesis*. The higher levels of the system are always implicit in the lower levels.

Ultimately, therefore, we come to the apex, or

unknowable, they reasoned, then it is unthinkable, and if it is unthinkable, why, it just plain *isn't*.

Reality is not, however, the expression of *your* thought or ours or any other particular person's, they said, for neither you nor we nor any other person created the world of independent external things that exist around us. Rather, reality is the expression of *infinite* or *absolute* thought or reason. And when you and we think or philosophize about reality, this is the rational process becoming aware of itself, that is, becoming infinite.

So, from the perspective of Hegel, the cosmos and its history are the concrete expression of thought, and thus everything that happens and every field of human inquiry are the proper domain of the philosopher, who alone can understand and interpret the true relationship of each aspect of reality to the Whole. **Absolute Idealism,** as this philosophy is called, attempted to achieve a complete and unified conception of all reality, a conception that gave meaning to each and every aspect in rela-

highest triad, of Hegel's system: the synthesis of "Idea" and "Nature" in "Spirit." And Idea and Nature are each, in turn, the synthesis of two lower opposing concepts. Thus, Idea is the synthesis of subjectivity (that which thinks) and objectivity (that which is thought of). What Hegel means by "Idea" is self-conscious thought, which is exactly what you would expect to be the synthesis of that which thinks and that which is thought of. "The absolute Idea," Hegel wrote, "alone is being, eternal life, self-knowing truth, and it is all truth."

The antithesis of Idea is Nature. In other words, on one hand there is self-knowing or self-conscious thought ("Idea"), and on the other there is what we might call the independent world (Nature), the external expression of Idea, or Idea outside itself. (It is in his philosophy of Nature that Hegel attempted to integrate the various concepts of science into his system.)

Nature and Idea, as thesis and antithesis, have their own synthesis. This is the synthesis of the main triad of Hegel's entire system, and is what Hegel called "Spirit." We might translate "Spirit" as "thought knowing itself both as thought and as object" or as "the Idea returning into itself." We didn't say Hegel is easy.

The philosophy of Spirit also has three main subdivisions: subjective spirit and its antithesis objective spirit, with the synthesis as Absolute Spirit. Subjective spirit is the realm of the human mind; objective spirit is the mind in its external manifestation in social institutions. Hegel's analysis of objective spirit contains his social and political philosophy, in which Hegel attempts to display the relationships (always more or less triadic) among such various concepts as property, contract, crime, punishment, right, personality, family, society, and the state.

In the end, therefore, we come to know the part played by every aspect of reality in the whole, and we are led to understand that the highest conception of the Absolute is as Spirit.

So Hegel's system is really a grandiose vision of the history of the universe and the history of human consciousness as a necessary unfolding of infinite reason. It purports to be a complete conceptual framework for each aspect of reality and for every component of human thought and history. This system represents the towering summit of metaphysical speculation.

---

tionship to the sum total. It was the towering pinnacle of metaphysical speculation, and virtually everything that happened subsequently in metaphysics happened in reaction to it, as we are about to see. In a nearby box we explain the main themes of Hegel's philosophy.

The following brief selection will give you the flavor of Absolute Idealism.

▶ S E L E C T I O N 3.5

From Georg Hegel, THE PHILOSOPHY OF HISTORY

The only Thought which Philosophy brings with it to the contemplation of History, is the simple conception of *Reason*; that Reason is the Sovereign of the World; that the history of the world, therefore, presents us with a rational process. This conviction and intuition is a hypothesis in the domain of history as such. In that of Philosophy it is no hypothesis. It is there provided by speculative cognition, that Reason—and this term may here suffice us, without investigation the relation sustained by the Universe to the Divine Being—is *Substance*, as well as *Infinite Power;* its own *Infinite Material* underlying all the natural and spiritual life which it originates, as also the *Infinite Form*— that which sets this Material in motion. On the one hand, Reason is the *substance* of the Universe; viz., that by which and in which all reality has its being and subsistence. On the other hand, it is the *Infinite Energy* of the Universe; since Reason is not so powerless as to be incapable of producing anything but a mere ideal, a mere intention— having its place outside reality, nobody knows where; something separate and abstract, in the heads of certain human beings. It is *the Infinite complex of things,* their entire Essence and Truth. It is its own material which it commits to its own Active Energy to work up; not needing, as finite action does, the conditions of an external material of given means from which it may obtain its support, and the objects of its activity. It supplies its own nourishment, and is the object of its own operations. While it is exclusively its own basis of existence, and absolute final aim, it is also the energizing power realizing this aim; developing it not only the phenomena of the Natural, but also of the Spiritual Universe—the History of the World. That this "Idea" or "Reason" is the *True,* the *Eternal,* the absolutely *powerful* essence; that it reveals itself in the World, and that in that World nothing else is revealed but this and its honor and glory—is the thesis which, as we have said, has been proved in Philosophy, and is here regarded as demonstrated.

Checklist

To help you review, here is a checklist of the key philosophers and concepts of this chapter. The brief descriptive sentences that appear with each philosopher summarize one of his leading ideas. Keep in mind that some of these summary statements represent terrific oversimplifications of complex positions.

Philosophers

- **René Descartes** "Father" of modern philosophy. Dualist; said there are two separate and distinct substances: material substance and mind.
- **Thomas Hobbes** The first great modern materialist: held that all that exists is bodies in motion.
- **Benedictus de Spinoza** Neutralist. Maintained that thought and extension are attributes of a single substance.
- **George Berkeley** Idealist. Denied the existence of material substance.
- **David Hume** Held there is no metaphysical knowledge; maintained that knowledge is limited to what we experience.

- **Immanuel Kant** Believed that the mind imposes a certain form and order on experienceable objects. Held that there can be no knowledge of things "as they are in themselves," independent of experience.

- **Georg Hegel** Premier exponent of Absolute Idealism. Rejected concept of the "thing-in-itself." Held that all reality is the expression of thought or reason.

Concepts

dualism

materialism

idealism

neutralism

epistemological detour

extension as the essential attribute of material substance

thought as the essential attribute of mind

problems of dualism

problems of materialism

parallelism

Absolute Idealism

phenomenon

noumenon

Ding-an-sich

Questions for Discussion and Review

1. "Material things, including one's own body, are completely subject to physical laws." "The immaterial mind can move one's body." Are these two claims incompatible? Explain.

2. "Modern science undermines metaphysical dualism." Explain this remark.

3. What is parallelism?

4. Explain how all mental activity reduces to matter in motion, according to Hobbes.

5. "The things that really are in the world outside us are those motions by which these seemings [i.e., objects and their qualities] are caused." Explain and critically evaluate this assertion by Hobbes.

6. What is the relationship of the mind to the body, according to Spinoza?

7. Explain Berkeley's reasons for saying that sensible objects exist only in the mind.

8. Are the qualities of sensible objects (e.g., size, color, taste) all equally "relative to the observer"?

9. Does Berkeley's philosophy make everything into a dream?

10. "Everything depends on grasping the truth not merely as Substance but as Subject as well." Who said this and what does it mean?

11. Define or explain dualism, materialism, idealism, and neutralism.

12. "We can think. This proves we are not just mere matter." Does it?

13. Is your brain your mind? Explain.

14. Do you see any difficulties with supposing that a nonmaterial mind could make things happen in a brain?

15. Psychokinesis is the mental power by which psychics claim to make changes in the external physical world—to bend spoons, to cause balls to roll, and so on. Is there any difference between using your mind to bend a spoon and using your mind to bend your arm? Explain.

Suggested Further Readings

George Berkeley, *Principles of Human Knowledge/Three Dialogues*, Roger Woolhouse, ed. (New York: Penguin Books, 1988). These are Berkeley's main works. He is so much fun, once you get used to the initial strangeness of his position, that we think it would be a mistake to limit yourself to mere excerpts or "selections."

E. O. Burtt, *The English Philosophers from Bacon to Mill* (New York: Modern Library, 1939). A general book on modern philosophy.

René Descartes, *Philosophical Works*, in two volumes. E. S. Haldane and G. R. T. Ross, trans. (Cambridge: The University Press, 1968). This is what you need to read Descartes.

C. J. Ducasse, *A Critical Examination of the Belief in Life After Death* (Springfield: Charles C Thomas, 1974). The first part of the book contains an excellent elementary discussion of the various theories of mind.

G. W. F. Hegel, *The Phenomenology of Mind* (New York: Harper & Row, 1967). Hegel's first major work and a brilliant reinterpretation of Western philosophy through the eyes of an Absolute Idealist. Not easy reading, though.

W. T. Jones, *Kant and the Nineteenth Century*, 2nd ed. (New York: Harcourt Brace Jovanovich, 1975). Jones's section on Hegel contains enough original material for the introductory student and explains it all very nicely, too.

Immanuel Kant, *Prolegomena to Any Future Metaphysics*, P. Carus, trans. (Indianapolis: Hackett, 1977). This is Kant's own (relatively) simplified introduction to his thinking about metaphysics and epistemology. After you read what we have to say about Kant in Part 2, you should be able to go directly to this work.

J. Loewenberg, ed., *Hegel Selections* (New York: Scribners, 1929). Hegel is very, very difficult.

J. Wild, ed., *Spinoza Selections* (New York: Scribners, 1930). This contains enough original material for the introductory student.

F. J. E. Woodbridge, ed., *Hobbes Selections* (New York: Scribners, 1930). Here, too, we think that selected original material will be sufficient for the introductory student.

The Rejection of Absolute Idealism

The question is: Why is there any being at all and not rather Nothing?

—MARTIN HEIDEGGER

Absolute Idealism left distinct marks on many facets of Western culture. True, science was indifferent to it, and common sense was more or less stupefied by it. Still, the greatest political movement of the nineteenth and twentieth centuries, Marxism, was to a significant degree an out-growth of Absolute Idealism (Bertrand Russell remarked some place that Marx was nothing more than Hegel mixed with British economic theory); and nineteenth- and twentieth-century literature, theology, and even art also fell under its spell. The great Romantic composers of the nineteenth century, for example, with their fondness for expanded form, vast or-chestras, complex scores, and soaring melodies, searched for the all-encompassing musical statement and in doing so mirrored the efforts of the metaphysicians, whose vast and imposing systems were sources of inspiration to many artists and composers.

As we have said, a great deal of what happened in philosophy after Hegel happened either in continuation of his work or in reaction to it, mostly the latter. On the continent of Europe, the assault on idealism was begun by the nihilistic attacks of Schopenhauer and Nietzsche and by the religious anti-idealism of Søren Kierkegaard. (**Nihilism** is the rejec-tion of traditional values and beliefs.) Anti-Hegelianism reached its sum-mit in the twentieth century in the philosophy known as *existentialism*, according to which life is not only not perfectly rational, it is fundamen-tally irrational and absurd. Though we devote an entire chapter to post-Hegelian philosophy on the European continent, including existentialist philosophy, we will say something briefly about it here.

In England Hegel was ignored at first, but then, in the later part of the nineteenth century, neo-Hegelianism became the dominant philosophical school even in that country. But around the turn of the century there arose a great opposition to Hegelian-type idealism, and this reaction was the point of departure in the early twentieth-century for what is known as *analytic philosophy*. Analytic philosophy, too, will receive its own chapter.

The Reaction on the Continent

On the continent of Europe the reaction to Hegel began with Schopenhauer, Nietzsche, and Kierkegaard.

Hegel, remember, rejected Kant's concept of the thing-in-itself; the concept of reality apart from thought and experience. What is, is knowable, Hegel said; and he regarded this proposition as expressing an identity between existence and thought.

Arthur Schopenhauer (1788–1860), the great pessimist of philosophy, thought Hegel mistaken in abandoning the thing-in-itself. But unlike Kant, Schopenhauer interpreted the thing-in-itself as a blind and purposeless impelling force that is manifested in humans as a *will to live*. It is this drive, this will, that determines human behavior, not reason. Thus the human being is not fundamentally rational but willful.

The conflict between individual wills is the cause of endless strife and suffering, Schopenhauer believed. The world is torment, and people are driven in endless pursuit of unattainable goals, or goals that, if attained, bring only temporary satisfaction. Through sex and "love" we succeed only in introducing more people to this grim rock, and it is for this reason we think of sex as shameful, he said.

Schopenhauer's pessimistic portrayal of humans tossed about by will in an irrational world is a sharp rejection of the metaphysics of Hegel, according to which actuality equates with rationality.

Friedrich Nietzsche (1844–1900), of whom everyone has heard because of his proclamation that God is dead, carried this abandonment of Hegelian metaphysics even further. Nietzsche is famous for his biting denunciation of Western civilization and its values, which he found perverse and decadent; and especially for his excoriation of Christian "slave morality," which he viewed as a morality of unhappiness and unfulfillment. The underlying source of this cultural degeneracy, according to Nietzsche, is nothing less than metaphysics, which he perceived to be a spurning of this world for a supposedly higher and unchanging world of pure spirit. Metaphysics, for Nietzsche, is stupid and hopeless, an abandonment of the changing here and now for pursuit of a nonexistent fixed world of being.

Metaphysics rests, Nietzsche thought, on an unfounded belief in the principle of identity, according to which (loosely speaking) a single thing is the same as itself. Neitzsche held the contrary view, that everything is

Profile: Arthur Schopenhauer (1788–1860)

The adult Schopenhauer had few friends, was never married, had a low opinion of women, found his mother intolerable, despised most other philosophers of his time, and was, in general, a grump.

Schopenhauer's father died when Schopenhauer was a young man and left him a modest inheritance that he acquired after he came of age. His mother, who was a literary person and succeeded in becoming a novelist of minor note, did not particularly care for Schopenhauer and was inclined to be critical of her son's literary efforts. When he told her that his dissertation, "The Fourfold Root on the Sentence Concerning Sufficient Reason" was to be published, she told him that the title sounded like a druggist's prescription and predicted that the printed copies of the work would never be sold. Schopenhauer retorted that his works would be read long after hers gathered dust in forgotten corners. Both predictions were correct.

Schopenhauer's relationship with his mother deteriorated even further over the years and no doubt explains his very low regard for women and, perhaps, his own pessimistic nature. He regarded life as an ongoing deception, generally full of misery and wretchedness, a place where survival is a merciless struggle that leaves humans without virtue or honor or decency or merit. His only companions were his poodle, his cigars, and a loaded revolver, for Schopenhauer was not disposed to love or trust his fellow creatures.

Despite being almost totally ignored by the academic professors of philosophy, whom he loathed, Schopenhauer had not the least doubt that he was the "emperor of philosophy" of his time. Fortunately, later in his life he did receive some recognition, though this he thought only his due.

Schopenhauer's principal work was *The World as Will and Idea* (1818).

---

constantly changing; therefore it isn't really valid to talk about "things" in the first place. The concept of thingness itself, according to Nietzsche, presupposes a something that remains permanent and enduring while its properties change; but this presupposition, he believed, is quite invalid. Concepts of unchanging entities, like subject, object, and ego, are utterly arbitrary creations of human thought that have no foundation in reality.

According to Nietzsche, out of the unceasing change and apparent chaos that is this world, the "overman," whose "will-to-power" distinguishes him from the inferior masses, creates a new morality beyond conventional standards of good and evil. Only by fully embracing the will-to-power may a human being become truly alive, Nietzsche held. The warrior carves out his own values with the sword.

This attack on idealist metaphysics reached something of an apex during the almost rabid anti-Hegelianism of the Danish religious philosopher **Søren Kierkegaard** (1813–1855). Kierkegaard despised what seemed to him to be Hegel's overly optimistic, rational system of absolute truth. He thought that such idealism papered over the irrational nature of human life and merely masked the anxiety and despair that are life's "sickness unto death." Kierkegaard's own melancholy life, too, he described as full of dread and foreboding and as a search for a handhold in the night.

Kierkegaard, however, found nothing in the finite world that could give him peace of mind and came to believe that the only adequate escape lies in committing oneself to God. Reason, Kierkegaard held, cannot justify the belief in God, especially given the paradox that God's creation is an irrational world. Therefore he believed that we are called on to go against and beyond reason by a leap of faith. Only through a passionate commitment of ourselves to God and to the infinite can we achieve peace and freedom from dread, self-loathing, and despair.

In calling for this leap of faith into the abyss beyond reason Kierkegaard reinforced the belief in the primacy of will as established by Schopenhauer and reiterated by Nietzsche.

In viewing the world as a fundamentally absurd place, Kierkegaard, Nietzsche, and Schopenhauer foreshadowed the coming of the existentialist movement of the twentieth century. It remained for future existentialist thinkers to examine more closely the irrationality that, they believed, is to be found at the core of existence. This is a story for a later chapter.

The Reaction in England

In England, too, by around the turn of the century, idealist metaphysical systems were being rejected, but in an entirely different way and for entirely different reasons.

From the point of view of mainstream English philosophy, whose point of departure was also a rejection of idealist metaphysics, the thoughts of a Kierkegaard or Nietzsche are more nearly the ravings of a neurotic needing clinical help than the products of reasoned philosophical inquiry. But then the metaphysical alternatives proposed by English philosophers would have impressed Kierkegaard, Schopenhauer, and Nietzsche as even more sterile than Hegel's system.

At the center of the English reaction to idealism was **Bertrand Russell** (1872–1970), the most celebrated British philosopher of this century, and the preeminent practitioner of the method of philosophical analysis, about which more later.

Russell was a mathematician and turned to philosophy to find some reason to believe in the truth of mathematics, or so he said. Though early in his adult life Russell was himself a sort of idealist in the British neo-Hegelian tradition, when he read Hegel for himself he found reason to reject idealism completely. In the first place, he perceived that what Hegel said about mathematics was "muddle-headed nonsense." And in the second place, he came to believe that metaphysical idealism rested on an outdated and indefensible logic.

To consider the second point, idealism, according to Russell, rested

Profile: Bertrand Russell (1872–1970)

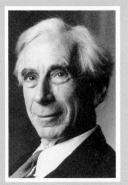

Bertrand Russell came from a distinguished background. His grandfather, Lord John Russell, was twice prime minister, his godfather was John Stuart Mill, of whom much mention is made in later chapters, and his parents were prominent freethinkers. Because his parents died when he was young, Russell was brought up in the household of Lord Russell. This side of the family was austerely Protestant, and Russell's childhood was solitary and lonely. As a teenager he had the intuition that God did not exist and found this to be a great relief.

In the fall of 1890, Russell went to Cambridge to study mathematics and philosophy at a time when several other brilliant philosophers were present. Many of Russell's important works in philosophy and mathematics were written during his association with Cambridge, first as a student then as a fellow and lecturer. His association with Cambridge ended in 1916 when he was dismissed for pacifist activities during World War I. He was restored as a fellow at Cambridge, however, in 1944.

Russell was dismayed by the enthusiasm among ordinary people for the war, and his own pacifism created much resentment. After he was dismissed from Cambridge, he was imprisoned for six months for his pacifism; thereafter, he held no academic position again until he began to teach in the United States in 1938.

Russell thought that without a proper education a person is caught in the prison of prejudices that make up common sense, and he wanted to create a kind of education that would be not only philosophically sound but also non-threatening, enjoyable, and stimulating. To this end he and his wife Dora founded the Beacon Hill School in 1927, which was influential in the founding of similar schools in England and America.

In addition to writing books on education during the period between the wars, Russell wrote extensively on social and political philosophy. His most infamous popular work, *Marriage and Morals* (1929), was very liberal in its attitude toward sexual practices and caused the cancelation of his appointment to City College of New York in 1940. He was taken to court by the mother of a CCNY student, and the court revoked Russell's appointment "for the sake of public health, safety, and morals." Apparently the most damaging part of the evidence against Russell was his recommendation in the book that a child caught masturbating should not be physically punished.

World War II and the Nazi onslaught caused Russell to abandon his pacifism. In 1961, however, he was again imprisoned, this time for activity in demonstrations against nuclear weapons, and in 1967 he organized the so-called "war crimes tribunal" directed against American activities in Vietnam.

Russell received the Nobel Prize for Literature in 1950, one of many honors bestowed on him. In his autobiography he said that three passions had governed his life: the longing for love, the search for knowledge, and unbearable pity for the suffering of mankind. Throughout his life Russèll exhibited intellectual brilliance and extraordinary personal courage.

on a false notion that was unconsciously assumed by the idealist meta-physicians, namely, that "relations are internal." Whether relations are internal or, as Russell thought, "external" is a technical issue of some importance in analytic metaphysics, but the basic idea is pretty easy to understand.

Here is Kenneth, and there is Brooke, and Kenneth is older than Brooke. In other words, Kenneth stands in an "older than" relationship to Brooke. To believe that relations are internal is to believe that a thing's relations to other things are a part of the essence or nature of the related things. It is to believe, for example, that the property of being older than Brooke belongs to the nature of Kenneth (and to the nature of Brooke). That's the view that relations are "internal."

Because each thing is related in some way or another to every other thing, this apparently innocent doctrine that relations are internal has as its consequence that each thing contains as part of its nature every other thing and thus that there exists in fact only one thing, the all-encompassing Whole.

Further, because to *think* of a thing is to be related to it, it follows that the all-encompassing whole is contained within thought. So you can see that, if you believe that relations are internal, you end up in idealism.

This doctrine of **internal relations,** in Russell's opinion, was uncon-sciously held by the idealists and was what generated their metaphysics. But—*why* did they unconsciously assume that relations are internal, if it is true they did? In Russell's opinion, the idealists assumed that rela-tions are internal because they were the unwitting victims of the anti-quated and inadequate system of *logic* under which they operated.

In this outdated logic, every proposition was thought to be of the subject-predicate form. That is, every proposition was thought to attribute a characteristic (*predicate*) to a thing that has it. Thus, from this anti-quated point of view, the proposition "Ken is older than Brooke" has as its subject "Ken" and attributes to Ken the characteristic or predicate of being older than Brooke. Russell came to think that, if you hold that every proposition is of the subject-predicate form, then you are logically obliged to say that mathematics is impossible. Russell's reasoning is far too tech-nical to go into here, but the upshot was that, because mathematics clearly is not impossible, the "old" logic, and the idealist metaphysics that fol-lows from it, must be in error.

Russell's discovery that the fundamental logical principles you accept commit you to a certain brand of metaphysics was an event of major importance in his life, and in philosophy.

In Selection 4.1 later, Russell explains some of the confusion that, in his view, underlies Hegel's philosophy.

Logical Atomism and Logical Positivism

Russell's metaphysics evolved considerably over the years, but for a major part of his life he subscribed to what is known as **logical atomism.** The world, he believed, is not an all-encompassing Oneness, as Hegelians would have it, but a collection of *atomic facts*.

To say that the world consists ultimately of *facts* is to say that it does not consist just simply of *things*, but of things that have properties and stand in various relations to one another. Your study area, for example, does not just consist of a chair and a desk and a lamp, for these things must stand in a certain relationship to one another if they are to comprise your study area. These things *in their relationship to each other* do not make up just another thing; their being in this relationship is not a thing but a *fact*. Even your desk is not just a *thing*; it is a thing with properties, and that it has the properties it has is a fact. Likewise the world, the universe, reality, does not consist just simply of things, but more precisely of facts.

And the basic or most fundamental facts, Russell believed, are *atomic*. To say that they are *atomic* is not to relate them to nuclear physics or the scientific atomic theory, but rather to indicate two things: (1) The basic facts are absolutely *simple*: they can be components of more complicated or "molecular" facts, but they are not themselves resolvable into more basic components. (2) Each basic fact is logically independent of every other: any given basic fact could remain exactly the same even if all the other facts were different. For example, even if the world were entirely different, the fact that the top of your desk is rectangular could remain unchanged, assuming that that fact is a basic fact.

Russell believed that metaphysical truth is dictated simply by the fact that we can form propositions about the world, some more complex than others. Complex propositions, he thought, must in principle be resolvable into simpler propositions. As an example, the proposition, "America elected a Republican to be its president," is resolvable, in principle, into propositions about individual people and their actions, most especially the action of voting. But when people vote, they are really just doing certain things with their bodies, and so a proposition about a person voting is resolvable, in principle, into propositions about these doings— about going into an enclosed booth, picking up a pencil, marking a piece of paper, depositing the paper in an envelope, etc., etc. Even a proposition such as, "John Smith picked up a yellow pencil," is theoretically resolvable into propositions about John Smith's bodily motions and a piece of wood that has certain properties; and indeed we are still quite far from reaching the end of this theoretical process of resolving complex propositions into more elementary propositions.

Because complex propositions, Russell thought, must in principle be resolvable into simpler propositions (performing this resolution is what Russell meant by "analysis"), there must therefore be fundamental and absolutely uncomplex (i.e., simple) propositions that cannot be resolved further. Corresponding to these absolutely simple "atomic" propositions are the fundamental or atomic facts. Because any atomic fact may hold regardless of what is true about the rest of the world, including what we think about it, Hegel was mistaken (Russell said) in believing that the only thing that is true is the Totality. Individual atomic propo-

Tractatus Logico-Philosophicus

In a later chapter, too, we shall discuss Russell's student, **Ludwig Wittgenstein** (1889–1951), who in many ways was as important as Russell himself. In his great metaphysical treatise, *Tractatus Logico-Philosophicus*, Wittgenstein also attempted to determine what the basic metaphysical structure of the world must be, given that language, as well as thought about the world, exists. His final conclusion, however, pointed up a possibly serious difficulty in this "linguistic" approach to metaphysics, in which inferences are made to the structure and nature of the world from the manner in which language is said to be related to the world.

That we can represent the world to ourselves in language entailed, according to Wittgenstein, a metaphysics that is very much like Russell's logical atomism, and the bulk of the *Tractatus* boldly set forth this metaphysics with majestic logic. To derive the metaphysics entailed by language's linkage to the world, however, Wittgenstein had to discuss just *how* language links itself to the world, and his discussion of how language represents the world was itself expressed in language. This placed Wittgenstein in the paradoxical situation of having used language to represent how language represents the world. And this, he concluded, could not be done—despite the fact that he had just done it. Language, he said, may be used to represent the world but cannot be used to represent how language represents the world. "What expresses itself in language, we cannot express by means of language."

Thus, Wittgenstein concluded the *Tractatus* with an outrageous paradox: "My propositions serve as elucidations in the following way," he wrote, "Anyone who understands me eventually recognizes them as nonsensical, when he has used them—as steps—to climb up beyond them. (He must, so to speak, throw away the ladder after he has climbed up it.)"

sitions may be true in isolation from all other propositions because the facts they depict are logically unrelated to all other facts.

Now, you may want an example or two of an atomic fact. Just what *is* a basic fact? Are these facts about minds or matter or neutrons or quarks or what? you will ask.

But the logical atomists, remember, were *logical* atomists, and this means that they were not much concerned with what *actually are* the atomic facts. They were concerned with setting forth what logically must be the basic structure of reality and left it to others to determine the actual content of the universe. Determining the logical structure of reality was enough, and was no little task in its own right.

And anyway, Russell was always less concerned about what actually exists than with what we must *suppose* exists. For all he knew, he said, all the Gods of Olympus exist. But the essential point, he said, is that we have no reason whatsoever to suppose that this is so.

As for what we *must* suppose exists, Russell changed his mind over the course of his long life. Around 1920, he came to think that the bare minimum that must be supposed to exist does *not* include physical objects, spatial points or temporal instants, numbers, atomic or subatomic particles, minds, ideas, selves, or any other thing conceived to exist by com-

Awareness Without a Subject?

If any single thing seems beyond doubt from a common-sense point of view, it is that sensory awareness requires a subject or "I" or "self" or "mind" that has that awareness. Russell, however, eventually came to think that *only the awareness itself* is present in experience.

The subject, he maintained, is *not* revealed to us by observation, and we only suppose that such a thing exists because it is demanded by language. When you report an experience by saying, "I heard a loud bang," for example, only the bang is given in experience. The "I" part is grammatically convenient, but it is not actually present in the experience. According to Russell, "if we are to avoid a perfectly gratuitous assumption, we must dispense with the subject as one of the actual ingredients of the world."

Thus Russell came to think that the distinction between the mental and the physical is entirely a matter of the way awarenesses are grouped. In one kind of grouping, an awareness belongs to the physical world and, in another, to the mental world. Take, for example, the sense-data you have when you look at a chair. According to Russell: "If one arranges together all those sense-data that appear to different people at a given moment and are such as we should ordinarily say are appearances of the same physical object, then that class of sense-data will give you something that belongs to physics, namely, the chair at this moment. On the other hand, if I take all the appearances that the different chairs in this room present to me at this moment, I get something belonging to psychology."

This "neutral monism" was derived from William James, and Russell's conviction that no "I" is given in experience is traceable to David Hume. Consider the matter yourself: Do the data of experience bring you in contact with a subject, or is the subject an inference you make from an assumed premise that consciousness cannot exist without a conscious subject?

mon sense or science. What we say and think and believe about such things as these, Russell came to maintain, can be expressed in propositions that refer only to *awarenesses* or **sense-data;** therefore, these are all we need suppose exist. Eventually Russell backed off somewhat from this position, which is a version of neutralism known as **neutral monism.** We will talk about it later.

▶ S E L E C T I O N   4.1

From Bertrand Russell,
OUR KNOWLEDGE OF THE EXTERNAL WORLD

Hegel and his followers widened the scope of logic in quite a different way—a way which I believe to be fallacious, but which requires discussion if only to show how their conception of logic differs from the conception which I wish to advocate. In their writings, logic is practically identical with metaphysics. In broad outline, the way this came about is as follows. Hegel believed that, by means of *a priori* reasoning, it could be shown that the world *must* have various important and interesting characteristics, since any world without these characteristics would be impossible and self-contradictory. Thus what he calls "logic" is an investigation of the nature of the universe, in so far as this can be inferred merely from the principle that the universe must be logically self-consistent. I do not myself believe that from this principle alone anything of importance can be inferred as regards the existing universe. But, however that may be, I should not regard Hegel's reasoning even if it were valid, as properly belonging to logic: it would rather be an application of logic to the actual world. Logic itself would be concerned rather with such questions as what self-consistency is, which Hegel, so far as I know, does not discuss. And though he criticises the traditional logic, and professes to replace it by an improved logic of his own, there is some sense in which the traditional logic, with all its faults, is uncritically and unconsciously assumed throughout his reasoning. It is not in the direction advocated by him, it seems to me, that the reform of logic is to be sought, but by a more fundamental, more patient, and less ambitious investigation into the presuppositions which his system shares with those of most other philosophers.

The way in which, as it seems to me, Hegel's system assumes the ordinary logic which it subsequently criticises, is exemplified by the general conception of "categories" with which he operates throughout. This conception is, I think, essentially a product of logical confusion, but it seems in some way to stand for the conception of "qualities of Reality as a whole." Mr. Bradley has worked out a theory according to which, in all judgment, we are ascribing a predicate to Reality as a whole; and this theory is derived from Hegel. Now the traditional logic holds that every proposition ascribes a predicate to a subject, and from this it easily follows that there can be only one subject, the Absolute, for if there were two, the proposition that there were two would not ascribe a predicate to either. Thus Hegel's doctrine, that philosophical propositions must be of the form, "the Absolute is such-and-such," depends upon the traditional belief in the universality of the subject-predicate form. This belief, being traditional, scarcely self-conscious, and not supposed to be important, operates underground, and is assumed in arguments which, like the refutation of relations, appear at first sight such as to establish its truth. This is the most important respect in which Hegel uncritically assumes the traditional logic. Other less important respects—though important enough to be the source of such essentially Hegelian conceptions as the "concrete universal" and the "union of identity in difference"—will be found where he explicitly deals with formal logic.[1]

---

[1] See the translation by H. S. Macran, *Hegel's Doctrine of Formal Logic*, Oxford, 1912. Hegel's argument in this portion of his "Logic" depends throughout on confusing the

"is" of predication, as in "Socrates is mortal," with the "is" of identity, as in "Socrates is the philosopher who drank the hemlock." Owing to this confusion, he thinks that "Socrates" and "mortal" must be identical. Seeing that they are different, he does not infer, as others would, that there is a mistake somewhere, but that they exhibit "identity in difference." Again, Socrates is particular, "mortal" is universal. Therefore, he says, since Socrates is mortal, it follows that the particular is the universal—taking the "is" to be throughout expressive of identity. But to say "the particular is the universal" is self-contradictory. Again Hegel does not suspect a mistake, but proceeds to synthesise particular and universal in the individual, or concrete universal. This is an example of how, for want of care at the start, vast and imposing systems of philosophy are built upon stupid and trivial confusions, which, but for the almost incredible fact that they are unintentional, one would be tempted to characterise as puns.

There are difficulties in the metaphysics of logical atomism, most of which Russell himself, with cheery openness, brought to the attention of his readers. And during a period of some thirty years, from about 1920 to 1950, an important movement arose within philosophy, known as **logical positivism,** which discarded *all* metaphysics as meaningless.

The logical positivists held, among other beliefs, a principle known as the **verifiability theory of meaning,** according to which if you make a factual statement but no one has any idea what empirical observations would verify it, then your words do not really express a genuine factual proposition. Your words may express something that is true by definition, such as, "A dog is a dog," but they do not say anything factually significant. And thus metaphysical utterances, the logical positivists held, because they are nonverifiable (and are not "true by definition"), are not genuine factual propositions. They are in fact, the positivists held, meaningless. Take, for example, Hegel's remark that "reason is the substance of the universe." How could this be verified? Well, it just couldn't. And it isn't true by definition. So it is meaningless. A selection from the writings of the late A. J. Ayer, a leading logical positivist, appears later.

Today logical positivism is almost universally rejected by philosophers. And, though metaphysics has not quite yet become as fashionable as it once was in England and other English-speaking countries, philosophers in these countries are again concerned with specific metaphysical issues. As it turns out, one of the issues they are most concerned with is the traditional problem of the ultimate nature of reality as mental, material, both, or neutral. In Part 6 on analytic philosophy we explain this. If you like, you can read that part now, for it too really deals with metaphysics.

Russell, who outlived logical positivism by about two decades, always did retain the following metaphysical beliefs. These beliefs are characteristic of logical atomism:

1. Relations are external.
2. The universe is plural, that is, it consists of particular facts that are logically independent of one another.
3. What makes a proposition true is its relationship to a fact.

4. An isolated empirical proposition is either true or false and is not partially true and partially false; and it does not depend on the Whole for its truth.

5. The universe could exist even in the absence of thought about it.

Throughout his life Russell was also concerned with the relationship between sensory experience and belief in the world outside the mind. He also steadfastly maintained that analysis is the proper method of philosophy.

Today many philosophers who call themselves "analytic" paradoxically do not in fact believe that analysis is the sole proper method of philosophy—but more about that, including just what analysis is, later. Also, many are not especially concerned with the relationship between sense experience and the "external world." Nevertheless, although there may be no single set of beliefs all philosophical analysts have in common, certainly the five metaphysical beliefs enumerated here are widely assumed within the analytic tradition, which has come to dominate philosophy in England and North America and Australia.

Perhaps enough has been said now for you to understand that the reactions to idealist metaphysics in England and on the continent of Europe were entirely different in focus and in spirit. Perhaps, too, you will understand why communication between "Continental" and analytic philosophers is so difficult. The existentialist thinks of the analytic philosopher as splitting linguistic hairs and as being preoccupied with sterile intellectual puzzles. The analytic philosopher, so the existentialist is inclined to think, just plain ignores what is truly important, namely, how we are to find a meaningful existence in an irrational world.

The analytic philosopher, on the other hand, is inclined to think that the existentialist has given up trying to answer traditional philosophical questions in order to respond to psychological needs, some of which are perhaps pathological.

Selection 4.2 is by **A. J. Ayer** (1910–1989), a leading logical positivist. In it Ayer states his view that metaphysical utterances are meaningless.

▶ S E L E C T I O N 4.2

From A. J. Ayer,
*LANGUAGE, TRUTH, AND LOGIC**

The traditional disputes of philosophers are, for the most part, as unwarranted as they are unfruitful. The surest way to end them is to establish beyond question what should be the purpose and method of a philosophical inquiry. And this is by no means so difficult a task as the history of philosophy would lead one to suppose. For if there are any questions which science leaves it to philosophy to answer, a straightforward process of elimination must lead to their discovery.

We may begin by criticizing the metaphysical thesis that philosophy affords us knowledge of a reality transcending the world of science and common sense. Later on, when we come to define metaphysics and account for its existence, we shall find that it is possible to be a metaphysician without believing in a transcendent reality; for we shall see that many metaphysical utterances are due to the commission of logical errors, rather than to a conscious desire on the part of their authors to go beyond the limits of experience. But it is convenient for us to take the case of those who believe that it is possible to have knowledge of a transcendent reality as a starting-point for our discussion. The arguments which we use to refute them will subsequently be found to apply to the whole of metaphysics.

One way of attacking a metaphysician who claimed to have knowledge of a reality which transcended the phenomenal world would be to inquire from what premises his propositions were deduced. Must he not begin, as other men do, with the evidence of his senses? And if so, what valid process of reasoning can possibly lead him to the conception of a transcendent reality? Surely from empirical premises nothing whatsoever concerning the properties, or even the existence, of anything super-empirical can legitimately be inferred. But this objection would be met by a denial on the part of the metaphysician that his assertions were ultimately based on the evidence of his senses. He would say that he was endowed with a faculty of intellectual intuition which enabled him to know facts that could not be known through sense-experience. And even if it could be shown that he was relying on empirical premises, and that his venture into a non-empirical world was therefore logically unjustified, it would not follow that the assertions which he made concerning this non-empirical world could not be true. For the fact that a conclusion does not follow from its putative premise is not sufficient to show that it is false. Consequently one cannot overthrow a system of transcendent metaphysics merely by criticizing the way in which it comes into being. What is required is rather a criticism of the nature of the actual statements which comprise it. And this is the line of argument which we shall, in fact, pursue. For we shall maintain that no statement which refers to a "reality" transcending the limits of all possible sense-experience can possibly have any literal significance; from which it must follow that the labours of those who have striven to describe such a reality have all been devoted to the production of nonsense. . . .

The criterion which we use to test the genuineness of apparent statements of fact is the criterion of verifiability. We say that a sentence is factually significant to any given person, if, and only if, he knows how to verify the proposition which it purports to express—that is, if he knows what observations would lead him, under certain conditions, to accept the proposition as being true, or reject it as being false. If, on the other hand, the putative proposition is of such a character that the assumption of its truth, or falsehood, is consistent with any assumption whatsoever concerning the nature of his future experience, then, as far as he is concerned, it is, if not a tautology, a mere pseudo-proposition. The sentence expressing it may be emotionally significant to him; but it is not literally significant. And with regard to questions the procedure is the same. We inquire in every case what observations would lead us to answer the question, one way or the other; and, if none can be discovered, we must conclude that the sentence under consideration does not, as far as we are concerned, express a genuine question, however strongly its grammatical appearance may suggest that it does. . . .

Such a metaphysical pseudo-proposition as "the Absolute enters into, but is itself incapable of, evolution and progress," is not even in principle verifiable. For one cannot conceive of an observation which would enable one to determine whether the Absolute did, or did not, enter into evolution and progress. Of course it is possible that the author of such a remark is using English words in a way in which they are not commonly used by English-speaking people, and that he does, in fact, intend to assert something which could be empirically verified. But until he makes us understand how the proposition that he wishes to express would be verified, he fails to communicate anything to us. And if he admits, as I think the author of the remark in question would have admitted, that his words were not intended to express either a tautology or a proposition which was capable, at least in principle, of being verified, then it follows that he has made an utterance which has no literal significance even for himself.

To make our position clearer, we may formulate it in another way. Let us call a proposition which records an actual or possible observation an experiential proposition. Then we may say that it is the mark of a genuine factual proposition, not that it should be equivalent to an experiential proposition, or any finite number of experiential propositions, but simply that some experiential propositions can be deduced from it in conjunction with certain other premises without being deducible from those other premises alone. . . .

An example of a controversy which the application of our criterion obliges us to condemn as fictitious is provided by those who dispute concerning the number of substances that there are in the world. For it is admitted both by monists, who maintain that reality is one substance, and by pluralists, who maintain that reality is many, that it is impossible to imagine any empirical situation which would be relevant to the solution of their dispute. But if we are told that no possible observation could give any probability either to the assertion that reality was one substance or to the assertion that it was many, then we must conclude that neither assertion is significant. We shall see later on that there are genuine logical and empirical questions involved in the dispute between monists and pluralists. But the metaphysical question concerning "substance" is ruled out by our criterion as spurious. . . .

As to the validity of the verification principle, in the form in which we have stated it, a demonstration will be given in the course of this book. For it will be shown that all propositions which have factual content are empirical hypotheses; and that the function of an empirical hypothesis is to provide a rule for the anticipation of experience. And this means that every empirical hypothesis must be relevant to some actual, or possible, experience, so that a statement which is not relevant to any experience is not an empirical hypothesis, and accordingly has no factual content. But this is precisely what the principle of verifiability asserts.

---

*Ayer's footnotes have been eliminated.

In the remainder of this chapter we will consider two other important twentieth-century philosophers who may be viewed as responding to Absolute Idealism.

Two Other Reactions

Dewey

The American philosopher of this century who is the most famous outside philosophy is **John Dewey** (1859–1952). Dewey's philosophy, known as **instrumentalism,** holds, roughly, that the forms of human activity, including thought, are instruments used by people to solve practical problems. In Dewey's view, thinking is not a search for "truth" but an activity aimed at solving individual and social problems, a means by which humans strive to achieve a satisfactory relationship with their environment.

From Dewey's perspective, metaphysics, like religious rites and cults, has been a means of "escape from the vicissitudes of existence." Instead of facing the uncertainties of a constantly changing world, metaphysicians have sought security by searching for fixed, universal, and immutable truth.

From Dewey's point of view, nature is experience. This is what he means. Objects are not fixed substances, but individual things ("existences" or "events," he called them) that are imbued with meanings. A piece of paper, for instance, means one thing to a novelist, another to someone who wants to start a fire, still another for an attorney who uses it to draw up a contract, still another for children making paper airplanes, and so on. A piece of paper is an instrument for solving a problem within a given context. What a piece of paper *is* is what it means within the context of some activity or other.

But when he held that an object is what it means within an activity, Dewey did not mean to *equate* the object with the thought about it. That

John Dewey

John Dewey (1859–1952) lived almost a century. He was born before the American Civil War, and he died during the Korean War. His influence on American life was profound.

Dewey was the third of four children in his family. His father owned a grocery business, and then a tobacco business, in Burlington, Vermont, where Dewey was raised. Dewey wasn't considered a brilliant mind as a high school student, but his discovery of philosophy as a junior at the University of Vermont awakened slumbering genius. He received his Ph.D. at Johns Hopkins and taught at Michigan, Minnesota, Chicago, and Columbia. He continued to write, publish, and lecture long after his retirement from Columbia in 1930.

Dewey exerted his greatest influence on society by virtue of his educational theories. He was an effective proponent of progressive education, which opposed formal, authoritarian methods of instruction in favor of having students learn by performing tasks that are related to their own interests. Today educational practice throughout the United States and in many areas across the world generally follows the fundamental postulates of Dewey's educational philosophy, though his belief that the school is the central institution of a democratic society is not always shared by American taxpayers.

A kind, generous, and modest man, Dewey was also an effective social critic and an influential participant in reform movements. He was utterly fearless in advocating democratic causes, even those, like women's suffrage, that were deeply unpopular. Despite having unreconcilable philosophical differences with Bertrand Russell, Dewey was active on Russell's behalf when Russell was denied permission to teach at the City College of New York in 1941 (see the profile on Russell). He was also one of the original founders of the American Civil Liberties Union.

Dewey was not the world's most inspiring public speaker, and one of his students said that you could understand his lectures only by reading your notes afterwards. Maybe the popularity of these lectures of his throughout the world despite the stylistic drawbacks is sound indication of the power of Dewey's ideas.

The bibliography of Dewey's works runs over 150 pages, and his writings touch on virtually every philosophical subject. All told, he wrote forty books and 700 articles. His thought dominated American philosophy throughout the first part of this century. He was and still is America's most famous philosopher.

We certainly can't list all Dewey's works, but among the most famous are *Reconstruction in Philosophy* (1920), *Human Nature and Conduct* (1922), *Experience and Nature* (1925), *The Quest for Certainty* (1929), *Art as Experience* (1934), *Freedom and Culture* (1939), and *Problems of Men* (1946).

was the mistake made by idealism, in Dewey's view. Idealism equated objects with thought about them and thus left out of the reckoning the particular, individual thing. Objects are not reducible to thought about objects, according to Dewey. Things have an aspect of particularity that idealism entirely neglects, he held.

But this does not mean that Dewey thought that there are fixed, immutable substances or things. The doctrine that "independent" objects exist "out there" outside the mind, objects that the mind contemplates and are what they are regardless of what the mind thinks about them, is known as realism, or, as Dewey also called it, the "spectator theory of knowledge." But this theory was no more acceptable to Dewey than idealism. On the contrary, his view was that, as the uses to which a thing is put changes, the thing itself changes. To refer to the earlier example, a piece of paper is *both* (1) a particular item, and (2) what is thought about it within the various and forever-changing contexts in which it is used.

Given this metaphysical perspective, from which abstract speculation about so-called eternal truths is mere escapism, it is easy to understand why Dewey was primarily interested in practical problems and actively participated in movements of social, political, and educational reform. He was effective as a social activist, too. Few individuals have had more impact on American educational, judicial, or legislative institutions than Dewey. The educational system in which you most probably were raised, which emphasized experimentation and practice rather than abstract learning and authoritarian instructional techniques, is the result of his influence.

In Selection 4.3, Dewey asserts that metaphysics, from the ancient Greeks onward, has been a quest for certain knowledge of a fixed and immutable realm of ultimate Being, a quest that has given practical activity and beliefs an inferior, second-citizen status in Western culture.

▶ S E L E C T I O N 4.3

From John Dewey,
THE QUEST FOR CERTAINTY

If one looks at the foundations of the philosophies of Plato and Aristotle as an anthropologist looks at his material, that is, as cultural subject-matter, it is clear that these philosophies were systematizations in rational form of the content of Greek religious and artistic beliefs. The systematization involved a purification. Logic provided the patterns to which ultimately real objects had to conform, while physical science was possible in the degree in which the natural world, even in its mutabilities, exhibited exemplification of ultimate immutable rational objects. Thus, along with the elimination of myths and grosser superstitions, there were set up the ideals of science and of a life of reason. Ends which could justify themselves to reason were to take the place of custom as the guide of conduct. These two ideals form a permanent contribution to western civilization.

But with all our gratitude for these enduring gifts, we cannot forget the conditions which attended them. For they brought with them the idea of a higher realm of fixed reality of which alone true science is possible and of an inferior world of changing things with which experience and practical matters are concerned. They glorified the invariant at the expense of change, it being evident that all practical activity falls within the realm of change. It bequeathed the notion, which has ruled philosophy ever since the time of the Greeks, that the office of knowledge is to uncover the antecedently real, rather than, as is the case with our practical judgments, to gain the kind of understanding which is necessary to deal with problems as they arise.

In fixing this conception of knowledge it established also, as far as philosophies of the classic type are concerned, the special task of philosophic inquiry. As a form of knowledge it is concerned with the disclosure of the Real in itself, of Being in and of itself. It is differentiated from other modes of knowing by its preoccupation with a higher and more ultimate form of Being than that with which the sciences of nature are concerned. As far as it occupied itself at all with human conduct, it was to superimpose upon acts ends said to flow from the nature of reason. It thus diverted thought from inquiring into the purposes which experience of actual conditions suggest and from concrete means of their actualization. It translated into a rational form the doctrine of escape from the vicissitudes of existence by means of measures which do not demand an active coping with conditions. For deliverance by means of rites and cults, it substituted deliverance through reason. This deliverance was an intellectual, a theoretical affair, constituted by a knowledge to be attained apart from practical activity. . . .

Thus the depreciation of practice was given a philosophic, an ontological, justification. Practical action, as distinct from self-revolving rational self-activity, belongs in the realm of generation and decay, a realm inferior in value as in Being. In form, the quest for absolute certainty has reached its goal. Because ultimate Being or reality is fixed, permanent, admitting of no change or variation, it may be grasped by rational intuition and set forth in rational, that is, universal and necessary, demonstration. I do not doubt that there was a feeling before the rise of philosophy that the unalterably fixed and the absolutely certain are one, or that change is the source from which comes all our uncertainties and woes. But in philosophy this inchoate feeling was definitely formulated. It was asserted on grounds held to be as demonstrably necessary as are the conclusions of geometry and logic. Thus the predisposition of philosophy toward the universal, invariant and eternal was fixed. It remains the common possession of the entire classic philosophic tradition. . . .

Although this Greek formulation was made long ago and much of it is now strange in its specific terms, certain features of it are as relevant to present thought as they were significant in their original formulation. For in spite of the great, the enormous changes in the subject-matter and method of the sciences and the tremendous expansion of practical activities by means of arts and technologies, the main tradition of western culture has retained intact this framework of ideas. Perfect certainty is what man wants. It cannot be found by practical doing or making; these take effect in an uncertain future, and involve peril, the risk of misadventure, frustration and failure. Knowledge, on the other hand, is thought to be concerned with a region of being which is fixed in itself. Being eternal and unalterable, human knowing is not to make any difference in it. It can be approached through the medium of the apprehensions and demonstrations of thought, or by some other organ of mind, which does nothing to the real, except just to know it.

Something must be said here about the final and perhaps ultimate critique of metaphysics in Continental philosophy, that made by **Martin Heidegger** (1889–1976). For Heidegger, metaphysics began with Plato and truth ended when metaphysics began. Western philosophy, according to Heidegger, is a systematic unfolding of Platonic idealism, the necessary stages of which passed from the early Greeks through to Descartes, Leibniz, Kant, and Hegel and finally to Nietzsche. In its essence, metaphysics, according to Heidegger, was a forgetting of Being-as-such. It was an attempt to establish human thought as the ultimate standard of truth. In Hegel's equation of Being with absolute subjectivity (i.e., the Absolute Idea or Spirit), this pre-eminence assigned to human thought reached its speculative culmination, according to Heidegger.

But the final chapter of metaphysics, for Heidegger, was written not by Hegel but by Nietzsche, who, ironically, thought himself to be a foe of Plato, of Hegel, and of metaphysics. For in Nietzsche's philosophy the "overman," through the will to power, absolutely determines the being of truth and the truth of being. Thus, in Nietzsche's philosophy, human thought, as embodied in the overman, becomes the absolute creator of value, truth, and being. Therefore Nietzsche, in Heidegger's opinion, was the ultimate Platonist, the ultimate subjectivist, who carried to its ultimate conclusion the Protagorean maxim (see next chapter) that man is the measure of all things. Nietzsche's supreme subjectivism, Heidegger thought, was the inevitable result of the whole history of metaphysics.

This neglect or forgetting of Being, according to Heidegger, has now led to an impoverished historical epoch, the contemporary world that is dominated by the "thoughtless" tyranny of technology over life. The world as we find it now represents a vulgarized version of Nietzsche's idea that man is the master of nature by strength of will alone. Heidegger foresaw the possibility that this kind of thinking might lead to further destructive activities, even to nuclear war.

Heidegger therefore emphasizes the absolute necessity of going beyond subjectivist metaphysics in order to re-find Being itself. We must abandon our presumed superiority and refrain from imposing our subjective "truths" on things. What this means is that we must *listen* to Being. We must not approach Being from without, as would a spectator. Instead, we must approach it from within and permit it to reveal itself to us.

More specifically, we must return to the pre-Platonic thought before Being was subordinated to thought and categorized and described. To undertake this task seriously would require that we could no longer arbitrarily impose our wills on everything else. Instead, we would be called on to obtain wisdom from Being as it manifests itself to us. Only in this way, Heidegger believed, will the fullness of Being be rediscovered.

Heidegger thus recommended a new kind of thinking, a way of thinking that is really a return to the oldest kind of thinking. It is not only like the thinking done by the pre-Socratics but also resembles the Eastern way

Extensions of Heidegger

Heidegger made a major impact on Western thought in fields other than philosophy. The first other area strongly influenced by his work was theology, especially through the writings of Rudolf Bultmann, Karl Rahner, and others. Heidegger provided a method of interpreting texts historically that initiated a whole new way of approaching scriptural studies. Key Heideggerian concepts such as openness, caring, being-in-the-world, bad faith, and authenticity entered into the theological dialogue among Catholic and Protestant theologians and contributed to the tenor and themes of the Second Vatican Council.

For many years Heidegger together with Medard Boss, author of *Psychoanalysis and Daseinanalysis*, held seminars for psychiatric residents in Switzerland. Heidegger's interpretation of the human situation became the basis of a new phenomenological approach to psychoanalysis and psychiatry. The current interest in holistic living and healing has also led some researchers to look to Heidegger for a way of understanding the human's relationship to the world as a whole.

Heidegger's critique of technology and the technological age has had widespread influence in the related areas of social critique, sociology, and political science. Because he grounds all questions of practice in an overall view of Being, Heidegger provides a context in which to ask meaningful questions about social and political existence. His idea that humans are directed toward the future has been of interest to futurologists.

Finally, Heidegger's method and theory of art have been widely used and developed in the fields of aesthetic and literary criticism.

---

of thinking found in Taoism and Zen—as we will see. From both perspectives, truth is attained by ridding oneself of the limitations and selfishness of human subjectivity and ego. If Heidegger is correct, the end of metaphysics may thus see the convergence of Eastern and Western, and of ancient and contemporary, philosophies.

▶ S E L E C T I O N 4.4

From Martin Heidegger, "LETTER ON HUMANISM"

We are still far from pondering the essence of action decisively enough. We view action only as causing an effect. The actuality of the effect is valued according to its utility. But the essence of action is accomplishment. To accomplish means to unfold something into the fullness of its essence, to lead it forth into this fullness—*producere*. Therefore only what already is can really be accomplished. But what "is" above all is Being. Thinking accomplishes the relation of Being to the essence of man. It does not make or cause the relation. Thinking brings this relation to Being solely as something handed over to it from Being. Such offering consists in the fact that in thinking Being comes to language. Language is the house of Being. In its home man dwells. Those who think and those who create with words are the guardians of this home. Their guardianship accomplishes the manifestation of Being insofar as they bring the manifestation to language and maintain it in language through their speech. Thinking does not become action only because some effect issues from it or because it is applied. Thinking acts insofar as it thinks. Such action is presumably the simplest and at the same time the highest, because it concerns the relation of Being to man. But all working or effecting lies in Being and is directed toward beings. Thinking, in contrast, lets itself be claimed by Being so that it can say the truth of Being. Thinking accomplishes this letting. Thinking is *l'engagement par l'Être pour l'Être* [engagement by Being for Being]. I do not know whether it is linguistically possible to say both of these ("*par*" and "*pour*") at once, in this way: *penser, c'est l'engagement de l'Être* [thinking is the engagement of Being]. Here the possessive form "*de l' . . .*" is supposed to express both subjective and objective genitive. In this regard "subject" and "object" are inappropriate terms of metaphysics, which very early on in the form of Occidental "logic" and "grammar" seized control of the interpretation of language. We today can only begin to descry what is concealed in that occurrence. The liberation of language from grammar into a more original essential framework is reserved for thought and poetic creation. Thinking is not merely *l'engagement dans l'action* for and by beings, in the sense of the actuality of the present situation. Thinking is *l'engagement* by and for the truth of Being. The history of Being is never past but stands ever before; it sustains and defines every *condition et situation humaine*. In order to learn how to experience the aforementioned essence of thinking purely, and that means at the same time to carry it through, we must free ourselves from the technical interpretation of thinking. The beginnings of that interpretation reach back to Plato and Aristotle. They take thinking itself to be a *techné*, a process of reflection in service to doing and making. But here reflection is already seen from the perspective of *praxis* and *poiésis*. For this reason thinking, when taken for itself, is not "practical." The characterization of thinking as *theoria* and the determination of knowing as "theoretical" behavior occur already within the "technical" interpretation of thinking. Such characterization is a reactive attempt to rescue thinking and preserve its autonomy over against acting and doing. Since then "philosophy" has been in the constant predicament of having to justify its existence before the "sciences." It believes it can do that most effectively by elevating itself to the rank of a science. But such an effort is the abandonment of the essence of thinking. Philosophy is hounded by the fear that it loses prestige and validity if it is not a science. Not to be a science is taken as a failing which is equivalent to being unscientific. Being, as the element of thinking, is abandoned by the technical interpretation of thinking. "Logic," beginning with the Sophists and Plato, sanctions this explanation. Thinking is judged by a standard that does not measure up to it. Such judgment may be compared to the procedure of trying to evaluate the nature and powers of a fish by seeing how long it can live on dry land. For a long time now, all too long, thinking has been stranded on dry land. Can then the effort to return thinking to its element be called "irrationalism"? . . .

Every humanism is either grounded in a metaphysics or is itself made to be the ground of one. Every determination of the essence of man that already presupposes an interpretation of being without asking about the truth of Being, whether knowingly or not, is metaphysical. The result is that what is peculiar to all metaphysics, specifically with respect to the way the essence of man is determined, is that it is "humanistic." Accordingly, every humanism remains metaphysical. In defining the humanity of man humanism not only does not ask about the relation of Being to the essence of man; because of its metaphysical origin humanism even impedes the question by neither recognizing nor understanding it. On the contrary, the necessity and proper form of the question concerning the truth of Being, forgotten in and through metaphysics, can come to light only if the question "What is metaphysics?" is posed in the midst of metaphysics' domination. Indeed every inquiry into Being, even the one into the truth of Being, must at first introduce its inquiry as a "metaphysical" one.

The first humanism, Roman humanism, and every kind that has emerged from that time to the present, has presupposed the most universal "essence" of man to be obvious. Man is considered to be an *animal rationale*. This definition is not simply the Latin translation of the Greek *zoon logon echon* but rather a metaphysical interpretation of it. This essential definition of man is not false. But it is conditioned by metaphysics. The essential provenance of metaphysics, and not just its limits, became questionable in *Being and Time*. What is questionable is above all commended to thinking as what is to be thought, but not at all left to the gnawing doubts of an empty skepticism.

Metaphysics does indeed represent beings in their Being, and so it thinks the Being of beings. But it does not think the difference of both. Metaphysics does not ask about the truth of Being itself. Nor does it therefore ask in what way the essence of man belongs to the truth of Being. Metaphysics has not only failed up to now to ask this question, the question is inaccessible to metaphysics as such. Being is still waiting for the time when it will become thought-provoking to man.

Checklist

To help you review, here is a checklist of the key philosophers and concepts of this chapter. The brief descriptive sentences that appear with each philosopher summarize one of his leading ideas. Keep in mind that some of these summary statements represent terrific oversimplifications of complex positions.

Philosophers

- **Arthur Schopenhauer**   Believed Hegel was mistaken in abandoning the thing-in-itself, which he held is manifested in humans as a will to live.
- **Friedrich Nietzsche**   Rejected metaphysics as a hopeless and stupid pursuit of a nonexistent fixed world of being and as an underlying source of cultural degeneracy.
- **Søren Kierkegaard**   Rejected metaphysics as papering over life's irrationality, which can be overcome only by a leap of faith in God.
- **Bertrand Russell**   Analytic philosopher; rejected Absolute Idealism as resting on an outdated logic and the false doctrine of internal relations.
- **Ludwig Wittgenstein**   Derived a metaphysics of logical atomism from a consideration of the relationship of language and the world.
- **A. J. Ayer**   Logical positivist. Held that metaphysical utterances are unverifiable, hence meaningless.
- **John Dewey**   Instrumentalist; said that thinking is not a search for "truth," but is aimed at solving practical problems. Believed that metaphysics is escapism.
- **Martin Heidegger**   Held that metaphysics neglects Being-as-such and is responsible for the tyranny of technology over life.

Concepts

nihilism

internal relations

subject-predicate form

logical atomism

analysis

logical positivism

atomic fact

neutral monism

verifiability theory of meaning

Instrumentalism

spectator theory of knowledge

listening to Being

Questions for Discussion and Review

1. "Much of twentieth-century metaphysics is a reaction to Absolute Idealism." Explain this remark, making reference to specific philosophers.
2. Give an example, other than the one in the book, of a proposition that is not of the subject-predicate form.
3. What does it mean to say there are "atomic" facts?
4. "If X might exist but we have no reason to suppose that it actually does exist, then as metaphysicians we should not concern ourselves with X." Evaluate this principle.
5. Apply the principle stated in 4 by letting X stand for God, ghosts, and space aliens.

6. "When you report an experience by saying, 'I heard a loud bang,' only a bang is given. The 'I' part is not actually present in experience." Evaluate this remark.

7. Explain the logical positivists' reasons for holding that all metaphysics is meaningless.

8. Could the universe exist even in the absence of thought about it? Is there any way we could know this?

9. "Everything doubled in size last night." Critically evaluate this remark.

10. "At least in part, a thing *is* what is thought about it within the various contexts in which it is used." Evaluate this claim.

Suggested Further Readings

A. J. Ayer, *Language, Truth and Logic*, 2nd rev. ed. (New York: Dover, 1946). Stimulating. Ayer explains the basic positivist position in strong language.

R. Bretall, ed., *A Kierkegaard Anthology* (Princeton: Princeton University Press, 1949). A useful collection.

John Dewey, *The Quest for Certainty* (New York: Minton Balch & Company, 1929). One of Dewey's most popular works. Portrays metaphysics as a quest for certainty.

Martin Heidegger, *An Introduction to Metaphysics*, Ralph Mannheim, trans. (New Haven: Yale University Press, 1959). Much more than an introduction to the metaphysical tradition, this is a careful exploration of the roots of metaphysics and the question of Being.

W. Kaufman, trans. and ed., *The Portable Nietzsche* (New York: Viking, 1968). Very "portable" and nicely arranged.

J. A. Passmore, *A Hundred Years of Philosophy* (London, 1959). Excellent, readable general history from Mill on.

D. F. Pears, *Bertrand Russell and the British Tradition in Philosophy* (New York: Random House, 1967). Traces the development of Russell's metaphysics from 1905 to 1919.

Bertrand Russell, "The Philosophy of Logical Atomism," in *Logic and Knowledge*, R. C. Marsh, ed. (London: George Allen & Unwin, 1956). Introductory students will find this difficult to read but not impossible.

Bertrand Russell, *My Philosophical Development* (London: George Allen & Unwin Ltd, 1959). Russell's philosophical development as told by Russell himself, and only 200 pages long. Quite spirited, especially in its "Some Replies to Criticism."

Bertrand Russell, *Autobiography*, 3 vols. (London: Allen and Unwin, 1967–1969). Candid and highly entertaining.

Arthur Schopenhauer, *World as Will and Representation*, 2 vols. (New York: Dover, 1966). Schopenhauer's exposition of will as the being-in-itself is clear, strong, deeply disquieting—and it has yet to be come to terms with.

Richard Taylor, *Metaphysics*, 3rd ed. (Englewood Cliffs, N.J.: Prentice-Hall, 1983). An easy introduction to popular metaphysical issues, including the "mind-body problem" and free will.

J. O. Urmson, *Philosophical Analysis* (London: Oxford, 1956). Surveys logical atomism and logical positivism. Not easy reading for introductory students, but detailed and complete.

SUMMARY AND CONCLUSION

If Dewey is correct, metaphysics is mere escapism, a diversion from the human need to cope with the ever-changing conditions of the environment. If, on the other hand, Heidegger is correct, metaphysics is a tyrannical subjugation of being-as-such, a way of thinking that infects the entire Western psyche and ultimately may threaten the very existence of the human species.

Probably it is an exaggeration to suppose that metaphysics may spell disaster for the species. On the other hand, if metaphysics has been a diversion, it has not been an inconsequential one.

Metaphysical speculation was essential to technological mastery of the world, for metaphysics began with those questions that must be asked if there is to be any deeper understanding of the natural order. These are the questions first raised by the pre-Socratics, who sought to comprehend and explain the complex world that we see in terms of a simpler underlying reality. This recognition is required for the full and fruitful development of science and technology.

Also, as we have seen, metaphysics was important to religion, especially the Christian religion. Christianity incorporates many metaphysical elements. Without the Platonic and Neoplatonic interpretations given to it by Augustine, and without the Aristotelean interpretations given to it by Aquinas, Christianity, if it had survived at all, would have done so in a far different form from that in which it did.

Metaphysical speculation, then, was essential to the emergence of science and was vital to the history of religion. It is scarcely surprising, therefore, that much of what today seems to be common sense is a by-product of metaphysics. For example, today's common-sense dualism, according to which both physical and nonphysical things exist, is really nothing more than Cartesian metaphysics. Descartes did not invent this metaphysics out of whole cloth, of course, for his dualism was essentially the two-worlds view of Plato that, with certain changes, had been incorporated into Christianity by Augustine and transmitted down through the ages to Descartes for further refinement and modification.

The history of metaphysics from Descartes onward, we suggested, can be viewed as a sustained effort to ascertain the validity of four metaphysical "perspectives" concerning the ultimate nature of reality. Nothing less is at stake here than our very souls, for belief in souls assumes that one of these perspectives, materialism, is false. Materialism, the theory that only physical things exist, also happens to be the metaphysics seemingly implied by science, and that fact is strong *prima facie* evidence of its validity.

Nevertheless, by the last half of the nineteenth century most philosophers favored not materialism but rather Hegelian Absolute Idealism. Absolute Idealism, we said, was the summit of metaphysical speculation. It purported to offer a grand vision of the universe and consciousness as the necessary unfolding of infinite reason and was meant to be a complete conceptual framework for each aspect of reality and for every component of human thought and history. Much of what happened subsequently in metaphysics was in reaction to Absolute Idealism, and it had a great impact on literature, theology, and even art.

In closing, we would like to point out that Absolute Idealism, and the direct reactions to it, are not the end of metaphysics. Philosophers have not given up all concern with the nature of reality as expressed in the theories of materialism, idealism, dualism, and neutralism. In recent years, philosophers from within the analytic tradition, with eyes turned toward developments in psychology, cognitive science, computer science, neuroscience, and linguistics, have reconsidered the issues and have demonstrated a clear preference for versions of materialism. That, however, is a story for our Part 6, on analytic philosophy.

Epistemology: Theory of Knowledge

Skepticism and Philosophy

The refutation of skepticism is the whole business of philosophy.

—RUSH RHEES

To philosophize is to doubt.

—MONTAIGNE

Epistemology is the branch of philosophy concerned primarily with the nature and possibility of knowledge. WHAT IS KNOWLEDGE? IS KNOWLEDGE POSSIBLE? These are the two most fundamental questions of epistemology, the questions to which most epistemological inquiries relate.

Despite widespread current interest in the first of these questions, historically most epistemologists have been more interested in issues related to the question: Is knowledge possible? So let's concentrate on the second question.

Skepticism

Is knowledge possible? Well, you say, "Of *course* it's possible. *Are you kidding? Lots of things are known.*"

But are they? We'll make a little wager: we'll bet that before you finish this chapter, you are not going to be so sure.

Now a person who questions or suspends judgment on the possibility of knowledge is a **skeptic**. This is a word you should remember. Generally, there are two kinds of skeptics, total skeptics and modified skeptics. **Total skeptics** maintain that nothing can be known or, alternatively, suspend judgment in all matters. Sounds preposterous? Well, we'll see.

A **modified skeptic** does not doubt that at least some things are known, but denies or suspends judgment on the possibility of:

1. Knowledge about some particular thing, such as God or the external world; or

2. Knowledge within some subject area, such as history or metaphysics; or

3. Knowledge from this or that source, such as reason or experience.

Thus, the question on which we are focusing—*Is knowledge possible?*—must be viewed as a summary in shorthand for several more specific questions that have concerned philosophers, such as these:

- Is knowledge of a world outside the self possible?
- Is it possible to have knowledge of future experience?
- Is there knowledge beyond what can be derived from experience?
- Can anything at all be known?

Let's examine how philosophical interest in some of these issues developed historically.

Early Skepticism

It is to the Greek philosophers who lived before Socrates—the pre-Socratic philosophers—that the roots of skepticism may be traced. **Xenophanes** (c. 570–c. 480 B.C.), for example, declared that even if truth were stated, it would not be known. Xenophanes, to fix dates, was born about two hundred years after the first Olympic games were held and alphabetic writing began in Greece, and about two hundred years before Alexander the Great demonstrated that it is possible to conquer the world, or what then passed for it in Alexander's circles. **Heraclitus** (c. 535–c. 475 B.C.), a contemporary of Xenophanes, had the theory that, just as you cannot step into the same river twice, everything is in flux, and this theory suggests that it is impossible to discover any fixed truth beyond what is expressed in the theory itself. (Heraclitus, however, did not himself deduce skeptical conclusions from his theory.) **Cratylus,** a younger contemporary of Socrates (469–399 B.C.), carried this view concerning flux even further and said that you cannot step even once into the same river, because both you and the river are continually changing. Because everything is changing, our words themselves change in their meaning as we speak them, and therefore communication, Cratylus maintained, is impossible.

Cratylus, by the way, is said to have refrained from conversation and merely to have wiggled his finger when someone spoke to him, figuring that his understanding of the words he heard must necessarily be different from the meaning intended by the speaker.

Plato's *Theaetetus*

Plato (c. 427–347 B.C.) played an important role in the history of epistemology, but we won't dwell on him in this chapter. That is because he was less interested in our question about the possibility of knowledge than in the nature of knowledge and its proper objects, and we just don't have the space to cover everything.

You should, however, be aware that in the *Republic* Plato argued that true knowledge must concern itself with what is truly real, and therefore the proper objects of true knowledge, he said, are the Forms. (Plato's Theory of Forms is explained in Chapter 2 of this book.) And you should be aware that Plato's most extensive treatment of knowledge was in his dialogue, *Theaetetus*, in which Plato imagines Socrates discussing knowledge with a young mathematician after whom the dialogue is named. In this dialogue Socrates and Theaetetus examine and reject some possible answers to the question: What is knowledge?

First, the notion that knowledge may be equated with sense perception is rejected, principally on the grounds that if you come to know about something, you can retain your knowledge even after you are no longer in sensory contact with the thing. Then the theory that knowledge is "correct thinking" or true belief is discarded: your true belief might be based on nothing better than hearsay evidence, for example. Knowledge, Theaetetus and Socrates finally conclude, must consist of "correct belief together with an account," which means, essentially, that correct belief, to qualify as knowledge, must be based on something solid; it must be more than a lucky guess. Nevertheless, Socrates and Theaetetus find themselves unable to clarify to their own satisfaction this concept of an "account." The dialogue leaves off on this unsatisfactory note. (For a closer look at the question, "What is knowledge?" see the appendix entitled "Knowledge.")

Plato is also important because he is one of the first *rationalists*, but this is a theme we will pick up later.

Skeptic themes may also be found in the pronouncements of the Sophists, those itinerant Greek teachers of the fifth century B.C. discussed in Chapter 7. At this time, if you were a citizen of Athens and wanted to be influential or, say, able to defend yourself in a court of law, you needed to be trained by a Sophist. The Sophists were essentially skilled debaters and speechwriters who could devise an argument to support any claim and were glad to try to teach you how to do the same—for a fee. Because they often argued against the accepted views, they are said to have produced a breakdown in traditional morals. And because they apparently could advance a plausible argument for any position, they seemed to show that any position is as valid as the next.

Gorgias (c. 485–c. 380 B.C.), one particularly famous Sophist, said this: There is no reality, and if there were, we could not know of it, and even if we could, we couldn't communicate our knowledge. This statement, obviously enough, parallels that of Xenophanes, just mentioned.

And the remark of perhaps the best-known Sophist philosopher of all, **Protagoras** (c. 490–c. 421 B.C.), that "man is the measure of all things," can be interpreted (and was so interpreted by Plato) as meaning that there is no absolute knowledge—that one person's beliefs about the world are

Aristotle and the Deaf

We don't emphasize Aristotle in this chapter because he wasn't as central to the history of skepticism as some other thinkers were. But let us note in passing that Aristotle had the idea that hearing is more important than sight in acquiring knowledge, and he believed that the blind are more intelligent than the deaf. Probably at least in part because of Aristotle's authority, it was not generally believed that the deaf were educable until after the Middle Ages. In fact, during the Middle Ages priests barred the deaf from churches on the ground that they could not have faith. Of course, schools for the deaf are only a relatively recent phenomenon, and the deaf are still subject to various forms of hard discrimination in American education.

as valid as the next person's. **Plato** (c. 427–347 B.C.) employed several arguments in his dialogue, *Theaetetus*, in an effort to refute this view.

The greatest skeptic of ancient times, however, and perhaps of all time, was **Sextus Empiricus** (second–third centuries A.D.), about whose life very little is known (which seems fitting enough). So far, you've heard several skeptical pronouncements, but with Sextus we get something more than bald pronouncements. We get some very interesting explicit *reasons* for *accepting* skepticism, and we're talking here about *total* skepticism. So let's bring Sextus into clearer focus.

Sextus Empiricus and Total Skepticism

In the Hellenistic and Roman periods after Plato, four principal philosophical "schools" developed: the Stoics, the Epicureans, the Skeptics, and the Neoplatonists. The Neoplatonists were mainly metaphysicians, so we talked about them in Chapter 2. The Stoics and Epicureans are most important for their ethical theories, so we consider them in the next part. Here we are interested in the Skeptics.

There were two kinds of Skeptics, and they were something like rivals: the **Academics** (who flourished during the third and second centuries B.C. in what had earlier been Plato's Academy), and the **Pyrrhonists** (stemming from Pyrrho of Elis, c. 360–270 B.C.). Sextus Empiricus, with whom we are concerned in this section, was the last great Pyrrhonist. He is also the principal source of information we have about classical skepticism.

Now the Academics, at least according to Sextus, maintained that "all things are inapprehensible," whereas the Pyrrhonists, he said—and he counted himself as a Pyrrhonist—suspend judgment on all issues.

All things are inapprehensible, said the Academics. If that means that nothing can be known, then it certainly sounds pretty totally skep-

Pyrrho

Not a great deal is known about **Pyrrho,** after whom the Pyrrhonist tradition is named, for he left no writings. Diogenes Laertius, a third-century Greek biographer (whose tales about the ancient philosophers, despite their gossipy and sometimes unreliable nature, are an invaluable source of history) reported that Pyrrho was totally indifferent to and unaware of things going on around him. A well-known story told by Diogenes Laertius is that once, when Pyrrho's dear old teacher was stuck in a ditch, Pyrrho passed him by without a word. (On the other hand, maybe this story indicates that Pyrrho was quite aware of things around him.)

According to other reports, Pyrrho was a moderate, sensible, and quite level-headed person.

It is at any rate true that Pyrrho held that nothing can be known about the hidden essence or true nature of things. He held this because he thought every theory can be opposed by an equally sound contradictory theory. Hence we must neither accept nor reject any of these theories, but rather must suspend judgment on all issues. The suspension of judgment, **epoche,** was said by Pyrrho to lead to **ataraxia,** tranquility or unperturbedness. Pyrrho's fame was apparently primarily a result of his exemplary **agoge** (way of living), though there are differences of opinion about what that way of life actually was.

tical. Actually, there is some controversy among recent scholars about whether or not the Academic skeptics really held this view, but this has been their reputation through the centuries (thanks to Sextus).

Is it true that nothing can be known? This is one of those philosophical questions that must be handled with a certain amount of care, for if it is true that nothing can be known, or if people came to believe that it is, then we might expect to see some fairly spectacular changes in lifestyles.

Sextus Empiricus

Pyrrho was the first of the great Pyrrhonist skeptics, and **Sextus Empiricus** was the last. (Note that the tradition endured fully five or six centuries.) Although Sextus's writings are extensive and constitute the definitive first-hand report on Greek skepticism, little is known about Sextus himself. We don't know where he was born or died, or even where he lived. We do know, however, that he was a physician.

In Sextus's writings may be found virtually every skeptical argument that has ever been devised. He too, like Pyrrho, emphasized suspension of judgment (*epoche*) as the way to attain unperturbedness (*ataraxia*).

Fortunately, there seems to be an obvious and conclusive objection to this notion that nothing can be known. First of all, the claim that nothing can be known appears to be a knowledge-claim. Thus the claim that nothing can be known seems to be self-canceling.

Second, if it is true that nothing can be known, then any argument used to establish that fact cannot be known, either. Apparently, the idea that nothing can be known is thus not only self-cancelingly unknowable but also cannot be established on any grounds that are themselves claimed to be known.

It is little wonder, then, that Sextus differentiated his own position from that of the Academics. Sextus, unlike the Academics, did not proclaim that nothing can be known. Instead, he said, in effect: "I suspend judgment in the matter. Also, I suspend judgment on all other issues that I have examined, too." His position was, in short, that *he did not know whether or not knowledge is possible.*

Sextus's version of total skepticism does not seem nearly so easy to refute as that attributed by him to the Academics. And even today (as we'll see later) Sextus's version of total skepticism has its adherents. Sextus did not affirm the possibility of knowledge of any sort, so it's fair to call him a skeptic. But by not making any judgments—that is, by not commiting himself to any claims whatsoever, including the claim that knowledge is impossible—he did not place himself in the self-defeating position of claiming to know that he could not know.

You're not totally convinced by Sextus? Perhaps, then, you have noticed that Sextus certainly *appears* to make judgments despite the fact that he says that he does not make them. For example, doesn't he make a judgment when he explains the position of the Academics? Doesn't he commit himself to a claim when he says that Pyrrhonists suspend judgment in all matters?

But Sextus said that none of the *apparent* judgments that came from his mouth were genuine claims of knowledge. He said, in effect, that

when it appeared that he was making a knowledge-claim he was merely expressing his momentary impressions of the way things seem. He wrote:

> It must be understood in advance that we make no assertions to the effect that they are absolutely true. We even say that they can be used to cancel themselves, since they are themselves included in those things to which they refer, just as purgative medicines not only remove the humors from the body but expel themselves together with the humors.

Think about that for a moment.

Sextus's Rationale

Now what was Sextus's rationale for suspending judgment on every issue? In his *Outlines of Pyrrhonism*, Sextus set forth the infamous "Ten Tropes," a collection of ten arguments by the ancient skeptics against the possibility of knowledge. The idea behind the Ten Tropes is this. Knowledge is possible only if we have good grounds for believing that the world is exactly as we think it is or perceive it to be. But we do not have good grounds for believing that the world is exactly as we think it is or perceive it to be. For one thing, we never are aware of any object as it is independently of us but only as it stands in its relationship to us. Therefore we cannot know how any object really is in itself. For another thing, the thoughts and perceptions of one person are different from those of the next and depend on the person's own circumstances. So who is to say that one person's thoughts and perceptions are more accurate than those of the next?

Sextus's main reason for thinking that one must suspend judgment on every issue, however, was that "to every argument an equal argument is opposed." If this is true, then wouldn't it indeed be rational to suspend

Sextus's Asterisk

In a play by the great French comic playwright Molière called *The Forced Marriage*, a skeptic is beaten in one scene. While he is being beaten the skeptic is reminded that skeptics can't be sure that they are being beaten or feel pain. Molière, evidently, did not view skepticism as a serious philosophy.

In defense of Sextus, we might mention that Sextus placed a small asterisk beside his skepticism. He said that he did not "deny those things which, in accordance with the passivity of our sense impressions, lead us involuntarily to give our assent to them." That I am in pain is an *involuntary* judgment on my part and therefore doesn't count, Sextus would say.

We'll leave it up to you and your instructor to determine if this tactic enables Sextus to escape Molière's criticism.

judgment on every issue? (Thus the balance scale, which represents the equally compelling force of two contradictory views, is the symbol of skepticism—as well as the scales of justice.)

Before you complain that Sextus was in no position to say what is true of *every* argument, you should remember that he restricted his remarks to arguments "I have examined."

Selection 5.1 is the "Third Trope" from Sextus's *Outlines of Pyrrhonism*. (In this translation, "mode" is used for "trope.")

▶ S E L E C T I O N 5.1

From Sextus Empiricus,
OUTLINES OF PYRRHONISM

Chapter 14—Concerning the Ten Modes

The *Third Mode* is, we say, based on differences in the senses. That the senses differ from one another is obvious. Thus, to the eye paintings seem to have recesses and projections, but not so to the touch. Honey, too, seems to some pleasant to the tongue but unpleasant to the eyes; so that it is impossible to say whether it is absolutely pleasant or unpleasant. The same is true of sweet oil, for it pleases the sense of smell but displeases the taste. So too with spurge: since it pains the eyes but causes no pain to any other part of the body, we cannot say whether, in its real nature, it is absolutely painful or painless to bodies. Rainwater, too, is beneficial to the eyes but roughens the wind-pipe and the lungs; as also does olive-oil, though it mollifies the epidermis. The crampfish, also, when applied to the extremities produces cramp, but it can be applied to the rest of the body without hurt. Consequently we are unable to say what is the real nature of each of these things, although it is possible to say what each thing at the moment appears to be.

A longer list of examples might be given, but to avoid prolixity, in view of the plan of our treatise, we will say just this. Each of the phenomena perceived by the senses seems to be a complex; the apple, for example, seems smooth, odorous, sweet and yellow. But it is non-evident whether it really possesses these qualities only; or whether it has but one quality but appears varied owing to the varying structure of the sense-organs; or whether, again, it has more qualities than are apparent, some of which elude our perception. That the apple has but one quality might be argued from what we said above regarding the food absorbed by bodies, and the water sucked up by trees, and the breath in flutes and pipes and similar instruments; for the apple likewise may be all of one sort but appear different owing to differences in the sense-organs in which perception takes place. And that the apple may possibly possess more qualities than those apparent to us we argue in this way. Let us imagine a man who possesses from birth the senses of touch, taste and smell, but can neither hear nor see. This man, then, will assume that nothing visible or audible has any existence, but only those three kinds of qualities which he is able to apprehend. Possibly, then, we also, having only our five senses, perceive only such of the apple's qualities as we are capable of apprehending; and possibly it may possess other underlying qualities which affect other sense-organs, though we, not being endowed with those organs, fail to apprehend the sense-objects which come through them.

"But," it may be objected, "Nature made the senses commensurate with the objects of sense." What kind of "Nature"? we ask, seeing that there exists so much unresolved controversy amongst the Dogmatists concerning the reality which belongs to Nature. For he who decides the question as to the existence of Nature will be discredited by them if he is an ordinary person, while if he is a philosopher he will be a party to the controversy and therefore himself subject to judgement and not a judge. If, however, it is possible that only those qualities which we seem to perceive subsist in the apple, or that a greater number subsist, or, again, that not even the qualities which affect us subsist, then it will be nonevident to us what the nature of the apple really is. And the same argument applies to all the other objects of sense. But if the senses do not apprehend external objects, neither can the mind apprehend them; hence, because of this argument also, we shall be driven, it seems, to suspend judgement regarding the external underlying objects.

Augustine

So much, then, for the Academics and Pyrrhonists. As mentioned earlier, total skepticism has its adherents even today, so we shall have an opportunity to return to these issues later. For the most part, however, until recently, skepticism after Sextus was of the "modified" variety, as we will now see.

During the Christianization of the Roman Empire, which we discussed in Chapter 2 (in case you want to review some history), skepticism waned. St. Augustine (354–430) discussed Academic skepticism, as it has been described by the Roman historian Cicero, and concluded that skepticism is refuted by the principle of noncontradiction. This principle is stated in various ways, but the basic concept is that a proposition and its contradictory cannot *both* be true, and one or the other *must* be true. The statements, "The world now exists" and "The world now doesn't exist," cannot both be true, and one must be true. Thus we know, presumably, that the world can't both exist and not exist.

Skepticism is also refuted by the very act of doubting, Augustine held, for the act of doubting discloses your existence as something that is absolutely certain: from the fact that *I am doubting* it follows automatically that *I am*.

What Is Truth?

To understand what knowledge is, and whether it is possible to have knowledge, mustn't I understand what truth is? After all, we can know something only if it is true.

It would take a chapter in its own right to tell the philosophical story of truth. For a summary version of that story, see Appendix 2, "Truth."

Furthermore, according to Augustine, even in sense perception there is a rudimentary kind of knowledge. Deception in sense perception occurs, he said, only when we "give assent to more than the fact of appearance." For example, an oar appears bent at the point it enters the water. And if we assent only to the appearance of the oar and say merely that it looks bent, we make no mistake. It is only if we judge that the oar actually is bent that we fall into error.

But Augustine did not particularly develop these three insights. He saw in them a refutation of skepticism and regarded this refutation as highly important. But he did not try to derive anything else of great importance from them. The most important truths, for Augustine, are received by revelation and held on faith, and this doctrine was (of course) assumed throughout the Christian Middle Ages. During this long period, insofar as there was epistemological inquiry at all, it was concerned mainly with how knowledge of universals (for an explanation of which, see Chapter 2) was possible. Skepticism was not taken very seriously.

During the Renaissance, however, the classical skeptical works, notably those by Sextus, were "rediscovered" and published, and were taken quite seriously (even contributing to the controversies during the Protestant Reformation about the knowability of religious beliefs).

In the sixteenth century, various new skeptical writings appeared, most importantly by Hervet, Sanches, and Montaigne. The themes of these three writers were similar and reduced mainly to this: Skeptical arguments are unanswerable, and thus the human understanding, unless aided by faith, is restricted to knowledge of appearances, at best.

In the early part of the seventeenth century, **Pierre Gassendi** (1592–1655) and **Marin Mersenne** (1588–1648) separately used a variety of skeptical arguments to establish the unknowability of the true nature of things, though both believed that a study of the appearances of things could yield information useful for living in this world.

This brings us once again to Descartes, the towering figure of the seventeenth-century skeptical debates and one of the greatest philosophers of all time. Many introductory courses in philosophy devote themselves almost entirely to the philosophy of this famous individual, and we emphasized him in Chapter 3.

Often called the father of modern philosophy, **René Descartes** (1596–1650) made important contributions as well to physiology, psychology, optics, and especially mathematics, in which he originated the Cartesian coordinates and Cartesian curves. This, remember from Chapter 3, was the seventeenth century, the first century of what is now called the Scientific Revolution, the century in which Galileo constructed a telescope and discovered mountains on the moon and satellites around Jupiter, the century in which Harvey figured out how blood circulates and in which Gilbert determined that the world is a gigantic magnet (and coined the word "electricity"), and in which scores of other scientific discoveries short-circuited the traditional way of looking at things. Descartes was in the thick of it all, and it is thanks to him that students now study analytic geometry, since he introduced it to the world.

Descartes's interest in mathematics strongly affected his philosophical reflections, and it was his more or less lifelong intention to formulate a unified science of nature that was as fully certain as arithmetic. Thus Descartes was no skeptic.

Skepticism as the Key to Certainty

Descartes did, however, employ skepticism as a method of achieving certainty. The idea is simple enough: I will doubt everything that can possibly be doubted, he reasoned, and if anything is left, then it will be absolutely certain. Then I will consider what it is about this certainty (if there is one) that places it beyond doubt, and that will provide me with a yardstick against which I can measure all other purported truths to see if they, too, are beyond doubt.

Let's see how Descartes's *doubting methodology* worked.

To doubt every proposition that he possibly could, Descartes employed two famous conjectures, the **dream conjecture** and the **evil demon conjecture.** For all I know, Descartes said, I might now be dreaming—that's Descartes's dream conjecture. And further, he said, for all I know, some malevolent demon devotes himself to deceiving me at every turn so that I regard as true and certain propositions that are in fact false. That supposition is Descartes's evil demon conjecture.

Yes, these two conjectures are totally bizarre, and Descartes was as aware of that as you are. But that's just the point. What Descartes was looking for was a measure of certainty that escapes even the most incredible and bizarre possibilities of falsehood.

And what he discovered, when he considered everything he thought he knew in the light of one or the other of these two bizarre possibilities, is that he could doubt *absolutely everything—save one indubitable truth:* "I think, therefore I am": **cogito, ergo sum.** Remember this phrase.

What Descartes meant is that any attempt to doubt one's existence as a thinking being is impossible, because to doubt is to think and to exist.

Descartes's Conjectures

For all I know, I might now be dreaming. This is Descartes's dream conjecture, and it's easy enough to disprove, correct? I just pinch myself. But then again . . . am I just dreaming that I pinched myself? Might not any evidence I have that I am now awake just be dream evidence? Can I really be certain that I won't find myself in a few moments *waking up* realizing that I have been dreaming? And thus can I really be sure that the things I see around me, this desk and book, these arms and legs, have any existence outside my mind?

Well, you may say, even if I am dreaming, there are still many things I cannot doubt; even if I am dreaming, I can't doubt, for instance, that two and three is five or that a square has four sides.

But then again—and this is where Descartes's evil demon conjecture comes in—of course, it *seems* absolutely certain to me that two and three make five and that a square has four sides. But *some* propositions that have seemed absolutely certain to me have turned out to be false. So how can I be sure that *these* propositions (that two and three make five and that a square has four sides), or any other proposition that seems certain to me, are not likewise false? For all I know, a deceitful and all-powerful intelligence has so programmed me that I find myself regarding as absolute certainties propositions that in fact aren't true at all.

Descartes thus thought that these two conjectures combined in this way to force him "to avow that there is nothing at all that I formerly believed to be true of which it is impossible to doubt."

Try for a moment to doubt your own existence, and you'll see what Descartes meant. The self that doubts its own existence must surely exist in order to be able to doubt in the first place.

Augustine, too, had found certain truth in his inability to doubt his own existence, but Descartes went further than this. He examined this one indubitable truth to see what guaranteed its certainty and ascertained that any other proposition that he apprehended with identical "clarity and distinctness" must likewise be immune to doubt. In other words, he had discovered in the certainty of his own existence an essential characteristic or "test" of truth: Anything else that was as clear and distinct as his own existence would also have to be certain.

Using this "clear and distinct" test, Descartes was then able to certify as beyond doubt his belief in a God who would not deceive him. And because it was certain that God would not deceive him, Descartes could then also certify as certain his belief that God would not permit him to be deceived in his belief in the existence of the world outside his mind. Thus Descartes ultimately found within the certainty of his own existence the grounds for certainty in the belief in God and the "external world." We will omit the details of this grand deduction, however.

What does all this accomplish? Descartes's doubting methodology is like the axiomatic method in logic and mathematics, in which a theorem whose truth initially seems likely but not *totally* certain is demonstrated to be certain by deriving it from basic axioms by means of rules of inference. Descartes's "axiom" is, in effect, "I think, therefore I am," and his "rule of inference" is clear and distinct perception.

What Descartes accomplished, or what he thought he accomplished, is therefore this: by employing his doubting methodology he was able to show, at least to his own satisfaction, that many of the things he had previously merely *believed*, such as that God exists and that there is a material world outside his own mind, he now *knew for certain.*

Selection 5.2 is from Descartes's most famous philosophical work, *Meditations on First Philosophy*. It is considered one of the most powerful skeptical arguments ever set forth. The trouble is, the argument is so powerful that it is by no means clear that even Descartes's *cogito, ergo sum* is immune to skeptical doubt. Descartes, of course, thought otherwise, and you may wish to consider the issue yourself.

▶ S E L E C T I O N   5.2

*From René Descartes, MEDITATIONS [I AND II] ON FIRST PHILOSOPHY.**

Reason persuades me that I ought no less carefully to withhold my assent from matters which are not entirely certain and indubitable than from those which appear to me manifestly to be false. . . .

All that up to the present time I have accepted as most true and certain I have learned either from the senses or through the senses; [and], although the senses sometimes deceive us concerning things which are hardly perceptible, or very far away, there are yet many others to be met with as to which we cannot reasonably have any doubt. . . .

For example, there is the fact that I am here, seated by the fire, attired in a dressing gown, having this paper in my hands and other similar matters. And how could I deny that these hands and this body are mine. . . [?]

At the same time I must remember that . . . I am in the habit of sleeping and in my dreams representing to myself the same things . . . How often has it happened to me that in the night I dreamt that I found myself in this particular place, that I was dressed and seated near the fire, whilst in reality I was lying undressed in bed! At this moment it does indeed seem to me that it is with eyes awake that I am looking at this paper . . . But in thinking over this I remind myself that on many occasions I have in sleep been deceived by similar illusions, and in dwelling carefully on this reflection I see . . . that there are no certain indications by which we may clearly distinguish wakefulness from sleep . . .

At the same time we must at least confess that . . . whether I am awake or asleep, two and three together always form five, and the square can never have more than four sides, and it does not seem possible that truths so clear and apparent can be suspected of any falsity.

Nevertheless . . . how do I know that I am not deceived every time that I add two and three, or count the sides of a square, or judge of things yet simpler, if anything simpler can be imagined? . . . Possibly God has not desired that I should be thus deceived, for He is said to be supremely good. . . . But let us . . . grant that all that is here said of a God is a fable . . . I shall then suppose, not that God who is supremely good and the fountain of truth, but some evil genius not less powerful than deceitful, has employed his whole energies in deceiving me; I shall consider that the heavens, the earth, colors, figures, sound, and all other external things are nought but the illusions and dreams of which this genius has availed himself in order to lay traps for my credulity; I shall consider myself as having no hands, no eyes, no flesh, no blood, nor any senses, yet falsely believing myself to possess all these things. . . .

[Yet even if] there is some deceiver or other, very powerful and very cunning, who ever employs his ingenuity in deceiving me[,] then without a doubt I exist also if he deceives me, and let him deceive me as much as he will, he can never cause me to be nothing so long as I think that I am something. So that after having reflected well and carefully examined all things, we must come to the definite conclusion that this proposition: I am, I exist, is necessarily true each time that I pronounce it, or that I mentally conceive it.

---

*Edited slightly for the modern reader.

The "Clear and Distinct" Criterion of Certainty

In Selection 5.2 we see Descartes finding supposedly certain knowledge in his own existence as a thing that thinks. He then reasons, as we have explained, as follows:

> I am certain that I am a thing which thinks; but do I not then likewise know what is requisite to render me certain of a truth? Certainly in this first knowledge there is nothing that assures me of its truth, excepting the clear and distinct perception of that which I state, which would not indeed suffice to assure me that what I say is true, if it could ever happen that a thing which I conceived so clearly and distinctly could be false; and accordingly it seems to me that already I can establish as a general rule that all things which I perceive very clearly and very distinctly are true.

In this way, then, Descartes found to his own satisfaction that he can regard as certain knowledge much of what he had initially cast in doubt. All he must do is ascertain which among his various beliefs he perceives

I THINK, THEREFORE
I AM, I THINK...

"clearly and distinctly" to be true. Those beliefs he now can regard as absolutely certain. This is the **clear and distinct criterion** of certainty.

Unfortunately, the least debatable part of Descartes's overall reasoning is the two skeptical arguments (the dream conjecture and the evil demon conjecture) that he advanced at the outset. When others read Descartes and followed his line of reasoning for themselves, they found themselves doubting everything—including the validity of Descartes's

Variations on a Theme

I feel, therefore I exist.
  —Thomas Jefferson

I rebel, therefore I am.
  —Albert Camus

I ought, therefore I can.
  —Immanuel Kant

I want, therefore I am.
  —Leo Tolstoy

Sometimes I think: and sometimes I am.
  —Paul Valéry

Only the first word of the Cartesian philosophy is true: it was not possible for Descartes to say *cogito, ergo sum,* but only *cogito.*
  —Moses Hess

I labor, therefore I am a man.
  —Max Stirner

There is, of course, the *cogito ergo sum* principle—perhaps the most famous of all philosophical theories . . . which, incidentally, is fallacious.
  —Barrows Dunham

Cogito, ergo sum . . . can only mean, "I think therefore I am a thinker." The truth is, *sum ergo cogito.*
  —Miguel de Unamuno

Rationalists and Empiricists

A doctrine that St. Thomas Aquinas (see Chapter 2) accepted and attributed to Aristotle, and that John Locke also accepted, is: **nihil in intellectu quod prius non fuerit in sensu,** that is, there's nothing in the intellect that wasn't first in the senses. Those who accept this doctrine are called **empiricists**. Others, however, known as **rationalists**, hold that the intellect contains important truths that weren't placed there by sensory experience. "Something never comes from nothing," for example, might count as one of these truths, because experience can tell you only that something has never come from nothing so far, not that it can never, ever happen. (Or so a rationalist might argue.) Sometimes rationalists believe in a theory of *innate ideas,* according to which these truths are "innate" to the mind—that is, they are part of the original dispositions of the intellect.

The empiricist is, in effect, a type of modified skeptic—he or she denies that there is any knowledge that doesn't stem from sensory experience. Most rationalists, by contrast, do not deny that some knowledge about the world can be obtained through experience. But other rationalists, such as Parmenides (check Chapter 2), deny that experience can deliver up any sort of true knowledge. This type of rationalist is also a type of modified skeptic.

Classical rationalism and empiricism in modern philosophy were mainly a product of the seventeenth and eighteenth centuries. Rationalism is associated most significantly during that time period with Descartes (1596–1650), Spinoza (1632–1677),

and Leibniz (1646–1716). These three, as already noted, are often called the Continental rationalists, and they are often contrasted with Locke (1632–1704), Berkeley (1685–1753), and Hume (1711–1776), the so-called British Empiricists. Philosophers from other periods, however, are sometimes classified as rationalists or empiricists depending on whether they emphasized the importance of reason or experience in knowledge of the world. Those earlier philosophers treated in this book who are usually listed as rationalists are, among others, Pythagoras, Parmenides, and Plato. Those who are often listed as empiricists are Aristotle, Epicurus, and Aquinas. Immanuel Kant (1724–1804), discussed in the next chapter, is said to have synthesized rationalism and empiricism because he believed that all knowledge *begins* with experience (a thesis empiricists agree with) but also believed that knowledge is not limited to what has been found in experience (a thesis rationalists agree with). The point is covered in the text.

Modern epistemology, as you will see, has been predominantly empiricist. This is because the Continental rationalists, and later rationalists too, were primarily metaphysicians. That is to say, they were generally less concerned with discussing the possibility of knowledge and related issues than with actually coming to propose some philosophically important theory about reality. The great exception is Descartes, a rationalist who concerned himself explicitly with the possibility of knowledge.

---

strategy for escaping doubt. Thus, what Descartes *really* accomplished was to render uncertain the entire edifice of what passes for human knowledge—or at least to make a live issue whether what passes for knowledge genuinely is knowledge.

The philosophers of the seventeenth century after Descartes therefore became divided about the power of reason in overcoming skepticism. On one hand, **Benedictus de Spinoza** (1632–1677) and **Gottfried Wilhelm, Baron von Leibniz** (1646–1716) both developed elaborate metaphysical systems that, in being grounded (or so they thought) on reason, were (in their opinion) impervious to skeptical attack. The three philosophers, Descartes, Spinoza, and Leibniz, are often referred to collectively as the **Continental rationalists.**

In contrast with the rationalists, **Pierre Bayle** (1647–1706), in his *Historical and Critical Dictionary* (1695 and 1697) found reason to be productive of doubt and uncertainty and thus inherently unreliable. Bayle marshaled arguments to dispute possibly every metaphysical, moral, scientific, mathematical, or historical affirmation that anyone had ever made. Because reason leaves "everything that is said and everything that is done" open to dispute and challenge, Bayle thought it best to turn to faith for guidance as to truth. Bayle makes interesting reading, but historically he is not as important as the Continental rationalists or as the group of philosophers we are about to consider.

An alternative to the rationalism of Descartes, Spinoza, and Leibniz as well as to the antirationalism of Bayle was the empiricism of **John Locke** (1632–1704), whose great epistemological work, *An Essay Concerning Human Understanding*, became available to the public at about the same time as Bayle's *Dictionary*. Locke, together with two of his successors, **George Berkeley** and **David Hume,** are often referred to as the **British empiricists** and are contrasted with the Continental rationalists, Descartes, Spinoza, and Leibniz. Having already discussed two rationalists, Descartes and Spinoza (see Chapter 3 for a discussion of Spinoza), we will now look closely at the three British empiricists.

John Locke's purpose in *An Essay Concerning Human Understanding*, he wrote, was to inquire into "the original, certainty, and extent of human knowledge." Many of Locke's views on these matters will almost certainly be shared by most readers of this book, so influential have his views been. Locke's epistemology is indeed so widely accepted that much of it is now thought to be so much common sense. You should be prepared, however. We're going to show you that terrible philosophical difficulties attend Locke's basic position, as common-sensical as it will probably seem.

The British Empiricists

John Locke and Representative Realism

All our ideas come from experience, Locke contended. The human mind at birth is essentially a **tabula rasa** or blank slate, he wrote, his metaphor to become famous. On this blank slate experience makes its imprint. External objects impinge on our senses, which convey into the mind ideas, or, as we might prefer to say today, perceptions, of these objects and their various qualities. In short, sensation furnishes the mind with all its contents. *Nihil in intellectu quod prius non fuerit in sensu—noth-*

ing exists in the mind that wasn't first in the senses. This, of course, is familiar and plausible.

Now these ideas or perceptions of some of the qualities of external objects are accurate copies of qualities that actually reside in the objects, Locke said. This is what he means. Think of a basketball. It has a certain size, shape, and weight, and when we look at and handle the ball our sensory apparatus provides us with accurate pictures or images or ideas or perceptions of these "primary" qualities, as Locke called them.

The basketball also has the power to produce in us ideas of "secondary" qualities such as the brown color, the leathery smell, the coolness that we feel when we hold it, and so forth. Are *these* qualities really in the basketball? Well, of course not, you will say. And that's exactly what Locke said. These secondary qualities are not really in the basketball—they are purely subjective and exist in us merely as ideas. In other words, in Locke's view—and we will bet that this is your view as well—if all sentient creatures were removed from the proximity of the basketball there would not *be* any brownness, leathery odor, or coolness, but only an object of a certain size and shape and weight, composed of minute particles that collectively would smell leathery and feel cool and look brown if any creatures with sense organs then came into existence and held and looked at and sniffed the ball.

Locke's Theory: According to Locke, when we say we are looking at an external object, what we are really doing is attending to the perceptions or "ideas" of the object that are in our mind. Some of these perceptions, like those of a basketball's size and shape, accurately represent qualities that are really in the object itself. Other perceptions, like those of the basketball's color and odor, don't represent anything that is really in the object; the color and shape are just subjective qualities that exist only within us.

This theory that Locke accepted is often called **representative realism.** In a sentence, it is the theory that we perceive objects *indirectly* by means of our "representations" or ideas or perceptions of them, some of which are accurate copies or representations or reflections of the real properties of "external" objects, of objects "outside the mind." This theory is widely held and is probably regarded by most people as self-evident. Open almost any introductory psychology text and you will behold implicit in its discussion of perception Locke's theory of representative realism.

Now we said a moment ago that terrible philosophical difficulties attend to this very nice, down-to-earth, common-sense theory known as representative realism, and it is time for us to explain ourselves. As justifiable as Locke's theory may seem, it is subject to a powerful objection, stated most eloquently by **George Berkeley** (1685–1753), an Irish bishop and philosopher.

George Berkeley

If Locke is correct, then we experience sensible things, things like basketballs and garden rakes, *indirectly*—that is, through the intermediary of our ideas or perceptions. But if that's true, Berkeley said, then we cannot know that *any* of our ideas or perceptions accurately represent the qualities of these sensible things. Why can't we know this? Because, Berkeley argued, if Locke is correct, we do not directly experience the basketball (or any other object) *itself*. Instead, what we directly experience is our *perceptions and ideas of the basketball.* And if we do not have direct experience of the basketball itself, then we cannot compare our perceptions or ideas of the basketball with the basketball itself to see if they "accurately represent" the basketball's qualities.

Indeed, given Locke's position, Berkeley said, we cannot really know that a thing like a basketball or a garden rake even *exists.* For according to Locke's theory it is not the *object* we experience, but rather our perceptions or ideas of it.

This, then, is Berkeley's criticism of Locke's theory. As satisfying as it might seem to common sense, Locke's position is the short road to skepticism. If we accept Locke's theory, then we cannot know that "sensible things," things like basketballs and rakes and even our own hands and feet, actually exist.

Fortunately, Berkeley is an orderly and compelling writer, and we may permit him to set forth his philosophy himself. In the following selection, Berkeley begins by noting that the objects of human knowledge are ideas of various sorts (e.g., ideas of sensation, emotion, memory, imagination, etc.), and that these ideas can only exist in the mind that perceives them. He then observes that there is a contradiction in the "strange opinion" that sensible objects (houses, mountains, rivers, etc.) exist outside the mind.

▶ S E L E C T I O N   5.3

From George Berkeley, TREATISE CONCERNING THE PRINCIPLES OF HUMAN KNOWLEDGE (1)

It is evident to anyone who takes a survey of the objects of human knowledge, that they are either ideas (1) actually imprinted on the senses, or else such as are (2) perceived by attending to the passions and operations of the mind, or lastly (3) ideas formed by help of memory and imagination, either compounding, dividing, or barely representing those originally perceived in the aforesaid ways. By sight I have the ideas of lights and colors, with their several degrees and variations. By touch I perceive hard and soft, heat and cold, motion and resistance, and of all these more and less either as to quantity or degree. Smelling furnishes me with odors, the palate with tastes, and hearing conveys sounds to the mind in all their variety of tone and composition. And as several of these are observed to accompany each other, they come to be marked by one name, and so to be reputed as one thing. Thus, for example, a certain color, taste, smell, figure, and consistence, having been observed to go together, are accounted one distinct thing, signified by the name "apple." Other collections of ideas constitute a stone, a tree, a book, and the like sensible things. . . .

2. But besides all that endless variety of ideas or objects of knowledge, there is likewise something which knows or perceives them, and exercises divers operations, as willing, imagining, remembering, about them. This perceiving, active being is what I call mind, spirit, soul, or myself. By which words I do not denote any one of my ideas, but a thing entirely distinct from them wherein they exist, or, which is the same thing, whereby they are perceived; for the existence of an idea consists in being perceived.

3. That neither our thoughts, nor passions, nor ideas formed by the imagination, exist without the mind, is what everybody will allow. And it seems no less evident that the various sensations or ideas imprinted on the sense, however blended or combined together (that is, whatever objects they compose), cannot exist otherwise than in a mind perceiving them. . . .

4. It is indeed an opinion strangely prevailing amongst men, that houses, mountains, rivers, and in a word all sensible objects, have an existence, natural or real, distinct from their being perceived by the understanding. But with how great an assurance and acquiescence soever this principle may be entertained in the world, yet whoever shall find in his heart to call it in question may, if I mistake not, perceive it to involve a manifest contradiction. For what are the forementioned objects but the things we perceive by sense? and what do we perceive besides our own ideas or sensations? and is it not plainly repugnant that any one of these, or any combination of them, should exist unperceived?

5. Light and colors, heat and cold, extension and figures—in a word the things we see and feel—what are they but so many sensations, notions, ideas, or impressions on the sense? And is it possible to separate, even in thought, any of these from perception?

Next, Berkeley sets forth and rejects the Lockian view that our ideas represent to us or copy or resemble the qualities of objects. The main thrust of Berkeley's argument is that whatever considerations suggest that the secondary qualities exist only in the mind apply equally to the so-called primary qualities; further, secondary and primary qualities are inseparately united and thus both exist only in the mind. In plain English, whatever makes you think that the leathery smell of a basketball is "subjective" or exists "only in the mind" will equally well serve to show that the size and shape of the ball also are subjective and exist only in the mind.

▶ S E L E C T I O N   5.4

From George Berkeley, *TREATISE CONCERNING THE PRINCIPLES OF HUMAN KNOWLEDGE* (2)

8. But, say you, though the ideas themselves do not exist without the mind, yet there may be things like them, whereof they are copies or resemblances, which things exist without the mind in an unthinking substance. I answer, an idea can be like nothing but an idea; a color or figure can be like nothing but another color or figure. . . . Again, I ask whether those supposed originals or external things, of which our ideas are the pictures or representations, be themselves perceivable or no? If they are, then they are ideas and we have gained our point; but if you say they are not, I appeal to anyone whether it be sense to assert a color is like something which is invisible; hard or soft, like something which is intangible; and so of the rest.

9. Some there are who make a distinction betwixt primary and secondary qualities. By the former they mean extension, figure, motion, rest, solidity or impenetrability, and number; by the latter they denote all other sensible qualities, as colors, sounds, tastes, and so forth. The ideas we have of these they acknowledge not to be the resemblances of anything existing without the mind, or unperceived, but they will have our ideas of the primary qualities to be patterns or images of things which exist without the mind, in an unthinking substance which they call matter. By matter, therefore, we are to understand an inert, senseless substance, in which extension, figure, and motion do actually subsist. But it is evident from what we have already shown, that extension, figure, and motion are only ideas existing in the mind, and that an idea can be like nothing but another idea, and that consequently

neither they nor their archetypes can exist in an unperceiving substance. Hence, it is plain that the very notion of what is called matter, or corporeal substance, involves a contradiction in it.

10. They who assert that figure, motion, and the rest of the primary or original qualities do exist without the mind in unthinking substances, do at the same time acknowledge that color, sounds, heat, cold, and such-like secondary qualities, do not; which they tell us are sensations existing in the mind alone . . . Now, if it be certain that those original qualities are inseparably united with the other sensible qualities, and not, even in thought, capable of being abstracted from them, it plainly follows that they exist only in the mind. But I desire anyone to reflect and try whether he can, by any abstraction of thought, conceive the extension and motion of a body without all other sensible qualities. For my own part, I see evidently that it is not in my power to frame an idea of a body extended and moving, but I must withal give it some color or other sensible quality which is acknowledged to exist only in the mind. In short, extension, figure, and motion, abstracted from all other qualities, are inconceivable. Where therefore the other sensible qualities are, there must these be also, to wit, in the mind and nowhere else.

11. Again, great and small, swift and slow, are allowed to exist nowhere without the mind, being entirely relative, and changing as the frame or position of the organs of sense varies. The extension therefore which exists without the mind is neither great nor small, the motion neither swift nor slow, that is, they are nothing at all. . . .

12. That number is entirely the creature of the mind, even though the other qualities be allowed to exist without, will be evident to whoever considers that the same thing bears a different denomination of number as the mind views it with different respects. Thus, the same extension is one, or three, or thirty-six, according as the mind considers it with reference to a yard, a foot, or an inch. Number is so visibly relative, and dependent on men's understanding, that it is strange to think how anyone should give it an absolute existence without the mind. . . .

14. It is said that heat and cold are affections only of the mind, and not at all patterns of real beings, existing in the corporeal substances which excite them, for that the same body which appears cold to one hand seems warm to another. Now, why may we not as well argue that figure and extension are not patterns or resemblances of qualities existing in matter, because to the same eye at different stations, or eyes of a different texture at the same station, they appear various, and cannot therefore be the images of anything settled and determinate without the mind? Again, it is proved that sweetness is not really in the sapid thing, because the thing remaining unaltered the sweetness is changed into bitter, as in case of a fever or otherwise vitiated palate. Is it not as reasonable to say that motion is not without the mind, since if the succession of ideas in the mind become swifter, the motion, it is acknowledged, shall appear slower without any alteration in any external object?

15. In short, let anyone consider those arguments which are thought manifestly to prove that colors and tastes exist only in the mind, and he shall find they may with equal force be brought to prove the same thing of extension, figure, and motion. . . . the arguments foregoing plainly show it to be impossible that any color or extension at all, or other sensible quality whatsoever, should exist in an unthinking subject without the mind, or in truth, that there should be any such thing as an outward object.

And now, in the final selection, Berkeley considers whether the existence of things outside the mind can be proved through reason. He thinks not. He then concludes by saying that he is willing to rest the whole question of whether things exist outside the mind on the results of one very simple test. We invite you to take Berkeley's test. If you can even *conceive* of a sensible thing existing outside the mind, Berkeley says, he will give up his argument.

▶ S E L E C T I O N 5.5

From George Berkeley, TREATISE CONCERNING THE PRINCIPLES OF HUMAN KNOWLEDGE (3)

18. But though it were possible that solid, figured, movable substances may exist without the mind, corresponding to the ideas we have of bodies, yet how is it possible for us to know this? Either we must know it by sense or by reason. As for our senses, by them we have the knowledge only of our sensations, ideas, or those things that are immediately perceived by sense, call them what you will; but they do not inform us that things exist without the mind. . . . It remains therefore that if we have any knowledge at all of external things, it must be by reason, inferring their existence from what is immediately perceived by sense. But what reason can induce us to believe the existence of bodies without the mind, from what we perceive. . . . it is granted on all hands (and what happens in dreams, frenzies, and the like, puts it beyond dispute) that it is possible we might be affected with all the ideas we have now, though there were no bodies existing without, resembling them. Hence, it is evident the supposition of external bodies is not necessary for the producing our ideas; since it is granted that they are produced sometimes, and might possibly be produced always in the same order we see them in at present, without their concurrence. . . .

20. In short, if there were external bodies, it is impossible we should ever come to know it; and if there were not, we might have the very same reasons to think there were that we have now. Suppose (what no one can deny possible) an intelligence without the help of external bodies, to be affected with the same train of sensations or ideas that

you are, imprinted in the same order and with like vividness in his mind. I ask whether that intelligence hath not all the reason to believe the existence of corporeal substances, represented by his ideas, and exciting them in his mind, that you can possibly have for believing the same thing?

22. I am content to put the whole upon this issue: if you can but conceive it possible for one extended movable substance, or, in general, for any one idea, or anything like an idea, to exist otherwise than in a mind perceiving it, I shall readily give up the cause. . . .

23. But, say you, surely there is nothing easier than for me to imagine trees, for instance, in a park, or books existing in a closet, and nobody by to perceive them. I answer, you may so, there is no difficulty in it; but what is all this, I beseech you, more than framing in your mind certain ideas which you call books and trees, and the same time omitting to frame the idea of anyone that may perceive them? But do not you yourself perceive or think of them all the while? . . . When we do our utmost to conceive the existence of external bodies, we are all the while only contemplating our own ideas.

Material Things as Clusters of Ideas

So Berkeley's view is that sensible things, such as tables, chairs, trees, books, frogs, and the like are not material things that exist outside the

Berkeley's Proofs of God

Berkeley's position is that sensible things cannot exist independent of perception—to be is to be perceived (**esse est percipi**). What, then, happens to this book and desk when everyone leaves the room? What happens to the forest when all the people go away? What, in short, according to Berkeley, happens to sensible things when no one perceives them?

Berkeley's answer is that the perceiving mind of God makes possible the continued existence of sensible things when neither you nor we nor any other people are perceiving them. Because sensible things do not depend on the perception of humans and exist independently of them, Berkeley wrote, "there must be some other mind wherein they exist." This other mind, according to Berkeley, is God.

That sensible things continue to exist when we don't perceive them is thus, for Berkeley, a short and simple proof of God's existence. It is also, perhaps, a proof you have not heard before.

Another, similar proof, in Berkeley's view, can be derived from the fact that we do not ourselves cause our ideas of tables and chairs and mountains and other sensible things. "There is therefore," he reasoned, "some other will or spirit that produces them"—God.

Berkeley was not unaware that his theory that what we call material things are ideas both in God's mind and in our own raises peculiar questions about the relationship between our ideas and minds and the ideas and mind of God. For example, if a mountain is an idea in God's mind and we perceive the mountain, does that mean we perceive or have God's ideas?

mind. Instead, according to Berkeley, so-called material things are in fact groups of ideas and, as such, are perceived directly and exist only within the mind. Because they are ideas, we can no more doubt their existence than we can doubt our own aches and pains (which too, indeed, are ideas).

Berkeley's view may, perhaps, sound eccentric, but he argues for it convincingly, as the selections may show. In a nearby box we present a paraphrase of Berkeley's argument. See if you can find a mistake in it.

David Hume

David Hume (1711–1776), arguably the most important epistemologist of all time, was also, like Berkeley, especially influenced by Locke and Bayle. But unlike Berkeley, Hume found no answer to Bayle's skepticism.

Hume's epistemology is a development of the empiricist thesis that all our ideas come from experience—that is, from sensation or inner

Berkeley's Argument Analyzed

Berkeley obviously did not just assert dogmatically, without reason, that sensible things are in fact groups of ideas. He had *arguments* for his view, as set forth above in the selections. His main arguments may be analytically summarized as follows:

1. The things we experience are sensations or ideas.

2. Among the things we experience are pain and pleasure, heat and cold, light and colors, size and shape.

3. Therefore, these are sensations or ideas.

4. Hence it is self-contradictory to say that objects do not have sensations or ideas but do have size and shape. [For size and shape are sensations or ideas.]

5. Hence objects, conceived of as things that don't have sensations or ideas but do have size and shape, cannot exist.

6. Thus, because objects, conceived in this way, cannot exist, they must just be clusters of ideas or sensations. To be, Berkeley wrote, is to be perceived: *esse est percipi*.

In this argument, (6) follows from (5), and (5) follows from (4), which follows from (3), which follows from (2) and (1). Because (2) seems indisputable, the entire argument rests on (1).

Can (1) be challenged? Well, try to do so. You might contend (a) that we never experience sensations or ideas. (But is this silly?) Or you might contend (b) that some of the items we experience are sensations or ideas but that others are not. (But then how would we distinguish one from the other?) Or finally, you might contend (c) that although the only things we experience are sensations or ideas, at least some of these *warrant the inference* that external bodies exist. Option (c), of course, is John Locke's representative realism, which leaves it entirely mysterious how our sensations do warrant such an inference, if, according to (c), we experience only sensations, never objects.

If you are not wholly satisfied with any of the options (a), (b), or (c), or with Berkeley's argument, you have company, including the next great philosopher after Berkeley, David Hume.

feelings. In some passages Hume displays total skepticism, but mostly he appears as a modified skeptic who focuses his attention on certain narrower issues, including, most importantly, the knowledge and nature of the self, causality, induction, God, and the external world. And these issues have tended to dominate epistemological inquiry since Hume's time.

Much of Hume's epistemology rests on four assumptions. To get full value from your reading, you should consider whether you accept them.

1. Thought, knowledge, belief, conception, and judgment each consist in having ideas.

2. All ideas are derived from, and are copies of, *impressions* of sense or inner feelings. (Hume's impressions are what we would call *perceptions*.)

3. Every claim that something exists is a factual claim. (That is, when you claim that something exists, you are expressing what you think is a fact.)

4. Factual claims can be established only by observation or by causal inference from what is observed. (For example, you can tell if an engine is knocking just by listening to it, but to know that it has worn bearings you have to make an inference to the cause of the knocking.)

Now, let's consider what these innocent little assumptions entail.

The Quarter Experiment

Let's begin with (3) and (4). First, go find a quarter and put it in front of you next to this book. You would claim that the quarter exists, correct? This claim, according to principle (4), can be established—that is, proved or justified, only by observation or by inference from what you observe, right?

But what is it you observe? The quarter? Well, no, as a matter of fact that doesn't seem quite right. Look at what you call the quarter. Leave it on your desk and get up and move around the room a bit, looking at the quarter all the while. Now, then: what you *observe*, as you move about, is a silverish expanse that constantly changes its size and shape as you move. Right now, for example, what you *observe* is probably elliptical in shape. But a *quarter* is not the sort of thing that constantly changes its size and shape, and a quarter is never elliptical (unless someone did something illegal to it.) *So what you observe changes its size and shape, but the quarter does not change its size and shape. It follows that what you observe is not the quarter.*

Here you might object. "What I'm seeing is a silver expanse from various distances and angles," you might say.

But in fact, if you consider carefully what you are observing, it is a silverish expanse that changes its size and shape. You do not see a silverish expanse that remains unchanged. What you see does change. Thus, it still follows, because the quarter does not change, that what you see is not the quarter.

What is it, then, that you observe? According to Hume, it is your *sense impressions* of the quarter. Thus, if your belief that the quarter exists is to be justified, that belief must be a causal inference from what you observe—that is, from your impressions—to something that is distinct from your impressions and causes them, namely, the quarter. But there is a major problem here: you never experience or are in any way in contact with anything that *is* distinct from your impressions. Thus you never observe a connection between your perceptions and *the quarter!* So how could you possibly establish that the quarter *causes* your impressions? And if you cannot establish that, then, according to Hume, you cannot regard your belief in the existence of the quarter as justified.

Of course, the same considerations apply to a belief in the existence of any external object whatsoever. Here's Hume expressing these considerations in his own words:

▶ S E L E C T I O N 5.6

From David Hume, A TREATISE OF HUMAN NATURE (1)

The only existences, of which we are certain, are perceptions. . . . The only conclusion we can draw from the existence of one thing to that of another, is by means of the relation of cause and effect, which shews, that there is a connection betwixt them. . . . But as no things are ever present to the mind but perceptions; it follows that we may observe a conjunction or a relation of cause and effect between different perceptions, but can never observe it between perceptions and objects. 'Tis impossible, therefore, that from the existence of any of the qualities of the former, we can ever form any conclusion concerning the existence of the latter.

Now, go back to innocent assumptions (1) and (2), on page 152. Notice that it follows directly from these two assumptions that there is no knowledge, belief, conception, judgment, thought about, or even idea of external objects, or things that are distinct from our sense impressions of them! Here again Hume explains:

▶ S E L E C T I O N 5.7

From David Hume, A TREATISE OF HUMAN NATURE (2)

Now, since nothing is ever present to the mind but perceptions, and since all ideas are derived from something antecedently present to the mind; it follows, that 'tis impossible for us so much as to conceive or form an idea of anything specifically different from ideas and impressions. Let us fix our attention out of ourselves as much as possible: Let us chase our imagination to the heavens, or to the utmost limits of the universe; we never really advance a step beyond ourselves, nor can conceive any kind of existence, but those perceptions, which have appeared in that narrow compass.

Hume on the Self

According to Hume, similar careful scrutiny of the notion of the self or mind, supposedly an unchanging nonmaterial substance within us, discloses that we have no knowledge of such a thing. Indeed, we do not really have even an *idea* of the mind, if the mind is defined as an unchanging nonmaterial substance within, Hume holds. For again, our ideas cannot go beyond our sense impressions, and we have no impressions of the mind, except perhaps as a bundle of impressions:

▶ S E L E C T I O N 5.8

From David Hume, A TREATISE OF HUMAN NATURE (3)

There are some philosophers, who imagine we are every moment intimately conscious of what we call our Self [or mind]; that we feel its existence and its continuance in existence; and are certain, beyond the evidence of a demonstration, both of its perfect identity and simplicity. ... Unluckily all these positive assertions are contrary to that very experience, which is pleaded for them, nor have we any idea of *self*, after the manner it is here explained. For from what impression could this idea be derived? ... It must be some one impression, that gives rise to every real idea. But self or person is not any one impression, but that to which our several impressions and ideas are supposed to have a reference. If any impression gives rise to the idea of self, that impression must continue invariably the same, through the whole course of our lives; since self is supposed to exist after that manner. But there is no impression constant and invariable. ... There is no such idea. ...

For my part, when I enter most intimately into what I call *myself*, I always stumble on some particular perception or other, of heat or cold, light or shade, love or hatred, pain or pleasure. I never can catch *myself* at any time without a perception, and never can observe any thing but the perception. ... The mind is a kind of theatre, where several perceptions successively make their appearance; pass, re-pass, glide away, and mingle in an infinite variety of postures and situations. There is properly no *simplicity* in it at one time, nor *identity* in different. ... The comparison of the theatre must not mislead us. They are the successive perceptions only, that constitute the mind.

Hume on Cause and Effect

Because any inference from the existence of one thing to that of another is founded, according to Hume, on the relation of cause and effect, Hume analyzed that relation carefully and discovered that experience reveals no necessary connection between a cause and an effect.

Do we see the pin *making* the balloon pop? Hume maintained that all he saw was just (1) the pin coming into spatial contact with the balloon, followed by (2) the balloon popping. He did not see the pin making the balloon pop.

Profile: David Hume (1711–1776)

David Hume died from cancer at the age of sixty-five. In the face of his own annihilation he retained his composure and cheerfulness, having achieved the goal of the ancient skeptics, *ataraxia* (unperturbedness). It may be questioned, though, whether his calm good nature resulted from his skepticism, for apparently he exhibited this trait of personality throughout his life.

Born in Edinburgh of a "good family," as he said in his autobiography, Hume was encouraged to study law, but "found insurmountable aversion to everything but the pursuits of philosophy and general learning." Before he was thirty, he published *A Treatise of Human Nature*, one of the most important philosophical works ever written. Yet at the time Hume's *Treatise* "fell dead-born from the press," as he put it, "without reaching such distinction as even to excite a murmur among the zealots." Convinced that the failure of the work was due more to form than content, he recast parts of it anew in *An Enquiry Concerning Human Understanding* and *An Enquiry Concerning the Principles of Morals*. The latter work, in Hume's opinion, was incomparably his best. Hume's last philosophical work, *Dialogues Concerning Natural Religion*, was published posthumously in 1779.

There are differences between Hume's *Treatise* and the *Enquiry*, his two works in epistemology, and philosophers disagree about the merits of each. In any case, during his lifetime Hume's reputation was primarily as a historian rather than as a philosopher. Nevertheless, his impact on subsequent philosophy, especially in Great Britain and other English-speaking countries, and on Kant, was significant.

In the passage that follows, Hume's friend Adam Smith quotes a letter from Hume's physician at the time of Hume's death and then adds a few thoughts of his own.

Dear Sir,

Yesterday, about four o'clock, afternoon, Mr. Hume expired. The near approach of his death became evident in the night between Thursday and Friday, when his disease became excessive, and soon weakened him so much, that he could no longer rise out of his bed. He continued to the last perfectly sensible, and free from much pain or feelings of distress. He never dropped the smallest expression of impatience; but when he

At first, this thesis—that we experience no necessary connection between a cause and its effect—seems straightforwardly false. The car going by *makes* the noise you hear, not so? The impact of the golf club *drives* the ball down the fairway. Disconnecting a spark plug *forces* the engine to idle roughly. The cue-ball *moves* the eight-ball when it hits it. What could be plainer than that in each case the cause *necessitates* the effect?

had occasion to speak to the people about him, always did it with affection and tenderness. . . . When he became very weak, it cost him an effort to speak; and he died in such a happy composure of mind, that nothing could exceed it.

Thus died our most excellent and never to be forgotten friend; concerning whose philosophical opinions men will, no doubt, judge variously . . . but concerning whose character and conduct there can scarce be a difference of opinion. His temper, indeed, seemed to be more happily balanced, if I may be allowed such an expression, than that perhaps of any other man I have ever known. Even in the lowest state of his fortune, his great and necessary frugality never hindered him from exercising, upon proper occasions, acts both of charity and generosity. It was a frugality bounded not upon avarice, but upon the love of independency. The extreme gentleness of his nature never weakened either the firmness of his mind or the steadiness of his resolutions. His constant pleasantry was the genuine effusion of good nature and good humor, tempered with delicacy and modesty, and without even the slightest tincture of malignity, so frequently the disagreeable source of what is called wit in other men. It never was the meaning of his raillery to mortify; and therefore, far from offending, it seldom failed to please and delight, even those who were frequently the objects of it; there was not perhaps any one of all his great and amiable qualities which contributed more to endear his conversation. And that gayety of temper, so agreeable in society, but which is so often accompanied with frivolous and superficial qualities, was in him certainly attended with the most severe application, the most extensive learning, the greatest depth of thought, and a capacity in every respect the most comprehensive. Upon the whole, I have always considered him, both in his lifetime and since his death, as approaching as nearly to the idea of a perfectly wise and virtuous man as perhaps the nature of human frailty will permit.

I ever am, dear sir,
Most affectionally yours,
Adam Smith

Yet by paying careful attention to what he actually experienced in an instance of so-called causation, Hume discovered that he did not experience the cause actually producing the effect. His experience of supposed causation, he discovered, consisted at best in awareness of the nearness in space and successiveness in time of the cause and effect along with recollection of a constant conjunction of similar things in past experience. You don't really *see* the cue-ball *moving* the eight-ball; what you see is just a sequence of events: first, you see the cue-ball in motion, then you see it hit the eight-ball, and then you see the eight-ball in motion. And though you recollect that there is a constant conjunction between a cue-ball's hitting another ball and the other ball's starting to move, you do not experience any *necessity* in the other ball's moving. Therefore, Hume wrote, "necessity is something in the mind, not in the objects."

In short, Hume observed that "there is nothing in any object, considered in itself, which can afford us a reason for drawing a conclusion beyond it." "The effect," he wrote, "is totally different from the cause, and consequently can never be discovered in it."

▶ S E L E C T I O N 5.9

From David Hume, A TREATISE OF HUMAN NATURE (4)

When I see, for instance a Billiard-ball moving in a straight line towards another; even suppose motion in the second ball should by accident be suggested to me, as the result of their contact or impulse; may I not conceive, that a hundred different events might as well follow from that cause? May not both these balls remain at absolute rest? May not the first ball return in a straight line, or leap off from the second in any line or direction? All these suppositions are consistent and conceivable. Why then should we give preference to one, which is no more consistent or conceivable than the rest? All our reasonings a priori will never be able to show us any foundation for this preference.

Further, according to Hume, even after we observe a frequent and constant conjunction between a cause and its effect, there is no rational justification for supposing that that conjunction will repeat itself in the future.

Here's an example. You have experienced a constant conjunction between flame and heat. Are you not then rationally justified in supposing that future experience will show a similar conjunction between flame and heat? Can you seriously doubt that this supposition is rationally justified?

Well, Hume's answer is that it is *not* rationally justified. If you say that the next flame you encounter will be accompanied by heat, it is because you suppose that *the future will resemble the past.* Indeed, all reasoning based on present and past experience rests on the supposition that the future will be like the past. But that means, Hume saw in a flash of brilliant insight, that the supposition itself cannot be proved by an appeal to experience. To attempt to prove the supposition by appealing to experience, he observed, "must evidently be going in a circle."

It is hard to exaggerate the significance of this finding, as a moment's thought will show. The fact that all inference from past and present expe-

Hume as a Total Skeptic

When Hume said that he was ready to reject all belief and reasoning and could look on no opinion even as more probable or likely than another, he was expressing the views of a total skeptic. You should be aware, though, that a true skeptic, Hume said, "will be diffident in his philosophical doubts, as well as of his philosophical conviction." In other words, a true (total) skeptic will doubt his doubts, too.

rience rests on an apparently unprovable assumption (that the future will resemble the past) leads to skeptical conclusions even more sweeping than Hume for the most part was willing to countenance. It means, for instance, that much of what we think we know we do not really know. Will food and water nourish you the next time you eat and drink? Will my name be the same this evening as it is now? Will the words in the beginning of this sentence have changed meaning by the time you get to the end of the sentence? Evidently the answers to these questions, while seemingly obvious, *are mere assumptions that we cannot really know*.

Perhaps you can now understand why, in the conclusion to Book I of *The Treatise of Human Nature*, Hume reflects that what he has written shows that

> the understanding, when it acts alone, and according to its most general principles, entirely subverts itself, and leaves not the lowest degree of evidence in any proposition, either in philosophy or common life.

Thus, Hume says, he is "ready to reject all belief and reasoning, and can look upon no opinion even as more probable or likely than another." This skepticism is not modified: it is uncompromisingly total.

Now that you have looked at the philosophy of David Hume, you will perhaps see why we have given this book the title it has. If Hume's ideas are correct, then must we not in the end despair as Cratylus did and watch the world from a distance, merely wiggling our fingers?

In the next chapter we will see whether anything can be left for philosophy after Hume.

To help you review, here is a checklist of the key philosophers and concepts of this chapter. The brief descriptive sentences that appear with each philosopher summarize one of his leading ideas. Keep in mind that some of these summary statements represent terrific oversimplifications of complex positions.

Checklist

Philosophers

- **Xenophanes** Said that even if truth were stated, it would not be known.
- **Heraclitus** Said that everything is in flux; you cannot step twice into the same river.
- **Cratylus** Held that because everything is changing, communication is impossible.
- **Gorgias** Said that there is no reality, and if there were, we could not know it, and even if we could, we couldn't communicate our knowledge.
- **Protagoras** Said that man is the measure of all things.
- **Plato** Believed that knowledge is correct belief together with an "account." Said that the proper objects of true knowledge are the Forms.
- **Diogenes Laertius** Third-century Greek biographer whose tales are usually intriguing but sometimes not fully reliable.
- **Pyrrho** Held that every theory can be opposed by an equally valid contradictory theory, so we must suspend judgment on all issues.
- **Sextus Empiricus** Most famous total skeptic. Held the position: I do not know whether or not knowledge is possible.
- **St. Augustine** Rejected skepticism; diagnosed the cause of error in sense perception.
- **René Descartes** Used doubting methodology to obtain certain knowledge. "Father" of modern philosophy.
- **Benedictus de Spinoza** Continental rationalist (see Chapter 3).
- **Baron Gottfried Wilhelm von Leibniz** Continental rationalist (see Chapter 11).
- **Pierre Bayle** Famous seventeenth-century skeptic; found reason to doubt just about everything.
- **John Locke** Held that we perceive objects indirectly by means of our perceptions of them, some of which he believed were accurate copies of the real properties of objects.
- **George Berkeley** Rejected distinction between primary and secondary qualities; held that sensible objects exist only in the mind.
- **David Hume** Summoned powerful arguments to question our supposed knowledge of the self, causality, God, and the external world.

Concepts

skepticism

total vs. modified skepticism

Sophists

Plato's Forms

Academics

Pyrrhonists

epoche

ataraxia

agoge

ten tropes (modes)

principle of noncontradiction

dream conjecture

evil demon conjecture

cogito, ergo sum

clear and distinct criterion

Continental rationalists

British empiricists

Nihil in intellectu quod prius non fuerit in sensu

theory of innate ideas

representative realism

tabula rasa

primary vs. secondary qualities

esse est percipi

constant conjunction

"The future will resemble the past."

---

1. Explain the difference between total and modified skepticism.

2. What are some of the questions that philosophers have been concerned with under the heading: Is knowledge possible?

3. "Everything is changing, so our words change in their meaning as we speak them. Therefore, true communication is impossible." Evaluate this argument.

4. Compare and contrast the views of the Academics and the Pyrrhonists.

5. "Nothing can be known." What is a powerful objection to this claim?

6. "I do not know whether or not knowledge is possible." Critically evaluate this claim.

7. Devise an argument, other than the two mentioned in the next item, to defend some version of total skepticism.

8. Explain and critically evaluate either Descartes's "dream conjecture" or his "evil demon conjecture."

9. "Descartes assumed that there cannot be thinking without an 'I' that does the thinking. Since he wanted to question everything, he should have questioned this assumption." Critically evaluate this remark.

10. Why, if all our knowledge comes from experience, is it difficult to maintain that we have knowledge of external objects?

11. Explain Berkeley's reasons for maintaining that it is a contradiction to hold that sensible objects exist outside the mind.

12. Do you ever observe anything other than your own perceptions? Explain.

13. Explain Hume's reasons for questioning the idea of the mind/self.

14. "Necessity is something in the mind, not in the objects." Explain what this means and what Hume's reasons were for holding it.

15. Will the future resemble the past? Can you *know* that it will, or must you merely *assume* that it will?

Questions for Discussion and Review

Suggested Further Readings

Julia Annas and Jonathan Barnes, *The Modes of Scepticism: Ancient Texts and Modern Interpretations* (Cambridge: Cambridge University Press, 1985). Another product of the recent interest in ancient skepticism. Excellent.

Augustine, *Against the Academicians*, vol. 3, Sister Mary Patricia Garvey, trans. (Milwaukee: Marquette University Press, 1957). Contains easy-to-understand arguments against skepticism.

George Berkeley, *Principles of Human Knowledge/Three Dialogues*, Roger Woolhouse, ed. (New York: Penguin Books, 1988). These are Berkeley's main works. As we said earlier, Berkeley is so much fun to read that there is no reason to turn to secondary sources or excerpts.

John Burnet, *Early Greek Philosophy*, 4th ed. (London: Macmillan, originally published in 1930). This is a standard work on early Greek philosophy.

René Descartes, *Meditations on First Philosophy*, in René Descartes, *Philosophical Works*, in two volumes. E. S. Haldane and G. R. T. Ross, trans. (Cambridge: Cambridge University Press, 1968). The dream conjecture and evil demon conjecture are both here.

Philip P. Hallie, ed., *Scepticism, Man, and God: Selections from the Major Writings of Sextus Empiricus* (Middletown, Conn.: Wesleyan University Press, 1964). Clear, readable, authoritative.

C. W. Hendel, Jr., *Hume Selections* (New York: Scribners, 1927). Hume's "Treatise" is the most skeptical of his works, and there are ample selections here from that work.

G. S. Kirk, J. E. Raven, and M. Schofield, *The Presocratic Philosophers: A Critical History with a Selection of Texts*, 2nd ed. (Cambridge: Cambridge University Press, 1983). This is a comprehensive recent treatment of the pre-Socratics.

S. Lamprecht, ed., *Locke Selections* (New York: Scribners, 1928). If you want to read about Locke's theory of knowledge in more detail, you must turn to his *An Essay Concerning Human Understanding*, in 2 vols., A. C. Fraser, ed. (New York: Dover, 1959). This (the Fraser edition) is a heavily annotated work.

Plato, *Theaetetus*, in E. Hamilton and H. Cairns, eds., *The Collected Dialogues of Plato* (New York: Bollingen Foundation, 1961). Plato's classic text on the nature of knowledge.

Epistemology After Hume

The quest for certainty has played a considerable part in the history of philosophy: it has been assumed that without a basis of certainty all our claims to knowledge must be suspect. Unless some things are certain, it is held, nothing can be even probable.

—A. J. AYER

In the last chapter we saw that epistemology reached a crisis in the philosophy of David Hume. By carefully examining such key concepts as self and causation, and by adhering very rigorously to the principle that all ideas are derived from impressions, Hume's philosophy seemed to show that human understanding "entirely subverts itself and leaves not the lowest degree of evidence in any proposition either in philosophy or in common life." Is epistemology possible after Hume? Is *philosophy* possible?

Immanuel Kant

It is time now to turn to **Immanuel Kant** (1724–1804). Most scholars regard Kant as one of the most brilliant intellects of all time. Unfortunately, they also consider him one of the most difficult of all philosophers to read. Difficult or not, Kant provided a significant and ingenious response to Hume's skepticism.

In a sentence, Kant believed that certain knowledge does indeed exist and set about to show how this could be possible, given Hume's various arguments that pointed in the opposite direction.

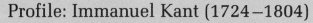

Profile: Immanuel Kant (1724–1804)

Kant was one of the first modern philosophers to earn his living as a professor of philosophy. Though he hardly ever left Königsberg, his birthplace, his ideas traveled far, and he is considered by many as the greatest philosopher, ever.

Kant's first works were in natural science and secured for him a substantial reputation before his appointment as professor of logic and metaphysics at Königsberg in 1770. After his appointment, he wrote nothing for ten years as he contemplated the issues that eventually appeared in his most important work, the *Critique of Pure Reason* (1781, 2nd ed. 1787). The actual writing of the book took "four or five months," he said, and was done "with the utmost attention to the contents, but with less concern for the presentation or for making things easy for the reader." Readers universally understand what he meant.

The reaction to the work was primarily one of confusion, and this led Kant to publish a shorter, more accessible version of his major work, entitled *Prolegomena to Any Future Metaphysics* (1783). This is an excellent book with which to begin the study of Kant's epistemology and metaphysics.

Two years after publication of the *Prolegomena*, Kant's first major treatise on ethics appeared, the *Foundations for the Metaphysics of Morals*. A comparatively brief work, it is nevertheless one of the most important books ever written on ethics.

Kant's second and third critiques, the *Critique of Practical Reason* (1788) and *Critique of Judgment* (1790), were concerned with morality and aesthetics, respectively. In addition to the three *Critiques*, the *Prolegomena*, and the *Foundations*, Kant wrote many other lesser works.

In his last years he suffered the indignity of hearing younger German philosophers say that he had not really understood what he had written, an unusually stupid idea that history has long since laid to rest.

The Ordering Principles of the Mind

Kant agreed with Hume that all knowledge *begins* with experience. But it does not follow, Kant maintained, that knowledge must therefore *arise from* experience. Experience is the occasion for the awakening of the knowing mind, Kant said; but the mind, thus awakened, is not limited in its knowledge to what it has found in experience.

Why is the mind not limited to what it has found in experience, according to Kant? Because the constituents of experience must themselves always be ordered and organized in certain ways even to count as experience. And it is possible to have knowledge of these underlying principles by means of which the constituents of experience are ordered and organized. Because this knowledge is of the universally applicable preconditions of experience, it is absolutely certain, he held.

An example may help make these difficult thoughts clearer. Suppose we were to suggest to you that someday you might encounter a fire that

Kant's Fundamental Insight

Kant called his most fundamental epistemological insight **the Copernican revolution in philosophy.** Copernicus (1473–1543) was the modern European credited with the heliocentric theory of planetary motion, according to which the old assumption that the sun and planets circle the earth must be replaced with a new assumption that the earth and other planets circle the sun. Only the new assumption could account for the observed motions of the heavenly bodies, Copernicans maintained.

In somewhat analogous manner, Kant said that the old assumption that our ideas, to be true, must conform to objects outside the mind, must be replaced with a new assumption that objects outside the mind must conform to that which the mind imposes on them in experiencing them. Only the new assumption could account for our knowledge of certain universally true principles, Kant maintained.

was not hot or a plant that had no fragrance whatsoever. We imagine that you would discount the possibility entirely. Still, if we pressed you a bit, you should concede that, well, it's not absolutely *certain* that you would never come across a cool fire or a plant that had absolutely no fragrance, though you would probably regard it as *almost* certain. (Having difficulty imagining the possibility of a cool fire or plants that don't smell at all? Think, for instance, of some strange new synthetic substance burning, say, in alcohol. Or think of a plant developed by genetic engineers to subsist on traces of methane rather than on water and air. Would such a plant have odor? Who knows?)

But suppose we were to suggest to you that someday you might encounter a fire or a plant that was not in *space or time.* Now, this suggestion you would find just plain *absurd.* You would not, indeed you *could* not, take us seriously. Whereas you cannot be *absolutely* certain that sometime in your lifetime you won't encounter a cool fire or a plant that has absolutely no fragrance, you can be absolutely certain that you will *never ever* encounter a fire or plant that will not be in space and time.

Clearly, therefore, a fundamental difference exists between the spatial-temporal qualities of things, on one hand, and qualities such as their warmth and fragrance, or their heaviness or color or texture, on the other. You know that each event you witness and each object you encounter *must* be experienced in space or in time (or both). But given Hume's principles, you could not absolutely know this, because (remember?) you cannot be certain that future experience will resemble past experience. So something must be wrong with Hume's principles.

Space and time are thus different from other qualities, and their universal applicability to experienced things can only be explained, according to Kant, on the supposition that they are necessary *preconditions* of experience. *To even qualify as experienced, a thing must be experienced as in space or time.*

Let's put it another way. Our certain knowledge that everything we encounter will be experienced in space or time cannot be *derived from* experience, for experience informs us only of the way things have been so far, and not of the way they *must* be. So our knowledge of space and time results from the fact that space and time are the *way* experienced items are experienced: they are the *form* under which experience takes shape. Sensation, we might say, provides the content of perception; space and time provide the form.

Perceptions Must Be Conceptualized and Unified

Now perceptions by themselves are "blind," according to Kant: they must be organized under concepts for genuine experience to occur. In other words, perception of unconceptualized entities is not experience—experience is perception of this *type* of thing—this *car*, this *person*, this *song*, this *piece of lead*, and so on.

To understand what Kant means, just think of an electric door or an auto-focus camera. They are able to process information that comes to them from the external world, but they do not really experience anything, for they do not *recognize* the information that comes to them. They "perceive" a person in front of them, but they do not *experience* a person, for they do not conceptualize what they perceive as a person or *as* anything else.

Further, Kant holds, perceptions, to qualify as experience, must be connected together or *unified* in one consciousness. But conceptualization and unification must conform to certain rules or principles of the understanding, just as perception must conform to spatial-temporal shaping. Thus, for instance, for experience to be possible things must be apprehended not merely as in space or time but as conforming to cause-and-effect relationships as well; and change must be experienced as the change of a permanent substance whose quantity in nature remains constant.

Things in Themselves

In substance, then, this was Kant's response to the challenge put to epistemology by David Hume. Yes, knowledge begins with experience. But no, knowledge does not all arise from experience. Because there are certain underlying principles and categories in terms of which the raw data of sensation must be ordered if these data are even to count as experience, we have universally valid knowledge of experienceable objects. We thus have certain knowledge that experienceable objects are in space and time, stand in causal relationships with one another, and must otherwise conform to other rules of the understanding. They must so conform, to repeat, because if they did not, they could not qualify as experienced.

So Kant showed that there can be epistemology after Hume.

Now one very important final point must be mentioned about Kant's epistemology. According to Kant, we cannot say that things *as they are in themselves*, as they are independently of experience, must also conform to these principles and rules of the understanding. Concerning the experienceable object we can have certain knowledge, because an object, to be experienced, must conform to these rules and principles. But concerning the other world, the world of the thing-in-itself, *das Ding-an-sich* (as it is said in German), complete skepticism is unavoidable, for Kant. And when rules that apply to the experienced world are applied to a reality-beyond-experience, contradictions and mistakes are the result.

So, relative to the experienceable world, Kant was not a skeptic, but relative to things-in-themselves he was.

In Selection 6.1 Kant asks, and then answers, the question, "What, then, is time?"

▶ S E L E C T I O N 6.1

From Immanuel Kant, *CRITIQUE OF PURE REASON**

Transcendental Aesthetic

Section II, Time

§ 4, Metaphysical Exposition of the Concept of Time

1. Time is not an empirical concept that has been derived from any experience. For neither coexistence nor succession would ever come within our perception, if the representation of time were not presupposed as underlying them *a priori.* . . .

2. Time is a necessary representation that underlies all intuitions. We cannot, in respect of appearances in general, remove time itself, though we can quite well think time as void of appearances. Time is, therefore, given *a priori.* In it alone is actuality of appearances possible at all. Appearances may, one and all, vanish; but time (as the universal condition of their possibility) cannot itself be removed.

3. . . . Time has only one dimension; different times are not simultaneous but successive (just as different spaces are not successive but simultaneous). These principles cannot be derived from experience, for experience would give neither strict universality nor apodeictic certainty. We should only be able to say that common experience teaches us that it is so; not that it must be so. These principles are valid as rules under which alone experiences are possible; and they instruct us in regard to the experiences, not by means of them.

4. Time is not a discursive, or what is called a general concept, but a pure form of sensible intuition. Different times are but parts of one and the same time . . . Moreover, the proposition that different times cannot be simultaneous is not to be derived from a general concept. . . .

§ 6, CONCLUSIONS FROM THESE CONCEPTS

(a) Time is not something which exists of itself, or which inheres in things as an objective determination, and it does not, therefore, remain when abstraction is made of all subjective conditions of its intuition. Were it self-subsistent, it would be something which would be actual and yet not an actual object. Were it a determination or order inhering in things themselves, it could not precede the objects as their condition. . . .

(b) Time is nothing but the form of inner sense, that is, of the intuition of ourselves and of our inner state. It cannot be a determination of outer appearances; it has to do neither with shape nor position, but with the relation of representations in our inner state. . . .

(c) Time is the formal *a priori* condition of all appearances whatsoever. Space, as the pure form of all *outer* intuition, is so far limited; it serves as the *a priori* condition only of outer appearances. But since all representations, whether they have for their objects outer things or not, belong, in themselves, as determinations of the mind, to our inner state; and since this inner state stands under the formal condition of inner intuition, and so belongs to time, time is an *a priori* condition of all appearance whatsoever. It is the immediate condition of inner appearances (of our souls), and thereby the mediate condition of outer appearances. Just as I can say *a priori* that all outer appearances are in space, and are determined *a priori* in conformity with the relations of space, I can also say, from the principle of inner sense, that all appearances whatsoever, that is, all objects of the senses, are in time, and necessarily stand in time-relations.

If we abstract from *our* mode of inwardly intuiting ourselves—the mode of intuition in terms of which we likewise take up into our faculty of representation all outer intuitions—and so take objects as they may be in themselves, then time is nothing. It has objective validity only in respect of appearances, these being things which we take *as objects of our senses.* . . .

Time is therefore a purely subjective condition of our (human) intuition (which is always sensible, that is, so far as we are affected by objects), and in itself, apart from the subject, is nothing.

---

*Kant's footnotes omitted.

The Nineteenth Century

Kant died in 1804, at the beginning of the nineteenth century. The first part of the nineteenth century was the Romantic era in European arts and letters, which rose up in revolt against the rationalism of the preceding century. This was the period that emphasized adventure and spiritual vision in literature, produced huge and noisy symphonies, and stressed exotic themes in the visual arts. Careful reasoning was out; emotional spontaneity was in.

In philosophy, although his successors didn't exactly repudiate what Kant had written, they certainly did stand it on its ear. This dramatic response to Kant was German Absolute Idealism, the philosophies of **Johann Gottlieb Fichte** (1762–1814), **Friedrich Wilhelm Joseph von Schelling** (1775–1854), and **Georg Wilhelm Friedrich Hegel** (1770–1831).

Kant had argued that the mind imposes certain categories on the objects of experience and that this is what makes it possible to have knowledge of the world of experience. His epistemological thesis, as we have seen, is that we can have knowledge *only* of the world of experience, and can have no knowledge of things "as they are in themselves." The Absolute Idealists, however, transformed this epistemological skepticism into metaphysical idealism. What could there be such that the mind could not know it?, they asked. Whatever *is*, they said, is *knowable*; therefore, they concluded, thought does not merely categorize reality, its categories *are* reality. There cannot be unknowable things-in-themselves, they said, for everything that is, is a product of the knowing mind.

Hegel, the most influential of the Absolute Idealists, and one of the most important philosophers of all time, set forth an account of consciousness in its various stages from sense perception to absolute knowledge. Knowledge of the world is ultimately self-knowledge, Hegel maintained; the object of thought is thought itself. This perplexing theory, which is really metaphysical rather than epistemological, was discussed in Chapter 3 (see pages 91–94).

If Hegel was the most famous German philosopher of the nineteenth century, **John Stuart Mill** (1806–1873) was perhaps the most widely known British philosopher. The Absolute Idealists, despite their differences with Kant, were greatly under Kant's influence. But Mill was unfazed. He accepted the basic empiricist premise of Locke, Berkeley, and Hume that all ideas and beliefs, and thus, too, all knowledge, derive from sense experience, and he tried to provide an account of how we come to know and believe some of the things we do, given this premise.

Mill distinguished between what is directly given to us in perception and what we know on the basis of inference. When we perceive a table, for instance, what is directly given to us is some sensations, but the table is more than just *these* sensations. From these sensations that we are actually having, we infer that if we were to move around a bit, we would experience new and additional sensations. Thus the table consists not only of the actual sensations but also of those sensations that we anticipate having if we were to move around the table, push it, put things on it, etc. The table, in short, Mill says, is a "permanent possibility of sensation." Mill's theory, you can see, was a not-too-distant cousin of Berkeley's, according to which tables and other "external objects" are groups or clusters of sensations.

Mill considered whether you could offer a parallel analysis of the mind as a permanent possibility of awareness. But he was not satisfied with this notion, because, in particular, he believed, the mind is some-

Profile: John Stuart Mill (1806–1873)

Many years ago, one of the authors came across a table of projected IQ scores for various historic "geniuses" in a psychology text. (Who knows how the scores were calculated?) At the top of the list, with some incredible score, was John Stuart Mill.

Mill began reading Greek at three and Latin at eight, and by adolescence had completed an extensive study of Greek and Latin literature, as well as of history, mathematics, and logic. Mill's education was administered by his father, who subjected young John to a rigorous regimen.

At fifteen Mill settled on his lifelong objective, to work for social and political reform, and it is as a reformer and ethical and political philosopher that he is most remembered. Mill championed individual rights and personal freedom, and advocated emancipation of women and proportional representation. His most famous work, *On Liberty* (1859), is thought by many to be the definitive defense of freedom of thought and discussion.

In ethics Mill was a utilitarian, concerning which we will have much to say in Chapter 8. He published *Utilitarianism* in 1863.

Mill's interests also ranged over a broad range of topics in epistemology, metaphysics, and logic. His *A System of Logic* (1843), which was actually read at the time by the man in the street, represented an empiricist approach to logic, abstraction, psychology, sociology, and morality. Mill's "methods of induction" is still standard fare in university courses in beginning logic.

When Mill was twenty-five, he met Harriet Taylor, a merchant's wife, and this was the beginning of one of the most celebrated love affairs of all time. Twenty years later, and three years after her husband died, Mrs. Taylor married Mill, on whose thought she had a profound influence. *On Liberty* was perhaps jointly written with her, and in any case was dedicated to her.

Harriet Taylor died in 1858. Mill spent his remaining years in Avignon, France, where she had died, to be near her grave.

Mill's *Autobiography*, also widely read, appeared in the year of his death. Mill still is the most celebrated English philosopher of his century.

---

times aware of its awareness. He proposed no other analysis of the nature of the mind, however.

It's hard to imagine two more divergent philosophies than those of Hegel and Mill. And so it is that in the twentieth century the philosophy that evolved from nineteenth-century idealism is starkly different from that which grew out of the empiricist tradition of Mill.

Early Twentieth-Century Epistemology

As we've noted in earlier chapters, in our century the predominant philosophical tradition in English-speaking countries is analytic, and the professional concerns of philosophers from within this tradition have been different from those of the existentialist and phenomenological traditions

In the remainder of this chapter we will focus on epistemology in the analytic tradition. This tradition reaches back much more to Locke, Berkeley, Hume, and Mill than to the German idealist philosophies that were an outgrowth of Kant. It also, unfortunately, tends to discount or even just simply ignore some of the important insights of Kant himself.

Bertrand Russell

Now, as we have seen, through the course of modern epistemology from Descartes onward, the question of the possibility of knowledge tended to become focused on the question of the possibility of knowledge of an external world, a world outside the mind. Here, on one hand, are the "data" actually given to us in sensation; there, on the other, are the external objects we strongly believe are out there. How do we get from knowledge of our sense-data to knowledge of the objects? This was still the fundamental question of early twentieth-century epistemology. Note that the early twentieth-century epistemologists, unlike the classic British empiricists, had also to deal with the fact that pretty convincing scientific reason was available for thinking that these external objects also included molecules, atoms, and subatomic particles.

According to the most famous British philosopher of the twentieth century, **Bertrand Russell** (1872–1970), what we truly *know* is the data of immediate experience, i.e., sense-data. Therefore, said Russell, what we *believe* exists (e.g., physical objects *and* scientific entities like atoms and electrons), must either be *inferred* from the data of immediate experience or—and this is the view Russell favored—they must in effect be *defined* in terms of the data of immediate experience. Are external objects to be viewed as *inferences* from sense-data, or are they to be regarded as *definable* in terms of sense-data? This is a distinction that we had better explain.

Russell's work in logic and the philosophy of mathematics showed him that discourse about numbers can be restated in terms of another more basic and undeniable kind of entity, namely, classes. Thus, numbers can in effect be *defined* in terms of classes. (A class is a group of things sharing common attributes.) In *Principia Mathematica* (1910–1913), Russell and **Alfred North Whitehead** (1861–1947) endeavored to show in detail how all of pure mathematics could be stated in terms of logic, employing as undefined terms not numbers but rather those required for logic, such as class membership and implication. The book has great significance for both philosophy and mathematics.

Thus similarly, Russell reasoned, our supposed knowledge of physical objects and scientific entities can be expressed, at least in theory, in propositions that make reference to less doubtable entities, namely, sense-impressions or sense-data. In other words, physical objects and scientific entities can be *defined* in terms of sense-data. In the language of philosophers, physical objects and scientific entities are **logical constructions** from sense-data.

Now if physical objects and, say, atoms or neutrons, are things the existence of which we *infer* from our sense-data, then we really cannot be certain about their existence, because inferences can always be mistaken. They can always go awry. But Russell said there is really no need to feel uncertain or skeptical about our beliefs in physical objects and atoms and other scientific entities because such entities can be defined in terms of sense-data: our beliefs in physical objects and scientific entities can be "reduced" to beliefs in a more unquestionable sort of entity—namely, our sense-data.

This position, of course, makes a certain amount of sense. Because we can understand a proposition only if it refers, directly or indirectly, to something we are acquainted with, and because it seems that ultimately we are acquainted only with sense-impressions, it seems to follow that we can *understand* discourse about physical objects and scientific entities only insofar as it is reducible to discourse about sense-impressions. And Russell spent a good deal of time and energy in showing how, in broad outline, this reduction might be done for discourse both about ordinary physical objects and about more exotic scientific entities.

In fact, after about 1920 Russell began to think that even the mind that received those sense-impressions might also be "reduced to" or "defined" in terms of the sense-impressions. Thus sense-data or impressions grouped one way would "constitute" a physical object, while grouped another way would be a part of the mind. We said more about this in Chapter 4.

Now in truth Russell was never *entirely* satisfied with the theory that all knowledge could be restated in purely experiential (sensorial) terms and believed increasingly in his later years that some aspects of our scientific and common-sense beliefs can only be viewed as inferences from what we are immediately given in sensation. His misgivings came to be shared by most other philosophers.

In Selection 6.2 Russell explains that the common-sense "thing" (physical object) can be defined as a series of aspects or appearances (sense-data).

▶ S E L E C T I O N   6.2

From Bertrand Russell, OUR KNOWLEDGE OF THE EXTERNAL WORLD

Among the objections to the reality of objects of sense, there is one which is derived from the apparent difference between matter as it appears in physics and things as they appear in sensation. Men of science, for the most part, are willing to condemn immediate data as "merely subjective," while yet maintaining the truth of the physics inferred from those data. But such an attitude, though it may be *capable* of justification, obviously stands in need of it; and the only justification possible must be one which exhibits matter as a logical construction from sense-data—unless, indeed, there were some wholly *a priori* principle by which unknown entities could be inferred from such as are known. It is therefore necessary to find some way of bridging the gulf between the world of physics and the world of sense, and it is this problem which will occupy us in the present lecture. Physicists appear to be unconscious of the gulf, while psychologists, who are conscious of it, have not the mathematical knowledge required for spanning it. The problem is difficult, and I do not know its solution in detail. All that I can hope to do is to make the problem felt, and to indicate the kind of methods by which a solution is to be sought.

Let us begin by a brief description of the two contrasted worlds. We will take first the world of physics, for, though the other world is given while the physical world is inferred, to us now the world of physics is the more familiar, the world of pure sense having become strange and difficult to rediscover. Physics started from the common-sense belief in fairly permanent and fairly rigid bodies—tables and chairs, stones, mountains, the earth and moon and sun. This common-sense belief, it should be noticed, is a piece of audacious metaphysical theorising; objects are not continually present to sensation, and it may be doubted whether they are there when they are not seen or felt. This problem, which has been acute since the time of Berkeley, is ignored by common sense, and has therefore hitherto been ignored by physicists. . . .

Common sense, and physics before the twentieth century, demanded a set of indestructible entities, moving relatively to each other in a single space and a single time. The world of immediate data is quite different from this. Nothing is permanent; even the things that we think are fairly permanent, such as mountains, only become data when we see them, and are not immediately given as existing at other moments. . . .

One task, if what has just been said is correct, which confronts us in trying to connect the world of sense with the world of physics, is the task of reconstructing the conception of matter without the *a priori* beliefs which historically gave rise to it. . . .

For this purpose, it is only necessary to take our ordinary common-sense statements and reword them without the assumption of permanent substance. We say, for example, that things change gradually—sometimes very quickly, but not without passing through a continuous or nearly continuous series of intermediate states. What this means is that, given any sensible appearance, there will usually be, *if we watch*, a continuous series of appearances connected with the given one, leading on by imperceptible gradations to the new appearances which common sense regards as those of the same thing. Thus a thing may be defined as a certain series of appearances, connected with each other by continuity and by certain causal laws. In the case of slowly changing things, this is easily seen. Consider, say, a wall-paper which fades in the course of years. It is an effort not to conceive of it as one "thing" whose colour is slightly different at one time from what it is at another. But what do we really *know* about it? We know that under suitable circumstances—i.e. when we are, as is said, "in the room"—we perceive certain colours in a certain pattern: not always precisely the same colours, but sufficiently similar to feel familiar. If we can state the laws according to which the colour varies, we can state all that is empirically verifiable; the assumption that there is a constant entity, the wall-paper, which "has" these various colours at various times, is a piece of gratuitous metaphysics. We may, if we like, *define* the wall-paper as the series of its aspects. These are collected together by the same motives which led us to regard the wall-paper as one thing, namely a combination of sensible continuity and causal connection. More generally, a "thing" will be defined as a certain series of aspects, namely those which would commonly be said to be *of* the thing. To say that a certain aspect is an aspect *of* a certain thing will merely mean that it is one of those which, taken serially, *are* the thing. Everything will then proceed as before: whatever was verifiable is unchanged, but our language is so interpreted as to avoid an unnecessary metaphysical assumption of permanence.

The above extrusion of permanent things affords an example of the maxim which inspires all scientific philosophising, namely "Occam's razor": *Entities are not to be multiplied without necessity.* In other words, in dealing with any subject-matter, find out what entities are undeniably involved, and state everything in terms of these entities. Very often the resulting statement is more complicated and difficult than one which, like common sense and most philosophy, assumes hypothetical entities whose existence there is no good reason to believe in. We find it easier to imagine a wall-paper with changing colours than to think merely of the series of colours; but it is a mistake to suppose that what is easy and natural in thought is what is most free from unwarrantable assumptions, as the case of "things" very aptly illustrates.

Phenomenalism

The theory we have been considering, that propositions that refer to physical objects ("physical-object propositions") can be expressed in propositions that make reference only to sense-data ("sense-data propositions") is known as **phenomenalism.** Russell, therefore, at one time was a phenomenalist, though over the years he had increasing misgivings about this position.

During the first forty or so years of this century many philosophers in English-speaking countries were phenomenalists, and the *burning issue* of epistemology during this time was whether phenomenalism is sound.

Why was this issue so important? After all, we are considering a period of time that included two world wars, a global depression, and Buchenwald. What could be so important about phenomenalism?

First, you must remember the seed of uncertainty planted by Descartes at the beginning of the Scientific Revolution and Hume's all-inclusive doubts. Can one really be certain of what passes for knowledge? In particular, can one really know of the continued existence of a realm of objects that exist outside the mind? These questions, from Descartes's time onward, *nagged* many philosophers. To epistemologists, they seemed perhaps the most fundamental of all theoretical questions. As Kant had remarked, it was absolutely scandalous that philosophy had been unable to prove that external, material objects exist.

And phenomenalism seemed *so* plausible as a way of certifying our supposed knowledge of external objects. Think once again of the quarter that we talked about in connection with Hume. At first glance it seems that you could, in a variety of ways, be mistaken when you think that there before you is a quarter. But it is easy to suppose that, even though your belief that you are seeing a *quarter* might be mistaken, you could not possibly be mistaken about your *sense-data*. That is, it is easy to suppose that a proposition that refers to your present sense-data, a proposition like, perhaps, "This seems to me to be a round silverish expanse," is **incorrigible**—that is, *incapable* of being false if you believe that it is true. (After all, could you possibly be mistaken about the way things *seem* to you?) Therefore, if the empirical meaning of a physical-object proposition, a proposition like, "There is a quarter," could in fact be captured by an incorrigible sense-data proposition, or set of such propositions, then the nagging skepticism about physical objects would have been answered for once and for all, finally.

So phenomenalism was interesting as a possible way around skepticism about the external world. It was interesting to epistemologists also simply because the precise nature of the *relationship* between, on one hand, our beliefs about the objects of everyday experience and science (i.e., physical objects and their constituents) and, on the other hand, the sensory information that comprises the stream of experience, has always been of interest to epistemologists. Phenomenalism is a theory about this relationship.

But at bottom, the question of whether phenomenalism is sound just simply is the question whether our supposed knowledge of an external world can be understood in purely sensory terms. It is the question, loosely speaking, of whether "reality" reduces to "appearances." The alternative, that it does not reduce, that it is somehow *inferred* from the appearances, seems to leave the mind uncomfortably severed from the world.

For these reasons phenomenalism was of much interest to epistemologists even while the world was at war. And the underlying issue of the relationship of appearance to reality was thought to have (and does have) enduring significance.

Selection 6.3 will help explain why phenomenalism found initial widespread acceptance.

▶ S E L E C T I O N 6.3

From C. H. Whiteley, "PHENOMENALISM: ITS GROUNDS AND DIFFICULTIES"

49. The Meaning of Words

When I am teaching a child the meaning of the word "table," I point to the table so that he sees it; I put his hand to it, so that he feels it; that is, I cause him to sense certain sense-data. Surely it is with these sense-data that he thereupon associates the sound "table"; when he sees and feels similar sense-data, he repeats "table." It is by the differences in what they look like and feel like that he distinguishes tables from chairs and apples and half-crowns. It is natural to conclude that when he uses the word "table" or "apple," he is using it to describe what he sees, feels, tastes, etc., rather than to propound some theory about an invisible and intangible material substance.

The word "table" *means* a certain visible squareness and brownness, a certain tangible hardness; i.e., it means a certain type of sense-experience. When I say "There is a table in this room" I am describing the sense-data which I am now sensing, and if I do not sense such sense-data, then, being a truthful person, I do not say that there is a table in the room. If someone else says that there is, I test his statement by looking and feeling, i.e., by finding out whether the appropriate sense-data are available; if they are not, I dismiss his statement as false. If I say "Socrates drank his companions under the table," I am not describing any sense-experiences which I have now, but I am describing sense-experiences which I suppose Socrates and his companions to have had at another time and place.

We cannot, of course, identify "the table" with any one single sense-datum; an experience which was entirely unique and did not recur would not be worth naming. The function of words is not to name everything we see or hear, but to pick out the recurrent patterns in our experience. They identify our present sense-data as being of the same group or type as others which we have sensed before. A word, then, describes, not a single experience, but a group or type of experiences; the word "table" describes all the various sense-data which we normally refer to as appearances or sensations "of" the table. So a material thing is not indeed identical with any sense-datum; but neither is it something different in kind from sense-data. It is a group, or class, or system of sense-data; and nothing but sense-data goes to constitute it. So this doctrine may be expressed by saying that every statement we make about a material thing is equivalent to another statement about sense-data.

This analysis of the notion of a material thing is called Phenomenalism, since it makes of a material thing a group of phenomena, appearances, instead of a transcendent reality distinct from appearances. It is a widespread view, and has been accepted by many philosophers who do not call themselves Idealists and are far from accepting Berkeley's view that the fundamental reality is Mind. The term "idealism" itself, however, though it has shifted in meaning since, does properly denote just this part of Berkeley's theory, that the material world—"the whole choir of heaven and furniture of the earth" says Berkeley—consists of what he calls "ideas" and I have been calling "sense-data." The word in this sense has nothing to do with ideals, and the theory would have been called "ideaism" but for considerations of pronunciation.

Phenomenalism, then, is the doctrine that all statements about material objects can be completely analysed into statements about sense-data. The analysis of any such statement must be very complex; and the value of the "material-object language" is that it enables us to refer in one word, such as "table," to a vast number of sense-data differing very much among themselves. The group of sense-data constituting the table includes all the different views I can obtain at different distances, from different angles, in different lights, no two of them exactly alike, but all of them variations on one central pattern; it includes sense-data of touch, and those of sound (though these last seem somewhat more loosely connected with the main visuo-tactual group); and with other kinds of material things, such as apples, sense-data of taste and smell form important constituents of the thing.

51. *Its Advantages*

This type of theory has certain clear advantages. On the representative theory, the very existence of a material world or of any given material object must always be in principle doubtful. I am directly aware of my sense-data, and so can be certain of their existence and character: but "material objects" are quite different—their existence and character can be known only by an inference, which cannot give the complete certainty which comes from observation. Descartes, for example, accepts this consequence of the theory, and will not allow himself to believe that there is a material world at all, until he has convinced himself that there exists an omnipotent and benevolent God who would never have led him to believe in the material world if it had not been real. But if Descartes really succeeded in keeping up this attitude of doubt for more than a moment, few men have been able to imitate him. We *cannot* believe that the existence of the table is in any way subject to doubt.

The phenomenalist theory, by making the existence of the table *the same thing* as the occurrence of certain sense-data, removes that doubt; for the system of sense-data constituting the table has beyond doubt come under my observation.

The theory not only removes the doubt, but makes it clear why we cannot seriously entertain it. The Plain Man was right after all: material things are seen and touched, are objects of direct awareness, and it is by seeing and touching that we know that they exist, though no material thing is straightforwardly identical with what I am seeing and touching *at this particular moment.*

So, by accepting the phenomenalist analysis, we escape being involved in any reference to an unobservable Matter. We can preserve our empiricism inviolate, and talk about the things we see and hear and smell and touch, and not about other hypothetical things beyond the reach of our observation. Science, the knowledge of nature, on this view becomes the recording, ordering and forecasting of human experiences. Therein lies its interest for us. If the physical world lay outside our experience, why should we be concerned with it?

The Discrediting of Phenomenalism

Today only a few philosophers would describe themselves as phenomenalists, thanks to the strong adverse criticism of phenomenalism that emerged around the middle of the century. This criticism is complex and technical, generally too much so to permit discussion of it in any great detail in an introductory textbook. To simplify, however, the main lines of criticism were these:

For one thing, it became generally accepted that there is no set of sense-data, the having of which logically entails that you are experiencing any given physical object. For another, it was unclear that physical-object propositions that mention specific times and places could find their

Why Phenomenalism Is So Plausible: Jones believes she is looking at a tomato, but if she is a philosopher, she will concede that she might be mistaken. So how can she determine whether or not her belief is correct? By examining what she sees, surely: by touching, tasting, smelling, and so on. In other words, she confirms (or disconfirms) her belief through her senses. Thus, because her belief that she is looking at a tomato is ultimately confirmed or disconfirmed by her sense-data, it is plausible to think that her belief must really just *be* about her sense-data, as phenomenalism maintains.

equivalents in propositions that refer only to sense-data. And finally, it was thought that phenomenalists had to believe in the possibility of what is called a private language, and it was questioned whether the idea of such a language is coherent (see box).

Private Languages?

"What I mean by 'book' or 'blue' might be entirely different from what you mean by those words, and you and I cannot really understand one another."

This thought, we'll bet, is one that has occurred to you. The empiricist in you may well think that all words ultimately derive their meaning from sense-impressions and that, because one person cannot have another person's sense-impressions, I can't really know what your words mean and vice versa. In short, we all speak **private languages,** right?

Let's pretend you are discussing the issue with a philosopher who is arguing that a private language is an impossibility. You begin with the obvious question.

YOU: And just why is it an impossibility?

PHILOSOPHER: Well, for something to be a word, you have to be able to tell whether you have used it consistently. If you have no way of telling whether you are using some sound to denote the same kind of thing each time you use it, then the sound would just be a noise, not a word.

YOU: So what follows from that?

PHILOSOPHER: Well, if no one else knew what you meant by your words, then *you* couldn't know if you had used them consistently. So then they wouldn't *be* words. They'd just be noises.

YOU: Yes, well, but *why* couldn't I know if I had used a word consistently under those circumstances?

PHILOSOPHER: Because you would only have your own memory to rely on. There would be no independent check for your belief that you used a sound like *book* to apply to the same thing today as you applied it to yesterday. Thus you would, in effect, be using *book* in any way you pleased. And a sound that you use as you please is not a word.

In this little discussion the philosopher is interpreting a sketchy argument against "private languages" laid out in Ludwig Wittgenstein's (1889–1951) *Philosophical Investigations* (published in 1953 and regarded by many as one of the most important philosophical works of this century). As mentioned in the text, phenomenalists were thought to be logically committed to the possibility of private languages. If, as was thought, Wittgenstein had shown a private language to be impossible, then phenomenalism was defective.

The question of whether a private language is impossible is interesting apart from its connection to phenomenalism, for the idea that one person really *doesn't* know what another person means by a given word is an idea that—thanks to the influence of the British empiricists on our thinking—most people find quite plausible, once they think about it. What we tend to believe is that a word stands for an idea, or some other sort of mental entity, that we think is the meaning of the word. And therefore, we think, because a word's meaning is locked up inside the mind, what each of us means by our words is private to each of us.

What Wittgenstein argued is that the whole notion of a "private language," and the theory of meaning on which it rests, is pure bunkum. The meanings of words lie not inside the mind, he said, but in their *uses*, and these uses are governed by rules. As these rules are not our own private rules, other people can check the correctness of our usage of a given word. We don't have private languages, and could not possibly have them, for in such "languages" the correctness of our usage of words is not subject to a public check. In a "private language" the "words" would just be *sounds* that one could use any way one pleased.

The World's Shortest Refutation of Skepticism

Suppose someone waved his hand in front of your face and said, "See? Here's a hand, a material object. What more do you want as disproof of skepticism?" That, in effect, was the refutation of skepticism set forth by **G. E. Moore** (1873–1958), a friend and colleague of Bertrand Russell. It is a sufficient refutation of skepticism, Moore said, simply to point to cases in which we know very well that we are dealing with a material object. He said:

> This, after all, you know, really is a finger: there is no doubt about it: I know it, and you all know it. And I think we may safely challenge any philosopher to bring forward any argument in favor either of the proposition that we do not know it, or of the proposition that it is not true, which does not at some point, rest upon some premise which is, beyond comparison, less certain than is the proposition which it is designed to attack.

The questions whether we do ever know such things as these, and whether there are any material objects, seem to me, therefore, to be questions which there is no need to take seriously: they are questions which it is quite easy to answer, with certainty, in the affirmative.

Moore (1873–1958) exerted a tremendous influence on twentieth-century philosophy, as we will see in a later chapter. His main epistemological concerns were the relationships between acts of consciousness and their objects, the ways in which we can be said to know things and what it is we can know in those ways, and the connection between sense-data and physical objects.

Many philosophers have not been entirely comfortable with his easygoing refutation of skepticism quoted here. Are you?

So much, then, for phenomenalism. The theory sounds good—yes, knowledge of the external world is indeed possible because to experience external objects just is to have sense-data—but alas, this response to skepticism is no longer widely regarded as viable.

Post-Phenomenalist Epistemology

If you step back for a second and consider the history of epistemology from Descartes onward, as we have now done, one way of characterizing this history is that it has really just been an extended search for *incorrigible foundations* for knowledge, especially knowledge of the external world. (An *incorrigible* proposition, recall, is one that is incapable of being false if you believe it is true.)

Actually, philosophers from before Socrates to the present have searched incessantly for these incorrigible foundations. They have looked everywhere for an unshakeable bedrock on which the entire structure of knowledge might be built. Augustine found the bedrock in revealed truth. Descartes thought that he had found it in the certainty of his own exis-

Nonpropositional Foundations

We have proceeded as if the only sort of thing that could qualify as a foundation for knowledge is some type of proposition. But could entities other than propositions serve as well? For example, could my existence *itself*, as distinct from the proposition that I exist, serve as a foundation for knowledge? Could my sense-data *themselves*, as distinct from propositions in which it is asserted that I am having them, serve as the foundations? Doesn't the elliptical silverish expanse that I am now seeing *itself* entail that I am seeing a quarter, and isn't the expanse itself therefore the foundation of my knowledge that I am seeing a quarter?

The difficulty here is that *things* don't entail anything, only propositions do. True, we do say such things as, "His laughter means he is amused," and that sounds as though his laugh, a thing, entails the proposition, "He is amused." In fact, though, it is the *proposition*, "He is laughing," that entails the proposition, "He is amused." His laugh, the thing, *verifies* the proposition "He is laughing" and thus may *show* or *indicate* or *confirm* or *suggest* that he is is amused, but it does not entail the proposition, "He is amused."

So no *thing* itself could be a foundation for my knowledge because absolutely nothing follows from a thing. Nothing whatsoever follows from the elliptical silver expanse I am now sensing, although from the proposition that I am sensing an elliptical silver the proposition that I am seeing a quarter may follow.

---

tence. Empiricists believed that the foundational bedrock of knowledge must somehow or other lie in immediate sensory experience. Kant found the foundation in principles supplied by the mind in the very act of experiencing the world.

But must a belief really rest on *incorrigible* foundations if it is to qualify as knowledge? More fundamentally, must it even rest on *foundations*? Recently philosophers have begun to question whether knowledge really requires foundations at all. Thus they have begun to question an assumption on which much of traditional epistemology rests.

The **foundationalist,** as someone who makes this assumption is called these days, holds that a belief qualifies as knowledge only if it logically follows from propositions that are incorrigible (incapable of being false if you believe that they are true). For example, take for one last time my belief that this before me is a quarter. According to a foundationalist from the empiricist tradition, I *know* that this before me is a quarter only if my belief that it is absolutely follows from the propositions that describe my present sense-data, because these propositions alone are incorrigible. But, the antifoundationalist argues, why not say that my belief that there is a quarter before me *automatically* qualifies as knowledge, unless there is some definite and special reason to think that it is mistaken?

The question of whether knowledge requires foundations is currently under wide discussion among epistemologists. It is too early to predict what the results of this discussion may be.

Many of those who attack the foundationalist position have been inclined, recently, to endorse what is called **naturalized epistemology.** This is the view that traditional epistemological inquiries should be replaced by psychological inquiries into the processes that are actually involved in the acquisition and revision of beliefs. This view, which in its strongest form amounts to saying that epistemology should be phased out in favor of psychology, is highly controversial. Nevertheless, much recent writing in epistemology has reflected a deep interest in developments in psychology.

Contemporary Discussions of Total Skepticism

When philosophers were considering, during the first half of the century, whether sense-data propositions could provide the incorrigible foundations of knowledge of the external world, some challenged the notion that such propositions were even incorrigible to begin with. Now it may well seem that I cannot possibly be mistaken about what it *seems* to me that I am seeing and that if I really believe that it *seems* to me that I am seeing a silverish circle, then what I believe cannot possibly be wrong. But some philosophers argued that I may be mistaken in even such a simple matter as this. For even such a guarded proposition as, "It seems to me that I am seeing a silverish circle," involves classifying or categorizing what it seems to me I am seeing, and any categorization I make could be a *mis*categorization and thus mistaken.

Accordingly, given that some philosophers began to think that even descriptions of the way things seem to one might be open to question, it isn't terribly surprising that in recent years some epistemologists have begun to reconsider the case that might be made for total skepticism. Thus, even though some recent philosophers have been arguing that knowledge does not require foundations and that therefore many beliefs qualify as knowledge, other philosophers have taken a rather different tack and have published strong defenses of total skepticism. Perhaps epistemology has come a full circle.

In Selection 6.4, which closes this chapter, Oliver Johnson advances an updated version of Pyrrhonism. A Pyrrhonist, remember, is someone like Sextus Empiricus, who does not proclaim that knowledge is impossible but rather suspends judgment on that and all other questions. The idea in the Johnson selection is that the *cognitivist*—that's someone like you who believes that knowledge is possible (do you still?)—cannot legitimately establish his case and thus loses the battle with what Johnson calls the negative skeptic. Johnson's **negative skeptic** is a total skeptic of the Pyrrhonist variety.

Though Johnson is not himself entirely satisfied with negative skepticism, as readers of his book will discover for themselves, it is nevertheless clear that total skepticism is not to be dismissed lightly, even from the elevated and enlightened perspective of the late twentieth century.

From Oliver Johnson,
SKEPTICISM AND COGNITIVISM

I think the skeptic may be able to carve out a third position, which I shall call negative skepticism. Let us see how he might go about doing so.

The cognitivist [one who says that knowledge exists], in contending that knowledge exists, is making a truth claim: that the proposition "Knowledge exists" is true. He is also making a knowledge claim: that he knows the proposition to be true, or, at least, that he has reasons for believing it to be true, which entails an implicit knowledge claim about his possession of reasons. In order to qualify as something he knows, the knowledge claim he makes must satisfy the general criteria of knowledge. It must be true and, more especially, he must be able to offer reasons in its support capable of establishing it to be true. If he can offer no reasons in its support, the claim is simply gratuitous, and if the reasons he offers do not establish its truth, he has not succeeded in making his case. In neither event has he been able to justify his thesis that knowledge exists. So we can ask the cognitivist: Can you give us any satisfactory reasons in support of your claim that knowledge exists? If you cannot, we can write your theory off as a failure. In such an event skepticism is triumphant, even though the critic of cognitivism has not revealed himself as a skeptic but has instead carefully refrained from asserting or attempting to defend any positive skeptical hypothesis at all. . . .

Let us look at the questions I have raised a little more closely.

The cognitivist claims that knowledge exists; thus he claims to know the proposition "Knowledge exists" to be true. But what reasons can he offer in support of this claim? . . . If we are to offer reasons capable of justifying us in claiming to know something, these reasons must consist of true propositions that entail the conclusion we are claiming as an item of knowledge . . . To qualify as good reasons, the reasons must in addition be such that (a) we know them to be true and (b) we know that they entail the conclusion we derive from them. The justification for this additional requirement is fairly clear. To see its necessity, let us suppose that it has not been fulfilled. We have offered reasons for claiming that knowledge exists; these reasons are in fact true and they do entail the existence of knowledge. However, we do not know that they are true or that they entail the existence of knowledge. Can we, under such circumstances, legitimately claim to know that knowledge exists? Clearly we cannot, for our claim would be gratuitous because we have no justification to offer for it. In order to support that claim it is necessary that we be able to establish that the reasons we offer on its behalf are both true and entail it. And to require that we be able to establish either of these things is to require that we know them to be true. It follows that in order to justify our cognitivistic claim that knowledge exists, we must employ an argument one of whose necessary presuppositions is that we know something.

That the negative skeptic, who has challenged the cognitivist to offer reasons in support of his claim that knowledge exists, should fail to be satisfied with the results of the analysis we have just completed is understandable, for the cognitivist's attempt to provide such reasons has led him into a circular argument in which, to establish the existence of knowledge, he must presuppose that he knows things. And this circularity inherent in the cognitivist's argument is enough to satisfy the negative skeptic. . . . He is justified in coming to the conclusion that the cognitivist has been unsuccessful in his attempt to show that knowledge does exist.

Looking at the results of the argument I have just offered, we might feel inclined to conclude that the opponents have arrived at an impasse, with neither one the victor. But this would not, I think, be correct, for the situation, as I have set it forth as a negative skeptic who has gone on the defensive, forces the cognitivist to assume the offensive. It is he who must bear the burden of proof. He is arguing for the existence of knowledge; the negative skeptic, on the contrary, is arguing for no position of his own at all. So an impasse, in which the cognitivist does not succeed in producing an argument that establishes that knowledge exists, becomes a victory for the skeptic. . . . We cannot, as cognitivists, legitimately claim that knowledge exists, unless we can offer an argument that is capable of supporting our claim. And such an argument, if the reasoning I have just offered is sound, is not to be found.

Checklist

To help you review, here is a checklist of the key philosophers and concepts of this chapter. The brief descriptive sentences that appear with each philosopher summarize one of his leading ideas. Keep in mind that some of these summary statements represent terrific oversimplifications of complex positions.

Philosophers

- **Immanuel Kant**   Believed that there is certain knowledge, namely, knowledge of the principles and categories by means of which the constituents of experience are ordered and organized by the mind.
- **Absolute Idealists**   Schelling, Fichte, and most importantly Hegel, who held that whatever is, is knowable, and that the object of thought is thought itself (see also Chapter 3).
- **John Stuart Mill**   Thoroughgoing empiricist; regarded external objects as permanent possibilities of sensation.
- **Bertrand Russell**   Sought the connection between the "hard" data actually given in experience (sense-data) and supposedly "external," physical (and scientific) objects.
- **G. E. Moore**   Was also concerned with the relationship between sense-data and physical objects; rejected skepticism on the basis of common sense.

- **Ludwig Wittgenstein** Argued that private languages are impossible, thus undermining phenomenalism.
- **Oliver Johnson** A contemporary analytic philosopher; one among several who has been concerned with the viability of total skepticism.

Concepts

principle that perceptions must be conceptualized and unified to qualify as experience

Copernican revolution in philosophy

the thing-in-itself/*das Ding-an-sich*

logical construction

sense-data

phenomenalism

foundationalism

incorrigible foundations of knowledge

private language

negative skeptic

---

1. If knowledge begins with experience, must it also rise from experience? Explain.
2. Is it possible that we may someday experience an event that is in neither space nor time? If not, why not?
3. Is it possible for extraterrestrial aliens to experience things that are not in space or time?
4. Do auto-focus cameras or electric doors have experience? Why not? Do infants? Cats? Fish? Why?
5. Can two different people ever have the identical experience? That is, can the experience of one person ever simultaneously be the experience of another person? Why or why not?
6. Can we have knowledge of things in themselves? Be sure to clarify what you mean by "things in themselves."
7. Explain what phenomenalism is and why so many philosophers accepted it as a sound theory.
8. Are physical objects just "clusters" of sensations? If so, why? If not, how do you know that they are not?
9. Can you know that physical objects exist when no one is perceiving them?
10. Does a photograph of an object taken when no one is looking at the object prove that it existed when no one was looking at it?

Questions for Discussion and Review

A. J. Ayer, *Foundations of Empirical Knowledge* (New York: St. Martin's, 1969). This is an easy-to-understand examination of the problem of our knowledge of the external world. It has been quite popular. Ayer takes a phenomenalist position.

Suggested Further Readings

Oliver Johnson, *Skepticism and Cognitivism* (Berkeley: University of California Press, 1978). A fine, in-depth treatment of practically every skeptical argument ever presented.

Immanuel Kant, *Prolegomena to Any Future Metaphysics*, P. Carus, trans. (Indianapolis: Hackett, 1977). This is Kant's own (relatively) simplified introduction to his thinking about metaphysics and epistemology. If you want to have a look at the *Critique of Pure Reason* itself, the Norman Kemp Smith translation is published by St. Martin's in New York (1965). If you need help with this difficult work, you cannot do better than H. J. Paton's *Kant's Metaphysics of Experience*, in 2 volumes (London, 1936). Paton's work covers only the first half of the *Critique*, but it explains it, sentence by difficult sentence, in clear English.

P. K. Moser and A. vander Nat, *Human Knowledge: Classical and Contemporary Approaches* (New York: Oxford University Press, 1987). Excellent anthology of readings, both classical and recent.

Arne Naess, *Scepticism* (London: George Allen & Unwin, 1968). A complete account of skepticism. Naess is quite sympathetic to Pyrrhonism.

Bertrand Russell, *Our Knowledge of the External World* (Chicago and London: Open Court, 1915). An excellent introduction to some of the epistemological questions that concerned Russell around the time of his logical atomism (see Chapter 4).

Bertrand Russell, *Human Knowledge, Its Scope and Limit* (New York: Simon & Schuster, 1948). This book is addressed to "the larger public which is interested in philosophical questions" and not primarily to professional philosophers.

Peter Unger, *Ignorance: A Case for Scepticism* (Oxford: Clarendon Press, 1975). Unger attempts to defend skepticism. Fun to read, though some arguments are complicated.

Michael Williams, *Groundless Belief: An Essay on the Possibility of Epistemology* (New Haven: Yale University Press, 1977). Written for philosophers, this book may be tough for the layperson. But it sets forth in clear detail some of the difficulties in "foundationalism."

Ludwig Wittgenstein, *Philosophical Investigations*, G. E. M. Anscombe, trans. (Oxford: Oxford University Press, 1953). Contains Wittgenstein's attack on private languages, but it is rather bewildering to the layperson (and to the professional philosopher, too). An easy introduction to Wittgenstein's philosophy is George Pitcher's *Wittgenstein, The Philosophical Investigations* (Garden City: Doubleday Anchor, 1966).

SUMMARY AND CONCLUSION

Are you still as sure as you once were that you really *know* that physical objects exist? That you have a mind? That there is even such a thing as knowledge? Or do you find yourself, as Hume once did, "ready to reject all belief and reasoning" and unable to look on one opinion "even as more probable or likely than another"?

If you find yourself thinking as Hume did, something else he said may interest you. When he found himself confounded with skepticism and "in the most deplorable condition imaginable, environed with the deepest darkness, and utterly deprived of the use of every member and faculty," Hume noticed this:

> Most fortunately it happens, that since reason is incapable of dispelling these clouds, nature herself suffices to that purpose, and cures me of this philosophical melancholy and delirium, either by relaxing this bent of mind, or by some avocation. . . . I dine, I play a game of back-gammon, I converse, and am merry with my friends; and when after three or four hours' amusement, I would return to these speculations, they appear so cold, and strained, and ridiculous, that I cannot find in my heart to enter into them any farther.

So if you now are weighing under with skeptical doubts, take heart: nature will care for you.

(Hume, by the way, also observed that it is "almost impossible for the mind of man to rest, like those of beasts, in that narrow circle of objects which are the subject of daily conversation and action" and that sometimes one just grows *weary* of amusement and company. For these times, Hume recommended philosophy.)

Now, to summarize:

In reading this part maybe you noticed that the historical development of inquiry concerning the possibility of knowledge has been neither continuous nor sequential. Philosophers do not always pick up where their predecessors leave off, and the focus of one philosopher is often quite different from that of his successor.

True, many of the philosophers covered in this part have been concerned with finding certain knowledge; but not all have. Kant, for example, had a tendency just to assume there is certain knowledge and mainly tried to explain how this fact is possible. But Descartes's primary epistemological undertaking was to ascertain whether certain knowledge could exist given the threat of total skepticism. Locke, too, was concerned with what can be known for certain, but the bulk of his *Essay* is in fact devoted to explaining the origin of our ideas and discerning the connection between ideas and words. Berkeley focused his attention on a relatively narrow issue, our supposed knowledge of the external world, whereas Hume actually spent far less time on that subject than on others. The early twentieth-century empiricists emphasized again the issue that vexed Berkeley.

There is, therefore, no simple or single philosophical answer, or one that evolved in a linear fashion, to the question: Is knowledge possible? That question is really a short way of asking several more specific questions like: Is knowledge of an external world possible? Is knowledge of the self possib e? Can I know anything about the future course of experience? Can anything at all be known? Most philosophers will respond affirmatively to such questions, as indeed will most everyone (though philosophers may be especially aware of the difficulties in the response). That is, relatively few philosophers have been skeptics.

But skepticism has nevertheless been of major importance in the history of philosophy. For, as Richard Popkin has said, skepticism keeps philosophers honest. Skepticism is an anonymous letter that arrives at your house and challenges your theories and suppositions. It is by striving to overcome the objection of imagined skeptical foes that philosophers succeed in establishing the tenability of their own positions.

PART 3

Ethics

Ethics Through Hume

Happiness, then, is something final and self-sufficient, and is the end of action.

—ARISTOTLE

Morality is not properly the doctrine how we should make ourselves happy, but how we should become worthy of happiness.

—IMMANUEL KANT

Advice is something you never stop getting, though good, sound advice is perhaps not too common.

Most advice you get—and give—is of a practical nature: "If you want to live longer," someone will say, "you should stop smoking." Or, "If I were you, I'd buy life insurance now while you're young."

But advice is not always intended to be merely practical. Sometimes it is moral advice. Someone—a friend, your minister, a relative—may suggest that you should do something not because it will be in your own best interest to do it, but because doing it is *morally right*. The suggestion expresses a moral judgment.

Ethics is the philosophical study of moral judgments—value judgments about what is virtuous and base, just and unjust, morally right and wrong, morally good and bad or evil, morally proper and improper. We say *morally* right and *morally* good and so on because terms like *right* and *good* and *proper* (and their negative correlates *wrong* and *bad* and *improper*) can be used in nonmoral value judgments, as when someone speaks of a bad wine or of the right or proper way to throw a pass.

Many questions can be asked about moral judgments, so ethical philosophers discuss quite a wide array of issues. One pretty basic question they ask is: What *is* a moral judgment? In other words, exactly what does it mean to describe something as morally right or wrong, good or evil;

what is it to say that one thing ought to be done and another thing ought not be done? Or, they might ask alternatively, what makes a moral judgment a *moral* judgment? How do moral judgments differ from other value judgments, factual assertions, and pieces of practical advice? What distinguishes reasoning about moral issues from reasoning about other things (from reasoning about the structure of matter, say, or about the qualities of good art)? These are some of the questions ethical philosophers ask.

The most important question of ethics, however, is just simply: Which moral judgments are correct? That is, what *is* good and just and the morally right thing to do? What is the "moral law," anyway? This question is important because the answer to it tells us how we should conduct our affairs. Perhaps it is the most important question not of ethics, but of philosophy. Perhaps it is the most important question, period.

A less obvious question of ethics, though logically more fundamental, is whether there is a moral law in the first place. In other words, do moral obligations even exist? Are there really such things as good and bad, right and wrong? And if there are, what is it that makes one thing right and another wrong? That is, what is the ultimate justification of moral standards?

In what follows we'll examine some of these issues, and related questions, as they have been treated through the history of philosophy.

That moral judgments must be supported by reasons is an idea we owe to the **Sophists,** those professional teachers of fifth-century-B.C. Greece, and to **Socrates** (C. 470–399 B.C.). The Sophists, who attacked the traditional moral values of the Greek aristocracy, demanded rational justification for rules of conduct, as did Socrates; and their demands, together with Socrates's skillful deployment of the dialectical method in moral discussions, mark the beginning of philosophical reasoning about moral issues.

Maybe it wasn't inevitable that a time came when someone would insist that moral claims be defended by reasons. When children ask why they should do something their parents think is right, they may be content to receive, and their parents content to give, the simple answer, "Because that is what is done." In some societies, evidently, values are accepted without much question and demands for justification of moral claims are not issued. In our society it is frequently otherwise, and this is the legacy of the Sophists and Socrates.

It was Socrates especially who championed the use of reason in moral deliberation and with it raised good questions about some still-popular ideas about morality, such as that good is what pleases, that might makes right, and that happiness comes only to the ruthless.

Socrates was also concerned with the meaning of words that signify moral virtues, words like *justice, piety,* and *courage.* Because a moral

Subjectivism

Subjectivism, along with relativism (see next chapter) and skepticism (which we already mentioned) is a very popular belief these days. The subjectivist holds that right and wrong, good and bad (i.e., ethical standards in general), depend entirely on the opinions of people: take away people's opinions about right and wrong and good and bad, and right and wrong, good and bad go away. Some ethical relativist doctrines (see the box "When in Rome . . ." on page 252) are subjectivist, too.

One currently popular subjectivist belief is that ethical standards are determined by what you yourself believe: what is right is what you believe is right. If you find this idea plausible (do you?), you should know this: although this idea is accepted by some philosophers and is very popular outside

the discipline, many other philosophers regard it as ridiculous.

For one thing, they say, the view entails the presumably absurd notion that an action is neither right nor wrong until *you* have thought about it. This would mean, among other things, that before your birth no acts were either right or wrong and no person was either moral or immoral. The view also entails, the critics say, another absurd notion: if what is right is what you believe is right, then when someone else makes a statement about what is right, what that person is really doing is making a statement about what you believe. It may come as a surprise to Queen Elizabeth, for example, to learn that her opinions about what is right are really just opinions about your beliefs.

term can be correctly applied to various specific acts—many different types of deeds count as courageous deeds, for example—Socrates believed that all acts characterized by a given moral term *must have something in common.* He therefore sought to determine (without notable success, we are sorry to report) what the essential commonality is. Socrates's assumption that a virtue has an essential nature, an essence that may be disclosed through rational inquiry, is still made by many philosophers and is central to several famous ethical theories, including Plato's, as you will shortly see.

Socrates also assumed that any sane person who possessed knowledge of the essence of virtue could not fail to act virtuously. He thus believed that ignoble behavior, if not the result of utter insanity, is always the product of ignorance. This is also a view that Plato shared and has its adherents today.

Plato

So Plato accepted the Socratic idea that all things named by a given term, including any given moral term, share a common essential or "defining" feature. For example, what is common to all things called *chairs* (yes, we know *chair* is not a moral term, but it will illustrate the point) is that feature by virtue of which a thing qualifies as a chair. What is common to all brave deeds is that feature that qualifies them all as brave. This essential or defining characteristic Plato referred to as the **Form** of the things in question; and, for various quite plausible reasons, he regarded this Form as possessing more reality than the particular things that exemplified it. We talked about this in Chapter 2, but let's look into Plato's reasoning again, for this will bear closely on Plato's ethics.

For a thing to be a chair, we think you must agree, it must possess that feature that qualifies a thing as a chair. That feature—let us call it *chairness*—is what Plato called the Form. And so, for a thing to qualify as a chair, it must possess chairness. Thus, the Form *chairness* must exist if anything at all is to qualify as a chair. So the Form is more fundamental and "real" than even the chair you're sitting on or any other chair.

Forms, Plato held, are not perceptible to the senses, for what the senses perceive are individual things: particular chairs, particular people, particular brave deeds, and so forth. Through the senses we just don't perceive the Forms. We can't see chairness; and we cannot reach out and grasp bravery or humanity. Thus Forms, he maintained, are known only through reason.

Further, according to Plato, the individual things that we perceive by sense are forever changing. Some things—rocks, for example—change very slowly. Other things, such as people, change a good bit more rapidly. That means that knowledge by sense perception is uncertain and unstable. Not so knowledge of the Forms. Knowledge of the Forms is certain and stable, for the objects known—the Forms—are eternal and unchanging.

Is the Objective World Value Neutral?

According to Plato, the Form of the Good is the source of all that is real. It is itself real, of course (according to Plato) and, moreover, has a reality independent of our minds. In other words, it has *objective* reality.

Many people these days are inclined to think of objective reality—reality as it exists outside our minds and perceptions—as morally neutral. So far as they've considered the issue at all, they regard values as subjective creations of the mind that the mind superimposes on events and objects, which things are themselves neither good nor bad, right nor wrong. It is very, very likely that this is your view.

Still, *if* it is a fact that the universe "as it is in itself" is value-neutral, this is not a fact that we *discovered* in the same way that we discovered the principles of physics, chemistry, and biology. Rather, it seems to be something we just *believe*. Is this belief more correct than the view of Plato, who thought that the good does not depend on our opinions but is set by, and is inherent in, a reality external to our minds?

If you think Plato is wrong, how would you establish that?

Now the various Forms, Plato maintained (and here we'll see what all this has to do with ethics)—the various Forms comprise a *hierarchy* in terms of their inherent value or worth. It's easy enough to understand his point. For example, doesn't the Form *beauty* (i.e., the essence of beautiful things) seem to you to be inherently of more worth than a Form like *wartness* (i.e., the essence of warts)?

At the apex of all Forms, Plato said, is the Form *goodness*, or (as it is often expressed) *the Good*, because it is the Form of highest value. Thus, for Plato, because

(a)   the Forms define true reality, and because

(b)   the Form of the Good is the uppermost of all Forms, it follows that

(c)   individual things are real only insofar as they partake of or exemplify this ultimate Form.

A corollary of (c) is that things are less "real" the less they partake of the Good. Another corollary is that evil is unreal. Make a mental note of this second idea. We will come across it again.

Because the Form of the Good is the source of all value and reality, Plato believed, we must strive to obtain knowledge and understanding of it. This notion seems reasonable enough, surely. Therefore, he maintained, because (remember) Forms can be apprehended only by reason, you and we should govern ourselves by reason. Similarly, the state should be ruled by intellectuals, he said, but more of this in the next chapter.

So, to summarize to this point, according to Plato the true reality of individual things consists in the Forms they exemplify, Forms that are apprehended by reason and not by the senses, and the Form highest in value is the Form of the Good. One should therefore strive for knowledge of the Good and hence be ruled by reason.

But now consider this moral edict that Plato has in effect laid down: "Be governed by reason!" Is this not a little too abstract? Does it not fail to enjoin anything *specific* about what the individual should or should not do?

Plato would have answered "no" to both questions. The human soul, he said (a couple of thousand years before Freud proposed an analogous theory), has three different elements, an element consisting of raw appetites, an element consisting of drives (like anger and ambition), and an intellectual element, (i.e., an element of thought or reason). For each of these elements there is an excellence or virtue that obtains when reason is in charge of that element, as is the case when you govern yourself by reason. When our *appetites* are ruled by reason, we exhibit the virtue of *temperance;* when our *drives* are governed by reason, we exhibit *courage,* and when the *intellect* itself is governed by reason, we exhibit *wisdom.*

Thus, Plato held, the well-governed person, the person ruled by reason, exhibits the four cardinal virtues of temperance, courage, wisdom, and "justice." How did justice get in the list? Justice is the virtue that obtains when all elements of the soul function as they should in obedience to reason.

So, given Plato's understanding of the soul, the principle, "Be governed by reason," which follows from the theory of Forms, dictates that you be temperate, courageous, wise, and "just." And what, in turn, *these* dictates mean more specifically was much discussed by Plato, though we won't go into the details. Further, he said, only by being virtuous—that is, by possessing these four virtues—can you have a *well-ordered soul* and thus have the psychological well-being that is true happiness. In this way Plato connected virtue with happiness, a connection we still acknowledge by saying, "Virtue is its own reward."

A Complete Ethical Theory

Plato's moral philosophy is often cited as a *complete* ethical theory.[1] It

- Identifies an *ultimate source of all value* (the Form of the Good).
- Sets forth a *metaphysical justification for accepting this source as ultimate* (the theory of Forms).

---

[1] For the concept of a complete ethical theory and this analysis of Plato's ethics as a complete ethical theory we are indebted to Professor Rollin Workman.

- Stipulates a *fundamental moral principle* ("Be governed by reason!").

- Provides a *rationale for accepting the principle as universally binding* (the Form of the Good is the source of all that is real).

- Specifies *how knowledge of the supreme intrinsic good is obtained* (only through reasoning).

- Finally, holds that *obedience to the moral principle is motivated.* For in being governed by reason, you meet the conditions that are necessary and sufficient for the well-being of the soul and thus for true happiness. An additional motivation to accept the governance of reason, according to Plato, is that in doing so you may obtain knowledge of the Forms. This knowledge is desirable to have because the Forms are unchanging and hence eternal, and that means that when you come to know them you gain access to immortality.

For these reasons, then, Plato's ethics is said to have provided philosophers with a standard of completeness. Measure your own ethics by this standard.

The following selection is from Plato's *Republic.* In it Socrates (Plato) explains the Form of the Good by analogy.

▶ S E L E C T I O N 7.1

From Plato, REPUBLIC, Books VI and VII

But, Socrates, what is your own account of the Good? Is it knowledge, or pleasure, or something else? . . .

For the moment let us leave the question of the real meaning of good; to arrive at what I at any rate believe it to be would call for an effort too ambitious for an inquiry like ours. However, I will tell you, though only if you wish it, what I picture to myself as the offspring of the Good and the thing most nearly resembling it.

Well, tell us about the offspring, and you shall remain in our debt for an account of the parent. . . .

First we must come to an understanding. Let me remind you of the distinction we drew earlier and have often drawn on other occasions, between the multiplicity of things that we call good or beautiful or whatever it may be and, on the other hand, Goodness itself or Beauty itself and so on. Corresponding to each of these sets of many things, we postulate a single Form or real essence, as we call it.

Yes, that is so.

Further, the many things, we say, can be seen, but are not objects of rational thought; whereas the Forms are objects of thought, but invisible.

Yes, certainly.

And we see things with our eyesight, just as we hear words with our ears and, to speak generally, perceive any sensible thing with our sense-faculties.

Of course.

Have you noticed, then, that the artificer who designed the senses has been exceptionally lavish of his materials in making the eyes able to see and their objects visible?

That never occurred to me.

Well, look at it in this way. Hearing and sound do not stand in need of any third thing, without which the ear will not hear nor sound be heard; and I think the same is true of most, not to say all, of the other senses. Can you think of one that does require anything of the sort?

No, I cannot.

But there is this need in the case of sight and its objects. You may have the power of vision in your eyes to try to use it, and colour may be there in the objects, but sight will see nothing and the colours will remain invisible in the absence of a third thing peculiarly constituted to service this very purpose.

By which you mean—?

Naturally I mean what you call light; and if light is a thing of value, the sense of sight and the power of being visible are linked together by a very precious bond, such as unites no other sense with its object.

No one could say that light is not a precious thing.

And of all the divinities in the skies is there one whose light, above all the rest, is responsible for making our eyes see perfectly and making objects perfectly visible?

There can be no two opinions: of course you mean the Sun.

And how is sight related to this deity? Neither sight nor the eye which contains it is the Sun, but of all the sense-organs it is the most sun-like; and further, the power it possesses is dispensed by the Sun, like a stream flooding the eye. And again, the Sun is not vision, but it is the cause of vision and also is seen by the vision it causes.

Yes.

It was the Sun, then, that I meant when I spoke of that offspring which the Good has created in the visible world, to stand there in the same relation to vision and visible things as that which the Good itself bears in the intelligible world to intelligence and to intelligible objects.

How is that? You must explain further.

You know what happens when the colours of things are no longer irradiated by the daylight, but only by the fainter luminaries of the night: when you look at them, the eyes are dim and seem almost blind, as if there were no unclouded vision in them. But when you look at things on which the Sun is shining, the same eyes see distinctly and it becomes evident that they do contain the power of vision.

Certainly.

Apply this comparison, then, to the soul. When its gaze is fixed upon an object irradiated by truth and reality, the soul gains understanding and knowledge and is manifestly in possession of intelligence. But when it looks towards that twilight world of things that come into existence and pass away, its sight is dim and it has only opinions and beliefs which shift to and fro, and now it seems like a thing that has no intelligence.

That is true.

This, then, which gives to the objects of knowledge their truth and to him who knows them his power of knowing, is the Form or essential nature of Goodness. It is the cause of knowledge and truth; and so, while you may think of it as an object of knowledge, you will do well to regard it as something beyond truth and knowledge and, precious as these both are, of still higher worth. And, just as in our analogy light and vision were to be thought of as like the Sun, but not identical with it, so here both knowledge and truth are to be regarded as like the Good, but to identify either with the Good is wrong. The Good must hold a yet higher place of honour.

You are giving it a position of extraordinary splendour, if it is the source of knowledge and truth and itself surpasses them in worth. You surely cannot mean that it is pleasure.

Heaven forbid, I exclaimed. But I want to follow up our analogy still further. You will agree that the Sun not only makes the things we see visible, but also brings them into existence and gives them growth and nourishment; yet he is not the same thing as existence. And so with the objects of knowledge: these derive from the Good not only their power of being known, but their very being and reality; and Goodness is not the same thing as being, but even beyond being, surpassing it in dignity and power.

Aristotle

The ultimate source of all value for Plato was the Form of the Good, an entity that is distinct from the particular things that populate the natural world, the world we perceive through our senses. This Platonic idea, that all value is grounded in a *nonnatural* source, is an element of Plato's philosophy that is found in many ethical systems and is quite recognizable in Christian ethics. But not every ethical system postulates a nonnatural source of value.

Those systems that do not are called *naturalistic ethical systems.* According to **ethical naturalism,** moral judgments are really judgments of fact about the natural world. Thus Aristotle, for instance, who was the first great ethical naturalist, believed that the good for us is defined by our natural objective.

Now, what would you say is our principal or highest objective by nature? According to Aristotle, it is the attainment of happiness, for it is

Philosophers' Attitudes Toward Women

Though philosophers are usually thought of as a fairly enlightened bunch, when it came to their attitudes toward women they did not, as a group, have much to brag about—at least not until recently. Many of the philosophers we discuss in this book expressed shockingly sexist views, and before the nineteenth century few had respect for women as rational beings. Plato was maybe the best of the old lot.

Here are some quotations. Notice the change in attitude that begins to appear by the time we get to John Stuart Mill (1806–1873). In fact, this change was not nearly so abrupt as a brief series of quotations makes it out to be. Certainly it was not the case that before Mill all philosophers were sexists and after Mill none was.

All the pursuits of man are the pursuits of women also, but in all of them a woman is inferior to a man.
—Plato (c. 427–347 B.C.)

The female is, as it were, a mutilated male.
—Aristotle (384–322 B.C.)

The courage of a man is shown in commanding, of a woman in obeying.
—St. Augustine (354–430)

But in a secondary sense, the image of God is found in man, and not in woman, for man is the beginning and end of woman, as God is the beginning and end of every creature.
—St. Thomas Aquinas (1225–1274)

They [women] must be trained to bear the yoke from the first, so that they may not feel it, to master their own caprices and to submit themselves to the will of others.
—Jean-Jacques Rousseau (1712–1778)

Laborious learning or painful pondering, even if a woman should greatly succeed in it, destroy the merits that are proper to her sex.
—Immanuel Kant (1724–1804)

Women are capable of education, but they are not made for activities which demand a universal faculty such as the more advanced sciences, philosophy, and certain forms of artistic production.
—Georg Wilhelm Friedrich Hegel (1770–1831)

Women are directly fitted for acting as the nurses and teachers of our early childhood by the fact that they are themselves childish, frivolous and short-sighted; in a word, they are big children all their life long.
—Arthur Schopenhauer (1788–1860)

The ideas and institutions by which the accident of sex is made the groundwork of an inequality of legal rights, and a forced dissimilarity of social functions, must . . . be recognized as the greatest hindrance to moral, social, and even intellectual improvement.
—John Stuart Mill (1806–1873)

The first class antagonism appearing in history coincides with the development of the antagonism of man and wife in monogamy, and the first class oppression with that of the female by the male sex.
—Friedrich Engels (1820–1895)

Woman wishes to be independent, and therefore she begins to enlighten men about "woman as she is"—this is one of the worst developments of the general *uglifying* of Europe.
—Friedrich Nietzsche (1844–1900)

It is plain that no man can call himself truly a democrat if he is in favor of excluding half the nation from all participation in public affairs.
—Bertrand Russell (1872–1970)

that alone that we seek for its own sake. And, because the attainment of happiness is naturally our highest objective, it follows that happiness is our highest good.

In what does happiness, our highest good, consist, according to Aristotle? To answer, we must consider man's function, he said. To discover what goodness is for an axe or a chisel or anything whatsoever, we must consider its function, what it actually does. And when we consider what the human animal does, as a *human* animal, we see that, most essentially, it (a) lives, and (b) reasons.

Thus happiness consists of two things, Aristotle concluded: *enjoyment (pleasure)* and the *exercise and development of the capacity to reason.* It consists in part of enjoyment because the human being, as a living thing, has biological needs and impulses the satisfaction of which is pleasurable. And it consists in part of developing and exercising the capacity to reason, because only the human being, as distinct from other living things, has that capacity. Because this capacity differentiates humans from other living things, its exercise is stressed by Aristotle as the most important component of happiness. Pleasure alone does not constitute happiness, he insists.

The exercise of our unique and distinctive capacity to reason is termed by Aristotle *virtue,* and there are two different kinds of virtues. To exercise actively our reasoning abilities, as when we study nature or cogitate about something, is to be *intellectually* virtuous. But we also exercise our rational capacity by moderating our impulses and appetites, and when we do this we are said by Aristotle to be *morally* virtuous.

The largest part of Aristotle's major ethical work, the *Nicomachean Ethics,* is devoted to analysis of specific moral virtues, which Aristotle held to be *the mean between extremes* (e.g., courage is the mean between fearing everything and fearing nothing). He emphasized as well that virtue is a matter of *habit:* just as an axe that is only occasionally sharp does not fulfill its function well, the human who exercises his rational capacities only occasionally does not fulfill his function, that is, is not virtuous.

Aristotle also had the important insight that a person's pleasures reveal his true moral character. "He who faces danger with pleasure, or, at any rate, without pain, is courageous," he observed, "but he to whom this is painful is a coward." Of course, we might object that he who is willing to face danger *despite* the pain it brings him is the most courageous, but this is a quibble.

So Aristotle's ethics were basically naturalistic: human good is defined by human nature. Plato's were nonnaturalistic: goodness in all its manifestations is defined by the Form of the Good. Despite these differences, Aristotle and Plato would doubtless have agreed to a great extent in their praise and condemnation of the activities of other people. Aristotle, too, deemed the cardinal moral virtues to be courage, temperance, justice, and wisdom, and both he and Plato advocated the intellectual life.

Nevertheless, it must be kept in mind that the ultimate source of all moral value—that is, the Good—was for Plato a nonnatural "Form," whereas

Instrumental and Intrinsic Ends

A distinction made by Aristotle of some importance is that between instrumental ends and intrinsic ends. An **instrumental end** is an act performed as a means to other ends. An **intrinsic end** is an act performed for its own sake.

For example, when we, Bruder and Moore, sat down to write this book, our end was to finish it. But that end was merely instrumental to another end: providing our readers with a better understanding of philosophy.

But now notice that the last goal, the goal of providing our readers with a better understanding of philosophy, is instrumental to a further end, namely, an enlightened society.

Notice, too, that when your teacher grades you and the other students in the class, this act is instrumental to their learning, and that end also is instrumental to an enlightened society.

As a matter of fact, all the activities in the university are aimed at producing an enlightened society. For example, your teacher may recently have received a promotion. Promotions are instrumental to effective teaching in your university, and effective teaching also is instrumental to an enlightened society.

But notice that that end, an enlightened society, is merely instrumental to another end, at least according to Aristotle. For why have an enlightened society? An enlightened society is good, Aristotle would say, because in such a society people will be able to fulfill their natural function as human beings. And therefore, he would say, when we understand what the natural function of people is, then we finally will know what is intrinsically good, good for its own sake. Then we will know what the "Good of Man" is.

Aristotle sought to define the good for humans in terms of what the human organism in fact naturally seeks, namely, happiness.

Ever since Aristotle's time ethical systems have tended to fall into one of two categories: those that find the supreme moral good as something that *transcends* nature and thus follow the lead of Plato and those that follow Aristotle by grounding morality *in* human nature.

▶ S E L E C T I O N 7.2

From Aristotle, THE NICOMACHEAN ETHICS

Leaving these matters, then, let us return once more to the question, what this good can be of which we are in search.

It seems to be different in different kinds of action and in different arts—one thing in medicine and another in war, and so on. What then is the good in each of these cases? Surely that for the sake of which all else is done. And that in medicine is health, in war is victory, in building is a house—, a different thing in each different case, but always in whatever we do and in whatever we choose, the end. For it is always for the sake of the end that all else is done.

If then there be one end of all that man does, this end will be the realizable good,—or these ends, if there be more than one.

Our argument has thus come round by a different path to the same point as before. This point we must try to explain more clearly.

We see that there are many ends. But some of these are chosen only as means, as wealth, flutes, and the whole class of instruments. And so it is plain that not all ends are final.

But the best of all things must, we conceive, be something final.

If then there be only one final end, this will be what we are seeking,—or if there be more than one, then the most final of them.

Now that which is pursued as an end in itself is more final than that which is pursued as means to something else, and that which is never chosen as means than that which is chosen both as an end in itself and as means, and that is strictly final which is always chosen as an end in itself and never as means.

Happiness seems more than anything else to answer to this description: for we always choose it for itself, and never for the sake of something else: while honour and pleasure and reason, and all virtue or excellence, we choose partly indeed for themselves (for, apart from any result, we should choose each of them), but partly also for the sake of happiness, supposing that they will help to make us happy. But no one chooses happiness for the sake of these things, or as a means to anything at all.

We seem to be led to the same conclusion when we start from the notion of self-sufficiency.

The final good is thought to be self-sufficing. In applying this term we do not regard a man as an individual leading a solitary life, but we also take account of parents, children, wife, and, in short, friends and fellow-citizens generally, since man is naturally a social being. Some limit must indeed be set to this; for if you go on to parents and descendants and friends of friends, you will never come to a stop. But this we will consider further on: for the present we will take self-sufficing to mean what by itself makes life desirable and in want of nothing. And happiness is believed to answer to this description.

And further, happiness is believed to be the most desirable thing in the world, and that not merely as one among other good things: if it were merely one among other good things, it is plain that the addition of the least of other goods must make it more desirable; for the addition becomes a surplus of good, and of two goods the greater is always more desirable.

Thus it seems that happiness is something final and self-sufficing, and is the end of all that man does.

But perhaps the reader thinks that though no one will dispute the statement that happiness is the best thing in the world, yet a still more precise definition of it is needed.

This will best be gained, I think, by asking, What is the function of man? For as the goodness and the excellence of a piper or a sculptor, or the practiser of any art, and generally of those who have any function or business to do, lies in that function, so man's good would seem to lie in his function, if he has one.

But can we suppose that, while a carpenter and a cobbler has a function and a business of his own, man has no business and no function assigned him by nature? Nay, surely as his several members, eye and hand and foot, plainly have each his own function, so we must suppose that man also has some function over and above all these.

What then is it?

Life evidently he has in common even with the plants, but we want that which is peculiar to him. We must exclude, therefore, the life of mere nutrition and growth.

Next to this comes the life of sense; but this too he plainly shares with horses and cattle and all kinds of animals.

There remains then the life whereby he acts—the life of his rational nature, with its two sides or divisions, one rational as obeying reason, the other rational as having and exercising reason.

But as this expression is ambiguous, we must be understood to mean thereby the life that consists in the exercise of the faculties; for this seems to be more properly entitled to the name.

The function of man, then, is exercise of his vital faculties on one side in obedience to reason, and on the other side with reason.

But what is called the function of a man of any profession and the function of a man who is good in that profession are generically the same, e.g. of a harper and of a good harper; and this holds in all cases without exception, only that in the case of the latter his superior excellence at his work is added, for we say a harper's function is to harp, and a good harper's to harp well.

Man's function then being, as we say, a kind of life—that is to say, exercise of his faculties and action of various kinds with reason—the good man's function is to do well and beautifully.

But the function of anything is done well when it is done in accordance with the proper excellence of that thing.

Putting all this together, then, we find that the good of a man is exercise of his faculties in accordance with excellence or virtue, or, if there be more than one, in accordance with the best and most complete virtue.

But there must also be a full term of years for this exercise; for one swallow or one fine day does not make a spring, nor does one day or any small space of time make a blessed or happy man.

This, then, may be taken as a rough outline of the good.

Epicureanism and Stoicism

In the Greek and Roman period following Aristotle, there were four main "schools" of philosophy, the **Epicureans,** the **Stoics,** the **Skeptics,** and the **Neoplatonists.** The Neoplatonists were discussed in the chapter on metaphysics.

The Skeptics, remember from Chapter 5, denied the possibility of all knowledge, and this denial included moral knowledge. They said that no judgments can be established, and it doesn't matter if the judgments are factual judgments or value judgments. Accordingly, they advocated tolerance toward others, detachment from the concerns of others, and caution in your own actions. Whether the Skeptics were *consistent* in advocating toleration, detachment, and caution while maintaining that no moral judgment can be established you might consider for yourself.

Epicureanism and Stoicism, which mainly concern us in this chapter, were both naturalistic ethical philosophies, and both had a lasting effect on philosophy and ethics. To this day, "taking things philosophically" means responding to disappointments as a Stoic would, and the word *epicure* has its own place in the everyday English found outside the philosophy classroom.

Epicureanism

Epicureanism began with **Epicurus** (341–270 B.C.), flourished in the second and first centuries B.C., spread to Rome, and survived as a school until almost the third century A.D. Though few today would call themselves Epicureans, there is no question that many people still subscribe to some of the central tenets of this philosophy. You may do so yourself. We do.

According to Epicurus, it is natural for us to seek a pleasant life above all other things; it follows, he reasoned (as perhaps you will, too), that we ought to seek a pleasant life above all other things. In this sense Epicurus was a naturalist in ethics.

The pleasant life, Epicurus said, comes to you when your desires are satisfied. And there are three kinds of desires, he maintained:

- Those that are *natural and must be satisfied* for one to have a pleasant life (such as the desire for food and shelter)
- Those that, *though natural, need not necessarily be satisfied* for a pleasant life (including, for example, the desire for sexual gratification)
- Those that are *neither natural nor necessary* to satisfy (such as the desire for wealth or fame)

The pleasant life is best achieved, Epicurus believed, by neglecting the third kind of desire and satisfying only desires of the first kind, though desires of the second kind may also be satisfied, he said, when doing so does not lead to discomfort or pain. It is *never* prudent to try to satisfy unnecessary/unnatural desires, he said, for in the long run trying to do so will produce disappointment, dissatisfaction, discomfort, or poor health. There is, surely, much that is reasonable in this philosophy, even though

At about the time Plato lived in Athens, another Greek, **Aristippus** (435–350 B.C.), who lived in Cyrene, espoused an ethical doctrine quite different from Plato's. Aristippus said our lives should always be dedicated to the acquisition of as many pleasures, preferably as intense as possible, as we can possibly obtain. Even when intense pleasures lead to subsequent pain, they should still be sought, he said, for a life without pleasure or pain would be unredeemingly boring. Pleasures are best obtained, according to Aristippus, when one takes control of a situation and other people and uses them to one's own advantage.

Perhaps you know people who agree with Aristippus.

Cyrenaicism, which is the name of this hedonistic (pleasure-seeking) philosophy, was the historical antecedent of Epicureanism. As you can see from the text, Epicurus's pleasure-oriented philosophy is considerably more moderate than Aristippus's. Epicurus recommended avoiding intense pleasure as producing too much pain and disappointment over the long run.

many people spend a good bit of time and energy in trying to satisfy precisely those desires that, according to Epicurus, are both unnecessary and unnatural.

As is evident, Epicurus favored the pleasant *life* over momentary pleasures and attached great importance to the avoidance of pain as the prime ingredient in the pleasant life. It is one of the great ironies of philosophy that the word *epicure* is often used to denote a person devoted to the indulgence of sensuous pleasures. Epicurus was certainly not an epicure in this sense, for he recommended a life of relaxation, repose, and moderation, and avoidance of the pleasures of the flesh and passions. He would not have been fond of lavish vacations or the typical Sunday afternoon tailgate party.

The Stoics

If Epicurus was not exactly an epicure (at least in one meaning of the word), were the Stoics stoical? A stoic is a person who maintains a calm indifference to pain and suffering, and yes, the Stoics were stoical.

The school was founded by **Zeno** (334–262 B.C.), who met his students on the *stoa* (Greek for "porch"). Stoicism spread to Rome and survived as a school until almost the third century A.D. Its most famous adherents, other than Zeno, were **Cleanthes** (303–233 B.C.), **Cicero** (106–43 B.C.), **Epictetus** (A.D. 60–117), **Seneca** (c. 4 B.C.–A.D. 65) and **Marcus Aurelius,** the Roman Emperor (A.D. 121–180).

Like the Epicureans, the Stoics believed that it is only natural for a person to seek a pleasant life and that therefore a person ought to seek

Diogenes the Dog

No ethics text would be complete without mention of the fourth-century-B.C. philosopher **Diogenes,** who is famous for having wandered about with a lantern in bright sunlight looking for an honest face.

Diogenes was a disciple of **Antisthenes** (though it is arguable that it was the other way around), who founded a school of philosophy known as the **Cynics** in Athens just after Socrates died. We mention the Cynics, whose most famous figure was Diogenes, because they were the precursors of the Stoics, who are discussed in the text.

According to the Cynics, who were fiercely individualistic, the wise person avoids even the most basic comforts and seeks total self-reliance by reducing all wants to a minimum and by forgoing any convenience or benefit offered by society. Diogenes, for example, is said to have dressed in rags and lived in an empty tub, and even to have thrown out his drinking cup when he observed a child drinking from his hands. It is reported that Alexander the Great, who admired Diogenes, made his way to the latter and announced that he would fill Diogenes's greatest need. Diogenes replied that he had a great need for Alexander to stop blocking his sunlight.

This answer, by the way, according to legend, moved Alexander to declare that the only person he would like to be if he were not Alexander was Diogenes. Maybe this says more about Alexander than about Diogenes. It certainly says something about Alexander's opinion of his teacher, Aristotle.

Diogenes is also reported to have masturbated in public while observing that it was too bad that hunger could not be relieved in similar fashion merely by rubbing your stomach. His point in part was simply to flout conventions, but it was apparently also to contrast sexual needs with the need for food.

According to another story, Diogenes visited the home of a wealthy man. The man asked Diogenes to avoid spitting on the floor or furnishings because the home was expensively appointed. Diogenes responded by spitting in the man's face, and commented that it was the only worthless thing in the room.

Whether these stories are true or not—and there are many other legends about Diogenes, some of which it wouldn't do for us to repeat—the indifference to material things that they portray was appreciated by the Stoics. Yet even though the Stoics saw the advantages to scaling back needs in the manner of the Cynics, they were not nearly so flamboyant in what they said and did. The Cynics were often willing to do or say something just to shock people.

Incidentally, as the word is most commonly used today, a cynic is one who sneers at sincerity, helpfulness, and other virtuous activity as inspired by ulterior motives. It's clear how the word acquired this meaning, given the contempt the Cynics had for traditional institutions and practices.

such a life. But the Stoics were much influenced by the Cynics (see box), who went *out of their way* to find hardship. The Stoics saw that the Cynics, by actively pursuing hardship, acquired the ability to remain untroubled by the pains and disappointments of life. They (the Stoics) thought there was some sense in this. It occurred to them that untroubledness or serenity is a desirable state indeed.

The Stoics, however, more than the Cynics, had a *metaphysical justification* for their ethics. All that occurs, the Stoics believed, occurs in accordance with natural law, which they equated with reason. **Natural**

law, they said, is the vital force that activates or (as we might say) energizes all things. It follows that

1. Whatever happens is the inevitable outcome of the logic of the universe.
2. Whatever happens, happens with a reason and therefore is for the best.

So, according to the Stoic philosophy, you can do nothing to alter the course of events because they have been fixed by the law of nature. Do not struggle against the inevitable, they said. Instead, understand that what is happening is for the best and accept it.

If you're wise, according to the Stoics, you'll approach life as an actor approaches his part. You'll realize that you have no control over the plot or assignment of roles and therefore you will distance yourself psychologically from all that happens to the character you play. Does the character you play grow ill in the play? Well, you will *act* the part to the best of your ability, but you certainly won't permit yourself to suffer. Do your friends die in the play? Do you die? It is all for the best because it is dictated by the plot.

Now perhaps you are thinking: Well, if I cannot control what happens to me, then how on earth can I control my attitude about what happens? If what happens is inevitable, then what happens to my attitudes is inevitable, too, right? Nevertheless, this was their doctrine: *You can control your attitude. Remain uninvolved emotionally in your fate, and your life will be untroubled.*

The Stoic philosophy also had a political ethic according to which the Stoic had a duty to serve his fellow men and respect their inherent worth as equals under natural law. So the Stoics thought that, although you should seek the untroubled life for yourself, your ethical concerns are not limited to your own welfare. Whether this social component of Stoicism is consistent with a philosophy of emotional noninvolvement, acceptance of the natural order, and seeking tranquility for yourself may be questioned, of course. In fact, whether a philosophy of self-interest is compatible with concern for the common good is one of the most important questions of ethics, and you know quite well that this is a very live issue even today.

Let's summarize this section: According to the Epicureans, one's ultimate ethical objective is to lead the pleasant life through moderate living. According to the Stoics, the objective is to obtain the serene or untroubled life through acceptance of the rational or natural order of things while remembering that one is obligated to be of service to one's fellow creatures.

Stoicism in particular had an impact on Christian thought, primarily through the philosophy of St. Augustine, to whom we shall turn in a moment.

Selections 7.3 and 7.4 are from, respectively, Epicurus and Epictetus. The latter was among the most famous of all Stoics. He also is unusual among philosophers in that he was sold as a slave when a child but was given an education and later freed, thereafter becoming an influential teacher of philosophy. *Be sure to compare the two selections.* As you might expect from what we have said about Stoicism and Epicureanism, the two philosophies are very similar (even though Epictetus thought he was recommending a way of life quite different from that of the Epicureans).

▶ S E L E C T I O N   7.3

From Epicurus, "EPICURUS TO MENOECEUS"

The things which I [unceasingly] commend to you, these do and practice, considering them to be the first principles of the good life. . . .

Become accustomed to the belief that death is nothing to us. For all good and evil consists in sensation, but death is deprivation of sensation. And therefore a right understanding that death is nothing to us makes the mortality of life enjoyable, not because it adds to it an infinite span of time, but because it takes away the craving for immortality. For there is nothing terrible in life for the man who has truly comprehended that there is nothing terrible in not living. . . . death, the most terrifying of ills, is nothing to us, since so long as we exist, death is not with us; but when death comes, then we do not exist. It does not then concern either the living or the dead, since for the former, it is not, and the latter are no more. . . .

We must then bear in mind that the future is neither ours, nor yet wholly not ours, so that we may not altogether expect it as sure to come, nor abandon hope of it, as if it will certainly not come.

We must consider that of desires some are natural, others vain, and of the natural some are necessary and others merely natural; and of the necessary some are necessary for happiness, others for the repose of the body, and others for very life. The right understanding of these facts enables us to refer all choices and avoidance to the health of the body and the soul's freedom from disturbance, since this is the aim of the life of blessedness. For it is to obtain this end that we always act, namely, to avoid pain and fear. And when this is once secured for us, all the tempest of the soul is dispersed, since the living creature has not to wander as though in search of something that is missing, and to look for some other thing by which he can fulfil the good of the soul and the good of the body. For it is then that we have need of pleasure, when we feel pain owing to the absence of pleasure; but when we do not feel pain, we no longer need pleasure. And for this cause we call pleasure the beginning and end of the blessed life. For we recognize pleasure as the first good innate in us, and from pleasure we begin every act of choice and avoidance, and to pleasure we return again, using the feeling as the standard by which we judge every good.

And since pleasure is the first good and natural to us, for this very reason we do not choose every pleasure, but sometimes we pass over many pleasures, when greater discomfort accrues to us as the result of them: and similarly we think many pains better than pleasures, since a greater pleasure comes to us when we have endured pains for a long time. Every pleasure then because of its natural kinship to us is good, yet not every pleasure is to be chosen: even as every pain also is an evil, yet not all are always of a nature to be avoided. Yet by a scale of comparison and by the consideration of advantages and disadvantages we must form our judgment on all these matters. For the good on certain occasions we treat as bad, and conversely the bad as good.

And again independence of desire we think a great good—not that we may at all times enjoy but a few things, but that, if we do not possess many, we may enjoy the few in the genuine persuasion that those have the sweetest pleasure in luxury who least need it, and that all that is natural is easy to be obtained, but that which is superfluous is hard. And so plain savours bring us a pleasure equal to a luxurious diet, when all the pain due to want is removed; and bread and water produce the highest pleasure, when one who needs them puts them to his lips. To grow accustomed therefore to simple and not luxurious diet gives us health to the full, and makes a man alert for the needful employments of life, and when after long intervals we approach luxuries disposes us better towards them, and fits us to be fearless of fortune.

When, therefore, we maintain that pleasure is the end, we do not mean the pleasures of profligates and those that consist in sensuality, as is supposed by some who are either ignorant or disagree with us or do not understand, but freedom from pain in the body and from trouble in the mind. For it is not continuous drinkings and revellings, nor the satisfaction of lusts, nor the enjoyment of fish and other luxuries of the wealthy table, which produce a pleasant life, but sober reasoning, searching out the motives for all choice and avoidance, and banishing mere opinions, to which are due the greatest disturbance of the spirit.

Of all this the beginning and the greatest good is prudence. Wherefore prudence is a more precious thing even than philosophy: for from prudence are sprung all the other virtues, and it teaches us that it is not possible to live pleasantly without living prudently and honourably and justly, nor, again, to live a life of prudence, honour and justice without living pleasantly. For the virtues are by nature bound up with the pleasant life, and the pleasant life is inseparable from them. For indeed who, think you, is a better man than he who holds reverent opinions concerning the gods, and is at all times free from fear of death, and has reasoned out the end ordained by nature?

From Epictetus, "THE ENCHEIRIDION"

1. Some things are under our control, while others are not under our control. Under our control are conception, choice, desire, aversion, and, in a word, everything that is our own doing; not under our control are our body, our property, reputation, office, and in a word, everything that is not our own doing. Furthermore, things under our control are by nature free, unhindered, and unimpeded; while the things not under our control are weak, servile, subject to hindrance, and not our own. Remember, therefore, that if what is naturally slavish you think to be free, and what is not your own to be your own, you will be hampered, will grieve, will be in turmoil, and will blame both gods and men; while if you think only what is your own to be your own, and what is not your own to be, as it really is, not your own, then no one will ever be able to exert compulsion upon you, no one will hinder you, you will blame no one, will find fault with no one, will do absolutely nothing against your will, you will have no personal enemy, no one will harm you, for neither is there any harm that can touch you. . . .

Make it, therefore, your study at the very outset to say to every harsh external impression, "You are an external impression and not at all what you appear to be." After that examine it and test it by these rules which you have, the first and most important of which is this: Whether the impression has to do with the things which are under our control, or with those which are not under our control; and, if it has to do with some one of the things not under our control, have ready to hand the answer, "It is nothing to me."

2. Remember that the promise of desire is the attainment of what you desire, that of aversion is not to fall into what is avoided, and that he who fails in his desire is unfortunate, while he who falls into what he would avoid experiences misfortune. If, then, you avoid only what is unnatural among those things which are under your control, you will fall into none of the things which you avoid; but if you try to avoid disease, or death, or poverty, you will experience misfortune. Withdraw, therefore, your aversion from all the matters that are not under our control, and transfer it to what is unnatural among those which are under our control. But for the time being remove utterly your desire; for if you desire some one of the things that are not under our control you are bound to be unfortunate; and, at the same time, not one of the things that are under our control, which it would be excellent for you to desire, is within your grasp. But employ only choice and refusal, and these too but lightly, and with reservations, and without straining. . . .

5. It is not the things themselves that disturb men, but their judgements about these things. For example, death is nothing dreadful, or else Socrates too would have thought so, but the judgment that death

is dreadful, this is the dreadful thing. When, therefore, we are hindered, or disturbed, or grieved, let us never blame anyone but ourselves, that means, our own judgments. It is the part of an uneducated person to blame others where he himself fares ill; to blame himself is the part of one whose education has begun; to blame neither another nor his own self is the part of one whose education is already complete. . . .

8. Do not seek to have everything that happens happen as you wish, but wish for everything to happen as it actually does happen, and your life will be serene. . . .

11. Never say about anything, "I have lost it," but only "I have given it back." Is your child dead? It has been given back. Is your wife dead? She has been given back. "I have had my farm taken away." Very well, this too has been given back. "Yet it was a rascal who took it away." But what concern is it of yours by whose instrumentality the Giver called for its return? So long as He gives it to you, take care of it as of a thing that is not your own, as travellers treat their inn. . . .

15. Remember that you ought to behave in life as you would at a banquet. As something is being passed around it comes to you; stretch out your hand and take a portion of it politely. It passes on; do not detain it. Or it has not come to you yet; do not project your desire to meet it, but wait until it comes in front of you. So act toward children, so toward a wife, so toward office, so toward wealth; and then some day you will be worthy of the banquets of the gods. But if you do not take these things even when they are set before you, but despise them, then you will not only share the banquet of the gods, but share also their rule. For it was by so doing that Diogenes and Heracleitus, and men like them, were deservedly divine and deservedly so called.

16. When you see someone weeping in sorrow, either because a child has gone on a journey, or because he has lost his property, beware that you be not carried away by the impression that the man is in the midst of external ills, but straightway keep before you this thought: "It is not what has happened that distresses this man (for it does not distress another), but his judgment about it." Do not, however, hesitate to sympathize with him so far as words go, and, if occasion offers, even to groan with him; but be careful not to groan also in the centre of your being.

17. Remember that you are an actor in a play, the character of which is determined by the Playwright; if He wishes the play to be short, it is short; if long, it is long; if He wishes you to play the part of a beggar, remember to act even this role adroitly; and so if your role be that of a cripple, an official, or a layman. For this is your business, to play admirably the role assigned you; but the selection of that role is Another's. . . .

20. Bear in mind that it is not the man who reviles or strikes you that insults you, but it is your judgment that these men are insulting you. Therefore, when someone irritates you, be assured that it is your own opinion which has irritated you. And so make it your first en-

deavour not to be carried away by the external impression; for if once you gain time and delay, you will more easily become master of yourself.

21. Keep before your eyes by day death and exile, and everything that seems terrible, but most of all death; and then you will never have any abject thought, nor will you yearn for anything beyond measure. . . .

33. Lay down for yourself, at the outset, a certain stamp and type of character for yourself, which you are to maintain whether you are by yourself or are meeting with people. And be silent for the most part, or else make only the most necessary remarks, and express these in few words. But rarely, and when occasion requires you to talk, talk indeed, but about no ordinary topics. Do not talk about gladiators, or horse-races, or athletes, or things to eat or drink—topics that arise on all occasions; but above all, do not talk about people, either blaming, or praising, or comparing them. If, then, you can, by your own conversation bring over that of your companions to what is seemly. But if you happen to be left alone in the presence of aliens, keep silence.

Do not laugh much, nor at many things, nor boisterously.

Refuse, if you can, to take an oath at all, but if that is impossible, refuse as far as circumstances allow. . . .

In things that pertain to the body take only as much as your bare need requires, I mean such things as food, drink, clothing, shelter, and household slaves; but cut down everything which is for outward show or luxury.

In your sex-life preserve purity, as far as you can, before marriage, and if you indulge, take only those privileges which are lawful. However, do not make yourself offensive, or censorious, to those who do indulge, and do not make frequent mention of the fact that you do not yourself indulge.

If someone brings you word that So-and-so is speaking ill of you, do not defend yourself against what has been said; but answer: "Yes, indeed, for he did not know the rest of the faults that attach to me; if he had, these would not have been the only ones he mentioned." . . .

41. It is a mark of an ungifted man to spend a great deal of time in what concerns his body, as in much exercise, much eating, much drinking, much evacuating of the bowels, much copulating. But these things are to be done in passing; and let your whole attention be devoted to the mind. . . .

44. The following statements constitute a non-sequitur: "I am richer than you are, therefore I am superior to you"; or, "I am more eloquent than you are, therefore I am superior to you." But the following conclusions are better: "I am richer than you are, therefore my property is superior to yours"; or, "I am more eloquent than you are, therefore my elocution is superior to yours." But you are neither property nor elocution. . . .

46. On no occasion call yourself a philosopher, and do not, for the most part, talk among laymen about your philosophic principles, but do what follows from your own principles.

Christianizing Ethics

Let us next turn to the way the Christian religion shaped the ancient idea of ethics, and the figure most responsible for that transformation.

St. Augustine

The greatness of **St. Augustine** (354–430) lay in this: he helped set forth the philosophical justification for believing that Christianity is not a mere superstition.

Augustine found this philosophical justification for Christianity in the metaphysics of Plato, as reinterpreted by the Neoplatonist, **Plotinus** (204–270). Christianity rests on the belief in a transcendent God, and with the assistance of Platonic metaphysics St. Augustine was able to make philosophically intelligible to himself the concept of a *transcendent realm,* a realm of being beyond the spatio-temporal universe that contains (or is) the source of all that is real and good. He also saw in Platonic and Neoplatonic doctrines the solution to the *problem of evil.* This problem can be expressed in a very simple question: How could evil have arisen in a world created by a perfectly good God?

One solution to this problem that Augustine considered was that evil is the result of a creative force other than God, a *force of darkness,* so to speak. But isn't there supposed to be just one and only one Creator? That's what Augustine believed, so this solution was not acceptable.

For Plato, remember, the Form of the Good was the source of all reality, and from this principle it follows that all that is real is good. Thus evil, given Plato's principle, *is not real.* This approach to the problem of evil St. Augustine found entirely satisfactory. Because evil is not something, it was not created by God.

This theory of evil is plausible enough as long as you're thinking of certain "physical" evils, like blindness or droughts (though others, like pain, seem as real as can be). Blindness, after all, is the absence of sight and droughts are the absence of water.

Unfortunately, however, the absence theory does not plausibly explain *moral* evil, the evil that is the wrongdoing of men and women. How did Augustine account for moral evil? His explanation of moral evil was a variation of another idea of Plato's, the idea that a person never knowingly does wrong, that evil actions are the result of ignorance of the good, of misdirected education, so to say. But Augustine added a new twist to this idea. Moral evil, he said, is not exactly a case of misdirected *education* but a case of misdirected *love.* This brings us to the heart of Augustine's ethics.

For Augustine, as for the Stoics, a natural law governs all morality and human behavior must conform to it. But for Augustine this is not an impersonal rational principle that shapes the destiny of the cosmos. The Augustinian natural law is, rather, the eternal law of God as it is written in the heart of man and woman and is apprehended by them in their conscience; and the eternal law is the "reason and will of God."

Thus the ultimate source of all that is good, for Augustine, is God, and God alone is intrinsically good. Our overriding moral imperative is therefore to love God, and the individual virtues are simply different aspects of the love of God.

Augustine didn't mean that you must love *only* God. He meant that while there is nothing wrong with loving things other than God, you must not love them as if they were good in and of themselves: for *only God is intrinsically good*. To love things other than God as if they were inherently good—e.g., to love money or success as if these things were good in and of themselves—is *disordered* love: it is to turn away from God, and moral evil consists in just this disordered love.

Now don't let any of this make you think that Augustine was unconcerned with happiness, for as a matter of fact he did indeed think we should seek happiness. But happiness, he argued, consists in having all you want and wanting no evil. This may seem to be an odd notion at first, but when you think about it, it is by no means absurd. In any event, the only conceivable way to have all you want and to want no evil, Augustine thought, is to make God the supreme object of your love.

So, for Augustine, moral evil arises when man or woman turns away from God. Thus *God* is not the creator of moral evil: it is *we* who create evil through our own free choice. But doesn't it then follow that *we* can create good? No, for God, remember, is the source of all that is good. Thus we can do good only *through* God, Augustine said. Whereas evil is caused by our free acts, goodness is the result of God's grace.

In sum, Augustine borrowed a theme from Plato by maintaining that physical evil can always be explained as the absence of something; and his concept of moral evil as arising from misdirected love can be viewed as a variation of Plato's idea of moral evil as ignorance of the good. In this way Augustine thought he had solved the problem of evil without doing damage to principles of Christian faith.

▶ S E L E C T I O N 7.5

From St. Augustine,
"OF THE MORALS OF THE CATHOLIC CHURCH"

Happiness is the enjoyment of man's chief good. Two conditions of the chief good: 1st, Nothing is better than it; 2d, it cannot be lost against the will.

How then, according to reason, ought man to live? We all certainly desire to live happily; and there is no human being but assents to this statement almost before it is made. But the title happy cannot, in my opinion, belong either to him who has not what he loves, whatever it may be, or to him who has what he loves if it is hurtful, or to him who does not love what he has, although it is good in perfection. For one who seeks what he cannot obtain suffers torture, and one who has got what is not desirable is cheated, and one who does not seek for what is worth seeking for is diseased. Now in all these cases the mind cannot but be unhappy, and happiness and unhappiness cannot reside at the same time in one man; so in none of these cases can the man be happy. I find, then, a fourth case, where the happy life exists,—when that which is a man's chief good is both loved and possessed. . . .

Man's chief good is not the chief good of the body only, but the chief good of the soul.

Now if we ask what is the chief good of the body, reason obliges us to admit that it is that by means of which the body comes to be in its best state. But of all the things which invigorate the body, there is nothing better or greater than the soul. The chief good of the body, then, is not bodily pleasure, not absence of pain, not strength, not beauty, not swiftness, or whatever else is usually reckoned among the goods of the body, but simply the soul. For all the things mentioned the soul supplies to the body by its presence, and, what is above them all, life. . . .

But if it follows, as it does, that the body which is ruled over by a soul possessed of virtue is ruled both better and more honourably, and is in its greatest perfection in consequence of the perfection of the soul which rightfully governs it, that which gives perfection to the soul will be man's chief good, though we call the body man. For if my coachman, in obedience to me, feeds and drives the horses he has charge of in the most satisfactory manner, himself enjoying the more of my bounty in proportion to his good conduct, can any one deny that the good condition of the horses, as well as that of the coachman, is due to me? So the question seems to me to be not, whether soul and body is man, or the soul only, or body only, but what gives perfection to the soul; for when this is obtained, a man cannot but be either perfect, or at least much better than in the absence of this one thing.

Virtue gives perfection to the soul; the soul obtains virtue by following God; following God is the happy life.

No one will question that virtue gives perfection to the soul. But it is a very proper subject of inquiry whether this virtue can exist by itself or only in the soul. . . . In either case, whether virtue can exist by itself without the soul, or can exist only in the soul, undoubtedly in the pursuit of virtue the soul follows after something. . . .

This something else, then, by following after which the soul becomes possessed of virtue and wisdom, is either a wise man or God. But we have said already that it must be something that we cannot lose against our will. No one can think it necessary to ask whether a wise man, supposing we are content to follow after him, can be taken from us in spite of our unwillingness or our persistence. God then remains, in following after whom we live well, and in reaching whom we live both well and happily.

Augustine fashioned a philosophical framework for Christian thought that was essentially Platonic. He found many Platonic and Neoplatonic themes that could be given a Christian interpretation, and thus is sometimes said to have Christianized Plato. Eight centuries later, **St. Thomas Aquinas** (1225–1274), in a somewhat different sense, Christianized the philosophy of Aristotle. Aquinas's task was perhaps the more difficult of the two, for the philosophy of Aristotle, with its this-worldly approach to things, was less congenial to a Christian interpretation. Thus it is customary to speak of Aquinas as having *reconciled* Aristotelianism with Christianity. In Aquinas's ethical philosophy, this amounted by and large to accepting both Christianity and the philosophy of Aristotle wherever that could be done without absurdity.

Think back for a moment to Aristotle. Aristotle said that the good for each kind of thing is defined with reference to the function or the nature of that kind of thing and is in fact the goal or purpose of that kind of thing. In the case of humans, goodness is happiness. Aquinas agreed. The natural (moral) law, which is God's eternal law as it is applied to man on earth, is apprehended by us in the dictates of our conscience and practical reasoning, which guide us to our natural goal, happiness on earth.

But there is also, according to Aquinas, an eternal, atemporal good— namely, happiness everlasting. The law that directs us to that end is God's divine law, which the Creator reveals to us through His grace.

Thus the **natural law** of Aquinas is the law of reason, which leads us to our natural end insofar as we follow it. The **divine law** is God's gift to us, revealed through His grace. Therefore, according to Aquinas, there are two sets of virtues: the "higher" virtues of faith, love, and hope, and the natural virtues such as courage, temperance, justice, and prudence, which are achieved when the will, directed by the intellect, moderates our natural drives, impulses, and inclinations. Thus did Aquinas accept both Aristotle and Christianity.

We shall return to Aquinas's concept of natural law in a later chapter.

In Selection 7.6, from one of his major works, the *Summa Contra Gentiles*, Aquinas sets out to prove that ultimate human happiness does not consist in wealth, worldly power, health, beauty, or strength, or the sensual pleasures, or anything else to be found in this life.

▶ S E L E C T I O N   7.6

From Thomas Aquinas, SUMMA CONTRA GENTILES

XVII. That All Things Are Directed to One End, Which Is God.

From the foregoing it is clear that all things are directed to one good as their last end.

For if nothing tends to something as its end, except insofar as this is good, it follows that good, as such, is an end. Consequently that which is the supreme good is supremely the end of all. Now there is but one Supreme good, namely God, as their end.

Again. That which is supreme in any genus, is the cause of everything in that genus: thus fire which is supremely hot is the cause of heat in other bodies. Therefore the supreme good, namely God, is the cause of goodness in all things good. Therefore He is the cause of every end being an end: since whatever is an end, is such, insofar as it is good. Now the cause of a thing being such is yet more so. Therefore God is supremely the end of all things. . . .

XXX. That Man's Happiness Does Not Consist in Wealth.

Hence it is evident that neither is wealth man's supreme good. For wealth is not sought except for the sake of something else: because of itself it brings us no good, but only when we use it, whether for the support of the body, or for some similar purpose. Now the supreme good is sought for its own, and not for another's sake. Therefore wealth is not man's supreme good. . . .

XXXI. That Happiness Consists Not in Worldly Power.

. . . Man's supreme good cannot be a thing that one can use both well and ill: for the better things are those that we cannot abuse. But one can use one's power both well and ill: for rational powers can be directed to contrary objects. Therefore human power is not man's supreme good. . . .

XXXII. That Happiness Consists Not in Goods of the Body.

. . . The soul is better than the body, which neither lives, nor possesses these goods, without the soul. Wherefore the soul's good, such as understanding and the like, is better than the body's good. Therefore the body's good is not man's supreme good. . . .

XXXIII. That Human Happiness is Not Seated in the Senses.

. . . Intellect is superior to sense. Therefore the intellect's good is better than the sense's. Consequently man's supreme good is not seated in the senses. . . .

XXXVII. That Man's Ultimate Happiness Consists in Contemplating God.

Accordingly if man's ultimate happiness consists not in external things, which are called goods of chance; nor in goods of the body;

nor in goods of the soul, as regards the sensitive faculty; nor as regards the intellective faculty, in the practice of moral virtue; nor as regards intellectual virtue in those which are concerned about action, namely art and prudence; it remains for us to conclude that man's ultimate happiness consists in the contemplation of the truth.

For this operation alone is proper to man, and none of the other animals communicates with him therein.

Again. This is not directed to anything further as its end: since the contemplation of the truth is sought for its own sake.

Again. By this operation man is united to things above him, by becoming like them: because of all human actions this alone is both in God and in separate substances. Also, by this operation man comes into contact with those higher beings, through knowing them in any way whatever. . . .

Now, it is not possible that man's ultimate happiness consists in contemplation based on the understanding of first principles: for this is most imperfect, as being universal and containing potential knowledge of things. Moreover, it is the beginning and not the end of human study, and comes to us from nature, and not through the study of the truth. Nor does it consist in contemplation based on the sciences that have the lowest things for their object: since happiness must consist in an operation of the intellect in relation to the highest object of intelligence. It follows then that man's ultimate happiness consists in wisdom, based on the consideration of divine things. It is therefore evident by way of induction that man's ultimate happiness consists solely in the contemplation of God. . . .

XLVIII. That Man's Ultimate Happiness Is Not in This Life.

Seeing then that man's ultimate happiness does not consist in that knowledge of God whereby he is known by all or many in a vague kind of opinion, nor again in that knowledge of God whereby he is known in science through demonstration; nor in that knowledge whereby he is known through faith, as we have proved above: and seeing that it is not possible in this life to arrive at a higher knowledge of God in His essence, or at least so that we understand other separate substances, and thus know God through that which is nearest to Him, so to say, as we have proved; and since we must place our ultimate happiness in some kind of knowledge of God, as we have shown; it is impossible for man's happiness to be in this life.

Again. Man's last end is the term of his natural appetite, so that when he has obtained it, he desires nothing more: because if he still has a movement towards something, he has not yet reached an end wherein to be at rest. Now, this cannot happen in this life: since the more man understands, the more is the desire to understand increased in him—this being natural to man—unless perhaps someone there be who understands all things: and in this life this never did nor can happen to anyone that was a mere man; seeing that in this life we are unable to know separate substances which in themselves are most intelligible, as we have proved. Therefore man's ultimate happiness cannot possibly be in this life. . . .

Further. All admit that happiness is a perfect good: else it would not bring rest to the appetite. Now perfect good is that which is wholly free from any admixture of evil: just as that which is perfectly white is that which is entirely free from any admixture of black. But man cannot be wholly free from evils in his state of life; not only from evils of the body, such as hunger, thirst, heat, cold and the like, but also from evils of the soul. For no one is there who at times is not disturbed by inordinate passions; who sometimes does not go beyond the mean, wherein virtue consists, either in excess or in deficiency; who is not deceived in something or another; or at least ignores what he would wish to know, or feels doubtful about an opinion of which he would like to be certain. Therefore no man is happy in this life.

Hobbes and Hume

We've seen that the naturalism found in Aristotle's ethics and the non-naturalistic ethics of Plato, with its conception of a transcendental source of ultimate value, flowed in separate streams through the philosophy of the centuries until the time of Aquinas. If it is not quite true to say that Aquinas channeled the waters from each of these two streams into a common bed, it may at least be said that he contrived to have them flow side by side, though in separate channels.

But the next philosopher we wish to discuss, **Thomas Hobbes** (1588–1679), drew exclusively from the Aristotelian channel. This is not surprising, for Hobbes was one of the first philosophers of the modern period in philosophy, a period marked by the emergence of experimental science, in which once again nature itself was an object of study, just as it had been for Aristotle. (You should be aware, nevertheless, that Hobbes, reacting to the Aristotelianism of his Oxford tutors, had harsh things to say about Aristotle.)

Hobbes

Hobbes's metaphysics was a relentless materialism. All that exists, he said, are material things in motion. Immaterial substance does not exist. There is no such thing as the nonphysical soul. Thoughts, emotions, feelings—all are motions of the matter within the brain, caused by moving things outside the brain. Even our reasoning and volition are purely physical processes.

As for values, according to Hobbes the words *good* and *evil* simply denote that which a person desires or hates. And Hobbes, like Aristotle, the Epicureans, the Stoics, and Aquinas, believed that we have a natural "end" or objective toward which all of our activity is directed. Hobbes specified this object of desire as the preservation of our own life. We seek personal survival above all other things, he held.

Now people live under one or another of two basic conditions, Hobbes said: a condition of *war,* in which they can harm each other, or a condition of *peace,* in which they cannot harm each other.

Notice that Hobbes did not define peace as a condition in which people *do not* harm each other, but as one in which people *cannot* harm each other. This is because Hobbes thought that people are fundamentally so selfish, mean, and stupid that they *will* harm each other unless they are *prevented* from doing so. But because their primary objective—survival—is better achieved under a condition of peace, people should seek peace if they are rational, he said. Fortunately, in Hobbes's opinion, people are possibly just barely rational enough to see that this is so.

But how is a condition of peace supposed to be kept, given the basic brutality, stupidity, and selfishness of the human race? Hobbes thought that a condition of peace could be sustained only if people agree or "contract" among themselves to transfer their collective strength to a sovereign power—an individual (or group of individuals) who would *compel* his subjects to honor their commitments and stand by their other agreements and contracts and thus to live peacefully. Without this third party to keep them in line, people will soon enough return to their original condition, a state of war of each against all.

Now, *justice* and *injustice*, he said, consist entirely in the keeping or breaking of covenants (i.e., agreements). If you keep our agreement, that's just. If you break it, that's unjust. But covenants are empty words, he observed, without this coercive power that can compel people to abide by the terms of the covenant. Thus, justice and injustice, according to Hobbes, really don't even exist until people become smart enough to entrust their power to the sovereign. Justice and morality begin and end with the sovereign, according to Hobbes.

There are difficulties in Hobbes's solution to the problems that arise from the supposed selfishness and brutality of people, but discussion will have to wait until Chapter 9, when we consider Hobbes's political philosophy. For now what is important is to see that for Hobbes, values (good and evil) are defined by desires and justice and injustice begin and end with the sovereign.

Given Hobbes's view of good and evil and justice and injustice, it seems surprising at first to find Hobbes affirming the existence of natural laws. For the concept of natural law that we have encountered so far in this chapter is the Stoic concept, which was introduced into Christian philosophy by Augustine and accepted as well by Aquinas. As these earlier philosophers used the concept, the natural law was a moral law; it was a principle of rationality that infused the universe and to which human behavior is morally obliged to conform. For the Christian thinker, of course, the natural law was decreed by God.

But for Hobbes, a natural law is simply a value-neutral principle, discovered by reason, of how best to preserve one's life. Hobbes's laws of nature are therefore nonmoral. When he says, for example, that according to natural law people ought to seek peace, he means only that this is what people ought to do if they want to save their skins.

Hobbes also speaks of **natural right** and affirms that we have a natural right to use all means to defend ourselves. Today we think of a natural right as a moral restriction placed on others in their actions relative to us. For example, when we think of ourselves as having a natural right to life, we mean that others should not act so as to deprive us of our life. But Hobbes meant something rather different when he said that when peace cannot be obtained we have a natural right to use all means to defend ourselves. He meant that in these conditions we suffer no moral restrictions whatsoever, and each person can use any methods he wishes—including murder—to ensure his own survival.

For Hobbes, therefore, there are natural laws, but these are not moral prescriptions. We have a natural right; but this right does not morally proscribe any activity. Good and evil exist, but these are defined subjectively, in terms of desires and aversions. Justice and injustice likewise are real things, but they are defined as the keeping or breaking of covenants.

Is Altruism Really Egoism?

The story is told of Hobbes that he was asked by a clergyman why he was giving alms to a beggar.

"Is it because Jesus has commanded you to do so?" the latter asked.

"No," came Hobbes's answer.

"Then why?"

"The reason I help the man," said Hobbes, "is that by doing so I end my discomfort at seeing his discomfort."

One moral that might be drawn from the story is that even the most altruistic and benevolent actions can be given an egoistic interpretation. Why did Hobbes help the beggar? To relieve his own discomfort. Why do saints devote their lives to relieving the suffering of others? Because it brings them pleasure to do so. Why did the soldier sacrifice his life to save his comrades? To end the distress he felt at thinking of his friends' dying—or maybe even because it pleased him to think of others praising him after his demise.

In short, because those who act to relieve their own discomfort or to bring pleasure to themselves are acting for their own self-interest, all these seemingly altruistic actions can be interpreted egoistically.

Are you convinced?

Well, if you are you should know that many philosophers are uncomfortable with this egoistic analysis of altruistic behavior. After all (they argue), it brings the saint pleasure to help others only if he is genuinely motivated to help others, right? Thus, if egoism is equated with the doctrine that we are never motivated to help others, it is false. If it is equated with the doctrine that we only act as we are motivated to act, it is true, but not particularly interesting.

Hobbes was important to the history of philosophy for several reasons. In metaphysics, as we have seen, he was the first modern exponent of a thorough-going materialism. In political philosophy, which we will get to later, Hobbes is important for his **contractarian** theory of justice and the state according to which justice and injustice and the state only come to exist when people contract among themselves to transfer their powers to a central agency that forces people to abide by their agreements.

In ethics, Hobbes is important, among other reasons, for his **descriptivism:** he did not attempt to determine how people ought to behave in some absolute sense; rather, he was concerned with describing how they ought to behave *if* they want best to secure their objective. A question Hobbes left for subsequent philosophers, therefore, and one that has not been resolved to this day, is this: If the universe is material, can there really *be* absolute values? Do good and evil, justice and injustice, exist in some *absolute* sense, or must they be regarded, as Hobbes so regarded them, as expressions of desires or the products of human agreements?

Selection 7.7 is from Hobbes's major work, *Leviathan*. A classic in political philosophy, it encompasses as well metaphysics, epistemology, ethics, and psychology, and secured for him a prime-time place in all histories of Western thought.

In Selection 7.7, Hobbes explains the "natural state" of mankind. This state, according to Hobbes, is a state of war, as explained, in which there is no right or wrong, justice or injustice.

▶ S E L E C T I O N   7.7

*From Thomas Hobbes, LEVIATHAN**

Of the Natural Condition of Mankind as Concerning Their Felicity and Misery

Nature has made men so equal, in the faculties of the body, and mind; as that though there be found one man sometimes manifestly stronger in body, or of quicker mind than another; yet when all is reckoned together, the difference between man, and man, is not so considerable, as that one man can thereupon claim to himself any benefit, to which another may not pretend, as well as he. For as to the strength of body, the weakest has strength enough to kill the strongest, either by secret machination, or by confederacy with others, that are in the same danger with himself.

And as to the faculties of the mind . . . I find yet a greater equality amongst men, than that of strength. . . . That which may perhaps make such equality incredible, is but a vain conceit of one's own wisdom, which almost all men think they have in a greater degree, than the vulgar; that is, than all men but themselves, and a few others, whom by fame, or for concurring with themselves, they approve. For such is the nature of men, that howsoever they may acknowledge many others to be more witty, or more eloquent or more learned; yet they will hardly believe there be many so wise as themselves; for they see their own wit at hand, and other men's at a distance. But this proves rather that men are in that point equal, than unequal. For there is not ordinarily a greater sign of the equal distribution of any thing, than that every man is contented with his share.

From this equality of ability, arises equality of hope in the attaining of our ends. And therefore if any two men desire the same thing, which nevertheless they cannot both enjoy, they become enemies; and in the way to their end, which is principally their own conservation, and sometimes their delectation only, endeavour to destroy, or subdue one another. And from hence it comes to pass, that where an invader has no more to fear, than another man's single power; if one plant, sow, build, or possess a convenient seat, others may probably be expected to come prepared with forces united, to dispossess, and deprive him, not only of the fruit of his labour, but also of his life, or liberty. And the invader again is in the like danger of another.

And from this diffidence of one another, there is no way for any man to secure himself, so reasonable, as anticipation; that is, by force, or wiles, to master the persons of all men he can, so long, till he see no other power great enough to endanger him: and this is no more than his own conservation requires, and is generally allowed. . . .

Again, men have no pleasure, but on the contrary a great deal of grief, in keeping company where there is no power able to over-awe them all. For every man looks that his companion should value him, at the same rate he sets upon himself: and upon all signs of contempt, or undervaluing, naturally endeavours, as far as he dares, (which amongst them that have no common power to keep them in quiet, is far enough to make them destroy each other), to extort a greater value from his condemners, by damage; and from others, by the example.

So that in the nature of man, we find three principal causes of quarrel. First, competition; secondly, diffidence; thirdly, glory.

The first, makes men invade for gain; the second, for safety; and the third, for reputation. The first use violence, to make themselves masters of other men's persons, wives, children, and cattle; the second, to defend them; the third for trifles, as a word, a smile, a different opinion, and any other sign of undervalue, either direct in their persons, or by reflection in their kindred, their friends, their nation, their profession, or their name.

Hereby it is manifest, that during the time men live without a common power to keep them all in awe, they are in that condition which is called war; and such a war, as is of every man, against every man. For WAR, consists not in battle only, or the act of fighting; but in a tract of time, wherein the will to contend by battle is sufficiently known: and therefore the notion of *time*, is to be considered in the nature of war; as it is the nature of weather. For as the nature of foul weather, lies not in a shower or two of rain; but in an inclination thereto of many days together; so the nature of war, consists not in actual fighting; but in the known disposition thereto, during all the time there is no assurance to the contrary. All other time is PEACE.

Whatsoever therefore is consequent to a time of war, where every man is enemy to every man; the same is consequent to the time, wherein men live without other security, than what their own strength, and their own invention shall furnish them withal. In such condition, there is no place for industry; because the fruit thereof is uncertain: and consequently no culture of the earth; no navigation, nor use of the commodities that may be imported by sea; no commodious building; no instruments of moving, and removing, such things as require much force; no knowledge of the face of the earth; no account of time; no arts; no letters, no society; and which is worst of all, continual fear, and danger of violent death; and the life of man, solitary, poor, nasty, brutish, and short.

It may seem strange to some man, that has not well weighed these things; that nature should thus dissociate, and render men apt to invade, and destroy one another; and he may therefore, not trusting to this inference, made from the passions, desire perhaps to have the same confirmed by experience. Let him therefore consider with himself, when taking a journey, he arms himself, and seeks to go well accompanied; when going to sleep, he locks his doors; when even in his house he locks his chests; and this when he knows there be laws, and public officers, armed, to revenge all injuries shall be done him; what opinion he has of his fellow-subjects, when he rides armed; of his fellow citizens, when he locks his doors; and of his children, and servants, when he locks his chests. Does he not there as much accuse mankind by his actions, as I do by my words? But neither of us accuse man's nature in it. The desires, and other passions of man, are in themselves no sin. No more are the actions, that proceed from those passions, till they know a law that forbids them: which till laws be made they cannot know: nor can any law be made, till they have agreed upon the person that shall make it. . . .

To this war of every man, against every man, this also is consequent; that nothing can be unjust. The notions of right and wrong, justice and injustice have there no place. Where there is no common power, there is no law: where no law, no injustice. Force, and fraud, are in war the two cardinal virtues. Justice and injustice are none of the faculties neither of the body, nor mind. If they were, they might be in a man that were alone in the world, as well as his senses, and passions. They are qualities that relate to men in society, not in solitude. It is consequent also to the same condition, that there be no propriety, no dominion, no *mine* and *thine* distinct; but only that to be every man's, that he can get; and for so long, as he can keep it. And thus much for the ill condition, which man by mere nature is actually placed in; though with a possibility to come out of it, consisting partly in the passions, partly in his reason.

The passions that incline men to peace, are fear of death, desire of such things as are necessary to commodious living; and a hope by their industry to obtain them. And reason suggests convenient articles of peace, upon which men may be drawn to agreement. These articles, are they, which otherwise are called the Laws of Nature: whereof I shall speak more particularly, in the two following chapters.

---

*Edited slightly for the modern reader.

Hume

Hobbes maintained that the idea of incorporeal or immaterial substance was a contradiction in terms, but he denied being an atheist. Nevertheless, he certainly did not rest his ethics on the authority of the Church. And although most of the major philosophers of the modern period shrank from Hobbes's extreme materialism, they, too—most of them—sought to discover the basic principles of morality elsewhere than in Scripture.

Some, such as Locke, though believing that these principles are decreed by God, held, like Hobbes, that they are discoverable—and provable— by reason.

But in the eighteenth century, **David Hume** (1711–1776) argued with some force that moral principles are neither divine edicts nor discoverable by reason. Hume's general position regarding God, as we shall see in Part 5, was that the order in the universe does offer some slight evidence that the universe has or had a creative force remotely analogous to human intelligence. But we certainly cannot affirm anything about the moral qualities of the creator, he held; and we cannot derive guidelines for our own actions from speculating about his (its) nature. Christianity Hume regarded as superstition.

Value Judgments Are Based on Emotion, Not Reason

Hume held likewise that moral judgments are not the "offspring of reason." Scrutinize an act of murder as closely as you can, he said. Do you find anything in the *facts of the case* that reveal that the act is morally wrong? The *facts*, he said, are simply that one person has terminated the life of another in a certain way at a particular time and place. Reasoning can disclose how long it took for death to occur, whether the victim suffered great pain, what the motives of the killer were as well as the answers to many other factual questions such as these. But it will not show the *moral wrongfulness* of the act. The judgment that an act is immoral, Hume maintained, comes not from reason but from *emotion*. Perhaps this idea has occurred to you as well.

It is the same, Hume believed, with all value judgments. Is the judgment that a portrait is beautiful founded on reason? Of course not. Reason can disclose the chemical composition of the paints and canvas, the

Cold-Blooded Murder

A fundamental principle of Hume's philosophy is that moral judgments are not the offspring of reason.

A consideration that might possibly favor Hume's thesis is that we tend to think of particularly heinous deeds, execution-style murders, for example, as "cold-blooded" and "heartless," not as "irrational." This is an indication that we view the murderer as lacking in *feeling* rather than as deficient in *reason*.

Is it hard to believe that an absolutely brilliant mind could commit murder? We think not. But is it hard to believe that someone with normal sensibilities could commit murder? We think that it is. These considerations favor Hume's principle.

monetary value of the work, and many similar factual things. But whether or not the portrait is beautiful is an issue that cannot be settled by reason.

Thus, for Hume, moral judgments, and all value judgments, are based on emotion. Actions that we find morally praiseworthy or blameworthy create within us feelings of pleasure or displeasure, respectively. Now, obviously, these feelings are different in kind from aesthetic pleasures and pleasures of the palate. Humans clearly have a capacity for moral pleasure as well as for other types of pleasure: we are *morally sensitive creatures*. Behavior that pleases our moral sensibilities elicits our approval and is deemed good, right, just, virtuous, and noble. Behavior that offends our moral sense is deemed bad, wrong, unjust, base, and ignoble.

Benevolence

But just what is it about behavior that elicits our moral approval? *What do virtuous, good, right, and noble acts have in common?* Hume's answer was that the type of act we deem morally praiseworthy is one taken by an agent *out of concern for others*. The act that pleases our moral sensibilities is one that reflects a *benevolent character* on the part of the agent, he said. By "agent," Hume meant the person who did the act.

Why does benevolence bring pleasure to us when we witness or read about or contemplate it? A cynical answer is that we imagine ourselves as benefiting from the benevolent activity and imagining this is pleasant. Do you get a warm glow when you read about someone coming to the aid of a fellow person? Well, according to the cynical view that's because you picture yourself on the receiving end of the exchange.

But this cynical theory is really quite unnecessarily complex, said Hume. The reason you get that pleasant feeling when you read about or see someone helping someone else is just simply that you *sympathize* with others. It just plainly upsets a normal person to see others suffering, and it pleases them to see others happy. True, there are J. R. Ewing types around who suffer from the emotional equivalent of color blindness and lack the capacity to sympathize with others. But these people aren't the norm. The normal human being is a sympathetic creature, maintained Hume.

This aspect of Hume's moral philosophy may well have some significance for us today. On one hand we tend to believe that you should care for others, but on the other hand that you must also certainly look out for yourself. And we are inclined to think that there is a problem in this because self-concern and other-concern seem mutually exclusive. But if Hume is correct, they are not. Looking out for your own interests includes doing that which brings you pleasure. And if Hume is correct, caring for others will bring you an important kind of pleasure. Indeed, if Hume is correct, when you praise an action as good, it is precisely because it brings you this kind of pleasure.

Hume's idea that goodness consists in traits and actions that promote the welfare of people was appropriated and developed in the nineteenth century by some of the most influential ethical theorists of all time, the utilitarians. There is every possibility that you yourself are a utilitarian; but of utilitarianism, more later.

Can There Be Ethics After Hume?

In sum, then, according to Hume, moral principles are neither divine edicts nor the "offspring of reason." Instead, *a judgment of moral approval is simply an expression of a particular kind of pleasure, a pleasure that we experience when confronted with behavior done out of concern for others.*

Now notice how severe Hume's break with tradition was. Earlier philosophers had asked questions like these: *What actions are virtuous and right and good, and why? What ought we do, and what determines this?* Hume, in contrast, asked questions like these: *What is a moral judgment? What are we doing when we praise something as morally good? What gives rise to our moral opinions? What do all acts considered to be morally praiseworthy have in common?* (This last question, of course, does have a very Socratic flavor.)

The questions asked by preceding philosophers, in short, tend to focus on this issue: What *is* good? Hume's questions, on the other hand, tend to focus on this question: What do we *mean* by "good"? The first question is a request for *norms*—that is, for standards or principles of right and wrong. Hume's question, in contrast, is a request for *facts* about what moral judgments are and about what sorts of things are deemed to be good.

It is plain why Hume's inquiries took him away from a consideration of norms or standards. For although other possible ultimate sources of values than God or reason exist, there may not be any as plausible as these two. So it is easy to suppose that, if ethical standards are set neither by God nor by reason, then there just *aren't* any ethical standards apart from those established by people. And if this is true, then you would have to think that there is no *meaning* in the question: What is good?, beyond what is revealed by considering what people *call* good.

This was, in effect, Hume's position. Neither God nor reason lay down the ethical law, and once you discover what people *mean* by "good," you have found out what *is* good.

As we shall see, Hume's empirical, nonnormative approach to ethics came to predominate contemporary ethical philosophy in English-speaking countries during the first half of the twentieth century.

Nevertheless, for many people today, especially those outside philosophy, the notion that there is nothing left for ethical philosophy beyond the consideration of the meaning of ethical terminology is equivalent to saying that ethics is sterile or dead. They might therefore be inclined to say that, if Hume is correct in maintaining that moral principles are neither divine edicts nor the "offspring of reason," then nothing of much significance is left for ethics.

Can there be ethical philosophy after Hume? In the next chapter we find out.

In Selection 7.8, Hume argues that "morality is not an object of reason."

▶ S E L E C T I O N   7.8

From David Hume,
A TREATISE OF HUMAN NATURE

But to make these general reflexions more clear and convincing, we may illustrate them by some particular instances, wherein this character of moral good or evil is the most universally acknowledged. Of all crimes that human creatures are capable of committing, the most horrid and unnatural is ingratitude, especially when it is committed against parents, and appears in the more flagrant instances of wounds and death. This is acknowledged by all mankind, philosophers as well as the people, the question only arises among philosophers, whether the guilt or moral deformity of this action be discovered by demonstrative reasoning or be felt by an internal sense, and by means of some sentiment, which the reflection on such an action naturally occasions. This question will soon be decided against the former opinion, if we can show the same relations in other objects, without the notion of any guilt or iniquity attending them. Reason or science is nothing but the comparing of ideas, and the discovery of their relations; and if the same relations have different characters, it must evidently follow, that those characters are not discovered merely by reason. To put the affair, therefore, to this trial, let us choose any inanimate object, such as an oak or elm; and let us suppose, that by the dropping of its seed, it produces a sapling below it, which springing up by degrees, at last overtops and destroys the parent tree: I ask, if in this instance there be wanting any relation, which is discoverable in parricide or ingratitude? Is not the one tree the cause of the other's existence; and the latter the cause of the destruction of the former, in the same manner as when a child murders his parent? It is not sufficient to reply, that a choice or will is wanting. For in the case of parricide, a will does not give rise to any *different* relations, but is only the cause from which the action is derived; and consequently produces the *same* relations, that in the oak or elm arise from some other principles. It is a will or choice, that determines a man to kill his parent; and they are the laws of matter and motion, that determine a sapling to destroy the oak, from which it sprung. Here then the same relations have different causes; but still the relations are the same: And as their discovery is not in both cases attended with a notion of immorality, it follows, that the notion does not arise from such a discovery.

But to choose an instance, still more resembling; I would fain ask any one, why incest in the human species is criminal, and why the very same action, and the same relations in animals have not the smallest moral turpitude and deformity? If it be answered, that this action is innocent in animals, because they have not reason sufficient to discover its turpitude, but that man, being endowed with that faculty, which *ought* to restrain him to his duty, the same action instantly becomes criminal to him; should this be said, I would reply, that this is evidently arguing in a circle. For before reason can perceive this turpitude, the turpitude must exist; and consequently is independent of the decisions of our reason, and is their object more properly than their affect. According to this system, then, every animal, that has sense, and appetite, and will; that is, every animal must be susceptible of all the same virtues and vices, for which we ascribe praise and blame to human creatures. All the difference is, that our superior reason may serve to discover the vice or virtue, and by that means may augment the blame or praise: But still this discovery supposes a separate being in these moral distinctions, and a being, which depends only on the will and appetite, and which, both in thought and reality, may be distinguished from the reason. Animals are susceptible of the same relations, with respect to each other, as the human species, and therefore would also be susceptible of the same morality, if the essence of morality consisted in these relations. Their want of sufficient degree of reason may hinder them from perceiving the duties and obligations of morality, but can never hinder these duties from existing; since they must antecedently exist, in order to their being perceived. Reason must find them, and can never produce them. This argument deserves to be weighed, as being, in my opinion, entirely decisive.

Nor does this reasoning only prove, that morality consists not in any relations, that are the objects of science; but if examined, will prove with equal certainty, that it consists not in any *matter of fact*, which can be discovered by understanding. This is the *second* part of our argument; and if it can be made evident, we may conclude, that morality is not an object of reason. But can there be any difficulty in proving, that vice and virtue are not matters of fact, whose existence we can infer by reason? Take any action allowed to be vicious: Wilful murder, for instance. Examine it in all lights, and see if you can find that matter of fact, or real existence, which you call *vice*. In whichever way you take it, you find only certain passions, motives, volitions and thoughts. There is no other matter of fact in the case. The vice entirely escapes you, as long as you consider the object. You never can find it, till you turn your reflexion into your own breast, and find a sentiment of disapprobation, which arise in you, towards this action. Here is a matter of fact; but it is the object of feeling, not of reason. It lies in yourself, not in the object. So that when you pronounce any action or character to be vicious, you mean nothing, but that from the constitution of your nature you have a feeling or sentiment of blame from the contemplation of it. Vice and virtue, therefore, may be compared to sounds, colours, heat and cold, which according to modern philosophy, are not qualities in objects, but perceptions in the mind: And this discovery in morals like that other in physics, is to be regarded as a considerable advancement of the speculative sciences; though like that too, it has little or no influence on practice. Nothing can be more real, or concern us more, than our own sentiments of pleasure and uneasiness; and if these be favourable to virtue, and unfavourable to vice, no more can be requisite to the regulation of our conduct and behaviour.

I cannot forbear adding to these reasonings an observation, which may, perhaps, be found of some importance. In every system of morality, which I have hitherto met with, I have always remarked, that the author proceeds for some time in the ordinary way of reasoning, and establishes the being of a God, or makes observations concerning human affairs, when of a sudden I am surprised to find, that instead of the usual copulations of propositions, *is*, and *is not*, I meet with no proposition that is not connected with an *ought*, or an *ought not*. This change is imperceptible, but is, however, of the last consequence. For as this *ought*, or *ought not*, expresses some new relation or affirmation, it is necessary that it should be observed and explained; and at the same time that a reason should be given, for what seems altogether inconceivable, how this new relation can be a deduction from others, which are entirely different from it. But as authors do not commonly use this precaution, I shall presume to recommend it to the readers, and am persuaded, that this small attention would subvert all the vulgar systems of morality, and let us see, that the distinction of vice and virtue is not founded merely on the relations of objects, nor is perceived by reason.

Checklist

To help you review, here is a checklist of the key philosophers and concepts of this chapter. The brief descriptive sentences that appear with each philosopher summarize one of his leading ideas. Keep in mind that some of these summary statements represent terrific oversimplifications of complex positions.

Philosophers

- **Sophists** Professional teachers of fifth-century B.C. Greece whose attack on traditional moral values marks the beginnings of ethical philosophy.

- **Socrates** Sought to discover the essences of moral virtues and championed the use of reason in moral deliberation.

- **Plato** Also sought the essences of moral virtues; identified these with the unchanging Forms, the highest of which he held to be the Form of the Good, the ultimate source of all value and reality.

- **Aristotle** Ethical naturalist; held that moral judgments are judgments of fact about the natural world. Said that happiness is our highest good.

- **Zeno** Founder of Stoicism.

- **Cleanthes, Cicero, Seneca, and Marcus Aurelius** Famous Stoics.

- **Aristippus** Held that life should be dedicated to the pursuit of intense pleasure.

- **Diogenes** Most famous Cynic, who taught by shocking example that the wise person reduces all wants and avoids all comforts.

- **Epicurus** An ethical egoist; held that one's highest objective is to lead the pleasant life through moderate living.

- **Epictetus** A leading Stoic; held that one's highest objective is to find a serene or untroubled life through acceptance of the rational natural order of things.

- **Saint Augustine** Used Platonic concepts to solve "the problem of evil"; held moral evil to be misdirected love; identified God as the supreme moral authority and source of all goodness.

- **Saint Thomas Aquinas** Reconciled Aristotelian ethical naturalism with Christianity.

- **Thomas Hobbes** Held that "good" and "evil" denote what a person desires or hates; maintained that our natural end is preservation of self.

- **David Hume** Held that moral principles are neither divine edicts nor discoverable by reason, and that value judgments are based on emotion. Said that the act that pleases our moral sensibilities is one that reflects the agent's benevolent character.

Concepts

ethics

value judgment

ethical skepticism

subjectivism

ultimate source of value

well-ordered soul

nonnatural source of value

ethical naturalism

mean between extremes

instrumental vs. intrinsic ends

Epicureans

Stoics

epicure

stoic

Cyrenaics

Cynics

misdirected/disordered love

descriptive egoism

prescriptive egoism

contractarian theory

descriptivism

altruism

benevolence

Questions for Discussion and Review

1. Is there some single thing that all morally good actions have in common? Defend your view.

2. "What is right is what you yourself believe is right." Critically evaluate this statement.

3. What is the connection between virtue and happiness, in the philosophy of Plato?

4. Explain how Plato's theory may be regarded as "complete."

5. In what does happiness consist, according to Aristotle? When can we be said to be virtuous, according to him?

6. What is the connection between habit and moral character, for Aristotle?

7. Compare and contrast the ethical philosophies of Epicureanism and Stoicism. Which do you think is a superior philosophy, and why?

8. Evaluate Aristippus's philosophy (see box).

9. Is it a sound policy to reduce all wants to a minimum and to achieve utter self-reliance by avoiding all the comforts of society?

10. Can you control your attitude if you cannot control your fate?

11. Explain Augustine's solution to the problem of evil and determine whether or not it is sound.

12. Explain and evaluate Aquinas's reasons for believing that ultimate human happiness does not consist in wealth, worldly power, or anything in this life (see Selection 7.6).

13. Do we seek personal survival above all other things?

14. Do we always act selfishly? Explain.

15. Explain and critically evaluate prescriptive egoism.

16. Does it make sense for a (prescriptive) egoist to advocate egoism?

17. Is altruism really disguised egoism?

18. Can reasoning disclose the moral wrongfulness of an act of murder?

19. Is Hume correct in saying that the type of act we deem morally praiseworthy is one done out of concern for others?

20. Is it abnormal not to have sympathy for others? Are J. R. Ewing types (i.e., selfish people) really admired in today's society?

Aristotle, *The Nicomachean Ethics*, Martin Ostwald, ed. (Indianapolis: Bobbs-Merrill, 1962).

John Burnet, *Early Greek Philosophy*, 4th ed. (London: Macmillan, originally published in 1930). A standard work on early Greek philosophy.

F. C. Copleston, *Aquinas* (Baltimore: Penguin Books, 1955). See Chapter 5.

Epicurus, *The Extant Remains*, C. Bailey, trans. (Oxford: Clarendon Press, 1962). For those who wish to read more from Epicurus.

Epictetus, *Discourses*. This contains other ethical works of Epictetus.

E. Hamilton and H. Cairns, eds., *The Collected Dialogues of Plato* (New York: Bollingen Foundation, 1961). This, as we said before, is what you need to acquaint yourself firsthand with Plato's dialogues. Be sure to read *The Republic*. The other dialogues especially relevant to ethics are *Gorgias*, *Meno*, *Philebus*.

R. D. Hicks, *Stoic and Epicurean* (New York: Russell and Russell, 1962). See chapters 3, 4, and 5.

J. Kemp, *Ethical Naturalism: Hobbes and Hume* (London: Macmillan, 1970). See chapters 2 and 3. For original works, try F. J. E. Woodbridge, *Hobbes Selections* and C. W. Hendel, Jr., *Hume Selections*, both published by Scribners in New York.

G. S. Kirk, J. E. Raven, and M. Schofield, *The Presocratic Philosophers: A Critical History with a Selection of Texts*, 2nd ed. (Cambridge: Cambridge University Press, 1983). This is a comprehensive recent treatment of the pre-Socratics.

E. Gilson, *The Christian Philosophy of St. Augustine* (New York: Random House, 1960). See the introduction and part II for relevant material.

J. Gould, *The Development of Plato's Ethics* (London: Cambridge University Press, 1955). Explains the important principles and concepts in Plato's ethics.

W. F. R. Hardie, *Aristotle's Ethical Theory* (Oxford: Clarendon Press, 1968). There are several reliable books on Aristotle's ethics. This is one of the most popular.

Suggested Further Readings

Ethics After Hume

The moral order is just as much part of the fundamental nature
of the universe as is the spatial or numerical structure expressed
in the axioms of geometry or arithmetic.

—W. D. ROSS

Hamlet: *There is nothing either good or bad, but thinking
makes it so.*

—SHAKESPEARE

In Part 2 we saw that David Hume said some things about what can be
known that marked a big turning point in the history of epistemology.
And now in Part 3 we see Hume's philosophy pointing out new directions
for ethics, too. "Morality," Hume said, "is more properly felt than judged
of." Ethical standards are not fixed by reason, he held; further, even if
there is a God, he maintained, it is quite impossible for us to gain moral
guidance from Him.

Loosely speaking, therefore, ethics after Hume seems generally to
have had these options: First, it might seek to establish that, despite
Hume, morality *can* be grounded on reason or God. This was the option
taken by Kant, who favored reason as the ultimate ground of morality. Or
second, it might try to find objective sources of moral standards other
than reason and God. This is what the utilitarians tried to do. Or third,
it might try to determine how one should conduct one's affairs given the
absence of objective moral standards. This is a primary concern of contemporary existentialists. Or fourth, it might abandon the search for moral
standards altogether and concentrate instead on such factual questions
as: What do people believe is good and right? What does it mean to say
that something is good or right? How do moral judgments differ from
other kinds of judgments? What leads us to praise certain actions as moral

and condemn others as immoral? These are some of the issues that have captured the attention of contemporary analytic philosophers.

Let's start with Kant, who survived Hume by twenty-eight years.

Kant

Immanuel Kant (1724–1804) disagreed entirely with Hume's discounting of the possibility that reason can settle whether or not an act is morally right. In Kant's opinion, reason and reason alone can settle this. Kant's argument, paraphrased and distilled, went like this:

1. *Scientific inquiry can never reveal to us principles that we know hold without exception.* For scientific inquiry is based on experience, and in the final analysis experience can only show how things have been to this point, not how they must be. For example, science reveals to us physical "laws" that hold true of the universe as it is now, but it cannot provide absolutely conclusive guarantees that these laws will forever hold true. (If you have difficulty understanding this point, rereading the section on Kant in Chapter 6 will help.)

2. *Moral principles, however, hold without exception.* For example, if it is wrong to torture helpless animals, then it would be wrong for anyone, at any time, to do so.

Thus, from these two premises—that moral principles hold without exception and that scientific investigations cannot reveal what holds without exception—it follows that:

3. *Moral principles cannot be revealed through scientific investigation.* Because Kant believed that any principle that holds without exception is knowable only through reason, he maintained that *reason alone can ascertain principles of morality.*

The Supreme Principle of Morality

Further, according to Kant, because a moral rule is something that holds without exception—that is, holds universally—you should act only on principles that could hold universally. For example, if you think you must cheat to pass an exam, then the principle on which you would act (if you were to cheat) would be this: *To obtain a passing grade, it is acceptable to cheat.* But now consider: If this principle were a universal law, then a passing grade would be meaningless, right? And in that case the principle itself would be meaningless. In short, the principle logically could not hold universally, and (this comes to the same thing) it would be irrational for anyone to want it to hold universally.

Now if it would be irrational for you to want the principle on which you act to be a universal law, then that principle is morally improper and the act should not be done. Thus, for Kant, *the supreme prescription of morality is to act always in such a way that you could, rationally, will the principle on which you act to be a universal law.*

Kant on Reason and Morals

A fundamental principle of Kant's moral philosophy is that reason alone can determine whether or not an act is morally right.

Why You Should Do What You Should Do

Now moral principles, Kant observes, may always be expressed in the imperative form: Do not steal! Be kind to others! Further, because moral imperatives must hold without exception, they are different from **hypothetical imperatives,** which state, in effect, that one ought to do something *if* such-and-such an end is desired.

For example, the imperatives, "If you wish to be healthy, then live moderately!" and "If you wish to secure your own survival, then surrender your rights to a sovereign power!" are both hypothetical imperatives. Neither is a **moral imperative,** for a moral imperative holds unconditionally or *categorically.* This means that a moral imperative commands obedience for the sake of no other end than its own rightness.

Thus, for Kant, what I should do I should do *because it is right.* Doing something for any other purpose—for the sake of happiness or the welfare of mankind, for example—is not to act morally. It is to act under the command of a hypothetical imperative, which is not unconditional, as a moral imperative must be. According to Kant, you should do your moral duty simply because it is your moral duty. You may well find this position difficult to accept, but we *challenge* you to find a flaw in the reasoning that led Kant to adopt it.

Is It Ever Right to Break a Promise?

According to Kant, if a universal law allowed breach of promise, then there would be no such thing as a promise. Thus the maxim, "Break promises!", if it were to become a universal law, would (as Kant says in Selection 8.1) "destroy itself."

But hold on. Suppose I promise to return your car at 4 o'clock. And suppose that shortly before 4 my wife becomes ill and must be rushed to the hospital—and the only transportation available is your car! Should I break my promise to you in order to save my wife's life? And if I did, which maxim would I be acting on, breaking promises or saving lives?

Kant's answer (of course) would be that the maxim I acted on is, "Break promises when doing so is required to save a life." And there would apparently be no inconsistency in willing this maxim to be a universal law.

For Kant, then, the maxim, "Break your promises!" cannot be universalized. But that doesn't mean that, given his principles, you should never break a promise.

Furthermore, according to Kant, it's not the *effects or consequences* of your acts that determine whether your act is good or not, for these are not totally within your control. What is within your control is the *intent* with which you act. Thus, what determines whether your act is good or bad is the intent with which it is taken: He wrote: "Nothing can possibly be conceived in the world, or even out of it, which can be called good, without qualification, except a good will."

And, because a morally good will is one that acts solely for the sake of doing what is right, it follows, in Kant's opinion, that *there is no moral worth* in, say, helping others because you are sympathetic or inclined to do so. There only is moral worth in helping others because it is right to do so.

Yes, this is an astonishing doctrine, but again we challenge you to find a mistake in Kant's reasoning.

Because to violate the supreme principle of morality, the supreme **categorical imperative,** is to be irrational, rationality may be said to be the source of all value, and hence the rational will alone is deemed inherently good by Kant. Accordingly, Kant offers an alternative formulation of the supreme categorical imperative: *Treat rational beings (i.e., humans) in every instance as ends and never just as means!*

That this is an alternative formulation of the same principle may be seen in the fact that if you were to violate the categorical imperative and do something that you could not rationally will to be a law for all, then in effect you would be treating the interests of others as subordinate to your own; that is, you would be treating others as means and not as ends. Kant, it is often said (for obvious reasons), was the first philosopher to provide a *rational basis* for the golden rule found in many religions: Do unto others as you would have them do unto you.

Did Kant provide a viable response to Hume's idea that reason cannot determine whether an act is morally right? You decide.

Selection 8.1 is from Kant's *Foundations of the Metaphysics of Morals.* In it, Kant considers in what the moral worth of an action lies. Compare Kant's views on the subject with those of the two philosophers we turn to next.

▶ S E L E C T I O N 8.1

From Immanuel Kant, *FOUNDATIONS OF THE METAPHYSICS OF MORALS*

Morals

Transition from the Common Rational Knowledge of Morals to the Philosophical

Nothing in the world—indeed nothing even beyond the world—can possibly be conceived which could be called good without qualification except a *good will*. Intelligence, wit, judgment, and the other talents of the mind, however they may be named, or courage, resoluteness, or perseverance as qualities of temperament are doubtless in many respects good and desirable. But they can become extremely bad and harmful if the will, which is to make use of these gifts of nature and which in its special constitution is called character, is not good. It is the same with the gifts of fortune. Power, riches, honor, even health, general well-being, and the contentment with one's condition which is called happiness make for pride and even arrogance if there is not a good will to correct their influence on the mind and on its principles of action, so as to make it universally conformable to its end. It need hardly be mentioned that the sight of a being adorned with no feature of a pure and good will yet enjoying uninterrupted prosperity can never give pleasure to a rational impartial observer. Thus the good will seems to constitute the indispensable condition even of worthiness to be happy.

Some qualities seem to be conducive to this good will and can facilitate its action, but, in spite of that, they have not intrinsic unconditional worth. They rather presuppose a good will, which limits the high esteem which one otherwise rightly has for them and prevents their being held to be absolutely good. Moderation in emotions and passions, self-control, and calm deliberation not only are good in many respects but even seem to constitute a part of the inner worth of the person. But however unconditionally they were esteemed by the ancients, they are far from being good without qualification. For, without the principles of a good will, they can become extremely bad, and the coolness of a villain makes him not only far from dangerous but also more directly abominable in our eyes than he would have seemed without it.

The good will is not good because of what it effects or accomplishes or because of its adequacy to achieve some proposed end; it is good only because of its willing, i.e., it is good of itself. And, regarded for itself, it is to be esteemed incomparably higher than anything which could be brought about by it in favor of any inclination or even of the sum total of all inclinations. Even if it should happen that, by a particularly unfortunate fate or by the niggardly provision of a stepmotherly nature, this will should be wholly lacking in power to accomplish its purpose, and if even the greatest effort should not avail it to achieve anything of its end, and if there remained, only the good will (not as a mere wish but as the summoning of all the means in our power), it would sparkle like a jewel in its own right, as something that had its full worth in itself. Usefulness or fruitlessness can neither diminish nor augment this worth. Its usefulness would be only its setting, as it were, so as to enable us to handle it more conveniently in commerce or to attract the attention of those who are not yet connoisseurs, but not to recommend it to those who are experts or to determine its worth.

Kant, we have seen, may well have offered a sound refutation of Hume's idea that moral principles are not determined by reason. It is therefore perhaps strange that two of the most celebrated ethical philosophers of the nineteenth century, the Englishmen **Jeremy Bentham** (1748–1832) and **John Stuart Mill** (1806–1873), largely ignored the rationalistic ethics of Kant, Bentham perhaps more so than Mill. Bentham and Mill did not, however, ignore Hume. Instead, they developed further Hume's idea that those traits and actions are virtuous that promote the welfare of people, the "general happiness."

Bentham and Mill were **utilitarians,** which means they believed that *the rightness of an action is identical with the happiness it produces as its consequence.* What's new or exciting about this? Didn't Aristotle and the Epicureans and Augustine and Aquinas also advocate pursuing happiness? The difference is that according to the latter philosophers, it is *your own happiness* that you should strive for.

By contrast, when the utilitarians said that the morally best act is the one that produces, as compared with all possible alternative acts, the greatest amount of happiness, they meant the greatest amount of happiness *with everyone considered.* Often the point is expressed (somewhat misleadingly, and perhaps incoherently) by saying that, according to the utilitarians, the right act is the one that produces the greatest happiness for the greatest number.

In short, the utilitarians held that when you are trying to produce happiness, you should not single out yourself for preferential treatment: your own happiness is *not* more important morally than that of others.

Notice, too, that for the utilitarians it is the *consequences* of an act that determine its rightness, a position that contrasts strongly with Kant's idea that the moral worth of an act depends on the "will" or motive with which it is taken.

Bentham

Bentham, the earlier of the two utilitarians, equated happiness with pleasure. "Nature," he wrote, "has placed mankind under the governance of two sovereign masters, *pain* and *pleasure.* It is for them alone to point out what we ought to do, as well as determine what we shall do."

The words *ought, right, good,* and the like only have meaning when defined in terms of pleasure, he said. This fact is evident, he argued, in that all other intelligible moral standards either must be interpreted in terms of the pleasure standard or are simply disguised versions of the pleasure standard in the first place.

For example, suppose you maintain that the right act is the one that is preferred by God. Well, said Bentham, unless we know God's preferences—that is, unless we know what, exactly, pleases God—what you

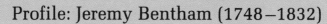

Profile: Jeremy Bentham (1748–1832)

You will find it easy to identify with Jeremy Bentham—if, that is, you studied Latin when you were four, started college when you were twelve, graduated by age fifteen, and finished law school and were admitted to the bar all while you were still a teenager.

Yes, Bentham was a sharp youth. When he was fifteen, he went to hear Sir William Blackstone, the famous English jurist. Bentham said that he instantly spotted errors in Blackstone's reasoning, especially on natural rights. Bentham came to believe that the whole notion of natural rights, including that found in the American Declaration of Independence, was just "nonsense on stilts." In 1776, he published his first book, *Fragment on Government*, a critique of Blackstone.

For David Hume and Hume's *Treatise on Human Nature*, however, Bentham had more respect, and he claimed that the work made the scales fall from his eyes about ethics. Bentham's own ethical philosophy reflects the great influence of Hume.

Though qualified to do so, Bentham never actually practiced law. He was much more interested in legal and social reform and wrote daily commentaries on English law and society. He advocated a simplified and codified legal system, and worked for prison and education reform and extension of voting rights. Bentham also published numerous pamphlets on such abuses as jury packing and extortionate legal fees, and his followers, the "Benthamites," were an effective political force that endured after his death.

Bentham was in the habit of not finishing books that he started to write, and the only major philosophical treatise that he published himself is the *Introduction to the Principles of Morals and Legislation* (1789). The title states exactly Bentham's main concern in life: applying sound principles of morality to the law.

If you want to know what Bentham looked like, don't stop with a picture. Bentham's embalmed body, complete with a wax head, and dressed just as he liked to, is there for you to see at the University College, London.

maintain is pretty meaningless, isn't it? And the only way "to know what is His pleasure," he said, is by "observing what is our own pleasure and pronouncing it to be His."

Or consider the theory that a moral obligation to obey the law stems from a "social contract" among members of society (see Part 4). That theory, said Bentham, is unnecessarily complicated. For when we have a moral obligation to obey the law, he said, that obligation is more simply explained by the fact that in that instance obedience to the law would result in more pleasure for more people than disobedience would.

Now Bentham believed that the pain and pleasure an act produces can be evaluated solely with reference to *quantitative* criteria. Which of

Hedonism

Hedonism is the pursuit of pleasure. Philosophers distinguish between the descriptive doctrine known as **psychological hedonism,** according to which the ultimate object of a person's desire is always pleasure, from the ethical doctrine known as **ethical hedonism,** according to which a person ought to seek pleasure over other things. You should remember these doctrines.

The descriptive doctrine may be plausible at first glance, but on closer inspection it appears somewhat doubtful. For we do seem to seek things beside pleasure—for example, food, good health, relaxation, rest, rightness in our actions, success, friends, and many other things, too. As the British moralist and clergyman Bishop **Joseph Butler** (1692–1752) observed, we couldn't seek pleasure at all unless we had desires for something other than pleasure, since pleasure consists in satisfying these desires. And then too, "the pleasure of virtue," as W. E. H. Lecky wrote, "is one which can only be obtained on the express condition of its not being the object sought." In other words, if your motive in acting virtuously is to obtain the pleasure that accompanies virtuous acts, then you aren't being virtuous and won't get that pleasure.

As for ethical hedonism, there are two kinds: *egoistic* ethical hedonism, according to which one ought to seek his or her own pleasure over other things, and *universalistic* ethical hedonism, otherwise known as **utilitarianism,** according to which one ought to seek the greatest pleasure for the greatest number of people, over other things.

One difficulty utilitarians face is in explaining why pleasure for *others* is something oneself should seek. One common answer is that only by seeking others' pleasure can I experience a full allotment of pleasure for myself. But this answer seems to assume that one's primary ethical duty is to oneself, after all.

MY PHILOSOPHY PROFESSOR TOLD US TODAY THAT WE SHOULD SEEK PLEASURE AND FORGET ABOUT EVERYTHING ELSE. I'M GOING FOR IT.

FINE. THEN I GUESS YOU WON'T WANT ANY SUPPER TONIGHT.

The cartoon implies that we cannot seek pleasure *by itself,* for such seeking has no direction to it. What we seek is food, shelter, companionship, sex, and so forth—we do not, strictly speaking, seek pleasure *per se.* And if you tried to seek pleasure, you would not know how to go about finding it. Your seeking must always be for something that is not *itself* pleasure, such as food.

two or more courses of action you should take should be determined by considering the probable consequences of each possible act with respect to the certainty, intensity, duration, immediacy, and extent (the number of persons affected) of the pleasure or pain it produces, and with respect to the other kinds of sensations it is likely to have as a result over the long run. This "calculus" of pleasure, as it is often called, represents a distinctive feature of Bentham's ethics. Bentham believed that by using these criteria one could and should calculate which of alternative courses of action would produce the greatest amount of pleasure and which, therefore, ought morally to be taken.

Through all of this you should be asking: But why ought I seek the *general* happiness and not give higher priority to my own? Bentham's answer was that my own happiness *coincides* with the general happiness: what brings pleasure to me and what brings pleasure to others fortunately go together.

You may wish to consider whether this answer is fully satisfactory.

Mill

John Stuart Mill, who claimed to have discovered in Bentham's ethical theory what he needed to give purpose to his own life, was also concerned with providing a philosophical justification for the utilitarian doctrine that it is the *general* happiness that one should aim to promote. The justification, according to Mill, lies in the fact that a *moral* principle by its very nature singles out no one for preferential treatment. Thus, Mill wrote, "as between his own happiness and that of others," the utilitarian is required "to be as strictly impartial as a disinterested and benevolent spectator." Compare Mill's justification with that of Bentham, just given. Mill's justification is sounder, isn't it?

Probably the most important difference between Mill and Bentham is that Mill believed that some pleasures are *inherently better* than others and are to be preferred even over a greater amount of pleasure of an inferior grade.

That some pleasures are better than others can be seen, Mill argued, in the fact that few people would be willing to trade places with an animal or even with a more ignorant person, even if the exchange guaranteed their having the fullest measure of an animal's or ignoramus's pleasure. Here is what he meant. Would *you* trade places with a pig or a lunkhead? Would you do it even if you knew that as a pig or lunkhead, you would have more pig or lunkhead pleasures than you now have pleasure as an intelligent human being?

Thus, for Mill, in determining the pleasure for which we should strive, we must consider the *quality* of the pleasure as well as the quantity. Choose the pleasure of the highest quality.

Now this is all very well, but what settles which of two pleasures is of higher quality?

Mill's answer is quite simple: Of two pleasures, if there is one to which most who have experienced both give a decided preference, that is the more desirable pleasure.

Notice what this answer seems to entail. It seems to entail that the pleasures preferred by the *intellectual* will be found to be of superior quality, for nonintellectuals "only know their own side of the question. The other party to the comparison knows both sides."

According to Mill, then, it is not simply the quantity of pleasure an act produces that determines its moral worth, for the quality of the pleasure produced must also be taken into account. Mill is thus said to have recognized implicitly (though not in so many words) a factor other than pleasure by which the moral worth of actions should be compared: the factor of quality. In other words, he is said to have proposed, in effect, a standard of moral worth other than pleasure, a standard of "quality" by

The Paradox of Hedonism.

means of which pleasure itself is to be evaluated. So he sometimes is said not to be a "pure" utilitarian, if a utilitarian is one who believes that the pleasure an act produces is the only standard of good.

It is not unusual, therefore, to find philosophers who think of Bentham's philosophy as more consistently utilitarian than Mill's, though everyone refers to both Mill and Bentham as "the" Utilitarians.

Selection 8.2 is from Bentham's influential *An Introduction to the Principles of Morals and Legislation* (1789).

▶ S E L E C T I O N 8.2

From Jeremy Bentham, AN INTRODUCTION TO THE PRINCIPLES OF MORALS AND LEGISLATION

Chapter I

Of the Principle of Utility

I. Nature has placed mankind under the governance of two sovereign masters, *pain* and *pleasure*. It is for them alone to point out what we ought to do, as well as to determine what we shall do. On the one hand the standard of right and wrong, on the other the chain of causes and effects, are fastened to their throne. They govern us in all we do, in all we say, in all we think: every effort we can make to throw off our subjection, will serve but to demonstrate and confirm it. In words a man may pretend to abjure their empire: but in reality he will remain a subject to it all the while. The *principle of utility* recognizes this subjection, and assumes it for the foundation of that system, the object of which is to rear the fabric of felicity by the hands of reason and of law. Systems which attempt to question it, deal in sounds instead of sense, in caprice instead of reason, in darkness instead of light.

But enough of metaphor and declamation: it is not by such means that moral science is to be improved.

II. The principle of utility is the foundation of the present work: it will be proper therefore at the outset to give an explicit and determinate account of what is meant by it. By the principle of utility is meant that principle which approves or disapproves of every action whatsoever, according to the tendency which it appears to have to augment or diminish the happiness of the party whose interest is in question: or, what is the same thing in other words, to promote or to oppose that happiness. I say of every action whatsoever; and therefore not only of every action of a private individual, but of every measure of government.

III. By utility is meant that property in any object, whereby it tends to produce benefit, advantage, pleasure, good, or happiness, (all this in the present case comes to the same thing) or (what comes again to the same thing) to prevent the happening of mischief, pain, evil, or unhappiness to the party whose interest is considered: if that party be the community in general, then the happiness of the community: if a particular individual, then the happiness of that individual.

IV. The interest of the community is one of the most general expressions that can occur in the phraseology of morals: no wonder that the meaning of it is often lost. When it has a meaning, it is this. The community is a fictitious *body*, composed of individual persons who are considered as constituting as it were its *members*. The interest of the community then is, what?—the sum of the interests of the several members who compose it.

V. It is in vain to talk of the interest of the community, without understanding what is the interest of the individual. A thing is said to promote the interest, or to be for the interest, of an individual, when it tends to add to the sum total of his pleasures: or, what comes to the same thing, to diminish the sum total of his pains.

VI. An action then may be said to be conformable to the principle of utility, or, for shortness sake, to utility, (meaning with respect to the community at large) when the tendency it has to augment the happiness of the community is greater than any it has to diminish it. . . .

X. Of an action that is conformable to the principle of utility one may always say either that it is one that ought to be done, or at least that it is not one that ought not to be done. One may say also, that it is right it should be done; at least that it is not wrong it should be done: that it is a right action; at least that it is not a wrong action. When thus interpreted, the words *ought*, and *right* and *wrong*, and others of the stamp, have a meaning: when otherwise, they have none.

XI. Has the rectitude of this principle been ever formally contested? It should seem that it had, by those who have not known what they have been meaning. Is it susceptible of any direct proof? it should seem not: for that which is used to prove every thing else, cannot itself be proved: a chain of proofs must have their commencement somewhere. To give such proof is as impossible as it is needless.

XII. Not that there is or ever has been that human creature breathing, however stupid or perverse, who has not on many, perhaps on most occasions of his life, deferred to it. By the natural constitution of the human frame, on most occasions of their lives men in general embrace this principle, without thinking of it: if not for the ordering of their own actions, yet for the trying of their own actions, as well as those of other men. There have been, at the same time, not many, perhaps, even of the most intelligent, who have been disposed to embrace it purely and without reserve. There are even few who have not taken some occasion or other to quarrel with it, either on account of their not understanding always how to apply it, or on account of some prejudice or other which they were afraid to examine into, or could not bear to part with. For such is the stuff that man is made of: in principle and in practice, in a right track and in a wrong one, the rarest of all human qualities is consistency.

XIII. When a man attempts to combat the principle of utility, it is with reasons drawn, without his being aware of it, from that very principle itself. His arguments, if they prove any thing, prove not that the principle is *wrong*, but that according to the applications he supposes to be made of it, it *is misapplied*. Is it possible for a man to move the earth? Yes; but he must first find out another earth to stand upon.

Early Analytic Ethics

According to Bentham, then, the rightness of an action is to be equated with the amount of pleasure it produces. Now consider for a moment what this means. Is it true that the rightness of an action is to be equated with the amount of pleasure it produces? If so, it logically follows that judgments of moral value—judgments that an act is right or ought to be taken or is proper or good—are really judgments of *fact*, judgments about the amount of pleasure the act has as a consequence.

Theories according to which moral judgments are really judgments of fact about the natural world are called *naturalistic* theories, as we've mentioned twice already. Naturalistic theories, you should remember, do not postulate a supernatural or "transcendental" source of value. They're not like Plato's theory, or Augustine's.

Now **G. E. Moore** (1873–1958), with whom contemporary ethical theory of the analytic branch of twentieth-century philosophy is often said to begin, took great issue with all naturalistic ethical theories, as we shall see in a moment. Analytic philosophy, as we have already mentioned in Parts 1 and 2, is the tradition of philosophy that came to predominate in the English-speaking world in the twentieth century.

Moore

Moore is regarded as the starting point of contemporary (analytic) ethics, because he opened up new issues for consideration and altered the focus of ethical discussion. Much of twentieth-century analytic ethics, at least until very recently, treated issues that either were raised by Moore or were raised by philosophers responding to him or to other respondents. Though analytic ethical philosophers discussed many questions that were not directly (or indirectly) considered by Moore, even these questions were raised along tributaries that can be traced back to the main waterway opened by Moore. Some people regret the influence Moore had on ethics. You will have to draw your own conclusions.

Moore believed that the task of the ethical philosopher is to conduct a "general inquiry into what is good." This seems reasonably straightforward and down to earth, surely. And useful. If you know what good or goodness *is* and if you know what things *are* good, then you also know what proper conduct is, right? For the morally right act is the one that produces the greatest amount of good, not so? This, at any rate, is what Moore maintained.

Now good, or goodness, which is the same thing, is a *noncomplex* and *nonnatural* property of good things, Moore argued. Goodness is noncomplex in that it cannot be broken down or "analyzed" into simpler constituents. It isn't at all like the property of being alive, for example. A thing's being alive consists in many simpler things, like having a beating heart and a functioning brain (at least for humans and other animals). But a thing's being *good* is rather more like a person's being in pain, at least with respect to the question of complexity. Pain is pain, and that's that. Pain cannot be broken down into simpler constituent parts (though how we come to have pain can be *explained*, but that is quite a different matter). Good, too, is simple, according to Moore: it is a property that cannot be further analyzed or broken down into simpler constituent parts. Thus good is also *indefinable*, he said; at least you cannot come up with a definition of good that states its constituent parts (because there aren't any). Good is good, and that's that.

Good is also a nonnatural property, Moore stated. This is what he meant. Suppose that you pronounce that something is good. Is what you are saying *equivalent* to saying that it is a certain size or shape or color or is pleasant or worth a lot of money? Of course not. Size, shape, color, pleasantness, and monetary value are all natural properties: they are a part of nature, construed broadly. They can be perceived. But good is not equivalent to these or any other natural properties, or so said Moore. Take something you regard as good, like an act of generosity, for instance. Now list all the natural properties (that is, all the properties that can be apprehended by sense) of this act. Do you find goodness on the list? Not at all. What you find are such items as the duration, location, causes, and consequences of the generous act. The *goodness* of the act is not identical

WHAT'S SO GREAT ABOUT AN EDUCATION ANYWAY?

DID YOU EVER MEET A PERSON WHO HAD ONE WHO'D TRADE PLACES WITH YOU?

OPSTEDAL

This idea comes straight from J. S. Mill, who observed that "no instructed person" would consent to become an ignoramus even if he were persuaded that as an ignoramus he would be happier than he presently is. Plato had a similar thing in mind when he said that a person who had found knowledge would rather be the slave of the poorest master than be ignorant.

When in Rome . . .

Relativism is a popular idea about ethics these days, and many people describe themselves as "relativists."

Now, there are various kinds of relativist doctrines. One very popular doctrine is **cultural relativism,** according to which the moral standards people subscribe to differ from culture to culture, and from society to society.

Cultural relativism may well be true, though that it is true is not as obvious as it might seem at first glance. For example, suppose one culture approves of abortion and another doesn't. Do they have different moral standards? Perhaps. But perhaps not. They both might accept the standard that it is wrong to kill a *living person* but just differ about whether a fetus counts as a living person. Different practices, in short, do not necessarily entail different standards.

Cultural relativism, however, is not really an ethical doctrine. It is a *descriptive* doctrine about differences in cultural beliefs and attitudes. A popular relativist *prescriptive* doctrine is **ethical relativism,** according to which what *is* right (as distinguished from what is *believed* to be right) depends on the culture. Thus, according to many who accept this doctrine, what you should do, ethically, is to abide by the moral standards of your culture or society: *When in Rome, do as the Romans do.*

Now there is no denying that this idea—that what morally you should do is to abide by the moral standards of your culture or society—is very popular, and we'd not be surprised in the least to learn that you accept it.

Be advised, then, that there is alleged to be a logical difficulty in the position of a relativist who says that you ought to abide by the standards of your culture. The difficulty is that the prescription, "Abide by the standards of your culture!" seems itself not to be a relativistic pronouncement at all. On the contrary, it seems very absolute and universalistic, because it is presumably supposed to apply to anyone, regardless of his or her culture.

Likewise (it is said), if you believe that it is immoral for one to impose one's own morality on people from another culture who have a different set of moral standards, then you are, in effect, laying down a universal, absolute, and nonrelative moral principle that one shouldn't impose one's standards on others.

Anyway, Moore was not an ethical relativist. When Moore said that something is good, he meant that it was good, period, and anyone who thought otherwise, regardless of culture, was just simply mistaken.

---

with any of these items. It is something quite different from the act's natural properties.

That goodness does not equate with any natural property is easily seen, Moore argued, in a passage that became one of the most famous in all of twentieth-century ethics. Think of any natural property, like, say, pleasantness. Now, it is certainly reasonable to ask if pleasantness is good. But if pleasantness were *equivalent* to good, then asking "Is pleasantness good?" would be the same as asking "Is good good?", and that is *not* a reasonable question. Because it is legitimate and intelligible to ask of any natural property, whether that property is good, it follows that good is not equivalent to any natural property.

Ethics and Metaethics

Being concerned with what is good or right or just is called **first-order thinking.** But you can also be concerned with thought and talk about what's good and right and just. That's **second-order thinking.**

Metaethics is second-order thinking. The metaethicist doesn't ask: What is good? Instead, he or she asks such questions as: What does it mean to call something good? How are judgments about the goodness of things and the rightness of acts related? How are moral judgments verified or validated? What is a value-judgment?

First-order moral thoughts result directly in normative claims, that is, in value judgments, such as "Generosity is good." Metaethical inquiries, by contrast, do not directly yield value judgments. Instead, they yield propositions such as this: "To say that 'generosity is good' is to attribute to generosity a nonnatural property."

Much of contemporary ethics in the analytic tradition has been metaethics.

You can see that Moore certainly did not agree with the utilitarians, who equated the goodness of an act with the pleasure it produced as a consequence.

Now Moore wanted especially to know which things that are good can we really hope to obtain. His answer? Personal affection and aesthetic enjoyments. Moore wrote: "Personal affection and aesthetic enjoyments include by far the greatest good with which we are acquainted." Note how different this answer is from any that would have been proposed by the other philosophers we have discussed.

But the remarkable thing is that it was not Moore's opinion about what things are good that interested other philosophers. Rather it was Moore's **metaethical** opinions that were most discussed. We'd better explain. *Is* goodness a simple, nonnatural, and indefinable property, as Moore argued? Is it *true*, as Moore asserted, that what makes an act right is that it produces the maximum amount of good? Notice that you can set forth an answer to each of these questions without commiting yourself one way or the other about what *actually is* right and wrong, good and bad, or ought and ought not be done. Answers to these questions are thus value neutral. The questions call not for value judgments as answers, but for judgments about the relationships between value judgments and between value judgments and factual judgments.

The philosophical investigation, of a value-neutral sort, into the logical relationships of moral value judgments, or into the sources, criteria, meaning, verification, or validation of such judgments (or of theories in which such judgments are proposed) is known as **metaethics.** And it was Moore's metaethical views and not his ethical claims about what actually is good that provoked the most discussion in the professional philosophical literature.

Further, much contemporary (analytic) ethical philosophy, which has grown out of the issues raised by Moore and by those who in turn responded to Moore, has been metaethical. Many people outside the field find this state of affairs just awful. Philosophers should propose theories about what people should do and about what things are good, they believe. But contemporary analytic ethical philosophers have often not attempted to do this, and their opinions on these matters, insofar as they have been given, are not often the subject of much discussion or debate in the professional literature or at professional meetings (though this has been changing during the last fifteen or so years).

Ross

Thus, for example, in an influential book, *The Right and the Good* (1930), **W. D. Ross** (1877–1970) defined his purpose as "to examine the nature, relations, and implications of three conceptions which appear to be fundamental in ethics—those of 'right,' 'good' in general, and 'morally good'." Ross's purpose, therefore, was to conduct a metaethical inquiry, and his work was devoted largely to criticism of certain metaethical ideas set forth by G. E. Moore. Let's consider Ross briefly to get the sense of what he, and metaethics generally, was about.

Moore, as we noted, believed that that which alone makes right actions right is that they produce more good than alternative actions. This seems reasonable enough, doesn't it? If a course of action is right, it must be because it is more productive of good than alternative courses of action. But Ross disagreed. Certainly, he wrote, it is right and morally obligatory and our duty (these expressions all mean the same, for Ross) to bring into existence as many good things as possible. But the production of maximum good is not the only thing that makes an act right: we have other duties than to bring about good results.

For example, it is your duty to keep promises, Ross said. What makes it right for you to do what you have promised to do is not that your doing it will produce more good, as Moore thought, but simply the fact that you promised to do it.

In short, according to Ross there exist **prima facie duties**—things it is our duty to do unless that duty is overridden by some other duty. Our *prima facie* duties include such actions as keeping promises, relieving distress, showing gratitude, improving ourselves, and being truthful. What makes it right to do these things is not that doing so produces the maximum good (though it may have this as a side benefit), but simply that it is right to do them.

According to Ross, our *prima facie* duties are not *absolute* duties—for example, though it is our duty to keep promises, we are justified in breaking a promise to save someone's life—but it *is* at any rate our duty to do them unless other moral considerations take precedence.

And further, according to Ross, that it is right to keep promises, return services rendered, and so forth, is *self-evident*, "just as a mathe-

Losing Sight of the Big Issues?

Much ethical inquiry in twentieth-century analytic philosophy has been *metaethical* inquiry. This is unfortunate, in the opinion of some people.

Many intellectuals and others expect philosophers to make pronouncements on the "big" issues, such as: What should we strive for? How should we live our lives? What is the fundamental good? What's wrong with the world, anyway? and so on. Some of these individuals view the focus of analytic philosophers on questions of metaethics with disappointment and disdain and believe that metaethics contrasts most unfavorably with existentialism, which seems clearly interested in important issues.

Certainly this disappointment in some cases is a product of noncomprehension, a failure to understand the importance of second-order inquiry to first-order inquiry, of metaethics to ethics. Take Moore's seemingly academic question, whether goodness is a simple, nonnatural, and indefinable property. The question may well seem trivial and uninteresting, but if Moore's answer is correct, then all who equate goodness with a natural property, as many have done for over twenty centuries, are mistaken in their values.

So metaethics is not completely trivial. In fact, it can be pretty important stuff.

matical axiom or the validity of a form of inference, is self-evident." "The moral order expressed in these propositions," Ross asserted, "is just as much part of the fundamental nature of the universe . . . as is the spatial or numerical structure expressed in the axioms of geometry or arithmetic."

Now Ross recognized not only *prima facie* duties but also *intrinsic goods*, specifically virtue, knowledge, and (with certain limitations) pleasure. We do indeed have a *prima facie* duty to produce as much of these good things as possible, Ross maintained.

But what we wish here to emphasize is that what other philosophers mainly discussed was *not* Ross's thoughts about what things actually are good or about what our duties actually are, but his *metaethical* theories. What was discussed was not any of the duties or ethical norms or standards that he advocated but rather such ideas as that *right is not reducible to good*, that *some true moral propositions are self-evident*, and that *some duties are "prima facie."*

Here, then, are two brief selections, one each from Moore and Ross.

▶ S E L E C T I O N 8.3

From G. E. Moore, PRINCIPIA ETHICA

6. What, then, is good? How is good to be defined? . . . my answer . . . may seem a very disappointing one. If I am asked "What is good?" my answer is that good is good, and that is the end of the matter. Or if I am asked "How is good to be defined?" my answer is that it cannot

be defined, and that is all I have to say about it. But disappointing as these answers may appear, they are of the very last importance. To readers who are familiar with philosophic terminology, I can express their importance by saying that they amount to this: That propositions about the good are all of them synthetic and never analytic; and that is plainly no trivial matter. And the same thing may be expressed more popularly, by saying that, if I am right, then nobody can foist upon us such an axiom as that "Pleasure is the only good" or that "The good is the desired" on the pretence that is "the very meaning of the word."

7. Let us, then, consider this position. My point is that "good" is a simple notion, just as "yellow" is a simple notion; that, just as you cannot, by any manner of means, explain to any one who does not already know it, what yellow is, so you cannot explain what good is. Definitions of the kind that I was asking for, definitions which describe the real nature of the object or notion denoted by a word, and which do not merely tell us what the word is used to mean, are only possible when the object or notion in question is something complex. You can give a definition of a horse, because a horse has many different properties and qualities, all of which you can enumerate. But when you have enumerated them all, when you have reduced a horse to his simplest terms, then you can no longer define those terms. They are simply something which you think of or perceive, and to any one who cannot think of or perceive them, you can never, by any definition, make their nature known. . . .

10. "Good," then, if we mean by it that quality which we assert to belong to a thing, when we say that the thing is good, is incapable of any definition, in the most important sense of that word. The most important sense of "definition" is that in which a definition states what are the parts which invariably compose a certain whole; and in this sense "good" has no definition because it is simple and has no parts. It is one of those innumerable objects of thought which are themselves incapable of definition, because they are the ultimate terms by reference to which whatever *is* capable of definition must be defined. That there must be an indefinite number of such terms is obvious, on reflection; since we cannot define anything except by analysis, which, when carried as far as it will go, refers us to something, which is simply different from anything else, and which by that ultimate difference explains the peculiarity of the whole which we are defining: for every whole contains some parts which are common to other wholes also. There is, therefore, no intrinsic difficulty in the contention that "good" denotes a simple and indefinable quality. There are many other instances of such qualities.

Consider yellow, for example. We may try to define it, by describing its physical equivalent; we may state what kind of light-vibrations must stimulate the normal eye, in order that we may perceive it. But a moment's reflection is sufficient to shew that those light-vibrations are not themselves what we mean by yellow. *They* are not what we perceive. Indeed we should never have been able to discover their existence, unless we had first been struck by the patent difference of quality between the different colours. The most we can be entitled to say of those vibrations is that they are what corresponds in space to the yellow which we actually perceive.

Yet a mistake of this simple kind has commonly been made about "good." It may be true that all things which are good are also something else, just as it is true that all things which are yellow produce a certain kind of vibration in the light. And it is a fact, that Ethics aims at discovering what are those other properties belonging to all things which are good. But far too many philosophers have thought that when they named those other properties they were actually defining good; that these properties, in fact, were simply not "other," but absolutely and entirely the same with goodness. . . .

13. . . . There are, in fact, only two serious alternatives to be considered, in order to establish the conclusion that "good" does denote a simple and indefinable notion. It might possibly denote a complex, as "horse" does; or it might have no meaning at all. Neither of these possibilities has, however, been clearly conceived and seriously maintained, as such, by those who presume to define good; and both may be dismissed by a simple appeal to facts.

(1) The hypothesis that disagreement about the meaning of good is disagreement with regard to the correct analysis of a given whole, may be most plainly seen to be incorrect by consideration of the fact that whatever definition be offered, it may be always asked, with significance, of the complex so defined, whether it is itself good. . . .

(2) And the same consideration is sufficient to dismiss the hypothesis that "good" has no meaning whatsoever. . . . whoever will attentively consider with himself what is actually before his mind when he asks the question "Is pleasure (or whatever it may be) after all good?" can easily satisfy himself that he is not merely wondering whether pleasure is pleasant. And if he will try this experiment with each suggested definition in succession, he may become expert enough to recognise that in every case he has before his mind a unique object, with regard to the connection of which with any other object, a distinct question may be asked. Every one does in fact understand the question, "Is this good?" When he thinks of it, his state of mind is different from what it would be, were he asked "Is this pleasant, or desired, or approved?" It has a distinct meaning for him.

▶ S E L E C T I O N   8.4

From W. D. Ross, THE RIGHT AND THE GOOD

II What Makes Right Acts Right?

[An] attractive theory has been put forward by Professor Moore: that what makes actions right is that they are productive of more *good* than could have been produced by any other action open to the agent. . . .

When a plain man fulfils a promise because he thinks he ought to do so, it seems clear that he does so with no thought of its total consequences, still less with any opinion that these are likely to be the best possible. He thinks in fact much more of the past than of the future. What makes him think it right to act in a certain way is the fact that he has promised to do so—that and, usually, nothing more. That his act will produce the best possible consequences is not his reason for calling it right. What lends colour to the theory we are examining, then, is not the actions (which form probably a great majority of our actions) in which some such reflection as "I have promised" is the only reason we give ourselves for thinking a certain action right, but the exceptional cases in which the consequences of fulfilling a promise (for instance) would be so disastrous to others that we judge it right not to do so. It must of course be admitted that such cases exist. If I have promised to meet a friend at a particular time for some trivial purpose, I should certainly think myself justified in breaking my engagement if by doing so I could prevent a serious accident or bring relief to the victims of one. And the supporters of the view we are examining hold that my thinking is due to my thinking that I shall bring more good into existence by the one action than by the other. A different account may, however, be given of the matter, an account which will, I believe, show itself to be the true one. It may be said that besides the duty of fulfilling promises I have and recognize a duty of relieving distress, and that when I think it right to do the latter at the cost of not doing the former, it is not because I think I shall produce more good thereby but because I think it the duty which is in the circumstances more of a duty. This account surely corresponds much more closely with what we really think in such a situation. If, so far as I can see, I could bring equal amounts of good into being by fulfilling my promise and by helping some one to whom I had made no promise, I should not hesitate to regard the former as my duty. Yet on the view that what is right is right because it is productive of the most good I should not so regard it.

In fact the theory of "ideal utilitarianism," if I may for brevity refer so to the theory of Professor Moore, seems to simplify unduly our relations to our fellows. It says, in effect, that the only morally significant relation in which my neighbours stand to me is that of being possible beneficiaries by my action. They do stand in this relation to me, and this relation is morally significant. But they may also stand to me in the relation of promisee to promiser, of creditor to debtor, of wife to husband, of child to parent, of friend to friend, of fellow countryman to fellow countryman, and the like; and each of these relations is the foundation of a *prima facie* duty, which is more or less incumbent on me according to the circumstances of the case. When I am in a situation, as perhaps I always am, in which more than one of these *prima facie* duties is incumbent on me, what I have to do is to study the situation as fully as I can until I form the considered opinion (it is never more) that in the circumstances one of them is more incumbent than any other; then I am bound to think that to do this *prima facie* duty is my duty *sans phrase* in the situation.

I suggest "*prima facie* duty" or "conditional duty" as a brief way of referring to the characteristic (quite distinct from that of being a duty proper) which an act has, in virtue of being of a certain kind (e.g. the keeping of a promise), of being an act which would be a duty proper if it were not at the same time of another kind which is morally significant. Whether an act is a duty proper or actual duty depends on *all* the morally significant kinds it is an instance of. . . .

There is nothing arbitrary about these *prima facie* duties. Each rests on a definite circumstance which cannot seriously be held to be without moral significance. Of *prima facie* duties I suggest, without claiming completeness or finality for it, the following division.[1]

(1) Some duties rest on previous acts of my own. These duties seem to include two kinds, (a) those resting on a promise or what may fairly be called an implicit promise, such as the implicit undertaking not to tell lies which seems to be implied in the act of entering into conversation (at any rate by civilized men), or of writing books that purport to be history and not fiction. These may be called the duties of fidelity. (b) Those resting on a previous wrongful act. These may be called the duties of reparation. (2) Some rest on previous acts of other men, i.e., services done by them to me. These may be loosely described as the duties of gratitude. (3) Some rest on the fact or possibility of a distribution of pleasure or happiness (or of the means thereto) which is not in accordance with the merit of the persons concerned; in such cases there arises a duty to upset or prevent such a distribution. These are the duties of justice. (4) Some rest on the mere fact that there are other beings in the world whose condition we can make better in respect of virtue, or of intelligence, or of pleasure. These are the duties of beneficence. (5) Some rest on the fact that we can improve our own condition in respect of virtue or of intelligence. These are the duties of self-improvement. (6) I think that we should distinguish from (4) the duties that may be summed up under the title of "not injuring others." No doubt to injure others is incidentally to fail to do them

---

[1] I should make it plain at this stage that I am assuming the correctness of some of our main convictions as to *prima facie* duties, or, more strictly, am claiming that we know them to be true. To me it seems as self-evident as anything could be, that to make a promise, for instance, is to create a moral claim on us in someone else. Many readers will perhaps say that they do *not* know this to be true. If so, I certainly cannot prove it to them; I can only ask them to reflect again, in the hope that they will ultimately agree that they also know it to be true. The main moral convictions of the plain man seem to me to be, not opinions which it is for philosophy to prove or disprove, but knowledge from the start; and in my own case I seem to find little difficulty in distinguishing these essential convictions from other moral convictions which I also have, which are merely fallible opinions based on an imperfect study of the working for good or evil of certain institutions or types of action.

good; but it seems to me clear that non-maleficence is apprehended as a duty distinct from that of beneficence, and as a duty of a more stringent character. It will be noticed that this alone among the types of duty has been stated in a negative way. . . .

The essential defect of the "ideal utilitarian" theory is that it ignores, or at least does not do full justice to, the highly personal character of duty. If the only duty is to produce the maximum of good, the question who is to have the good—whether it is myself, or my benefactor, or a person to whom I have made a promise to confer that good on him, or a mere fellow man to whom I stand in no such special relation—should make no difference to my having a duty to produce that good. But we are all in fact sure that it makes a vast difference.

If the objection be made, that this catalogue of the main types of duty is an unsystematic one resting on no logical principle, it may be replied, first, that it makes no claim to being ultimate. It is a *prima facie* classification of the duties which reflection on our moral convictions seems actually to reveal. And if these convictions are, as I would claim that they are, of the nature of knowledge, and if I have not misstated them, the list will be a list of authentic conditional duties, correct as far as it goes though not necessarily complete. The list of *goods* put forward by the rival theory is reached by exactly the same method—the only sound one in the circumstances—viz. that of direct reflection on what we really think. Loyalty to the facts is worth more than a symmetrical architectonic or a hastily reached simplicity. If further reflection discovers a perfect logical basis for this or for a better classification, so much better.

It may, again, be objected that our theory that there are these various and often conflicting types of *prima facie* duty leaves us with no principle upon which to discern what is our actual duty in particular circumstances. But this objection is not one which the rival theory is in a position to bring forward. For when we have to choose between the production of two heterogeneous goods, say knowledge and pleasure, the "ideal utilitarian" theory can only fall back on an opinion, for which no logical basis can be offered, that one of the goods is the greater; and this is no better than a similar opinion that one of two duties is more urgent.

Emotivism and Existentialism

The utilitarians, recall, defined the rightness of an action in terms of the happiness it produces as a consequence. Accordingly, moral judgments, for utilitarians, in effect are a type of *factual judgment*, a judgment about how much happiness some action produces.

Moore and Ross, though denying that the rightness of an act or the goodness of an end can be defined in terms of happiness or any other natural property or thing, and though disagreeing between themselves about the relationship between rightness and goodness, also (like the utilitarians) believed that moral judgments are a type of *factual judgment*. To say that an end is good or that an act is right, for Moore and Ross both, is to state a fact. It is to attribute a property to the thing in question, a "nonnatural" property. Whether a certain type of act possesses the property of rightness and whether a certain end possesses the property of goodness are questions of fact, even though the fact is nonempirical. That it is right to keep a promise, Moore and Ross would agree, is a *fact*: it is *true* that you should keep your promises, and *false* that you should break them.

A radically different view of moral judgments was set forth by the emotivists, a group of analytic philosophers who had read Moore and Ross and disagreed with them both.

The Emotivists

The **emotivists** maintained that *moral judgments have no factual meaning whatsoever*. Such judgments, according to the emotivists, *are not even genuine propositions*. In their view, the judgment, "It is right to keep your promises," is neither true nor false: the utterance is not really a proposition at all.

Thus, according to the emotivists, there is no question about what we are saying, if, for example, we state, "Abortion is wrong." For because we are not really asserting a genuine proposition, we are not really *saying* anything at all. The question therefore is only what we are *doing* when we open our mouths and voice an expression like, "Abortion is wrong."

And what we are doing, they said, is *expressing our distaste* for abortion and also, sometimes, *encouraging others to feel the same way*. Thus, **C. L. Stevenson,** an influential emotivist, maintained that an ethical judgment like, "Abortion is wrong," is a linguistic act by which the speaker expresses his or her attitude toward abortion and seeks to influence the attitude, and in turn the conduct, of the listener.

Can it really be that the rich and varied discourse in which human beings discuss ethical issues amounts to nothing more than expressions of attitude and emotion? Can it really be that the person who maintains, for example, that it is wrong for society not to care for the disadvantaged is merely *expressing distaste* for something? Selection 8.5, by **A. J. Ayer** (1910–1989), is an effective statement of this position.

▶ S E L E C T I O N 8.5

From A. J. Ayer, LANGUAGE, TRUTH AND LOGIC

The fundamental ethical concepts are unanalysable, inasmuch as there is no criterion by which one can test the validity of the judgements in which they occur. . . . We say that the reason why they are unanalysable is that they are mere pseudo-concepts. The presence of an ethical symbol in a proposition adds nothing to its factual content. Thus if I say to someone, "You acted wrongly in stealing that money," I am not stating anything more than if I had simply said, "You stole that money." In adding that this action is wrong I am not making any further statement about it. I am simply evincing my moral disapproval of it. It is as if I had said, "You stole that money," in a peculiar tone of horror, or written it with the addition of some special exclamation marks. The tone, or the exclamation marks, adds nothing to the literal meaning of the sentence. It merely serves to show that the expression of it is attended by certain feelings in the speaker.

If now I generalize my previous statement and say, "Stealing money is wrong," I produce a sentence which has no factual meaning—that is, expresses no proposition which can be either true or false. It is as if I had written "Stealing money!!"—where the shape and thickness of the exclamation marks show, by a suitable convention, that a special sort of moral disapproval is the feeling which is being expressed. It is clear that there is nothing said here which can be true or false. Another man may disagree with me about the wrongness of stealing, in the sense that he may not have the same feelings about stealing as I have, and he may quarrel with me on account of my moral sentiments. But he cannot, strictly speaking, contradict me. For in saying that a certain type of action is right or wrong, I am not making any factual statement, not even a statement about my own state of mind. I am merely expressing certain moral sentiments. And the man who is ostensibly contradicting me is merely expressing his moral sentiments. So that there is plainly no sense in asking which of us is in the right. For neither of us is asserting a genuine proposition.

What we have just been saying about the symbol "wrong" applies to all normative ethical symbols. Sometimes they occur in sentences which record ordinary empirical facts besides expressing ethical feeling about those facts: sometimes they occur in sentences which simply express ethical feeling about a certain type of action, or situation, without making any statement of fact. But in every case in which one would commonly be said to be making an ethical judgement, the function of the relevant ethical word is purely "emotive." It is used to express feeling about certain objects, but not to make any assertion about them.

It is worth mentioning that ethical terms do not serve only to express feeling. They are calculated also to arouse feeling, and so to stimulate action. Indeed some of them are used in such a way as to give the sentences in which they occur the effect of commands. Thus the sentence "It is your duty to tell the truth" may be regarded both as the expression of a certain sort of ethical feeling about truthfulness and as the expression of the command "Tell the truth." The sentence "You ought to tell the truth" also involves the command "Tell the truth," but here the tone of the command is less emphatic. In the sentence "It is good to tell the truth" the command has become little more than a suggestion. And thus the "meaning" of the word "good," in its ethical usage, is differentiated from that of the word "duty" or the word "ought." In fact we may define the meaning of the various ethical words in terms both of the different feelings they are ordinarily taken to express, and also the different responses which they are calculated to provoke.

We can now see why it is impossible to find a criterion for determining the validity of ethical judgements. It is not because they have an "absolute" validity which is mysteriously independent of ordinary sense-experience, but because they have no objective validity whatsoever. If a sentence makes no statement at all, there is obviously no sense in asking whether what it says is true or false. And we have seen that sentences which simply express moral judgements do not say anything. They are pure expressions of feeling and as such do not come under the category of truth and falsehood. They are unverifiable—because they do not express genuine propositions.

The Existentialists

The emotivist position in essence denies the existence of values, except as mere expressions of likes and dislikes. There is another important group of philosophers who also appear to deny the existence of values and who are therefore at least superficially like the emotivists. These are the **existentialists.**

Existentialism, however, in case you've forgotten what we said in Chapter 1, is an entirely different tradition of philosophy from the analytic tradition of Moore and Ross and Stevenson and Ayer. In a later chapter we provide a close-up of existentialism. Here you must keep in mind that the existentialists, unlike the emotivists, were not reacting to Moore and Ross. There is little evidence that they were even interested in Moore or Ross, or, for that matter, in the emotivists. They were on their own agenda, even though their philosophy superficially resembled that of the emotivists in seeming to deny the existence of values.

Jean-Paul Sartre (1905–1980) perhaps the most famous existentialist, rested his philosophy on the premise that God does not exist: because there is no God, he reasoned, "we do not find before us any values or orders which will justify our conduct." In other words, because there is no God, there is no objective good or evil, right or wrong: as the nineteenth-century Russian novelist Dostoyevsky said, "everything is permissible." And because there is no God, there is no fundamental reason why the world is the way it is and not some other way: the world is therefore irrational and absurd. And because there is no God, we experience ourselves as abandoned and are forlorn. How are we to exist in an absurd world? This is the fundamental human problem for Sartre.

Because values do not exist objectively, we create our own values, Sartre reasoned. We do so, he said, through our choices and decisions, through our actions. But we do so, he said, in *anguish*. Our choices are

Values Without God

In the last chapter, when we discussed Hume, we noticed how easy it would be to think that if neither God nor reason determine moral standards, then there just would not be any moral standards. But this is by no means certain. Naturalistic ethical theories, for instance, need not assume the existence of God, nor need they assume that reason dictates moral standards. Then, too, there are non-naturalistic ethical theories, like those of Plato and Moore, that do not require the existence of God and also do not suppose that reason sets the standard on what is right and wrong.

So we should not blithely assume without argument that God is required for there to be ethical standards. Even if we disregard such reason-based ethical theories as that of Kant, there may be other grounds for denying that without God "everything is permissible."

made in anguish, Sartre thought, for there is nothing objective to guide us, and also because in choosing, one acts as a *lawgiver for all mankind*: to choose a course of action is in effect to say what is right; that is, it is to say what all should do. The awesome responsibility of your choices, in which you in effect act the part of God, is experienced in anguish.

Anguish, thus, for Sartre, comes in the awareness of our freedom to choose in a universe that has no objective values. We may try to *hide* from our responsibility as moral lawgivers, we may try to *escape* anguish, by pretending that we do not impose our values on all people. Or we may try to hide from our responsibility by pretending that we are not free, by pretending that what we choose and do is determined by circumstances or by our heredity. But such pretenses, Sartre said, such pretenses are a self-deception, the mark of *inauthenticity* and *bad faith*. They are a self-deception, he reasoned, because the very attempt to conceal one's freedom presupposes this freedom exists.

You can now see that the resemblance between Sartre's ethics and the metaethics of the emotivists is very superficial indeed. There is an altogether different tone about Sartre's philosophy. It carries a sense of urgency that is entirely lacking in the writings of Ayer and Stevenson. Sartre would never have been content with setting forth some neutral description of the function or meaning of moral expressions. And the emotivists would never have felt comfortable discussing the existential plight of modern humans.

But even more to the point, Sartre's philosophy does not really suppose that there are no values or that "everything is permissible." For Sartre there is something dishonest, something *wrong*, about a way of life in which one seeks to avoid one's responsibility or disguise one's absolute freedom of choice. The notions of inauthenticity and bad faith are clearly pejorative. To act morally, for Sartre, is to act in good faith. Because each person determines his or her own morality, acting in good faith can only mean acting consistently within one's own moral standards.

From an emotivist point of view, therefore, Sartre's moral philosophy is *prescriptive*: it does make value judgments. Therefore, from the emotivist point of view, Sartre's philosophy is merely just one more expression of sentiment.

Selection 8.6 is from Sartre's *Existentialism and Humanism*. (You may wish to turn to Chapter 15 to read more of this essay.) In it Sartre gives a detailed examination of a case in which an important ethical decision must be made by an individual who yet must face the decision absolutely alone: no one can help the person choose and no doctrine can guide his way. In that respect he is like all of us, Sartre implies.

Notice how very different the flavor of this piece is from that of the Moore, Ross, and Ayer selections.

▶ S E L E C T I O N 8.6

From Jean-Paul Sartre, ## *EXISTENTIALISM AND HUMANISM*

Dostoyevsky has written, "If God did not exist, everything would be allowed." This is the point of departure for existentialism. Indeed, everything is allowed if God does not exist, and consequently man is abandoned, because neither in himself nor beyond himself does he find any possibility of clinging on [to something]. . . . Moreover, if God does not exist, we do not find before us any values or orders which will justify our conduct. So, we have neither behind us nor before us, in the luminous realm of values, any justifications or excuses. We are alone, without excuses. It is what I will express by saying that man is condemned to be free. Condemned, because he has not created himself, and nevertheless, in other respects [he is] free, because once [he is] cast into the world, he is responsible for everything that he does. . . .

To give you an example which [will] allow [you] to understand abandonment better, I will cite the case of one of my students who came to see me in the following circumstances. His father was on bad terms with his mother, and moreover, was inclined to be a collaborator. His older brother had been killed in the German offensive of 1940, and this young man, with feelings somewhat primitive but generous, wanted to avenge him. His mother lived alone with him, quite distressed by the semi-betrayal of his father and by the death of her eldest son, and found consolation only in him. This young man had the choice, at that time, between leaving for England and enlisting in the Free French Forces—that is to say, to forsake his mother—or to stay near his mother and to help her [to] live. He fully realized that this woman lived only for him and that his disappearance—and perhaps his death—would cast her into despair. He also realized that, in reality, [and] concretely, each action that he performed with regard to his mother had its surety in the sense that he was helping her to live, whereas each action that he might perform in order to leave and fight was an ambiguous action which could be lost in the sands, to answer no purpose. For example, leaving for England, he might remain indefinitely in a Spanish camp, while passing through Spain; he might arrive in England or in Algiers and be placed in an office to keep records. Consequently, he found himself facing two very different kinds of action: one concrete, immediate, but applying only to one individual; or else an action which applied to a whole [group] infinitely vaster, a national community but which was by that reason ambiguous, and which could be interrupted on the way. And, at the same time, he hesitated between two kinds of ethics. On the one hand, an ethic of sympathy, of individual devotion; and on the other hand a wider ethic but whose effectiveness was more questionable. He had to choose between the two. Who could help him to choose? Christian doctrine? No. Christian doctrine says: "be charitable, love your neighbor, devote yourself to others, choose the hardest way, etc. . . ." But which is the hardest way? Whom must we love as our brother, the soldier or the mother? Which has the greatest utility, the one [which is] definite, to help a definite individual to live? Who can decide it *a priori*? No one. No written ethic can tell him. The Kantian ethic says: "never treat others as [a] means, but as [an] end." Very well; if I remain near [with] my mother I will treat her as an end and not as means, but by this same action, I risk treating those who fight around me as a means; and conversely if I go to rejoin those who are fighting I will treat them as an end, and by this action I risk treating my mother as a means.

If these values are vague, and if they are still too broad for the specific and concrete case that we are considering, it remains for us only to rely on our instincts. This is what this young man tried to do; and when I saw him, he said: "basically, what counts is the sentiment; I ought to choose that which actually pushes me in a certain direction. If I feel that I love my mother enough to sacrifice everything else for her—my desire for vengeance, my desire for action, my desire for adventures—I [will] stay near her. If, on the contrary, I feel that my love for my mother is not sufficient, I [will] leave." But how [do we] judge the weight of a feeling? What constituted the worth of his feeling for his mother? Precisely the fact that he stayed for her. I may say, I love this friend enough to sacrifice such a [a certain] sum of money for him; I can say it, only if I have done it. I may say: I love my mother enough to remain with her, if I have remained with her. I can determine the worth of this affection only if, precisely, I have performed an action which confirms and defines it. Now, as I require this affection to justify my action, I find myself caught in a vicious circle.

Further, Gide has said very well, that a feeling which is acting and a feeling which is real are two nearly indiscernable things: to decide that I love my mother by remaining near her, or to act a part which will make me stay for my mother, is nearly the same thing. In other words, the feeling is constituted by the actions that we perform; I cannot then consult it in order to guide myself according to it. What that means is that I can neither seek for in myself the authentic state which will push me to act, nor demand from an ethic the concepts which will allow me to act. At least, you say, he went to see a professor to ask his advice. But, if you seek advice from a priest, for example, you have chosen this priest, you already knew, after all, more or less, what he was going to advise you. In other words, to choose the adviser is still to commit yourself. The proof of it is what you will say, if you are a Christian: consult a priest. But there are priests who are collaborators, priests who wait for the tide to turn, priests who belong to the resistance. Which [should you] choose? And if the young man chooses a priest who is a member of the resistance, or a priest who is a collaborator, he has already decided [on] the kind of advice he will receive. Thus, in coming to see me, he knew the reply that I was going to make to him, and I had only one reply to make: you are free, choose, that is to say, invent. No general ethic can show you what there is to do; there is no sign in the world. The Catholics will reply: "but there are signs." Let's admit it; it is myself in any case who chooses the meaning that they have.

Contemporary Ethics

Again, it must be stressed that Sartre was not an analytic philosopher. His ethical philosophy should not be construed as in any way a response to Moore or Ross or the emotivists, who came from a radically different tradition of philosophy. Ayer would not have regarded Sartre's moral pronouncements as coming under the categories of truth or falsehood, and perhaps as not being philosophical in the first place.

Until recently, most analytic philosophers did not pay much attention to existentialism. They were much more interested in getting clear on the purpose or function of moral judgments than in finding values in a world thought to be absurd. And though emotivism had strong adherents within analytic philosophy, it seemed to many other analytic philosophers that the emotivist analysis of ethical judgments was not essentially correct. To consider briefly one example, according to the contemporary British linguistic philosopher **R. M. Hare**, the function of moral discourse is not to express or influence attitudes. Rather, Hare said, the function of moral discourse is to *guide conduct*.

A moral judgment, according to Hare, is a kind of prescriptive judgment that is "universalizable": when I make a moral judgment such as, "You ought to give Smith back the book you borrowed," I am prescribing a course of conduct and my prescription is general and exceptionless (i.e., I believe that anyone else in the same or relevantly similar situation ought to conduct him or herself similarly).

That emotivism misrepresents, or indeed trivializes, moral discourse is now fairly widely accepted by contemporary philosophers. In Selection 8.7, **Gilbert Harman** discusses whether emotivism can account for moral reasoning.

From Gilbert Harman,
THE NATURE OF MORALITY

3. Advantages of Emotivism

Let me now briefly review what I have been saying. Emotivism is the theory that your moral judgments express your attitudes. In other words, your moral beliefs (if it is proper to speak of "beliefs" in this connection) are not cognitive but are themselves attitudes for or against something. According to emotivism, "I believe that this act is wrong" means roughly "I disapprove of this act." But "This act is wrong," by itself, cannot be equated with any purely naturalistic expression like "this act causes human suffering" unless there is a law of nature that to think that an act causes human suffering is to be against it—to disapprove of it. . . .

5. Moral Reasoning

Now let us consider a second objection, one that asks whether emotivism can account for moral reasoning. There is, evidently, such a thing as moral reasoning; and we sometimes adopt a particular moral opinion—if "opinion" is the right word—in consequence of such reasoning. Furthermore, it strikes us as appropriate to ask for someone's reasons for his moral opinion. If someone says that it is a good thing that the Oregon Taxpayers Union kidnapped Sally Jones, we will ask him why he supposes that it is. It would strike us as odd if he said that he had no reasons—that's just the way he feels about it. That would strike us as odd because his saying that the kidnapping was a good thing suggests or even implies that (he thinks that) there are reasons for supposing that the kidnapping is a good thing.

Reasoning is not relevant in the same way to feelings. You do not reason yourself into liking or disliking something. It is often true that you simply like something, or dislike it, without having a reason. Of course, you may like something in certain respects and not in others. But this is not the same thing as liking it for certain reasons or as the result of argument. . . .

The emotivist holds that moral judgments are expressions of feeling. But expressions of feeling do not depend on reasoning from general principles, nor do they require defense by appeal to principle, whereas moral judgments do depend on reasoning from general principles and do require defense by appeal to principle. Therefore, the emotivist would seem to be mistaken in treating moral judgments as expressions of feeling.

The emotivist might reply that "there are feelings and feelings." Some feelings, he might agree, are simple reactions, such as likes and dislikes. Other feelings, more properly called attitudes, he might continue, are more complex and involve principles and one's basic values. Moral beliefs cannot be identified with any feelings whatsoever—only with these more complex feelings and attitudes.

But, unless the emotivist says more than this, his view takes on an ad hoc character. For nothing has so far been said as to why certain feelings should differ from others in this way. It is obscure why a feeling or attitude is the sort of thing to which reasoning from principles could be relevant. But before we consider what more an emotivist might say about this, let us consider a third objection that reinforces the second.

You sometimes make a moral judgment that you later decide was mistaken. If your moral beliefs were simply feelings, it is not clear how they could be mistaken in this way. At one time you felt one way; now you feel another way. In what sense can you suppose that your first feeling was mistaken? Years ago you used to like sugar in your coffee; now you do not. But you would not say that you were mistaken to have once liked sugar. On the other hand, if you once thought that incest was wrong and now think that it is right, you do suppose you were mistaken before. How can this change in moral belief be simply a change in your feelings?

Harman's discussion, you should note, is metaethical. (Metaethics, remember, is the study of the meaning, justification, and logical interrelationships of moral judgments, and their relationship to factual judgments.) Now even though the Harman article is recent, discussions of metaethical issues no longer dominate in the analytic philosophical literature as they once did, and today many professors of ethics prefer to focus their courses on specific contemporary moral dilemmas such as abortion, equal rights, pornography, and so on. This trend may or may not be for the best.

We close this chapter with a selection from an essay that will give you an example of this recent literature in ethics. In the essay, **James Rachels** argues that our duty not to let people die of starvation is as strong as our duty not to kill them. In the excerpt here he defends a weaker point, that letting people die of starvation is much closer to killing than we normally assume.

▶ S E L E C T I O N   8.8

From James Rachels,
"KILLING AND STARVING TO DEATH"

Although we do not know exactly how many people die each year of malnutrition or related health problems, the number is very high, in the millions. By giving money to support famine relief efforts, each of us could save at least some of them. By not giving, we let them die.

Some philosophers have argued that letting people die is not as bad as killing them, because in general our "positive duty" to give aid is weaker than our "negative duty" not to do harm. I maintain the opposite: letting die is just as bad as killing. At first this may seem wildly implausible. When reminded that people are dying of starvation while we spend money on trivial things, we may feel a bit guilty, but certainly we do not feel like murderers. Philippa Foot writes:

> Most of us allow people to die of starvation in India and Africa, and there is surely something wrong with us that we do; it would be nonsense, however, to pretend that it is only in law that we make a distinction between allowing people in the underdeveloped countries to die of starvation and sending them poisoned food. There is worked into our moral system a distinction between what we owe people in the form of aid and what we owe them in the way of noninterference.

No doubt this would be correct if it were intended only as a description of what most people believe. Whether this feature of "our moral system" is rationally defensible is, however, another matter. I shall argue that we are wrong to take comfort in the fact that we *only* let these people die, because our duty not to let them die is equally as strong as our duty not to kill them, which, of course, is very strong indeed.

Obviously, this Equivalence Thesis is not morally neutral, as philosophical claims about ethics often are. It is a radical idea that, if true, would mean that some of our "intuitions" (our prereflective beliefs about what is right and wrong in particular cases) are mistaken and must be rejected. Neither is the view I oppose morally neutral. The idea that killing is worse than letting die is a relatively conservative thesis that would allow those same intuitions to be preserved. However, the Equivalence Thesis should not be dismissed merely because it does not conform to all our prereflective intuitions. Rather than being perceptions of the truth, our "intuitions" might sometimes signify nothing more than our prejudices or selfishness or cultural conditioning. Philosophers often admit that, in theory at least, some intuitions might be unreliable—but usually this possibility is not taken seriously, and conformity to prereflective intuition is used uncritically as a test of the acceptability of moral theory. In what follows I shall argue that many of our intuitions concerning killing and letting die *are* mistaken, and should not be trusted.

I

We think that killing is worse than letting die, not because we overestimate how bad it is to kill, but because we underestimate how bad it is to let die. The following chain of reasoning is intended to show that letting people in foreign countries die of starvation is very much worse than we commonly assume.

Suppose there were a starving child in the room where you are now—hollow-eyed, belly bloated, and so on—and you have a sandwich at your elbow that you don't need. Of course you would be horrified; you would stop reading and give her the sandwich or, better, take her to a hospital. And you would not think this an act of supererogation; you would not expect any special praise for it, and you would expect criticism if you did not do it. Imagine what you would think of someone who simply ignored the child and continued reading, allowing her to die of starvation. Let us call the person who would do this Jack Palance, after the very nice man who plays such vile characters in the movies. Jack Palance indifferently watches the starving child die; he cannot be bothered even to hand her the sandwich. There is ample reason for judging him very harshly; without putting too fine a point on it, he shows himself to be a moral monster.

When we allow people in faraway countries to die of starvation, we may think, as Mrs. Foot puts it, that "there is surely something wrong with us." But we most emphatically do not consider ourselves moral monsters. We think this, in spite of the striking similarity between Jack Palance's behavior and our own. He could easily save the child; he does not, and the child dies. We could easily save some of those starving people; we do not, and they die. If we are not monsters, there must be some important difference between him and us. But what is it?

One obvious difference between Jack Palance's position and ours is that the person he lets die is in the same room with him, while the people we let die are mostly far away. Yet the spatial location of the dying people hardly seems a relevant consideration. It is absurd to suppose that being located at a certain map coordinate entitles one to treatment that one would not merit if situated at a different longitude or latitude. Of course, if a dying person's location meant that we *could not* help, that would excuse us. But, since there are efficient famine relief agencies willing to carry our aid to the faraway countries, this excuse is not available. It would be almost as easy for us to send these agencies the price of the sandwich as for Palance to hand the sandwich to the child.

The location of the starving people does make a difference, psychologically, in how we feel. If there were a starving child in the same room with us, we could not avoid realizing, in a vivid and disturbing way, how it is suffering and that it is about to die. Faced with this realization our consciences probably would not allow us to ignore the child. But if the dying are far away, it is easy to think of them only abstractly, or to put them out of our thoughts altogether. This might explain why our conduct would be different if we were in Jack Palance's position, even though, from a moral point of view, the location of the dying is not relevant.

There are other differences between Jack Palance and us, which may seem important, having to do with the sheer numbers of people, both affluent and starving, that surround us. In our fictitious example Jack Palance is one person, confronted by the need of one other person. This makes his position relatively simple. In the real world our position is more complicated, in two ways: first, in that there are millions of people who need feeding, and none of us has the resources to care for all of them; and second, in that for any starving person we *could* help there are millions of other affluent people who could help as easily as we.

On the first point, not much needs to be said. We may feel, in a vague sort of way, that we are not monsters because no one of us could possibly save *all* the starving people—there are just too many of them, and none of us has the resources. This is fair enough, but all that follows is that, individually, none of us is responsible for saving everyone. We may still be responsible for saving someone, or as many as we can. This is so obvious that it hardly bears mentioning, yet it is easy to lose sight of, and philosophers have actually lost sight of it. In his article "Saving Life and Taking Life," Richard Trammell says that one morally important difference between killing and letting die is "dischargeability." By this he means that, while each of us can discharge completely a duty not to kill anyone, no one among us can discharge completely a duty to save everyone who needs it. Again, fair enough; but all that follows is that since we are only bound to save those we can, the class of people we have an obligation to save is much smaller than the class of people we have an obligation not to kill. It does *not* follow that our duty with respect to those we can save is any less stringent. Suppose Jack Palance were to say: "I needn't give this starving child the sandwich because, after all, I can't save everyone in the world who needs it." If this excuse will not work for him, neither will it work for us with respect to the children we could save in India or Africa.

The second point about numbers was that, for any starving person we *could* help, there are millions of other affluent people who could help as easily as we. Some are in an even better position to help since they are richer. But by and large these people are doing nothing. This also helps explain why we do not feel especially guilty for letting people starve. How guilty we feel about something depends, to some extent, on how we compare with those around us. If we were surrounded by people who regularly sacrificed to feed the starving and we did not, we would probably feel ashamed. But because our neighbors do not do any better than we, we are not so ashamed.

But again, this does not imply that we should not feel more guilty or ashamed than we do. A psychological explanation of our feelings is not a moral justification of our conduct. Suppose Jack Palance were only one of twenty people who watched the child die; would that decrease his guilt? Curiously, I think many people assume it would.

Many people seem to feel that if twenty people do nothing to prevent a tragedy, each of them is only one-twentieth as guilty as he would have been if he had watched the tragedy alone. It is as though there is only a fixed amount of guilt, which divides. I suggest, rather, that guilt multiplies, so that each passive viewer is fully guilty, if he could have prevented the tragedy but did not. Jack Palance watching the girl die alone would be a moral monster; but if he calls in a group of his friends to watch with him, he does not diminish his guilt by dividing it among them. Instead, they are all moral monsters. Once the point is made explicit, it seems obvious.

The fact that most other affluent people do nothing to relieve hunger may very well have implications for one's own obligations. But the implication may be that one's own obligations *increase* rather than decrease. Suppose Palance and a friend were faced with two starving children, so that, if each did his "fair share," Palance would only have to feed one of them. But the friend will do nothing. Because he is well-off, Palance could feed both of them. Should he not? What if he fed one and then watched the other die, announcing that he has done *his* duty and that the one who died was his friend's responsibility? This shows the fallacy of supposing that one's duty is only to do one's fair share, where this is determined by what would be sufficient *if* everyone else did likewise.

To summarize: Jack Palance, who refuses to hand a sandwich to a starving child, is a moral monster. But we feel intuitively that we are not so monstrous, even though we also let starving children die when we could feed them almost as easily. If this intuition is correct, there must be some important difference between him and us. But when we examine the most obvious differences between his conduct and ours—the location of the dying, the differences in numbers—we find no real basis for judging ourselves less harshly than we judge him. Perhaps there are some other grounds on which we might distinguish our moral position, with respect to actual starving people, from Jack Palance's position with respect to the child in my story. But I cannot think of what they might be. Therefore, I conclude that if he is a monster, then so are we—or at least, so are we after our **rationalizations** and thoughtlessness have been exposed.

This last qualification is important. We judge people, at least in part, according to whether they can be expected to realize how well or how badly they behave. We judge Palance harshly because the consequences of his indifference are so immediately apparent. By contrast, it requires an unusual effort for us to realize the consequences of our indifference. It is normal behavior for people in the affluent countries not to give to famine relief, or if they do give, to give very little. Decent people may go along with this normal behavior pattern unthinkingly, without realizing, or without comprehending in a clear way just what this means for the starving. Thus, even though those decent people may act monstrously, we do not judge them monsters. There is a curious sense, then, in which moral reflection can transform decent people into indecent ones; for if a person thinks things through, and realizes that he is, morally speaking, in Jack Palance's position, his continued indifference is more blameworthy than before.

The preceding is not intended to prove that letting people die of starvation is as bad as killing them. But it does provide strong evidence that letting die is much worse than we normally assume, and so that letting die is much *closer* to killing than we normally assume. These reflections also go some way towards showing just how fragile and unreliable our intuitions are in this area. They suggest that, if we want to discover the truth, we are better off looking at arguments that do not rely on unexamined intuitions.

Checklist

To help you review, here is a checklist of the key philosophers and concepts of this chapter. The brief descriptive sentences that appear with each philosopher summarize one of his leading ideas. Keep in mind that some of these summary statements represent terrific oversimplifications of complex positions.

Philosophers

- **Immanuel Kant** Held that the supreme prescription of morality is to act always in such a way that you could rationally will the principle on which you act to be a universal law. Believed that what you should do you should do not because it promotes some end but simply because it is right.

- **Jeremy Bentham** A utilitarian; held that the rightness of an action is identical with the pleasure it produces as its consequence and said that pleasure can be evaluated quantitatively.

- **John Stuart Mill** A utilitarian; held that the rightness of an action is identical with the happiness that it produces as its consequence and said that plea-sure—a part of happiness—must be measured in terms of quality as well as quantity.

- **G. E. Moore** Most important early figure in contemporary analytic ethics and metaethics. Held that goodness is an undefinable, noncomplex, and non-natural property of good things. Said that what makes right actions right is that they produce more goodness than alternative actions.

- **W. D. Ross** Held that the production of maximum good is not the only thing that makes an act right; some things are just simply our moral duty to do.

- **C. L. Stevenson** An emotivist; held that ethical judgments are linguistic acts by which we express our own attitudes and seek to influence those of others.

- **A. J. Ayer** Important emotivist; held that ethical judgments are not genuine assertions.

- **Jean-Paul Sartre** An existentialist; held that there are no necessary ethical absolutes and that the fundamental problem of existence is to know how to live, given this fact.

- **R. M. Hare** British analytic philosopher; held that moral judgments are "universalizable" prescriptions whose function is to guide conduct.

- **Gilbert Harman** American analytic philosopher concerned with various metaethical issues, e.g., whether emotivism can account for moral reasoning.

- **James Rachels** American analytic philosopher concerned with such ethical issues as the extent of our duty to remedy starvation.

Concepts

Kant's supreme principle of morality

hypothetical imperative

categorical imperative

treating humans as ends and not as means

utilitarianism

general happiness

hedonism

psychological hedonism

ethical hedonism

egoistic ethical hedonism

universalistic ethical hedonism

paradox of hedonism

quality vs. quantity of pleasure

naturalistic ethical theories

noncomplex property

nonnatural property

cultural relativism

ethical relativism

first-order thinking

second-order thinking

metaethics

absolute duty

prima facie duty

factual judgment

emotivism

prescriptive judgment

1. Is it true that moral principles hold without exception? Explain.

2. Is it true that moral principles cannot be revealed through scientific investigation?

3. Suppose you stole something that didn't belong to you. Could you rationally will the principle on which you acted to be a universal law? Explain.

4. Explain the difference between a hypothetical imperative and a categorical imperative.

Questions for Discussion and Review

5. Which is it: Do the consequences of an act determine whether it is good, or the intent with which the act has been taken? Or something else altogether?

6. Kant held that there is no moral worth in helping others out of sympathy for them. What reasons are there for holding this view? Are they sound?

7. What does it mean to say that rational beings should be treated as ends and not as means? Give an example of treating another as a means.

8. Is happiness identical with pleasure?

9. Is your own happiness more important morally than that of others? ("It is to me" does not count as an answer.)

10. Was Bentham correct in saying that *ought, right, good,* and the like only have meaning when defined in terms of pleasure?

11. Explain the difference between psychological hedonism and ethical hedonism.

12. Is it true that the ultimate object of a person's desire is always pleasure? Explain.

13. Was Mill correct in saying that some pleasures are inherently better than others?

14. How does Mill propose to establish which of two pleasures is qualitatively better? Can you think of a better way of establishing this?

15. Explain the paradox of hedonism.

16. Is Moore correct in saying that good is a simple property that cannot be analyzed or broken down into simpler constituent parts or defined?

17. What does it mean to say that good is a nonnatural property? Explain in your own words Moore's reasons for saying that good is not equivalent to any natural property.

18. Explain the difference between cultural and ethical relativism. Can an ethical relativist answer "yes" to question 1?

19. Are moral value judgments merely expressions of taste? Explain.

20. "There cannot be moral values if there is no God." Critically evaluate this assertion.

Suggested Further Readings

A. J. Ayer, *Language, Truth and Logic*, 2nd rev. ed. (New York: Dover, 1946). See chapter 6 for this important emotivist treatment of ethics.

J. Bentham, *An Introduction to the Principles of Morals and Legislation* (New York: Methuen, 1982). Bentham's principal work.

R. M. Hare, *The Language of Morals* (Oxford: Clarendon Press, 1952). An important treatise on the logic of moral discourse.

Immanuel Kant, *Foundations of the Metaphysics of Morals*, R. P. Wolff, ed. (Indianapolis: Bobbs-Merrill, 1959). Contains Kant's most important moral philosophy together with commentary by Kant scholars on assorted problems.

S. Korner, *Kant* (Baltimore: Penguin Books, 1955). See chapters 6 and 7. A standard work on Kant.

J. S. Mill, *Utilitarianism* (Baltimore: Penguin Books, 1982). A classic. Short and very readable.

G. E. Moore, *Principia Ethica* (New York: Cambridge University Press, 1903). A work of major importance in ethics. Not terribly difficult to read.

W. D. Ross, *The Right and the Good* (London: Oxford University Press, 1930). Clearly written. An important book; good example of metaethics.

W. D. Ross, *Kant's Ethical Theory* (Oxford: Oxford University Press, 1954). Brief, excellent.

J. P. Sartre, *Existentialism and Humanism* (London: Methuen, 1948). The classic shorter treatment of ethics by Sartre.

Henry Sidgwick, *Outlines of the History of Ethics* (Boston: Beacon, 1960) and *The Methods of Ethics* (New York: Dover, 1874). These are classic works in ethics. Many standard ethical concepts, principles, and distinctions originated with Sidgwick, and his treatment of Utilitarianism is complete and penetrating.

C. L. Stevenson, *Ethics and Language* (New Haven: Yale University Press, 1944). The most influential emotivist analysis of ethics.

M. Warnock, *Ethics Since 1900* (London: Oxford University Press, 1960). A brief but useful general treatment of analytic ethics in the first half of this century. Chapter 2 is a critical exposition of Moore's ethics. See also her *Existentialist Ethics* (London: Macmillan, 1967) for an introduction to existentialist ethics.

James E. White, *Contemporary Moral Problems*, 2nd ed. (St. Paul: West, 1988). A good anthology of recent literature on contemporary moral issues.

SUMMARY AND CONCLUSION

Ethics, the philosophical study of moral judgments, began with the Sophists and Socrates. But the first complete ethical theory was Plato's, which grounded all ethical values on a nonnatural or "transcendent" source, the Form of the Good. Aristotle's ethics, by contrast, were naturalistic: human good is defined by the highest natural human objective, happiness.

Epicureanism and Stoicism too were naturalistic ethical philosophies. According to the Epicureans, the individual's ultimate ethical goal is to lead the pleasant life through moderate living, and according to the Stoics the goal is to lead a serene or untroubled life through acceptance of your fate.

Augustine, who endeavored to find philosophical justification for Christianity in Platonic metaphysics, interwove Platonic ethical themes with the Christian doctrine that God is the ultimate source of all that is good. Within the nonnaturalistic framework of Augustinian ethics, to love God as the sole intrinsic good is the fundamental ethical imperative.

Thomas Aquinas, who is said to have reconciled Aristotelianism with Christianity and who accepted the Aristotelian naturalistic premise that the good for each kind of thing is set by the goal or objective of that kind of thing, thought that there are two sets of virtues. One set, the natural virtues, are those actions that help us achieve our natural objective of happiness on earth; the other set, the higher virtues, direct us to our eternal good, happiness everlasting.

One of the most important contributions of Aquinas to philosophy lies in his use of the Stoic concept of the natural (moral) law, a matter that we touched on briefly in this part and will develop more fully in Part 4. According to Aquinas, the natural law is God's eternal law as it applies to human actions, and it is apprehended by us through conscience and practical reasoning. For Thomas Hobbes, too, there is a natural law, or rather there are natural laws, but these laws he held to be descriptive, nonnormative rational principles of how best to preserve one's life. According to Hobbes, good and evil are to be defined in terms of desires and aversions, and justice and injustice are to be defined as the keeping or breaking of covenants.

In the eighteenth century David Hume argued that moral principles are not divine prescripts; nor, he said, are they founded on reason. A judgment of moral approval, he held, is in effect an expression of the pleasure we experience when we are presented with an instance of benevolent behavior.

Many of the themes, ideas, and concerns of later ethical philosophers may be found in the philosophy of Hume. Although Immanuel Kant rejected Hume's idea that moral principles are not founded on reason in favor of the opposite view that reason alone can determine what one ought to do, the Utilitarians, in the nineteenth century, developed another of Hume's ideas, that goodness consists in behavior and traits that promote the general happiness. The interest in metaethics that runs so strongly through twentieth-century analytic philosophy ultimately has its roots in Hume, too, as does the emotivist doctrine that moral value judgments are expressions of likes and dislikes. Even the ethical philosophy of Sartre owes much to Hume, because it rests on the premise that God does not exist: as we shall see in Chapter 11, Hume was a powerful champion of religious skepticism.

G. E. Moore, with whom twentieth-century analytic ethics began, believed that the task of the ethical philosopher is to conduct a general inquiry into what is good. However, though Moore offered his view on what things are good, his metaethical opinions were most influential, especially his opinions that (1) goodness is a simple, nonnatural, and indefinable property; that (2) what makes an act right is that it produces the maximum amount of good; and that (3) whether something is good is a true/false question of nonempirical fact.

This third view of Moore's was vigorously rejected by the emotivists, who held that questions of values are not questions of fact and that moral judgments are not even genuine propositions. The emotivist position in effect denies that there are values, except as expressions of likes and dislikes, and thus is superficially like the existentialist philosophy of Jean-Paul Sartre. But Sartre, though saying "everything is permissible," does not set forth a value-neutral metaethical analysis of the meaning or function of moral judgments, as the emotivists did.

Finally, recent years have seen something of a decline in metaethical discussions in the Anglo-American philosophical literature in favor of examinations of specific contemporary moral issues.

Let us say this, then, in conclusion. The questions that arise in connection with an introduction to ethical philosophy include some of the most difficult, and yet some of the most important, questions that might be asked. What is the highest human good? Happiness? In what does happiness consist? What is the best means of attaining happiness? What is the relation between happiness and pleasure? Are some pleasures of a better or higher quality than others? Do people search for things other than their own pleasure or happiness? Should they? How important ethically is the happiness of others as compared with one's own happiness? Is the golden rule sound? Why?

Is our ethical first priority even determined by what humans naturally seek? Or is it determined by something else—duty, perhaps, or natural law, or God's wishes? If there is no God, can there be any absolute ethical standards? Are ethical standards determined by one's culture? By one's own opinion? Are moral judgments mere expressions of personal likes and dislikes? What role does reason play in the determination of what is right and good? What is the relationship between what is right and what is good? Are any moral truths self-evident? Is moral knowledge even possible?

These are easy questions not to answer. This is because they are not easy questions to answer. If you want to bring a casual conversation or even a serious discussion to a rapid close, try asking one of them. People really don't know what to say about these issues, or even what to think.

Yet this surely is unfortunate, for making an ethically proper decision about most anything depends on such matters as these. What you have read in this part certainly won't, by itself, give you answers to these questions. But it might make it possible for you to begin to think about them in a systematic way. Knowing something about what important philosophers have thought about these issues may be that big first step toward finding your own sound answers.

In the next part we discuss political philosophy, an area closely related to ethics.

Political Philosophy

Classical Theory

Man, when perfected, is the best of all animals, but, when sepa-
rated from law and justice, he is the worst of all. . . . Justice is
the bond of men in states.

—ARISTOTLE

That one human being will desire to render the person and
property of another subservient to his pleasures, notwithstand-
ing the pain or loss of pleasure which it may occasion to that
individual, is the foundation of government.

—JAMES MILL

While the state exists there is no freedom. Where there is free-
dom, there will be no state.

—VLADIMIR I. LENIN

Ethics, we explained in Part 3, is the philosophical study of moral judgments. But many moral judgments are at the same time political judgments.

Should goods be distributed equally? Or should they be distributed
according to need? Or perhaps according to merit, or according to contribution to production, or to existing ownership, or to something else?

Is it justifiable for a government to restrict the liberty of its citizens
and, if so, in what measure?

When, if ever, is fine or imprisonment legitimate? And what is the
purpose of fine and imprisonment: Punishment? Deterrence? Re-
habilitation?

Are there natural rights that all governments must respect? What
form of political society or state is best? Should there even be a state?

285

The answers to these questions are moral judgments of a political variety. Political philosophy considers such issues and the concepts that are involved in them.

More generally, political philosophy seeks to find the best form of political existence. It is concerned with determining the state's right to exist, its ethically legitimate functions and scope, and its proper organization. Political philosophy also seeks to describe and understand the nature of political relationships and political authority, though scholars whose inquiries are focused within the purely descriptive branch of political philosophy now usually call themselves political scientists.

Plato and Aristotle

Let's start with Plato and Aristotle, because they were the first to try to build a political philosophy from the ground up.

Plato

According to Plato's *Republic*, the human soul has three different elements, one consisting of raw appetites, another consisting of drives (such as anger and ambition), and a third consisting of thought or intellect. In the virtuous or "just" person, each of these three elements fulfills its own unique function and does so under the governance of reason. Likewise, according to Plato, in the ideal or "just" state there are also three elements, each of which fulfills its unique function and does so in accordance with the dictates of reason.

The lowest element in the soul—the appetitive element—corresponds in the well-ordered state to the class of *craftsmen*. The soul's drive element corresponds in the state to the class of *police-soldiers,* who are auxiliaries to the *governing class.* This last class, in the well-ordered state, corresponds to the intellectual, rational element of the soul.

The governing class, according to Plato, is comprised of a select few of highly educated and profoundly rational individuals, including women so qualified. Though an individual becomes a member of a class by birth, he or she will move to a higher or lower class according to aptitude.

In the healthy state, said Plato, as in the well-ordered soul, the rational element is in control. Thus, for Plato, the ideal state is a class-structured aristocracy ruled by "philosopher kings."

Unlike the craftsmen, the ruling elite and their auxiliaries who jointly are the guardians of society have neither private property nor even private families: property, wives, and children are all possessions held in common. Reproduction among the guardians is arranged always to improve the blood line of their posterity in intelligence, courage, and other qualities apt for leadership. The guardians not only must be trained appro-

Plato's Forms of Government

In Book VIII of the *Republic* Plato identifies five forms of government. The preferred form, of course, is an *aristocracy*, governed by rational philosopher-kings.

According to Plato, however, even if this ideal state could be achieved, it would in time degenerate into a *timocracy* in which the ruling class is motivated by love of honor rather than by love for the common good.

A timocracy in turn gives way to a *plutocracy*, which is rule by men who primarily desire riches. Under a plutocracy, society becomes divided between two classes, the rich and the poor, Plato thinks.

Nevertheless, this form of government, Plato says, is preferable to the next degeneration, *democracy*, which results because "a society cannot hold wealth in honor and at the same time establish self-control in its citizens." (Perhaps we will eventually see if Plato is correct that a society that honors wealth cannot maintain self-control.) Within Plato's democracy people's impulses are unrestrained, and the result is lack of order and direction. "Mobocracy" is what we would call Plato's "democracy" today.

Tyranny, the last form of government in Plato's classification, results when the democratic mob submits itself to a strongman, each person selfishly figuring to gain from the tyrant's rule and believing that the tyrant will end democracy's evil. In fact, Plato thinks, the tyrant will acquire absolute power and enslave his subjects. Further, he, the tyrant, will himself become a slave to his wretched craving for power and self-indulgence.

Plato was not always an optimist.

---

priately for soldiering, but must also be given a rigorous intellectual education that, for the few whose unique abilities allow it, prepares them for advanced work in mathematics, dialectic (that is, the Socratic method; see Chapter 2), and philosophy. These few, at age fifty, and after many years of public service, advance to membership in the ruling aristocracy and to leadership of the state. Such is Plato's vision of the ideal political structure.

It is important to be aware that from Plato's perspective the state, like the person, is a *living organism* whose well-being must be sought by its subjects. Although he assumed that the healthy state is best for the individuals in it, Plato believed that the health or well-being of the state is something that is *desirable for its own sake*. And just as a person's health or well-being requires the proper functioning and coordination of the elements of the soul under the overarching rule of reason, the state's health or well-being lies in the proper functioning and coordination of its elements under the rule of the reasoning elite. The ideal state, according to Plato, is well ordered in this way, and its being well ordered in this way is something that is intrinsically desirable.

We, of course, are more likely to evaluate Plato's prescriptions solely according to what they would do for the general welfare—that is, the welfare of all the citizens or subjects of the state. And so it may occur to you that, if the citizens are satisfied with their class level and do not think that their natural abilities warrant higher placement, then they might well like Plato's form of government. After all, the division of power, responsibility, and labor among classes as envisioned by Plato might maximize (as he thought it would) the productivity of the state; and the unavailability of private property to the ruling elite could conceivably remove acquisitive temptations so that they would devote their efforts to the public good rather than to personal gain. A state governed by a wise and enlightened aristocracy that seeks the betterment of its citizens might well do much to enhance the public welfare and happiness, even if it sometimes may be difficult for a ruling aristocracy to understand the needs and desires of the populace. In short, you may be disposed to give Plato a passing grade on his state, at least with reference to what it would do for the welfare of its subjects. You would probably not be inclined to think of the state as an organism in its own right whose well-being is something desirable for its own sake.

The Platonic idea of the state as an organism whose well-being is desirable for its own sake has been exploited, as we will see, as justification for the more totalitarian premise that the individual must sacrifice his or her own well-being for that of the state. Plato himself, we add hurriedly, was not advocating tyrannical rule.

In Selection 9.1, from the *Republic*, Plato has just explained that the guardians of society must live together, must not possess private property, and must hold all possessions in common. The question thus arises, Plato thinks, of the status of women within the circle of guardians. In this excerpt he gives his views. The main speaker ("I") is "Socrates" (Plato), and he is talking to Plato's two brothers, Glaucon and Adeimantus.

▶ S E L E C T I O N   9.1

From Plato, REPUBLIC

[Explain, said Glaucon,] how this communion of wives and children among our guardians will be managed, and also about the rearing of the children while still young in the interval between birth and formal schooling which is thought to be the most difficult part of education. Try, then, to tell us what must be the manner of it. . . .

Well, said I . . . our endeavor, I believe, was to establish these men in our discourse as the guardians of a flock?

Yes.

Let us preserve the analogy, then, and assign them a generation and breeding answering to it, and see if it suits us or not.

In what way? he said.

In this. Do we expect the females of watchdogs to join in guarding what the males guard and to hunt with them and share all their pursuits or do we expect the females to stay indoors as being incapacitated by the bearing and the breeding of the whelps while the males toil and have all the care of the flock?

They have all things in common, he replied, except that we treat the females as weaker and the males as stronger.

Is it possible, then, said I, to employ any creature for the same ends as another if you do not assign it the same nurture and education?

It is not possible.

If, then, we are to use the women for the same things as the men, we must also teach them the same things.

Yes.

Now music together with gymnastics was the training we gave the men.

Yes.

Then we must assign these two arts to the women also and the offices of war and employ them in the same way.

It would seem likely from what you say, he replied. . . .

Can it be denied then that there is by nature a great difference between men and women? Surely there is. Is it not fitting, then, that a different function should be appointed for each corresponding to this difference of nature? Certainly. How, then, can you deny that you are mistaken and in contradiction with yourselves when you turn around and affirm that the men and the women ought to do the same thing, though their natures are so far apart? Can you surprise me with an answer to that question?

Not easily on this sudden challenge, he replied.

Come then, consider, said I, if we can find a way out. We did agree that different natures should have differing pursuits and that the natures of men and women differ. . . . We meant, for example, that a man and a woman who have a physician's mind have the same nature. Don't you think so?

I do.

But that a man physician and a man carpenter have different natures?

Certainly, I suppose.

Similarly, then, said I, if it appears that the male and the female sex have distinct qualifications for any arts or pursuits, we shall affirm that they ought to be assigned respectively to each. But if it appears that they differ only in just this respect that the female bears and the male begets, we shall say that no proof has yet been produced that the woman differs from the man for our purposes, but we shall continue to think that our guardians and their wives ought to follow the same pursuits.

And rightly, said he.

Then, is it not the next thing to bid our opponent tell us precisely for what art or pursuit concerned with the conduct of a state the woman's nature differs from the man's? . . . Come then, we shall say to him, answer our question. Was this the basis of your distinction between the man naturally gifted for anything and the one not so gifted—that the one learned easily, the other with difficulty, that the one with slight instruction could discover much for himself in the matter studied, but the other, after much instruction and drill, could not even remember what he had learned, and that the bodily faculties of the one adequately served his mind, while, for the other, the body was a hindrance? Were there any other points than these by which you distinguish the well-endowed man in every subject and the poorly endowed?

No one, said he, will be able to name any others. . . .

Then, [said I,] there is no pursuit of the administrators of a state that belongs to a woman because she is a woman or to a man because he is a man. But the natural capacities are distributed alike among both creatures, and women naturally share in all pursuits and men in all—yet for all the woman is weaker than the man.

Assuredly.

Shall we, then, assign them all to men and nothing to women?

How could we?

We shall rather, I take it, say that one woman has the nature of a physician and another not, and one is by nature musical, and another unmusical?

Surely.

Can we, then, deny that one woman is naturally athletic and warlike and another unwarlike and averse to gymnastics?

I think not.

And again, one a lover, another a hater, of wisdom? And one high-spirited, and the other lacking spirit?

That also is true.

Then it is likewise true that one woman has the qualities of a guardian and another not. Were not these the natural qualities of the men also whom we selected for guardians?

They were.

The women and the men, then, have the same nature in respect to the guardianship of the state, save in so far as the one is weaker, the other stronger.

Apparently.

Women of this kind, then, must be selected to cohabit with men of this kind and to serve with them as guardians since they are capable of it and akin by nature.

By all means.

And to the same natures must we not assign the same pursuits?

The same. . . .

For the production of a female guardian, then, our education will not be one thing for men and another for women, especially since the nature which we hand over to it is the same.

There will be no difference. . . .

All that precedes has for its sequel, [said I,] the following law.

What?

That these women shall all be common to all these men, and that none shall cohabit with any privately, and that the children shall be common, and that no parent shall know its own offspring nor any child its parent. . . . they, having houses and meals in common, and no private possessions of that kind, will dwell together, and being commingled in gymnastics and in all their life and education, will be conducted by innate necessity to sexual union. Is not what I say a necessary consequence?

Not by the necessities of geometry, he said, but by those of love, which are perhaps keener and more potent than the other to persuade and constrain the multitude.

They are, indeed, I said. But next, Glaucon, disorder and promiscuity in these unions or in anything else they do would be an unhallowed thing in a happy state and the rulers will not suffer it.

It would not be right, he said.

Obviously, then, we must arrange marriages, sacramental so far as may be. And the most sacred marriages would be those that were most beneficial.

By all means.

How, then, would the greatest benefit result? Tell me this, Glaucon. I see that you have in your house hunting dogs and a number of pedigreed cocks. Have you ever considered something about their unions and procreations?

What? he said.

In the first place, I said, among these themselves, although they are a select breed, do not some prove better than the rest?

They do.

Do you then breed from all indiscriminately, or are you careful to breed from the best?

From the best.

And, again, do you breed from the youngest or the oldest, or, so far as may be, from those in their prime?

From those in their prime.

And if they are not thus bred, you expect, do you not, that your birds' breed and hounds will greatly degenerate?

I do, he said.

And what of horses and other animals? I said. It is otherwise with them?

It would be strange if it were, said he.

Gracious, said I, dear friend, how imperative, then, is our need of the highest skill in our rulers, if the principle holds also for mankind. . . . the best men must cohabit with the best women in as many cases as possible and the worst with the worst in the fewest, and . . . the offspring of the one must be reared and that of the other not, if the flock is to be as perfect as possible.

Aristotle as Political Scientist

We would not wish to imply, by pointing out Aristotle's fondness for observing the world around him, including the political world, that he was a purely neutral describer of political systems. It should be noted, for example, that Aristotle did enunciate principles in terms of which various forms of government can be evaluated. Also, when he listed monarchy, aristocracy, and polity as proper forms of government and tyranny, oligarchy, and democracy as their corresponding improper forms, he was not merely describing these forms, as a modern-day political scientist might, but also was evaluating them, as a political philosopher will do.

Nor is Aristotle a historian of political systems. You would have no inkling, from reading Aristotle's *Politics*, that the Greek city-state system of government went out of existence forever during his lifetime.

Aristotle

Aristotle, too, regarded the state as an organism, as a living being. The state as a living being, he thought, exists for some end, for some purpose. That purpose, he believed, is to promote the good life for humans. Thus, Aristotle offers a standard of evaluation of the state different from Plato's. For Aristotle, a state is good only to the degree to which it enables its citizens themselves to achieve the good life, whereas for Plato a state is good to the extent that it is well ordered.

Aristotle, who had studied the constitutions, or basic political structures, of numerous Greek city and other states, was a practical thinker. He insisted that the form of the ideal state depends on, and can change with, circumstances. And unlike Plato, Aristotle did not set forth a recipe for the ideal state. A state, he said, can be ruled properly by one person; but it can also be ruled properly by a few people or by many. When a state is properly ruled by one person, he said, it is a *monarchy;* improper rule by one is *tyranny.* Proper rule by the few is *aristocracy,* improper rule *oligarchy.* Proper rule by the many is a *polity* and improper rule by them is a *democracy.* Good forms of government tend to degenerate into bad, he thought, as Plato also did. Aristocracies become oligarchies, monarchies become tyrannies, polities become democracies.

Though Aristotle thought that states may be good or bad irrespective of their form, he observed that political societies always have three classes: a lower class of laborers and peasants, a middle class of craftsmen, farmers, and merchants, and an upper class of aristocrats. He further observed that political power rested in one or another of these social classes or was shared by them variously, irrespective of the form of the state.

Aristotle, like Plato, is no egalitarian. (An egalitarian believes that all humans are equal in their social, political, and economic rights and privileges.) But even though Plato's ideal state has no slaves, Aristotle held that some people are by nature suited for slavery, whereas others by nature are suited for freedom. Even freemen are not equals, Aristotle held. Those who, like laborers, do not have the aptitude (or time) to participate in governance should not be citizens. But, he said, beware: the desires of lesser men for equality are the "springs and fountains" of revolution and are to be so recognized by a properly functioning government, which takes precautions to avoid revolt.

Selection 9.2, from Aristotle's *Politics*, has two parts; the first concerns the origin and purpose of the state, and the second concerns a degenerate form of government—tyranny. Notice how very descriptive of actual political facts Aristotle is, as compared with Plato. Because of his descriptivism, Aristotle is sometimes called the first political scientist. But be sure to see the nearby box, "Aristotle as Political Scientist."

▶ S E L E C T I O N   9.2

From Aristotle, POLITICS

When several villages are united in a single complete community, large enough to be nearly or quite self-sufficing, the state comes into existence, originating in the bare needs of life, and continuing in existence for the sake of a good life. And therefore, if the earlier forms of society are natural, so is the state, for it is the end of them, and the nature of a thing is its end. For what each thing is when fully developed, we call its nature, whether we are speaking of a man, a horse, or a family. Besides, the final cause and end of a thing is the best, and to be self-sufficing is the end and the best.

Hence it is evident that the state is a creation of nature, and that man is by nature a political animal. And he who by nature and not by mere accident is without a state, is either a bad man or above humanity. . . .

Further, the state is by nature clearly prior to the family and to the individual, since the whole is of necessity prior to the part; for example, if the whole body be destroyed, there will be no foot or hand, except in an equivocal sense, as we might speak of a stone hand; for when destroyed the hand will be no better than that. But things are defined by their working and power; and we ought not to say that they are the same when they no longer have their proper quality, but only that they have the same name. The proof that the state is a creation of nature and prior to the individual is that the individual, when isolated, is not self-sufficing; and therefore he is like a part in relation to the whole. But he who is unable to live in society, or who has no need because he is sufficient for himself, must be either a beast or a god; he is no part of a state. A social instinct is implanted in all men by nature, and yet he who first founded the state was the greatest of benefactors. . . .

A state exists for the sake of a good life, and not for the sake of life only: if life only were the object, slaves and brute animals might form a state, but they cannot, for they have no share in happiness or in a life of free choice. Nor does a state exist for the sake of alliance and security from injustice, nor yet for the sake of exchange and mutual intercourse. . . . Virtue must be the care of a state which is truly so called, and not merely enjoys the name: for without this end the community becomes a mere alliance which differs only in place from alliances of which the members live apart; and law is only a convention, "a surety to one another of justice," as the sophist Lycophron says, and has no real power to make the citizens good and just. . . . It is clear then that a state is not a mere society, having a common place, established for the prevention of mutual crime and for the sake of exchange. These are conditions without which a state cannot exist; but all of them together do not constitute a state, which is a community of families and aggregation of families in well-being, for the sake of a perfect and self-sufficing life. Such a community can only be established among those who live in the same place and intermarry. Hence arise in cities family connections, brotherhoods, common sacrifices, amusements which draw men together. But these are created by friendship, for the will to live together is friendship. The end of the state is the good life, and these are the means towards it. And the state is the union of families and villages in a perfect and self-sufficing life, by which we mean a happy and honourable life.

Our conclusion, then, is that political society exists for the sake of noble actions, and not of mere companionship. Hence they who contribute most to such a society have a greater share in it than those who have the same or a greater freedom or nobility of birth but are inferior to them in political virtue; or than those who exceed them in wealth but are surpassed by them in virtue. . . .

As to tyrannies, they are preserved in two most opposite ways. One of them is the old traditional method in which most tyrants administer their government. Of such arts Periander of Corinth is said to have been the great master, and many similar devices may be gathered from the Persians in the administration of their government. There are firstly the prescriptions mentioned some distance back, for the preservation of a tyranny, in so far as this is possible; viz. that the tyrant should lop off those who are too high; he must put to death men of spirit; he must not allow common meals, clubs, education, and the like; he must be upon his guard against anything which is likely to inspire either courage or confidence among his subjects; he must prohibit literary assemblies or other meetings for discussion, and he must take every means to prevent people from knowing one another (for acquaintance begets mutual confidence). Further, he must compel all persons staying in the city to appear in public and live at his gates; then he will know what they are doing: if they are always kept under, they will learn to be humble. In short, he should practise these and the like Persian and barbaric arts, which all have the same object. A tyrant should also endeavour to know what each of his subjects says or does, and should employ spies, like the "female detectives" at Syracuse, and the eavesdroppers whom Hiero was in the habit of sending to any place of resort or meeting; for the fear of informers prevents people from speaking their minds, and if they do, they are more easily found out. Another art of the tyrant is to sow quarrels among the citizens; friends should be embroiled with friends, the people with the notables, and the rich with one another. Also he should impoverish his subjects; he thus provides against the maintenance of a guard by the citizens, and the people, having to keep hard at work, are prevented from conspiring. The Pyramids of Egypt afford an example of this policy; also the offerings of the family of Cypslus, and the building of the temple of Olympian Zeus by the Psisistratidae, and the great Polycratean monuments at Samos; all these works were alike intended to occupy the people and keep them poor. Another practice of tyrants is to multiply taxes, after the manner of Dionysius at Syracuse, who contrived that within five years his subjects should bring into the treasury their whole property. The tyrant is also fond of making war in order that his subjects may have something to do and be always in want of a leader. And whereas the power of a king is preserved by his friends, the characteristic of a tyrant is to distrust his friends, because he knows that all men want to overthrow him, and they above all have the power.

Natural Law Theory and Contractarian Theory

Aristotle, recall from Part 3 on ethics, was an **ethical naturalist.** For answers to questions about what *ought* to be the case, he looked around him (i.e., he turned to "nature") to see what *is* the case. To determine what the purpose of the state ought to be, he considered what the purpose of existing states actually is. Ought all people be equal in freedom? In citizenship? Aristotle's answers to these and other questions of political ethics were grounded on what he observed. In this instance, the apparent natural inequality of people he perceived prompted him to answer negatively.

Because of his naturalism Aristotle is sometimes viewed as the source of **natural law political theory.** According to this theory, questions of political ethics are to be answered by reference to the so-called natural law, which alone supposedly determines what is right and wrong, good and bad, just and unjust, proper and improper.

As we saw in Chapter 7, however, the first relatively clear concept of natural law per se is probably found not in Aristotle's writings but later, in Stoic philosophy, in which the natural law is conceived as an impersonal principle of reason that governs the cosmos. But the Stoics were not primarily political philosophers. So it is to the celebrated Roman statesman **Cicero** (106–43 B.C.) that one turns for the classic expression of the Stoic concept of natural law as applied to political philosophy: "True law," wrote Cicero,

> is right reason in agreement with Nature; it is of universal application, unchanging and everlasting . . . there will not be different laws at Rome and at Athens; or different laws now and in the future, but one eternal and unchangeable law will be valid for all nations and all times.

In other words, Cicero is proposing that there is only one valid law, the natural law of reason, which holds eternally and universally. This is a bold idea, and to a certain extent we still accept it today.

Augustine and Aquinas

In the thought of **Augustine** (354–430) and **Aquinas** (1225–1274), the natural law as conceived by the Stoics, which according to Cicero was the only valid basis for human law, was *Christianized*. **Natural law** was conceived by these Church philosophers to be the eternal moral law of *God* as it is apprehended by humans through the dictates of their conscience and reason.

With Augustine and Aquinas two vital questions were raised: the relationship of secular law to the natural law of God and, correspondingly, the relationship of state to Church. According to both thinkers, the laws of the state must be just, which meant for them that the laws of the state

Aquinas's Conception of Law

One of Aquinas's most distinctive contributions to political philosophy is his discussion of law. Aquinas distinguished among four kinds of law.

Most fundamental is **eternal law,** which is, in effect, the divine reason of God that rules over all things at all times.

Then there is **divine law,** which is God's gift to man, apprehended by us through revelation rather than through conscience or reason, and which directs us to our *supernatural* goal, eternal happiness.

Natural law is God's eternal law as it applies to man on earth; in effect, it is the fundamental principles of morality, as apprehended by us in our conscience and practical reasoning. Natural law directs us to our *natural* goal, happiness on earth.

Finally, **human law** is the laws and statutes of society that are derived from man's understanding of natural law. A rule or decree of a ruler or government must answer to a higher authority, said Aquinas: it must conform to natural law. Any rule or statute that does not, he said, should not be obeyed: "we ought to obey God rather than men."

Aquinas's conception of law, especially of natural law and human law, bears widely on our own conceptions.

must accord with God's natural law. If secular laws do not accord, they held, they are not truly laws, and there is no legitimate state. For Augustine, the purpose of the state is to take "the power to do hurt" from the wicked; for Aquinas, it is to attend to the common good (which, for Aquinas, meant much more than merely curbing human sinfulness). For both, the Church provides for man's spiritual needs, and, though the state does have rights and duties within its own sphere, it is subordinate to the Church, just as its laws are subordinate to natural law.

Hobbes

Whereas Augustine, Aquinas, and other Christian thinkers conceived of the natural law as the moral law of God, **Thomas Hobbes** (1588–1679), who was discussed in the section on ethics, construed the natural law as neither the law of God nor moral law. In fact, Hobbes's conception of natural law amounts to discarding the older religious concept.

Hobbes did not speak of *the* natural law in the singular, as did the classical and Church philosophers, but of natural laws in the plural. These, for Hobbes, are simply rational principles of prudent action, prescriptions for best preserving your own life. According to Hobbes, who was a naturalist and in this respect resembled Aristotle, there is no higher authority beyond nature that passes judgment on the morality or immorality of human deeds. You obey the laws of nature insofar as you act rationally, and insofar as you don't, you don't live long.

Hobbes's first law of nature is *to seek peace as far as you have any hope of obtaining it, and when you cannot obtain it to use any means you can to defend yourself.* As you can see, this "law" is indeed simply a prescription of rational self-interest.

And it is easy to understand why Hobbes regarded this as the first law of nature. From Hobbes's perspective, the question of how best to prolong one's life was a pressing issue for most people. Historians emphasize the importance of the Scientific Revolution in the seventeenth century, which included the discoveries of Gilbert, Kepler, Galileo, Harvey, Boyle, Huygens, Newton, and others. The seventeenth century, in fact, reads like a *Who's Who* of scientific discoverers. But most seventeenth-century Europeans, plain folk and ruling aristocrats alike, had never even *heard* of these discoveries, and even if they had, they would have considered them uninteresting and irrelevant. That's because this was also a century of political chaos and brutal warfare both in England and on the Continent. The Thirty Years' War, a very ugly spectacle, happened during this century, and most Europeans were somewhat preoccupied with the safety of their skins. For most of them, the question of personal survival was of more than academic interest.

Hobbes's second law is *to be content, for the sake of peace and self-preservation, provided others are also content, with only so much liberty "against other men" as you would allow other men against yourself.* And the third law is *"that men perform their covenants made."* (A covenant is an agreement or contract, a compact.)

But nobody, Hobbes said, is so stupid as to live up to an agreement that turns out not to be in his own best interest. So, if you want people to live by their agreements, you have to make sure that they will *suffer* if they try to break them. This means you have to have some third power to enforce them. "Without the terror of some power to cause them to be observed," Hobbes wrote, covenants are only words.

In light of these considerations, Hobbes concluded, if you apply the "laws of nature" listed here to real-life situations, what they mean is this: For their own welfare, people should transfer both their collective strength and their right to use whatever is necessary to defend themselves to a sovereign power that will use the acquired power to *compel* all citizens to honor their commitments to one another and to live together peacefully. This is the best road to peace and security, according to Hobbes. Without this central power to make them honor their agreements and keep them in line, people live in a "state of nature," a state of unbridled war of each against all, a state of chaos, mistrust, deception, meanness, and violence in which each person stops at nothing to gain the upper hand, and life is "solitary, poor, nasty, brutish, and short."

The central sovereign power to which people will transfer their power and rights, if they are smart enough to see that it is in their own self-interest to do so, is called by Hobbes the **Leviathan.** When people transfer their power and rights to the Leviathan, they in effect create a **social contract.** It is this contract that delivers people from the evils of the natural state to civil society and a state of peace.

The social contract is thus an agreement between individuals who, for the sake of peace, are willing to make this absolutely unconditional and irrevocable transfer of right and power to the sovereign or Leviathan.

HAVE I GOT THIS STRAIGHT? PLATO SAID THAT IF PEOPLE AREN'T SMART, THEY'LL WIND UP VOLUNTARILY SUBMITTING TO A STRONGMAN. HOBBES SAID THAT IF PEOPLE **ARE** SMART, THAT'S EXACTLY WHAT THEY'LL DO.

YES. AND STALIN SAID THAT HOBBES AND PLATO WERE BOTH RIGHT.

According to Hobbes, only when people have contracted among themselves and created the Leviathan is there *law* or *justice*, and Hobbes is now speaking of civil laws, not natural laws. *Justice* and *injustice* Hobbes defined as the keeping and breaking of covenants. Because covenants and laws are meaningless unless there is a Leviathan to enforce them, law and justice can only exist under a Leviathan.

Now the original social covenant or contract that creates the Leviathan is not a contract *between* the Leviathan and its subjects, Hobbes stressed. It is a contract among the subjects themselves. There is and cannot be any covenant *between* the Leviathan and its subjects. Here's why: because the Leviathan holds all the power, it would be free to break any pledge, promise, agreement, commitment, contract, or covenant that it made. And that means that a covenant between the Leviathan and its subjects would be unenforceable and hence would be empty words.

Therefore, because logically there cannot be any covenant between the Leviathan and its subjects, and because justice is defined by Hobbes as the keeping of a covenant, it is *impossible* for the Hobbesian sovereign or Leviathan to act unjustly toward its subjects. Likewise, the Leviathan's laws—and the Leviathan's laws are the only laws, for they alone can be enforced—cannot be unjust. The Leviathan, according to Hobbes, has the

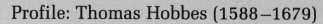

Profile: Thomas Hobbes (1588–1679)

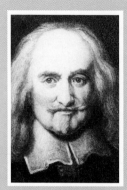

Scientific discovery, geometry, and the violence of civil war and anarchy—these were the major influences on Hobbes's philosophy.

A graduate of Oxford, Hobbes became a tutor in the influential Cavendish family, in which role he was able to meet many of the important intellectual figures of his day, including Gassendi, Galileo, and Bacon. Through his acquaintance with the work of these and other early scientists, it occurred to him that everything that happens does so as the result of physical matter in motion. This perception became the basis of his entire philosophy, including his metaphysics and political thought.

Amazingly, it was not until his early forties that Hobbes chanced on a copy of Euclid's *Elements*. This work influenced him to think that all knowledge could be derived deductively from axioms based on observation. Consequently he devised a comprehensive plan, which he never fully completed, to apply the Euclidean deductive method to all questions of physical nature, human nature, and the nature of society.

Hobbes's political philosophy, however, has earned him the greatest fame. The basic themes of his political writings—that man is by nature violent, self-serving, and at war with all other men, and that for their own defense against their natural predaciousness people must submit to a strong power capable of enforcing peace—are clear reflections of the political turbulence of the times. During Hobbes's lifetime, the Thirty Years' War on the European continent struck down half the population, and in England a state of anarchy followed the Civil War and the rule of Oliver Cromwell. Moreover, the plague ravaged England no less than four times during Hobbes's long life. Hobbes was no stranger to death, destruction, chaos, and the willingness of men to sacrifice others for their own ends.

right to lay down any laws it can enforce (although, as we see shortly, it cannot require us to take our own lives), and we are not only physically but also morally obliged to obey them, for only through its laws are we kept from anarchy.

That no covenant exists between the Leviathan and its subjects means that the Leviathan has no legal or moral obligation to them. That it has no legal or moral obligation to the subjects means that they are *gambling* when they agree among themselves unconditionally to transfer all power and rights to it; they are gambling that life under its rule (conditions of "peace") will be better than it would be under the conditions of anarchy that otherwise would obtain. Perhaps a rational sovereign is likely to see that it is not in his own self-interest to destroy or abuse his subjects, but there is always a chance that he won't.

Hobbes, obviously, thought the gamble a wise one. Were people to live without a common power, he wrote, a power "to keep them all in awe," their innate viciousness would preclude the development of any commerce, industry, or culture, and there would be "no knowledge on the face of the earth; no account of time; no arts; no letters; no society." There would only be, he wrote, "continual fear, and danger of violent death." In Hobbes's view, given the alternatives of anarchy and dictatorship (the Leviathan)—and these are the only alternatives—the most reasonable choice is dictatorship, even if it does involve the risk of despotism.

The political establishment of the Leviathan, however, Hobbes makes subject to certain minimal safeguards of its subjects. If the Leviathan fails to provide security to its subjects, they may transfer their allegiance to another sovereign. Further, because no one has the right to take his own life, this right is not among those transferred to the Leviathan at the time of the social contract of its subjects. Therefore the Leviathan cannot rightfully compel a subject to take his or her own life, according to Hobbes.

Critics of Hobbes, not too surprisingly, scoff at such "safeguards," because as a practical matter the Leviathan, having been given the collective power of its subjects, is able to do whatever it pleases with its subjects. As Locke said, with Hobbes you trade the chance of being ravaged by a thousand men acting independently for the chance of suffering the same fate at the hands of one person who has a thousand men at his command.

We have spent some time here on Hobbes. This is because Hobbes, in basing the creation and power of the Leviathan on a social contract, is the first philosopher to enunciate systematically the concept that the state, and with it justice, is created through an agreement or "contract" among the people who comprise the state. This is, of course, a very familiar notion to Americans, because the American constitution, about which more will be said later, is the social contract that brought the United States into existence.

So Hobbes really did more than reject the principle of natural law as representing God's will and its corollary that the laws of the state, and the state itself, derive their *legitimacy* from their harmony with this divine natural law. According to Hobbes, the legitimacy of the state and its laws derives from an initial consent of those governed (though keep in mind that this consent is "required" by those principles of practical reason that Hobbes refers to as natural laws). With Hobbes begins an important tradition in Western political philosophy, the so-called **contractarian theory** of justice and the state. We'll encounter other contractarian theories as we proceed, beginning with the philosophy of John Locke.

In Selection 9.3, Hobbes explains two of the laws of nature, as well as the transference of power to the Leviathan. You may also wish to reread Selection 7.7 from Hobbes in Part 3 at this time.

▶ S E L E C T I O N   9.3

From Thomas Hobbes, LEVIATHAN*

Chapter XIV. Of the First and Second Natural Laws, and of Contracts

THE RIGHT OF NATURE, which writers commonly called *Jus Naturale*, is the liberty each man has to use his own power as he will himself, for the preservation . . . of his own life; and consequently of doing anything which in his own judgment and reason he shall conceive to be apt.

By LIBERTY is understood, according to the proper significance of the word, the absence of external impediments: which impediments may often take away part of a man's power to do what he would, but cannot hinder him from using the power left him, according as his judgment and reason shall dictate to him.

A LAW OF NATURE (*Lex Naturalis*), is a precept or general rule, found out by reason, by which a man is forbidden to do that which is destructive of his life or takes away the means of preserving the same; and to omit that by which he thinks it may be best preserved. For though they that speak of this subject confound *Jus* and *Lex*, right and law; yet they ought to be distinguished; because right consists in liberty to do or to forbear; whereas law determines and binds to one of them: so that law and right differ as much as obligation and liberty; which in one and the same matter are inconsistent.

And because the condition of man (as has been declared in the preceding chapter) is a condition of war of everyone against everyone; in which case everyone is governed by his own reason; and there is nothing he can make use of, that may not be a help to him, in preserving his life against his enemies; it follows that in such a condition every man has a right to everything; even to one another's body. And therefore, as long as this natural right of every man to everything endures, there can be no security to any man (how strong or wise he is) of living out the time which nature ordinarily allows men to live. And consequently it is a precept or general rule of reason, *that every man ought to endeavor peace, as far as he has hope of obtaining it; and when he cannot obtain it he may seek and use all helps and advantages of war.* The first branch of which rule contains the first and fundamental law of nature; which is *to seek peace and follow it.* The second, the sum of the Right of Nature; which is, *by all means we can, to defend ourselves.*

From this fundamental law of nature, by which men are commanded to endeavor peace, is derived this second law; *that a man be willing, when others are also, as far as for peace, and defense of himself he shall think it necessary, to lay down this right to all things; and be contented with so much liberty against other men, as he would allow other men against himself.* For as long as every man holds this right of doing anything he likes; so long are all men in the condition of war. But if other men will not lay down their right, as well as he; then there is not reason for anyone to divest himself of his: For that would be to expose himself to prey (which no man is bound to) rather than to dispose himself to peace. This is that law of the gospel; *whatsoever you require that others should do to you, that do to them.* . . .

To lay down a man's right to anything, is to divest himself of the liberty of hindering another of the benefit of his own right to the same. For he that renounces or passes away his right, gives not to any other man a right which he had not before; because there is nothing to which every man had not right by nature: but only stands out of his way that he may enjoy his own original right without hindrance from him; not without hindrance from another. So that the effect which reverberates to one man by another man's defect of right, is but so much diminution of impediments to the use of his own right original.

Right is laid aside, either by simply renouncing it; or by transferring it to another. By simply RENOUNCING; when he cares not to whom the benefit thereof reverberates. By TRANSFERRING; when he intends the benefit thereof to some certain person or persons. And when a man has in either manner abandoned or granted away his right; then is he said to be OBLIGED or BOUND not to hinder those to whom such right is granted or abandoned, from the benefit of it: and that he ought, and it is his DUTY, not to make void that voluntary act of his own: and that such hindrance is INJUSTICE and INJURY, as being *sine jure*; the right being before renounced or transferred. . . .

When a man transfers right or renounces it; it is either in consideration of some right reciprocally transferred to himself; or for some good he hopes for. For it is a voluntary act: and of the voluntary acts of every man, the object is good to himself. And therefore there are some rights which no man can be understood by any words or other signs to have abandoned or transferred. As first: a man cannot lay down the right of resisting them that assault him by force to take away his life; because he cannot be understood to aim thereby at good to himself. The same may be said of wounds and chains and imprisonment; both because there is no benefit consequent to such patience; as there is to the patience of suffering another to be wounded or imprisoned: as also because a man cannot tell, when he sees men proceeding against him by violence, when they intend his death or not. And the motive and end for which this renouncing and transferring of right is introduced is nothing else but the security of a man's person, in his life and in the means of so preserving life as not to be weary of it. And therefore if a man by words or other signs seems to rob himself of the end for which those signs were intended; he is not to be understood as if he meant it or that it was his will; but that he was ignorant of how such words and actions were to be interpreted.

The mutual transferring of right, is that which men call CONTRACT. . . .

Chapter XVII. Of the Causes, Generation, and Definition of a Commonwealth

The final cause, end, or design of men (who naturally love liberty and dominion over others) in the introduction of that restraint upon themselves (in which we see them live in commonwealths) is the foresight of their own preservation and of a more contented life; that is to say, of getting themselves out from that miserable condition of war, which is necessarily consequent (as has been shown) to the natural passions of men, when there is no visible power to keep them in awe, and tie them by fear of punishment to the performance of their covenants, and observation of those laws of nature set down in the fourteenth and fifteenth chapters.

For the laws of nature (as justice, equity, modesty, mercy, and, in sum, doing to others as we would be done to) of themselves, without the terror of some power to cause them to be observed, are contrary to our natural passions, that carry us to partiality, pride, revenge, and the like. And covenants, without the sword, are but words, and of no strength to secure a man at all. Therefore notwithstanding the laws of nature (which everyone has then kept, when he has the will to keep them, when he can do it safely) if there be no power erected, or not great enough for our security; every man will, and may lawfully rely on his own strength and art, for caution against all other men. . . .

The only way to erect such a common power as may be able to defend them from the invasion of foreigners and the injuries of one another and thereby to secure them in such a way as that by their own industry, and by the fruits of the earth, they may nourish themselves and live contentedly; is to confer all their power and strength upon one man or upon one assembly of men, that may reduce all their wills, by plurality of voices, unto one will: which is as much as to say, to appoint one man or assembly of men to bear their person. . . .

This is more than consent or concord; it is a real unity of them all in one and the same person, made by covenant of every man with every man, in such manner as if every man should say to every man, I authorize and give up my right of governing myself to this man or to this assembly of men, on this condition that you give up the right to him and authorize all his actions in like manner. This done, the multitude so united in one person, is called a COMMON-WEALTH, in Latin, *Civitas*. This is the generation of that great LEVIATHAN, or rather (to speak more reverently) of that mortal God to which we owe under the immortal God our peace and defense. For by this authority, given him by every particular man in the commonwealth, he has the use of so much power and strength conferred on him, that by terror thereof, he is enabled to form the wills of them all, to peace at home, and mutual aid against their enemies abroad. And in him consists the essence of the commonwealth; which (to define it) is *one person, of whose acts a great multitude by mutual covenants one with another have made themselves every one the author, to the end he may use the strength and means of them all, as he shall think expedient, for their peace and common defense.*

And he that carries this person, is called SOVEREIGN, and said to have sovereign power; and everyone besides, his SUBJECT.

The attaining to this sovereign power, is by two ways. One, by natural force; as when a man makes his children submit themselves and their children to his government, as being able to destroy them if they refuse; or by war subdues his enemies to his will, giving them their lives on that condition. The other is when men agree amongst themselves, to submit to some man, or assembly of men, voluntarily on confidence to be protected by him against all others. This latter may be called a political commonwealth, or commonwealth by institution; and the former a commonwealth by acquisition.

---

*Edited slightly for the modern reader.

Two other contractarian theorists from the modern period were very important to the history of political philosophy. Both influenced American political thought, especially the earlier of the two, John Locke.

Two Other Contractarian Theorists

Locke

Hobbes lived much of his life during a time of rather unpleasant turmoil, and quite reasonably thought that civil peace should be a primary objective for people. **John Locke** (1632–1704), who was born some forty or so years later, responded in his writing to a threat other than that of anarchy and chaos, namely, the threat posed by a Roman Catholic monarch in Anglican England. To avoid getting lost in the maze known as English history, let's just say that this Catholic monarch, James II, was a blunderer of the first rank who not only suspended laws against fellow Catholics but also did his best to populate higher offices with them. The end result was that English aristocrats invited the Netherlands head of state, the Protestant William of Orange, to take the throne (which, of course, he was only too happy to do). When William landed in England, James was forced to flee to France, and in 1688 the throne was offered jointly to William and his wife Mary, who, incidentally, was James's daughter.

This switch was known as the Glorious Revolution, and its relationship to Locke's writings was this: Locke wished to define a right to resistance within a theoretical framework that wouldn't at the same time undermine the state's power to govern effectively. Although Locke wrote his *Two Treatises of Government* before the Glorious Revolution, he published them in 1690 and they were regarded as the philosophical justification of the Glorious Revolution.

Profile: John Locke (1632–1704)

Locke, like Hobbes, was educated at Oxford. Though he became a lecturer there, he turned to the study of medicine and, as the physician, friend, and advisor of Lord Ashley (who later was the Earl of Shaftesbury and Lord Chancellor of the realm), Locke became an influential man of state.

When Shaftesbury, who was involved in a plot to overthrow King Charles II, was forced to leave England, Locke found himself suspected by the king of disloyalty and went into exile in Holland in 1683. Five years later, when Prince William and Princess Mary of Orange were called to the throne in the Glorious Revolution, Locke returned to England as part of the entourage of the future Queen Mary.

Locke's two most important works, *Two Treatises of Government* and *An Essay Concerning Human Understanding*, were published in 1690, by which time Locke already was a famous philosopher and respected political advisor. In his last years he withdrew from political affairs and devoted himself to religious contemplation and study of the Epistles of St. Paul.

His contributions to epistemology and political theory were of major and lasting significance, and he is recognized as an articulate advocate of natural rights and religious freedom as well as a strong opponent of the divine right of kings.

Locke's *Two Treatises of Government* were published anonymously. During his life, rumors correctly reported that Locke was the author of these works, but Locke always denied this.

Locke's treatises, and especially the *Second Treatise*, are essentially an outline of the aims and purposes of the state. They have affected democratic theory at least as much as anything else that has ever been written. At the time of the American Revolution, Locke's political thought was well known to American political leaders and had become considerably incorporated in American popular political thought as well. It had a marked impact on the contents and wording of the Declaration of Independence, the Constitution, and the Bill of Rights and has had a continued substantial impact on American political thought and political institutions to this day. All Americans are directly or indirectly influenced by John Locke.

Locke, unlike Hobbes, believed there is a natural moral law that is more than a set of practical principles for survival. According to Locke, we are all made by God and are his "property." It logically follows that we are obliged to preserve ourselves and, as far as possible, the rest of humankind. Accordingly, except for the sake of just punishment, no person may take away or impair another's "life, liberty, health, limbs or goods," or anything on which these various items may depend.

Tacit Consent

For Locke the legitimacy of the state and its governing of its citizens rests on their prior consent to its existence, authority, and power. Without that prior consent, it is a violation of a person's natural rights for the state to exercise political power over him. Because men are "by nature all free, equal and independent," he wrote, "no one can be . . . subjected to the political power of another without his consent."

It is plain, however, that most people in most states have never explicitly given their consent to be governed by the state. Do you recall ever having given such consent? Can't it therefore be argued that existing states, by having laws and punishing lawbreakers, in effect violate the natural rights of their citizens?

Locke resolves this problem by maintaining that if we accept any of the advantages of citizenship—if, for instance, we own property or rely on the police or travel on a public highway—we have given **tacit consent** to the state to make and enforce laws, and we are obliged to obey these laws. In this way Locke can maintain that states do not violate the natural rights of citizens (and others subject to their authority) by exercise of governmental authority over them even though they have never explicitly expressed their consent to that authority.

That no person may destroy or impair another's life, liberty, and property requires, according to Locke, that each person has inalienable *natural rights* and duties. They are inalienable and natural in that their existence is entailed by the fact that we our God's creations.

Locke was considerably less gloomy than Hobbes in his opinion of people and was not nearly so pessimistic about what they might do to one another in the absence of civil society (i.e., in a hypothetical "state of nature"). Nevertheless, he thought it plainly advantageous to individuals to contract among themselves to establish a state to govern them, because the state, chiefly through its laws, offers the means to protect the right to property and to ensure "the peace, safety, and public good of the people."

Thus Locke, as well as Hobbes, held that the state is created and acquires its legitimacy by an agreement or social compact on the part of its citizens and subjects. For both philosophers the purpose of the social compact is to ensure the "public good," but for Locke the purpose is also to protect natural rights. For Hobbes, each subject *gives up* his rights to the Leviathan in exchange for, or rather in hopes of obtaining, peace and security. For Locke, the subject *entrusts* his rights to the state for safeguarding.

Locke and the Right to Property

That people have a natural right to property Locke regarded as evident. Because all people are created by God and thus (as explained earlier)

According to Locke, what's yours is what you mix your labor with (subject to certain provisos mentioned in the text). But here is a problem: Just *what* is the astronaut mixing his labor with?—the entire planet? Or just with what he has walked on? Or maybe just with the sign and the ground in which it is pounded? Also, *whose* labor is involved here, only the astronaut's?

have a right to their body (their "limbs"), it follows, Locke reasoned, that they have a right to their body's labor, and thus to whatever things they "mix their labor with." That is, they have a right to these things provided that they do not already belong to or are needed to sustain someone else, and provided that they do not exceed in amount what can be used before spoiling. Because money (specie) is durable, a person may "heap up as much of it" as he can, said Locke.

Locke's theory of property implies that, *though all people equally have a right to property, they do not all have a right to equal property,* because how much property a person lawfully has will depend on his ingenuity and industriousness. Yes, Bruder and Moore are equals in the right to acquire property. But no, it doesn't follow that Bruder and Moore have a right to have equal property, in Locke's view. This distinction is important because it can go some ways toward justifying an unequal distribution of wealth.

Separation of Power

When people agree to unite themselves in a state, Locke said, they consent to entrust to it the power to make and enforce laws and punish transgressors, and they consent to submit to the will of the majority. The majority must decide for itself what form of government is best—that is, whether it (the majority) will run the government itself or will delegate its ruling power to a select few, or even to one, or will adopt yet some other arrangement. The body to which the power is delegated (or the majority itself if the power is not delegated to anyone) is the *legislative* or law-making branch of the government.

Law making is the central function of government, in Locke's opinion, for it is only through law that people are assured of equal, fair, and impartial treatment and are protected from the arbitrary exercise of power by the government.

But, Locke thought, the persons who make the laws should not themselves execute them, and so, he said, the government should have an *executive* branch as well. Further, in addition to the legislative and executive branches of government, there must, he believed, be a *federative* branch with the power to make war and peace. Though Locke believed it essential that there be a judiciary to settle disputes and fix the degree of punishment of lawbreakers, the idea that the judiciary should be a separate branch of government was not his but the influential French jurist **Montesquieu's** (1689–1755).

So Locke's political theory also contrasts sharply with Hobbes's in that, for Hobbes, political power is *surrendered* to an *executive authority*, whereas for Locke, political power is *delegated* to the *legislature*. Also, as we have seen, Locke, unlike Hobbes, called for a division of governmental authority.

Because, according to Locke, the power of the government is entrusted to it by the people of the state, the government is the *servant* of the people. Whenever in the view of the people the government acts contrarily to that trust, the people may dismiss their servant. In other words, when this violation of trust is perceived to have happened, rebellion is justified.

It is plain, then, that several basic concepts of the American democratic form of government are found in the political theory of John Locke. These include the ideas that people have natural rights that government cannot infringe on, that the government is the servant of the people and its power is entrusted to it by them, that law rather than force is the basis of the government, that the will of the people is determined by majority vote, and that the government should be divided into separate branches.

In Selection 9.4, Locke sets forth the ends of political society and government.

▶ S E L E C T I O N   9.4

From John Locke,
SECOND TREATISE OF CIVIL GOVERNMENT

CHAPTER 9: Of the Ends of Political Society and Government

123. If man in the state of Nature be so free as has been said, if he be absolute lord of his own person and possessions, equal to the greatest and subject to nobody, why will he part with his freedom, this empire, and subject himself to the dominion and control of any other power? To which it is obvious to answer, that though in the state of

Nature he hath such a right, yet the enjoyment of it is very uncertain and constantly exposed to the invasion of others; for all being kings as much as he, every man his equal, and the greater part no strict observers of equity and justice, the enjoyment of the property he has in this state is very unsafe, very insecure. This makes him willing to quit this condition which, however free, is full of fears and continual dangers; and it is not without reason that he seeks out and is willing to join in society with others who are already united, or have a mind to unite for the mutual preservation of their lives, liberties and estates, which I call by the general name—property.

124. The great and chief end, therefore, of men uniting into commonwealths, and putting themselves under government, is the preservation of their property; to which in the state of Nature there are many things wanting.

Firstly, there wants an established, settled, known law, received and allowed by common consent to be the standard of right and wrong, and the common measure to decide all controversies between them. For though the law of Nature be plain and intelligible to all rational creatures, yet men, being biased by their interest, as well as ignorant for want of study of it, are not apt to allow of it as a law binding to them in the application of it to their particular cases.

125. Secondly, in the state of Nature there wants a known and indifferent judge, with authority to determine all differences according to the established law. For every one in that state being both judge and executioner of the law of Nature, men being partial to themselves, passion and revenge is very apt to carry them too far, and with too much heat in their own cases, as well as negligence and unconcernedness, make them too remiss in other men's.

126. Thirdly, in the state of Nature there often wants power to back and support the sentence when right, and to give it due execution. They who by any injustice offended will seldom fail where they are able by force to make good their injustice. Such resistance many times makes the punishment dangerous, and frequently destructive to those who attempt it.

127. Thus mankind, notwithstanding all the privileges of the state of Nature, being but in an ill condition while they remain in it are quickly driven into society. Hence it comes to pass, that we seldom find any number of men live any time together in this state. The inconveniencies that they are therein exposed to by the irregular and uncertain exercise of the power every man has of punishing the transgressions of others, make them take sanctuary under the established laws of government, and therein seek the preservation of their property. It is this makes them so willingly give up every one his single power of punishing to be exercised by such alone as shall be appointed to it amongst them, and by such rules as the community, or those authorised by them to that purpose, shall agree on. And in this we have the original right and rise of both the legislative and executive power as well as of the governments and societies themselves.

128. For in the state of Nature to omit the liberty he has of innocent delights, a man has two powers. The first is to do whatsoever he thinks fit for the preservation of himself and others within the permission of the law of Nature; by which law, common to them all, he and all the rest of mankind are one community, make up one society distinct from all other creatures, and were it not for the corruption and viciousness of degenerate men, there would be no need of any other, no necessity that men should separate from this great and natural community, and associate into lesser combinations. The other power a man has in the state of Nature is the power to punish the crimes committed against that law. Both these he gives up when he joins in a private, if I may so call it, or particular political society, and incorporates into any commonwealth separate from the rest of mankind.

129. The first power—viz., of doing whatsoever he thought fit for the preservation of himself and the rest of mankind, he gives up to be regulated by laws made by the society, so far forth as the preservation of himself and the rest of that society shall require; which laws of the society in many things confine the liberty he had by the law of Nature.

130. Secondly, the power of punishing he wholly gives up, and engages his natural force, which he might before employ in the execution of the law of Nature, by his own single authority, as he thought fit, to assist the executive power of the society as the law thereof shall require. For being now in a new state, wherein he is to enjoy many conveniences from the labour, assistance, and society of others in the same community, as well as protection from its whole strength, he is to part also with as much of his natural liberty, in providing for himself, as the good, prosperity, and safety of the society shall require, which is not only necessary but just, since the other members of the society do the like.

131. But though men when they enter into society give up the equality, liberty, and executive power they had in the state of Nature into the hands of the society, to be so far disposed of by the legislative as the good of the society shall require, yet it being only with an intention in every one the better to preserve himself, his liberty and property (for no rational creature can be supposed to change his condition with an intention to be worse), the power of the society or legislative constituted by them can never be supposed to extend farther than the common good, but is obliged to secure every one's property by providing against those three defects above mentioned that made the state of Nature so unsafe and uneasy. And so, whoever has the legislative or supreme power of any commonwealth, is bound to govern by established standing laws, promulgated and known to the people, and not by extemporary decrees, by indifferent and upright judges, who are to decide controversies by those laws; and to employ the force of the community at home only in the execution of such laws, or abroad to prevent or redress foreign injuries and secure the community from inroads and invasion. And all this to be directed to no other end but the peace, safety, and public good of the people.

Rousseau

According to Hobbes and Locke, people are better off in the properly constituted state than they are or were in the "state of nature." Quite a different point of view was expressed by **Jean-Jacques Rousseau** (1712–1778), at least in his early political writings.

In the **state of nature,** in which there was neither state nor civilization, people were essentially innocent, good, happy, and healthy, maintained Rousseau in his *Discourse on the Origin and Foundation of the Inequality among Men* (1754). Further, in the state of nature, he said, people enjoyed perfect freedom. But with the advent of private property, this all changed. "The first man who, having enclosed a piece of ground, bethought himself of saying *This is mine,* and found people simple enough to believe him, was the real founder of civil society," which brought with it the destruction of natural liberty and which, "for the advantage of a few ambitious individuals, subjected all mankind to perpetual labor, slavery and wretchedness."

To put this in some sort of perspective, Rousseau wrote this indictment of civilization in 1754. This was fully sixty-seven years after Newton had published his *Principia.* It was two years after Benjamin Franklin, with key and kite, had proved that lightning is electricity. Thirty years earlier, Fahrenheit had devised his thermometer. Bach had been dead four years, and it had been twenty-three years since he had completed the Brandenburg Concertos, a masterpiece of mathematical reasoning expressed in music. This, in short, was the eighteenth century, the Enlightenment, the age of light, the Age of Reason. Civilization was *stuffed* with benefits. Philosophers were (as always) critical, but *this* critical? Civilization a step in retrograde? Rousseau was regarded as insane.

But Rousseau later came to think that, in the proper society, people would surrender their individual liberty for a different and more important *collective* liberty. Through a social compact a people may agree, in effect, to unite into a collective whole, called "the state" or "the sovereign," and through the state or sovereign enact laws reflective of the *general will.* An important point to be aware of here is that, for Rousseau, the state or sovereign is *an entity in its own right,* a "moral person" (as Rousseau says), a nonbiological organism that has its own life and its own *will.* Rousseau's concept of the **general will**—that is, the will of a politically united people, the will of the state—is his most important contribution to political philosophy (see the box).

If you have difficulty conceiving of a state as a person or organic entity, remember that Plato also viewed the state as an organism. Or think of a football team, which can easily be regarded as something "over and beyond" the individual players that make it up, or of a corporation, which the law regards as a person.

The general will, according to Rousseau, defines what is to the common good, and thus determines what is right and wrong and should and should not be done. And the state or sovereign (i.e., the people as a collective agent) expresses this general will by passing laws.

Profile: Jean-Jacques Rousseau (1712–1778)

> He [Rousseau] is surely the blackest and most atrocious villain, beyond comparison, that now exists in the world; and I am heartily ashamed of anything I ever wrote in his favor.   —David Hume

Rousseau—philosopher, novelist, and composer, loved many women and eventually became paranoid to the point of madness—was born a watchmaker's son in Geneva. In his early teens he was apprenticed to an engraver but ran away from his master. When he was about sixteen, he met Baroness Louise de Warens, who became his patroness and later his lover. With her he spent most of his time until he was thirty, attempting through wide reading to remedy the deficiencies in his education. In 1742, he went to Paris by himself to make his fortune, which he failed to do, with a new system of musical notation he had invented. There he became a close associate of several important literary figures of the time, including, most significantly, Denis Diderot (editor of the *Encyclopédie*, the crowning jewel of eighteenth-century rationalism). There he also met Thérèse Le Vasseur, an almost illiterate servant girl, who became his common-law wife.

In 1749, Rousseau won first prize in a contest sponsored by the Academy of Dijon, for his essay on the question: Has the progress of the sciences and art contributed to the corruption or to the improvement of human conduct? His answer, startling to the sensibilities of the French Enlightenment, was an attack on the corrupting effects of civilization and instantly made him famous. A second essay, *Discourse on the Origin and Foundation of Inequality among Men* (1754), which again portrayed the evils brought to man by civilization, was also highly controversial. Voltaire, to whom Rousseau had sent a copy of the work, thanked him for his "new book against the human race."

At this time Rousseau, disillusioned with Paris, went briefly to Geneva to regain his Genevan citizenship, but he soon returned to Paris and retired to the estate of yet another woman, one Madame d'Epinay. Always emotional, temperamental, suspicious, and unable to maintain constant friendships, however, he suspected his friends—Diderot, Mme. d'Epinay, and others—of conspiring to ruin him. He departed and became the guest of the Duc de Luxembourg, at whose chateau he finished *La Nouvelle Heloise* (1761), written under the influence of his love for (yes!) the sister-in-law of Mme. d'Epinay.

The Social Contract, and his treatise on education, *Emile*, both published the following year, were so offensive to ecclesiastic authorities that Rousseau had to leave Paris. He fled to Neuchatel and then to Bern. Finally, in 1766, he found a haven with David Hume in England. But after a year, Rousseau, who by this time had become deeply paranoid, quarreled with Hume, whom he thought was plotting against him. In fact, Hume had been trying to procure a royal pension for Rousseau. (Hume's last opinion of Rousseau is stated above.)

Rousseau now returned to France, and eventually to Paris, even though he was in danger of arrest. He was left undisturbed, however, and spent his last years copying music, wandering about reading his *Confessions* out loud, and insulting the curious throngs that came to look at him.

Still, few philosophers have had as much impact, either on political philosophy and politics or on education or literature, as Rousseau.

The General Will

Rousseau's concept of the general will is essentially the same as such familiar concepts as the "sentiment of a nation" and the "aspirations of a people." The idea is that a group of people may *collectively* or *as a group* desire or wish or want something, and that this collective desire, though it may coincide with the desires of the individuals in the group, is a metaphysically distinct entity.

Two questions about the general will, and all similar notions of a collective sentiment, are controversial to this day. First, what is it? Let's suppose, for example, that every member of a group of people believe that the federal deficit should be reduced. We may say, then, that the general will is that the federal deficit should be reduced. But can saying this possibly mean otherwise than simply that every individual in the group believes that it should be reduced? In this instance, that is, the general will seems no different from the wills of all individuals.

Let's suppose now that 60 percent of the group believes that the deficit should be reduced. If we now say that the general will is that the federal deficit should be reduced, can we mean anything other than that 60 percent believes that way? In this instance, then, the general will seems no different from the individual wills of 60 percent.

Suppose, finally, that 50 percent believes in raising taxes to reduce the federal deficit and 50 percent believes in cutting taxes to reduce the federal deficit. If we ignore the differences about how the deficit should be reduced (these, Rousseau might say, are "pluses and minuses that cancel each other") and say that the general will is that the federal deficit should be reduced, do we mean anything other than what we did in the first instance, namely, that everyone believes that it should be reduced?

Thus, if the general will is supposedly something other than the will of all or the will of the majority—which clearly is Rousseau's view because he envisions circumstances in which the majority will and the will of all may actually run counter to the general will—the question is: What is it?

And the second question is: Even granting that a group may have a general will that is distinct from the will of all and the will of the majority, how is one to determine the specific propositions it endorses? Polls and elections disclose the will of all and the will of the majority; what discloses the general will?

Further, the general will, the will of the people taken collectively, represents the *true* will of each person. Thus, insofar as the individual's actions coincide with the common will, he is acting as he "really" wants to act, and to act as you really want to act is to be free, says Rousseau. Compelling a person to accept the general will by obeying the laws of the state is *forcing him to be free,* Rousseau wrote in a famous passage. So we may lose individual or "natural" liberty when we unite to form a collective whole, but we gain this new type of "civil" liberty, "the freedom to obey a law which we prescribe for ourselves." Thus, he writes, "it is to law alone that men owe justice and [civil] liberty."

The question arises, of course, just how do we know what the general will is? Rousseau's answer: If we, the citizens, are enlightened and are not allowed to influence one another, then a majority vote determines what the general will is:

The general will is found by counting votes. When, therefore, the opinion which is contrary to my own prevails, this proves neither more nor less than that I was mistaken, and that what I thought to be the general will was not so.

Rousseau, however, distinguishes between the "will of all" and the general will. The former, Rousseau writes,

> is indeed but a sum of private wills: but remove from these same wills the pluses and minuses that cancel each other, and then the general will remains as the sum of the differences.

According to Rousseau, it makes no sense to think of either delegating or dividing the general will. Therefore, he calculated, in the state there cannot validly be a division of powers (in contrast to what Locke thought), and, though we may commission some person or persons to administer or enforce the law, these individuals act only as our *deputies*, not as our representatives.

Rousseau maintained that the citizens of the state have the right at any time to terminate the social contract. He also held that they have the right at any time to depose the officials of the state. The implication of the right of the citizenry to terminate the social contract at any time and of their right to remove officials of the state at any time is that the citizenry have a right of revolution and a right to resume anarchy at any time. Thus Rousseau is thought to have provided a philosophical justification for anarchy and revolution.

Did Rousseau also unwittingly establish a philosophical basis for totalitarianism? Some think that this is the case because he said that "the articles of the social contract [reduce] to this single point: the total alienation of each associate, and all his rights, to the whole community." If the

According to Rousseau, when you force a person to accept the general will, you are forcing him to be free.

community is regarded not just as the sum total of its members but as an entity somehow over and above the individuals in it, an entity with its own life and will that can itself do no wrong and must always be obeyed, then Rousseau's words do have an ominous ring, as does what he writes near the end of *The Social Contract* (1762):

> If any one, after he has publicly subscribed to these dogmas [which dispose a person to love his duties and be a good citizen], shall conduct himself as if he did not believe them, he is to be punished by death.

Selection 9.5 is from *The Social Contract*, which contains Rousseau's mature political philosophy.

▶ S E L E C T I O N   9.5

From Jean-Jacques Rousseau, *THE SOCIAL CONTRACT**

Chapter VI Of the Social Compact

I will suppose that men in the state of nature are arrived at that crisis when the strength of each individual is insufficient to overcome the resistance of the obstacles to his preservation. This primitive state can therefore subsist no longer; and the human race would perish unless it changed its manner of life.

As men cannot create for themselves new forces, but merely unite and direct those which already exist, the only means they can employ for their preservation is to form by aggregation an assemblage of forces that may be able to overcome the resistance, to be put in motion as one body, and to act in concert.

This assemblage of forces must be produced by the concurrence of many; but as the force and the liberty of each man are the chief instruments of his preservation, how can he engage them elsewhere without danger to himself, and without neglecting the care which is due himself? This difficulty, which leads directly to my subject, may be expressed in these words:

"Where shall we find a form of association which will defend and protect with the whole common force the person and the property of each associate, and by which every person, while uniting himself with all, shall obey only himself and remain as free as before?" Such is the fundamental problem of which the Social Contract gives the solution.

The articles of this contract are so unalterably fixed by the nature of the act that the least modification renders them vain and of no effect; so that they are the same everywhere, and are everywhere tacitly understood and admitted, even though they may never have been formally announced; until, the social compact being violated, each individual is restored to his original rights, and resumes his native liberty, while losing the conventional liberty for which he renounced it.

The articles of the social contract will, when clearly understood, be found reducible to this single point: the total alienation of each associate, and all his rights, to the whole community; for, in the first place as every individual gives himself up entirely, the condition of every person is alike; and being so, it would not be to the interest of any one to render that condition offensive to others.

Nay, more than this, the alienation being made without any reserve, the union is as complete as it can be, and no associate has any further claim to anything: for if any individual retained rights not enjoyed in general by all, as there would be no common superior to decide between him and the public, each person being in some points his own judge, would soon pretend to be so in everything; and thus would the state of nature be continued and the association necessarily become tyrannical or be annihilated.

Finally, each person gives himself to all, and so not to any one individual; and as there is no one associate over whom the same right is not acquired which is ceded to him by others, each gains an equivalent for what he loses, and finds his force increased for preserving that which he possesses.

If, therefore, we exclude from the social compact all that is not essential, we shall find it reduced to the following terms:

Each of us places in common his person and all his power under the supreme direction of the general will; and as one body we all receive each member as an indivisible part of the whole.

From that moment, instead of as many separate persons as there are contracting parties, this act of association produces a moral and collective body, composed of as many members as there are votes in the assembly, which from this act receives its unity, its common self, its life, and its will. This public person, which is thus formed by the union of all other persons, took formerly the name of "city," and now takes that of "republic" or "body politic." It is called by its members "State" when it is passive, "Sovereign" when in activity, and, whenever it is compared with other bodies of a similar kind, it is denominated "power." The associates take collectively the name of "people," and separately, that of "citizens," as participating in the sovereign authority, and of "subjects" because they are subjected to the laws of the State. . . .

Chapter VII Of the Sovereign

It appears from this formula that the act of association contains a reciprocal engagement between the public and individuals, and that each individual, contracting, as it were, with himself, is engaged under a double character; that is, as a member of the Sovereign engaging with individuals, and as a member of the State engaged with the Sovereign. But we cannot apply here the maxim of civil right, that no person is bound by any engagement which he makes with himself; for there is a material difference between an obligation to oneself individually, and an obligation to a collective body of which oneself constitutes a part.

It is necessary to observe here that public deliberation, which can bind all the subjects to the Sovereign, in consequence of the double character under which the members of that body appear, cannot, for the opposite reason, bind the Sovereign to itself; and consequently that it is against the nature of the body politic for the sovereign power to impose on itself any law which it cannot break. Being able to consider itself as acting under one character only, it is in the situation of an individual forming a contract with himself; and we see therefore that there neither is nor can be any kind of fundamental law obligatory for the body of the people, not even the social contract itself. But this does not mean that this body could not very well engage itself to others in any manner which would not derogate from the contract; for, with respect to what is external to it, it becomes a simple being, an individual. But the body politic, or the Sovereign, which derives its existence from the sacredness of the contract, can never bind itself, even towards outsiders, in anything that would derogate from the original act, such as alienating any portion of itself, or submitting to another Sovereign. To violate the contract by which it exists would be to annihilate itself; and that which is nothing can produce nothing.

As soon as this multitude is united in one body, you cannot offend one of its members without attacking the body; much less can you offend the body without incurring the resentment of all the members. Thus duty and interest equally oblige the two contracting parties to lend aid to each other; and the same men must endeavour to unite under this double character all the advantages which attend it.

Further, the Sovereign, being formed only of the individuals who compose it, neither has, nor can have, any interest contrary to theirs; consequently, the sovereign power need give no guarantee to its subjects, because it is impossible that the body should seek to injure all its members; and we shall see presently that it can do no injury to any individual in particular. The Sovereign, by its nature, is always everything it ought to be.

But this is not so with the relation of subjects towards the Sovereign, which, notwithstanding the common interest, has nothing to make them responsible for the performance of their engagements if some means is not found of ensuring their fidelity.

In fact, each individual may, as a man, have a private will, dissimilar or contrary to the general will which he has as a citizen. His own private interest may dictate to him very differently from the common interest; his absolute and naturally independent existence may make him regard what he owes to the common cause as a gratuitous contribution, the omission of which would be less injurious to others than the payment would be burdensome to himself; and considering the moral person which constitutes the State as a creature of the imagination, because it is not a man, he may wish to enjoy the rights of a citizen without being disposed to fulfil the duties of a subject. Such an injustice would in its progress cause the ruin of the body politic.

In order, therefore, to prevent the social compact from becoming an empty formula, it tacitly comprehends the engagement, which alone can give effect to the others—that whoever refuses to obey the general will shall be compelled to it by the whole body; this in fact only forces him to be free; for this is the condition which, by giving each citizen to his country, guarantees his absolute personal independence, a condition which gives motion and effect to the political machine. This alone renders all civil engagements justifiable, and without it they would be absurd, tyrannical, and subject to the most enormous abuses.

Chapter VIII Of the Civil State

The passing from the state of nature to the civil state produces in man a very remarkable change, by substituting justice for instinct in his conduct, and giving to his actions a moral character which they lacked before. It is then only that the voice of duty succeeds to physical impulse, and a sense of what is right, to the incitements of appetite. Man, who had till then regarded none but himself, perceives that he must act on other principles, and learns to consult his reason before he listens to his inclinations. Although he is deprived in this new state of many advantages which he enjoyed from nature, he gains in return others so great, his faculties so unfold themselves by being exercised, his ideas are so extended, his sentiments so exalted, and his whole mind so enlarged and refined, that if, by abusing his new condition, he did not sometimes degrade it even below that from which he emerged, he ought to bless continually the happy moment that snatched him forever from it, and transformed him from a circumscribed and stupid animal to an intelligent being and a man.

In order to draw a balance between the advantages and disadvantages attending his new situation, let us state them in such a manner that they may be easily compared. Man loses by the social contract his *natural* liberty, and an unlimited right to all which tempts him, and which he can obtain; in return he acquires *civil* liberty, and proprietorship of all he possesses. That we may not be deceived in the value of these compensations, we must distinguish natural liberty, which knows no bounds but the power of the individual, from civil liberty which is limited by the general will; and between possession, which is only the effect of force or of the right of the first occupant, from property, which must be founded on a positive title. In addition we might add to the other acquisitions of the civil state that of moral liberty, which alone renders a man master of himself; for it is *slavery* to be under the impulse of mere appetite, and *freedom* to obey a law which we prescribe for ourselves. But I have already said too much on this head, and the philosophical sense of the word "liberty" is not at present my subject.

---

*Rousseau's footnotes have been omitted.

Classic Liberalism and Marxism

We turn now to the nineteenth century, the century ushered in by Romanticism in art, music, and literature; grandiose metaphysical speculations in philosophy; and (to mention something non-European for a change) the accession of Muhammad Ali (the pasha of Egypt, not the boxer). It was the century that saw spreading industrialization and nationalism, Darwin and Freud, the Suez Canal, civil war in America, the emergence of Italy and Germany as states, and the invention of photography and the automobile. The two major political philosophies were liberalism and Marxism. They still are, for the most part.

First liberalism, then Marxism.

Mill

John Stuart Mill (1806–1873), like Locke and Rousseau, was much concerned with liberty. Mill, you'll recall from Part 3, was a utilitarian. He believed that happiness not only is good but also is *the* good, the ultimate end of all action and desire: "Actions are right in proportion as they tend to promote happiness, wrong as they tend to produce the reverse of happiness," he wrote. But remember that utilitarians are not egoists, and Mill believed that it is not *one's own* happiness that one should seek but instead the greatest amount of happiness altogether—that is, the general happiness.

Unlike Rousseau, Mill does not view a community, a society, a people, or a state as an organic entity separate and distinct from the sum of the people in it. When Mill said that one should seek the general happiness, he is not referring to the happiness of the community as some kind of organic whole. For Mill, the general happiness is just the sum total happiness of the individuals in the group.

Now Mill, following Bentham and Hume, and like Rousseau, rejected Locke's theory that people have God-given natural rights. But he maintained that the general happiness requires that all individuals enjoy personal liberty to the fullest extent consistent with the liberties of others. "The only part of the conduct of anyone, for which he is amenable to society, is that which concerns others. In the part which merely concerns himself, his independence is . . . absolute."

Liberalism (from the Latin word for "liberty") is precisely the philosophy articulated by Mill in his treatise, *On Liberty*:

> The sole end for which mankind are warranted, individually or collectively, in interfering with the liberty of action of any of their number, is . . . to prevent harm to others. His own good, either physical or moral, is not a sufficient warrant.

Mill regarded personal liberty, including freedom of thought and speech, as essential to the general happiness. It is essential, he argued, because

Utilitarianism and Natural Rights

Jeremy Bentham, as discussed in Part 3, considered the notion of natural rights nonsense, and utilitarian philosophy in general does not easily accommodate a belief in natural rights. Why? Well, consider a possible natural right, for example, the right to keep what you've honestly earned. If taking from you what you have honestly earned and distributing it to people who are poorer than you increases the sum total of happiness, utilitarianism apparently requires that we do this, despite your "natural right." Utilitarianism seems to require violating any so-called natural right if doing so increases the total happiness.

Utilitarians often attempt to accommodate our intuitions about natural rights by maintaining that in civilized society more happiness results when what are called natural rights are respected than when they are not. They say that natural rights should, in effect, be regarded as secondary rules of conduct that must be obeyed for the sake of the general happiness. In viewing natural rights as a system of moral rules productive of the general happiness, however, utilitarians do not clearly explain why such rules should not be infringed on or overridden when doing so better promotes the general happiness. It is difficult for utilitarians to provide such an explanation.

---

truth and the development of the individual's character and abilities are essential to the general happiness, and only if there is personal liberty can truth be ascertained and each individual's capacities developed. It therefore follows that an individual should enjoy unrestrained personal liberty up to the point where his activities may harm others.

Of course, it is a difficult question as to when an action may be said to harm others. Liberalism places the burden of proof on the person who claims that harm to others will be done. That the burden must be so placed is Mill's position.

The best form of government, according to Mill, is that which, among all realistic and practical alternatives, produces the greatest benefit. The form of government best suited to do this, he maintained, is representative democracy. But Mill was especially sensitive to the threat to liberty posed in democracies by the tyranny of public opinion as well as by the suppression by the majority of minority points of view. For this reason he emphasized the importance of safeguards such as proportional representation, universal suffrage, and enforcement of education by the state.

Now promoting the general happiness would seem sometimes to justify (if not explicitly to require) restrictions on personal liberty. Zoning ordinances, antitrust laws, and motorcycle helmet laws, to take modern examples, are, arguably, restrictions of this sort. Mill recognized the dilemma that potentially confronts anyone who wishes both to promote the general happiness and to protect personal liberty. His general position is this: The government should not do anything that could be done more effectively by private individuals themselves; and even if something could

Adam Smith

The most important classical liberal economic theorist was **Adam Smith** (1723–1790), a contemporary of David Hume. The basic principle of Smith's economic theory is that in a laissez-faire economy, each individual, in seeking his own gain, is led "by an invisible hand" to promote the common good, though doing so is not his intention. As an exponent of the benefits for everyone of **capitalism** (which is a system of private ownership of property and the means of production and distribution) and a **free market economy** (in which individuals may pursue their own economic interests without governmental restrictions on their freedom) Smith's thinking resembles that of some contemporary American conservatives. His *An Inquiry into the Nature and Causes of the Wealth of Nations* (1776) has become a classic in economics.

be done more effectively by the government, if the government's doing it would deprive individuals of an opportunity for development or education, the government should not do it. In short, Mill was opposed to enlarging the power of the government unnecessarily.

Here, then, is a brief selection from *On Liberty* (1859). Following that, we shall close this chapter on classical political theory by looking at the other great political philosopher of the nineteenth century, Karl Marx.

▶ S E L E C T I O N 9.6

From John Stuart Mill, ON LIBERTY

Chapter 1. Introductory

The object of this Essay is to assert one very simple principle, as entitled to govern absolutely the dealings of society with the individual in the way of compulsion and control, whether the means used be physical force in the form of legal penalties or the moral coercion of public opinion. That principle is, that the sole end for which mankind are warranted, individually or collectively, in interfering with the liberty of action of any of their number, is self-protection. That the only purpose for which power can be rightfully exercised over any member of a civilized community, against his will, is to prevent harm to others. His own good, either physical or moral, is not a sufficient warrant. He cannot rightfully be compelled to do or forbear because it will be better for him to do so, because it will make him happier, because, in the opinions of others, to do so would be wise, or even right. There are good reasons for remonstrating with him, or reasoning with him, or

The All-Male Club

In Part 3 we noted a beginning of a change in attitude toward women on the part of philosophers, first clearly articulated in the philosophy of J. S. Mill. So it is appropriate here, where we've come to Mill once again, to say something about feminism.

Feminism is organized activity on behalf of women's rights and interests. The first great feminist publication was Mary Wollstonecraft's *Vindication of the Rights of Women* in 1792.

In the nineteenth and early twentieth centuries, feminists were concerned primarily with women's suffrage in Europe and the United States, and feminism was a political movement. The focus of the feminist "movement" was political equality.

Then, with the publication of Simone de Beauvoir's *The Second Sex* (1949), in which de Beauvoir argued that woman has been the Other to man's Self, the focus of feminism began to shift to an issue perhaps more basic than equality, namely, freedom: the freedom to choose one's life work and situation as well as to make of oneself what one wills. Because women have been oppressed, they must examine and transcend the obstacles to their freedom. The women's liberation movement had begun.

Recently, feminist thinkers have been examining the historical roots and logic of what Joyce Trebilcot calls evaluative dualism—the assignment of "superiority" and "inferiority" as a justification for the "superior" exercising power over the "inferior." Thus feminist perspectives have been introduced in all areas of philosophical inquiry in which value judgments are made—in social, legal, and political philosophy; in aesthetics, philosophy of religion, ethics, and—for gender bias figures even here—in metaphysics and epistemology.

Some specific issues investigated have been the questions of woman's "nature"; women as an economic class; violence against women; gender roles; problems for women-of-color/ethnicity issues; procreative issues; friendship, love, and sexuality (between women and between women and men); war and peace; concepts of self and morality, women and religion; and sexism in aesthetic expression and artistic criticism.

Now you will probably have noticed that virtually every philosopher mentioned in this book has been male (and this book carries through to the late twentieth century!). The major figures in the history of philosophy have been males, and despite the fact that a few of them—such as Mill and his godson Bertrand Russell—were "feminists" in the very broad sense in which we defined that term, it is clear that philosophy has been dominated by a male perspective. Through recent feminist philosophy we are now beginning dimly to comprehend what that fact has meant for our civilization.

persuading him, or entreating him, but not for compelling him, or visiting him with any evil, in case he do otherwise. To justify that, the conduct from which it is desired to deter him must be calculated to produce evil to some one else. The only part of the conduct of any one, for which he is amenable to society, is that which concerns others. In the part which merely concerns himself, his independence is, of right, absolute. Over himself, over his own body and mind, the individual is sovereign.

It is, perhaps, hardly necessary to say that this doctrine is meant to apply only to human beings in the maturity of their faculties. We are not speaking of children, or of young persons below the age which the law may fix as that of manhood or womanhood. Those who are still in a state to require being taken care of by others, must be protected against their own actions as well as against external injury. For the same reason, we may leave out of consideration those backward states of society in which the race itself may be considered as in its nonage. The early difficulties in the way of spontaneous progress are so great, that there is seldom any choice of means for overcoming them; and a ruler full of the spirit of improvement is warranted in the use of any expedients that will attain an end, perhaps otherwise unattainable. Despotism is a legitimate mode of government in dealing with barbarians, provided the end be their improvement, and the means justified by actually effecting that end. Liberty, as a principle, has no application to any state of things anterior to the time when mankind have become capable of being improved by free and equal discussion. Until then there is nothing for them but implicit obedience to an Akbar or a Charlemagne, if they are so fortunate as to find one. But as soon as mankind have attained the capacity of being guided to their own improvement by conviction or persuasion (a period long since reached in all nations with whom we need here concern ourselves), compulsion, either in the direct form or in that of pains and penalties for non-compliance, is no longer admissible as a means to their own good, and justifiable only for the security of others.

It is proper to state that I forgo any advantage which could be derived to my argument from the idea of abstract right, as a thing independent of utility. I regard utility as the ultimate appeal on all ethical questions; but it must be utility in the largest sense, grounded on the permanent interests of man as a progressive being. Those interests, I contend, authorize the subjection of individual spontaneity to external control, only in respect to those actions of each, which concern the interest of other people. If any one does an act hurtful to others, there is a prima facie case for punishing him, by law, or, where legal penalties are not safely applicable, by general disapprobation. There are also many positive acts for the benefit of others, which he may rightfully be compelled to perform; such as, to give evidence in a court of justice; to bear his fair share in the common defence, or in any other joint work necessary to the interest of the society of which he enjoys the protection; and to perform certain acts of individual beneficence, such as saving a fellow creature's life, or interposing to protect the defenceless against ill-usage, things which whenever it is obviously a man's duty to do, he may rightfully be made responsible to society for not doing. A person may cause evil to others not only by his actions but by his inaction, and in either case he is justly accountable to them for the injury. The latter case, it is true, requires a much more cautious exercise of compulsion than the former. To make any one answerable for doing evil to others, is the rule; to make him answerable for not preventing evil, is comparatively speaking, the exception. Yet there are many cases clear enough and grave enough to justify that exception. In all things which regard the external relations of the individual, he is *de jure* amenable to those whose interests are concerned, and if need be, to society as their protector. There are often good reasons for not holding him to the responsibility; but these reasons must arise from the special expediencies of the case: either because it is a kind of case in which he is on the whole likely to act better, when left to his own discretion, than when controlled in any way in which society have it in their power to control him, or because the attempt to exercise control would produce other evils, greater than those which it would prevent. When such reasons as these preclude the enforcement of responsibility, the conscience of the agent himself should step into the vacant judgment-seat, and protect those interests of others which have no external protection; judging himself all the more rigidly, because the case does not admit of his being made accountable to the judgment of his fellow-creatures.

But there is a sphere of action in which society, as distinguished from the individual, has, if any, only an indirect interest; comprehending all that portion of a person's life and conduct which affects only himself, or, if it also affects others, only with their free, voluntary, and undeceived consent and participation. When I say only himself, I mean directly, and in the first instance: for whatever affects himself, may affect others *through* himself; and the objection which may be grounded on this contingency, will receive consideration in the sequel. This, then, is the appropriate region of human liberty. It comprises, first, the inward domain of consciousness, demanding liberty of conscience, in the most comprehensive sense; liberty of thought and feeling; absolute freedom of opinion and sentiment on all subjects, practical or speculative, scientific, moral, or theological. The liberty of expressing and publishing opinions may seem to fall under a different principle, since it belongs to that part of the conduct of an individual which concerns other people; but, being almost of as much importance as the liberty of thought itself, and resting in great part on the same reasons, is practically inseparable from it. Secondly, the principle requires liberty of tastes and pursuits; of framing the plan of our life to suit our own character; of doing as we like, subject to such consequences as may follow; without impediment from our fellow-creatures, so long as what we do does not harm them, even though they should think our conduct foolish, perverse, or wrong. Thirdly, from this liberty of each individual, follows the liberty, within the same limits, of combination among individuals; freedom to unite, for any purpose not involving harm to others: the persons combining being supposed to be of full age, and not forced or deceived.

No society in which these liberties are not, on the whole, respected, is free, whatever may be its form of government; and none is completely free in which they do not exist absolute and unqualified. The only freedom which deserves the name, is that of pursuing our own good in our own way, so long as we do not attempt to deprive others of theirs, or impede their efforts to obtain it. Each is the proper guardian of his own health, whether bodily, or mental and spiritual. Mankind are greater gainers by suffering each other to live as seems good to themselves, than by compelling each to live as seems good to the rest.

Marx

According to **Karl Marx** (1818–1883), philosophers have only tried to understand the world, whereas the real point is to change it. Accordingly, Marx viewed his own work not merely as an attempt to understand and interpret the world but as an effort to transform it. In fact, he did not regard his work as philosophy. So it would be wrong for us to view his writings *solely* as efforts accurately to understand or describe the human social and political condition. Marx did not himself present his understanding of social reality as the absolute and final truth. This caution must be kept in mind throughout the following discussion.

Means of Production vs. Productive Relations   For Marx, the ideal society will have no economic classes, no wages, no money, no private property, and no exploitation. Each person will not only be provided a fully adequate material existence but will also be given the opportunity to develop freely and completely his physical and mental faculties. The alienation (estrangement) of the individual from the world around will be minimal.

Furthermore, according to Marx, this type of society will ultimately arise as the result of the historical process. Here's why.

Man, Marx believed, is a social animal with physical needs, needs that are satisfied when he develops the means to satisfy them. These means of producing the satisfaction of needs are called the **means** or **forces of production.** The utilization of any one set of means of production leads to fresh needs and therefore to further means of production. For example, the invention of iron tools (a new means of production) for the cultivation of needed crops leads to still a newer need—for iron—and therewith to the means for satisfying this newer need.

Thus, human history consists of successive stages of development of various means of production.

Furthermore, the utilization of any given means of production, whether it is a simple iron tool or a complex machine, necessarily involves certain social relationships, especially those involving property. These social relationships (or, as we might say, institutions or practices) are called the **productive relations.** Thus, the social relationships (the productive relations) depend on the stage of evolution of the forces of production.

Profile: Karl Marx (1818–1883)

When one of the authors was in high school, his civics teacher stated that the four most important figures in history were (alphabetically) Einstein, Freud, Jesus Christ, and Marx. The same teacher was also the football coach, and he gave a different list to the team.

His Western bias notwithstanding, this teacher was certainly right about the preeminence of these four, especially Jesus and Marx. Of course, the followers of Marx probably outnumber even the followers of Jesus (and by a good margin). Some people, moreover, regard themselves as both Marxists and Christians.

Marx was the son of a Jewish lawyer who converted to Lutheranism despite having descended from generations of rabbis; Marx was thus raised as a Protestant. He studied at Bonn, Berlin, and Jena, first in law and then in philosophy. His Ph.D. at Jena (received when he was only twenty-three) was based on a completely ordinary dissertation on Democritus and Epicurus.

While in Berlin, Marx had come under the sway of Hegelianism and a group of radical Hegelians, but later, strongly influenced by the philosophy of Ludwig Feuerbach, he rejected idealism for materialism and his own theory of history as the outworking of economic factors.

Marx's radical views prevented him from occupying an academic post. In 1842, he became editor of a Cologne newspaper that, during his tenure, became much too radical for the authorities and was suppressed. The twenty-five-year-old Marx then went to Paris, where he mingled with many famous radicals and established another radical periodical. In Paris he also met his future collaborator, Friedrich Engels.

In about one year Marx was expelled from Paris, and from 1845 to 1848 he lived in Brussels. While there, he helped form a worker's union that, together with other similar groups, became known as the Communist League. It was for this organization that he and Engels wrote their famous and stirring *Communist Manifesto* (1848). Marx spent a brief period again in Paris and then in Cologne, participating in both the French and German revolutions of 1848. He was, however, expelled once again from both countries. In 1849, Karl Marx went to London and stayed there for the rest of his life.

In London, Marx required financial help from Engels, for, just as some men are addicted to gambling, Marx was addicted to reading and writing, and these activities did not produce much of an income. Despite Engels's help and the small amount of money he received for articles he wrote for the New York Tribune, he lived in poverty, illness, and—when his children and wife died one by one—immense sadness.

During this period Marx wrote the *Critique of Political Economy* (1859) and, more important, the work destined to become the primary document of international communism, *Capital* (vol. 1, 1867; vols. 2 and 3, edited by Engels, 1885 and 1894). In 1864, he helped create the International Workingmen's Association (the so-called First International), which he later led. The famous clash between Marx and the anarchist Mikhail Bakunin, however, led to its dissolution within about ten years. Marx died in London when he was sixty-five, of pleurisy.

Marxism and Liberalism

"Classical" liberalism and "orthodox" Marxism both drew from the Enlightenment (the eighteenth century, remember) belief that the natural order produces perfection. Both looked forward to a future of ever-increasing human freedom and happiness and placed great faith in human goodness.

To highlight some of the similarities and differences between these philosophies we'll list ten doctrines that many orthodox Marxists accept, together with comments on how a group of classical liberals might respond to them.

1. *Ideally, society should provide for human beings as much happiness, liberty, opportunity for self-development, and dignity as possible.*

   Liberals would agree to this claim, and who wouldn't? Utilitarian liberals, however, would emphasize the importance of happiness over the latter three values, or would regard the latter as a part of happiness.

2. *The only society that can provide these ends is a socialized society,* that is, one in which both ownership and production are socialized.

   Many nineteenth- (and twentieth-) century liberals would not have denied that their ultimate ethical objectives could be achieved within a socialist society, but most would have denied that socialism *alone* could accommodate these objectives. Most also thought that these objectives are more likely to be achieved within a constitutionally based representative democracy with a market economy.

3. *In nonsocialist societies the function of the state is to serve and protect the interests of the powerful.*

   Liberals maintained that in nonsocialist societies it is possible for the state to serve and protect the interests and rights of all its subjects, both strong and weak, even though few states, if any, were thought effectively to have done so.

4. *A group's interests can be protected only through exercise of its power.*

   A common liberal response is that a group's interests can be and are best protected through *law.* Marxists would say in rejoinder that, ever since Locke the "rule of law" has been slanted toward protecting property and the propertied class.

5. *Human essence is defined historically, and economic factors largely determine history.*

The forces of production at a given stage, however, develop to the point where they come into conflict with the existing social relationships, which are then destroyed and replaced by new social relationships. For example, the need at the end of the Middle Ages to supply the new markets in the Far East and the colonies in the New World required new methods of manufacture and commerce, which brought with their development societal changes incompatible with the feudal social structure of the Middle Ages.

The new social relationships then endure until new needs arise and a new stage is reached in the evolution of the forces of production.

This *dialectical process* repeats itself over and over again and is the history of man, economics, and society. To put this another way, *history is the result of man's productive activity in interplay with his social*

Liberals also emphasized the importance of economics to social history and evolution but stressed that certain fundamental human characteristics (e.g., having rights, desiring pleasure) are unalterable by history.

6. *The value of a commodity is determined by the amount of labor required for its production.*

   Liberals regarded this thesis as an oversimplification and maintained that many factors affect the value of a commodity.

7. *Capitalist societies necessarily are exploitative of a laboring class.*

   Private ownership, many liberals believed (and still do), is not inherently or necessarily exploitative, though individual capitalists may exploit their workers. Exploitation, they say, may be eliminated through appropriately formulated laws, and a society in which a great unevenness in the distribution of wealth exists may nevertheless permit equal freedom and opportunity for all.

8. *A capitalist state cannot be reformed for two reasons: (a) It is inherently exploitative. (b) True reforms are not in the interest of the ruling class, which therefore will not permit* them. *Because such a state cannot be reformed, it must be replaced.*

   Liberals thought (and still think) that through reform many states, including most capitalist states, can gradually be improved. They did not deny the appropriateness of revolutionary overthrow of dictatorships. Contemporary Marxists insist that liberal reforms in the United States are made possible through exploitation of Third World nations.

9. *The redistribution of goods through welfare, taxation, and similar means is mere tokenism serving only to pacify the exploited classes in order to protect the exploiting class from uprising and revolt.*

   Liberals thought (and still think) that measures like these, if they benefit the less well-off, are required by principles of fairness, justice, or utilitarian considerations.

10. *The philosophy of liberalism, with all its talk of fairness and justice, is merely an attempt to rationalize and legitimize capitalist oppression.*

    Liberals regard this as an *argumentum ad hominem.* Liberal claims must be evaluated on their own merits, they say.

relationships. According to Marx, this interplay accounts not only for man's socio-economic-political situation but for his morality, law, and religion, and, to a greater or lesser extent, even his philosophy and art.

Class Struggle   As already stated, according to Marx the critical social relationships involve property. With the advent of private property, society became divided into basically two classes: those with property and those without.

Hostility between the two classes was, and is, inevitable, he said. Those with property, of course, are the dominant class, and government and morality are always the instruments of the dominant class. When the forces of production create conflict with the existing social relationships, class struggle becomes acute; revolution results, and a new dominant class seizes control of the organs of state and imposes its ethic. This dialectical process repeats itself until private property and the division of society into opposed classes disappears.

Capitalism and Its Consequences   In modern capitalist societies, what has happened, according to Marx, is that the means of production are primarily concentrated in large factories and workshops in which a group of individual workers cooperatively produce a product. They collectively "mix their labor with the product," as Locke would say. But the product they mix their labor with is not owned by them. Rather, it is appropriated by the owners of the factories, who thus in effect also own the workers. Out of this circumstance comes the fundamental conflict of capitalist society: *production is socialized but ownership is not.*

Furthermore, Marx argued, the capitalist obviously must sell what his workers produce for more than he pays them to make it. The laborers thus produce goods that are worth more than their wages. This exploitation of the workers is inevitable as long as the conflict between socialized means of production and nonsocialized ownership continues. It is a necessary part of the capitalist system and is not a result of wickedness or inhumanity on the part of the capitalist.

There are two further unavoidable consequences of continuing capitalism, in Marx's opinion. First, the longer the capitalist system continues, the smaller and wealthier the possessing class becomes. This is simply the result of the fact that the surplus value of products—that's the value of a product less its "true" cost, which is the cost of the labor put into it—continues to accrue to the capitalists. Further, as smaller capitalists cannot compete, and as a result fail in their enterprise and sink into the ranks of the workers, society's wealth becomes increasingly concentrated: fewer and fewer people control more and more of it.

Alienation   The second consequence of continued capitalism, according to Marx, is the increasing alienation of the workers. The more wealth the worker produces, the poorer he becomes, relatively speaking, for it is not

Anarchism

"Every man should be his own government, his own law, his own church, a system within himself."

—Josiah Warren

"Our first work must be the annihilation of everything as it now exists."

—Mikhail Bakunin

Anarchists deny that the state is necessary for peace, justice, equality, the optimum development of human capacities, or, indeed, for any other worthwhile thing. In the nineteenth century, anarchism was the main philosophical alternative to liberalism and Marxism.

Pierre Joseph Proudhon (1809–1865), the so-called "father of anarchism," was among the first in modern times to call himself an anarchist. Proudhon believed that all authoritarian political institutions hinder human development and should be replaced by social organizations founded on the free and voluntary agreement of individuals, organizations in which no person has power over another. The existence of private property, he argued, creates social inequalities and injustice and gives rise to government; both it and government should be eliminated, though not through violent means. Communists were much influenced by Proudhon's attack on the idea of private property.

The famous Russian anarchist communists **Mikhail Bakunin** (1814–1876) and **Prince Piotr Kropotkin** (1842–1921) both emphasized the intrinsic goodness of the individual and viewed law and government as the instruments of the privileged classes and the true source of human corruption (both Bakunin and Kropotkin were aristocrats, incidentally). Kropotkin, much influenced by Charles Darwin, held that humans have a biologically grounded propensity to cooperate that will hold society together even in the absence of government. Bakunin—who, unlike Proudhon and Kropotkin, advocated the violent overthrow of all government—was active in the communist First International (see the box on Marxism and Communism). A clash between Marx and Bakunin, and more generally between Marxist communists and anarchist communists concerning the necessity of a transitional dictatorship of the proletariat, led to the demise of that organization.

The slogan, "From each according to his means, to each according to his needs," came from the anarchist communists.

---

he who retains this wealth. So the result of increased productivity for the worker is, paradoxically (but inevitably), his *devaluation* in his own eyes and in fact. He has become a mere commodity.

In addition, because the worker produces through his labor what belongs to another person, neither his labor nor the product he makes is his own. They are both as alien things that dominate him. Thus, he feels at home with himself only during his leisure time and in eating, drinking, and having sex. His presence at work is not voluntary but imposed and, whenever possible, avoided. Because he has put his life into what belongs to another, he is abject, debased, physically exhausted, and overcome with malaise. And, because the relation of man to himself "is first realized and expressed in the relationship between each man and other men," he is alienated from his fellow man.

The Inhuman Conditions

According to Marx, humans are different from other animals because only humans can produce the means of satisfying their needs; that is, they can creatively alter the environment for their own purposes. Therefore, to be fully human one must have the freedom to "objectify" oneself through creative interaction with the environment, that is, through creative labor. It follows for Marx that, because under capitalist conditions the product of one's labor is appropriated by another, a laborer does not have this freedom and cannot attain full humanness. Alienation, as discussed in the text, is what results from this unnaturalness in human relationships.

Capitalism Self-Liquidating The situation Marx describes is, in his view, self-liquidating. The capitalist system of property ownership is incompatible with the socialized conditions of production and ultimately destined to failure. Inevitable overproduction will result in economic crises, a falling rate of profit, and increased exploitation of the working class, which will increasingly become conscious of itself and its own intolerable condition, the inadequacy of capitalism, and the inevitability of history. The revolution of the proletariat (working class), leading to a dictatorship of the proletariat, will follow. In this instance, however, the overturning of the existing social order will eventually result in the classless society just described, for property, as well as the means of production, will have become socialized. The disappearance of classes will mark the end of class struggle and also, therefore, the end of political power, because the sole function of political power is the suppression of one class at the expense of another.

Selection 9.7 is from one of the most famous political documents of all time, the *Communist Manifesto*. We will begin the next chapter by considering the philosophy of a contemporary Marxist philosopher.

▶ S E L E C T I O N 9.7

From Karl Marx and Friedrich Engels, *COMMUNIST MANIFESTO**

I. Bourgeois and Proletarians

The history of all hitherto existing society is the history of class struggles.

Freeman and slave, patrician and plebian, lord and serf, guild-master and journeyman, in a word, oppressor and oppressed, stood in

Marxism and Communism

By the end of the nineteenth century most European socialist parties were committed to Marxism, but a split developed between the *revolutionists*, those who believed (as for the most part had Marx) that a violent revolution was necessary to set in place the collective ownership of the means of production and distribution of goods, and the *revisionists* or *evolutionary socialists*, those who thought that these ends could be achieved through peaceful (and piecemeal) reform.

Although evolutionary socialism became strong in Great Britain and survives in the socialist parties of many nations to the present day, the revolutionists gained ascendency in the Second International, the successor to Marx's International Workingmen's Association or the First International (though in deed, as opposed to word, the "revolutionists" were not particularly revolutionary). Under the leadership of Lenin, the revolutionist Bolsheviks came to control the Russian Social Democratic Labor party and seized control of Russia itself in the Revolution of 1917, becoming in 1918 the Communist party of the USSR.

Though the Russian Communists withdrew from the Second International and founded the Third International or Comintern in 1919 in order to gain leadership of the world socialist movement, most European Socialist parties disassociated themselves from the Communists. The term **Communism,** with a capital "C," today denotes the Marxist-Leninist ideology of the parties founded under the banner of the Comintern and is to be distinguished from small-C **communism,** which denotes any form of society in which property or other important goods are held in common by the community.

constant opposition to one another, carried on an uninterrupted, now hidden, now open fight, a fight that each time ended either in a revolutionary reconstitution of society at large or in the common ruin of the contending classes.

In the earlier epochs of history we find almost everywhere a complicated arrangement of society into various orders, a manifold gradation of social rank. In ancient Rome we have patricians, knights, plebians, slaves; in the Middle Ages, feudal lords, vassals, guildmasters, journeymen, apprentices, serfs; in almost all of these classes, again, subordinate gradations.

The modern bourgeois society that has sprouted from the ruins of feudal society has not done away with class antagonisms. It has but established new classes, new conditions of oppression, new forms of struggle in place of the old ones.

Our epoch, the epoch of the bourgeoisie, possesses, however, this distinctive feature: it has simplified the class antagonisms. Society as a whole is splitting up more and more into two great hostile camps, into two great classes directly facing each other: Bourgeoisie and Proletariat.

From the serfs of the Middle Ages sprang the chartered burghers of the earliest towns. From these burgesses the first elements of the bourgeoisie were developed.

The discovery of America, the rounding of the Cape, opened up fresh ground for the rising bourgeoisie. The East Indian and Chinese markets, the colonization of America, trade with the colonies, the increase in the means of exchange and in commodities generally, gave to commerce, to navigation, to industry, an impulse never before known, and thereby, to the revolutionary element in the tottering feudal society, a rapid development.

The feudal system of industry, under which industrial production was monopolized by closed guilds, now no longer sufficed for the growing wants of the new markets. The manufacturing system took its place. The guild-masters were pushed on one side by the manufacturing middle class; division of labor between the different corporate guilds vanished in the face of division of labor in each single workshop.

Meantime the markets kept ever growing, the demand ever rising. Even manufacture no longer sufficed. Thereupon, steam and machinery revolutionized industrial production. The place of manufacture was taken by the giant, Modern Industry, the place of the industrial middle class by industrial millionaires—the leaders of whole industrial armies, the modern bourgeois.

Modern industry has established the world market, for which the discovery of America paved the way. This market has given an immense development to commerce, to navigation, to communication by land. This development has, in its turn, reacted on the extension of industry; and in proportion as industry, commerce, navigation, railways extended, in the same proportion the bourgeoisie developed, increased its capital, and pushed into the background every class handed down from the Middle Ages.

We see, therefore, how the modern bourgeoisie is itself the product of a long course of development, of a series of revolutions in the modes of production and of exchange.

Each step in the development of the bourgeoisie was accompanied by a corresponding political advance of that class. An oppressed class under the sway of the feudal nobility, an armed and self-governing association in the medieval commune, here independent urban republic (as in Italy and Germany), there taxable "third estate" of the monarchy (as in France), afterward, in the period of manufacture proper, serving either the semi-feudal or the absolute monarchy as a counterpoise against the nobility, and, in fact, cornerstone of the great monarchies in general, the bourgeoisie has at last, since the establishment of Modern Industry and of the world market, conquered for itself, in the modern representative State, exclusive political sway. The executive of the modern State is but a committee for managing the common affairs of the whole bourgeoisie.

The bourgeoisie, historically, has played a most revolutionary part.

The bourgeoisie, wherever it has got the upper hand, has put an end to all feudal, patriarchal, idyllic relations. It has pitilessly torn asunder the motley feudal ties that bound man to his "natural superiors," and has left remaining no other nexus between man and man than naked self-interest, than callous "cash payment."....

The bourgeoisie cannot exist without constantly revolutionizing the instruments of production, and thereby the relations of production, and with them the whole relations of society....

The need of a constantly expanding market for its products chases the bourgeoisie over the whole surface of the globe. It must nestle everywhere, settle everywhere, establish connections everywhere....

In place of the old wants, satisfied by the production of the country, we find new wants, requiring for their satisfaction the products of distant lands and climes. In place of the old local and national seclusion and self-sufficiency, we have intercourse in every direction, universal interdependence of nations....

The bourgeoisie, by the rapid improvement of all instruments of production, by the immensely facilitated means of communication, draws all, even the most barbarian, nations into civilization. The cheap prices of its commodities are the heavy artillery with which it batters down all Chinese walls, with which it forces the barbarians' intensely obstinate hatred of foreigners to capitulate. It compels all nations, on pain of extinction, to adopt the bourgeois mode of production; it compels them to introduce what it calls civilization into their midst, i.e., to become bourgeois themselves. In a word, it creates a world after its own image.

The bourgeoisie has subjected the country to the rule of the towns. It has created enormous cities, has greatly increased the urban population as compared with the rural, and has thus rescued a considerable part of the population from the idiocy of rural life. Just as it has made the country dependent on the towns, so it has made barbarian and semi-barbarian countries dependent on the civilized ones, nations of peasants on nations of bourgeois, the East on the West.

The bourgeoisie keeps doing away more and more with the scattered state of the population, of the means of production, and of property. It has agglomerated population, centralized means of production, and has concentrated property in a few hands. The necessary consequence of this was political centralization....

The bourgeoisie during its rule of scarce one hundred years has created more massive and more colossal productive forces than have all preceding generations together. Subjection of nature's forces to man, machinery, application of chemistry to industry and agriculture, steam navigation, railways, electric telegraphs, clearing of whole continents for cultivation, canalization of rivers, whole populations conjured out of the ground—what earlier century had even a presentiment that such productive forces slumbered in the lap of social labor?

We see then: the means of production and of exchange, on the foundation of which the bourgeoisie built itself up, were generated in feudal society. At a certain stage in the development of these means of production and of exchange, the conditions under which feudal society produced and exchanged, the feudal organization of agriculture and manufacturing industry, in a word, the feudal relations of property became no longer compatible with the already developed productive forces; they became so many fetters. They had to be burst asunder; they were burst asunder.

Into their place stepped free competition, accompanied by a social and political constitution adapted to it and by the economic and political sway of the bourgeois class.

A similar movement is going on before our own eyes. Modern bourgeois society with its relations of production, of exchange and of property, a society that has conjured up such gigantic means of production and of exchange, is like the sorcerer who is no longer able to control the powers of the nether world whom he has called up by his spells. For many a decade past the history of industry and commerce is but the history of the revolt of modern productive forces against modern conditions of production, against the property relations that are the conditions for the existence of the bourgeoisie and of its rule. It is enough to mention the commercial crises that by their periodical return put on trial, each time more threateningly, the existence of the entire bourgeois society. In these crises a great part not only of the existing products, but also of the previously created productive forces, are periodically destroyed. In these crises there breaks out an epidemic that in all earlier epochs would have seemed an absurdity—the epidemic of over-production. Society suddenly finds itself put back into a state of momentary barbarism; it appears as if a famine, a universal war of devastation had cut off the supply of every means of subsistence; industry and commerce seem to be destroyed; and why? Because there is too much civilization, too much means of subsistence, too much industry, too much commerce. The productive forces at the disposal of society no longer tend to further the development of the conditions of bourgeois property; on the contrary, they have become too powerful for these conditions, by which they are fettered, and as soon as they overcome these fetters, they bring disorder into the whole of bourgeois society, endanger the existence of bourgeois property. The conditions of bourgeois society are too narrow to comprise the wealth created by them. And how does the bourgeoisie get over these crises? On the one hand by enforced destruction of a mass of productive forces; on the other, by the conquest of new markets and by the more thorough exploitation of the old ones. That is to say, by paving the way for more extensive and more destructive crises and by diminishing the means whereby crises are prevented.

The weapons with which the bourgeoisie felled feudalism to the ground are now turned against the bourgeoisie itself.

But not only has the bourgeoisie forged the weapons that bring death to itself; it has also called into existence the men who are to wield those weapons—the modern working class, the proletarians.

---

*The authors' footnotes have been omitted.

To help you review, here is a checklist of the key philosophers and concepts of this chapter. The brief descriptive sentences that appear with each philosopher summarize one of his leading ideas. Keep in mind that some of these summary statements represent terrific oversimplifications of complex positions.

Philosophers

- **Plato**   Held that the best or "just" state is a class-structured aristocracy ruled by "philosopher-kings."

- **Aristotle**   Held that a state is good to the degree to which it enables its citizens to achieve the good life and believed that the form of the ideal state depends on the circumstances.

- **Cicero**   Roman statesman who defined the classic Stoic position on natural law: there is only one valid law, the natural law of reason, and it holds universally.

- **St. Augustine and St. Thomas Aquinas**   Christianized the concept of natural law; were concerned with the relationship of secular law to natural law and of the state to the church. Aquinas distinguished four kinds of law; this was one of his most important contributions to political philosophy.

- **Thomas Hobbes**   Contractarian theorist who held that civil society, civil laws, and justice come into existence when people contract among themselves to transfer their power and rights to a sovereign power who compels people to live in peace and honor their agreements. Hobbes believed the transfer is "commanded" by natural law, which he held to be a set of rational principles for best ensuring self-preservation.

- **Niccolò Machiavelli**   Author of *The Prince*, which sets forth the measures by which a prince may best gain and maintain power.

- **John Locke**   Held that people have God-given natural rights and that the state is created for the protection of these rights by mutual agreement among its citizens, who entrust their rights to the state for safeguarding.

- **Charles-Louis de Secondat, baron de Montesquieu**   French jurist who held that the judiciary should be a separate branch of government.

- **Jean-Jacques Rousseau**   Another contractarian, who held that through a social compact people may agree to unite into a state and through the state to enact laws reflective of the general will. He believed that people neither give up their rights to the state nor entrust them to it, for they *are* the state.

- **John Stuart Mill**   Classical liberal theorist; held that the function of the state is to promote the general happiness (not to safeguard natural rights) and said that a person's liberty may be interfered with only to prevent harm to others.

- **Adam Smith**   Classical liberal economic theorist, exponent of capitalism and a laissez-faire economy.

- **Karl Marx**   Held that human history is a dialectical interplay between social relationships and economic productive activity that involves class warfare but ultimately leads to an ideal society lacking classes, wages, money, private property, or exploitation.

- **Pierre Joseph Proudhon**   Important anarchist; held that all social organizations must be founded on the free and voluntary agreement of individuals.

- **Mikhail Bakunin and Prince Piotr Kropotkin** Russian anarchist communists; held that law and the state are the instruments of the privileged classes. Bakunin advocated the violent overthrow of all government.

Concepts

philosopher-king

egalitarian

aristocracy

timocracy

plutocracy

democracy

tyranny

monarchy

oligarchy

polity

descriptivism

ethical naturalism

natural law political theory

eternal law

divine law

human law

Leviathan

covenant

sovereign

social contract/contractarian theory

justice/injustice in Hobbes's theory

natural rights

tacit consent

division of powers

general will

forcing someone to be free

general happiness

utilitarianism

liberalism

capitalism

laissez-faire economy

feminism

means (forces) of production

productive relations

alienation

class struggle

anarchism

proletariat

bourgeoisie

revolutionists

revisionists (evolutionary socialists)

communism

Communism

Comintern/Third International

---

1. According to Plato, the ideal state consists of three classes. What are they, what are their functions, and how is class membership determined?

2. Is the well-being of the state desirable in its own right, apart from what it contributes to the welfare of its citizens?

3. Evaluate Aristotle's idea that people who do not have the aptitude or time to participate in governance should not be citizens.

4. Explain the four types of law distinguished by Aquinas.

5. In the absence of civil authority, would anyone live up to an agreement that turns out not to be in his or her own best interest?

6. Would it be wise for people, for their own good, to transfer their collective strength to a sovereign power? Explain.

7. Why can't a covenant between the Leviathan and its subjects be made, and why is it impossible for Hobbes's Leviathan to act unjustly toward its subjects?

8. Which is better, in your view, dictatorship or anarchy? Why?

9. Why doesn't the Leviathan have the right to take your life, according to Hobbes?

10. Compare and contrast the purpose of the state and the relationship between it and its subjects for Hobbes, Locke, and Rousseau.

11. What is Locke's argument for saying that each person has inalienable natural rights?

12. Explain the concept of tacit consent.

13. "All people equally have a right to property, but they do not all have a right to equal property." Critically evaluate this claim.

14. Critically evaluate Locke's concept of private property.

15. What is the general will and how do we know what it is?

16. "The only part of the conduct of anyone, for which he is amenable to society, is that which concerns others. In the part which merely concerns himself, his independence is absolute." Critically evaluate this assertion.

17. What, for utilitarians, are "natural rights"?

18. Compare and contrast classical liberalism and orthodox Marxism.

19. What, according to Marx, are the consequences of capitalism and why are they consequences?

20. Does alienation exist? Defend your answer.

Questions for Discussion and Review

Suggested Further Readings

Julia Annas, *An Introduction to Plato's "Republic"* (Oxford: Clarendon Press, 1981). A systematic introduction to Plato's most important work.

Aristotle, *Politics*, in J. Barnes, ed., *The Complete Works of Aristotle*, vol. 2 (Princeton: Princeton University Press, 1984).

E. Barker, *The Political Thought of Plato and Aristotle* (New York: Putnam, 1906). Old but still good.

Cicero, *De re publica*, and *De legibus*, both translated by C. W. Keyes (and both London: Loeb Classical Library, 1928). See book III of each of these classic works.

E. Gilson, *The Christian Philosophy of St. Thomas Aquinas*, L. Shook, trans. (New York: Random House, 1956). See part III, ch. 1, sect. 4 for Aquinas's concept of law.

J. Locke, *The Second Treatise of Government*, Thomas P. Peardon, ed. (Indianapolis: Bobbs-Merrill, 1952). Features a short and critical introduction by the editor.

N. Machiavelli, *The Prince*, C. Detmold, trans. (New York: Airmont, 1965). Required reading for political science students as well as philosophy students.

D. McLellan, *The Thought of Karl Marx* (New York: Macmillan, 1977). Excellent analytic treatment of Marx's philosophy. For an authoritative biography of Marx, see McLellan's *Marx: His Life and Thought* (New York: Harper & Row, 1973). Finally, for Marx readings, see McLellan's *Selected Writings* (New York: Oxford University Press, 1977).

J. S. Mill, *On Liberty*, E. Rapaport, ed. (Indianapolis: Hackett, 1978). The statement of classic liberalism.

Plato, *Republic*, in E. Hamilton and H. Cairns, eds., *The Collected Dialogues of Plato* (New York: Bollingen Foundation, 1961). Plato's classic.

J. J. Rousseau, *The Social Contract*, C. Frankel, trans. and ed. (New York: Hafner, 1966). Few political philosophers are easier to read and understand than Rousseau.

F. J. E. Woodbridge, ed., *Hobbes Selections* (New York: Scribners, 1930). By this time you may wish to have a look at the complete *Leviathan*. There is a good edition by M. Oakeshott with an introduction by R. S. Peters (New York: Collier: 1962).

R. P. Wolff, *In Defense of Anarchism* (New York: Harper & Row, 1970). Also contains critiques of Rousseau and Locke.

Contemporary Theory

*The passion for freedom of the mind is strong and everlasting,
which is fortunate, because so is the passion to squelch it.*

—A. M. ROSENTHAL

*The truth, apparent to everyone whose eyes are not blinded by
dogmatism, is that men are perhaps weary of liberty. They have
had a surfeit of it.*

—BENITO MUSSOLINI

In the last chapter, we explained classical political theory, ending with
Marxism, one of the two great political philosophies of the nineteenth
century. The thought of Karl Marx has been interpreted, expanded, and
amended by his many followers, conspicuously so, of course, by the
Communist party, and today Marxism, like Christianity (as Sidney Hook
has said), is a *family* of doctrines that is continually being renewed and
revived. It is more appropriate to treat the details of the further evolution
of Marxism in a text on political history than in this summary overview
of political philosophy. Still, because Marxism has been very important
in contemporary political philosophy, we shall begin this chapter by
describing briefly the views of a contemporary Marxist. Later in the chapter we shall also discuss the philosophy of a contemporary liberal theorist.

A Contemporary Marxist: Marcuse

In the late 1960s, the most famous philosopher in the United States was
Herbert Marcuse (1898–1979). This was the era of tumultuous social and
political unrest, the era of the New Left, Vietnam protest, "people power,"
militant black and feminist disaffection, hippies, acid, four-letter words,
and Woodstock. Marcuse was in.

Marcuse in Southern California

What may sometimes be the penalty for advocating an unpopular political philosophy is illustrated by the treatment Herbert Marcuse received during his stay in Southern California in the late 1960s.

Marcuse left Germany after Hitler's rise to power and became a U.S. citizen in 1940. He obtained work for the Office of Strategic Services and the State Department and thereafter held positions at Harvard, Columbia, and Brandeis. Later, in 1965, he accepted a postretirement appointment at the University of California, San Diego, where he was a quiet but popular professor. Although he had acquired by then a worldwide reputation among leftists and radicals for his social criticism, in San Diego he was not widely known beyond the campus.

In 1968, however, it was reported in the national media that Marcuse had invited "Red Rudi" Dutschke, a notorious West German student radical, to visit him in San Diego. After this, the local populace quickly informed itself about Marcuse. The outcry against any possible Dutschke visit and against the perceived radicalism of Marcuse in that conservative naval community was vigorous and strident. In thundering editorials the *San Diego Union* denounced Marcuse and called for his ouster. Thirty-two American Legion posts in San Diego County demanded termination of his contract and offered the regents of the University of California the money to buy it out. Marcuse began receiving death threats and hate mail, and his student followers armed themselves with guns to protect him.

When his appointment neared its end in 1969, the question of reappointment arose and attracted nationwide attention. With the strong support of the faculty but in face of strenuous opposition from the *Union*, the Legion, and other powerful groups, university chancellor John McGill decided to offer Marcuse a one-year contract of reappointment. When the regents of the University of California met to discuss McGill's decision, they had to do so under the protection of the San Francisco Police Department's Tactical Force. Though a substantial number strongly dissented, the majority supported McGill. Marcuse was reappointed.

By the expiration of the reappointment contract Marcuse had passed the age of mandatory retirement. Nevertheless, he was permitted to keep his office and to teach informally.

Marcuse's reputation on the street arose from his book, *One-Dimensional Man* (1964), a Marxist-oriented appraisal of contemporary industrial society. For the New Left the book was a clear statement of deficiencies in American society.

As we have seen, it is a Marxist doctrine (or, at any rate, a doctrine of orthodox Marxists) that a disenfranchised working class is the inevitable instrument of social change. But according to Marcuse, the working class has been *integrated* into advanced capitalist society. Indeed, it has been integrated so well that it "can actually be characterized as a pillar of the establishment," he said. This integration has been effected, he believed, through the overwhelming efficiency of technology in improving the standard of living. Because today's workers share so largely in the comforts of consumer society, they are far less critical of the status quo than if they had been indoctrinated through propaganda or even brainwashed.

In fact, Marcuse said, today's workers don't merely share these comforts: they actually "*recognize themselves* in their commodities." "They find their soul in their automobile, hi-fi set, split-level home, kitchen equipment." Their needs have been determined by what are, in effect, new forms of social control, such as advertising, consumerism, the mass media, and the entertainment industry, all of which produce and enforce conformity in what people desire, think, and do.

Thus, according to Marcuse, in the West with its advanced capitalist societies the workers have lost their individual autonomy, their capacity to choose and act for themselves, to refuse and to dissent and to create. Yes, needs are satisfied, but the price the workers pay for satisfaction of need is loss of ability to think for themselves. Further, the perceived needs that are satisfied, in Marcuse's opinion, are *false* needs, needs stimulated artificially by producers to sell new products, needs whose satisfaction promotes insane wastefulness and does not lead to true fulfillment of the individual or release from domination.

Marcuse emphasized that the integration of the working class into the advanced capitalist society by the satisfaction of false needs created by advertising, television, and other does not mean that society has become classless. Despite the fact that their "needs" are satisfied, members of the working class are still in effect slaves, because they remain mere instruments of production that capitalists use for their own purposes. Further, he wrote,

> if the worker and his boss enjoy the same television program and visit the same resorts, if the typist is as attractively made up as the daughter of her employer . . . if they all read the same newspaper, then this assimilation indicates not the disappearance of classes, but the extent to which the needs and satisfactions that serve the preservation of the Establishment are shared by the underlying population.

Thus the working class in advanced capitalist societies, according to Marcuse, has been transformed from a force for radical change into a force for conservatism and the status quo.

The neutralizing of possible sources of radical social change through the integration of the working class into a one-dimensional society is visible everywhere to Marcuse. In the political sphere the one-dimensionalization of society is apparent in the unification of labor and capital against Communism in a "welfare and warfare state," in which the cold war and arms race unite all against the Communist threat while simultaneously stimulating the economy through the production of weapons.

Likewise, he said, a one-dimensional quality pervades contemporary art, language, philosophy, and science and all of contemporary culture. Thus, for example, art has lost its power to criticize, challenge, and transcend society and has been integrated as mere entertainment mass produced in paperbacks, records, and television shows. As such, art now serves to promote conformity in thought, aspiration, and deed. The same is true of philosophy and science, he believed. The elite classes can tolerate free speech simply because such conformity of thought in art, philosophy, science, and politics is present.

Thus, as Marcuse saw it, advanced capitalist society has managed to assimilate and integrate into itself the forces that oppose it and to "defeat or refute all protest in the name of the historical prospects of freedom from toil and domination." Still, at the very end of *One-Dimensional Man* Marcuse acknowledged that there is a slim chance of revolutionary change at the hands of a substratum of the outcasts of society, such as persecuted ethnic minorities and the unemployed and unemployable.

In his later thought, moreover, Marcuse perceived a weakening of the integration of the working classes into society and a growing awareness on the part of workers, students, and the middle class that consumer prosperity has been purchased at too high a price, and that a society without war, exploitation, repression, poverty, or waste is possible. The revolution that will produce this society, Marcuse said—and only through revolution can it be created, he maintained—will be born not of privation but of "disgust at the waste and excess of the so-called consumer society."

We shall see.

Selection 10.1 is from *One-Dimensional Man*.

▶ S E L E C T I O N   10.1

From Herbert Marcuse,
ONE-DIMENSIONAL MAN

Does not the threat of an atomic catastrophe which could wipe out the human race also serve to protect the very forces which perpetuate this danger? The efforts to prevent such a catastrophe overshadow the search for its potential causes in contemporary industrial society. These causes remain unidentified, unexposed, unattacked by the public because they recede before the all too obvious threat from without—to the West from the East, to the East from the West. Equally obvious is the need for being prepared, for living on the brink, for facing the challenge. We submit to the peaceful production of the means of destruction, to the perfection of waste, to being educated for a defense which deforms the defenders and that which they defend.

If we attempt to relate the causes of the danger to the way in which society is organized and organizes its members, we are immediately confronted with the fact that advanced industrial society becomes richer, bigger, and better as it perpetuates the danger. The defense structure makes life easier for a greater number of people and extends man's mastery of nature. Under these circumstances, our mass media have little difficulty in selling particular interests as those of all sensible men. The political needs of society become individual needs and aspirations, their satisfaction promotes business and the commonwealth, and the whole appears to be the very embodiment of Reason.

And yet this society is irrational as a whole. Its productivity is destructive of the free development of human needs and faculties, its peace maintained by the constant threat of war, its growth dependent on the repression of the real possibilities for pacifying the struggle for existence—individual, national, and international. This repression, so different from that which characterized the preceding, less developed stages of our society, operates today not from a position of natural and technical immaturity but rather from a position of strength. The capabilities (intellectual and material) of contemporary society are immeasurably greater than ever before—which means that the scope of society's domination over the individual is immeasurably greater than ever before. Our society distinguishes itself by conquering the centrifugal social forces with Technology rather than Terror, on the dual basis of an overwhelming efficiency and an increasing standard of living. . . .

The fact that the vast majority of the population accepts, and is made to accept, this society does not render it less irrational and less reprehensible. The distinction between true and false consciousness, real and immediate interest still is meaningful. But this distinction itself must be validated. Men must come to see it and to find their way from false to true consciousness, from their immediate to their real interest. They can do so only if they live in need of changing their way of life, of denying the positive, of refusing. It is precisely this need which the established society manages to repress to the degree to which it is capable of "delivering the goods" on an increasingly large scale, and using the scientific conquest of nature for the scientific conquest of man.

Fascism

The term *fascist* is sometimes applied today to any totalitarian state that does not pay lip service to Marxism, but it is historically more correct to regard fascism as the political philosophy of the Mussolini government in Italy from 1922 to the Allied invasion of Italy in World War II. Unlike Marxism, fascism, so regarded, is not a systematic political philosophy, but certain fundamental tenets of fascist thought do distinguish it from other sets of political beliefs.

The first tenet of fascism is that the rights of the state, as distinct from the rights of the individual, are supreme. Liberalism and Marxism both in effect regard the ultimate good as that which benefits individual people, but in fascist thought the ultimate good is that which benefits the state. The fascist state is considered an organic whole, with its own purpose and destiny, to which the interests of the individual are always

Twentieth-Century Isms

Liberalism, Communism, socialism, capitalism, fascism, conservatism—these ill-defined terms are sometimes thought to denote mutually exclusive alternative forms of government. Actually, they do not stand for parallel alternatives at all.

Liberals are not in principle wedded to any particular form of government, though many or most happen to favor some sort of representative democracy. The basic concept of **liberalism** is that each individual should have the maximum freedom consistent with the freedom of others. People who regard themselves as liberals tend to be more open to political reform than those who call themselves conservatives.

Conservatism was originally a reaction to the social and political upheaval of the French Revolution. Conservatives, as the word suggests, desire to conserve past social and political traditions and practices as representing the wisdom of a society's experience and are opposed to widespread social reform or experimentation. Even so, **Edmund Burke**, 1729–1797, the most eloquent and influential conservative writer of the eighteenth century, if not of all time, advocated many liberal and reform causes. Burke considered "society" as a contract among the dead, the living, and those to be born, and each social contract of each state but a clause in the great primeval contract of eternal society.

Contemporary American conservatism is in large measure a defense of private enterprise, laissez-faire or free-market economic policies and a narrow or strict or literal interpretation of the American Constitution. Critics charge that conservatives do not want to have individual liberty protected by the state against economic forces or exploitation, but conservatives themselves say that individual liberty is best protected by limiting the scope of government, especially in economic matters, and by dispersing its power. In emphasizing both personal freedom and free-market economics and in distrusting centralized power, modern conservatism is very similar to nineteenth-century laissez-faire liberalism.

Communists (with a capital C), as explained in an earlier box, accept the social, political, and economic ideology of the Communist party, including the idea that the dictatorship of the proletariat will come about only through revolution; **communism** (small C), on the other hand, is simply a form of economic organization in which the primary goods (usually the means of production and distribution) are held in common by a community. The definitions of **socialism** and communism are essentially the same, and Communists, of course, are advocates of communism.

Capitalism is an economic system in which ownership of the means of production and distribution is maintained primarily by private individuals and corporations. Capitalism, therefore, is an opposite to socialism and communism.

And **fascism,** as you've seen, is the totalitarian political philosophy espoused by the Mussolini government, which emphasized the absolute primacy of the state and leadership by an elite who embody the will and intelligence of the people.

subservient. Because political activity must redound to the benefit of the state rather than to the individual, the primary virtues for the citizen are service and sacrifice. True liberty, in fascism, consists not in doing what you please, but in accepting the authority of the state.

A corollary of this premise is that the state is morally unlimited by anything exterior to itself in its relationship to its citizens. The state does not exist primarily to protect the rights of its citizens, as is the case in liberal theory; on the contrary, individual citizens exist for the sake of the state. Therefore the state cannot wrong the individual by its actions. (The word *fascist* derives from the Latin *fasces*, a bundle of rods containing an ax with its blade projecting. These were carried by the attendants of the Roman magistrates and symbolized the power of the state to flog or behead any who challenged its decrees.)

A second tenet of fascism is that the destiny and ideals of the state are embodied in its leader, whose authority is, therefore, absolute, but who, in the exercise of his authority, protects the citizenry from mob rule and anarchy. (Mussolini's seizure of power in 1922 was widely condoned by wealthy landowners, industrialists, the military, the Catholic Church, and many workers as well, because he appeared able to provide protection of the social order against anarchy and communism.) The leader governs with the assistance of an elite that embodies the genius of the people and that alone has the intelligence and knowledge to understand the problems that affect the entire nation.

This elitism of fascism contrasts sharply with the egalitarianism of democracy and the rule of the proletariat under communism. (Racism and anti-Semitism, central tenets of Nazism, were not particularly espoused by Italian fascists until it became advisable to do so to please Hitler.)

A third tenet of fascism is that the Darwinian concept of survival of the fittest applies to the state. Because only the fittest state will survive, only the aggressive, self-serving state will win out in the struggle for survival. Imperialism and militarism thus become prominent features of the fascist state. Corollaries of this aggressive nationalism are the rejection of pacifism, disarmament, and "universal embraces" with neighboring nations along with glorification of the "virtues" of war to maximize human potential for the benefit of the state.

Another tenet of fascism is that the best economic system is that known as the "corporative state," in which the state has unlimited rights to intervene in the economy without owning all property and means of production outright. In Italy, the interests of landowning and monied classes were well protected, and the complaints of workers nullified or silenced, under a system of "corporations" composed of both capitalists and workers, one corporation for each branch of business or industry, that were permitted, under state leadership, to set policy for that business or industry.

Fascism asserts the power of the state to be opportunistic in its own interest as it pleases. In 1919, Mussolini stated, "We allow ourselves the luxury of being aristocratic and democratic, reactionary and revolutionary, legalistic and illegalistic, according to the circumstances of place, time and environment." Although fascism was never especially democratic except perhaps within some very small confines, this comment is otherwise true and helps explain why a list of the essential tenets of fascism is so short. The fascists were always prepared to change policies to suit their convenience.

Selection 10.2 contains some so-called "fundamental ideas" of fascism, as stated by Mussolini.

▶ S E L E C T I O N 10.2

From Benito Mussolini,
FASCISM: DOCTRINES AND INSTITUTIONS

Fascism does not, generally speaking, believe in the possibility or util-ity of perpetual peace. It therefore discards pacifism as a cloak for cowardly supine renunciation in contra-distinction to self-sacrifice. War alone keys up all human energies to their maximum tension and sets the seal of nobility on those peoples who have the courage to face it. All other tests are substitutes which never place a man face to face with himself before the alternative of life or death. Therefore, all doc-trines which postulate peace at all costs are incompatible with Fascism. Equally foreign to the spirit of Fascism, even if accepted as useful in meeting special political situations—are all internationalistic or League superstructures which, as history shows, crumble to the ground when-ever the heart of nations is deeply stirred by sentimental, idealistic or practical considerations. Fascism carries this anti-pacifistic attitude into the life of the individual. "I don't care a damn" (*[Non] me ne frego*)—the proud motto of the fighting squads scrawled by a wounded man on his bandages, is not only an act of philosophic stoicism, it sums up a doctrine which is not merely political: it is evidence of a fighting spirit which accepts all risks. . . .

Fascism [is] the resolute negation of the doctrine underlying so-called scientific and Marxian socialism, the doctrine of historic mate-rialism which would explain the history of mankind in terms of the class-struggle and by changes in the processes and instruments of pro-duction, to the exclusion of all else.

That the vicissitudes of economic life—discoveries of raw mate-rials, new technical processes, scientific inventions—have their importance, no one denies; but that they suffice to explain human history to the exclusion of other factors is absurd. Fascism believes now and always in sanctity and heroism, that is to say in acts in which no economic motive—remote or immediate—is at work. . . . Fascism also denies the immutable and irreparable character of the class strug-gle which is the natural outcome of this economic conception of his-tory; above all it denies that the class struggle is the preponderating agent in social transformations. . . .

After socialism, Fascism trains its guns on the whole block of democratic ideologies, and rejects both their premises and their prac-tical applications and implements. Fascism denies that numbers, as such, can be the determining factor in human society; it denies the right of numbers to govern by means of periodical consultations; it asserts the irremediable and fertile and beneficent inequality of men who cannot be levelled by any such mechanical and extrinsic device as universal suffrage. Democratic régimes may be described as those under which the people are, from time to time, deluded into the belief that they exercise sovereignty, while all the time real sovereignty resides in and is exercised by other and sometimes irresponsible and secret forces. Democracy is a kingless régime infested by many kings who are sometimes more exclusive, tyrannical, and destructive than one, even if he be a tyrant. . . .

The key-stone of the Fascist doctrine is its conception of the State, of its essence, its functions, and its aims. For Fascism the State is absolute, individuals and groups relative. Individuals and groups are admissable in so far as they come within the State. Instead of directing the game and guiding the material and moral progress of the community, the liberal State restricts its activities to recording results. The Fascist State is wide awake and has a will of its own. For this reason it can be described as "ethical." At the first quinquennial assembly of the régime, in 1929, I said:

"The Fascist State is not a night-watchman, solicitous only of the personal safety of the citizens; nor is it organised exclusively for the purpose of guaranteeing a certain degree of material prosperity and relatively peaceful conditions of life; a board of directors would do as much. Neither is it exclusively political, divorced from practical realities and holding itself aloof from the multifarious activities of the citizens and the nation. The State, as conceived and realised by Fascism, is a spiritual and ethical entity for securing the political, juridical, and economic organisation of the nation, an organisation which in its origin and growth is a manifestation of the spirit. The State guarantees the internal and external safety of the country, but it also safeguards and transmits the spirit of the people, elaborated down the ages in its language, its customs, its faith. The State is not only the present, it is also the past and above all the future. Transcending the individual's brief spell of life, the State stands for the immanent conscience of the nation. The forms in which it finds expression change, but the need for it remains . . .

The Fascist State lays claim to rule in the economic field no less than in others; it makes its action felt throughout the length and breadth of the country by means of its corporative, social, and educational institutions, and all the political, economic, and spiritual forces of the nation, organised in their respective associations, circulate within the State.

A State based on millions of individuals who recognize its authority, feel its action, and are ready to serve its ends is not the tyrannical state of a mediaeval lordling. . . . Far from crushing the individual, the Fascist State multiplies his energies, just as in a regiment a soldier is not diminished but multiplied by the number of his fellow soldiers. . . .

Imperial power, as understood by the Fascist doctrine, is not only territorial, or military, or commercial; it is also spiritual and ethical. An imperial nation, that is to say a nation which directly or indirectly is a leader of others, can exist without the need of conquering a single square mile of territory. Fascism sees in the imperialistic spirit—i.e.

in the tendency of nations to expand—a manifestation of their vitality. In the opposite tendency, which would limit their interests to the home country, it sees a symptom of decadence. People who rise or rearise are imperialistic; renunciation is characteristic of dying peoples. The Fascist doctrine is that best suited to the tendencies and feelings of a people which, like the Italian, after lying fallow during centuries of foreign servitude, is now reasserting itself in the world.

But imperialism implies discipline, the coordination of efforts, a deep sense of duty and a spirit of self-sacrifice. This explains many aspects of the practical activity of the régime, and the direction taken by many of the forces of the State, as also the severity which has to be exercised towards those who would oppose this spontaneous and inevitable movement of XXth century Italy by agitating outgrown ideologies of the XIXth century, ideologies rejected wherever great experiments in political and social transformations are being dared.

Never before have the peoples thirsted for authority, direction, order, as they do now.

Two Recent Analytic Political Philosophers

We turn now to the political philosophy of two contemporary American analytic philosophers. Analytic philosophy, as we have mentioned in each part of this book so far, has been the predominant tradition of philosophy in English-speaking countries during the twentieth century. Part 6 is devoted entirely to analytic philosophy.

A Contemporary Liberal: Rawls

In the opinion of many, the most important theoretical publication in political philosophy in recent years is John Rawls's *A Theory of Justice* (1971). Rawls (1921–   ) is a professor of philosophy at Harvard. The book just mentioned is his only book, though Rawls has written many journal articles.

A Theory of Justice is a lengthy and systematic attempt to establish, interpret, and illuminate the fundamental principles of justice, to apply them to various central issues in social ethics, to use them for appraising social, political, and economic institutions, and to examine their implications for duty and obligation. We'll focus our discussion on the principles themselves.

The Fundamental Requirements of the Just Society   According to Rawls, because society is typically characterized by a conflict as well as an identity of interests, it must have a set of principles for assigning basic rights and duties and for determining the appropriate distribution of the benefits and burdens of social cooperation. These are the *principles of distributive or social justice.* They specify the kinds of social cooperation that can be entered into and the forms of government that can be established. (It is here that Rawls's theory of justice intersects with traditional philosophical questions about the ethically legitimate functions and organization of the state.) For Rawls, a society (or a state) is not well ordered unless (1) its members know and accept the same principles of social justice, and (2) the basic social institutions generally satisfy and are generally known to satisfy these principles.

If a society is to be well ordered, its members must determine by rational reflection what are to be their principles of justice, says Rawls. If the principles selected are to be reasonable and justifiable, they must be selected through a procedure that is *fair.* (Hence Rawls's book is an elaboration on a 1958 paper he wrote entitled "Justice as Fairness.")

The Veil of Ignorance and the Original Position   Now if the selection of principles of justice is to be fair, the possibility of bias operating in their selection must be removed, correct? Ideally, therefore, in our selection of the principles none of us should have insider's knowledge. We should all be ignorant of one another's—and our own—wealth, status, abilities, intelligence, inclinations, aspirations, and even beliefs about goodness.

Of course, no group of people ever were or could *really* be in such a state of ignorance. Therefore, says Rawls, we must select the principles *as if* we were behind such a **veil of ignorance.** This is to ensure that nobody is advantaged or disadvantaged in the choice of principles by his or her own unique circumstances.

If from behind a veil of ignorance we were to deliberate on what principles of justice we would adopt, we would be in what Rawls calls the **original position** (or sometimes the *initial situation*). Like Locke and Rousseau's state of nature, the original position is an entirely hypothetical condition: as noted, people never were and never could be in such a condition of ignorance. Rawls's concepts of a veil of ignorance and an original position are intended "simply to make vivid to ourselves the restrictions that it seems reasonable to impose on arguments for principles of justice, and therefore on these principles themselves." Determining our principles of justice by imagining ourselves in the original position simply ensures that we do not tailor our conception of justice to our own case.

In short, according to Rawls the basic principles of justice are those to which we will agree if we are thinking rationally and in our own self-interest and eliminate irrelevant considerations. Because the basic principles of justice are those to which we will agree, Rawls's theory of justice is said to be a *contractarian* theory, as were the theories of Hobbes, Locke, and Rousseau.

The Two Principles of Social Justice   The principles we would select in the original position, if we are thinking rationally and attending to our own self-interest, are two, Rawls says.

The *first*, which takes precedence over the second when questions of priority arise, requires that *each person has an equal right to "the most extensive basic liberty compatible with a similar liberty for others."*

And the *second* requires that *social and economic inequalities be arranged "so that they are both (a) reasonably expected to be to everyone's advantage and (b) attached to positions and offices open to all."*

These two principles, writes Rawls, are a special case of a more general conception of justice to the effect that: *all social goods (e.g., liberty, opportunity, income, etc.) are to be distributed equally unless an unequal distribution is to everyone's advantage.*

We are led to this concept, Rawls writes, when we decide to find a concept of justice that "nullifies the accidents of natural endowment and the contingencies of social circumstances as counters in quest for political and economic advantage."

It follows from these principles, of course, that an unequal distribution of the various assets of society—wealth, for instance—*can* be just, as long as these inequalities are to everyone's benefit. (For example, it may be to everyone's benefit that physicians are paid more than, say, concrete workers.)

It also follows from the priority of the first principle over the second that, contrary to what utilitarian theory seems to require, someone's personal liberty *cannot* be sacrificed for the sake of the common good. Does the pleasure of owning slaves bring more happiness to the slave owners than it brings unhappiness to the slaves? If so, then the total happiness of society may well be greater with slavery than without it, and thus slavery would be to the common good and utilitarianism would require that it should be instituted. Of course, utilitarians may well maintain that slavery or other restrictions of liberties will *as a matter of fact* diminish the sum total of happiness in a society and for this reason cannot be condoned, but they must nevertheless admit that, *as a matter of principle*, violations of liberty would be justified for the sake of the happiness of the many. According to Rawls's principles, such violations for the sake of the general happiness are not justified.

The Rights of Individuals   Although Rawls does not explicitly discuss the "rights" of individuals as a major topic, his theory obviously can be interpreted as securing such rights (see, for example, Rex Martin's 1985 book, *Rawls and Rights*). Many have believed that without God talk of rights is pretty much nonsense; Rawls does not discuss God and it seems plain that he would not need to do so in order to speak meaningfully of a person's rights. Rawls in effect attempts to derive social ethics from a basis in rational self-interest rather than from God, natural law, human nature, utility, or other ground.

Why Should I Accept That?   If Rawls's theory is correct, he has spelled out in plain language the fundamental requirements of the just society. Furthermore, if his theory is correct, these are the requirements that self-interested but rational people would, on reflection, accept.

This means that Rawls's theory provides a strong answer to the person who asks of any provision entailed by one or the other of the two principles just stated, "Why should *I* accept this provision?"

Let's say, for example, that you want to know what is wrong with enslaving another person. The answer is that the wrongfulness of slavery logically follows from the two principles of social justice. But why *should you agree* to these principles? The answer is that you *would* agree to them. For they are the principles that would be selected by self-interested but rational people playing on a level playing field—one, that is, on which no one has an unfair advantage. They are the principles that would be selected by self-interested but rational people if the procedure through which they are selected is unbiased by anyone having insider's knowledge of his or her or anyone else's unique circumstances. They are, in short, the principles that self-interested but rational people would select if the procedure by which they are selected is a *fair* one.

So, then, the reason you *should* accept that slavery is wrongful is because you *would* accept the principles from which the wrongfulness of slavery logically follows.

Few philosophical works by analytic philosophers have received such widespread attention and acclaim outside the circles of professional philosophers as Rawls's *A Theory of Justice*. Though uncompromisingly analytical, it dealt with current issues of undeniable importance and interest and did so in the light of recent work in economics and the social sciences. The book was reviewed not merely in philosophical journals but in the professional literature of other disciplines and very widely in the popular press and in magazines of opinion and social commentary, and it became the focal point of numerous conferences, many of them interdisciplinary. The concern of analytic philosophers with concrete issues of morality and public policy, so visible in recent years, dates from the publication of this book. Here is a brief selection from it.

▶ S E L E C T I O N   10.3

*From John Rawls, A THEORY OF JUSTICE**

My aim is to present a conception of justice which generalizes and carries to a higher level of abstraction the familiar theory of the social contract as found, say, in Locke, Rousseau, and Kant. In order to do this we are not to think of the original contract as one to enter a particular society or to set up a particular form of government. Rather, the guiding idea is that the principles of justice for the basic structure of society are the object of the original agreement. They are the principles that free and rational persons concerned to further their own interests would accept in an initial position of equality as defining the fundamental terms of their association. These principles are to regulate all further agreements; they specify the kinds of social cooperation that can be entered into and the forms of government that can be established. This way of regarding the principles of justice I shall call justice as fairness.

Thus we are to imagine that those who engage in social cooperation choose together, in one joint act, the principles which are to assign basic rights and duties and to determine the division of social benefits.

Men are to decide in advance how they are to regulate their claims against one another and what is to be the foundation charter of their society. Just as each person must decide by rational reflection what constitutes his good, that is, the system of ends which it is rational for him to pursue, so a group of persons must decide once and for all what is to count among them as just and unjust. The choice which rational men would make in this hypothetical situation of equal liberty, assuming for the present that this choice problem has a solution, determines the principles of justice.

In justice as fairness the original position of equality corresponds to the state of nature in the traditional theory of the social contract. This original position is not, of course, thought of as an actual historical state of affairs, much less as a primitive condition of culture. It is understood as a purely hypothetical situation characterized so as to lead to a certain conception of justice. Among the essential features of this situation is that no one knows his place in society, his class position or social status, nor does any one know his fortune in the distribution of natural assets and abilities, his intelligence, strength, and the like. I shall even assume that the parties do not know their conceptions of the good or their special psychological propensities. The principles of justice are chosen behind a veil of ignorance. This ensures that no one is advantaged or disadvantaged in the choice of principles by the outcome of natural chance or the contingency of social circumstances. Since all are similarly situated and no one is able to design principles to favor his particular condition, the principles of justice are the result of a fair agreement or bargain. For given the circumstances of the original position, the symmetry of everyone's relations to each other, this initial situation is fair between individuals as moral persons, that is, as rational beings with their own ends and capable, I shall assume, of a sense of justice. The original position is, one might say, the appropriate initial status quo, and thus the fundamental agreements reached in it are fair. This explains the propriety of name "justice as fairness": it conveys the idea that the principles of justice are agreed to in an initial situation that is fair. The name does not mean that the concepts of justice and fairness are the same, any more than the phrase "poetry as metaphor" means that the concepts of poetry and metaphor are the same.

Justice as fairness begins, as I have said, with one of the most general of all choices which persons might make together, namely, with the choice of the first principles of a conception of justice which is to regulate all subsequent criticism and reform of institutions. Then, having chosen a conception of justice, we can suppose that they are to choose a constitution and a legislature to enact laws, and so on, all in accordance with the principles of justice initially agreed upon. Our social situation is just if it is such that by this sequence of hypothetical agreements we would have contracted into the general system of rules which defines it. . . .

I shall maintain . . . that the persons in the initial situation would choose two rather different principles: the first requires equality in the assignment of basic rights and duties, while the second holds that social and economic inequalities, for example inequalities of wealth and authority, are just only if they result in compensating benefits for everyone, and in particular for the least advantaged members of society. These principles rule out justifying institutions on the grounds that the hardships of some are offset by a greater good in the aggregate. It may be expedient but it is not just that some should have less in order that others may prosper. But there is no injustice in the greater benefits earned by a few provided that the situation of persons not so fortunate is thereby improved. The intuitive idea is that since everyone's well-being depends upon a scheme of cooperation without which no one could have a satisfactory life, the division of advantages should be such as to draw forth the willing cooperation of everyone taking part in it, including those less well situated. Yet this can be expected only if reasonable terms are proposed. The two principles mentioned seem to be a fair agreement on the basis of which those better endowed, or more fortunate in their social position, neither of which we can be said to deserve, could expect the willing cooperation of others when some workable scheme is a necessary condition of the welfare of all. Once we decide to look for a conception of justice that nullifies the accidents of natural endowment and the contingencies of social circumstance as counters in quest for political and economic advantage, we are led to these principles. They express the result of leaving aside those aspects of the social world that seem arbitrary from a moral point of view.

---

*Rawls's footnotes have been omitted.

Robert Nozick's Libertarianism

If any other book by an analytic philosopher attracted as much attention as *A Theory of Justice*, it was Robert Nozick's *Anarchy, State, and Utopia*, published three years later. By this time (thanks largely to Rawls) it was not unusual to find analytic philosophers speaking to "big" issues, and Nozick certainly did that.

The reaction to *Anarchy, State, and Utopia* was more mixed than that to Rawls's book, and, though many reviewers acclaimed it enthusiastically, others condemned it, often vehemently. These negative reactions are easily understandable in view of Nozick's vigorous espousal of principles of political philosophy not very popular with many contemporary liberal political theorists.

The basic question asked in *Anarchy, State, and Utopia* is, simply: Should there even be a political state, and if so, why? Nozick's answer is worked out in elaborate detail through the course of his book, but it consists essentially of three claims:

1. a minimal state, limited to the narrow functions of protection against force, theft, fraud, enforcement of contracts, and so on, is justified;
2. any more extensive state will violate persons' rights not to be forced to do certain things, and is unjustified; and
3. the minimal state is inspiring as well as right.

To each of these three claims Nozick devotes one part of his book. We won't spend time on his last claim.

A Minimal State Is Justified   The first claim, that a minimal state is justified, will seem so obvious to many as hardly to require lengthy argument. The basic idea accepted by political theorists in the liberal political tradition, from John Locke through Mill and up to and including Rawls, is that the political state, as compared with a state of anarchy or "the state of nature," "advances the good of those taking part of it" (to quote Rawls). But *does* it?

If, as Nozick believes, "individuals have rights, and there are things no person or group may do to them (without violating their rights)," then it may well be true, as anarchists believe, that "any state necessarily

Animals and Morality

One interesting side discussion in *Anarchy, State, and Utopia* concerns the moral status of animals.

Animals are not mere objects, Nozick says: the same moral constraints apply to what one may do to animals as to what one may do to people. Even a modern utilitarian, who holds that the pleasure, happiness, pain, and suffering that an action produces determines its moral worth, must count animals in moral calculations to the extent they have the capacities for these feelings, Nozick suggests.

Furthermore, he argues, utilitarianism isn't adequate as a moral theory concerning animals (or humans) to begin with. In his view, neither humans nor animals may be used or sacrificed against their will for the benefit of others; that is, neither may be treated as means (to use Kant's terminology) but only as ends. Nozick's argument for this view is a negative argument that challenges a reader to find an acceptable ethical principle that would prohibit the killing or hurting or sacrificing or eating of humans for the sake of other ends that would not equally pertain to animals. Can you think of one?

Here is a good place to mention that the question of animal rights has been widely discussed by contemporary philosophers, and the animal rights movement of recent years, which frequently makes headlines, has received strong theoretical support from several of them. Others do not think that animals have rights in the same sense in which humans have them, and they are not philosophically opposed to medical experimentation involving animals or to eating them. (As far as we know, Nozick has not been an activist in the animal rights movement.)

violates people's moral rights and hence is intrinsically immoral." In the first part of his book, Nozick considers carefully whether this anarchist belief is true. His conclusion is that it is not. To establish this conclusion, he attempts to show that a minimal state can arise by the mechanism of "an invisible hand" (see box) from a hypothetical state of nature without violating any natural rights. As intuitively plausible as Nozick's conclusion is on its face, his defense of it is controversial, and the issue turns out to be difficult.

Only the "Night-Watchman" State Doesn't Violate Rights   The main claim advanced by Nozick in the second part of his book, and by far the most controversial claim of the work as a whole, is that any state more powerful or extensive than the minimal "night-watchman" state that protects its citizens from force and fraud and like things impinges on the individual's natural rights to his or her holdings and therefore is not legitimate or justifiable. It is further a corollary to this claim that concepts of justice that mandate the distribution of assets in accordance with a formula (e.g., "to each according to his _____") or in accordance with a goal or objective (e.g., to promote the general happiness) always require re-distributing the goods of society and thus require taking from some individuals the goods that are rightfully theirs. Such concepts of justice are therefore illegitimate, according to Nozick.

Taking from the Rich and Giving to the Poor

According to Nozick's view of social justice, taking from the rich without compensation and giving to the poor is never just (assuming the rich didn't become rich through force or fraud, etc.). This would also be *Locke's* view. According to the strict *utilitarian* view, by contrast, doing so *is* just if it is to the greater good of the aggregate of people (as would be the case, for example, if through progressive taxation you removed from a rich person's income an amount that he or she would miss but little and used it to prevent ten people from starving). Finally, according to *Rawls's* view of justice, taking from the rich and giving to the poor is just if it is to the greater good of the aggregate, *provided* it does not compromise anyone's liberty (which, in the case just envisioned, it arguably would not).

Nozick's own concept of justice rests on an idea that comes naturally to many people (at least until they imagine themselves in Rawls's "initial situation" behind a "veil of ignorance" about their own assets and abilities). The idea is that *what's yours is yours:* redistributing your income or goods against your wishes for the sake of the general happiness or to achieve any other objective is unjust. Nozick defends this idea. *A person is entitled to what he or she has rightfully acquired, and justice consists in each person's retaining control over his or her rightful acquisitions.* This is Nozick's "entitlement" concept of social justice.

Nozick does not clarify or attempt to defend his entitlement concept of social justice to the extent some critics would like (he basically accepts a refined version of Locke's theory of property acquisition, according to which, you'll remember, what's yours is what you mix your labor with). Instead, he mainly seeks to show that alternative conceptions of social justice, conceptions that ignore what a person is entitled to by virtue of rightful acquisition, are defective. According to Nozick, social justice, that is, justice in the distribution of goods, is not achieved by redistributing these goods in order to achieve some objective but by permitting them to remain in the hands of those who have legitimately acquired them:

> Your being forced to contribute to another's welfare violates your rights, whereas someone else's not providing you with things you need greatly, including things essential to the protection of your rights, does not *itself* violate your rights, even though it avoids making it more difficult for someone else to violate them.

The Rights of Individuals   In the opening sentence of his book Nozick asserts that individuals have rights, and indeed his entire argument rests on that supposition, especially those many aspects that pertain to property rights. Unfortunately, Nozick's theoretical justification of the supposition is very obscure: it has something to do, evidently, with a presumed inviolability of individuals that prohibits their being used as means to ends, and perhaps also with the necessary conditions for allowing them to give meaning to their lives. If Nozick has not made his thought entirely clear in this area, he has set forth very plainly the implications for social theory, as he sees them, of assuming that natural rights exist. In addition, his work contains many interesting and provocative side discussions, including critical discussions of Marx's theory of exploitation, but we must pass over these.

Selection 10.4, from *Anarchy, State, and Utopia*, is one of these side discussions in which Nozick criticizes the "principle of fairness" defended by John Rawls and Herbert Hart.

▶ S E L E C T I O N   10.4

From Robert Nozick,
ANARCHY, STATE, AND UTOPIA

A principle suggested by Herbert Hart, which (following John Rawls) we shall call the *principle of fairness,* would be of service here if it were adequate. This principle holds that when a number of persons engage in a just, mutually advantageous, cooperative venture according to rules and thus restrain their liberty in ways necessary to yield advantages for all, those who have submitted to these restrictions have a right to similar acquiescence on the part of those who have benefited from their submission. Acceptance of benefits (even when this is not a giving of express or tacit undertaking to cooperate) is enough, according to this principle, to bind one. . . .

The principle of fairness, as we stated it following Hart and Rawls, is objectionable and unacceptable. Suppose some of the people in your neighborhood (there are 364 other adults) have found a public address system and decide to institute a system of public entertainment. They post a list of names, one for each day, yours among them. On his assigned day (one can easily switch days) a person is to run the public address system, play records over it, give news bulletins, tell amusing stories he has heard, and so on. After 138 days on which each person has done his part, your day arrives. Are you obligated to take your turn? You *have* benefited from it, occasionally opening your window to listen, enjoying some music or chuckling at someone's funny story. The other people *have* put themselves out. But must you answer the call when it is your turn to do so? As it stands, surely not. Though you benefit from the arrangement, you may know all along that 364 days of entertainment supplied by others will not be worth your giving up *one* day. You would rather not have any of it and not give up a day than have it all and spend one of your days at it. Given these preferences, how can it be that you are required to participate when your scheduled time comes? It would be nice to have philosophy readings on the radio to which one could tune in at any time, perhaps late at night when tired. But it may not be nice enough for you to want to give up one whole day of your own as a reader on the program. Whatever you want, can others create an obligation for you to do so by going ahead and starting the program themselves? In this case you can choose to forgo the benefit by not turning on the radio; in other cases the benefits may be unavoidable. If each day a different person on your street sweeps the entire street, must you do so when your time comes? Even if you don't care that much about a clean street? Must you imagine dirt as you traverse the street, so as not to benefit as a free rider? Must you refrain from turning on the radio to hear the philosophy readings? Must you mow your front lawn as often as your neighbors mow theirs?

At the very least one wants to build into the principle of fairness the condition that the benefits to a person from the actions of the others are greater than the costs to him of doing his share. . . .

If the principle of fairness were modified so as to contain this very strong condition, it still would be objectionable. The benefits might only barely be worth the costs to you of doing your share, yet others might benefit from *this* institution much more than you do; they all treasure listening to the public broadcasts. As the person least benefited by the practice, are you obligated to do an equal amount for it? Or perhaps you would prefer that all cooperated in *another* venture, limiting their conduct and making sacrifices for *it*. It is true, given that they are not following your plan (and thus limiting what other options are available to you), that the benefits of their venture *are* worth to you the costs of your cooperation. However, you do not wish to cooperate, as part of your plan to focus their attention on your alternative proposal which they have ignored or not given, in your view at least, its proper due. (You want them, for example, to read the Talmud on the radio instead of the philosophy they are reading.) By lending the institution (their institution) the support of your cooperating in it, you will only make it harder to change or alter.

On the face of it, enforcing the principle of fairness is objectionable. You may not decide to give me something, for example a book, and then grab money from me to pay for it, even if I have nothing better to spend the money on. You have, if anything, even less reason to demand payment if your activity that gives me the book also benefits you; suppose that your best way of getting exercise is by throwing books into people's houses, or that some other activity of yours thrusts books into people's houses as an unavoidable side effect. Nor are things changed if your inability to collect money or payments for the books which unavoidably spill over into others' houses makes it inadvisable or too expensive for you to carry on the activity with this side effect. One cannot, whatever one's purposes, just act so as to give people benefits and then demand (or seize) payment. Nor can a group of persons do this. If you may not charge and collect for benefits you bestow without prior agreement, you certainly may not do so for benefits whose bestowal costs you nothing, and most certainly people need not repay you for costless-to-provide benefits which yet *others* provided them. So the fact that we partially are "social products" in that we benefit from current patterns and forms created by the multitudinous actions of a long string of long-forgotten people, forms which include institutions, ways of doing things, and language (whose social nature may involve our current use depending upon Wittgensteinian matching of the speech of others), does not create in us a general floating debt which the current society can collect and use as it will.

Perhaps a modified principle of fairness can be stated which would be free from these and similar difficulties. What seems certain is that any such principle, if possible, would be so complex and involuted that one could not combine it with a special principle legitimating *enforcement* within a state of nature of the obligations that have arisen under it. Hence, even if the principle could be formulated so that it was no longer open to objection, it would not serve to obviate the need for other persons' *consenting* to cooperate and limit their own activities.

American Constitutional Theory

In closing this chapter, we want to discuss briefly American constitutional political philosophy. We'll conclude with excerpts from two recent Supreme Court decisions concerning the right to privacy and a woman's right to an abortion. The connection between this material and other topics covered in this chapter will become clear immediately.

Before the American constitution, philosophers had theorized about a social compact as the foundation of the state, but there had been only a few instances of written constitutions and these were of no lasting importance. England was the only great power that had ever had one, lasting a few months in the Cromwell period. Thus, the first significant experience with written constitutions was the American constitution.

The main trend in American political thought has been embodied in the development of theory pertaining to the Constitution. This trend relates essentially to *natural law* and *natural rights* and to the incorporation in the federal and state constitutions of a *social contract* to establish or control a political state. You now know something about the history of these concepts before the founding of the United States.

Natural Law and Rights in the Declaration of Independence

In 1776, the Declaration of Independence had proclaimed the doctrine of natural or divine law and of natural or God-given rights. The Declaration had asserted that there are "Laws of Nature and of Nature's God," and the framers had appealed "to the Supreme Judge of the World for the rectitude of our intentions." It had also asserted that it is "self-evident" that "all men are created equal, that they are endowed by their Creator with certain unalienable rights, that among these are Life, Liberty and the pursuit of happiness." The framers of the Declaration also stated that "it is the Right of the People to alter or abolish" any form of government, whenever that form of government becomes destructive of "its ends to secure" the unalienable rights with which men are endowed by their creator.

In thus proclaiming the existence of natural or divine law and of natural and God-given rights, the Declaration of Independence incorporates what had become widespread political theory in the colonies by the time of the American Revolution, prevalent among those who opposed the British king and parliament. This political theory was rooted in (1) familiarity with the writings of European political theorists, particularly British, and in (2) the constant preaching of the clergy in the colonies, who had been dominant in civil and political as well as in religious matters, that the moral code reflected divine law and should determine civil law and rights.

But as for the philosophically vexing question of who should say what natural or divine law ordains and what God-given rights are *in particular*, it was no longer generally conceded, by the time of the Declaration, that this power belonged primarily in the clergy. Instead, it was recognized that the power lies ultimately in the people and mediately in the legislative branch of government subject (some people thought) to judicial review.

Natural Law and Rights in the U.S. Constitution

The original Constitution itself, before the adoption of the Bill of Rights constituted by the first ten amendments to the Constitution, makes scant allusion to natural law or divine rights. It does so implicitly only in its preamble in stating its purpose to "establish Justice, insure domestic tranquility, provide for the common defense, promote the General Welfare, and secure the Blessings of Liberty." Although it can plausibly be argued that these purposes are those of natural law and that the "Blessings of Liberty" include natural rights, nevertheless the original Constitution was directed toward establishing law and order and not toward guaranteeing natural rights. Nor is there any explicit reference to divine law or God-given rights in the original.

Ratification of the original Constitution was attained only by assurance that a Bill of Rights would immediately be adopted by amendment, which indeed occurred when the first ten amendments were ratified on December 15, 1791. This Bill of Rights arguably limits the federal government in ways dictated by natural law and arguably guarantees rights in ways dictated by the existence of natural rights. And undoubtedly, the rights explicit (and implicit) in the Bill of Rights were regarded by the framers of the Constitution and by the American people in general as the unalienable rights to which the Declaration of Independence alluded.

Under Section 1 of the Fourteenth Amendment, ratified July 9, 1869, most of the limitations on government and guarantees of rights contained in the Bill of Rights became applicable to the states as well as to the federal government. The relationship of the authority of the states to the authority of the federal government has always been a central issue in American constitutional philosophy.

Now in *Marbury v. Madison*, decided by the Supreme Court in 1803 under Chief Justice John Marshal, and in Supreme Court cases in its wake, it became firmly established that the Supreme Court has the power under the Constitution to declare void federal and state laws that violate it. Thus, the extent to which what may in effect be called natural law and rights are incorporated in the Constitution is for the Supreme Court to determine.

The Right to Privacy

Today there is much discussion about whether or not the Constitution protects a right to "privacy." Because it is the Supreme Court that decides such things, the views of potential (and actual) members of the Supreme Court on this important question are of widespread concern to the American people. In 1987, for instance, President Ronald Reagan's nominee to the Supreme Court, Robert H. Bork, was rejected by the U.S. Senate, mainly because of Bork's views on the question of whether there is a constitutional right to privacy. The question is especially controversial because in its landmark decision in *Roe v. Wade* the Supreme Court upheld a woman's right to abortion as included within the right to privacy.

Whether or not the U.S. Constitution protects a right to privacy is perhaps not a purely philosophical question. But it bears on the larger issue of the legitimate scope and authority of the state, and that issue is a philosophical one.

Selection 10.5 is from Mr. Justice Douglas's opinion of the Court in *Griswold v. Connecticut*, 381 US 579, decided June 7, 1965, holding that a Connecticut statute making it criminal to use contraceptives was unconstitutional because it violated the right of privacy. The second selection is from Mr. Justice Blackmun's opinion of the Court in *Roe v. Wade*, 410 US 113, decided January 22, 1973, finding that the right to privacy includes a woman's right to terminate her pregnancy subject to the power of the state appropriately to regulate that right, and that until the end of the first trimester of pregnancy, the attending physician, in consultation with the woman, is free to determine, without regulation by the state, that in his or her medical judgment the woman's pregnancy should be terminated.

From Mr. Justice Douglas's opinion of the Court in GRISWOLD V. CONNECTICUT, 381 US 479, decided June 7, 1965.

The foregoing cases suggest that specific guarantees in the Bill of Rights have penumbras, formed by emanations from those guarantees that help give them life and substance. . . . Various guarantees create zones of privacy. The right of associations contained in the penumbra of the First Amendment is one, as we have seen. The Third Amendment in its prohibitions of the quartering of soldiers "in any house" in time of peace without the consent of the owner is another facet of that privacy. The Fourth Amendment explicitly affirms the "right of people to be secure in their persons, houses, papers, and effects, against unreasonable searches and seizures." The Fifth Amendment in its Self-Incrimination Clause enables the citizens to create a zone of privacy which government may not force him to surrender to his detriment. The Ninth Amendment provides: "The Enumerations in the Constitution, of certain rights, shall not be construed to deny or disparage others retained by the people." . . .

We have had many controversies over these penumbral rights of "privacy and repose." . . . These cases bear witness that the right of privacy which presses for recognition here is a legitimate one.

The present case, then, concerns a relationship lying within a zone of privacy created by several fundamental constitutional guarantees. . . . Would we allow the police to search the sacred precincts of marital bedrooms for telltale signs of the use of contraceptives? The very idea is repulsive to the notion of privacy surrounding the marriage relationship.

We deal with a right of privacy older than the Bill of Rights—older than our political parties, older than our school system.

From the dissenting opinion of Mr. Justice Black, in which Mr. Justice Stewart joined, in GRISWOLD V. CONNECTICUT.

The Court talks about a constitutional "right of privacy" as though there is some constitutional provision or provisions forbidding any law ever to be passed which might abridge the "privacy" of individuals. But there is not. There are, of course, guarantees in certain specific constitutional provisions which are designed to protect privacy at certain times and places with respect to certain activities. . . .

One of the most effective ways of diluting or expanding a constitutionally guaranteed right is to substitute for the crucial word or words of a constitutional guarantee another word or words more or less flexible and more or less restricted in meaning. This fact is well illustrated by the use of the term "right to privacy" as a comprehensive substitute for the Fourth Amendment's guaranty against "unreasonable searches and seizures." Privacy is a broad, abstract and ambiguous concept which can easily be shrunken in meaning but which can also, on the other hand, easily be interpreted as a ban against many things other than searches and seizures. . . . I like my privacy as well as the next one, but I am nevertheless compelled to admit that government has a right to invade it unless prohibited by some specific constitutional provision. For these reasons I cannot agree with the Court's judgment and the reasons it gives for holding this Connecticut law unconstitutional.

This brings me to the arguments made by my Brothers Harlan, White and Goldberg [in opinions concurring in the judgment of the Court] for invalidating the Connecticut law. Brothers Harlan and White would invalidate it by the Due Process Clause of the Fourteenth Amendment, but Brother Goldberg, while agreeing with Brother Harlan, relies also on the Ninth Amendment. . . . My disagreement with the Court's opinion . . . is a narrow one, relating to the application of the First Amendment to the facts and circumstances of this particular case. But my disagreement with Brothers Harlan, White and Goldberg is more basic. I think that if properly construed neither the Due Process Clause nor the Ninth Amendment, nor both together, could under any circumstances be a proper basis for invalidating the Connecticut law. . . .

The due process argument which my Brothers Harlan and White adopt here is based, as their opinions indicate, on the premise that this Court is vested with power to invalidate all state laws that it considers to be arbitrary, capricious, unreasonable or oppressive, or this Court's belief that a particular state law under scrutiny has no "rational or justifying" purpose, or is offensive to a "sense of fairness and justice." If these formulas based on "natural justice," or others which mean the same thing, are to prevail, they require judges to determine what is or not constitutional on the basis of their own appraisal of what laws are unwise or unnecessary. . . .

My brother Goldberg has adopted the recent discovery that the Ninth Amendment as well as the Due Process Clause can be used by this Court as authority to strike down all state legislation which this Court thinks violates "fundamental principles of liberty and justice," or is contrary to the "traditions and conscience of our people." He also states, without proof satisfactory to me, that in making decisions on this basis judges will not consider "their personal and private notions." One may ask how they can avoid considering them. . . . one would certainly have to look far beyond the language of the Ninth Amendment to find that the framers vested in this Court any such awesome veto power over law-making, either by the States or by Congress. . . . the Ninth Amendment was intended to protect against the idea that "by enumerating particular exceptions to the grant of power" to the Federal Government, "those rights which were not singled out, were intended to be assigned into the hands of the General Government [the United States], and were consequently insecure." That Amendment was passed, not to broaden the powers of this Court or any other department of "the General Government," but, as every student of history knows, to assure the people that the Constitution in all its provisions was intended to limit the Federal Government to the powers granted expressly or by necessary implications.

From Mr. Justice Blackmun's opinion of the Court in ROE V. WADE, 410 US 113, decided January 22, 1973.

The Constitution does not explicitly mention any right of privacy. In a line of decisions, however, going back as far as . . . (1891), the Court has recognized that a right of personal privacy, or a guarantee of certain areas or zones of privacy, does exist under the Constitution. In varying contexts, the Court or individual Justices have, indeed, found at least the roots of that right in the First Amendment . . . ; in the Fourth and Fifth Amendments . . . ; in the penumbras of the Bill of Rights . . . ; in the Ninth Amendment . . . ; or in the Fourteenth Amendment. These decisions make it clear that only personal rights that can be deemed "fundamental" or "implicit in the concept of ordered liberty . . . are included in this guarantee of personal privacy." They also make it clear that the right has some extensions to activities relating to marriage . . . ; procreation . . . ; contraception . . . ; family relationships . . . ; and child rearing and education. . . .

This right of privacy, whether it is founded in the Fourteenth Amendment's concept of personal liberty, as we feel it is, or, as the District Court determines, in the Ninth Amendment's reservations of rights in the people, is broad enough to encompass a woman's decision whether or not to terminate her pregnancy. . . . The Court's decisions recognizing a right of privacy also acknowledge that some state regulation in areas protected by that right is appropriate. . . . The privacy right . . . cannot be said to be absolute. In fact, it is not clear to us that the claim asserted by some amici that one has an unlimited right to do with one's body as one pleases bears a close relationship to the right of privacy previously articulated in the Court's decisions. The Court has refused to recognize an unlimited right of this kind in the past.

To help you review, here is a checklist of the key philosophers and concepts of this chapter. The brief descriptive sentences that appear with each philosopher summarize one of his leading ideas. Keep in mind that some of these summary statements represent terrific oversimplifications of complex positions.

Checklist

Philosophers

- **Herbert Marcuse**   Marxist; held that the working class has been transformed from a force for radical change into a force for preserving the status quo because of the satisfaction of false needs created by consumerism and advertising.

- **Benito Mussolini**   Italian dictator and leader of the Fascist movement.

- **Edmund Burke**   Eighteenth-century conservative political writer.

- **John Rawls**   Analytic (liberal) political philosopher; attempted to establish the fundamental principles of distributive justice through consideration of a hypothetical "original position" in which people's choice of principles is not biased by their individual unique circumstances; held that all social goods are to be distributed equally unless an unequal distribution is to everyone's advantage.

- **Robert Nozick**   Analytic (libertarian) political philosopher; held that a limited "night-watchman" state is ethically justified but that any more extensive state violates people's rights.

Concepts

false needs

fascism

fasces

socialism

conservatism

Nazism

corporative state

principles of distributive justice

veil of ignorance

original position

invisible hand mechanism

night-watchman state

entitlement concept of social justice

Bill of Rights

Marbury v. Madison

Roe v. Wade

Griswold v. Connecticut

Questions for Discussion and Review

1. Critically discuss Marcuse's theory that the needs satisfied by advanced capitalist societies are to a large extent false needs.

2. Are our needs determined by advertising, consumerism, the mass media, and the entertainment industry?

3. "A revolution will come, born of disgust at the waste and excess of consumer society." Is this very likely? Explain.

4. "The state does not exist primarily to protect the rights of its citizens; citizens exist for the sake of the state." Evaluate this claim.

5. Explain the differences among liberalism, communism, socialism, capitalism, fascism, and conservatism.

6. Is it true that a state is not "well ordered" unless both (a) its members know and accept the same principles of social justice and (b) the basic social institutions generally satisfy and are generally known to satisfy these principles? Does the United States meet these conditions?

7. Do you agree that the principles of justice stated by Rawls are those to which we will agree if we are thinking rationally and in our own self-interest and are not influenced by irrelevant considerations? Explain.

8. Can an unequal distribution of the various assets of society be just? Explain.

9. Would it be right and proper to legalize human slavery if that resulted in an increase of overall happiness of society? Why or why not?

10. "Any state necessarily violates people's moral rights and hence is intrinsically immoral." Give some reason for thinking that this is true. Then give some reasons for thinking that it is false.

11. Can you think of an ethical principle that would prohibit the killing, hurting, sacrificing, or eating of humans for the sake of other ends that would not equally pertain to animals?

12. Compare and contrast the concepts of social justice proposed by Rawls and Nozick.

13. Can you think of any justification for the principle that people have natural rights other than that proposed by Locke in the preceding chapter?

14. Is self-respect the most important good, as Rawls says?

15. In Selection 10.4, Nozick criticizes the "principle of fairness." State that principle and summarize Nozick's reasons for finding it unacceptable.

Suggested Further Readings

R. Gettell, *History of Political Thought* (New York: The Century Co., 1924). The best single-volume history of political theory available.

R. Gettell, *History of American Political Thought* (New York: The Century Co., 1928). Excellent.

H. Marcuse, *One-Dimensional Man* (Boston: Beacon Press, 1964). Marcuse's searing indictment of advanced technological societies.

R. Martin, *Rawls and Rights* (Lawrence, Kan.: University Press of Kansas, 1985). Rawls's theory of justice explained, and given an interpretation in terms of rights.

B. Mussolini, *Fascism: Doctrines and Institutions* (New York: Howard Fertig, 1968).

J. Paul, ed. *Reading Nozick: Essays on "Anarchy, State, and Utopia"* (Totowa, N.J.: Rowman & Littlefield, 1981). A collection of essays that explain and criticize Nozick's political philosophy.

J. Rawls, *A Theory of Justice* (Cambridge: Harvard University Press, 1971). An important work; very clearly written.

R. Stewart, *Readings in Social and Political Philosophy* (Oxford: Oxford University Press), 1986. An excellent anthology of classic and contemporary readings in social and political philosophy.

R. Taylor, *Freedom Anarchy, and the Law: An Introduction to Political Philosophy*, 2nd ed. (Buffalo: Prometheus Books, 1982). A general introduction to political philosophy.

SUMMARY AND CONCLUSION
Political Philosophy

To review briefly: Political philosophy began with Plato's *Republic*, in which Plato set forth his vision of the ideal state. Plato conceived the state to be an organism whose health consists in its being well ordered in a manner similar to that in which the human soul, when it is healthy, is well ordered. In the well-ordered state, according to Plato, society is divided into three classes, one of which, an aristocracy of philosopher kings, rules the state.

Aristotle, in contrast to Plato, thought that the form or structure taken by an ideal state depends on circumstances, though he insisted that a state is praiseworthy only to the extent to which it enables its citizens to achieve the good life. Neither Plato nor Aristotle thought highly of democracies, and neither considered humans to be equal either in ability or in their right to social, political, or economic privileges.

Though Aristotle, because of his naturalism, is often thought of as the father of natural law political theory, the first clear concept of natural law itself—an impersonal principle of reason that governs the universe— is found in the philosophy of the Stoics and was first applied to political philosophy by Roman legal theorists such as Cicero.

Later, the concept of natural law was Christianized in the thought of Augustine and Aquinas and other Christian thinkers. The natural law, they held, is the moral law of God as it is apprehended by people through conscience and reason. No human law that fails to accord with the natural law is valid, they said, and no state whose laws fail to accord is legitimate.

For Hobbes, the natural law is merely a set of rational principles for best preserving one's life. Following these principles, according to Hobbes, would lead people to agree or contract among themselves to transfer their rights and power to a central authority, the Leviathan, that would deliver people from the anarchy of the state of nature by forcing them to honor their commitments and to live peacefully. Hobbes was the first major exponent of social contract theory, the theory that the legitimacy of the state and its laws is derived from an initial consent of its subjects.

Locke and Rousseau also held that the legitimacy of the state and its laws is derived from the consent of its subjects, though Locke, unlike Hobbes, maintained that these subjects delegate (rather than surrender) their power to the legislature (rather than to an executive authority). Locke also emphasized that the will of the people is determined by majority rule and that the government must be divided into separate branches. For Rousseau, the people united into a collective whole that expresses the general will *is* the state, and it is not possible for the people so united either to surrender or to delegate or to divide their power, though they

371

may commission deputies to administer and enforce any laws that they enact.

The two main political philosophies of the nineteenth century were liberalism, as represented most importantly by John Stuart Mill, and Marxism. For Mill, the purpose of the state is to promote the happiness of its citizens, a goal that is achieved only when each individual has the fullest freedom compatible with the freedom of others, to think, speak, act, and otherwise develop his or her own capacities as he or she sees fit.

Marx, too, stressed the importance of individual freedom to develop one's physical and mental abilities, and maintained that the only society in which this is possible is a society in which there is no exploitation, and hence a society with no economic or social classes, no money, wages, or private property. Marx believed that the dialectical interplay between social institutions and the forces of production will result in the overthrow of capitalism by the proletariat and the eventual creation of this classless society. According to the contemporary Marxist Herbert Marcuse, however, in advanced capitalist societies the proletariat has been transformed from a force for radical social change into a pillar of conservatism by insidious new forms of social control as found in advertising and consumerism.

For part of the twentieth century, fascism was equal in importance to Marxism and liberalism. Fascism was not a systematic political philosophy, but fascist thinkers were aggressive nationalists who also believed that the interests of the state supersede the interests of its subjects and who emphasized the absolute authority of the leader of the state as one who embodies its ideals and may justifiably use any means to fulfill its destiny.

According to one of the most important liberal philosophers of recent years, John Rawls, the basic social institutions of the well-ordered state, including its constitution, must satisfy the fundamental principles of social justice. These principles, which Rawls states are those that self-interested but rational persons would choose for the role of justice if they were to make the choice in a situation in which irrelevant considerations could not influence their choice, require all social goods to be distributed equally unless an unequal distribution is to everyone's advantage, but also require, unlike utilitarian-based liberal philosophies, that personal liberty never be sacrificed for the common good.

But if personal liberty may never be sacrificed for the common good, can *any* state be morally legitimate? According to Nozick, one and only one type of state, the minimal night-watchman state, can arise without violating any individual rights. Any other state, he argues, requires a redistribution of assets and thus is not morally legitimate.

A quick check of almost any university library will show more holdings in political philosophy possibly than in all the other areas and fields of philosophy combined. Nevertheless, familiarity with what has been written in this part will be a good first step toward understanding some of the more important basic issues and concepts in political philosophy.

Philosophy of Religion

Traditional Proofs of God

It is morally necessary to assume the existence of God.

—IMMANUEL KANT

We ought not to speak about religion to children, if we wish them to possess any.

—JEAN-JACQUES ROUSSEAU

What is the difference between a theologian and a philosopher of religion? Let's back up about four steps and get a running start at the question.

If you subscribe to a religion, and the opinion polls say you most likely do, then you also accept certain purely philosophical doctrines. For example, if you believe in a nonmaterial God, then you believe that not all that exists is material, and that means you accept a metaphysics of immaterialism. If you believe that you should love your neighbor because God said you should, then you are taking sides in the debate among ethical philosophers concerning ethical naturalism. You have committed yourself to a stand against naturalism.

Your religious beliefs commit you as well to certain epistemological principles. A lot of people who make no claim to have seen, felt, tasted, smelled, or heard God still say they know that God exists. So they must maintain that you can have knowledge not gained through sense experience. To maintain this is to take sides in an important epistemological issue, as you know from Part 2.

These and many other metaphysical, ethical, and epistemological points of view and principles are assumed by and incorporated in religion, and it is the business of the philosophy of religion to understand and rationally evaluate them.

Of course, *theology*, too, seeks clear understanding and rational evaluation of the doctrines and principles found in religion, including those that are metaphysical, ethical, and epistemological. But for the most part theologians start from premises and assumptions that are themselves

The Metaphysician and the Theologian

An old saying goes that the difference between a metaphysician and a theologian is this: The metaphysician looks in a dark room for a black cat that isn't there. The theologian looks in the same place for the same thing. And finds it.

religious tenets. The philosopher of religion, in contrast, does not make religious assumptions in trying to understand and evaluate religious beliefs.

The religions of the world differ in their tenets, of course. Therefore, a philosopher of religion usually focuses on the beliefs of a specific religion or religious tradition, and in fact it is the beliefs of the Judaeo-Christian religious tradition that have received the most discussion by Western philosophers. But though philosophers of religion may focus on the beliefs of a specific religion, they will not proceed in their inquiries from the *assumption* that these beliefs are true, though they may in fact accept them as a personal matter.

What are some of the metaphysical, ethical, and epistemological beliefs of the Judaeo-Christian tradition that philosophers have sought to understand and evaluate? Many of these beliefs have to do with *God*: that He exists, that He is good, that He created the universe and is the source of all that is real, that He is a personal deity, that He is a transcendent deity, and so forth. Many have to do with *humans*: that humans were created in the image of God, that they have free will, that they can have knowledge of God's will, that the human soul is immortal, and so on. Others have to do with *features of the universe*: for example, that there are miracles, that there is supernatural reality, that there is pain and suffering (a fact thought to require reconciliation with the belief in a good and all-powerful God). And still others have to do with *language*: that religious language is intelligible and meaningful; that religious utterances are (or are not) factual assertions or are (or are not) metaphorical or analogical; that terminology used in descriptions of God means the same (or does not mean the same) as when it is used in descriptions of other things.

This is a long list of issues. To simplify things, we will concentrate here on the philosophical consideration of the Christian belief in the existence of God. Let's begin with two Christian greats, Saints Anselm and Aquinas.

Two Christian Greats

Our other chapters have started with discussions of ancient Greek philosophers. We could have begun this chapter, too, with the ancient Greeks, for many modern religious beliefs contain ideas that were discussed by, and in some cases originated with, the Greeks. But we've narrowed focus here to the philosophical consideration of the Judaeo-Christian belief in God's existence, and it is appropriate to begin with the man who was abbot of Bec and later archbishop of Canterbury.

Anselm

St. Anselm (c. 1033–1109) was among the first to evaluate the belief in the Christian God from a purely philosophical perspective, that is, from a perspective that does not make religious assumptions from the outset. Nonetheless, Anselm never entertained the slightest doubt about whether God exists. Further, he made no distinction between philosophy and theology, and he thought it impossible for anyone to reason about God or God's existence without already believing in Him.

Still, Anselm was willing to evaluate *on its own merit and independently of religious assumptions* the idea that God does *not* exist.

The Ontological Argument　This idea, that God does not exist, is attributed in Psalms 14:1 to the "fool," and Anselm thought it plain that anyone who would deny God's existence is *logically* mistaken and is indeed an utter fool. Anselm reasoned that the fool is in a self-contradictory position. The fool, Anselm thought, is in the position of saying *that he can conceive of a being greater than the greatest being conceivable.* This may sound like a new species of doubletalk, so we must consider Anselm's reasoning carefully.

Anselm began with the premise that by "God" is meant "the greatest being conceivable," or, in Anselm's exact words, "a being than which nothing greater can be conceived."

Now the fool who denies that God exists at least *understands* what he denies, said Anselm charitably. Thus God at least exists in the fool's understanding. But, Anselm noted, a being that exists both in the understanding and outside in reality is greater than a being that exists only in the understanding. (That's why people prefer real houses and cars and clothes and vacations to those they just think about.)

But this means, Anselm said, that the fool's position is absurd. For his position is that God exists only in the understanding but not in reality. So the fool's position, according to Anselm, is that "the very being, than which nothing greater can be conceived, is one, than which a greater can be conceived." And yes, this silliness is something like doubletalk; but Anselm's point is that the denial of God's existence leads to this silliness. Hence God exists: to think otherwise is to be reduced to self-contradiction and mumbo jumbo.

This line of argument, according to which it follows from the very *concept* of God that God exists, is known as the **ontological argument**. It represents Anselm's most important contribution to the philosophy of religion. If Anselm's argument is valid, if Anselm did establish that it is self-contradictory to deny that God exists and hence established that God does exist, then he did so without invoking any religious premises or

Reductio Proofs

If a claim logically entails something that is absurd, nonsensical, or just plain false, you reject the claim, correct?

For example, if the claim that the butler killed Colonel Mustard in the kitchen means that the butler was in two different places at the same time (because it is known that he was in the library at the time of the murder), then you reject the claim that the butler killed Colonel Mustard in the kitchen.

This type of proof of a claim's denial is known as *reductio ad absurdum*: by demonstrating that a claim reduces to an absurdity or just to something false, you prove the denial of the claim. By showing that claim *C* entails falsehood *F*, you prove *not-C*.

Reductios, as they are called, are encountered frequently in philosophy and in real life. Anselm's ontological argument is a **reductio proof.** Here the claim, *C*, is that

> *God doesn't exist.*

This claim, argued Anselm, entails that falsehood, *F*, that

> *the very being, than which nothing greater can be conceived, is one, than which a greater can be conceived.*

The conclusion of the argument is thus *not-C*, that

> *God does exist.*

---

making any religious presuppositions. True, he made in effect an assumption about the *concept* of God, but even a non-Christian or an atheist, he thought, must concede that what is *meant* by "God" is "the greatest being conceivable." Thus, if the argument is valid, even those who are not moved by faith or are otherwise religious must accept its conclusion. Anselm in effect argued that the proposition, "God exists," is *self-evident* and can no more be denied than can the proposition, "A square has four sides," and anyone who thinks otherwise is either a fool or just doesn't quite grasp the concept of God.

Anselm gave another version of the ontological argument that goes like this: Because God is that, than which nothing greater can be conceived, God's nonexistence is inconceivable. For anything whose nonexistence *is* conceivable is not as great as one whose nonexistence is *not* conceivable, and thus is not God.

Are you convinced? Many are not. Many regard the ontological argument in any version as a cute little play on words that proves absolutely nothing.

Gaunilon's Objection   One who found the argument unconvincing was a Benedictine monk from the Abbey of Marmontier, a contemporary of Anselm whose name was **Gaunilon.** One of Gaunilon's objections was to the first version of the argument, which, he argued, could be used to prove ridiculous things. For example, Gaunilon said, consider the most perfect island. Because it would be more perfect for an island to exist both in reality and in the understanding, the most perfect island must exist in reality, if Anselm's line of reasoning is sound. For if this island did not exist in reality, then (according to Anselm's reasoning) any island that did exist in reality would be more perfect than it; that is, would be more perfect than the most perfect island, which is impossible. In other words, Gaunilon used Anselm's reasoning to demonstrate the necessary existence of the most perfect island, implying that any pattern of reasoning that can be used to reach such an idiotic conclusion must obviously be defective.

Anselm, however, believed that his reasoning applied only to God: Because God is that than which a greater cannot be conceived, God's nonexistence is inconceivable; whereas, by contrast, the existence of islands and all other things is conceivable.

As you will see in Selection 11.1, which contains the first version of his ontological argument, Anselm was able to express his thought with elegant simplicity. You may find it a challenge to figure out what, if anything, is wrong with his reasoning.

▶ S E L E C T I O N 11.1

From St. Anselm, PROSLOGION

Lord, who gives understanding to faith give to me as much as you deem suitable, that I may understand that You are as we believe You to be, and that You are what we believe You to be. Now we believe that You are something than which nothing greater can be thought. But perhaps there is no such nature since "the fool hath said in his heart: There is no God?" But surely this very same fool, when he hears what I say: "something than which nothing greater can be thought," understands what he hears, and what he understands is in his mind, even if he does not understand that it exists. For it is one thing for a thing to be in the mind, but something else to understand that a thing exists. For when a painter pre-thinks what is about to be made, he has it in mind but he does not yet understand that it exists because he has not yet made it. But when he has already painted it, he both has it in his mind and also understands that it exists because he has already made it. Hence, even the fool is convinced that something exists in the mind than which nothing greater can be thought, because when he hears this he understands and whatever is understood is in the mind. But surely that than which a greater cannot be thought cannot exist merely in the mind. For if it exists merely in the mind, it can be thought to exist also in reality which is greater. So if that than which a greater cannot be thought exists merely in the mind, that very same thing than which a greater cannot be thought is something than which a greater can be thought. But surely this cannot be. Hence, without doubt, something than which a greater cannot be thought exists both in the mind and in reality.

Indeed, it exists so truly that it cannot be thought not to be. For something can be thought to exist which cannot be thought not to exist, which is greater than what can be thought not to exist. So, if that than which a greater cannot be thought can be thought not to exist, that very thing than which a greater cannot be thought, is not that than which a greater cannot be thought; which is impossible. So there exists so truly something than which a greater cannot be thought that it cannot be thought not to exist.

You are that very thing, Lord our God.

Aquinas

About a century and a half after Anselm died, **St. Thomas Aquinas** (c. 1225–1274), whom we discussed in earlier chapters, interpreted Aristotelean philosophy from a Christian perspective. Aristotle, as we've had occasion to mention before, emphasized the importance to philosophy of direct observation of nature. In keeping with his empiricist, Aristotelean leanings, Aquinas regarded the ontological argument as invalid. You cannot prove that God exists, he said, merely by considering the word *God*, as the ontological argument in effect supposes. For that strategy to work, you would have to presume to know God's essence. The proposition, "God exists," he said, unlike "A square has four sides," is not self-evident to us mere mortals. Although you can prove God's existence in several ways, he asserted, you cannot do it just by examining the concept of God. You have to consider what it is about nature that makes it manifest that it requires God as its original cause.

The ways in which the existence of God can be proved are in fact five, according to Aquinas. Although Aquinas's theological and philosophical writings fill many volumes and cover a vast range of topics, he is most famous for his "Five Ways" (but some philosophers—e.g., Richard Swinburne, discussed later—don't regard Aquinas's proofs of God as his best philosophy).

It would be surprising if you were not already familiar with one or another of Aquinas's Five Ways in some version or other.

The First Way   The *first way* to prove that God exists, according to Aquinas, is to consider the fact that natural things are in motion. As we look around the world and survey moving things, it becomes clear that they didn't put themselves into motion. But if every moving thing were moved by another moving thing, then there would be no first mover; if no first mover exists, there would be no other mover, and nothing would be in motion. Because things are in motion, a first mover must therefore exist that is moved by no other, and this, of course, is God.

We should note here that Aquinas is usually understood as meaning something quite broad by "motion"—something more like *change in general*—and as including under the concept of movement the coming into and passing out of existence. Thus, when he says that things don't put

Profile: St. Thomas Aquinas (1225–1274)

It is time we gave a little background information on Thomas Aquinas, the Angelic Doctor, one of the most important of Roman Catholic saints.

Aquinas, the son of a count of Aquino, studied for many years with Albertus Magnus (i.e., "Albert the Great"). Albertus, who had the unusual idea that Christian thinkers should be knowledgeable about philosophy and science, wished to make all of Aristotle's writings available in Latin. His fondness for Aristotle was a strong influence on his pupil, Aquinas.

Aquinas eventually received his doctorate from the University of Paris in his late twenties and soon acquired a substantial reputation as a scholar. For ten years in his thirties and early forties he was a professor for the Papal Court and lectured in and about Rome.

Now, the thirteenth century was a time of considerable intellectual controversy between the Platonists and the Aristoteleans. Some theologians believed that the teachings of Aristotle could not be harmonized with Christian doctrines. This belief was in part a reaction to Averroes (1126–1198), an absolutely brilliant Arabian philosopher, and his followers, whose philosophy was built entirely around the thought of Aristotle. The Averroist philosophy conflicted with Church doctrine on creation and personal immortality, making Aristotle odious to some Christian theologians.

But Aquinas was no Averroist and defended his own version of Aristotle with inexorable logic. He returned to Paris in 1268 and became involved in a famous doctrinal struggle with the Averroists, which he won. Although some factions within the Church voiced strong opposition to his philosophy, opposition that lasted for many years after his death, slowly but surely Aquinas's thinking became the dominant system of Christian thought. He was canonized in 1323 and made a Doctor of the Church in 1567.

Aquinas was a stout fellow, slow and deliberate in manner. He was thus nicknamed the Dumb Ox. But he was a brilliant and forceful thinker and his writings fill many volumes and cover a vast array of theological and philosophical topics. His most famous works are the *Summa Contra Gentiles* (1258–1260) and the *Summa Theologica* (1267–1273), a systematic theology grounded on philosophical principles. He was, in addition, a most humane and charitable man.

In 1879, Pope Leo XIII declared Aquinas's system to be the official Catholic philosophy.

themselves into motion, don't suppose that he thought that you can't get up out of your chair and walk across the room. He means that things don't just bring themselves into existence.

The Second Way Aquinas's *second way* of proving God's existence is very similar to the first. In the world of sensible things nothing causes

itself. But if everything were caused by something else, then there would
be no first cause, and if no first cause exists, there would be no first effect.
In fact, there would be no second, third, or fourth effect, either: if no first
cause exists, there would be no effects, period. So we must admit a first
cause, to wit, God.

Note that Aquinas did not say anything in either of the first two proofs
about things being moved or caused by *earlier* motions or causes. The various motions and causes he is talking about are simultaneous in time. His
argument is not the common one you hear that things must be caused by
something earlier, which must be caused by something earlier, and so on,
and that because this chain of causes cannot go back infinitely there must
be a first cause, God. In Aquinas's opinion, there is no philosophical reason
that the chain of causes could not go back infinitely. But there cannot be an
infinite series of *simultaneous* causes or movers, he thought.

The Third Way   Aquinas's *third way* is easily the most complicated of
the five ways. Many consider it his finest proof, though Aquinas himself
seemed to prefer the first.

Many paraphrasings of the third proof are not faithful to what Aquinas actually said, which is essentially this:

In nature some things are such that it is possible for them not to exist.
Indeed, everything you can lay your hands on belongs to this "need-not-
exist" category: whatever it is, despite the fact that it does exist, it need
not have existed.

Now that which need not exist, said Aquinas, at some time did not
exist. Therefore if everything belongs to this category, then at one time
nothing existed, and then it would have been impossible for anything to
have begun to exist—and thus even now nothing would exist. Thus,
Aquinas reasoned, not everything is such that it need not exist: "There
must exist something the existence of which is *necessary*."

This isn't quite the end of the third proof, however, for Aquinas
believed that he had not yet ruled out the possibility that the necessity
of this necessary being might be caused by another necessary being, whose
necessity might be caused by another, and so on and so on. So, he asserted,
"It is impossible to go on to infinity in necessary things which have their
necessity caused by another." Conclusion: There must be some necessary
being that has its own necessity, and this is God.

We said the third way was complicated.

The Fourth and Fifth Ways   Aquinas's *fourth way* to prove God is to
consider the fact that all natural things possess degrees of goodness, truth,
nobility, and all other perfections. Therefore, there must be that which is
the source of these perfections, namely, pure goodness and truth, and so
on, and this is what we call God.

And the *fifth way* or proof of God's existence is predicated on the
observation that natural things act for an end or purpose. That is, they
function in accordance with a plan or design. Accordingly, an intelligent

being exists by which things are directed toward their end, and this intelligent being is God.

Aquinas's first three proofs of God's existence are versions of what today is called the **cosmological argument**. The cosmological argument is actually not one argument but a type of argument. Proponents of arguments of this type think that the existence of *contingent* things, things that could possibly not have existed, points to the existence of a noncontingent or *necessary* being, God, as their ultimate cause, creator, ground, energizer, or source of being. Note the difference between cosmological arguments and ontological arguments, which endeavor to establish the existence of God just by considering His nature or analyzing the concept of God, as we saw attempted by Anselm.

Aquinas's fourth proof, which cites the existence of goodness or good things, is called the **moral argument.** Here again, the term does not refer to just one argument but to a type of argument, and, as we will see, some of the "versions" of the moral argument resemble one another only vaguely.

Arguments like Aquinas's fifth proof, according to which the apparent purposefulness or orderliness of the universe or its parts or structure point to the existence of a divine designer, are called **arguments from design** or **teleological arguments.**

Too much terminology? Then let's summarize all this. The main point is that Anselm and Aquinas between them introduced what have turned out to be the four principal arguments for God's existence. These are:

- the ontological argument
- the cosmological argument
- the teleological or design argument
- the moral argument

Notice that none of these four arguments rests on any religious assumptions. They should therefore require the assent of every nonreligious person, if they are sound.

To a certain extent, the history of the philosophy of religion is a continuing discussion of various versions and aspects of these four arguments, as we will now learn. Therefore, just to understand each type of argument is already to have a good grasp of the basics of the philosophy of religion.

▶ S E L E C T I O N   11.2

From St. Thomas Aquinas, *SUMMA THEOLOGICA*

The existence of God can be proved in five ways.

The first and more manifest way is the argument from motion. It is certain, and evident to our senses, that in the world some things are in motion. Now whatever is moved is moved by another, for nothing can be moved except it is in potentiality to that towards which it is moved; whereas a thing moves inasmuch as it is in act. For motion is nothing else than the reduction of something from potentiality to actuality. But nothing can be reduced from potentiality to actuality, except by something in a state of actuality. Thus that which is actually hot, as fire, makes wood, which is potentially hot, to be actually hot, and thereby moves and changes it. Now it is not possible that the same thing should be at once in actuality and potentiality in the same respect, but only in different respects. For what is actually hot cannot simultaneously be potentially hot; but it is simultaneously potentially cold. It is therefore impossible that in the same respect and in the same way a thing should be both mover and moved, i.e., that it should move itself. Therefore, whatever is moved must be moved by another. If that by which it is moved be itself moved, then this also must needs be moved by another, and that by another again. But this cannot go on to infinity, because then there would be no first mover, and, consequently, no other mover, seeing that subsequent movers move only inasmuch as they are moved by the first mover; as the staff moves only because it is moved by the hand. Therefore it is necessary to arrive at a first mover, moved by no other; and this everyone understands to be God.

The second way is from the nature of efficient cause. In the world of sensible things we find there is an order of efficient causes. There is no case known (neither is it, indeed, possible) in which a thing is found to be the efficient cause of itself; for so it would be prior to itself which is impossible. Now in efficient causes it is not possible to go on to infinity, because in all efficient causes following in order, the first is the cause of the intermediate cause, and the intermediate is the cause of the ultimate cause, whether the intermediate cause be several, or one only. Now to take away the cause is to take away the effect. Therefore, if there be no first cause among efficient causes, there will be no ultimate, nor any intermediate, cause. But if in efficient causes it is possible to go on to infinity, there will be no first efficient cause, neither will there be an ultimate effect, nor any intermediate efficient causes; all of which is plainly false. Therefore it is necessary to admit a first efficient cause, to which everyone gives the name of God.

The third way is taken from possibility and necessity, and runs thus. We find in nature things that are possible to be and not to be, since they are found to be generated, and to be corrupted, and consequently, it is possible for them to be and not to be. But it is impossible for these always to exist, for that which can not-be at some time is not. Therefore, if everything can not-be, then at one time there was nothing in existence. Now if this were true, even now there would be nothing in existence, because that which does not exist begins to exist only through something already existing. Therefore, if at one time nothing was in existence, it would have been impossible for anything to have begun to exist; and thus even now nothing would be in existence—which is absurd. Therefore, not all beings are merely possible, but there must exist something the existence of which is necessary. But every necessary thing either has its necessity caused by another, or not. Now it is impossible to go on to infinity in necessary things which have their necessity caused by another, as has been already proved in regard to efficient causes. Therefore we cannot but admit the existence of some being having of itself its own necessity, and not receiving it from another, but rather causing in others their necessity. This all men speak of as God.

The fourth way is taken from the gradation to be found in things. Among beings there are some more and some less good, true, noble, and the like. But *more* and *less* are predicated of different things according as they resemble in their different ways something which is the maximum, as a thing is said to be hotter according as it more nearly resembles that which is hottest; so that there is something which is truest, something best, something noblest, and consequently, something which is most being, for those things that are greatest in truth are greatest in being. . . . Now the maximum in any genus is the cause of all in that genus, as fire, which is the maximum of heat, is the cause of all hot things, as is said in the same book. Therefore there must also be something which is to all beings the cause of their being, goodness, and every other perfection; and this we call God.

The fifth way is taken from the governance of the world. We see that things which lack knowledge, such as natural bodies, act for an end, and this is evident from their acting always, or nearly always, in the same way, so as to obtain the best result. Hence it is plain that they achieve their end, not fortuitously, but designedly. Now whatever lacks knowledge cannot move towards an end, unless it be directed by some being endowed with knowledge and intelligence; as the arrow is directed by the archer. Therefore some intelligent being exists by whom all natural things are directed to their end; and this being we call God.

Seventeenth-Century Believers

For our purposes here, we can now pass lightly over some three hundred years from the Middle Ages through the Renaissance to the seventeenth century. This is not to suggest that the time was unimportant for the history of religion. Europe had seen a mixture not only of enlightenment and religious revolution, but also of reaction and intolerance; it had brought forth not only printed books and open discussion, but also gunpowder and the stake. Luther had challenged the very foundations of Catholic doctrine, and Protestantism had spread throughout Europe. In England, Henry VIII had forced creation of the Anglican Church so he could marry young Anne Boleyn, and had remained neutral in the conflict between Luther and the Pope by giving the followers of each equal opportunity to be executed. A new disorder had been rung in by the time of Descartes's birth, and before his death modern science was offering its own challenge to the established orthodoxy.

But all this, though of great significance to the history of religion, was only indirectly important to the history of the philosophy of religion. The main point for our purposes is that the seventeenth century was the age of scientific discovery amid intellectual uncertainty and political and religious instability, an age in which past authorities and institutions and truths were questioned and often rejected or discarded.

Descartes

The next major figure in the philosophy of religion after Aquinas was, in fact, **René Descartes** (1596–1650). Descartes, longing for an unshaking intellectual footing, made it his primary business to devise what he thought was a new method for attaining certainty in his turbulent age. When he employed his new method, however, it revealed to him the certain existence of God.

As we saw in Parts 1 and 2, Descartes's method was to challenge every belief, no matter how plausible it seemed, in order to ascertain which of his beliefs, if any, were absolutely unassailable. Employing this method, Descartes found that he could not doubt his existence as a thing that thinks: *cogito, ergo sum*, I think, therefore I am. He also found that he could not doubt the existence of God, for basically three reasons. These three reasons are Descartes's proofs of God.

Descartes's First Proof   Having established as absolutely certain his own existence as a thinking thing, Descartes found within his mind the idea of God, the idea of an infinite and perfect being. Further, he reasoned, because there must be a cause for his idea, and because there must be as much reality or perfection in the cause of an idea as there is in the content of the idea, and because he himself therefore certainly could not be the cause of the idea, it follows, he concluded, that God exists.

Let's call this Descartes's first proof. It's really quite a simple proof, though Descartes makes it seem somewhat complicated because he has to explain *why* his idea of God could not have arisen from a source other than God, and, of course, it is difficult to do this.

As you can see, Descartes's first proof is sort of a combination onto-logical-cosmological argument. It's ontological in that the mere idea of God is held by Descartes to entail that God exists. It's cosmological in that the existence of some contingent thing—Descartes's idea of God—is considered by Descartes to require God as its ultimate cause.

Descartes's Second Proof   Descartes had two other proofs of God's existence. His second proof is only subtly different from the first and is basically this:

1. I exist as a thing that has an idea of God.
2. Everything that exists has a cause that brought it into existence and that sustains it in existence.
3. The only thing adequate to cause and sustain me, a thing that has an idea of God, is God.
4. Therefore God exists.

In this second proof, note, God is invoked by Descartes as the cause of *Descartes*, a being that has the idea of God; whereas in the first proof God is invoked by Descartes as the cause of Descartes's *idea* of God. In the second proof Descartes also utilizes the important notion that a thing needs a cause to *conserve* or *sustain* it in existence. We will encounter this idea again.

Descartes's Third Proof   Descartes's third proof, in contrast with the first two, is a straightforward and streamlined version of the ontological argument:

1. My conception of God is the conception of a being that possesses all perfections.
2. Existence is a perfection.
3. Therefore I cannot conceive of God as not existing.
4. Therefore God exists.

Now, assuming that this argument successfully gets you to conclusion (3), how about that move from (3) to (4)? Descartes had no difficulty with that move and said simply, "From the fact that I cannot conceive God without existence, it follows that existence is inseparable from Him, and hence that He really exists." He also offered what he thought was a parallel argument to support the move, and it was to this effect: Just as the fact that you cannot conceive of a triangle whose angles do not equal 180° means that a triangle must have angles that equal 180°, the fact that you cannot conceive of God as not existing means that God must exist.

Are you convinced?

Descartes's three proofs may certainly be novel, but certain objections may instantly spring to mind. A common criticism made of the first two proofs is that it seems possible to devise plausible alternative explanations for one's having an idea of God, explanations other than that given by Descartes. As we already said and as you will see from Selection 11.3, Descartes himself anticipates this objection and endeavors to show why the most likely alternative explanations fail. We think you should consider carefully whether Descartes has really eliminated alternative explanations of his idea of God.

The third proof—Descartes's version of the ontological argument—is more difficult to criticize, but about one hundred fifty years later Immanuel Kant formulated what became the classic refutation of ontological arguments. More about this when we turn to Kant.

A different sort of objection to Descartes's proofs is that, given Descartes's method—according to which he vowed not to accept any claim that is in the least bit doubtable—Descartes should not have accepted without question either the principle that he and his ideas must be caused, or the principle that there must be as much perfection and reality in the cause as in the effect. Although Descartes regarded his proofs of God as providing certainty, they seem to rest on principles that many people would think of as less than certain; yet Descartes seems to accept these principles without hesitation.

Nevertheless, Descartes's proofs are important in the history of our subject, for they raise the important question—at least the first two proofs raise this question—just how *does* a person come to have the idea of an *infinite* being?

In Selection 11.3 Descartes summarizes what we have called his first proof, and then considers and rejects three alternative explanations of how he could come to have the idea of God. If you have difficulty following it, refer back to our summary description of the argument.

▶ S E L E C T I O N 11.3

From René Descartes, MEDITATIONS

But of my ideas . . . [one] represents a God . . . concerning which we must consider whether it is something which cannot have proceeded from me myself. By the name God I understand a substance, that is infinite [eternal, immutable], independent, all-knowing, all-powerful, and by which I myself and everything else, if anything else does exist, have been created. Now all these characteristics are such that the more diligently I attend to them, the less do they appear capable of proceeding from me alone; hence, from what has been already said, we must conclude that God exists.

For although the idea of substance is within me owing to the fact that I am substance, nevertheless I could not have the idea of an infinite substance—since I am finite—if it had not proceeded from some substance which was veritably infinite.

Nor should I imagine that I do not perceive the infinite by a true idea, but only by the negation of the finite . . . for . . . I see that there is manifestly more reality in infinite substance than in finite. . . .

And we cannot say that this idea of God is perhaps materially false and that consequently I can derive it from nought . . . for . . . as this idea is very clear and distinct and contains within it more objective reality than any other, there can be none which is of itself more true, nor any in which there can be less suspicion of falsehood. . . .

But possibly I am something more than I suppose myself to be, and perhaps all those perfections which I attribute to God are in some way potentially in me . . . [For example,] I am already sensible that my knowledge increases little by little, and I see nothing which can prevent it from increasing more and more into infinitude. . . .

At the same time I recognize that this cannot be. For, in the first place, although it were true that every day my knowledge acquired new degrees of perfection, and that there were in my nature many things potentially which are not yet there actually, nevertheless these excellences do not pertain to [or make the smallest approach to] the idea which I have of God in whom there is nothing merely potential. . . . And further, although my knowledge grows more and more, nevertheless I do not for that reason believe that it can ever be actually infinite, since it can never reach a point so high that it will be unable to attain to any greater increase.

Leibniz

Many recent scholars, who are people qualified to make such a judgment, think that the most brilliant intellect of his age was **Gottfried Wilhelm, Baron von Leibniz** (1646–1716). This judgment is made specifically with the fact in mind that Leibniz was the contemporary of a very bright light, Sir Isaac Newton (1642–1727). Leibniz and Newton, independently of each other, developed the calculus, and at the time there was bitter controversy over who did so first. Leibniz's calculus was published in 1684, a few years before Newton's, but Newton had been slow in publishing his work.

Leibniz's philosophy is highly technical and difficult to characterize or summarize in a brief passage. Basically, it is a detailed metaphysical system according to which the ultimate constituents of reality are indivisible atoms. But Leibniz's atoms are not tiny pieces of matter, and they have no size or shape. Instead, they are what Leibniz called **monads,** which are indivisible points of force or energy. Here Leibniz anticipated by a couple of centuries the views of contemporary physics, according to which material particles are a form of energy. Leibniz, however, believed the monads to be entirely nonphysical and often referred to them as "souls," though he distinguished them from souls in the ordinary sense.

Leibniz's entire metaphysical system is derivable by logic from a few basic and plausible assumptions or basic principles. One of these principles is known as the **principle of sufficient reason,** according to which there is a sufficient reason that things are exactly as they are and are not otherwise. This principle is also used by Leibniz as a proof of God.

To see how the proof works, consider any occurrence whatsoever—say, the leaves falling from the trees in autumn. According to the principle in question, there must be a sufficient reason for that occurrence. Now a *partial* reason for any occurrence is that something else happened, or is happening, that caused or is causing the occurrence—in our example, the days turning cold. But that happening is only a *partial* reason for the occurrence in question, because it too requires a sufficient reason for happening. Why did the days turn cold?

So it is plain, thought Leibniz, that as long as you seek the sufficient reason for an occurrence from within the sequence of happenings or events, you never get the complete, final, sufficient reason for the occurrence. You only get to some other event, and that event itself needs a reason for having happened. (The days turned cold because of a shift

The Problem of Evil

Unfortunately, there is a great deal of pain and suffering in the world, not to mention disease, murder, torture, poverty, rape, child abuse, droughts, earthquakes, floods, wars, hijackings, and many other unpleasant things. Now, given that these things exist, it follows either that (1) God cannot do anything about them, which means that God is not all powerful, or that (2) God does not mind that they exist, which means either that (a) God is not good, or (b) these things are really good things in disguise. One further option is (3) God does not exist.

Assuming that these are the only options—and if you can think of another option, we would like to hear about it—then if you believe that God exists and is good and all powerful, you will choose option (2b) and say that these things are really good things in disguise. Of course, you might not put it exactly that way: you might say that these things are evil, all right, but the existence of some evil is required for the greater good. But that's saying that these things serve a purpose and to that extent are not *purely* evil.

Theodicy is the defense of God's goodness and omnipotence (all-powerfulness) in view of apparent evil. Many theologians and philosophers have written theodicies. But one of the most important

theodicies was that of Leibniz. For Leibniz subscribed to the principle of sufficient reason (see text), and that principle means (according to Leibniz) that God exists. It also means that the reason this world, this state of affairs, exists, and not some other world, some other state of affairs, is that this must be the best of all possible worlds (for otherwise God would not have chosen it for existence). So, according to Leibniz, this is the best or most perfect of all worlds possible, and he is thus especially obligated to explain how apparent evil fits into it.

Leibniz's explanation, briefly, is that, for God to create things other than Himself, the created things logically must be limited and imperfect. Thus, to the extent that creation is imperfect, it is not wholly good, and thus it is "evil."

Further, Leibniz argues, you have to look at the entire painting. You can't pronounce it bad if you look at this or that small part, for if you do that all you will see is a confused mass of colors. Likewise, you have to look at the world from a global perspective and not focus in on this or that unpleasant aspect of it.

Not everyone, of course, will find this explanation of evil satisfactory.

---

southward in the jet stream. The jet stream shifted southward because of a reduction in solar radiation. The solar radiation was reduced because of changes in the earth's orientation relative to the sun. And so forth.) So, unless there is something *outside* the series of events, some reason for the *entire* series *itself*, there is no sufficient reason for *any* occurrence.

Therefore, reasoned Leibniz, because there *is* a sufficient reason for every occurrence, it follows that there *is* something outside the series of events that is its own sufficient reason. And this "something outside," of course, is God.

Further, because God is a sufficient reason for God's own existence, God is a *necessary* being, argued Leibniz.

In this way, then, the principle of sufficient reason, coupled with the fact that something has occurred or is occurring, leads straightaway to a necessary being, God—at least according to Leibniz.

The Best of All Possible Worlds?

The optimism expressed in Leibniz's dictum that this is the best of all possible worlds (see the box, "The Problem of Evil") was skewered with dripping sarcasm by Voltaire (1694–1778) in his famous novel *Candide*. Leibniz was of the opinion that one must look at evil from a global perspective, from which unfortunate events might be perceived as a part of a larger fabric that, taken as a whole, is a perfect creation. This notion, in Voltaire's opinion, is meaningless from the standpoint of the individual who suffers a dreadful misfortune, and Voltaire had no difficulty in ridiculing it. If you look at the events of the world with a sober eye, Voltaire suggested, you will see anything but a just, harmonious, and ordered place. What you are more likely to see is injustice, strife, and rampant disorder.

"When death crowns the ills of suffering man, what a fine consolation to be eaten by worms, " he wrote. You get the idea.

This proof is, you can see, yet another cosmological argument, and it is very much like Aquinas's third way. In fact, there is a tendency in the literature to interpret Aquinas's third way in this Leibnizian mode. Further, Leibniz's "argument from sufficient reason" is thought by many to be the soundest cosmological argument, and soundest proof of God of any type, ever put forward. As we will see directly when we turn to David Hume, however, not everyone is impressed with the argument.

Later we will mention that Kant thought that the cosmological argument depends on the ontological argument. Kant thought this, apparently, because Leibniz's version ends up seeming to prove the existence of a necessary being, and it is the concept of God as a necessary being that is the foundation of the ontological argument. But it does seem doubtful that Leibniz's argument *depends* on the ontological argument or in any way *assumes* the existence of a necessary being. Instead, the argument seems to *prove* the existence of a necessary being.

Leibniz thought other proofs of God were sound, including an amended version of Descartes's ontological argument and a couple of others that rest on Leibniz's metaphysics. Leibniz, however, is most noted for the cosmological argument we have explained here, which he presents in Selection 11.4.

▶ S E L E C T I O N 11.4

From Gottfried Wilhelm, Baron von Leibniz, THE MONADOLOGY

36. But there must also be a *sufficient reason* for *contingent truths,* or those of *fact*,—that is, for the sequence of things diffused through the universe of created objects—where the resolution into particular

reasons might run into a detail without limits, on account of the immense variety of the things in nature and the division of bodies *ad infinitum*. There is an infinity of figures and of movements, present and past, which enter into the efficient cause of my present writing, and there is an infinity of slight inclinations and dispositions, past and present, of my soul, which enter into the final cause.

37. And as all this *detail* only involves other contingents, anterior or more detailed, each one of which needs a like analysis for its explanation, we make no advance: and the sufficient or final reason must be outside of the sequence or *series* of this detail of contingencies, however infinite it may be.

38. And thus it is that the final reason of things must be found in a necessary substance, in which the detail of changes exists only eminently, as in their source; and this is what we call God.

39. Now this substance, being a sufficient reason of all this detail, which also is linked together throughout, *there is but one God, and this God is sufficient.*

40. We may also conclude that this supreme substance, which is unique, universal and necessary, having nothing outside of itself which is independent of it, and being a pure consequence of possible being, must be incapable of limitations and must contain as much of reality as is possible.

41. Whence it follows that God is absolutely perfect, *perfection* being only the magnitude of positive reality taken in its strictest meaning, setting aside the limits or bounds in things which have them. And where there are no limits, that is, in God, perfection is absolutely infinite.

Recall now Aquinas's fifth way, a version of the *teleological argument*, which also often is called the *argument from design*. The basic idea of this type of proof of God's existence is that the world and its components act for a purpose and thus exhibit design; therefore the world was created by an intelligent designer. One of the most famous criticisms of the design argument was made by the British empiricist David Hume.

Eighteenth-Century Doubters

Hume

David Hume (1711–1776) was born some sixty years after Descartes died, during a period of European history that saw the very clear emergence of two rivals, science and religion. Between Descartes's *Meditations* and Hume's writings on religion, science had made strong advances, notable especially in 1687 with the publication of Sir Isaac Newton's *Principia Mathematica*. Although Newton himself did not question God's exis-

tence, his system seemed to confirm scientifically what Hobbes earlier
had concluded philosophically (see Part 1) and what Descartes seemed
most to fear: the universe is an aggregate of matter in motion that has no
need of and leaves no room for God. Hume's case-hardened doubts about
religion made blood pressures soar, but by the time Hume put them in
print they were by no means considered capital offenses.

Hume's empiricist epistemological principles (if valid) in fact rule
out the possibility of any meaningful ontological argument. But this is
complicated business and needn't detain us, because it is Hume's harsh
criticisms of the cosmological and especially the teleological arguments
that have been most influential in the philosophy of religion. The most
important criticism of the ontological argument comes from Kant, anyway.

Hume stated the teleological argument, that is, the argument from
design, as follows. You should judge for yourselves whether this is a fair
statement of that argument, because Hume goes on to criticize it severely,
as will be seen.

▶ S E L E C T I O N   11.5

From David Hume,
DIALOGUES CONCERNING NATURAL RELIGION

Look round the world; contemplate the whole and every part of it: you
will find it to be nothing but one great machine, subdivided into an
infinite number of lesser machines, which again admit of subdivisions,
to a degree beyond what human senses and faculties can trace and
explain. All these various machines, and even their most minute parts,
are adjusted to each other with an accuracy, which ravishes into admiration all men, who have ever contemplated them. The curious adapt-
ing of means to ends, throughout all nature, resembles exactly, though
it much exceeds, the productions of human contrivance; of human
design, thought, wisdom, and intelligence. Since therefore the effects
resemble each other, we are led to infer, by all the rules of analogy, that
the causes also resemble; and that the Author of Nature is somewhat
similar to the mind of men; though possessed of much larger faculties,
proportioned to the grandeur of the work, which he has executed. By
this argument *a posteriori*, and by this argument alone, do we prove
at once the existence of a Deity, and his similarity to human mind and
intelligence.

Now note that in this proof of God, as stated by Hume, the reasoning
is from an *effect* (the "world," i.e., the universe) and its parts, to its *cause*
(God). Further, the argument is one by *analogy*, in which the effect (the
world or universe) is likened to a human contrivance, the cause is likened
to a human creator, and the mechanism of creation is likened to human

Miracles

Some Christians regard miracles as evidence of divine action. Hume, however, was highly skeptical of reports of miracles.

A miracle, he reasoned, is a violation of a natural law—for example, that water flows downhill, that fire consumes wood. Thus, before it is reasonable to accept a report of a miracle as true, the evidence that supports the report must be even stronger than that which has established the natural law.

Because the evidence that a natural law holds is the uniform experience of humankind, it is almost inconceivable that any report of a miracle could be true. Therefore, before it would be reasonable to accept such a report, it would have to be a miracle in its own right for the report to be false. In fact, the report's being false would have to be a greater miracle than the miracle it reports.

"No testimony," wrote Hume, "is sufficient to establish a miracle, unless the testimony be of such a kind, that its falsehood would be more miraculous than the fact that it endeavors to establish."

Thomas Paine once asked which is more likely, that a person would lie or that a river would flow upstream? Hume's point is that before you accept some person's report of a river flowing upstream, it must be even more unlikely that the person would be mistaken than that a river would indeed flow upstream.

"When anyone tells me, that he saw a dead man restored to life, I immediately consider with myself, whether it be more probable that this person should either deceive or be deceived, or that the fact which he relates should really have happened. I weigh the one miracle against the other; and always reject the greater miracle. If the falsehood of his testimony would be more miraculous than the event which he relates; then, and not till then, can he pretend to command my belief or opinion."

thought and intelligence. Hume's criticisms of the proof are mainly related to (1) the appropriateness of these analogies, and (2) the legitimacy of this particular instance of effect-to-cause reasoning.

Hume began his criticism by noticing that in an effect-to-cause proof we cannot attribute to the supposed cause any qualities over and beyond those required for the effect. For example, is the world absolutely perfect? Is it free from every error, mistake, or incoherence? No? Then you cannot say that its cause is absolutely perfect, either. Does the world reflect infinite wisdom and intelligence? Hume's own opinion is that at best the world reflects these qualities to *some degree*; and therefore, though we perhaps can infer that the cause has these qualities to a similar degree, we are unauthorized to attribute to it these qualities in a higher degree; and we certainly are not authorized to attribute to it these qualities in an *infinite* degree.

We also are not authorized to attribute to it *other* qualities, such as pure goodness or infinite power. The existence of evil and misery, in Hume's opinion, certainly do *not* indicate that the cause of the world is pure goodness coupled with infinite power. His point was not that the existence of pain and misery necessarily mean that the creator of the world is *not* good or omnipotent. Rather, his point was just that, given the existence of evil and misery in the world, we cannot legitimately try to prove that the creator is all good and all powerful *by looking at the world*. To do that is to attribute something other to the cause than is found in the effect.

Hume also questioned whether we even *know* how perfect or good the world is. Given the limitations of our position, can we be sure that the world doesn't contain great faults? Are we entitled to say that the world deserves considerable praise? If an ignorant chucklehead pronounces the only poem he has ever heard to be artistically flawless, does his opinion count for much? And isn't our experience with worlds as limited as this ignoramus's experience with poetry?

Further, he noted, in the design proof of God a cause is inferred from a single effect, namely, the world. But, Hume asked, is it legitimate to infer a cause from a *single* effect? If I learn (to take a modern illustration of the point) that a certain weird kind of sound is caused by a new type of electronic instrument, then when I hear that kind of sound again, I can infer that it was caused by a similar instrument. But if it's the first time I hear the sound, I can't say much at all about its cause, save perhaps that it was not made by a trombone or guitar, etc. In other words, if we have experience of only a single instance of the effect, as seems to be the case with the world, then it is not clear "that we could form any conjecture or inference at all concerning its cause."

Of course, we have had experience with the building of machines and ships and houses and so forth. But can the world really be compared to any of these? Can we pretend to show much similarity between a house and the universe? To speak of the origin of *worlds*, wrote Hume, "it is not sufficient, surely, that we have seen ships and cities arise from human art and contrivance."

Hume laid a great deal of emphasis on the limitedness of our viewpoint. We, who are but a part of the universe, use our intelligence and thought to build cities and machines. And so we suppose that there must be a divine creator who used thought and intelligence to create the universe. But we and our creations are but a tiny aspect of the universe, and

A Verbal Dispute?

One startling idea proposed by Hume is that the dispute between theists and atheists in certain respects is merely verbal. This is his reasoning:

Theists say that the universe was created by the divine will. But they concede that there is a great and immeasurable difference between the creative activity of the divine mind and mere human thought and its creative activity.

But what do atheists say? They concede that there is some original or fundamental principle of order in the universe, but they insist that this principle can bear only some remote analogy to everyday creative and generative processes, or to human intelligence.

Thus atheist and theist are very close to saying the same thing!

The main difference between them seems to lie only in this, Hume said: The theist is most impressed by the necessity of there being or having been a fundamental principle of order and generation in the universe, whereas the atheist is most impressed by how wildly different such a principle must be from any creative activity with which we are familiar. But then the more pious the theist, the more he will emphasize the difference between divine intelligence and human intelligence; the more he will insist that the workings of God are incomprehensible to mere mortals. The more pious the theist, in short, the more he will be like the atheist!

human thought and intelligence are just one of hundreds of known principles of activity. Is it legitimate, Hume asked, for us to suppose that the mechanism by which one small aspect of the universe rearranges little bits of wood and steel and dirt is the very same mechanism by which *the entire universe* was originally created? We would be amused by an ignorant peasant supposing that the principles that govern the world economy are the same as those by which he runs his household. Yet we in effect suppose that the principles by which we build our houses and cities are those that govern the creation of the universe!

Further, even if we can liken the creation of the world to the building of a house or boat, there is this further problem, said Hume: If we survey a ship, we would be tempted to attribute a great deal of ingenuity to its builder, when in fact its builder may be a beef-brained clod who only copied an art that was perfected over the ages by hundreds of people working through a series of trials, mistakes, corrections, and gradual improvements. Can we be sure the world was not the result of a similar process of trial and error and even intermittent bungling, involving a multitude of lesser "creators"?

For that matter, Hume said, is it even proper to liken the world to a ship or watch or machine or other human artifact? Isn't the world arguably as much like a living organism as a machine? And aren't living organisms produced by processes radically different from those by which human artifacts are made?

This, then, is the substance of Hume's complaints about the design argument. Given what seemed to him to be its several difficulties, Hume's own conclusion about the argument, and evidently about God, was just this: There is an apparent order in the universe, and this apparent order provides some slight evidence of a cause or causes bearing some remote analogy to human intelligence. But that's all the evidence warrants, Hume thought. The manifestation of order is no evidence whatsoever for the existence of the God worshipped by people.

As for the cosmological argument, Selection 11.6 will explain Hume's position on the matter. A cosmological argument, in the version Hume examines, says that anything that exists must have a cause (or reason or explanation) that is different from itself; but, because the series of causes cannot go to infinity, there must be a first uncaused cause, God. A variation of the basic argument allows that the causal series can go to infinity but still stands in need of an uncaused cause that causes the whole infinite series. In either case, the uncaused cause cannot *not* exist. Thus, the uncaused cause is a **necessary being.**

Now Selection 11.6 features three characters: Demea, Cleanthes, and Philo. First, Demea states the cosmological argument. Then Cleanthes rips into it. At the end of the piece Philo brings forth an additional consideration against the argument.

▶S E L E C T I O N   11.6

From David Hume,
*DIALOGUES CONCERNING NATURAL RELIGION**

The argument, replied Demea, which I would insist on is the common one. Whatever exists must have a cause or reason of its existence, it being absolutely impossible for anything to produce itself or be the cause of its own existence. In mounting up, therefore, from effects to causes, we must either go on in tracing an infinite succession, without any ultimate cause at all, or must at least have recourse to some ultimate cause that is *necessarily* existent. Now that the first supposition is absurd may be thus proved. In the infinite chain or succession of causes and effects, each single effect is determined to exist by the power and efficacy of that cause which immediately preceded; but the whole eternal chain or succession, taken together, is not determined or caused by anything, and yet it is evident that it requires a cause or reason, as much as any particular object which begins to exist in time. The question is still reasonable why this particular succession of causes existed from eternity, and not any other succession or no succession at all. If there be no necessarily existent being, any supposition which can be formed is equally possible; nor is there any more absurdity in nothing's having existed from eternity than there is in that succession of causes which constitutes the universe. What was it, then, which determined *something* to exist rather than *nothing*, and bestowed being on a particular possibility, exclusive of the rest? *External causes*, there are supposed to be none. *Chance* is a word without a meaning. Was it *nothing*? But that can never produce anything. We must, therefore, have recourse to a necessarily existent Being who carries the *reason* of his existence in himself, and who cannot be supposed not to exist, without an express contradiction. There is, consequently, such a Being—that is, there is a Deity.

I shall not leave it to Philo, said Cleanthes, though I know that the starting objections is his chief delight, to point out the weakness of this metaphysical reasoning. It seems to me so obviously ill-grounded, and at the same time of so little consequence to the cause of true piety and religion, that I shall myself venture to show the fallacy of it.

I shall begin with observing that there is an evident absurdity in pretending to demonstrate a matter of fact, or to prove it by any arguments *a priori*. Nothing is demonstrable unless the contrary implies a contradiction. Nothing that is distinctly conceivable implies a contradiction. Whatever we conceive as existent, we can also conceive as non-existent. There is no being, therefore, whose non-existence implies a contradiction. Consequently there is no being whose existence is demonstrable. I propose this argument as entirely decisive, and am willing to rest the whole controversy upon it.

It is pretended that the Deity is a necessarily existent being; and this necessity of his existence is attempted to be explained by asserting that, if we knew his whole essence of nature, we should perceive it to be as impossible for him not to exist, as for twice two not to be four. But it is evident that this can never happen, while our faculties remain the same as at present. It will still be possible for us, at any time, to conceive the non-existence of what we formerly conceived to exist; nor can the mind ever lie under a necessity of supposing any object to remain always in being; in the same manner as we lie under a necessity of always conceiving twice two to be four. The words, therefore, *necessary existence* have no meaning or, which is the same thing, none that is consistent.

But further, why may not the material universe be the necessarily existent Being, according to this pretended explication of necessity? We dare not affirm that we know all the qualities of matter; and, for aught we can determine, it may contain some qualities which, were they known, would make its non-existence appear as great a contradiction as that twice two is five. I find only one argument employed to prove that the material world is not the necessarily existent Being; and this argument is derived from the contingency both of the matter and form of the world. "Any particle of matter," it is said, "may be *conceived* to be annihilated, and any form may be *conceived* to be altered. Such an annihilation or alteration, therefore, is not impossible." But it seems a great partiality not to perceive that the same argument extends equally to the Deity, so far as we have any conception of him, and that the mind can at least imagine him to be non-existent or his attributes to be altered. It must be some unknown, inconceivable qualities which can make his non-existence appear impossible or his attributes unalterable; and no reason can be assigned why these qualities may not belong to matter. As they are altogether unknown and inconceivable, they can never be proved incompatible with it.

Add to this that in tracing an eternal succession of objects it seems absurd to inquire for a general cause or first author. How can anything that exists from eternity have a cause, since that relation implies a priority in time and a beginning of existence?

In such a chain, too, or succession of objects, each part is caused by that which preceded it, and causes that which succeeds it. Where then is the difficulty? But the *whole*, you say, wants a cause. I answer that the uniting of these parts into a whole, like the uniting of several distinct countries into one kingdom, or several distinct members into one body, is performed merely by an arbitrary act of the mind, and has no influence on the nature of things. Did I show you the particular causes of each individual in a collection of twenty particles of matter, I should think it very unreasonable should you afterwards ask me what was the cause of the whole twenty. This is sufficiently explained in explaining the cause of the parts.

Though the reasonings which you have urged, Cleanthes, may well excuse me, said Philo, from starting any further difficulties, yet I cannot forbear insisting still upon another topic. It is observed by arithmeticians that the products of 9 compose always either 9 or some lesser product of 9 if you add together all the characters of which any of the former products is composed. Thus, of 18, 27, 36, which are products of 9, you make 9 by adding 1 to 8, 2 to 7, 3 to 6. Thus 369 is a product also of 9; and if you add 3, 6, and 9, you make 18, a lesser product of 9. To a superficial observer so wonderful a regularity may be admired as the effect either of chance or design; but a skillful algebraist immediately concludes it to be the work of necessity, and demonstrates that it must for ever result from the nature of these numbers. Is it not probable, I ask, that the whole economy of the universe is conducted by a like necessity, though no human algebra can furnish a key which solves the difficulty? And instead of admiring the order of natural beings, may it not happen that, could we penetrate into the intimate nature of bodies, we should clearly see why it was absolutely impossible they could ever admit of any other disposition? So dangerous is it to introduce this idea of necessity into the present question! and so naturally does it afford an inference directly opposite to the religious hypothesis!

---

*Hume's footnotes have been omitted.

This brings us to **Immanuel Kant** (1724–1804), whose contribution to the philosophy of religion equals in importance his work in epistemology and ethics. But please note: though we've titled this section of the chapter "Eighteenth-Century Doubters," Kant was not himself a doubter. Furthermore, he also invented one of the most famous moral arguments for God's existence. Nevertheless, Kant's criticisms of traditional proofs of God have seemed to many commentators to be more cogent than his proof, and in any case they are among the most important criticisms in the literature.

According to Kant, there are only three (traditional) ways of proving God's existence, and none of them work.

What's Wrong with the Ontological Proof   First, there is the ontological argument. Remember that according to *Anselm's* version of the argument, God is the greatest being conceivable; hence, if you suppose that God does not exist, you are supposing that the greatest being conceivable is not the greatest being conceivable, and that's nonsense. According to *Descartes's* version, God possesses all perfections, and, because existence is a perfection, God exists.

Now we are sure that you will agree that there is something very sneaky about the ontological argument, in any version. It seems intuitively wrong, somehow, yet it is difficult to pin down exactly what the problem is.

Kant provided a criticism that withstood the test of time, though in recent years there have been challenges to it. What's wrong with the argument, Kant said, is that it assumes that *existence is a "predicate," that is, a characteristic or attribute.* Because Anselm assumed that existence is a characteristic, he could argue that a being that lacked existence lacked an important characteristic and thus could not be the greatest being conceivable. Because Descartes assumed that existence is a characteristic, he could argue that God, who by definition possesses all perfections, necessarily possesses the characteristic of existence.

But existence, said Kant, is not a characteristic at all. Rather, it's a *precondition* of having characteristics. Is there any difference between a warm day and an *existing* warm day? If you state that the potato salad is salty, do you further characterize the salad if you state that it is salty *and exists*? If you tell the mechanic that your tire is flat, do you further enlighten him if you add that the tire also exists? The answer to all such questions, in Kant's view, is obviously "no." To say of something that it exists is not to characterize it: existence is not a predicate.

So, to apply this lesson first to Descartes: Existence is *not* a perfection or any other kind of characteristic. Certainly, *if* there *is* a being that possesses all perfections, then God exists, for existence is a precondition of something's having any perfections at all. But this fact does not mean that God actually exists.

And, to apply this lesson to Anselm: Existence is not a characteristic and so it is not one that belongs to greatness. Certainly, *if* the greatest being conceivable exists, then God exists, because God by definition is that being, and something cannot possess any aspect of greatness without existing. But that fact doesn't mean that such a being exists.

If Kant hadn't written another word about God, what he said about the ontological argument would itself have secured his high rank in the philosophy of religion.

What's Wrong with the Cosmological and Teleological Proofs   The second way of proving God's existence, according to Kant, is the cosmological argument, which, he asserts, reduces to this: If something exists, an absolutely necessary being must likewise exist. I, at least, exist. Therefore, an absolutely necessary being exists.

This is certainly a simple and streamlined version of the cosmological argument compared with those set forth by Aquinas and Descartes and Leibniz and Hume. Unfortunately, Kant, who generally did not try to make things easy for his reader, made up for this unusual lapse into simplicity and clarity by submitting the argument to several pages of exceedingly subtle and confusing analysis.

His basic criticisms of the cosmological argument, however, are two: First, the argument really rests on the ontological argument. Kant's explanation of why and how this is so is notoriously obscure, probably unsound, and let's just let it go. Second, and more important anyway, the argument employs a principle (that everything contingent has a cause) that has significance only in the *experienced* world. The argument then uses that

Kant argued that existence is not a characteristic and that you don't enlarge a description of a thing to say that it exists. Of course, you may wish to assert that something, God, say, or ghosts, or sexism, exists; but this sort of assertion is not really a description, Kant would maintain.

principle, Kant maintained, to arrive at a conclusion that goes beyond experience. (Kant, as we tried to make clear in Part 2, believed that causality is a concept applicable only to things-as-experienced. Why Kant held this position is too complicated to repeat here, but his case against the cosmological argument rests on his being correct about causality, which some people are inclined to doubt.)

The third and final way of trying to prove God's existence, according to Kant, is the teleological argument, the argument that cites the purposiveness and harmonious adaptation of nature as proof of the divine designer. Kant's main criticism is that at best the argument proves only an *architect* who works with the matter of the world, and not a creator. A similar line of thinking was found in Hume, as we saw.

Belief in God Rationally Justified   Despite Kant's criticisms of the three traditional proofs for God's existence, Kant believed in God. Further, amazingly to some, he thought this belief is rationally justified for any moral agent. Here, as almost always, his thinking is complicated, but what he had in mind was this:

Although we do not have theoretical or metaphysical knowledge of God, although we cannot prove or demonstrate that God exists, we must view the world *as if* it were created by God. Why? Because, Kant said, only if we assume the existence of God can we believe that virtue will be rewarded with happiness. Virtue, Kant held, is worthiness to be happy and is the supreme good. But without believing in God, the virtuous individual cannot be certain that the happiness of which he is worthy will in fact be his or that, in general, a person's happiness will be proportionate to his moral worth.

Thus, in Kant's opinion, God's existence cannot be proved, but can and must rationally be assumed by a moral agent. That God exists, he said, is a postulate of *practical* reason.

This particular argument for assuming that God exists is another version of the moral argument that we first encountered with Aquinas. In a moment we will turn to yet a third version of this argument.

In Selection 11.7, taken from the *Critique of Pure Reason* (1781), Kant argues that existence is not a predicate. This will be a good stopping point for this chapter, for the basic arguments and standard objections have now been explained.

▶ S E L E C T I O N   11.7

From Immanuel Kant,
THE CRITIQUE OF PURE REASON

My answer is as follows. There is already a contradiction in introducing the concept of existence—no matter under what title it may be disguised—into the concept of a thing which we profess to be thinking solely in reference to its possibility. . . .

"Being" is obviously not a real predicate; that is, it is not a concept of something which could be added to the concept of a thing. It is merely the positing of a thing, or of certain determinations, as existing in themselves. Logically, it is merely a copula of a judgment. The proposition, "God is omnipotent," contains two concepts, each of which has its object—God and omnipotence. The small word "is" adds no new predicate, but only serves to posit the predicate *in its relation* to the subject. If, now, we take the subject (God) with all its predicates (among which is omnipotence), and say "God is," or "There is a God," we attach no new predicate to the concept of God, but only posit the subject in itself with all its predicates, and indeed posit it as being an *object* that stands in relation to my *concept*. The content of both must be one and the same; nothing can have been added to the concept, which expresses merely what is possible, by my thinking its object (through the expression "it is") is given absolutely. Otherwise stated, the real contains no more than the merely possible. A hundred real thalers do not contain the least coin more than a hundred possible thalers. For as the latter signify the concept, and the former the object and the positing of the object, should the former contain more than the latter, my concept would not, in that case, express the whole object, and would not therefore be an adequate concept of it. My financial position is, however, affected very differently by a hundred real thalers than it is by the mere concept of them (that is, of their possibility). . . . The conceived hundred thalers are not themselves in the least increased through thus acquiring existence outside my concept.

By whatever and by however many predicates we may think a thing—even if we completely determine it—we do not make the least addition to the thing when we further declare that this thing *is*. Otherwise, it would not be exactly the same thing that exists, but something more than we had thought in the concept; and we could not, therefore, say that the exact object of my concept exists. If we think in a thing every feature of reality except one, the missing reality is not added by my saying that this defective thing exists. On the contrary, it exists with the same defect with which I have thought it, since otherwise what exists would be something different from what I thought. When, therefore, I think a being as the supreme reality, without any defect, the question still remains whether it exists or not.

Checklist

To help you review, here is a checklist of the key philosophers and concepts of this chapter. The brief descriptive sentences that appear with each philosopher summarize one of his leading ideas. Keep in mind that some of these summary statements represent terrific oversimplifications of complex positions.

Philosophers

- **St. Anselm**   Author of the ontological argument.

- **Gaunilon**   A Benedictine monk, contemporary of Anselm and critic of the ontological argument.
- **St. Thomas Aquinas**   Author of the Five Ways of proving God's existence.
- **René Descartes**   Offered three proofs of God, including a streamlined version of the ontological argument.
- **Gottfried Wilhelm, Baron von Leibniz**   Proposed one of the most effective versions of the cosmological argument.
- **David Hume**   Religious skeptic; provided classic criticisms of the teleological and cosmological arguments.
- **Immanuel Kant**   Criticized the ontological, cosmological, and teleological proofs of God and thought that God's existence cannot be proved, yet believed that God's existence must be assumed by the rational, moral individual.

Concepts

theology vs. philosophy

ontological argument

reductio proof

Aquinas's criticism of the ontological argument

Five Ways

something whose existence is necessary

cosmological argument

moral argument

argument from design/teleological argument

first mover

first efficient cause

something that conserves or sustains something in existence

perfection

monad

principle of sufficient reason

problem of evil

best of all possible worlds

argument by analogy

existence—a predicate?

1. Explain in your own words Anselm's two ontological proofs of God.
2. What is a *reductio* proof? Give an example other than one mentioned in the text.
3. Summarize Gaunilon's objection to Anselm's argument. Evaluate Anselm's response to that objection.
4. State, in your own words, Aquinas's first, second, and third ways. Which of these arguments seems to you the soundest, and why?

Questions for Discussion and Review

5. Compare Descartes's version of the ontological argument with one or another of Anselm's. Which version is the soundest, and why?

6. In your own words, state Leibniz's proof of God's existence. Can you find anything wrong with it?

7. Critically evaluate Leibniz's solution to the problem of evil.

8. In your own words, summarize Hume's criticisms of the teleological argument. Are these criticisms sound? Why or why not?

9. Explain Hume's reasoning for remaining skeptical of reports of miracles. Is this reasoning sound?

10. Hume maintained that if you explain the cause of each event in a series by reference to earlier events in the series, there is no sense in then trying to find a single cause for the entire series of events. Is this right? What does it have to do with the question of God's existence?

Suggested Further Readings

Anselm, *Basic Writings*, S. N. Deane, trans. (Lasalle: Open Court, 1974). This work contains Anselm's basic writings, though what we have already given you in this text may well be sufficient for most purposes.

Aquinas, *Basic Writings of Saint Thomas Aquinas*, 2 vols., A. C. Pegis, ed. (New York: Random House, 1945). You have read the Five Ways, but you might also wish to consult the sections of *Summa Theologica* that deal with the nature and attributes of God, and also part 1, questions 48 and 49 and the first part of part 2, question 79, for the classical Christian discussion of evil.

D. R. Burrill, ed., *The Cosmological Argument* (Garden City: Doubleday Anchor, 1967). Selected readings on the cosmological arguments, for and against.

A. Flew, *Hume's Philosophy of Belief: A Study of His First Inquiry* (London: Routledge & Kegan Paul, 1961). Contains an analysis of Hume's treatment of the "religious hypothesis."

C. W. Hendel, Jr., *Hume Selections* (New York: Scribners, 1927). See especially pp. 143–282 and 284–401.

I. Kant, *Critique of Practical Reason*, L. W. Beck, trans. (New York: Liberal Arts, 1956). See book II, chap. II, sect. V.

I. Kant, *Critique of Pure Reason*, N. K. Smith, trans. (New York: St. Martin's, 1965). Check the index under "God." The most important material is in the chapter entitled "The Ideal of Pure Reason."

A. Kenny, *Five Ways: St. Thomas Aquinas's Proofs of God's Existence* (London: Routledge & Kegan Paul, 1969). Good critical discussion of the Five Ways.

G. Leibniz, *Theodicy*, E. M. Huggard, trans. and A. Farrer, ed. (Lasalle: Open Court, 1952).

J. L. Mackie, *The Miracle of Theism: Arguments For and Against the Existence of God* (Oxford: Clarendon Press, 1982). Excellent commentary on all the traditional proofs of God's existence.

R. J. Moore and B. N. Moore, *The Cosmos, God and Philosophy* (New York: Peter Lang, 1988). Contains discussion of modern science on traditional proofs of God.

N. Pike, ed., *God and Evil: Readings on the Theological Problem of Evil* (Engle-wood Cliffs, N.J.: Prentice-Hall, 1964). A popular anthology on the subject.

A. Platinga, *The Ontological Argument from St. Anselm to Contemporary Phi-losophers* (New York: Doubleday Anchor, 1965). Contains relevant articles writ-ten mainly by analytic philosophers. Some are very tough.

B. Russell and F. C. Copleston, "The Existence of God: A Debate Between Bertrand Russell and Father F. C. Copleston." This lively debate touches on several lines of proof of God, and Copleston's version of Leibniz's cosmological argument is pretty effectively worded. The debate has been anthologized in many places. See, e.g., E. L. Miller, *Philosophical and Religious Issues: Classical and Con-temporary Statements* (Encino, Calif.: Dickenson, 1971).

God in the Age of Science

"God is dead."—Nietzsche
"Nietzsche is dead."—God
    — GRAFFITI

Religion and science are two high authorities in Western civilization. Unfortunately, they are not always comfortable with each other. Religion understands the world as requiring a deity; science apparently does not. Science portrays the universe as self-sustaining and self-sufficient. God does not figure into the equations of science and scientists never refer to a nonphysical agency in their professional work. Religion must wager that in some way or another a purely scientific understanding of the world will prove to be incomplete or else be prepared to explain why an intelligent person should adopt the religious perspective.

This tension between science and religion provides the backdrop to the philosophy of religion for the last two centuries. During this period we find philosophers increasingly concerned with whether or not the age of science leaves room for a belief in God. Some philosophers, you will see, viewed the complexity of the world as revealed by science as a reason *for* believing in God.

Three Nineteenth-Century Philosophers

Despite the criticism made by Kant and the more sustained barrage leveled at it by Hume, the design argument had (and still has) many defenders. One of these was the English philosopher **William Paley** (1743–1805), sometimes called "Pigeon Paley" during his own day because of his satirical account of some pigeons owning private property.

Paley had a high reputation in the late eighteenth and early nineteenth centuries as a moral philosopher, but he is best remembered now for his clever presentation of the argument from design. Paley is usually thought of as a late eighteenth-century philosopher, but his most important work came out early in the nineteenth century, so we will include him in this discussion.

In *A View of the Evidences of Christianity* (1794), Paley argued against Hume's thesis that reports of miracles are inherently untrustworthy, and in his most famous and important work, *Natural Theology* (1802), he in effect took issue with Hume's attack on the argument from design. We say "in effect" because in this book he did not argue against Hume explicitly, as he had in the earlier book; instead, he tendered his own very effectively worded version of the argument from design.

In Paley's opinion, you will see, dismissing the argument from design makes no sense whatsoever. Suppose you found a watch lying on the ground somewhere. Would you suppose that it had *just been lying there forever*, like a stone? Obviously not. The watch gives too much evidence of design; it obviously had a maker and was not produced by random forces. But now consider living organisms and their organs. These are things considerably more subtle and intricate in their composition than a mere watch. Are we seriously to suppose that they give no more evidence of intelligent design than a stone? In short, Paley suggests that dismissing the argument from design is a patent absurdity, akin to supposing that watches just happen to come into existence.

As you read Selection 12.1, you may wish to consider whether Paley's version of the argument is subject to Hume's criticism.

The speaker seems nutty because he regards something that obviously was made by an intelligent craftsperson as just a rock—something that was created by natural physical processes. From Paley's point of view, it is equally nutty to think that an organ like the eye could be the result of natural physical processes.

From William Paley, NATURAL THEOLOGY

A Watch Implies a Watchmaker

In crossing a heath, suppose I pitched my foot against a *stone*, and were asked how the stone came to be there; I might possibly answer, that, for anything I knew to the contrary, it had lain there forever: nor would it perhaps be very easy to show the absurdity of this answer. But suppose I had found a *watch* upon the ground, and it would be inquired how the watch happened to be in that place: I should hardly think of the answer which I had given before, that, for anything I knew, the watch might have always been there. Yet why should not this answer serve for the watch as well as for the stone? Why is it not as admissible in the second case, as in the first?

For this reason, and for no other, viz. that, when we come to inspect the watch, we perceive (what we could not discover in the stone) that its several parts are framed and put together for a purpose, e.g., that they are so formed and adjusted as to produce motion, and that motion so regulated as to point out the hour of the day; that if the different parts had been differently shaped from what they are, of a different size from what they are, or placed after any other manner, or in any other order . . . either no motion at all would have been carried on in the machine, or none which would have answered the use that is now served by it . . . The inference, we think, is inevitable; that the watch must have had a maker; that there must have existed, at sometime, and at some place or other, an artificer or artificers, who formed it for the purpose which we find it actually to answer; who comprehended its construction, and designed its use.

Nor would it, I apprehend, weaken the conclusion, that we had never seen a watch made. . . .

Neither, secondly, would it invalidate our conclusion, that the watch sometimes went wrong, or that it seldom went exactly right. . . . It is not necessary that a machine be perfect, in order to show with what design it was made: still less necessary, where the only question is, whether it were made with any design at all. . . .

Nor, thirdly, would it bring any uncertainty into the argument, if there were a few parts of the watch, concerning which we could not discover, or had not yet discovered, in what manner they conduced to the general effect. . . .

Nor, fourthly, would any man in his senses think the existence of the watch, with its various machinery, accounted for, by being told that it was one out of possible combinations of material forms. . . .

Nor, fifthly, would it yield to his inquiry more satisfaction to be answered, that there existed in things a principle of order, which had disposed the parts of the watch into their present form and situation.

He [cannot] even form to himself an idea of what is meant by a principle or order distinct from the intelligence of the watchmaker.

Sixthly, he would be surprised to hear that the mechanism of the watch was no proof of contrivance, only a motive to induce the mind to think so . . .

Neither, lastly, would our observer be driven out of his conclusion . . . by being told that he knew nothing at all about the matter. He knows enough for his argument. . . .

Even a "Self-Reproducing" Watch Implies a Watchmaker

Suppose, in the next place, that the person who found the watch, should, after sometime, discover, that, in addition to all the properties which he had hitherto observed in it, it possessed the unexpected property of producing, in the course of its movement, another watch like itself (the thing is conceivable), that it contained within it a mechanism, a system of parts, a mould for instance, or a complex adjustment of lathes, files, and other tools, evidently and separately calculated for this purpose; let us inquire, what effect ought such a discovery to have upon his former conclusion. . . .

If it be said, that upon the supposition of one watch being produced from another in the course of that other's movements, and by means of the mechanism within it, we have a cause for the watch in my hand, viz. the watch from which it proceeded: I deny, that for the design, the contrivance, the suitableness of means to an end, the adaptation of instruments to a use we have any cause whatever. It is in vain, therefore, to assign a series of such causes, or to allege that a series may be carried back to infinity; for I do not admit that we have yet any cause at all of the phenomena, still less any series of causes either finite or infinite. Here is contrivance, but no contriver: proofs of design, but no designer.

The conclusion which the *first* examination of the watch . . . suggested, was, that it must have had, for the cause and author of that construction, an artificer, who understood its mechanism, and designed its use. This conclusion is invincible. A *second* examination presents us with a new discovery. The watch is found, in the course of its movement, to produce another watch, similar to itself: and not only so, but we perceive in it a system or organization, separately calculated for that purpose. What effect would this discovery have or ought it to have, upon our former inference? What . . . but to increase, beyond measure, our admiration of the skill which had been employed in the formation of such a machine! Or shall it, instead of this, all at once turn us round to an opposite conclusion, viz. that no art or skill whatever has been concerned in the business, although all other evidences of art and skill remain as they were, and this last and supreme piece of art be now added to the rest? Can this be maintained without absurdity? Yet this is atheism.

This is atheism: for every indication of contrivance, every manifestation of design, which existed in the watch, exists in the works of nature; with the difference, on the side of nature, of being greater and more, and that in a degree which exceeds all computation. I mean, that the contrivances of nature surpass the contrivances of art, in the complexity, subtlety, and curiosity of the mechanism; and still more, if possible, do they go beyond them in number and variety; yet, in a multitude of cases, are not less evidently mechanical, not less evidently contrivances, not less evidently accommodated to their end, or suited to their office, than are the most perfect productions of human ingenuity.

The Eye and the Telescope

I know no better method of introducing so large a subject, than that of comparing a single thing with a single thing; an eye, for example, with a telescope. As far as the examination of the instrument goes, there is precisely the same proof that the eye was made for vision, as there is that the telescope was made for assisting it. They are made upon the same principles; both being adjusted to the laws by which the transmission and reflection of rays of light are regulated. . . . For instance; these laws require, in order to produce the same effect, that the rays of light, in passing from water into the eye, should be refracted by a more convex surface than when it passes out of air into the eye. Accordingly we find, that the eye of a fish, in that part of it called the crystalline lens, is much rounder than the eye of terrestrial animals. What plainer manifestation of design can there be than this difference? What could a mathematical instrument-maker have done more, to show his knowledge of this principle, his application of that knowledge, his suiting of his means to his end . . . [?]

Further Evidence of Design in the Eye

In considering vision as achieved by the means of an image formed at the bottom of the eye, we can never reflect without wonder upon the smallness, yet correctness, of the picture, the subtlety of the touch, the fineness of the lines. A landscape of five or six square leagues is brought into a space of half an inch diameter. . . . A stagecoach, travelling at its ordinary speed for half an hour, passes, in the eye, only over one-twelfth of an inch, yet is this change of place in the image distinctly perceived throughout its whole progress. . . .

Besides that conformity to optical principles which its internal constitution displays . . . there is to be seen, in everything belonging to it and about it, an extraordinary degree of care. . . . It is lodged in a strong, deep, bony socket. . . . Within this socket it is embedded in fat, of all animal substances the best adapted both to its repose and motion. It is sheltered by the eyebrows; an arch of hair, which like a thatched penthouse, prevents the sweat and moisture of the forehead from running down into it.

But it is still better protected by its lid. . . . It defends the eye; it wipes it; it closes it in sleep. Are there, in any work of art whatever, purposes more evident than those which this organ fulfills? or an apparatus for executing those purposes more intelligible, more appropriate, or more mechanical? . . .

In order to keep the eye moist and clean . . . a wash is constantly supplied by a secretion for the purpose; and the superfluous brine is conveyed to the nose through a perforation in the bone as large as a goose-quill. When once the fluid has entered the nose, it spreads itself upon the inside of the nostril, and is evaporated by the current of warm air, which, in the course of respiration, is continually passing over it. Can any pipe or outlet for carrying off the waste liquor from a dye-hour or a distillery, be more mechanical than this is? It is easily perceived, that the eye must want moisture: but could the want of the eye generate the gland which produces the tear, or bore the hole by which it is discharged—a hole through a bone? . . .

Were there no example in the world of contrivance except that of the eye, it would be alone sufficient to suppose the conclusion which we draw from it, as to the necessity of an intelligent Creator. . . . If other parts of nature were inaccessible to our inquiries, or even if other parts of nature presented nothing to our examination but disorder and confusion, the validity of this example would remain the same. If there were but one watch in the world, it would not be less certain that it had a maker. . . . The argument is cumulative, in the fullest sense of that term. The eye proves [divine agency] without the ear; the ear without the eye. The proof in each example is complete; for when the design of the part, and the conduciveness of its structure to that design is shown, the mind may set itself at rest; no future consideration can detract anything from the force of the example.

Newman

Few intellectuals have been as highly esteemed in their own time as **John Henry Newman** (1801–1890) was. Newman, deeply religious from his youth, had been ordained in the Church of England and was made vicar of St. Mary's, Oxford. But in early middle age he revised his views on Roman Catholicism and was received into the Roman Catholic Church, eventually becoming a cardinal and inspiring many other Anglicans to convert as well. Newman was therefore a churchman, but he was also a philosopher.

Newman was much concerned with the differences between formal logic and actual real-life, or as he called it, "concrete" reasoning—and especially with the principles that validate the latter. He came to believe

Kierkegaard

One of the great achievements in the history of religious thought is the philosophy of **Søren Kierkegaard** (1813–1855). In this chapter, however, we are focusing on proofs of God's existence, and as Kierkegaard offered no proofs we will not concentrate on him except in this box.

No, Kierkegaard did not think you could prove that God exists. Quite the opposite. For Kierkegaard, "to exist" is to be engaged in time and history. Because God is an eternal and immutable being, "existence" does not even apply to God. But God as Christ existed, for Kierkegaard. Christ, however, is a paradox that the human intellect cannot comprehend, for in Christ the immutable became changing, the eternal became temporal, and what is beyond history became historical.

In short, Kierkegaard thought that God is beyond the grasp of reason and that the idea that God came to us as a man in the person of Jesus is intellectually absurd. Yet at the same time Kierkegaard's primary mission was to show what it is to be a Christian, and he was himself totally committed to Christianity. How can this be?

First, the notion that we can sit back and weigh objectively the evidence about God's existence pro and contra, that we can conduct an impartial investigation of the issue and arrive at the "truth," is totally rejected by Kierkegaard. He would not have bothered reading this chapter.

In fact, Kierkegaard mocks the whole idea of objective truth. Truth, he said, is subjective. Truth lies not in *what* you believe, but in *how you live*. Truth is passionate commitment.

For example, think of a person who worships the "true" God but does so merely as a matter of routine, without passion or commitment. Compare this person with one who worships a mere idol but does so with the infinite commitment of his soul. In fact, said Kierkegaard, "the one prays in truth to God though he worships an idol; the other prays falsely to the true God, and hence worships in fact an idol."

Second, Kierkegaard rejected completely the Aristotelean idea that the essential attribute of humans is their capacity to reason. For Kierkegaard, the most important attribute of man is not thought but *will*. Man is a being that *makes choices*.

But if truth is not objective, then there are no external principles or criteria that are objectively valid and against which one might judge one's choices. How, then, are we to choose, if there are no objective, rational criteria and we have only our own judgment to rely on? This problem—the problem of knowing how and what to choose in the absence of objective truth—became, after Kierkegaard, the central problem of existentialism.

Kierkegaard's answer is that we must commit ourselves totally to God. Salvation can be had only through a *leap of faith*, through a nonintellectual, passionate, "infinite" commitment to Christianity. "Faith constitutes a sphere all by itself, and every misunderstanding of Christianity may at once be recognized by its transforming it into a doctrine, transferring it to the sphere of the intellectual."

What Kierkegaard said must not be confused with what earlier Christian thinkers had maintained. Earlier Christian thinkers had said that faith precedes understanding and had held that you must have faith in God before rational thought about Him can begin. But thinkers such as Augustine and Anselm had still looked for, and had fully expected there to be, rational grounds for confirming what they already accepted in faith. Kierkegaard, in contrast, thought that no such rational grounds exist: God is an intellectual absurdity.

Further, he held that rational grounds for believing in God, if there were any, would actually be *incompatible* with having faith. "If I wish to preserve myself in faith I must constantly be intent upon holding fast to the *objective uncertainty* [of God]," he said. The objective uncertainty of God, for Kierkegaard, is thus *essential* to a true faith in Him. Only if there is objective uncertainty, he wrote, can "[I] remain out upon the deep, over seventy thousand fathoms of water, still preserving my faith."

that whenever we concern ourselves with concrete matters of fact, our conclusions may not have the status of logical certainties, but we can nevertheless attain certitude, as a state of mind, about them. In particular, he held, we can achieve certitude in our religious faith.

Now it is by virtue of our experience of *conscience*, according to Newman, that we find certitude about God. Conscience, he said, can be relied on exactly as much as we rely on memory or reason. And feelings of conscience lead us to affirm an intelligent being as their cause, he held. Conscience is a sense of responsibility and duty that points toward something beyond the realm of people, toward a Supreme Governor or Judge whose dictates we are ashamed or fear to violate and whose approval we seek. In short, in the experience of conscience we find ourselves undeniably *answerable* to an intelligence beyond ourselves.

Newman thus endorsed a moral argument for God, but it is rather unlike Kant's moral argument. According to Kant, to assume that one can act morally is to assume that there is justice; it is to assume, that is, that moral uprightness will be rewarded with happiness. And this in turn is to assume the existence of a God who ensures that there is justice. In other words, if what ought to be is, then God exists. The requirements of morality thus lead us to *postulate* God, according to Kant.

But according to Newman, we are simply unable to doubt God's existence, given the experience of conscience. Newman's proof is much more direct, in other words. That God exists is as indisputable as our awareness that we are answerable to Him, and this awareness we find in the dictates of conscience.

Selection 12.2, from Newman's most important book, *A Grammar of Assent* (1870), gets to the heart of Newman's view.

▶ S E L E C T I O N   12.2

From John Henry Newman,
A GRAMMAR OF ASSENT

I have already said I am not proposing here to prove the Being of a God; yet I have found it impossible to avoid saying where I look for the proof of it. For I am looking for that proof in the same quarter as that from which I would commence a proof of His attributes and character—by the same means as those by which I show how we apprehend Him, not merely as a notion, but as a reality. The last indeed of these three investigations alone concerns me here, but I cannot altogether exclude the two former from my consideration. However, I repeat, what I am directly aiming at, is to explain how we gain an image of God and give a real assent to the proposition that He exists. And next, in order to do this, of course I must start from some first principle;—and that first principle, which I assume and shall not attempt to prove, is that which I should also use as a foundation in those other two inquiries, viz. that we have by nature a conscience.

I assume then, that Conscience has a legitimate place among our mental acts; as really so, as the action of memory, of reasoning, of imagination, or as the sense of the beautiful; that, as there are objects which, when presented to the mind, cause it to feel grief, regret, joy, or desire, so there are things which excite in us approbation or blame, and which we in consequence call right or wrong; and which, experienced in ourselves, kindle in us that specific sense of pleasure or pain, which goes by the name of a good or bad conscience. This being taken for granted, I shall attempt to show that in this special feeling, which follows on the commission of what we call right or wrong, lie the materials for the real apprehension of a Divine Sovereign and Judge. . . .

Conscience too, considered as a moral sense, an intelligent sentiment, is a sense of admiration and disgust, of approbation and blame: but it is something more than a moral sense; it is always, what the sense of the beautiful is only in certain cases; it is always emotional. No wonder then that it always implies what that sense only sometimes implies; that it always involves the recognition of a living object, towards which it is directed. Inanimate things cannot stir our affections; these are correlative with persons. If, as is the case, we feel responsibility, are ashamed, are frightened, at transgressing the voice of conscience, this implies that there is One to whom we are responsible, before whom we are ashamed, whose claims upon us we fear. If, on doing wrong, we feel the same tearful, broken-hearted sorrow which overwhelms us on hurting a mother; if, on doing right, we enjoy the same sunny serenity of mind, the same soothing, satisfactory delight which follows on our receiving praise from a father, we certainly have within us the image of some person, to whom our love and veneration look, in whose smile we find our happiness, for whom we yearn, towards whom we direct our pleadings, in whose anger we are troubled and waste away. These feelings in us are such as require for their exciting cause an intelligent being: we are not affectionate towards a stone, nor do we feel shame before a horse or a dog; we have no remorse or compunction on breaking mere human law: yet, so it is, conscience excites all these painful emotions, confusion, foreboding, self-condemnation; and on the other hand it sheds upon us a deep peace, a sense of security, a resignation, and a hope, which there is no sensible, no earthly object to elicit. "The wicked flees, when no one pursueth;" then why does he flee? whence his terror? Who is it that he sees in solitude, in darkness, in the hidden chambers of his heart? If the cause of these emotions does not belong to this visible world, the Object to which his perception is directed must be Supernatural and Divine; and thus the phenomena of Conscience, as a dictate, avail to impress the imagination with the picture of a Supreme Governor, a Judge, holy, just, powerful, all-seeing, retributive, and is the creative principle of religion, as the Moral Sense is the principle of ethics. . . .

Until we account for the knowledge which an infant has of his mother or his nurse, what reason have we to take exception at the doctrine, as strange and difficult, that in the dictate of conscience, without previous experiences or analogical reasoning, he is able gradually to perceive the voice, or the echoes of the voice, of a Master, living, personal, and sovereign?

I grant, of course, that we cannot assign a date, ever so early, before which he had learned nothing at all, and formed no mental associations, from the words and conduct of those who have the care of him. But still, if a child of five or six years old, when reason is at length fully awake, has already mastered and appropriated thoughts and beliefs, in consequence of their teaching, in such sort as to be able to handle and apply them familiarly, according to the occasion, as principles of intellectual action, those beliefs at the very least must be singularly congenial to his mind, if not connatural with its initial action. And that such a spontaneous reception of religious truths is common with children, I shall take for granted, till I am convinced that I am wrong in so doing. The child keenly understands that there is a difference between right and wrong; and when he has done what he believes to be wrong, he is conscious that he is offending One to whom he is amenable, whom he does not see, who sees him. His mind reaches forward with a strong presentiment to the thought of a Moral Governor, sovereign over him, mindful, and just. It comes to him like an impulse of nature to entertain it.

James

Paley's main work appeared at the very beginning of the nineteenth century, and Newman's was published about two-thirds of the way through. The next philosopher we consider, William James, published his first major work, *The Will to Believe and Other Essays*, in 1897, at the end of the century. So James and Paley were really turn-of-the-century philosophers, at different ends of the same century.

One big difference between James's end of the nineteenth century and Paley's lay in the marked increase in agnosticism by the year 1900. There is an antagonism between the religious view of the world as a divinely created paradise planned for the sake of human spiritual growth and the supposedly scientific view of the cosmos as a blind churning of material particles in accordance with physical laws, and for the past two hundred years the blind-churning view had become more and more congenial to Western intellectuals. Around mid-century, Darwin had explained how the origin of species need not be divine and Karl Marx had pronounced religion to be the opium of the people. If the power of Hume's and Kant's reasoning did not force philosophers to take seriously their criticisms of the old proofs of God, the spirit of the times did, and before the end of the century **Friedrich Nietzsche** (1844–1900) could proclaim that God was dead.

God Is Dead

By his infamous remark that God is dead, Friedrich Nietzsche did not mean that God once existed and now no longer does. He meant that all people with an ounce of intelligence would now perceive that there is no intelligent plan to the universe or rational order in it: they would now understand that there is no reason why things happen one way and not another and that the harmony and order we imagine to exist in the universe is merely pasted on by the human mind.

Nietzsche, however, would have regarded very few people as having this required ounce of intelligence, and he in fact had a way of denigrating everyone in sight. For the mass of people, Nietzsche thought, God certainly is not dead. But these people, in Nietzsche's opinion, are pathetic wretches governed by a world view inculcated by religion, science, and philosophy, a world view that in Nietzsche's opinion makes them feeble losers who are motivated mainly by resentment. They view the world as a rational, law-governed place and adhere to a slave morality that praises the man who serves his fellow creatures with meekness and self-sacrifice.

In Nietzsche's opinion, the negative morality of these pitiful slaves—the mass of humankind, ordinary people—must be reevaluated and replaced by life-affirming values. The new morality will be based on the development of a new kind of human being, whom Nietzsche calls the "overman" or "superman" (*Übermensch*). Such a one not only accepts life in all its facets, including all its pain, but also makes living into an art. Among the forerunners of the overman he cites Alexander the Great and Napoleon.

Neitzsche's thesis that there is no God and its apparent corollary that there are no absolute and necessary criteria of right and wrong were accepted by such twentieth-century existentialist philosophers as Albert Camus and Jean-Paul Sartre. For these thinkers, *the* fundamental problem of philosophy is how to live one's life, given the absence of objectively valid standards by which to evaluate one's choices and decisions.

Nietzsche, Kierkegaard, and some existentialists would all have agreed that the various rational discussions about God's existence to which this chapter is devoted are impotent and meaningless.

But God wasn't, and isn't, dead for everyone. In fact, the question of God's existence was at the time, and still is, for very many (1) a *live* issue, and furthermore (2) a *momentous* one. For William James it is both. It is also, in addition, according to James, (3) *forced*, which means that you cannot suspend judgment in the matter. For James, to profess agnosticism and to pretend to suspend judgment is in fact "backing the field against the religious hypothesis."

Now James argued for deciding this issue (of God's existence) in favor of God. He began his argument, not a simple one, by noting that "*our non-intellectual nature does influence our convictions.*" Indeed, usually our convictions are *determined* by our nonintellectual nature, he maintained. Rarely does pure reason settle our opinion. What settles our opinion usually is our wishing and willing and sentimental preferences, our fears and hopes, prejudices and emotions, and even the pressure of our friends. It is our "passional nature" that settles our opinion, he said.

Sometimes we even deliberately will what we believe, James held. Need proof that he is correct? Probably you would prefer not to accept claims that are based on pitifully insufficient evidence (we hope). So when someone asserts something that is based on insufficient evidence, what do you do? You *try not to believe it*. And often you are successful in not accepting the poorly supported claim. When you are, then haven't you in fact *willed* yourself not to accept what the person has asserted? Your will, your desire not to accept unsupported claims, has influenced your beliefs.

Of course, if you are like most of us, you may find yourself accepting what the person says anyway. But if you consider the matter carefully, isn't your acceptance also a case of something other than cold reason influencing your beliefs? You may *hope* that what the person has said is true. You may simply *want* to believe it, *despite* its having been poorly supported. If so, your hope that what has been said is true has simply *overcome* your desire not to accept unsupported claims. So here again your "passional nature" settled your opinion.

Having argued that our non-intellectual nature influences our opinions, James next distinguished between the *two commandments* of rational thinkers. These are

1. To believe the truth
2. To avoid errors

Some individuals, James noted, favor (2) over (1): they would rather avoid errors than find the truth. "Better go without belief forever than believe a falsehood," is the creed dictated to them by their passional nature: better dead than misled.

But favoring (2) over (1) is not James's creed. There are worse things than falling into error, he said. In some cases, he argued, it is best to regard "the chase for truth as paramount, and the avoidance of error as secondary."

Consider moral questions, where you must either act or not act and cannot wait for objective, definitive proof that one choice is right. In such cases, it is not possible to suspend judgment, because not to act is itself to make a judgment. In such cases, you make the best decision you can. Furthermore, according to James, it is *legitimate* to do this, even though you have no guarantee that your decision is correct.

And it is the same in religious matters, he said. At least it is the same if religion for you is a live and momentous issue that you cannot resolve through intellect alone. If it is, you cannot escape the issue by remaining skeptical and waiting for more information. To remain skeptical, James said, is tantamount to saying that it is better to yield to the fear of being in error than to yield to the hope that religion is true.

In fact, James argued, when it comes to religion, the other way is better: it is better to yield to the hope that all of it may be true than to give way to the fear of being in error. If you permit the fear of error to

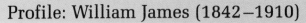

Profile: William James (1842–1910)

Few philosophers have been better writers than William James, whose catchy phrases gave life and succulence to even the driest philosophical subjects. James had a knack for words, and he was able to state complex ideas with easy elegance. This is to be expected, because James was the older brother of Henry James, the great American novelist.

The James children were raised by their wealthy and eccentric theologian father in an intellectually stimulating atmosphere that promoted their mental development. The Jameses benefited from diverse educational experiences in several schools both in America and in Europe and were largely free to pursue their own interests and develop their own capacities. They became refined and cosmopolitan.

William James had wide-ranging interests. Though fascinated with science, he decided, at age eighteen, to try to become a painter (and not the kind that paints houses). But he was also wise enough to see very soon that his artistic urge exceeded his ability.

So James went off to Harvard and studied science. Then he entered the college's medical school, though he did not intend to practice medicine, and in his late twenties he received his medical degree. A few years later, he joined the Harvard faculty as a lecturer on anatomy and physiology and continued to teach at Harvard until 1907. From 1880 on, he was a member of the Harvard department of philosophy and psychology. You shouldn't think that James got interested in philosophy all of a sudden. He had always been fond of the subject and tended to give a philosophical interpretation to scientific questions.

James suffered from emotional crises until he was able to resolve the question of free will and to answer the compelling arguments for determinism. Around 1870, he found in the ideas of the French philosopher Charles Renouvier philosophical justification for believing in free will, and with it, apparently, the cure to his episodes of emotional paralysis.

In 1890, James published his famous *Principles of Psychology*, thought by many to be his major work. Equally important, from a purely philosophical standpoint, was his *The Will to Believe and Other Essays in Popular Philosophy* (1897). This work is where to find James's solution to the problem of free will, in the essay, "The Dilemma of Determinism." Other important works include *The Varieties of Religious Experience* (1902), *Pragmatism* (1907), *A Pluralistic Universe* (1909), *The Meaning of Truth* (1909), *Some Problems in Philosophy* (1911), and *Essays in Radical Empiricism* (1912).

William James was perhaps the most famous American intellectual of his time. Yet today some philosophers think of him as a lightweight—a popularizer of philosophical issues who failed to make a substantial contribution to technical philosophy (whatever that is). He is thought to bear the same relation to Hume or Kant, say, that Tchaikovsky bears to Mozart or Bach, the philosophical equivalent of the composer who only cranks out pretty melodies. But this is all a mistake. The discerning reader will find in James a great depth of insight.

The Consequences of Belief

James's philosophy was a species of **pragmatism,** according to which, at least in its Jamesian version, the true is "only the expedient in our way of thinking." Confronted with competing views or theories both of which are more or less equally supportable rationally, you choose the viewpoint that works most beneficially. Instead of inquiring whether God exists, for example, the (Jamesian) pragmatist considers "what definite difference it will make to you and me" if we believe or disbelieve that he does. As can be seen from the text, James argued that the practical benefits of the theistic viewpoint are superior to those of the agnostic or atheistic viewpoint.

Applying the same strategy to the question of whether or not we have free will, James focused not directly on the question itself but on the outcomes that attend acceptance of the alternative viewpoints. Acceptance of determinism is unworkable, James believed, because it entails never regretting what happens: because what happened had to happen (according to determinism), it is illogical to feel that it should not have happened. Thus acceptance of determinism is inconsistent with the practices of moral beings, who perceive themselves as making genuine choices that can affect the world for better or for worse.

---

rule you and say to yourself, "Avoid error at any cost!" then you will withhold assent to religious beliefs. Doing so will, of course, *protect* you from being in error—if the religious beliefs are incorrect. But if you withhold your assent to religious beliefs, then you will also *lose the benefits* that come from accepting those beliefs. And it is worse, James thought, to lose the benefits than to gain the protection.

Further, if the religious beliefs are *true* but the evidence for them is insufficient, then the policy, "Avoid error at any cost!" effectively cuts you off from an opportunity to make friends with God. Thus, in James's opinion, the policy, "Avoid error at all cost!", when applied to religion, is a policy that keeps you from accepting certain propositions even if those propositions are really true; and that means that it is an *irrational* policy.

In short, because even as a rational thinker you will be influenced by your passional nature and thus will be led to give way either to the hope that the belief in God, and associated religious beliefs, are true, or to the fear that if you accept these beliefs you will be in error, it is better to give way to the hope.

Now James stressed that he was *not* saying that you should believe what, as he put it, "you know ain't true." His strategy applies, he said, only to *momentous* and *living* issues that cannot be resolved by the intellect itself. It applies only to issues like God's existence.

Selection 12.3 is taken from James's essay, "The Will to Believe." It ought to be clear why the essay had this title.

▶ S E L E C T I O N   12.3

From William James, "THE WILL TO BELIEVE"

What then do we now mean by the religious hypothesis? Science says
things are; morality says some things are better than other things; and
religion says essentially two things.

First, she says that the best things are the more eternal things, the
overlapping things, the things in the universe that throw the last stone,
so to speak, and say the final word. "Perfection is eternal,"—this phrase
of Charles Secrétarian seems a good way of putting this first affirmation
of religion, an affirmation which obviously cannot yet be verified scientifically at all.

The second affirmation of religion is that we are better off even
now if we believe her first affirmation to be true.

Now, let us consider what the logical elements of this situation
are *in case the religious hypothesis in both its branches be really true.*
(Of course, we must admit that possibility at the outset. If we are to
discuss the question at all, it must involve a living option. If for any
of you religion be a hypothesis that cannot, by any living possibility
be true, then you need go no farther. I speak to the "saving remnant"
alone.) So proceeding, we see, first, that religion offers itself as a
momentous option. We are supposed to gain, even now, by our belief,
and to lose by our nonbelief, a certain vital good. Secondly, religion is
a *forced* option, so far as that good goes. We cannot escape the issue
by remaining sceptical and waiting for more light, because, although
we do avoid error in that way *if religion be untrue,* we lose the good,
if it be true, just as certainly as if we positively chose to disbelieve. It
is as if a man should hesitate indefinitely to ask a certain woman to
marry him because he was not perfectly sure that she would prove an
angel after he brought her home. Would he not cut himself off from
that particular angel-possibility as decisively as if he went and married
some one else? Scepticism, then, is not avoidance of option; it is option
of a certain particular kind of risk. *Better risk loss of truth than chance
of error,*—that is your faith-vetoer's exact position. He is actively playing his stake as much as the believer is; he is backing the field against
the religious hypothesis, just as the believer is backing the religious
hypothesis against the field. To preach scepticism to us as a duty until
"sufficient evidence" for religion be found, is tantamount therefore to
telling us, when in presence of the religious hypothesis, that to yield
to our fear of its being error is wiser and better than to yield to our
hope that it may be true. It is not intellect against all passions, then;
it is only intellect with one passion laying down its law. And by what,
forsooth, is the supreme wisdom of this passion warranted? Dupery
for dupery, what proof is there that dupery through hope is so much
worse than dupery through fear? I, for one, can see no proof; and I

simply refuse obedience to the scientist's command to imitate his kind of option, in a case where my own stake is important enough to give me the right to choose my own form of risk. If religion be true and the evidence for it be still insufficient, I do not wish, by putting your extinguisher upon my nature (which feels to me as if it had after all some business in this matter), to forfeit my sole chance in life of getting upon the winning side,—that chance depending, of course, on my willingness to run the risk of acting as if my passional need of taking the world religiously might be prophetic and right.

All this is on the supposition that it really may be prophetic and right, and that, even to us who are discussing the matter, religion is a live hypothesis which may be true. Now, to most of us religion comes in a still further way that makes a veto on our active faith even more illogical. The more perfect and more eternal aspect of the universe is represented in our religions as having personal form. The universe is no longer a mere *It* to us, but a *Thou*, if we are religious; and any relation that may be possible from person to person might be possible here. For instance, although in one sense we are passive portions of the universe, in another we show a curious autonomy, as if we were small active centers on our own account. We feel, too, as if the appeal of religion to us were made to our own active good-will, as if evidence might be forever withheld from us unless we met the hypothesis half-way. To take a trivial illustration: just as a man who in a company of gentlemen made no advances, asked a warrant for every concession, and believed no one's word without proof, would cut himself off by such churlishness from all the social rewards that a more trusting spirit would earn,—so here, one who should shut himself up in snarling logicality and try to make the gods extort his recognition willy-nilly, or not get it at all, might cut himself off forever from his only opportunity of making the gods' acquaintance. This feeling, forced on us we know not whence, that by obstinately believing that there are gods (although not to do so would be so easy both for our logic and our life) we are doing the universe the deepest service we can, seems part of the living essence of the religious hypothesis. If the hypothesis *were* true in all its parts, including this one, then pure intellectualism, with its veto on our making willing advances, would be an absurdity; and some participation of our sympathetic nature would be logically required. I, therefore, for one, cannot see my way to accepting the agnostic rules for truth-seeking, or wilfully agree to keep my willing nature out of the game. I cannot do so for this plain reason, that *a rule of thinking which would absolutely prevent me from acknowledging certain kinds of truth if those kinds of truth were really there, would be an irrational rule.* That for me is the long and short of the formal logic of the situation, no matter what the kinds of truth might materially be.

This Century

James's essay elicited much criticism. Skeptics and believers both took issue with it. Skeptics thought James had elevated wishful thinking to the status of proof, and believers questioned James's implicit assumption that God's existence cannot be established. Still others said that belief grounded in James's way was not the uncompromising and unqualified faith in God demanded by religion. From their perspective, James's belief in God amounted to a gamble (and indeed James seemed to concede this) rather than to true religious acceptance of God.

James, in any event, brings us into our own century, and we shall now consider three twentieth-century discussions of God's existence. The first is a revised and rather sophisticated version of the argument from design.

The second is something like an argument that God does not exist, but in actuality it is an argument that the whole issue is pretty meaningless to begin with.

The third is an extended argument in favor of God that combines elements of the traditional proofs of God.

We will close the chapter by considering the consequences of accepting atheism, according to an important twentieth-century atheistic philosopher of religion.

F. R. Tennant's Argument from Design

F. R. Tennant (1866–1957), a Cambridge philosopher of religion, set forth a striking version of the argument from design. His argument, far more subtle than those used by Paley and Hume, takes developments in science, including evolutionary theory, fully into account.

Now at the heart of traditional design-type arguments for God's existence is the fact that organisms and their component parts are amazingly well suited to their environment, and vice versa. The heart, for example, is remarkably well suited to pump blood under just the sort of conditions under which creatures with hearts are found. In this respect the heart is just like a machine that was designed to perform a certain task under certain conditions, and so it is easy to conclude that the heart was designed by a grand designer.

Whole organisms, too, are remarkably well suited to live in their environment; fish, for example, which can swim and breathe in water, are very nicely suited to live in oceans, rivers, and lakes. Thus the fact that fish are so nicely adapted to their environment suggests that they, too, were created with their environment in mind; similar reasoning pertains to any other species of animal.

And looking at things from a slightly different angle, the environment itself seems very well suited for its inhabitants, as if it had been designed for their comfort and development.

In sum, organisms and their parts are adapted to or fit their environment, and vice versa, and this fact gives rise to the argument from design.

Now Tennant thought that the fit between organisms and the physical universe, when considered carefully, exhibits much more subtlety and complexity than traditional design arguments acknowledge.

For one thing, said Tennant, there is the fact that the world is *intelligible*. It is a cosmos and not a chaos. It can be *comprehended*. There is thus a fit between the world and *human thought* that must be considered as evidence of design.

For another, there is the evolutionary process, which operating through natural selection accounts for the adaptation of organisms to their environment. This process is very well suited to produce such adaptation. Further, it exhibits progressiveness. Thus the evolutionary process is *itself* a manifestation of divine purpose. For Tennant, the fact of evolution did not undermine the argument for God; it strengthened this argument.

It must also be considered, he wrote, that the *inorganic* world is remarkably well suited for the emergence and persistence of life. That the basic inorganic conditions could be just the right ones to give rise to life and intelligence and to sustain them is unlikely to have been a chance occurrence, he argued.

For still another thing, the world is not only intelligible to the intellect; it is pleasing and stimulating to the human sense of beauty and proportion. There is a clear fit between the natural order and human aesthetic sensibilities: the world is a bearer of aesthetic value.

And for still another, the world is also suited to foster the intellectual and moral development of humankind. "The whole process of Nature is capable of being regarded as instrumental to the development of intelligent and moral creatures."

Furthermore, according to Tennant, these various instances of fit must be considered not *separately* but *collectively*. So viewed, they make it less reasonable to suppose that existing life, especially human life with its intellectual, moral, and aesthetic aspects, is the result of "cumulative groundless coincidence" (as the blind-churning view mentioned earlier would have it). Tennant thus advances a version of the argument from design that seems fully compatible with such scientific views as the theory of evolution and the idea that life arose from a soup of inorganic chemicals.

In fact, from Tennant's perspective, a teleological explanation of the world is really a *continuation by extrapolation* of science and is verified in the same sort of way that scientific theories are—namely, it provides the most plausible explanation of the given empirical facts. Tennant did not think that the adaptation of life to the physical world, and vice versa, and the appropriateness of the natural conditions to give rise to life and to biological, intellectual, moral, and aesthetic progress, provide a *conclusive demonstration*, as might be found in logic or mathematics, for theism. But he thought that they do offer grounds for *reasonable belief.*

Selection 12.4 is from Tennant's *Philosophical Theology* (1928).

▶ S E L E C T I O N   12.4

From F. R. Tennant, PHILOSOPHICAL THEOLOGY

(I)

The classical proofs of the being of God sought to demonstrate that there is a Real counterpart to a preconceived idea of God, such as was moulded in the course of the development of religion, or constructed by speculative philosophy aloof from religious experience and from avowedly anthropic interpretation, or obtained by both these methods combined. The empirically-minded theologian adopts a different procedure. He asks how the world, inclusive of man, is to be explained. He would let the Actual world tell its own story and offer its own suggestions: not silence it while abstractive speculation, setting out with presuppositions possibly irrelevant to Actuality, weaves a system of thought which may prove to conflict with facts. . . . He will thus entertain, at the outset, no such presuppositions as that the Supreme Being, to which the world may point as its principle of explanation, is infinite, perfect, immutable, suprapersonal, unqualifiedly omnipotent or omniscient. The attributes to be ascribed to God will be such as empirical facts and their sufficient explanation indicate or require. . . .

The main fields of fact in which adaptation is conspicuous, and which have severally afforded data for particular arguments of the teleological kind and of restricted scope, are those of the knowability or intelligibility of the world (or the adaptation of thought to things), the internal adaptedness of organic beings, the fitness of the inorganic to minister to life, the aesthetic value of Nature, the world's instrumentality in the realisation of moral ends, and the progressiveness in the evolutionary process culminating in the emergence of man with his rational and moral status. A brief examination of these fields in turn will not only enable us to estimate the respective strengths of the more or less independent arguments derived from them severally, but also to appreciate the interconnections within the world, and the comprehensive teleology which such interconnectedness suggests. . . .

(II)

The adaptiveness that is so abundantly evinced in the organic world has already been discussed. . . . So long as organisms were believed to have originated, in their present forms and with all their specialised organs "ready made," the argument that adaptation of part to whole, of whole to environment, and of organ to function, implied design, was forcible. But its premise became untenable when Darwin shewed that every organic structure had come to be what it now is through a long series of successive and gradual modifications. . . . The sting of Darwinism . . . lay in the suggestion that proximate and "mechanical" causes were sufficient to produce the adaptations from which the teleology of the eighteenth century had argued to God. Assignable proximate causes, whether mechanical or not, are sufficient to dispose of the particular kind of teleological proof supplied by Paley. But the fact of organic evolution, even when the maximum of instrumentality is accredited to what is figuratively called natural selection, is not incompatible with teleology on a grander scale. . . . This kind of teleology does not set out from the particular adaptations in individual organisms or species so much as from considerations as to the progressiveness of the evolutionary process and as to the organic realm as a whole. . . .

The survival of the fittest presupposes the arrival of the fit, and throws no light thereupon. Darwin did not account for the origin of variations; their forthcomingness was simply a datum for him. . . The discovery of organic evolution has caused the teleologist to shift his ground from special design in the products to directivity in the process, and plan in the primary collocations. It has also served to suggest that the organic realm supplies no better basis for teleological arguments of the narrower type than does inorganic Nature. . . .

. . . It has been argued . . . that the inorganic environment is as plainly adapted to life as living creatures are to their environment. The vast complexity of the physico-chemical conditions of life on the earth suggests to common sense that the inorganic world may retrospectively receive a biocentric explanation . . . we may say that if science is to be trusted when it regards the organic realm as later in time than the inorganic world, and when it asserts that the processes, which made the emergence and persistence of life possible, would have been precisely the same had life not emerged at all, then there would seem to be a development of this fitness for life, involving convergence of innumerable events towards a result, as if that result were an end to which the inorganic processes were means. The fitness of our world to be the home of living beings depends upon certain primary conditions, astronomical, thermal, chemical, etc., and on the coincidence of qualities apparently not causally connected with one another, the number of which would doubtless surprise anyone wholly unlearned in the sciences. . . . Unique assemblages of unique properties on so vast a scale being thus essential to the maintenance of life, their forthcomingness makes the inorganic world seem in some respects comparable with an organism. It is suggestive of a formative principle . . .

Such is the teleological appeal of this field of facts to commonsense reasonableness, or mother-wit, which regards the "probability," that the apparent preparedness of the world to be a theatre of life due to "chance," as infinitesimally small. It remains to ask whether either science or logic is able to abate the forcibleness of this appeal.

Science does not seem to lessen the convincingness of the argument now before us when it suggests that (as if organic chemistry were irrelevant), had the conditions upon which life, as we know it, depends been wholly or partly different, other forms of organism might equally well have emerged, adapted to the altered environment: silicon perhaps replacing carbon in another kind of protoplasm, and iron replacing calcium phosphate in skeletons. For the point is that, for the existence of any forms of life that we may conceive, the necessary environment, whatever its nature, must be complex and dependent on a multiplicity of coincident conditions, such as are not reasonably attributable to blind forces or to pure mechanism. Nor, again, can science explain the adaptation of the inorganic environment to life after the manner in which Darwinism, its sufficiency being assumed, explains progressive adaptations in organisms without resort to design. Of a struggle for existence between rival worlds, out of which ours has survived as the fittest, we have no knowledge upon which to draw. Natural selection cannot here be invoked; and if the term "evolution" be applicable at all to the whole world-process, it must have a different meaning from that which it bears in Darwinian biology. Presumably the world is comparable with a single throw of dice. And common sense is not foolish in suspecting the dice to have been loaded.

Flew's Simple Central Questions

In the late 1920s, a group of philosophers, mathematicians, and scientists, led by Moritz Schlick, a philosopher at the University of Vienna, set forth a group of ideas known as logical positivism. A central tenet of this **Vienna Circle,** and of logical positivism, as we saw in Chapter 4, is the **verifiability principle,** according to which the meaning of a proposition is the experience you would have to have to know that it is true. What does it mean to say, "The sprinkler is on"? Well, to find out if that prop-

The Big Bang

The view now accepted by most scientists is that the universe is an explosion, known as the Big Bang. Unlike other explosions, the Big Bang does not expand outward into space, like a dynamite or bomb explosion, nor does it have a duration in external time, as do all other explosions, because all space and all time are located within it. The beginning of the Big Bang is the beginning of space and time and of matter and energy, and it is, in fact, the beginning of our expanding universe.

The most prevalent view among the qualified experts who have an opinion on the matter is that it is impossible to know what transpired in the Big Bang before 10^{-43} seconds after zero time, when the Big Bang began. But, for various reasons that we need not go into here, most of these experts do apparently believe that there was a zero time, that the universe did have an absolute beginning, that there was a first physical event.

Now the first physical event, assuming that such a thing did take place, either is explainable or it is not. On one hand, it is difficult to believe that the first physical event has no explanation, for that amounts to saying that the entire universe, with its incredible size and complexity, was just a chance occurrence, a piece of good luck. But on the other hand, if the first physical event is explicable, then it would seem that the explanation must refer to some sort of nonphysical phenomenon, which certainly could be called "God."

Thus, the Big Bang theory, if true—and there seems to be much reason for supposing that it is true—may well require philosophers to make a hard choice between an unexplainable universe and one explainable only by reference to something nonphysical.

---

osition is true, you'd have to look out the window or go out into the yard or otherwise do some checking. The experience required to do the checking is what the proposition means, according to the verifiability principle.

What this principle entails is that a pronouncement that is not verifiable has no meaning. Take the remark, "The sprinkler stopped working due to fate." What kind of checking would you do to see if this is true? There isn't any kind of experience a person might have that would verify this remark. Therefore, it's meaningless, the logical positivists would say.

Of course, some propositions are true by virtue of what their words mean, such as, "You are older than everyone who is younger than you." Such *analytic propositions,* as they are called, are rendered true by definition rather than by experience, according to the logical positivists. But the proposition, "The sprinkler stopped working due to fate," isn't like that. It's not an analytic proposition, so it has to be verifiable in experience if it is to have meaning. And because it isn't, it doesn't.

So, according to the logical positivists, the good many philosophical assertions from metaphysics, epistemology, and ethics that are neither analytic nor verifiable are meaningless. These assertions may perhaps express emotional sentiments, but they are neither true nor false and in fact are cognitively meaningless. **Rudolph Carnap** (1891–1970), one of

Is This Atheism?

Logical positivists, who dismissed the utterance, "God exists," as meaningless, were usually perceived as denying God's existence. But were they? A person who denies God exists believes God does not exist. But the positivist position was not that God does not exist. It was that the utterance, "God exists," is *meaningless*. Equally, they held, the proposition, "God does not exist," is meaningless, too. The debate between believers and doubters, they maintained, cannot be settled by sense experience and is therefore stuff and nonsense.

the most famous members of the Vienna Circle, even declared, "We reject *all* philosophical questions, whether of Metaphysics, Ethics or Epistemology."

The verificationist principle has its difficulties, most famous of which is that the principle itself isn't verifiable and thus must either be meaningless or a mere analytic verbal truth. Perhaps more important, at least to the logical positivists, is that even assuming that the principle is not meaningless, what it actually says is unclear. Does it require that a proposition must be *conclusively* verifiable? But in that case universal claims, such as those that state the laws of physics, would be meaningless. And if absolute verifiability is not required, to what extent is partial verifiability required?

Today few philosophers would call themselves logical positivists. But most philosophers would still maintain that *empirical or factual* propositions must in *some* sense and to *some* extent be verifiable by experience.

So what, then, about such assertions as, "God exists," or, "God created the world"? These look like factual propositions. But are they in any sense verifiable?

Selection 12.5 is by Professor **Antony Flew.** The influence of positivist thinking on his thought will be very clear to you.

▶ S E L E C T I O N   12.5

From Antony Flew,
*"THEOLOGY AND FALSIFICATION"**

Let us begin with a parable. It is a parable developed from a tale told by John Wisdom in his haunting and revelatory article "Gods." Once upon a time two explorers came upon a clearing in the jungle. In the clearing were growing many flowers and many weeds. One explorer says, "Some gardener must tend this plot." The other disagrees, "There is no gardener." So they pitch their tents and set a watch. No gardener is ever seen. "But perhaps he is an invisible gardener." So they set up a barbed-wire fence. They electrify it. They patrol with bloodhounds. (For they remember how H. G. Wells's "invisible man" could be both smelt and touched though he could not be seen.) But no shrieks ever suggest that some intruder has received a shock. No movements of the wire ever betray an invisible climber. The bloodhounds never give cry. Yet still the Believer is not convinced. "But there is a gardener, invisible, intangible, insensible to electric shocks, a gardener who has no scent and makes no sound, a gardener who comes secretly to look after the garden which he loves." At last the Sceptic despairs, "But what remains of your original assertion? Just how does what you call an invisible, intangible, eternally elusive gardener differ from an imaginary gardener or even from no gardener at all?"

In this parable we can see how what starts as an assertion, that something exists or that there is some analogy between certain complexes of phenomena, may be reduced step by step to an altogether different status, to an expression perhaps of a "picture preference." The Sceptic says there is no gardener. The Believer says there is a gardener (but invisible, etc.). One man talks about sexual behavior. Another man prefers to talk of Aphrodite (but knows that there is not really a superhuman person additional to, and somehow responsible for, all sexual phenomena). The process of qualification may be checked at any point before the original assertion is completely withdrawn and something of that first assertion will remain (Tautology). Mr. Wells's invisible man could not, admittedly, be seen, but in all other respects he was a man like the rest of us. But though the process of qualification may be, and of course usually is, checked in time, it is not always judiciously so halted. Someone may dissipate his assertion completely without noticing that he has done so. A fine brash hypothesis may thus be killed by inches, the death by a thousand qualifications.

And in this, it seems to me, lies the peculiar danger, the endemic evil, of theological utterance. Take such utterances as "God has a plan," "God created the world," "God loves us as a father loves his children." They look at first sight very much like assertions, vast cosmological assertions. Of course, this is no sure sign that they either are, or are intended to be, assertions. But let us confine ourselves to the cases where those who utter such sentences intend them to express assertions. (Merely remarking parenthetically that those who intend or interpret such utterances as crypto-commands, expressions of wishes, disguised ejaculations, concealed ethics, or as anything else but assertions, are unlikely to succeed in making them either properly orthodox or practically effective.)

Now to assert that such and such is the case is necessarily equivalent to denying that such and such is not the case. Suppose then that we are in doubt as to what someone who gives vent to an utterance is asserting, or suppose that, more radically, we are sceptical as to whether he is really asserting anything at all, one way of trying to understand (or perhaps it will be to expose) his utterance is to attempt to find what he would regard as counting against, or as being incompatible with, its truth. For if the utterance is indeed an assertion, it will necessarily be equivalent to a denial of the negation of that assertion. And anything which would count against the assertion, or which would induce the speaker to withdraw it and to admit that it had been mistaken, must be part of (or the whole of) the meaning of the negation of that assertion. And to know the meaning of the negation of an assertion is, as near as makes no matter, to know the meaning of that assertion. And if there is nothing which a putative assertion denies then there is nothing which it asserts either: and so it is not really an assertion. When the Sceptic in the parable asked the Believer, "Just how does what you call an invisible, intangible, eternally elusive gardener differ from an imaginary gardener or even from no gardener at all?" he was suggesting that the Believer's earlier statement had been so eroded by qualification that it was no longer an assertion at all.

Now it often seems to people who are not religious as if there was no conceivable event or series of events the occurrence of which would be admitted by sophisticated religious people to be a sufficient reason for conceding "There wasn't a God after all" or "God does not really love us then." Someone tells us that God loves us as a father loves his children. We are reassured. But then we see a child dying of inoperable cancer of the throat. His earthly father is driven frantic in his efforts to help, but his Heavenly Father reveals no obvious sign of concern. Some qualification is made—God's love is "not a merely human love" or it is "an inscrutable love," perhaps—and we realize that such sufferings are quite compatible with the truth of the assertion that "God loves us as a father (but, of course . . .)." We are reassured again. But then perhaps we ask: what is this assurance of God's (appropriately qualified) love worth, what is this apparent guarantee really a guarantee against? Just what would have to happen not merely (morally and wrongly) to tempt but also (logically and rightly) to entitle us to say "God does not love us" or even "God does not exist"? I therefore put to the succeeding symposiasts the simple central questions: "What would have to occur or to have occurred to constitute for you a disproof of the love of, or of the existence of, God?"

---

*Flew's footnotes have been omitted.

Swinburne's Extended Argument for God

A lengthy argument for the existence of God was proposed not too long ago by **Richard Swinburne,** professor of philosophy at the University of Keele, in *The Existence of God* (1979). This entire book is in fact an extended single argument for God's existence.

Swinburne concedes that the main traditional proofs of God do not establish God's existence with certainty. Most of what Swinburne views as the main proofs are variations of the proofs we've talked about in this chapter—that is, the cosmological, teleological, and moral proofs. His list includes some others, too, that we haven't mentioned, including one based on "history and miracles," and another based on the experiences of God many people seem to have had. Swinburne carefully presents his versions of these several proofs and then evaluates them.

Proofs of God Are "Personal Explanations" Now all these proofs are alike in that each is an *explanation*: each cites specific features of the world that need explaining, and each then provides the needed explanation by referring to God. Thus, to evaluate these arguments, Swinburne examines at length the general criteria by which explanations may be evaluated. He includes in his examination both scientific explanations and "personal explanations," which are given when we explain something as resulting from the intentional actions of a rational agent. The main traditional proofs of God are all personal explanations in Swinburne's sense.

Ordinarily, these proofs are considered in isolation from one another, according to Swinburne. This, he insists, is improper. In fact, he maintains, the various arguments back each other up and are interrelated in such a manner that collectively they show that it is "more probable than not" that there is a God who made and sustains people and the universe. Thus, Swinburne's proof of God's existence is in actuality a complicated interweaving of some of the traditional proofs, after he has "knocked them into clear shape" (as he puts it).

The Evidence for God's Existence Let's get to the essentials. The evidence for God's existence, according to Swinburne, and here we condense what he says, is this: a universe exists in which there is great order, in that (e.g.) physical things obey the same principles and have identical properties throughout a vast region of space and time; and in which there are conscious beings. This category of things includes people, who are agents of limited power and knowledge but who have the ability to grow in these capacities; who can marvel at the order in nature and can worship God; who are subject to desires, many of which are biologically useful but some of which are not; who are therefore subject to temptations; who are able to choose whether or not to act rightly and can develop, or fail to develop, a morally good character; who are interdependent and capable of increasing each other's power, knowledge, freedom, and happiness; and who, because they are subject to birth and death, know responsibility to distant generations. The world is also providential in permitting people to satisfy their needs; and though it contains suffering, this evil may be increased or diminished by human activity and "is necessary if men are to have knowledge of the evil consequences of possible actions." And finally, within this world there have been prophets and wise men who encourage all people to worship God, and there is some slight evidence of miraculous occurrences having happened in religious contexts.

The preceding paragraph, which focuses on certain key features of the world, describes, as we said, the *evidence* for God's existence. Each feature of the world mentioned there, says Swinburne, adds to the probability that there is God. But merely *adding to the probability* that something is so, he says, doesn't automatically show that *it is probable* that it is so. You *add to the probability* that you will die of heart disease if you smoke and drink, but even if you do it still isn't *probable* that you will die that way. So what Swinburne wants to know is this: Does this evidence show that it is *probable* that there is a God? Does it show that the God hypothesis is probable?

Evaluating Explanatory Hypotheses   When we consider how probable an explanatory hypothesis is in the light of the evidence in its favor, we must consider several things, Swinburne notes. First, we must consider whether the hypothesis would enable us to *predict* that evidence.

Here's a simple example of the principle: Suppose, knowing that our car won't start, we hypothesize that our battery is dead. This hypothesis is not unsound, because it would lead us to *expect* that the car wouldn't start. In other words, if we had supposed that the battery was dead, we would have predicted that the car wouldn't start. Our hypothesis would have enabled us to *predict* the evidence for it.

When we evaluate a hypothesis, then, we must consider its predictive power.

But we must consider something else as well when we are trying to ascertain the probability of a hypothesis. Before we can accept the dead-battery hypothesis, we have to consider whether other possible conditions would make the car not start, and how likely it is that one of them existed. If the dead-battery hypothesis is to be accepted, then the *prior probability* that the car wouldn't start even if the battery were good would have to be low. If, for instance, the spark plugs aren't working, then there would be a high probability that the car wouldn't start even if the battery were good. Knowing that the spark plugs aren't working obviously would give us reservations about the dead-battery hypothesis.

So we have to consider not only the predictive power of a hypothesis, but also the prior probability that what we are viewing as evidence would have existed even if the hypothesis is false.

But we must also consider how complicated the hypothesis is. Here is the car, and it won't start. One explanatory hypothesis is that the battery is dead. Another explanatory hypothesis is that the car won't start because the dog wasn't fed: the dog went out looking for food under the car and caused a wire to the starter to short out. But this dog hypothesis is altogether too complicated. The first hypothesis about the dead battery is shorter, simpler, better.

So the more complicated the hypothesis is, the lower its intrinsic probability.

Let's now apply these three principles to the hypothesis that God exists. We must consider:

1. The *predictive power* of the hypothesis: whether that hypothesis would warrant the prediction that the universe would be as just described, with order and people and so on. We must also consider:

2. The *prior probability* of the universe as just described: how likely it is that the universe would be that way even if God didn't exist. And we must consider

3. The *complexity* of the hypothesis.

Evaluating the God Hypothesis   In regard to the first principle, Swinburne thinks that the supposition that God exists does *not* warrant a very secure prediction that the universe would be as it is. We leave out the details of his argument, but his thesis is that, given God, the universe might well be as described above, but it certainly isn't necessary that it would be that way.

In regard to the second principle, however, Swinburne argues that it is even less likely that the universe would be as described if God didn't exist.

And in regard to the third principle, the explanation of the world as caused by God is extremely uncomplicated, Swinburne argues. His reason for saying that this hypothesis is simple rather than complicated is this: God is hypothesized to be unlimited in his powers. Now, if that which explains the universe had any limitations those limitations would themselves have to be explained. Because God doesn't have limitations, the God explanation is a simple one.

When we put all this together, what we find, he says, is that the probability that God exists, given the way the universe is, is neither 1 (certain), nor 0 (impossible). It's not a certain hypothesis, because it does not have much predictive power. On the other hand, the prior probability of the universe happening by itself is very low, and the God hypothesis is very uncomplicated. Thus the hypothesis is not a 0, either.

No Scientific Explanation of the Universe Is Possible   But even though the hypothesis that God exists is not certain—Swinburne then argues—it does nevertheless provide the only possible explanation of the universe as just described. Why? There can be no scientific explanation of the universe, he says, because science can only explain how one state of the universe is brought about by a past state; it cannot explain why the basic laws of physics are what they are and are not different. And the possibility that the universe has no explanation at all Swinburne discounts on the grounds of the universe's immense complexity.

The Testimony of Witnesses   Now, as a final consideration, many witnesses have testified to having had apparent experience of God, Swinburne says. This testimony, from so many individuals, makes the existence of God probable, *provided*, he says, there is no reason for thinking God's existence is very improbable. Because, according to what he's just shown, there is no such reasoning, Swinburne's final conclusion is that, yes, the combined evidence makes the hypothesis that God exists "more probable than not."

IF YOU ARE REAL, GOD, WHY DID YOU LET THE DEMOCRATS WIN THE ELECTION?

This, of course, is a variation of the problem of evil (see box in preceding chapter) from a Republican's viewpoint.

So that's Swinburne's argument. You have to work to follow it, but the basic idea is not difficult to grasp. Certain features of the world give evidence of God as a probable explanation for their existence, if you consider what is really involved in an explanation's probability.

By focusing on Swinburne's overall argument, we have glossed over what to many reviewers is most original and exciting in Swinburne's approach, namely, his use of the technical apparatus of probability and confirmation theory. If you are interested, you have only to read his book.

Selection 12.6 is from a chapter in Swinburne's book called "The Argument from Providence." Swinburne argues that a God has reason to make a world containing mortal beings and that there is thus some probability that he would make such a world. This is one of his less technical chapters.

▶ S E L E C T I O N   12.6

From Richard Swinburne, *THE EXISTENCE OF GOD*

Birth is fine, but what about death? Does a God have reason to make a world in which either by natural causes or by the action of agents, there is death? I believe that he does have a number of reasons to make mortal agents. The first is that if all agents are immortal, there is a certain harm (of a qualitatively different kind to other harms) which agents cannot do either to themselves or to others—they cannot deprive of existence. However much I may hate you or myself, I am stuck with you and me. And in this vital respect humanly free agents would not share the creative power of God. In refusing them this power, a God would refuse to trust his creatures in a crucial respect. To let a man have a gun is always a mark of profound trust. Secondly, a world without death is a world without the possibility of supreme self-sacrifice and courage in the face of absolute disaster. The ultimate sacrifice is the sacrifice of oneself, and that would not be possible in a world without death. ("Greater love hath no man than this, that a man lay down his life for his friends.") Supreme generosity would be impossible. So too would cheerfulness and patience in the face of absolute disaster. For in a world without death the alternatives would always involve continuance of life and presumably too the possibility that others would rescue one from one's misfortunes. There would be no absolute disaster to be faced with cheerfulness and patience.

Thirdly, a world with natural death would be a world in which an agent's own contribution would have a seriousness about it because it would be irreversible by the agent. If I spent all my seventy years doing harm, there is no time left for me to undo it. But if I live for ever, then whatever harm I do, I can always undo it. It is good that what people do should matter, and their actions matter more if they have only a limited time in which to reverse them. Fourthly, a world with birth but without natural death would be a world in which the young would never have a free hand. They would always be inhibited by the experience and influence of the aged.

The greatest value of death however seems to me to lie in a fifth consideration which is in a way opposite to my second one. I wrote earlier of the great value which lies in agents having the power to harm each other. Only agents who can do this have real power. Yet it may seem, despite the arguments which I gave earlier, unfair that creatures should be too much subject to other agents. Clearly for the sake of the potential sufferer, there must be a limit to the suffering which an agent can inflict on another. It would, I believe that we would all judge, be morally wrong for a very powerful being to give *limitless* power to one agent to hurt another. Giving to agents the power to kill is giving vast power of a qualitatively different kind from other power; but it involves the end of experience. It is very different from a power to produce endless suffering. Clearly the parent analogy suggests that it would be morally wrong to give limitless power to cause suffering. A parent, believing that an elder son ought to have responsibility, may give him power for good or ill over the younger son. But a good parent will intervene eventually if the younger son suffers too much—for the sake of the younger son. A God who did not put a limit to the amount of suffering which a creature can suffer (for any good cause, including that of the responsibility of agents) would not be a good God. There need to be limits to the intensity of suffering and to the period of suffering. A natural death after a certain small finite number of years provides the limit to the period of suffering. It is a boundary to the power of an agent over another agent. For death removes agents from that society of interdependent agents in which it is good that they should play their part. True, a God could make a temporal limit to the harm which agents could do to each other without removing them from each other's society. But that would involve agents being in mutual relation with each other while being immunized from each other's power for good or ill—and that arrangement has its own disadvantages in that the deep mutual interdependence of creatures would not hold there.

I could conclude that God would have reason to make what I shall call a World–IV. In a World–IV agents are born and die and during their life give birth, partly through their own choice, to other agents. They can make a difference to the world; but there is endless scope for improvement to it, and each generation can only forward or retard its well-being a little. Agents can make each other happy or unhappy, and can increase or decrease each other's power, knowledge, and freedom. Thereby they can affect the happiness and morality of generations distant in time. Our world is clearly a World–IV. A God has reason for making such a world.

In it there is the possibility of agents damaging each other over a number of generations until they fall badly down the ladder of ascent to divinity. Such a fall is described in a pictorial form in Genesis 3. Many modern commentators seem to me to have missed the point of this story. The point is not just that we are in a mess (of course we are), but that many of us are in a mess which is not largely of our making but which is due to others, our ancestors (and that is of course also fairly evidently so). Many, perhaps all, of the tragic situations—the hatreds and the violence—in the world today result largely from the choices of generations long past—Ireland, South Africa, the Iron Curtain, and so on. And those bad choices of centuries ago themselves were partly facilitated by bad choices of centuries before that, and so on until we reach back close to the early morally conscious choices of man.

But also in a World–IV there is the possibility of man's gradual ascent up the evolutionary scale, of man gradually developing his moral and religious awareness, and of each generation handing on to the next some new facet of that awareness. Man may grow in understanding moral truths and in applying them to the care of the less fortunate; he may grow in sensitivity to aesthetic beauty and in the creation and appreciation of works of art; in the acquisition of scientific knowledge and in its application to the betterment of the human condition and to the exploration and comprehension of the universe.

Although a God would have reason to make a World–IV, such a world is obviously a very unsatisfactory one in the crucial respect that lives capable of flourishing happily for years to come, if not for ever, are cut short, deprived of future experiences and choices. God would have reason to intervene in the process to preserve in existence in some other part of this world agents who cease to exist in our part (and of course Christian theism claims that he has so intervened). But if the advantages of a world with death are to remain, the mutual interdependence in this world must cease after a finite period (to give a limit to the suffering allowed herein) and the future existence must in no way be foreknown for certain by agents (else there would be no opportunity in our part of the world for choices of great seriousness). If God did intervene in this way, our part of the world would still be, as far as appears to its inhabitants, much like a World–IV.

J. L. Mackie's Atheism

We shall close this chapter with a selection from another English philosopher, **J. L. Mackie,** of Oxford University. In *The Miracle of Theism* (1982), Mackie examines his own list of the main arguments for God, which includes all those we have talked about here, all those considered by Swinburne, and some others besides. Mackie's finding is that "the balance of probabilities comes out strongly against the existence of a god." And his conclusion, we might note, takes into account Swinburne's strategy of joining the various arguments into a larger combined proof.

Mackie considers in detail and dismisses the theory that reports of miracles and apparent experiences of God are good evidence of a God. There are better naturalistic explanations for these things. (A *naturalistic explanation* is one that depends on no theistic or other supernaturalist assumptions.) Mackie also argues that, given that the natural world permits life to evolve, there are "no additional improbabilities" in the circumstance of conscious beings coming to exist and possessing moral values.

Now Mackie is willing to concede that a naturalistic explanation of the universe does make three things seem improbable, namely, (1) that there are regularities of cause and effect in the universe, (2) that the basic physical laws and constants are what they are and are not otherwise, and (3) that there even is a universe to begin with.

But, argues Mackie, it also seems improbable that if there were a god he would create a universe with causal laws and one with our specific laws and physical constants. For that matter, he says, it is incomprehensible how a god *could* do this. Further, that there is a God is itself improbable, he maintains. Granted, the naturalist cannot explain why there is a world, but the theist is equally embarrassed by an inability to explain why there is a god. Whatever improbability there is in the existence of an unexplained world possessing the regularities and constants that the world has, there is a greater improbability, Mackie argues, in the existence of an unexplained God capable of creating that world.

So the hypothesis that God exists is, in Mackie's view, unnecessary: it doesn't help explain anything and doesn't advance our understanding of why there is universe, of why there is something instead of nothing at all.

These points are perhaps not original with Mackie. But the argument by which he arrives at them is creative, detailed, and comprehensive.

Mackie ends his book by discussing the "lingering notion" that acceptance of atheism "would be morally and practically disastrous." Here's an excerpt, and it will conclude this chapter.

▶ S E L E C T I O N   12.7

From J. L. Mackie, THE MIRACLE OF THEISM*

(c) The Moral Consequences of Atheism

What differences would it make to morality if there were, or if there were not, a god, and again if people associated, or did not associate, their morality with religious belief?

The unsatisfactory character of the first, divine command, view of morality was pointed out by Plato, whose objections have been echoed many times. If moral values were constituted *wholly* by divine commands, so that goodness *consisted* in conformity to God's will, we could make no sense of the theist's own claims that God is good and that he seeks the good of his creation. However, it would be possible to hold coherently that while the goodness of some states of affairs— for example, of one sort of human life as contrasted with others—is independent of God's will, it is only his commands that supply the prescriptive element in morality. Or they could be seen as supplying an additional prescriptive element. A religious morality might then be seen as imposing stronger obligations.

Both these variants, however, as Kant pointed out, tend to corrupt morality, replacing the characteristically moral motives—whether these are construed as a rational sense of duty and fairness, or as specific virtuous dispositions, or as generous, co-operative, and sympathetic feelings—by a purely selfish concern for the agent's own happiness, the desire to avoid divine punishments and to enjoy the rewards of God's favour, in this life or in an afterlife. This divine command view can also lead people to accept, as moral, requirements that have no discoverable connection—indeed, no connection at all—with human purposes or well-being, or with the well being of any sentient creatures. That is, it can foster a tyrannical, irrational, morality. Of course, if there were not only a benevolent god but also a reliable revelation of his will, then we might be able to get from it expert moral advice about difficult issues, where we could not discover for ourselves what are the best policies. But there is no such reliable revelation. . . . .

It is widely supposed that Christian morality is particularly admirable. Here it is important to distinguish between the original moral teachings of Jesus, so far as we can determine them, and later developments in the Christian tradition. Richard Robinson has examined the synoptic gospels (Matthew, Mark, and Luke) as the best evidence for Jesus' own teaching, and he finds in them five major precepts: "love God, believe in me, love man, be pure in heart, be humble." The reasons given for these precepts are "a plain matter of promises and threats": they are "that the kingdom of heaven is at hand," and that "those who obey these precepts will be rewarded in heaven, while those who disobey will have weeping and gnashing of teeth." Robinson notes that "Certain ideals that are prominent elsewhere are rather conspicuously absent from the synoptic gospels." These include beauty, truth, knowledge, and reason. . . .

The later tradition of Christian ethics has tended to add to Jesus' teaching some deplorable elements, such as hostility to sex, and many more admirable ones, such as concern with justice and the other requirements for the flourishing of human life in society, and ideals of beauty, truth, knowledge, and (up to a point) reason. But it has in general retained the concern with salvation and an afterlife, and the view that disbelief, or even doubt, or criticism of belief, is sinful, with the resulting tendencies to the persecution of opponents—including, of course, the adherents of rival Christian sects and rival religions—the discouragement of discussion, hostility (even now in some places) to the teaching of well-confirmed scientific truths, like the theory of evolution, and the propagation of contrary errors, and the intellectual dishonesty of trying to suppress one's own well-founded doubts. Many people are shocked at the way in which the Unification Church ("the Moonies") entraps converts and enslaves their minds and emotions; but the same methods have been and are used by many more orthodox sects. Religion has, indeed, a remarkable ability to give vices the air of virtues, providing a sanctified outlet for some of the nastiest human motives. It is fashionable to ascribe the horrors of Nazism to an atheistic nationalism; but in fact the attitudes to the Jews which it expressed had long been established within the Christian tradition in Germany and elsewhere (sanctioned, for example, by Luther's writings), and the Old Testament itself reports many atrocities as having been not merely approved but positively demanded by God and his spokesmen. And while, following Robinson, I have spoken here particularly of Christian ethics, it is only too obvious that Islamic fundamentalism displays today, more clearly than Christianity has done recently, the worst aspects of religious morality. We do not need to go back in history to illustrate the dictum of Lucretius: *Tantum religio potuit suadere malorum* (So great are the evils that religion could prompt!). By contrast, there is a long tradition of an essentially humanist morality, from Epicurus to John Stuart Mill and modern writers, including Richard Robinson himself, centered on the conditions for the flourishing of human life and stressing intellectual honesty, tolerance, free inquiry, and individual rights.

There are, then, some marked dangers in a distinctively religious morality. . . .

But are there no corresponding dangers in a distinctively non-religious morality? Admittedly, there are. . . .

An alleged weakness, not of non-religious moralities in general, but specifically of moralities explained and understood in the naturalistic way outlined above, is that different groups of people can develop different moral views, which will produce conflict when these groups are in contact with one another, and that there is, on this basis, no clear way of resolving such conflicts. This is true. But it is not a *distinctive* weakness of the naturalistic approach. Absolutist and objectivist moralities, including ones with religious attachments, also differ from one another, and there is no clear way of resolving their conflicts either. That each party *believes* that some one morality is objectively right is no guarantee that they will be able to agree on what it is. Indeed, conflicts between rival absolutists were likely to be less resolvable than conflicts between those who understood morality in a naturalistic way, for the latter can more easily appreciate the merits of compromises and adjustment, or of finding, for the areas of contact, a *ius gentium*, a common core of principles on which they can agree. . . .

---

*Mackie's footnotes have been omitted.

To help you review, here is a checklist of the key philosophers and concepts of this chapter. The brief descriptive sentences that appear with each philosopher summarize one of his leading ideas. Keep in mind that some of these summary statements represent terrific oversimplifications of complex positions.

Checklist

Philosophers

- **William Paley**   Concocted one of the most effective pre-Darwin design arguments.

- **John Henry Newman**   Famous nineteenth-century religious thinker; held that God's existence is evidenced by the experience of conscience.

- **Søren Kierkegaard**   Held that God is beyond reason's grasp, that truth is subjective, and that salvation can be attained only through a leap of faith to Christianity.

- **Friedrich Nietzsche**   Believed that the masses are ruled by a slave morality inculcated by religion, science, and philosophy. His statement, "God is dead," meant that there is no rational order, not that people don't believe in God.

- **William James**   Held that it is rationally justifiable to yield to your hope that a God exists.

- **Blaise Pascal** Seventeenth-century French mathematician whose "wager" was that it is prudent to bet that God exists.
- **F. R. Tennant** Twentieth-century religious thinker who proposed a subtle version of the design argument that takes into account contemporary science and evolutionary theory.
- **Antony Flew** Contemporary analytic philosopher; argued that talk about God is unverifiable and hence meaningless.
- **Richard Swinburne** Contemporary analytic religious thinker; believed that God is an inductively sound explanatory hypothesis.
- **J. L. Mackie** Contemporary analytic critic of theism.

Concepts

Paley's watch

leap of faith

"God is dead"

overman

live, momentous, and forced issues

James's "two commandments" of rationality

pragmatism

Pascal's wager

verifiability principle

Vienna Circle

logical positivism

Big Bang

personal explanation

explanatory hypothesis

predictive power

prior probability

complexity

God's foreknowledge vs. free will

naturalistic explanation

God's gender?

Questions for Discussion and Review

1. Explain and critically evaluate Paley's design argument. Is it crazy to think that an organ like the eye is anything other than strong evidence of God?

2. Does the world/universe—or something or another in it—give evidence of divine design? Explain.

3. Does the theory of evolution undermine the design argument?

4. Is Newman correct in thinking that the existence of God is given to us in the experience of conscience? Explain.

5. Explain James's argument for God. Is it a version of Pascal's wager? Is it sound? Why?

6. Is James correct in saying that you cannot really suspend judgment about God's existence?

7. Is the question of God's existence live and momentous, as James says?

8. Is it rare for people to decide things on the basis of reasoned argument? Is it possible for them to do so?

9. Which is "better," to doubt everything that is less than certain or highly probable, or to believe falsehoods?

10. "It is impossible for normal people to believe that free will does not exist. Therefore it does exist." Evaluate this remark. "It is impossible for normal people to believe that free will does not exist. Therefore it is reasonable to believe that it does exist." Evaluate this remark.

11. "Most people believe in God; therefore God must exist." Evaluate this claim.

12. Is the fact that the world is intelligible evidence of divine design?

13. "He died because God called on him." "The sprinkler stopped working due to fate." Are these claims equally meaningless? Explain. Is the claim, "God exists," verifiable or falsifiable? Are any (other) claims made about God verifiable?

14. Assuming that there is scientific evidence that the universe had an absolute beginning, does that evidence also prove the existence of God? Explain.

15. Is the belief that the proposition, "God exists," is meaningless a form of atheism?

16. "The features of the world add to the probability that God exists, but do not automatically make it probable that God exists." Explain this remark.

17. Can you logically believe both that God knows everything and that there is free will? Explain the difficulty.

18. How valid as proof of God's existence are purported eye-witness reports of miracles?

19. "Even assuming that the existence of God explains why there is a world, what explains why there is a God?" Does this question contain a valid criticism of the cosmological proof of God? Is Mackie correct in saying that the explanation of the universe as caused by God doesn't advance our understanding of why there is a universe?

20. Would universal acceptance of atheism be morally disastrous for society?

21. In what sense is it legitimate rationally to think of God as male?

A. Flew and A. MacIntire, eds., *New Essays in Philosophical Theology* (New York: Macmillan, 1984). A popular anthology covering a range of topics. For a follow-up to the article by Flew excerpted in this text, see the pieces by F. Hare and B. Mitchell entitled "Theology and Falsification."

W. James, *The Will to Believe and Other Essays in Popular Philosophy*, ed. Frederick H. Burkhardt (Cambridge, Mass.: Harvard University Press, 1979). James is among the most pleasurable of philosophers to read.

Suggested Further Readings

W. T. Jones, *A History of Western Philosophy*, 2nd ed., vol. 6 (New York: Harcourt Brace Jovanovich, 1975). See chapter 6 for a good discussion of Kierkegaard and Nietzsche.

W. Kaufmann, *Nietzsche* (New York: Meridian, 1956). Good introduction to Nietzsche's philosophy.

J. Hick, "Theology and Verification," in *Theology Today*, vol. 17, no. 1 (April, 1960). A response to verificationist attacks of religious language.

J. L. Mackie, *The Miracle of Theism: Arguments For and Against the Existence of God* (Oxford, Clarendon Press, 1982). Excellent commentary on all the traditional and recent proofs (and other discussions) of God's existence.

R. J. Moore and B. N. Moore, *The Cosmos, God and Philosophy* (New York: Peter Lang, 1988).

W. Paley, *Natural Theology: Selections*, ed. Frederick Ferré (Indianapolis: Bobbs-Merrill, 1963). There is more to Paley than his famous stone and watch analogy, as the reader of this book will discover.

J. H. Newman, *A Grammar of Assent*, C. F. Harrold, ed. (New York: Longmans, Green and Co., 1947). Newman's most important book.

I. Ramsey, *Religious Language* (New York: Macmillan, 1963). A discussion of the questions surrounding the meaning of religious language.

R. Swinburne, *The Existence of God* (Oxford: Clarendon Press, 1979). Contains (or is) Swinburne's original "inductive" proof of God.

F. R. Tennant, *Philosophical Theology*, vol. 2 (New York: Cambridge University Press, 1928).

J. Thompson, *Kierkegaard* (Garden City, N.Y.: Doubleday, 1972). A collection of essays on Kierkegaard that were selected "so as to give the reader some sense of the shape and direction of recent Kierkegaardian criticism."

SUMMARY AND CONCLUSION

Let's just take stock of all this. Anselm, with whose philosophy we began this part, thought it follows from the very concept of God that God exists. This was the ontological argument.

The ontological argument was rejected by Aquinas, who said you can prove God's existence only by considering God's work, that is, by considering the world we perceive around us. Aquinas laid out five ways in which God can be inferred to exist from the evidence presented to us by the world. Three of these are forms of what is called the cosmological argument, according to which God may be deduced as the first cause or ultimate explanation of the world. Another of Aquinas's proofs was a version of the teleological argument, which reasons from the appearance of design in the world around us to the existence of God as its designer. And the remaining proof infers God from the existence of goodness; this is a type of moral argument for God's existence.

Descartes thought that once you consider the matter closely, you will see that the existence of your own idea of God proves that God exists. He also found a version of the ontological argument compelling. Leibniz argued that there must always be an explanation of why things are exactly as they are and are not otherwise, and this simple fact entails absolutely that there exists a necessary being, God.

With Hume and Kant we saw the other side of the coin, for both attacked the teleological and cosmological arguments as unsound. Kant also raised a fundamental objection to the ontological argument, though he nevertheless believed that the belief in God is rationally justified for any moral agent.

William Paley, we saw, ignored Hume's and Kant's criticisms of the design argument and published a version of the design argument that has remained popular to this day. Somewhat later, John Henry Newman, who was concerned with real-life or "concrete" reasoning, believed that in the experience of conscience we can attain certitude that God exists.

William James approached the issue from a different perspective. Does God exist? Well, said James, if you are like I am in finding that the unaided intellect just does not settle whether God does or does not exist, and if you consider what attaches to believing in God on the one hand and disbelieving in him on the other, then you shall find it makes good sense to believe in God.

In the twentieth century, we found F. R. Tennant proposing yet another version of the design argument. Tennant's careful and complex rendering of the argument emphasized the richness, subtlety, and beauty of the fit between human beings and their physical environment and, unlike Paley's, took into account the theory of evolution. Another complex argument for God was proposed in recent years by Richard Swinburne, an argument that draws on probability theory to reach the final conclusion that, when all the evidence that bears on the matter one way or the other is duly considered, the hypothesis that God exists is more probable than not.

But again on the other side of the coin, in this century A. N. Flew suggested that assertions about God are in fact meaningless, and J. L. Mackie criticized the hypothesis that God exists as improbable and unenlightening. Suffice it to say that the jury is still out on God, at least among professional philosophers.

Now not terribly long ago a student of one of the authors told him that the section on philosophy of religion in his introductory course had significantly affected her life. "How so?" he asked. "Did the course change your opinion about God?"

The student said, no, she had believed in God before the course, and still believed in God. But she now felt that there was a *rational justification* for believing in God. That discovery, she said, was very important to her. It had made her comfortable with her belief. It had given moorings to her faith.

Of course, her experience might have had a different outcome. She might have concluded that there really is no rational support for a belief in God. Many people who read in the philosophy of religion have come to that conclusion, after all. Coming to that conclusion, we suspect, would have been equally momentous to this student.

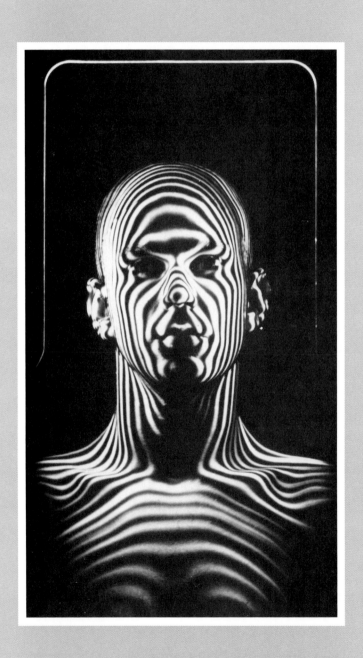

Analytic Philosophy

CHAPTER 13

The Proper Method of Philosophy

*[Philosophical analysis] seemed to have accomplished precisely
what speculative metaphysics had for so long failed to do: it
had led to significant progress in the resolution of outstanding
philosophical problems, and it had provided a basis for sub-
stantive philosophical agreement.*

—GEORGE D. ROMANOS

*Linguistic analysis . . . is at best entirely inconsequential. And,
at worst, it is an escape into the non-controversial, the unreal,
into that which is only academically controversial.*

—HERBERT MARCUSE

The twentieth century—the century of world wars, nuclear weapons,
television, space travel, genetic engineering, and spring riots in Fort Lau-
derdale. In art and literature traditional structures and approaches were
cast aside with abandon. Schoenberg and Stravinsky brought the world
music that lacked tonality; Cage brought it music that lacked sound. In
Russia and China the followers of Marx declared an end to the existing
order, and in Europe existentialist philosophers proclaimed the absurdity
of the human predicament. Meanwhile, in England and America, as we
saw in Chapter 6, philosophers lectured quietly in ivy-covered buildings
about—what? *Sense-data?* We'd best have a closer look at twentieth-
century philosophy in English-speaking countries.

Twentieth-century Anglo-American philosophy was profoundly influenced by Bertrand Russell, G. E. Moore, Ludwig Wittgenstein, John

Twentieth-Century Philosophy

Twentieth-century philosophy has three "traditions." One, **analytic philosophy,** developed from the work of primarily British philosophers who thought that analysis is the proper method of philosophy. The majority of those who teach philosophy in English-speaking countries hail from the analytic tradition. **Existentialism** and **phenomenology,** in contrast, evolved in continental Europe and, to somewhat a lesser extent, Latin America; most university-level appointments in philosophy in these areas of the world are held by those whose background is in one or the other or both of these traditions. (Sometimes Marxism is listed as a fourth tradition in twentieth-century philosophy, but in this book we treat Marxism as a field of political philosophy: see Part 4.)

Any brief statement of the differences among analytic philosophy, existentialism, and phenomenology is bound to be an oversimplification. Nevertheless, perhaps this much may be said in anticipation of more detailed discussion in this and the next chapter: Analysts emphasize linguistic and conceptual clarification as a method for resolving philosophical problems. Existentialists are concerned with finding meaningful existence for the twentieth-century individual, who, they believe, lives in an absurd world. And phenomenologists seek a rigorous yet purely descriptive methodology for studying a chosen subject. For Edmund Husserl, a leading phenomenologist discussed in Part 7, this took the form of a presuppositionless investigation of subjective conscious experience. Phenomenology and existentialism have been so interactive that they often are lumped together as *Continental philosophy.* Neither school has been particularly interactive with analytic philosophy, though this situation may be changing.

The differences between analytic philosophy, on one hand, and existentialism and phenomenology, on the other, seem to us to call for different approaches to explaining them to you. In Chapters 13 and 14 we introduce analytic philosophy by focusing on a particular set of issues that has been of concern to many analytic philosophers. In Part 7, which is Chapter 15, instead of focusing on a specific issue we consider the basic thought of two famous existentialists and two famous phenomenologists.

Wisdom, Gilbert Ryle, A. J. Ayer and other philosophers who, during the first thirty-five or forty years of the century regarded **analysis** as the proper method of philosophy. Thus philosophy in the English-speaking world during this century, which is largely an outgrowth of the discussions and writings of these and other analysts, is often called **analytic philosophy** in contrast with the philosophy that has evolved in Europe and Latin America, which we'll discuss later in Part 7, on existentialism and phenomenology.

What Analysis Is Just what is analysis, anyway? Quite simply put, *philosophical analysis resolves complex propositions or concepts into simpler ones.*
Let's take an elementary example. The proposition,

might be resolved by analysis into the simpler proposition,

"No squares are circular."

This second proposition is "simpler" philosophically because it refers only to squares and their lack of circularity, whereas the first proposition refers to two distinct classes of entities, square circles and nonexistent things.

Moreover, the first proposition is very troubling philosophically. It is certainly an intelligible proposition. Hence it would seem that square circles and nonexistent things must (somehow and amazingly) exist in some sense or another. For if they did not exist, then the proposition would be about nothing and thus would not be intelligible. (It is precisely this reasoning that has led some philosophers to conclude that every object of thought must exist "in some sense," or "subsist.")

So the second sentence contains the same information as the first but does not have the puzzling implications of the first. Not only is it simpler than the second, it is also clearer. Once the first sentence is recast or analyzed in this way, we can accept what the first sentence says without having to concede that square circles and nonexistent things exist "in some sense."

This very simple example of analysis will perhaps help make it clear why many analytic philosophers have regarded analysis as having great importance for the field of metaphysics. Be sure that you understand the example and everything we have said about it before you read any further.

Why Analysis Became Important

To understand better why analysis became so important as a method of philosophy, think back to Kant (Part 2). Kant thought that knowledge is possible if we limit our inquiries to things as they are experienceable, because the mind imposes categories on experienceable objects. The Absolute Idealists then expanded on Kant's theory and held that the categories of thought *are* the categories of being.

But this notion, that the categories of thought are the categories of being, is open to a certain amount of abuse and can in fact throw open the doors to the grandiose metaphysical speculation that Kant himself was anxious to combat. And consider this problem: What the categories of thought are to metaphysician A may not be the categories recognized by metaphysician B. So the question arises: How do you determine whose metaphysical system is correct, A's or B's? Granted, if A's system is in some respect self-contradictory, that would be a decisive reason for rejecting it. But even if A's and B's system are both internally consistent (not self-contradictory), they may still be vastly different. Just how do you determine whose system is correct?

So the situation by the late nineteenth century was this: on one hand, *science* was making great and striking advances, advances conceded to be genuine by scientists and nonscientists alike. But the situation seemed quite different in *philosophy*, at least in the late stages of Absolute Idealism. Those who worked from within a given metaphysical system could claim that significant headway had been made, but adherents of competing systems were usually of a different opinion about the significance or even the genuineness of the touted advances. So to the lay public generally, which could not possibly judge the alternatives or even understand them, the situation in metaphysical philosophy seemed *just awful*. Philosophy, apart from political philosophy and ethics, seem mired in hopeless and verbose speculation. To many scientists and scientifically or mathematically trained philosophers, metaphysics had become a tedious and even repellent mass of trifling verbiage.

One of these scientifically-trained individuals was **Bertrand Russell** (1872–1970), a Cambridge mathematician and philosopher. Russell began his philosophical career as a British Hegelian but came to regard Hegel's metaphysics as resting essentially on a silly verbal confusion and as of no more intrinsic philosophical interest or merit than a pun. When he read what Hegel had to say in the philosophy of mathematics, Russell was horrified, finding it both ignorant and stupid.

To anyone familiar with and sympathetic to nineteenth century German and British idealistic metaphysics, Russell's opinion of the tradition will seem unduly harsh. But Russell, rightly or wrongly, came to the conclusion that the idealistic metaphysics of his predecessors largely rested on mistakes and confusions rather like that described in our opening paragraphs, in which someone concludes from the fact that square circles can be talked about that they exist.

When Russell turned his attention to the philosophy of mathematics, he demonstrated, through the careful use of *analysis*, that mathematical truths could be derived from principles of logic (something that other philosophers had thought was true but had not demonstrated) and that propositions about numbers could be resolved into propositions about classes of classes. The importance of this achievement, of this apparent reduction of number theory to set theory, seemed undeniable to anyone who cared to consider it and was indisputably a stunning intellectual achievement. Russell had in effect shown that there was no more need to credit existence to numbers as something over and above and distinct from classes than there is to credit existence to square circles.

The same method of analysis was then applied by Russell and others to other notorious philosophical problems. The resulting solutions, unlike many so-called solutions of the idealists, however, seemed definitive to those who considered them. The method of analysis, in short, to those who familiarized themselves with it, seemed to yield substantial and demonstrable results, results very much like those achieved by science. In contrast to what seemed true of the apparently futile disputations of the nineteenth-century metaphysicians, philosophy was perceived at last *to be getting somewhere.*

The Evolution of Analytic Philosophy

Over the first half of the twentieth century, analysis became different things to different people and was used with different purposes in mind. For some, an analysis of an expression was in effect a mere paraphrase that, it was thought, was in some sense less misleading philosophically than the original. Some philosophers, such as **Gilbert Ryle**, thought the principal business of philosophy was to use such techniques of paraphrase to resolve or dissolve traditional philosophical problems, which were asserted largely to rest on "linguistic confusions." Analysis, on this view, was a sort of linguistic therapy for those who were troubled by these traditional problems.

Others, among them Russell, had a larger vision and thought that analysis was the means by which philosophy could actually disclose the ultimate logical constituents of reality, their interrelations, and their relationship to the world of experience. Russell's student, **Ludwig Wittgenstein** (1889–1951), thought the goal of analysis was to reduce all complex descriptive propositions to their ultimately simple constituent propositions. These latter propositions would consist of "names" in combination, which would represent the ultimate simple constituents of reality.

And, yes, many philosophers, for the reasons noted in Part 2, thought a prime objective of philosophy should be the analysis of propositions about physical objects into propositions about sense-data.

In the 1920s, Moritz Schlick, a philosopher at the University of Vienna, formed a group known as the Vienna Circle, the members of which were much impressed by the work of Russell and Wittgenstein. Calling themselves the **logical positivists,** the group held that philosophy is not a theory but an activity whose business is the logical clarification of thought. The logical positivists proclaimed a "verifiability criterion of meaning," according to which genuine propositions are either tautologies or are empirically verifiable (i.e., testable through observation). The pro-

Profile: Ludwig Wittgenstein (1889–1951)

So many discussions of Wittgenstein's philosophy were submitted to philosophy journals in the 1950s and 1960s that for a while some journals declined to accept further manuscripts on his ideas. No other philosopher of this century, save perhaps Bertrand Russell, has had as great an impact on philosophy in Great Britain and in the United States.

Wittgenstein was born in Vienna into a wealthy family and studied to become an engineer. From engineering his interests led him to pure mathematics and then to the philosophical foundations of mathematics. He soon gave up engineering to study philosophy with Russell at Cambridge in 1912–1913. The following year he studied philosophy alone and in seclusion in Norway, partly because he perceived himself as irritating others by his nervous personality. During World War I he served in the Austrian army; it was in this period that he completed the first of his two major works, the *Tractatus Logico-Philosophicus* (1921).

Wittgenstein's father had left Wittgenstein a large fortune, which after the war Wittgenstein simply handed over to two of his sisters, and he became an elementary school teacher. Next, in 1926, he became a gardener's assistant, perhaps a surprising walk of life for one of the most profound thinkers of all time. He did, however, return to Cambridge in 1929 and received his doctorate, the *Tractatus* serving as his dissertation. In 1937, he succeeded G. E. Moore in his chair of philosophy.

During World War II Wittgenstein found himself unable to sit idly by, so he worked for two years as a hospital orderly and for another as an assistant in a medical lab. Time and again Wittgenstein, an heir to a great fortune and a genius, placed himself in the humblest of positions.

In 1944, Wittgenstein resumed his post at Cambridge but, troubled by what he thought was his harmful effect on students and disturbed by their apparent poor comprehension of his ideas, he resigned in 1947. His second major work, the *Philosophical Investigations*, was published in 1953, two years after his death.

Reportedly, when he became seriously ill in April 1951 and was told by his physician that he was about to die, his response was, simply, "Good." When he died a few days later his last words were, "Tell them I've had a wonderful life."

nouncements of metaphysics and theology, they said, because these pronouncements cannot be tested empirically, are meaningless, a type of windy nonsense. Moral and value statements, they held, are merely expressions of emotion. Philosophy, they said, has as its only useful function the analysis of both everyday language and scientific language—it has no legitimate concern with the world apart from language or even with the connection between language and the world.

Wittgenstein's Turnaround

Wittgenstein's philosophy divides into two phases. Both had a great influence on his contemporaries, yet the philosophy of the second phase, that of the *Philosophical Investigations* (1953), is largely a rejection of the central ideas of the first, that of the *Tractatus* (1921). This is an unusual but not a unique occurrence in the history of philosophy, for other philosophers have come to reject their earlier positions.

In both works Wittgenstein was concerned with the relationships between language and the world. The *Tractatus* assumes a single, essential relationship; the *Investigations* denies this assumption.

In the *Tractatus*, Wittgenstein portrays the function of language as that of describing the world and is concerned with making it clear just how language and thought hook onto reality in the first place.

Well, just how does language hook onto reality? According to Wittgenstein, a proposition (or a thought) *pictures* the fact it represents. It can picture it, he said, because both it and the fact share the same *logical form*, a form that can be exhibited by philosophical analysis. All genuine propositions, he held, are reducible to logically elementary propositions, which, he said, are composed of *names* of absolutely simple objects. A combination of these names (i.e., a proposition), pictures a combination of *objects* in the world (i.e., a fact). The *Tractatus* is devoted in large measure to explaining and working out the implications of this picture theory of meaning across a range of philosophical topics.

But in the *Investigations*, Wittgenstein casts off completely this picture theory of meaning and the underlying assumption of the *Tractatus* that there is some universal function of language. After all, he notes in the later work, how a picture is *used* determines what it is a picture of—one and the same picture could be a picture of a man holding a guitar, or of how to hold a guitar, or of what a guitar looks like, or of what Bill Jones's fingers look like, and so on. Similarly, what a sentence means is determined by the use to which it is put within a given context or "language-game." Further, says the later Wittgenstein, there is nothing that the various uses of language have in common, and there is certainly no set of ideal elementary propositions to which all other propositions are reducible. In short, according to the later work the earlier work is completely wrongheaded.

When philosophers ignore the "game" in which language is used—Wittgenstein says in the *Investigations*—when they take language "on a holiday" and try to strait-jacket it into conformity with some idealized and preconceived notion of what its essence must be, the result is the unnecessary confusion known as a philosophical problem. From this perspective, the history of philosophy is a catalog of confusions that result from taking language on a holiday.

The Vienna Circle dissolved when the Nazis took control of Austria in the late 1930s, but to this day many people still equate analytic philosophy with logical positivism. This is true despite the fact that nowadays very few philosophers who refer to themselves as analysts subscribe to the verifiability criterion of meaning or accept many other of the basic assumptions of logical positivism.

In fact, today it's extremely doubtful whether many of those who would call themselves analytic philosophers would even describe analysis as the only proper method of philosophy. Indeed, few would even describe their daily philosophical task as primarily one of analysis. There are other philosophical tasks one might undertake than analysis, and some who would still not hesitate to call themselves "analysts" have simply lost interest in analysis in favor of these other tasks. Others, like Wittgenstein, for example, have explicitly repudiated analysis as the proper method of philosophy. Wittgenstein's about-face (see box) was published in 1953 in his enormously influential *Philosophical Investigations*.

Further, it is now widely held that many philosophically interesting claims and expressions cannot intelligibly be regarded as complexes subject to resolution into simpler and less misleading expressions. Certainly, the intent to recast the meaning of an expression into a less misleading form can be carried out only if its "real" or "true" meaning can be ascertained by the analyst. But concerns have been raised, perhaps most notably by **W. V. O. Quine**, about whether it is ever possible to say in some absolute, nonrelativistic sense what the meaning of an expresson is. And for many expressions it seems inappropriate in the first place to speak of their "meaning"; clearer understanding of many expressions seems to be achieved when we ask how the expression is used or what it is used to do, rather than what it means, unless the latter question is taken as being equivalent to the two former questions, as it often is.

So it has become accepted that there are many useful philosophical methods and techniques other than the analysis of language, and it is pretty widely thought that good, substantial philosophical work is by no means always the result of analysis of some sort. Many of today's analytic philosophers would deny being directly concerned with language (though most are concerned with expressing themselves in clear language). Nor could it be said that all analytic philosophers mean the same thing when they speak of analysis. In its broadest sense, a call for "analysis" today is just simply a call for clarification, and certainly today's analytic philosophers exhibit (or hope they exhibit) a concern for clarity of thought and expression. Most, too, would be inclined to say that at least some opinions expressed by earlier philosophers reflect linguistic confusions if not outright logical errors, but beyond this it is not the case that all analytic philosophers use some common unique method of philosophizing or have the same interests or share an identifiable approach to philosophical problems. In today's world philosophers are apt to call themselves "analytic" to indicate that they do not have much training or interest in existentialism or phenomenology as much as for any other reason.

So, then, a history of analytic philosophy is, for all intents and purposes, a history of a predominant strain of twentieth-century philosophy in English-speaking countries that has evolved from the philosophical writings and discussions of Russell, Moore, Wittgenstein, and others. We'll not endeavor to provide an entire history of analytic philosophy in this broad sense and instead will focus on one subject that has received much attention at the hands of those who have called themselves analysts or were so called by others. This subject is known as the philosophy of mind. In focusing on the philosophy of mind, we'll be able to illustrate some of the alternative things philosophers have meant by "analysis."

The Paradox of Analysis

An analysis of a proposition involves restating the proposition in different words, as you've seen. Thus, for example, you might analyze, "Square circles are nonexisting things," as, "Nothing is both square and circular." In other words, according to this analysis: *To say that square circles are nonexisting things is to say that nothing is both square and circular.*

The italicized sentence states the analysis of the proposition, "Square circles are nonexisting things." Now think about what the italicized sentence means. If it is true, then the sentence, "Square circles are nonexisting things," is identical with the sentence, "Nothing is both square and circular." And if these last two sentences are identical, then you can substitute one for the other whenever either appears, right? So let's make such a substitution in the second half of the italicized sentence.

The result is this sentence: *To say that square circles are nonexisting things is to say that square circles are nonexisting things.*

In other words, the first italicized sentence, if true, is identical with the second italicized sentence. But the second italicized sentence is trivial! Hence the first italicized sentence is also trivial. And that means that our analysis is trivial, because the first italicized sentence expresses our analysis.

This is the paradox of analysis. For an analysis of a given proposition to be correct, the proposition and its analysis must be equivalent. But if they are equivalent, then sentences that express the equivalence are mere trivial truisms. In short, analyses are either incorrect or trivial.

G. E. Moore, an analyst for over a half century, professed an inability to resolve this ugly paradox to his satisfaction. Can you resolve it?

A discussion of this subject will also serve very nicely to highlight some of the differences between analytic philosophy on one hand and existentialism and phenomenology on the other. These other two "types" of philosophical inquiry are also concerned with issues related to the human mind, though their perspective and concerns, as you will see, are quite different from those of analytic philosophers.

Checklist

To help you review, here is a checklist of the key philosophers and concepts of this chapter. The brief descriptive sentences that appear with each philosopher summarize one of his leading ideas. Keep in mind that some of these summary statements represent terrific oversimplifications of complex positions.

Philosophers

- **Bertrand Russell** Most influential early practitioner of the analytic method in philosophy. Applied techniques of analysis to mathematics and philosophy.

- **G. E. Moore** Another important early analytic philosopher; emphasized the paradox of analysis but was unable to resolve it.

- **Gilbert Ryle** Held that traditional philosophical problems were linguistic confusions that could be resolved by analysis.

- **Ludwig Wittgenstein**   Russell's student; ultimately thought by many to be the most profound of twentieth-century philosophers. Advanced the picture theory of meaning, then later rejected it.
- **Moritz Schlick**   Formed the Vienna Circle of logical positivists.
- **W. V. O. Quine**   American analytic philosopher; questioned whether it is possible to specify the meaning of an expression in an absolute sense.

Concepts

analysis

verifiability criterion of meaning

logical positivism

Vienna Circle

picture theory of meaning

the paradox of analysis

**Questions for
Discussion
and Review**

1. How would you go about determining which of two competing metaphysical systems is "correct"?

2. What does philosophical analysis do? In other words, define philosophical analysis.

3. What is accomplished by the use of philosophical analysis?

4. "Square circles are nonexistent things." "No squares are circles." Which of these two propositions is simpler, philosophically, and why?

5. What is the verifiability criterion of meaning?

6. Do all analytic philosophers regard analysis as *the* proper method of philosophy? Do all accept the verifiability criterion of meaning?

7. Explain, in your own words, the paradox of analysis.

8. "The first woman president of the United States is unmarried." Is this sentence true or false or neither? Explain why.

**Suggested Further
Readings**

A. J. Ayer, *Language, Truth and Logic*, 2nd rev. ed. (New York: Dover, 1946). Stimulating. Ayer explains the basic positivist position in easy-to-understand yet powerful language.

A. J. Ayer, ed., *Logical Positivism* (Glencoe, Ill.: Free Press, 1959). An important anthology that contains essays both sympathetic and critical of analytic philosophy and positivism, and an excellent bibliography.

John Hospers, *An Introduction to Philosophical Analysis* (Englewood Cliffs, N.J.: Prentice-Hall, 1953). This is what you should read as the next step in acquainting yourself with analytic philosophy.

Norman Malcolm, "Wittgenstein's Philosophical Investigations," *Philosophical Review* 47 (1956). A reasonably readable explication of important aspects of Wittgenstein's difficult work.

George D. Romanos, *Quine and Analytic Philosophy* (Cambridge, Mass.: Bradford, 1983). Good, brief history of analytic philosophy; fine bibliography.

Richard Rorty, ed., *The Linguistic Turn* (Chicago: The University of Chicago Press, 1967). An anthology of important essays in analytic philosophy.

J. O. Urmson, *Philosophical Analysis* (London: Oxford University Press, 1956). Surveys logical atomism and logical positivism. Not easy reading for introductory students, but detailed and complete.

G. Warnock, *English Philosophy Since 1900* (London: Oxford University Press, 1958). Brief and readable history of analytic philosophy in England.

Case Study in Analysis: Mind

I am, I exist; that is certain.

   —RENÉ DESCARTES

[The self, the "I"] is introduced, not because observation reveals it, but because it is linguistically convenient and apparently demanded by grammar. Nominal entities of this sort may or may not exist, but there is no good ground for supposing that they do.

   —BERTRAND RUSSELL

The philosophy of mind is a vast area of analytic philosophy that deals not with a single problem but with a host of interrelated issues and concerns. These issues and concerns have become so numerous, complicated, and involved, that many philosophers now treat the philosophy of mind as a separate major philosophical area in its own right, like epistemology and the philosophy of religion. What follows is only a brief overview.

The **philosophy of mind** is concerned primarily with the nature of consciousness, mental states (or psychological states, these being the same), and the mind. The approach usually taken (as you might expect from what we've said about analytic philosophy) is to look at everyday psychological vocabulary—with its reference to mental states of various sorts, including beliefs, desires, fears, suspicions, hopes, ideas, preferences, choices, thoughts, motives, urges, and so forth—and ask what this psychological vocabulary means, or how it is to be analyzed. In recent years these inquiries have broadened to encompass the research and findings of psychologists, neuroscientists, computer scientists, linguists, artificial intelligence researchers, and other specialists. The philosophy of mind is no longer the preserve of the professional philosopher.

A good approach to this large subject is to ask whether the mind is physical (material), nonphysical, both, or neither?

Let's begin by noting that many—perhaps most—members of Western societies take the position that a person has a nonmaterial mind or soul or spirit associated with his or her physical body. You may well take this position. And, as you may recall from Part 1 on metaphysics, this position is known as dualism. Let's take a closer look at it.

Dualism

According to the dualist, every existing thing (except for abstract items, e.g., geometric points, numbers, and brotherhood) is either *physical* (or material, these terms being used interchangeably here) or *nonphysical* (or immaterial or incorporeal, these terms also being interchangeable).

Physical things possess physical properties (like density, velocity, charge, temperature, mass, and, most fundamentally, spatial occupancy), and nonphysical things possess nonphysical properties. These latter properties are difficult to specify, though dualists would say that only nonphysical entities can have conscious states or exercise volition. Both physical and nonphysical things can have neutral properties. For example, physical and nonphysical things both have temporal properties, both may be numerous, belong to groups, and so forth.

A human being, according to the dualist, has (or is) both a physical body and a nonphysical mind (or soul or spirit). Further, according to

Popular Reasons for Believing that We Are Not Purely Physical Things

Why believe that a human being is not a thing purely physical (material, corporeal)? Here are some popular reasons.

- There's a world of difference between people and physical objects. People, unlike physical objects, have feelings, emotions, thoughts, and beliefs and can perform lots of acts purely physical things cannot. The best explanation of these facts is that people have something that purely physical things don't have, something nonphysical.

- People, unlike physical objects, have free will, which they wouldn't have if their minds were mere physical things.

- People are artistically (and otherwise) creative and have aesthetic sensibility—impossibilities for mere blind material things.

- People can sometimes override the constraints of physics. An example is overcoming a terminal disease through the exertion of will. Even leaving aside such questionable things as extrasensory perception, out-of-body travel, and walking on burning coals, people often demonstrate the power of mind over matter.

- People can have knowledge of nonmaterial things, like the truths of mathematics. Therefore they are not themselves totally physical.

- It is possible to doubt the existence of any given physical thing, as Descartes made clear. But it is not possible to doubt the existence of your own mind (as Descartes also made clear). Therefore your mind is not a physical thing.

- Beliefs and thoughts have properties that physical things by definition cannot have. Beliefs, for instance, are true or false. Physical things are not. So beliefs and thoughts are not physical. Conversely, physical things have properties that beliefs and thoughts cannot have, properties like location, density, temperature, and so forth. The same conclusion follows.

- I have knowledge of my mental states, but it is not gained through observation. Physical things, on the other hand, I find out about only through observation. So physical things and my mind states are essentially different.

Further considerations possibly supportive of dualism are mentioned in the text. Can you think of any others yourself?

(Most analytic philosophers, incidentally, would dispute the cogency of all these reasons.)

the dualist, a person's nonphysical and physical components are *interactive:* if someone comes along and gives you a *shove,* you may well become angry. In other words, the shoving of your physical body causes anger to arise in your nonphysical mind. Or—to run things in reverse—when you decide to do something, your body normally follows through; that is, your nonphysical mind causes your physical body to walk or run or speak or whatever it is you want your body to do.

Actually, a dualist doesn't have to believe that the immaterial mind and the material body interact, but most dualists do, so when we talk about dualism here we mean **interactionist dualism.**

Now to the extent that many people have ever thought about it, it seems pretty nearly self-evident that a human being has a nonphysical component of some sort, be it called a mind, soul, spirit, or something else. Do you believe this? Then you should be aware that there are reasons to suppose otherwise (see box). The difficulties in dualism have led many analytic philosophers to doubt whether dualism is a viable theory at all, and they have cast about for more attractive alternatives.

Let's now consider four **physicalist** (nondualist) analytic philosophies of the mind and mental states, in rough chronological order, beginning with the theory called neutral monism. Then we will close the chapter with a brief look at some of the issues that are now current in physicalist discussions of the mind.

Four Nondualist Theories of Mind

Theory 1: Neutral Monism

Recall that for Bertrand Russell analysis meant resolving a complex proposition into simpler propositions, propositions that do not make reference to unnecessary or questionable categories of things. Indeed, for Russell, the process of analysis is itself the proper method by which the metaphysician determines which categories of things are necessary to assume in the first place. Thus, as we've seen, propositions about numbers can be resolved into propositions about classes, according to Russell. We could express the same point by saying that, for Russell, numbers are *reducible* to classes.

Russell believed that other metaphysically important reductions could be achieved through analysis. In particular, he held that such entities of physics as points, instants, and particles, indeed physical objects in general, are reducible to sense-data. He also maintained that minds are likewise reducible to sense-data, and this is the point of interest here.

What does it mean to say that one kind of thing is "reducible" to another kind of thing, and why on earth would anyone think it important to make such reductions in the first place?

To **reduce** something, a physical object, for example, to something else, sense-data, for example, is (as we've noted) to replace a sentence about the physical object by a set of sentences about sense-data, a set of sentences that mean the same thing as the original sentence. Thus, the sentence, "I am eating an apple," theoretically might be replaced by a set of sentences that refer to a certain set of sense-data of taste, smell, touch, and sight (those sense-data that you have when you eat an apple). To replace the original sentence in this way would be to "reduce" the apple to sense-data.

What is gained by this procedure? The reduction reveals that what

Reasons for Doubting that the Mind Is Nonphysical

- First is the *characterization problem*. An immaterial mind and its states tend always to be characterized negatively, e.g., as not being divisible, as not being in space, as not being tangible, and so forth. A thing characterized only negatively is difficult to distinguish from nothingness.

- Second is the *individuation problem*. Two people cannot share a single mind. So let us consider what would account for this fact. If the mind were a *physical* thing like a brain, what would account for it is that a physical thing like a brain cannot be in two separate locations at the same time. But if the mind is nonphysical, then the fact that one mind cannot be shared by two people seems just inexplicable.

- Third is the *emergence problem*. If minds are immaterial, then at some stage in the evolution of human beings immaterial minds first made their appearance. But the selection of a point in the evolutionary history of humans at which minds first emerged could never be determined, even in principle. Further, for the immaterial mind to have emerged, it must have had some advantage in regard to the survival of the species. To account for the survival of the human species, however, it is not necessary to postulate the existence of an immaterial mind: the development of the brain and nervous system is sufficient for this purpose.

- Fourth is the *dependency problem*: there is an apparent dependency of mental states on brain states. For example, that my thoughts or beliefs or any of my mental states might change without something changing within my brain is unimaginable. Again, the effects of physical injury, alcohol, narcotics, psychotropic chemicals, and nerve-tissue degeneration on consciousness—via their effects on the brain—are obvious. Further, specific cognitive failings have been tied to damage of specific areas of the brain. In addition, learning is known to be accompanied by physical and chemical changes within the brain, changes without which it apparently would not occur. And other evidence of apparent dependency of mind processes on brain processes is abundant. The simplest explanation of this dependency is that the affected mental processes and the physical brain processes with which they are associated are in reality not two things but one.

we think we know when we say, "I am eating an apple," can be expressed without even mentioning apples; it can be expressed without assuming the existence of anything beyond our sense-data. In short, *the analysis reveals that our belief in the existence of the apple we are eating is in fact a belief in the existence of nothing beyond sense-data.* The reduction *simplifies* our metaphysics; it shortens the list of entities that we are obliged to credit with existence. The reduction thus has metaphysical significance.

The reduction also has epistemological significance. As we saw in Part 2, skeptics have powerful arguments for saying that you really don't know that physical objects exist. But it's harder for them to argue that you don't know that your sense-data exist. By reducing apples to sense-data, we place our belief in the existence of apples on a much surer epistemological footing.

- Fifth is the *no-necessity problem*. If the mind and mental states are immaterial things that play any sort of role in what we say and think and do and feel, then we would expect them to exert some sort of detectable influence on the brain, since what we say and think and do and feel is traceable to what happens in the brain. But brain scientists never find it necessary to postulate the existence of the mind to explain and account for what happens in the brain. There is, in short, no necessity to postulate the existence of immaterial causes to account for what happens in the brain, contrary to what we would expect if an immaterial mind is involved in human thought and behavior.

- Sixth is the *interaction problem*. If an immaterial mind is involved in human thought and behavior, then it must interact with the brain, as explained already. But it is difficult even to conceptualize how such interaction could occur. An immaterial mind could not push, pull, tug on, spin, or divide physical things within the brain, for pushing, pulling and the like are physical activities. Nor, for the same reason, could it pulverize, energize, electrify, or magnetize things within the brain. In other words, how an immaterial mind could exert an influence on the brain is most unclear, because such exertion would, apparently, have to be nonphysical, and the idea of nonphysical exertion or activation is most unclear.

- Last is the *understanding problem*. Anything that under any circumstances whatsoever could be experienced by more than one person is a physical thing, according to the usual concept of a physical thing. Thus, if mental things, things like beliefs, thoughts, ideas, and the like, are nonphysical, it would be impossible for them to be experienced by more than one person. Therefore, if my thoughts and beliefs and so forth are nonphysical, then I alone could experience them. But if you alone can experience your mental states, then it is difficult to see how we have come to understand one another when we speak of our mental states.

Although none of these objections to dualism is thought to be decisive, collectively they are thought to have much force as showing that it is (1) unnecessary and (2) unduly perplexing to suppose that the human being has a nonphysical mind or mental states.

Russell eventually thought that minds, too (just like apples and other physical objects), could be reduced to (i.e., analyzed in terms of) sense-data. In other words, what I say about my mind could, at least in theory, be expressed by sentences that refer only to sense-data. Thus, according to Russell, my body (which, like an apple, is a physical object) and my mind are both reducible to the same kind of thing, sense-data.

This doctrine, that mind and matter are both reducible to the same kind of thing, which is itself neither mental nor material, is called **neutral monism.** *Monism* means "one-ism." Neutral monism is therefore a rejection of dualism, which is "two-ism." Materialism (the doctrine that reality is ultimately physical or "material") and idealism (the doctrine that reality is ultimately nonphysical or "ideal" mind-stuff) are types of monism, too.

Yes, a theory like Russell's, that minds and bodies *both* are reducible to sense-data could (and sometimes is) viewed as a kind of idealism. But Russell held that sense-data are neither mental nor physical, for the very good reason that they are what mental things and physical things both reduce to. For this reason, he held that sense-data are *neutral* as between mind and matter; hence this philosophy is known as *neutral* monism. The American philosopher **William James** and the British analytic philosopher **A. J. Ayer,** who was a member of the Vienna Circle mentioned in Chapter 13, were also, at one point or another during their careers, neutral monists.

Selection 14.1 is a nontechnical exposition of this neutral monist position excerpted from Russell's *The Philosophy of Logical Atomism.*

From Bertrand Russell,
THE PHILOSOPHY OF LOGICAL ATOMISM

You all know the American theory of neutral monism, which derives really from William James and is also suggested in the work of Mach, but in a rather less developed form. The theory of neutral monism maintains that the distinction between the mental and the physical is entirely an affair of arrangement, that the actual material arranged is exactly the same in the case of the mental as it is in the case of the physical, but they differ merely in the fact that when you take the thing as belonging in the same context with certain other things, it will belong to psychology, while when you take it in a certain other context with other things, it will belong to physics, and the difference is as to what you consider to be its context, just the same sort of difference as there is between arranging the people in London alphabetically or geographically. So, according to William James, the actual material of the world can be arranged in two different ways, one of which gives you physics and the other psychology. It is just like rows or columns: in an arrangement of rows and columns, you can take an item as either a member of a certain row or a member of a certain column; the item is the same in the two cases, but its context is different.

If you will allow me a little undue simplicity I can go on to say rather more about neutral monism, but you must understand that I am talking more simply than I ought to do because there is not time to put in all the shadings and qualifications. I was talking a moment ago about the appearances that a chair presents. If we take any one of these chairs, we can all look at it, and it presents a different appearance to each of us. Taken all together, taking all the different appearances that that chair is presenting to all of us at this moment, you get something that belongs to physics. So that, if one takes sense-data and arranges together all those sense-data that appear to different people at a given moment and are such as we should ordinarily say are appearances of the same physical object, then that class of sense-data will give you something that belongs to physics, namely, the chair at this moment. On the other hand, if instead of taking all the appearances that that chair presents to all of us at this moment, I take all the appearances that the different chairs in this room present to me at this moment, I get quite another group of particulars. All the different appearances that different chairs present to me now will give you something belonging to psychology, because that will give you my experiences at the present moment. Broadly speaking, according to what one may take as an expansion of William James, that should be the definition of the difference between physics and psychology.

We commonly assume that there is a phenomenon which we call seeing the chair, but what I call my seeing the chair according to neutral monism is merely the existence of a certain particular, namely the particular which is the sense-datum of that chair at that moment. And I and the chair are both logical fictions, both being in fact a series of classes of particulars, of which one will be that particular which we call my seeing the chair. That actual appearance that the chair is presenting to me now is a member of me and a member of the chair, I and the chair being logical fictions. . . . There is no simple entity that you can point to and say: this entity is physical and not mental. . . .

I ought to proceed to tell you that I have discovered whether neutral monism is true or not, because otherwise you may not believe that logic is any use in the matter. But I do not profess to know whether it is true or not. I feel more and more inclined to think that it may be true. I feel more and more that the difficulties that occur in regard to it are all of the sort that may be solved by ingenuity. But nevertheless there *are* a number of difficulties; there are a number of problems, some of which I have spoken about in the course of these lectures. . . .

Theory 2: Behaviorism

Another influential analyst concerned with the philosophy of mind was **Gilbert Ryle**, who, in *The Concept of Mind* (1949), one of the most widely read books of twentieth-century analytic philosophy, argued for what we will call the behaviorist analysis of the mind.

Before we begin, however, *caution:* the word *behaviorism* is notoriously ambiguous. **Behaviorism** in one sense is a *methodological principle of psychology,* according to which fruitful psychological investigation confines itself to such psychological phenomena as can be behaviorally defined. *Philosophical behaviorism* is the doctrine we'll now explain that we are attributing to Ryle. Ryle denied being a behaviorist, incidentally. Still, *The Concept of Mind* is regarded as one of the most powerful expositions of (philosophical) behaviorism ever written. (Hereafter, when we refer to behaviorism, we'll mean *philosophical* behaviorism.)

According to Ryle, when we refer to someone's mental states (and this someone might be oneself), when we refer, for example, to a person's beliefs or thoughts or wishes, we are *not,* contrary to what is ordinarily supposed, referring to the immaterial states of a nonphysical mind. There is indeed no such thing as a nonphysical mind. There is, Ryle says, *no ghost within the machine.* A person is only a complicated—a very highly complicated—physical organism, one capable of doing the amazing sorts of things that people are capable of doing. When we attribute a so-called mental state to a person, we are in fact attributing to him or her a *propensity* or *disposition* to act or behave in a certain way.

For example, when you attribute to your friend the belief that it is going to rain, it might *seem* that you view her as having or possessing a nonphysical thing of some sort, termed a *belief,* a nonphysical, intangible, and unobservable entity that exists within her mind. But in fact, argues Ryle, to say that someone believes it is going to rain is merely to attribute to her a propensity or disposition to do things like close the windows and cover the barbecue and say things like "It's going to rain," and not to do certain other sorts of things like wash the car and hang out the sheets.

It is likewise when we credit someone with a thought or an idea. Thoughts and ideas, like beliefs, are not nonmaterial things, says Ryle. They are not even *things* at all. To be sure, "Thought," "idea," and "belief" are words for things, that is, *thing-words*. But these thing-words are (to borrow an expression Ryle used in a different context) *systematically misleading*. Because they are thing-words, they mislead or tempt us into thinking that there must be things for which they stand. And because there seem to be no physical things for which they stand, we are tempted to conclude that they stand for nonphysical things.

In fact, however, when we say that someone has a specific thought, all we can really be doing is attributing to him or her a propensity to say or do certain things, a propensity to behave in certain ways. It's rather like what we mean when we say that someone has mechanical knowledge. "Mechanical knowledge" is a thing-word, too. But we really don't think that someone who has mechanical knowledge possesses a *thing* that's out there in the tool box alongside the screwdriver and adjustable crescent; nor do we think that mechanical knowledge is a ghostly nonphysical thing that is hidden away in the person's "mind." When we say that some-

Although "ego" is a thing-word, when we say that someone has a big ego, we do not really mean that there is a thing, a big ego, that he or she keeps around someplace. We just mean that the person has a tendency or a disposition to do such things as brag, talk excessively about himself, never admit mistakes, and so forth.

Behaviorism, Pro and Con

Behaviorism makes plain how it is that we could come to understand and use expressions that refer to mental phenomena. These expressions do not refer to private, behind-the-scenes states and episodes within an immaterial mind but rather to publicly witnessable behavior and behavior tendencies.

Nevertheless, the philosophical literature is filled with objections to behaviorism, including the following:

1. Even if some behavioral dispositions could be correlated with a particular mental state, say, experiencing sorrow, it seems more plausible to view that state—the sorrow—as the *cause* of the behavior than to *equate it* with the behavior. We say a person is crying because he is saddened. We don't say or think his crying (among other behaviors) *is* his sadness.

2. Consider two people with their motor nerves severed, one of whom has also had his pain fibers cut. Because they would both have the same behavioral dispositions, according to the behaviorist either both would feel pain or neither would feel pain. Neither alternative is plausible.

3. To believe in behaviorism, you in effect have to believe people are anaesthetized, for only someone who is anaesthetized could think that a mental image or a sensation of pain are no more than behavioral dispositions.

4. What about paralysis? A paralyzed person can certainly have mental states—even though he or she would not have any particular behavioral dispositions.

As always, these objections are not definitive, and philosophers have devised ways, usually somewhat complicated, of meeting them. You should evaluate them for yourself.

---

one has mechanical knowledge, all we mean is that he or she is able, and apt, to do certain things in certain situations.

In short, references to someone's beliefs, ideas, thoughts, knowledge, motives, and to other mental "things" must be analyzed or understood as references to the ways the person is apt to behave given certain conditions.

Might not Ryle strengthen his case by providing an *actual analysis* of a mental-state expression, a translation into behavioral language of a simple mental-state proposition like, "She believes that it is time to go home"? Indeed Ryle could *not* strengthen his case in this way, for it is not his position that such translations could be made. According to behaviorists, there is no definite and finite list of behaviors and behavioral propensities that we are attributing to someone when we say, "She believes it is time to go home." Instead, we are referring in an *oblique and loose way* to an indefinite and open set of behaviors and behavioral tendencies.

This, then, is **philosophical behaviorism:**

- There is no such thing as a nonphysical mind.

- Mental-state thing-words do not really denote things at all. A statement in which such words appear is a kind of loose short-hand reference to behaviors (including verbal behaviors) and behavioral propensities.

- Statements about a person's mental states cannot actually be translated into some set of statements about the person's behavior and behavioral propensities, because the sets of behaviors and behavioral propensities to which they in fact refer are indefinite and open and depend on the situations in which the person happens to be.

Thus, behaviorism too is a kind of monism, a materialistic kind of monism. And as a monistic theory it escapes one dilemma faced by a dualist, noted in a box somewhere near here, the dilemma of how two such different things as nonphysical minds and physical bodies can have an effect on each other.

It also nicely accounts for another problem facing dualism, namely, explaining why it is that brain- and neuroscientists just never do have to postulate the existence of nonphysical mental states to explain the causes and origin of our behavior. The reason they never have to postulate such things, according to the behaviorist, is because there *aren't* such things.

▶ S E L E C T I O N   14.2

From Gilbert Ryle,
"WHICH SHOULD NOT BE SET IN GENERAL TERMS"

The story is told of some peasants who were terrified at the sight of their first railway-train. Their pastor therefore gave them a lecture explaining how a steam-engine works. One of the peasants then said, "Yes, pastor, we quite understand what you say about the steam-engine. But there is really a horse inside, isn't there?" So used were they to horse-drawn carts that they could not take in the idea that some vehicles propel themselves.

We might invent a sequel. The peasants examined the engine and peeped into every crevice of it. They then said, "Certainly we cannot see, feel, or hear a horse there. We are foiled. But we know there is a horse there, so it must be a ghost-horse which, like the fairies, hides from mortal eyes."

The pastor objected, "But, after all, horses themselves are made of moving parts, just as the steam-engine is made of moving parts. You know what their muscles, joints, and blood-vessels do. So why is there a mystery in the self-propulsion of a steam-engine, if there is none in that of a horse? What do you think makes the horse's hooves go to and fro?" After a pause a peasant replied, "What makes the horse's hooves go is four extra little ghost-horses inside."

Poor simple-minded peasants! Yet just such a story has been the official theory of the mind for the last three very scientific centuries. Several, though not all, of the scientists in this series have automatically posed their problem in this very way. I think that Lord Samuel still accepts the whole story, and that Professor Ayer would like to reject it, but does not see how to do so. For the general terms in which the scientists have set their problem of mind and body, we philosophers have been chiefly to blame, though we have been obsessed, not by the rustic idea of horses, but by the newer idea of mechanical contrivances. The legend that we have told and sold runs like this. A person consists of two theatres, one bodily and one non-bodily. In his Theatre A go on the incidents which we can explore by eye and instrument. But a person also incorporates a second theatre, Theatre B. Here there go on incidents which are totally unlike, though synchronized with those that go on in Theatre A. These Theatre B episodes are changes in the states, not of bits of flesh, but of something called "consciousness," which occupies no space. Only the proprietor of Theatre B has first-hand knowledge of what goes on in it. It is a secret theatre. The experimentalist tries to open its doors, but it has no doors. He tries to peep through its windows, but it has no windows. He is foiled.

We tend nowadays to treat it as obvious that a person, unlike a newt, lives the two lives, life A and life B, each completely unlike, though mysteriously geared to the other. Ingrained hypotheses do feel obvious, however redundant they may be. The peasants in my story correctly thought that a steam-engine was hugely different from a cart and automatically but incorrectly explained the difference by postulating a ghost-horse inside. So most of us, correctly thinking that there are huge differences between a clock and a person, automatically but incorrectly explain these differences by postulating an extra set of ghost-works inside. We correctly say that people are not like clocks, since people meditate, calculate, and invent things; they make plans, dream dreams, and shirk their obligations; they get angry, feel depressed, scan the heavens, and have likes and dislikes; they work, play, and idle; they are sane, crazy, or imbecile; they are skilful at some things and bunglers at others. Where we go wrong is in explaining these familiar actions and conditions as the operations of a secondary set of secret works.

Everybody knows quite well when to describe someone as acting absent-mindedly or with heed, as babbling deliriously or reasoning coherently, as feeling angry but not showing it, as wanting one thing but pretending to want another, as being ambitious, patriotic, or miserly. We often get our accounts and estimates of other people and of ourselves wrong; but we more often get them right. We did not need to learn the legend of the two theatres before we were able to talk sense about people and to deal effectively with them. Nor has this fairly new-fangled legend helped us to do it better.

When we read novels, biographies, and reminiscences, we do not find the chapters partitioned into Section A, covering the hero's "bodily" doings, and Section B, covering his "mental" doings. We find unpartitioned accounts of what he did and thought and felt, of what he said to others and to himself, of the mountains he tried to climb and the problems he tried to solve. Should an examiner mark the paper written by the candidate's hand but refuse to assess the candidate's wits? Theorists themselves, when actually describing people, sensibly forget Theatre A and Theatre B. Sir Charles Sherrington paid a well-deserved compliment to Professor Adrian, but he did not pay one cool compliment to Professor Adrian A and another warmer compliment to Professor Adrian B.

In saying that a person is not to be described as a mind coupled with a body I am not saying, with some truculent thinkers, that people are just machines. Nor are engines just wagons or live bodies just corpses. What is wrong with the story of the two theatres is not that it reports differences which are not there but that it misrepresents differences which are there. It is a story with the right characters but the wrong plot. It is an attempt to explain a genuine difference—or rather a galaxy of differences—but its effect, like that of the peasants' theory, is merely to reduplicate the thing to be explained. It says, "The difference between a machine like a human body on the one hand and a human being on the other, is that in a human being, besides the organs which we do see, there is a counterpart set of organs which we do not see; besides the causes and effects which we can witness, there is a counterpart series of causes and effects which we cannot witness." So now we ask, "But what explains the differences between what goes on in the Theatre B of a sane man and what goes on in that of a lunatic? A third theatre, Theatre C?"

No, what prevents us from examining Theatre B is not that it has no doors or windows, but that there is no such theatre. What prevented the peasants from finding the horse, was not that it was a ghost-horse, but that there was no horse. None the less, the engine *was* different from a wagon and ordinary people *are* different not only from machines, but also from animals, imbeciles, infants, and corpses. They also differ in countless important ways from one another. I have not begun to show how we should grade these differences. I have only shown how we should not grade them.

One last word. In ordinary life (save when we want to sound knowing) we seldom use the noun "mind" or the adjective "mental" at all. What we do is talk of people, of people calculating, conjuring, hoping, resolving, tasting, bluffing, fretting, and so on. Nor, in ordinary life, do we talk of "matter" or of things being "material." What we do is to talk of steel, granite, and water; of wood, moss, and grain; of flesh, bone, and sinew. The umbrella-titles "mind" and "matter" obliterate the very differences that ought to interest us. Theorists should drop both these words. "Mind" and "matter" are echoes from the hustings of philosophy, and prejudice the solutions of all problems posed in terms of them.

Behaviorism

The general trend of this book [*The Concept of Mind*] will undoubtedly, and harmlessly, be stigmatised as "behaviourist." So it is pertinent to say something about Behaviourism. Behaviourism was, in the beginning, a theory about the proper methods of scientific psychology. It held that the example of the other progressive sciences ought to be followed, as it had not previously been followed, by psychologists; their theories should be based upon repeatable and publicly checkable observations and experiments. But the reputed deliverances of consciousness and introspection are not publicly checkable. Only people's overt behaviour can be observed by several witnesses, measured and mechanically recorded. The early adherents of this methodological programme seem to have been in two minds whether to assert that the data of consciousness and introspection were myths, or to assert merely that they were insusceptible of scientific examination. It was not clear whether they were espousing a not very sophisticated mechanistic doctrine, like that of Hobbes and Gassendi, or whether they were still cleaving to the Cartesian para-mechanical theory, but restricting their research procedures to those that we have inherited from Galileo; whether, for example, they held that thinking just consists in making certain complex noises and movements or whether they held that though these movements and noises were connected with "inner life" processes, the movements and noises alone were laboratory phenomena.

However, it does not matter whether the early Behaviourists accepted a mechanist or a para-mechanist theory. They were in error in either case. The important thing is that the practice of describing specifically human doings according to the recommended methodology quickly made it apparent to psychologists how shadowy were the supposed "inner-life" occurrences which the Behaviourists were at first reproached for ignoring or denying. Psychological theories which made no mention of the deliverances of "inner perception" were at first likened to *Hamlet* without the Prince of Denmark. But the extruded hero soon came to seem so bloodless and spineless a being that even the opponents of these theories began to feel shy of imposing heavy theoretical burdens upon his spectral shoulders.

Novelists, dramatists and biographers had always been satisfied to exhibit people's motives, thoughts, perturbations and habits by describing their doings, sayings, and imaginings, their grimaces, gestures and tones of voice. In concentrating on what Jane Austen concentrated on, psychologists began to find that these were, after all, the stuff and not the mere trappings of their subjects. They have, of course, continued to suffer unnecessary qualms of anxiety, lest this diversion of psychology from the task of describing the ghostly might not commit it to tasks of describing the merely mechanical. But the influence of the bogy of mechanism has for a century been dwindling because, among other reasons, during this period the biological sciences have established their title of "sciences." The Newtonian system is no longer the sole paradigm of natural science. Man need not be degraded to a machine by being denied to be a ghost in a machine. He might, after all, be a sort of animal, namely, a higher mammal. There has yet to be ventured the hazardous leap to the hypothesis that perhaps he is a man.

Theory 3: Identity Theory

The third of the four nondualistic analytic philosophies of the mind is identity theory. According to identity theory, so-called mental phenomena are all physical phenomena within the brain and central nervous system. A thought, for example, according to identity theory, is in fact some sort of occurrence within the brain/nervous system, though we do not yet know enough about the brain or central nervous system to stipulate which particular occurrence it is.

Notice that the identity theorist does not say merely that thinking (or any other mental occurrence) is *correlated* with or *involves* a neural process of some sort. The claim is rather that thinking *is* a neural process. Just as light *is* electromagnetic radiation (and is not just "involved in" or "correlated with" electromagnetic radiation), and just as heat *is* movement of molecules, thinking and all other mental phenomena, according to identity theory, *are* physical states and happenings within the brain and central nervous system.

Beginning philosophy students sometimes have a difficult time distinguishing behaviorism from identity theory, usually, we think, for two reasons.

First, behaviorism and identity theory are both physicalistic (materialistic) theories in the sense that, according to both, you and we and all other people are completely physical organisms: neither theory countenances the existence of the nonmaterial or nonphysical soul, spirit, or mind; and neither theory thinks that mental-state thing-words denote nonmaterial or nonphysical things.

Second, few theorists are *pure* behaviorists or identity theorists. Most philosophers who call themselves identity theorists do in fact accept a behavioristic analysis of at least some assertions about mental states, and most behaviorists do likewise accept identity theory with respect to some mental states.

But the two theories really should not be confused. *Identity theory* holds that mind-states are brain-states, that when we speak of a person's beliefs, thoughts, hopes, ideas, and the like, we are in fact referring to events and processes and states within his or her brain and nervous system. Philosophical *behaviorism* holds that when we use our everyday psychological vocabulary to describe someone, we are really just talking in a shorthand way about his or her behavioral propensities.

Of course, all three of the theories discussed so far have points of intersection. As already noted, the behaviorist and identity theorist both accept the premise that a human being is an entirely physical organism. Further, if Russell is correct and propositions about physical things can in principle be resolved into (more complicated but philosophically more basic) propositions about sense-data, then propositions about behavior and propositions about brain/nervous system states both also can in principle be resolved into propositions about sense-data. Thus both the behaviorist and the identity theorist could accept neutral monism, if they were willing to accept Russell's thesis that physicalist propositions are reducible to sense-data propositions. (In fact, for the reasons explained in Part 2, most behaviorists and identity theorists would probably not be inclined to accept this condition.)

In Selection 14.3 Australian philosopher J. J. C. Smart explains a version of identity theory and then considers some objections to it.

▶ S E L E C T I O N   14.3

From J. J. C. Smart,
"SENSATIONS AND BRAIN PROCESSES"

It seems to me that science is increasingly giving us a viewpoint whereby organisms are able to be seen as physico-chemical mechanisms: it seems that even the behavior of man himself will one day be explicable in mechanistic terms. There does seem to be, so far as science is concerned, nothing in the world but increasingly complex arrangements of physical constituents. All except for one place: in consciousness. That is, for a full description of what is going on in a man you would have to mention not only the physical processes in his tissue, glands, nervous system, and so forth, but also his states of consciousness: his visual, auditory, and tactual sensations, his aches and pains. That these should be *correlated* with brain processes does not help, for to say that they are *correlated* is to say that they are something "over and above." You cannot correlate something with itself. You correlate footprints with burglars, but not Bill Sikes the burglar with Bill Sikes the burglar. So sensations, states of consciousness, do seem to be the one sort of thing left outside the physicalist picture, and for various reasons I just cannot believe that this can be so. That everything should be explicable in terms of physics (together of course with descriptions of the ways in which the parts are put together—roughly, biology is to physics as radio-engineering is to electro-magnetism) except the occurrence of sensations seems to me to be frankly unbelievable. . . .

Why should not sensations just be brain processes of a certain sort? There are, of course, well-known (as well as lesser-known) philosophical objections to the view that reports of sensations are reports of brain-processes, but I shall try to argue that these arguments are by no means as cogent as is commonly thought to be the case.

Let me first try to state more accurately the thesis that sensations are brain processes. It is not the thesis that, for example, "after-image" or "ache" means the same as "brain process of sort X" (where "X" is replaced by a description of a certain sort of brain process). It is that, in so far as "after-image" or "ache" is a report of a process, it is a report of a process that *happens to be* a brain process. It follows that the thesis does not claim that sensation statements can be *translated* into statements about brain processes. Nor does it claim that the logic of a sensation statement is the same as that of a brain-process statement. All it claims is that in so far as a sensation statement is a report of something, that something is in fact a brain process. Sensations are nothing over and above brain processes. Nations are nothing "over and above" citizens, but this does not prevent the logic of nation statements being very different from the logic of citizen statements, nor does it insure the translatability of nation statements into citizen statements. . . .

Remarks on identity. When I say that a sensation is a brain process or that lightning is an electric discharge, I am using "is" in the sense of strict identity. (Just as in the—in this case necessary—proposition "7 is identical with the smallest prime number greater than 5." . . .

I shall now discuss various possible objections to the view that the processes reported in sensation statements are in fact processes in the brain. Most of us have met some of these objections in our first year as philosophy students. All the more reason to take a good look at them. Others of the objections will be more recondite and subtle.

Objection 1. Any illiterate peasant can talk perfectly well about his after-images, or how things look or feel to him, or about his aches and pains, and yet he may know nothing whatever about neurophysiology. . . .

Reply. You might as well say that a nation of slug-abeds, who never saw the morning star or knew of its existence, or who had never thought of the expression "the Morning Star," but who used the expression "the Evening Star" perfectly well, could not use this expression to refer to the same entity as we refer to (and describe as) "the Morning Star." . . .

Consider lightning. Modern physical science tells us that lightning is a certain kind of electrical discharge due to ionization of clouds of water-vapor in the atmosphere. This, it is now believed, is what the true nature of lightning is. Note that there are not two things: a flash of lightning and an electrical discharge. There is one thing, a flash of lightning, which is described scientifically as an electrical discharge to the earth from a cloud of ionized water-molecules. . . .

In short, the reply to Objection 1 is that there can be contingent statements of the form "A is identical with B," and a person may well know that something is an A without knowing that it is a B. An illiterate peasant might well be able to talk about his sensations without knowing about his brain processes, just as he can talk about lightning though he knows nothing of electricity.

Objection 2. It is only a contingent fact (if it is a fact) that when we have a certain kind of sensation there is a certain kind of process in our brain. Indeed it is possible, though perhaps in the highest degree unlikely, that our present physiological theories will be as out of date as the ancient theory connecting mental processes with goings on in the heart. It follows that when we report a sensation we are not reporting a brain-process.

Reply. The objection certainly proves that when we say "I have an after-image" we cannot *mean* something of the form "I have such and such a brain-process." But this does not show that what we report (having an after-image) is not *in fact* a brain process. . . .

Now how do I get over the objection that a sensation can be identified with a brain process only if it has some phenomenal property, not possessed by brain processes, whereby one-half of the identification may be, so to speak, pinned down?

My suggestion is as follows. When a person says, "I see a yellowish-orange after-image," he is saying something like this: "*There is something going on which is like what is going on when* I have my eyes open, am awake, and there is an orange illuminated in good light in front of me, that is, when I really see an orange." . . .

Objection 4. The after-image is not in physical space. The brain-process is. So the after-image is not a brain-process.

Reply. This is an *ignoratio elenchi.* I am not arguing that the after-image is a brain-process, but that the experience of having an after-image is a brain-process. It is the *experience* which is reported in the introspective report. Similarly, if it is objected that the after-image is yellowy-orange but that a surgeon looking into your brain would see nothing yellowy-orange, my reply is that it is the experience of seeing yellowy-orange that is being described, and this experience is not a yellowy-orange something. So to say that a brain-process cannot be yellowy-orange is not to say that a brain-process cannot in fact be the experience of having a yellowy-orange after-image. . . .

Objection 5. It would make sense to say of a molecular movement in the brain that it is swift or slow, straight or circular, but it makes no sense to say this of the experience of seeing something yellow.

Reply. So far we have not given sense to talk of experiences as swift or slow, straight or circular. But I am not claiming that "experience" and "brain-process" mean the same or even that they have the same logic. "Somebody" and "the doctor" do not have the same logic, but this does not lead us to suppose that talking about somebody telephoning is talking about someone over and above, say, the doctor. . . .

Objection 6. Sensations are private, brain processes are *public.* If I sincerely say, "I see a yellowish-orange after-image" and I am not making a verbal mistake, then I cannot be wrong. But I can be wrong about a brain-process. The scientist looking into my brain might be having an illusion. Moreover, it makes sense to say that two or more people are observing the same brain-process but not that two or more people are reporting the same inner experience.

Reply. This shows that the language of introspective reports has a different logic from the language of material processes. It is obvious that until the brain-process theory is much improved and widely accepted there will be no *criteria* for saying "Smith has an experience of such-and-such a sort" *except* Smith's introspective reports. So we have adopted a rule of language that (normally) what Smith says goes.

Objection 7. I can imagine myself turned to stone and yet having images, aches, pains, and so on.

Reply. . . . I can imagine that the Evening Star is not the Morning Star. But it is. All the objection shows is that "experience" and "brain-process" do not have the same meaning. It does not show that an experience is not in fact a brain process.

Difficulties

There are important difficulties within each of these three nondualistic theories. The *neutral monist* idea that mental-state statements and physicalist statements can both be resolved into sense-data statements is vulnerable to the objections to phenomenalism, discussed in Part 2 on pages 178–179.

The *behaviorist* thesis, on the other hand, the thesis that mental-state statements are really disguised references to behavioral propensities, may seem plausible enough for *some* mental-state statements. For example, it doesn't sound terribly unreasonable to maintain that, when we attribute to someone *insane jealousy*, or credit him or her with having *an understanding of computers*, we are in fact saying something about the sorts of things he or she is apt and able to do (and say). But think for a moment about *mental images*. For example, picture in your mind Robert Redford. Is it really plausible to regard a statement like, "I can picture Redford's face very clearly," as a remark about your behavioral propensities? Or consider *specific thoughts*. Can it seriously be supposed that the statement, "I am thinking about my new Honda," is really a shorthand for a series of behavioral propensities? Doesn't it seem much more plausible to view mental images and specific thoughts as *brain/nervous-system events* of some sort and to regard statements about them not as references to behavioral propensities but as unscientific language for certain neurophysiological phenomena?

There also are theoretical difficulties involved in the third theory, *identity theory*, too, as will become clear in our next selection, from philosopher Paul Churchland.

Nevertheless, despite these difficulties, though some analytic philosophers remain dualists, most are physicalists; that is, most would deny that a living human being has a nonphysical component and most would deny that mental-state thing-words designate nonphysical states. For them the question is not whether physicalism is true but which version of physicalism is true.

In Selection 14.4 two *apparent* difficulties in identity theory are presented and rejected by Paul Churchland. The objections are similar to, but not exactly the same as, those discussed by J. J. C. Smart in Selection 14.3.

▶ S E L E C T I O N   14.4

From Paul Churchland,
"ARGUMENTS AGAINST THE IDENTITY THEORY"

It may be urged that one's brain states are more than merely not (yet) known by introspection: they are not know*able* by introspection under any circumstances. Thus,

1. My mental states are knowable by introspection.
2. My brain states are *not* knowable by introspection. Therefore, by Leibniz' Law [If x is identical with y, then x and y have the same properties],
3. My mental states are not identical with my brain states.

. . . Now the materialist is in a position to insist that the argument contains a false premise—premise (2). For if mental states are indeed brain states, then it is really brain states we have been introspecting all along, though without fully appreciating what they are. And if we can learn to think of and recognize those states under mentalistic descriptions, as we all have, then we can certainly learn to think of and recognize them under their more penetrating neurophysiological descriptions. At the very least, premise (2) simply begs the question against the identity theorist. The mistake is amply illustrated in the following parallel argument:

1. Temperature is knowable by feeling.
2. Mean molecular kinetic energy is *not* knowable by feeling. Therefore, by Liebniz' Law,
3. Temperature is not identical with mean molecular kinetic energy.

This identity, at least, is long established, and this argument is certainly unsound: premise (2) is false. Just as one can learn to feel that the summer air is about 70° F, or 21° C, so one can learn to feel that the mean KE of its molecules is about 6.2×10^{-21} joules, for whether we realize it or not, that is what our discriminatory mechanisms are keyed to. Perhaps our brain states are similarly accessible. . . .

Consider now a final argument, again based on the introspectible qualities of our sensations. Imagine a future neuroscientist who comes to know everything there is to know about the physical structure and activity of the brain and its visual system, of its actual and possible states. If for some reason she has never actually had a sensation-of-red (because of color blindness, say, or an unusual environment), then there will remain something she does *not* know about certain sensations: *what it is like to have a sensation-of-red.* Therefore, complete knowledge of the physical facts of visual perception and its related brain activity still leaves something out. Accordingly, materialism cannot give an adequate account of all mental phenomena, and the identity theory must be false.

The identity theorist can reply that this argument exploits an unwitting equivocation on the term "know." Concerning our neuroscientist's utopian knowledge of the brain, "knows" means something like "has mastered the relevant set of neuroscientific propositions". Concerning her (missing) knowledge of what it is like to have a sensation-of-red, "knows" means something like "has a prelinguistic representation of redness in her mechanisms for noninferential discrimination." It is true that one might have the former without the latter, but the materialist is not committed to the idea that having knowledge in the former sense automatically constitutes having knowledge in the second sense. The identity theorist can admit a duality, or even a plurality, of different *types of knowledge* without thereby committing himself to a duality in *types of things known.* The difference between a person who knows all about the visual cortex but has never enjoyed the sensation-of-red, and a person who knows no neuroscience but knows well the sensation-of-red, may reside not in *what* is respectively known by each (brain states by the former, nonphysical *qualia* by the latter), but rather in the different *type*, or *medium*, or *level* of representation each has of exactly the same thing: brain states.

In sum, there are pretty clearly more ways of "having knowledge" than just having mastered a set of sentences, and the materialist can freely admit that one has "knowledge" of one's sensations in a way that is independent of the neuroscience one may have learned. Animals, including humans, presumably have a prelinguistic mode of sensory representation. This does not mean that sensations are beyond the reach of physical science. *It just means that the brain uses more modes and media of representation than the mere storage of sentences.* All the identity theorist needs to claim is that those other modes of representation will also yield to neuroscientific explanation.

The identity theory has proved to be very resilient in the face of these predominantly antimaterialist objections. But further objections, rooted in competing forms of materialism, constitute a much more serious threat.

Theory 4: Functionalism

Now, to close the chapter, we will consider the last of the four nondualist theories of mind, functionalism, and then say something about current issues in the philosophy of mind.

Physicalist philosophers do not believe that people have nonphysical minds and they deny that mental-state thing-words stand for states or processes of a nonphysical variety. But many physicalists question the identity theory, according to which each distinct mental state or process equates with one and only one brain state or process. It is possible, these physicalists say, that the selfsame psychological (mental) state could be correctly ascribed to quite different physiological systems.

For example, there may be beings in a far distant galaxy whose brains and nervous systems are radically different from our own but who nevertheless have thoughts and beliefs and desires and motives and other mental states. This certainly is not a terribly far-fetched possibility. Now if there are such beings, it's quite possible that when they believe something, what goes on in their "brains" and "nervous systems" may not be the same thing at all as what goes on in ours when we believe something. (They might not even have what we would call brains!)

For that matter, the belief process in a brain-damaged *human* may not be quite the same as in a normal human. And some day thinking robots may be created (at least physicalists must admit that this is theoretically possible) with "brains" made out of silicon and plastic. Though these robots will think, in all probability somewhat different physical processes will be involved when they do than are involved when we think.

In the light of such examples as these it seems unwise to say that each distinct mental phenomenon equates with one and only one brain/nervous-system phenomenon, as does identity theory. It seems sounder philosophically to say that a given mental state is identical with *some* brain/nervous-system phenomenon *or other.*

This is what so-called functionalists say. According to **functionalism** a mental state is defined by its *function*. For example, you may believe it is going to rain. If you do, your belief will have been caused by certain sensory stimuli in conjunction with other beliefs that you have, and it (your belief that it is going to rain) will in turn have an effect on your behavior and other beliefs. In short, the belief will interact with your other mental states (including sensations) and your behavior in a way that is unique to just that belief. To play just that causal role it does play in this network of relationships is the *function* of that belief.

Thus, according to the functionalist, *any* physical process (regardless of what type of organism or physical system it occurs in) that has that precise function *is* that belief.

For the functionalist, therefore, a mental state is analogous to a mousetrap or a garage door opener or a word processor or anything else that is *defined by its function.* Mousetraps (or garage door openers or word processors) are not defined by what they are made of or how they are put together. Mousetraps may actually be made of *most anything* and put together in indefinitely many ways. Hence they are not defined by what they are made of or how they are assembled but by their functions, that is, by what they do. Anything that has the function of a mousetrap, no matter how it is assembled and out of what it is made, is a mousetrap. The same holds true for garage door openers and word processors, and, according to the functionalist, the same holds for beliefs, thoughts, ideas, and other mental states and processes. Beliefs and the like, they say, are defined by their *function*—the role they play in affecting behavior and in affecting and being affected by other mental states.

Therefore, according to the functionalist, beliefs and other mental phenomena must be analyzed functionally, *not reductively*. You can't *reduce* talk about mousetraps to talk about what they are made of. If someone were to ask what a mousetrap *is*, you would explain what a mousetrap *does*; what its unique function is. Beliefs and other mental phenomena, according to the functionalist, are likewise to be explained in terms of their unique functions—the specific roles they play relative to sensory data and other mental states and to behavioral output.

Thus, says the functionalist, though it is true that nothing nonphysical happens to you when you have a belief, that doesn't mean that we could somehow "translate" statements about your beliefs into statements about neurological processes. And conversely, the fact that we cannot translate talk about your beliefs into talk about neurological processes doesn't mean that beliefs are nonphysical.

So you can see that functionalism explains nicely why psychology—whether of the common sense ("folk") or the scientific variety—has resisted reduction to neurology. It has been resistant not because psychological states are nonphysical but because they are functional. Functionalism is therefore thought to provide a conceptual framework for psychological research that, on one hand, does not commit the researcher to murky and questionable dualistic metaphysical notions and, on the other, also does

Theories of Mind

DUALISM

interactionism | noninteractionism

NONDUALISM

neutral monism | physicalism | idealism

behaviorism
identity theory
functionalism

Note: Noninteractionist dualism, according to which a person's nonphysical and physical components do not interact causally with one another, and idealism, according to which only mind (thought) exists, have not generally been regarded as serious options by analytic philosophers.

not commit the researcher to the implausible idea that psychology, just like chemistry, "reduces" to physics.

A brief comment seems in order here. It has been the fond thought of many a philosopher that anything that happens could, in principle, be expressed in the language of physics. Let's call this thought **straightforward reductivist physicalism.** The thought is this: Just as chemistry is really just a matter of physics—that is, is reducible to physics—biology and neurophysiology are reducible to chemistry and physics, and hence ultimately are reducible just to physics. Further (according to straightforward reductivist physicalism), because psychology is really just a matter of neurophysiology, ultimately it, too, reduces to physics. Sociology and the other social sciences (according to straightforward reductivist physicalism) likewise ultimately reduce to the psychology of groups and hence, ultimately, they too reduce to physics. And hence, if the Grand Reduction of physics itself to a single force and/or particle is achieved, as some physicists apparently believe it will, everything from human thoughts and political elections to interactions of leptons and quarks will be reduced to and explained by a single physical factor (the physical version, perhaps, of God). If functionalism is correct, however, though everything that happens may indeed be physical, a thoroughgoing reduction of *everything* to physics is most unlikely.

Neutral monism, behaviorism, identity theory, and functionalism, then, are four (physicalist) theories of mind that have been developed by analytic philosophers in this century. As we said earlier, these days perhaps most analytic philosophers of mind (not to mention cognitive psychologists and artificial intelligence researchers) accept some physicalist theory of the mind (usually functionalism). Nevertheless, they are aware of several philosophical problems that physicalist theories encounter, as we see in the final section of this chapter.

So, as we just said, most contemporary analytic philosophers who study the philosophy of mind tend to accept some sort of physicalism, according to which a human being is an entirely physical organism that has no nonphysical, nonmaterial components or features.

But physicalist theories are not without their difficulties and we shall now briefly list the most important of these. Contemporary work in analytical philosophy that is concerned with the mind is usually related to one or another of these issues.

Final Authority Problem

Through introspection you gain knowledge of your own conscious states. It also seems that you are the *final authority* on what these states are. If you think that something looks brown to you, then you would be startled if we tried to tell you that it looks blue to you. If you say you are thinking of hiking in the mountains, it would be peculiar for us to say, "Oh no, in fact you are thinking of the Panama Canal Treaty."

It would be odd for us to say these things because everyone appreciates that only oneself is the final authority on one's own conscious states. Provided others think you can speak English, that you are honestly reporting your states, and that you haven't made a slip of the tongue, they would not consider correcting you. The notion that someone else might speak with equal authority about your conscious states seems not only false, but nuts.

But if conscious states are physical processes (as per identity theory), or are functional states of some physical system or other (as per functionalism), or are behavioral dispositions (as per behaviorism), then it would seem that, at least in principle, others could speak as authoritatively about your conscious states as you can. Whether (and in what sense) one truly is the final authority on his or her own conscious states, and how, if he or she is the final authority, physicalistic theories can accommodate that fact, are issues of current controversy.

Intentionality and Related Issues

Thinking, it seems, is not merely a process, for thinking is always about something. Thinking has content or an object that is thought about. Let's consider an example. Take two thoughts, let's say one about *Santa Claus* and the other about *the tooth fairy*. How are these two thoughts different?

Well, they differ from one another by virtue of their *objects*, namely, Santa Claus and the tooth fairy. Thoughts are thus said to have the property of **intentionality,** which is merely a way of saying that they "point to" or "contain" an object beyond themselves. This kind of intentionality has nothing to do with doing something deliberately, by the way.

According to some philosophers, *intentionality is the mark of mental phenomena.* Desires, beliefs, ideas, plans, doubts, imaginings—many (if not all) mental things are characterized by their objects. You don't just desire, you desire *something,* and one desire differs from the next because of its object. The same holds true for beliefs and the rest. A good bit of work is currently being done by philosophers of mind in grappling with whether and how a purely physical system can have intentional states.

Notice, too, that the objects that apparently characterize and define beliefs, desires, and the like may be completely *imaginary.* Consider the two thoughts just mentioned. How is it that nonexistent things, Santa Claus and the tooth fairy, can distinguish two thoughts from one another and from other mental states? The problem seems especially troublesome for physicalists.

Another way to approach the problem of intentionality is to note that thoughts, desires, beliefs, and the like are *propositional attitudes,* which is a philosopher's way of saying that to have a thought or desire or belief is to hold some proposition to be true. For example, when you think about Santa Claus, in fact your thought in large measure consists of the propositions you are thinking, such as that Santa Claus wears a red suit, that he has a white beard, or whatever it is that you are thinking. How is it, then, that a purely physical system can have states that are propositional—that is, true or false?

Look at it this way. A computer can cause sentences to be printed on a sheet of paper or flashed on a video screen in response to electric signals that are typed in on a keyboard. Inside the computer all that is going on is electrical processes of one sort or other. The signals, sentences, and processes are all physical things, flashes of light or bits of ink or bursts of electricity. These physical things can become true or false propositions to us, but are they true or false to the computer? What do you think?

If you are uncomfortable saying that they are true or false to the computer, then you can appreciate the problem presented to physicalists by the propositional nature of mental states. For, according to the physicalist, when a person is thinking, all that is going on internally is electrochemical processes of some sort. These processes are not the same processes as go on in a computer, but they, like those in the computer, are entirely physical (or so says the physicalist). How can these supposedly purely physical things be propositional? You can see that this is a problem.

A related issue is this. Through thought the world is *represented* to us. Thus, two questions arise. The first question has to do with the representing. How does a purely physical thing, whether it is ink marks, electrical impulses, flashes of light, bioelectric signals, neurological processes, or any other physical thing, come to *represent* anything? And the second question has to do with the "us." Surely, representations do not understand themselves: to be representations they must be understood *by* a consciousness, by an "us" that is *distinct* from the represen-

Brentano and Intentionality

To say that conscious states are "intentional" just means that they have objects (you don't just imagine, you imagine *something*; you don't just hope, you hope for something). The thesis that they are intentional is attributed to the German philosopher and psychologist **Franz Brentano** (1838–1917).

The objects of conscious states, Brentano noted, have "intentional inexistence," which means that they (the objects) need not exist. For instance, you can think about someone even if that person no longer exists and even if there never did exist such a person. Thus, *thinking* about someone seems to be quite fundamentally different from, say, *helping* someone, because you can't help someone unless he or she exists.

That conscious states are intentional was a fundamental tenet of Brentano's "descriptive psychology," which, in the hands of his student Edmund Husserl, evolved into phenomenology (which is discussed in the next chapter). Husserl asserted that if it weren't for Brentano's thesis of the intentionality of conscious states, phenomenology could not have come into being.

Contemporary *analytic philosophers* are endeavoring to understand how, if humans are purely physical entities, their conscious states could be intentional. The *phenomenologists'* interest in intentionality is entirely different, as will become clear in the next chapter. Phenomenology is not especially concerned with the issue of whether a physical system could have intentional states.

tations. Assuming that neurological processes do have representational capabilities, how do they become understood and what is it that understands them?

What Is It Like to Read This Book?

Let's move on to one more issue of concern for contemporary philosophy of mind. Let's consider: *What is it like for you to read this book?*

Most people would be inclined to say that what it is like for *me* to read this book is something *you* could never know. After all, you can only know what it is like for you to read it. What another person's experience is like when he or she reads a book, or sees a grape (see box on inverted spectrum), or daydreams, or thinks about summer plans; what it is like for a dog to hear a sound inaudible to human ears or for a cat to see a world of motions instead of objects; what, in short, experience—mental life in general—is *really* like for someone or something else is something no person can know. Experiences, it is often said, are private to the subject that has them. Until physicalist theories can explain *why* experiences are private, why they have a subjective dimension that remains inaccessible to outside scrutiny, or why it is a *mistake* to say that experiences are private and inaccessible to others, these theories will be incomplete. The

The Inverted Spectrum

You've probably heard of what Paul Churchland calls the **inverted spectrum** conjecture, though maybe not by that name. It's the idea that, for all you or I know, when we both look at objects that we call, say, orange, we may have different color experiences altogether. For all we know, oranges may give me the color experience that you get when you look at spinach, and spinach may give me the color experience you have when you look at an orange. The difference in our experience can never be detected because both of us always identify the same things as orange and the same things as green. That we might have "inverted" color experiences compared to each other thus seems entirely possible.

The possibility of our having inverted color experiences is said to pose a problem for functionalism. According to that theory, my experiencing of color is a functional state. Therefore, because my color experience on seeing an orange *is* functionally equivalent to your color experience on seeing an orange, then our color experiences (according to that theory) are the same, by definition. Thus functionalism rules out as impossible what seems clearly possible, an inverted color experience as here described. Therefore (it is said) functionalism has something wrong with it.

"privacy problem," as this issue might be called, is another current topic of discussion.

In sum, the final authority problem, the problem of intentionality, and the privacy problem are all currently unresolved issues in the philosophy of mind. All three issues are especially perplexing from a physicalist perspective.

In Selection 14.5 John Searle argues from the physicalist perspective that the solution to the mind-body problem is really much simpler than philosophers have made it out to be. Searle applies his solution to four subsidiary problems that fall under the mind-body problem, but our space limitations prevent us from reproducing his entire essay.

▶ S E L E C T I O N 14.5

From John Searle,
MINDS, BRAINS AND SCIENCE

I want to plunge right into what many philosophers think of as the hardest problem of all: What is the relation of our minds to the rest of the universe? This, I am sure you will recognize, is the traditional mind-body or mind-brain problem. In its contemporary version it usually takes the form: how does the mind relate to the brain?

I believe that the mind-body problem has a rather simple solution, one that is consistent both with what we know about neurophysiology and with our commonsense conception of the nature of mental states—pains, beliefs, desires, and so on. But before presenting that solution, I want to ask why the mind-body problem seems so intractable. . . .

There are four features of mental phenomena which have made them seem impossible to fit into our "scientific" conception of the world as made up of material things. . . .

The most important of these features is consciousness. I, at the moment of writing this, and you, at the moment of reading it, are both conscious. It is just a plain fact about the world that it contains such conscious mental states and events, but it is hard to see how mere physical systems could have consciousness. How could such a thing occur? How, for example, could this grey and white gook inside my skull be conscious? . . .

The second intractable feature of the mind is what philosophers and psychologists call "intentionality," the feature by which our mental states are directed at, or about, or refer to, or are of objects and states of affairs in the world other than themselves. . . . Now the question about intentionality is much like the question about consciousness. How can this stuff inside my head be *about* anything? How can it *refer* to anything? . . .

The third feature of the mind that seems difficult to accommodate within a scientific conception of reality is the subjectivity of mental states. This subjectivity is marked by such facts as that I can feel my pains, and you can't. I see the world from my point of view; you see it from your point of view. I am aware of myself and my internal mental states, as quite distinct from the selves and mental states of other people. . . .

Finally, there is a fourth problem, the problem of mental causation. We all suppose, as part of common sense, that our thoughts and feelings make a real difference to the way we behave, that they actually have some *causal* effect on the physical world. I decide, for example, to raise my arm and—lo and behold—my arm goes up. But if your thoughts and feelings are truly mental, how can they affect anything physical? . . . These four features, consciousness, intentionality, subjectivity, and mental causation are what make the mind-body problem seem so difficult. . . .

The first thesis I want to advance toward "solving the mind-body problem" is this:

Mental phenomena, all mental phenomena whether conscious or unconscious, visual or auditory, pains, tickles, itches, thoughts, indeed, all of our mental life, are caused by processes going on in the brain. . . .

To our first claim . . . we need to add a second claim:

Pains and other mental phenomena just are features of the brain (and perhaps the rest of the central nervous system).

One of the primary aims of this chapter is to show how *both* of these propositions can be true together. . . . To do this, I will turn away from the relations between mind and brain for a moment to observe some other sorts of causal relationships in nature.

A common distinction in physics is between micro- and macro-properties of systems—the small and large scales. Consider, for example, the desk at which I am now sitting, or the glass of water in front of me. Each object is composed of micro-particles. The micro-particles have features at the level of molecules and atoms as well as at the deeper level of sub-atomic particles. But each object also has certain properties such as the solidity of the table, the liquidity of the water, and the transparency of the glass, which are surface or global features of the physical systems. Many such surface or global properties can be causally explained by the behavior of elements at the micro-level. For example, the solidity of the table in front of me is explained by the lattice structure occupied by the molecules of which the table is composed. Similarly, the liquidity of the water is explained by the nature of the interactions between the H_2O molecules. Those macro-features are causally explained by the behavior of elements at the micro-level.

I want to suggest that this provides a perfectly ordinary model for explaining the puzzling relationships between the mind and the brain. In the case of liquidity, solidity, and transparency, we have no difficulty at all in supposing that the surface features are *caused by* the behavior of elements at the micro-level, and at the same time we accept that the surface phenomena *just are* features of the very systems in question. I think the clearest way of stating this point is to say that the surface feature is both *caused by* the behavior of micro-elements, and at the same time is *realised in* the system that is made up of the micro-elements. There is a cause and effect relationship, but at the same time the surface features are just higher level features of the very system whose behavior at the micro-level causes those features. . . .

If we apply these lessons to the study of the mind, it seems to me that there is no difficulty in accounting for the relations of the mind to the brain in terms of the brain's functioning to cause mental states. Just as the liquidity of the water is caused by the behavior of elements at the micro-level, and yet at the same time it is a feature realised in the system of micro-elements, so in exactly that sense of "caused by" and "realised in" mental phenomena are caused by processes going on in the brain at the neuronal or modular level, and at the same time they are realised in the very system that consists of neurons. . . . Nothing is more common in nature than for surface features of a phenomenon to be both caused by and realised in a micro-structure, and those are exactly the relationships that are exhibited by the relation of mind to brain.

To help you review, here is a checklist of the key philosophers and concepts of this chapter. The brief descriptive sentences that appear with each philosopher summarize one of his leading ideas. Keep in mind that some of these summary statements represent terrific oversimplifications of complex positions.

Checklist

Philosophers

- **René Descartes** Interactionist dualist.
- **Bertrand Russell** Neutral monist (at one point in his life).
- **A. J. Ayer and William James** Other neutral monists.
- **Gilbert Ryle** Held that when we talk about a person's psychological states, we are referring not to the immaterial states of a nonphysical mind but to the person's behavioral dispositions.
- **Franz Brentano** Held that conscious states have intentional inexistence.

Concepts

dualism
interactionist dualism
neutral monism
characterization problem
individuation problem
emergence problem
dependency problem
necessity problem
interaction problem
understanding problem
philosophical reduction
philosophical behaviorism
identity theory
functionalism
straightforward reductivist physicalism
final authority problem
intentionality
intentional inexistence

Questions for Discussion and Review

1. Present some reasons for believing that a human being is not a purely physical thing.
2. If humans are purely physical things, could they have free will? Explain.
3. Does the fact that a person can have knowledge of nonmaterial things, such as the truths of mathematics, demonstrate that humans are not purely physical?

4. Assuming that it is possible to doubt the existence of physical things but not your own mental states, does that show that your mental states are not physical things?

5. "Beliefs are true or false; physical things are not. So beliefs are not physical things." Evaluate this argument.

6. "My mental states are knowable by introspection, but my brain states are not; therefore my mental states are not brain states." Evaluate this argument.

7. Can a mind be characterized only "negatively," that is, as not divisible, as not existing in space, and so on?

8. Explain and try to resolve, in favor of dualism, either the emergence problem or the individuation problem.

9. Explain and try to resolve, in favor of dualism, either the dependency problem, the understanding problem, or the no-necessity problem.

10. Explain and try to resolve, in favor of dualism, the interaction problem.

11. Explain philosophical reduction. What is the connection between reduction and analysis?

12. What are sense-data, and are they physical, mental, or what?

13. What is philosophical behaviorism? Make clear in your explanation what a "disposition" is.

14. Do all thing-words refer to things?

15. Must the behaviorist say that actors feigning pain must actually be in pain?

16. Explain the difference between identity theory and behaviorism.

17. Do mental states reduce to brain states, according to the functionalist? Explain. Do functionalists believe that the mind and mental states are nonphysical?

18. "A brain scientist could never tell from looking at my brain what I am thinking. Therefore my thoughts are not brain states." Discuss this argument.

19. What does it mean to say, "intentionality is the mark of the mental"?

20. When all is said and done, which of the theories of mind discussed in this chapter do you think is the soundest, and why?

Suggested Further Readings

David Armstrong, *A Materialist Theory of the Mind* (London: Routledge and Kegan Paul, 1968). An important statement of a materialist position.

N. Block, *Readings in Philosophy of Psychology* (Cambridge, Mass.: Harvard University Press, 1980). A good collection of (not always easy-to-read) essays in the philosophy of mind.

C. D. Broad, *The Mind and Its Place in Nature* (New York: The Humanities Press, 1951). You won't find a better introduction to the subject, though it was originally written in 1925.

Keith Campbell, *Body and Mind* (London: Macmillan, 1970). This slender volume clearly sets forth the basic positions on this subject.

Paul M. Churchland, *Matter and Consciousness* (Cambridge, Mass.: Bradford, 1984). Excellent critical introduction to philosophy of mind. Slightly more difficult than Campbell.

Gilbert Ryle, *The Concept of Mind* (New York: Barnes and Noble, 1949). An important work, very readable.

Daniel Dennett, *Brainstorms* (Montgomery, Vt.: Bradford Books, 1978). A widely read anthology that contains sometimes difficult, but always well-written and entertaining essays on the mind and psychology.

Bertrand Russell, *The Analysis of Mind* (London: George Allen & Unwin, 1921). From Russell's "neutral monist" phase.

John Searle, *Minds, Brains, and Science* (Cambridge, Mass.: Harvard University Press, 1984). This short book raised hackles throughout cognitive science. Read it and find out why. The argument is very easy to follow.

Peter Smith and O. R. Jones, *The Philosophy of Mind* (Cambridge: Cambridge University Press, 1986). Another recent introductory text on the subject, with a fairly good bibliography.

SUMMARY AND CONCLUSION

We've talked some in this part about analytic philosophy in general and then looked at analytic philosophy at work in trying to understand the mind.

Though few philosophers today who call themselves analysts regard analysis as the only proper method of philosophy or even agree on what analysis is, most would say that many traditional philosophical problems were the result of linguistic confusions, and most place great value on careful, clear, and precise expression as essential to philosophical progress.

The main concern of analytic philosophers who have been concerned with the mind has been to find a proper understanding, or "analysis," if you will, of everyday discourse about the mind and its states. By "proper" is meant (roughly) one that is consistent, intelligible, and unconfused; one that is consonant with our scientific knowledge of the brain and human behavior and psychology (and with the findings of computer science and artificial intelligence research as well); and one that is not too at odds with our common-sense opinions about human psychology.

The overall objective might alternatively be described as one of seeking to delineate the interconnections between "folk psychology"—our "common-sense" understanding of the mind and its states and processes—and what brain science and psychology (and computer science and artificial intelligence research) tell us about consciousness, intelligence, and the internal causes of human behavior.

Beginning students sometimes wonder, *why not just get on with it* and study the mind and its states directly, and forget trying to understand mere *talk* about the mind? The answer to this question is as follows. If the concepts of the mind and mental phenomena were like the concepts of the sun and the brain and the Rocky Mountains, you could do that. You already know what objects you must study if you wish to study the sun, the brain, or the Rocky Mountains. But there is no similar understanding yet of just what the mind and its states are. You don't yet quite know just what you must undertake to examine if you wish to examine the mind or its states. By seeking to clarify the concept of mind, analytic philosophers of the mind strive to produce this understanding. Thus, their objective might also be described as trying to provide understanding of what the mind and its states are, no small task.

What we've written here is supposed to give you some comprehension of one important set of issues addressed by analytic philosophers as well as some understanding of an analytic approach to philosophy. But it's best to keep in mind that philosophy of mind is just one of many areas of investigation by analysts.

In the next part we turn to phenomenology and existentialism, the two other main focuses or traditions in twentieth-century philosophy. As you will shortly see, the concerns of phenomenologists and existentialists are quite different from those of analysts.

Continental Philosophy

The Continental Philosophers

The existentialist says at once that man is anguish.

—JEAN-PAUL SARTRE

Existentialism and phenomenology are philosophical movements from continental Europe. Both have their roots in the nineteenth century (though many of their themes can be traced back to Socrates and even to the pre-Socratics). And each has influenced the other to such an extent that two of the most famous and influential continental European philosophers of this century, **Martin Heidegger** (1889–1976) and **Jean-Paul Sartre** (1905–1980), are important figures in both movements, though Heidegger is primarily a phenomenologist and Sartre primarily an existentialist.

Between analytic philosophy on one hand and existentialism and phenomenology on the other yawns a great chasm. The focus and concerns of existentialism and phenomenology, and let's just refer to these jointly as *Continental philosophy*, are quite radically different from those of analytic philosophy—so much so that beginning students are amazed to learn that analytic philosophers and Continental philosophers both call themselves philosophers. It amazes some philosophers, too. It's not just that analytic philosophers and Continental philosophers come up with different answers. They basically don't even ask the same questions. And they really don't talk to each other all that much, though this has been changing in recent years. We regard this change as an encouraging development.

Existentialism

Many of the themes of existentialism had already been introduced by those dark thinkers of the nineteenth century, **Søren Kierkegaard** (1813–1855), and **Friedrich Nietzsche** (1844–1900), two of the most important forerunners of existentialism. Both men had a strong distaste for the optimistic idealism of Hegel and for metaphysical systems in general. Such philosophy, they thought, ignored the human predicament. For both Kierkegaard and Nietzsche, the universe, including its human inhabitants, is seldom rational, and philosophical systems that seek to make everything seem rational are just futile attempts to overcome pessimism and despair. This point of view will become clearer as we proceed.

For Kierkegaard, existence in this earthly realm must lead a sensitive person to despair. Despair, Kierkegaard held, is the inevitable result of the individual's having to confront momentous concrete ethical and religious dilemmas *as an individual*. It is the result of the individual's having to make, *for himself and alone*, choices of lasting significance.

According to Kierkegaard, despair is the *sickness-unto-death* and is the central philosophical problem. Is there anything in this world or outside it to which the individual can cling in order to keep from being swept away by the dark tides of despair? This, for Kierkegaard, is the fundamental question. His eventual conclusion was that nothing earthly can save a person from despair. Only a subjective commitment to the infinite and to God, not based on abstract intellectualizing or theoretical reasoning can grant relief.

Kierkegaard emphasized the theme of the irrationality of the world in opposition to Hegel's belief in its utter rationality. The earth, he thought, is a place of suffering, fear, and *dread*. Of these three, dread, according to Kierkegaard, is the worst because it has *no identifiable object or specifiable cause*. Dread renders us almost helpless to resist it. Kierkegaard regarded the idea that philosophy should be concerned with general or ideal "truths" and abstract metaphysical principles with disdain. Philosophy must speak to the anguished existence of the individual who lives in an irrational world and who must make important decisions in that world.

If Kierkegaard found Hegel's philosophy of absolute reason unpalatable, **Arthur Schopenhauer** (1788–1860), who must be mentioned in prelude to Nietzsche, found it beneath contempt. For Schopenhauer, Hegel's "reason" was an exercise in philistine self-deception; his attempt to paint the world in rational terms a part of a larger conspiracy. The sciences and humanities have all been mustered, he believed, to picture the universe as reasonable, governed by law, and under the mastery of the rational human intellect. Reality, he maintained, is very different.

Specifically, human beings are for Schopenhauer in fact rarely rational in their actions. On the contrary, they are blindly driven by their wills in pursuit of selfish desires. Reason is invoked after the fact as a way of rationalizing what has been done from impulse, he held. Schopenhauer's

Profile: Søren Kierkegaard (1813–1855)

Søren Kierkegaard, Danish philosopher and religious thinker, was virtually unknown outside Denmark until the twentieth century. Ultimately, however, his thought had a profound impact on existentialist philosophy and Protestant theology.

Kierkegaard's life was outwardly unexciting. He attended the universities of Copenhagen and Berlin and was much influenced by German culture, though he made polemical attacks on Hegel, whose metaphysics he regarded as totally inapplicable to the individual.

As for his inward life, Kierkegaard professed himself to have been, since childhood, "under the sway of a prodigious melancholy," and his grim outlook was made even gloomier by the confession of his father—himself no carefree spirit—that he had sinned and had even cursed God. Finding himself without moorings, Kierkegaard regarded dread and despair as the central problems of his life, and he learned that he could escape their grasp only through a passionate commitment of faith to God and the infinite.

Although Kierkegaard became engaged to marry, he found it necessary to break off the engagement, apparently because God occupied the "first place" in his life, though his own writing about the subject is murky. The episode, at any rate, was so momentous that even the sketchiest biography of Kierkegaard is obliged to mention the woman's name: Regine Olsen. The agony of choosing between God and Regine, a choice Kierkegaard felt he had to make, affected him profoundly.

Kierkegaard defined three types of life: the aesthetic, the ethical, and the religious. These correspond to what Professor Ray Billington has called the life of the observer, the life of the follower, and the life of the initiator. The "aesthetic" life is dominated by impulse, emotions, and sensual pleasures, and does not truly involve making choices. The "ethical" life does involve making choices, but those who live this life make choices on the basis of some kind of moral code, which they in effect fall back on as a sort of crutch. But at a higher and much more difficult plane, that of the "religious," the individual realizes that he must decide all issues for himself. He faces the agony of having to rely on his own judgment while never knowing whether his judgment is correct. The despair one faces at this level is overcome only by a "leap of faith," that total and infinite commitment to God.

Some of Kierkegaard's most important philosophical works, *Either/Or* (1843), *Philosophical Fragments* (1844), and *The Concluding Unscientific Postscript* (1846) were published under pseudonyms.

world is peopled with vicious little men who commit atrocities in pursuit of trifling objects. It is a world in which no one can be trusted and security requires sleeping with a loaded pistol underneath the pillow. Their willfulness makes humans a violent part of a grotesque scenario that has neither sense nor reason, in Schopenhauer's view.

Dostoyevsky's *Notes from the Underground*

In his 1864 novel *Notes from the Underground*, **Fyodor Dostoyevsky** (1821–1881) told how an imperfect society can waste the lives of its best members. The "underground man" lives in a society that prefers and rewards mediocrity. Hence his intelligence, sensitivity, and strength of character are neither needed nor wanted. He is condemned to watch second-rate compatriots surpass him and achieve success while his own superior talents languish unused. He is left with a life of bitterness, hopelessness, and shame. His sole pleasure consists in acts of spite and revenge, more imaginary than real. A passage:

"I was ashamed," he said; "I got to the point of feeling a sort of secret abnormal, despicable enjoyment in returning home to my corner on some disgusting Petersburg night, acutely conscious that that day I had committed a loathesome action again, that what was done could never be undone, and secretly, inwardly gnawing, gnawing at myself for it, tearing and consuming myself till the last of the bitterness turned into a sort of sweetness and at last into positive real enjoyment!

"I insist upon that . . . the enjoyment was just from the too intense consciousness of one's own degradation; it was from feeling oneself that one had reached the last barrier, that it was horrible, but that it could not be otherwise; that there was no escape for you: that you could never become a different man."

Dostoyevsky said in *The Brothers Karamazov* (1879–1880) that "the world stands on absurdities." It is just possible (is it not?) that a sense of uselessness is the most humiliating absurdity one can encounter.

Friedrich Nietzsche (1844–1900) further developed Schopenhauer's astringent critique of the blind optimism of rationalist idealists. According to Nietzsche, Western society had become increasingly decadent. People had come to lead lives largely devoid of joy or grandeur. They were enslaved by a morality that says "no" to life and to all that affirms it. They had become part of a herd, part of a mass that is only too willing to do what it is told. The herd animal, he held, is cowardly, reactionary, fearful, desultory, and vengeful. The mediocrity of Western civilization, he believed, was a reflection of these qualities. Nietzsche was under no illusions about the fate of the mass of mankind: only the rare and isolated individual is likely to escape a trivial life and pathetic fate, he maintained.

These writers gave signal that the smug self-satisfaction of nineteenth-century European philosophy—and culture—camouflaged emptiness and decadency. Their concern for the situation of the individual person; their disdain for abstract, remote, and (in their view) meaningless systems of thought; their denial of the rationality of the world and the people within it; their awareness of a vacuity, triviality, and pettiness within human existence; their efforts to find a reason for not despairing entirely—these themes spread rapidly into *belles lettres* (literature) as a whole in the late nineteenth and early twentieth centuries.

Sigmund Freud, for example, regarded the human being as a sexual animal from birth, one moved by drives that are unconscious and irra-

Profile: Friedrich Wilhelm Nietzsche (1844–1900)

Nietzsche, too, like Kierkegaard, was the son of a Lutheran minister. His father died of insanity when Nietzsche was four, and Nietzsche was raised until he was fourteen in a household of women, consisting of his mother, sister, grandmother, and two maiden aunts.

After studying at the universities of Bonn and Leipzig, Nietzsche, whose genius was evident from the beginning, was appointed associate professor of classical philology at the University of Basel at the unheard-of young age of twenty-four without even having written a doctoral thesis. Within two years he had become a full professor. In 1879, however, he was forced by ill health to resign his chair, and by 1889, he, like his father earlier, had become irretrievably insane. Nietzsche's insanity, however, may have been caused by medication.

Two of the principal intellectual influences on Nietzsche's life were the writings of Schopenhauer and the music of Richard Wagner, which Nietzsche compared to hashish in its ability to relieve mental pressure. For a period Nietzsche and Wagner—one of the century's most brilliant philosophers and one of its most brilliant composers—were friends, though this friendship did not last.

Nietzsche's writings have been enormously influential in Continental philosophy. Nietzsche saw himself as an active nihilist whose role was to tear down the old "slave morality" of Christian civilization. He looked to the "overman" whose "will to power" would set him beyond conventional standards of morality, a line of thought that later was seized upon, misinterpreted, and misused by defenders of Nazism.

Nietzsche's widespread popularity outside philosophical circles owes much to the power of thought expressed in numerous infamous quotations. "Which is it," Nietzsche asked in one of these, "is man one of God's blunders or is God one of man's?"

---

tional and over which there is little intelligent control. Art movements like *Dadaism, Surrealism,* and *Expressionism* expressed disenchantment with the established life of the bourgeoisie and its culture and values and sought to break out of the straightjacket of worn-out ideas and safe lifestyles. A sense that life is meaningless and empty, that the individual is alone and isolated and unable to communicate with others except on the most trivial of levels, permeated the thinking of the intellectuals and *literati* of the time and has persisted in art, literature, and philosophy to the present day.

In *The Bald Soprano* (1950), to take one example, **Eugene Ionesco** (1912–), a playwright in the dramatic tradition known as the *theater of the absurd,* has two strangers meeting at a dinner party and entering into

"The Death of Ivan Ilyich"

Leo Tolstoy (1828–1910) provides a powerful and moving example of the meaninglessness and futility of life in the story, "The Death of Ivan Ilyich" (1884).

Ivan Ilyich had led what he thought was a successful, busy, ambitious life. But then he learns that, though still in the prime of life, he has an incurable disease and will soon die. Quite naturally, he begins to look more closely at his life.

He notices that his wife and family members are really only concerned about the inheritance, and that his fellow workers have already begun jockeying to replace him. He sees that no one really cares about him or has any genuine sympathy for his situation. In short, his whole life seems to be a meaningless game. He finds that he cannot understand the insincerity and cruelty of others, including his own family. He also cannot understand God's cruelty and His absence in time of need. Above all, he cannot understand why he is so *alone*, abandoned to suffer and die. Has he done something deserving of such punishment? "'I am not guilty,' he exclaims, 'but he is not certain it is so.'"

"Life," wrote Tolstoy, "a series of increasing sufferings, flies further and further towards its end—the most terrible suffering." One of the implications of the story is that only when an individual faces the horror and suffering in life will he or she begin to understand its meaning—or lack of it.

a conversation. Slowly they discover that they had sat in the same train compartment five weeks earlier, live in the same city and house, and both have a daughter with one red eye and one white eye. Ultimately, to their delight, they discover that they are husband and wife.

The inability of humans to communicate with one another is also a principal theme of the Irish playwright **Samuel Beckett** (1906–). In *Waiting for Godot* (1953), the two principal characters wait in a desertlike environment for someone to arrive who will tell them what to do. They talk only to pass the time, not because they have anything to say. They seem often to be talking at the same time on entirely different subjects without either one noticing. And it doesn't matter, for it doesn't interrupt the emptiness of the words.

Another powerful depiction of the inability of people to reach one another can be found in the films of the Swedish director, **Ingmar Bergman** (1918–). In film after film, Bergman delineates the silence that exists between husband and wife, son and father, sister and sister. He further shows how the frustration and loneliness of the inner being lead to deep feelings of anger, resentment, and desire for revenge. Much time and energy is expended by Bergman's isolated characters in carefully hiding these feelings from themselves and others. Our separation and estrangement from others, Bergman implies, leaves our lives tragically and intolerably unfulfilled.

Another theme present in twentieth-century literature pertains to the horror of coping in an absurd world—a world in which there is no apparent reason why things happen one way and not another. The characters in the stories and novels of **Franz Kafka** (1883–1924), a Czech Jew whose mother tongue and language in which he wrote was German (a fact itself suggestive of human dislocation), invariably find themselves thrust into a situation they do not comprehend but in which they must nevertheless act and be judged for their actions. Nor are they certain that the situation in which they find themselves is not one of their own making. Kafka's parable, "The Metamorphosis," for example, tells of an ordinary salesman who supports his sister and aging parents. One day the salesman awakens at home to find that his body has been changed into a giant insect. He does not know why this has happened, and he will die without finding out. At first he is treated compassionately by the other family members, on whom he is of course dependent, but soon they resent his not supporting them and eventually come to regard him as a nuisance as well as an unwelcome family secret. At one point, pieces of fruit thrown by a frustrated and irate sister become embedded in his body and grow infected. Slowly but inevitably, the metamorphosized man loses heart and dies. Kafka presumably thought the story represented to some extent the fate of all human beings.

The themes we have been alluding to here, which began to surface in the nineteenth century and were developed throughout our own century (and give little indication of dying out today), are among the main themes of **existentialism.** The most important existentialist philosophers, about whom we shall say more later, only achieved worldwide recognition and notoriety just after World War II. But the ideas essential to existentialism were shared by many artists, novelists, poets, dramatists, and theologians much before this time.

Specifically, these main themes of existentialism (or at any rate some of them) may be listed as follows:

- Traditional and academic philosophy is sterile and remote from the concerns of real life.

- Philosophy must focus on the individual in his or her confrontation with the world.

- The world as found is irrational (or in any event beyond total comprehending or accurate conceptualizing through philosophy).

- It (the world) also is absurd, in the sense that no ultimate explanation can be given for why it is the way it is.

- Senselessness, emptiness, triviality, separation, and inability to communicate pervade human existence, giving birth to anxiety, dread, self-doubt, and despair.

- The individual confronts, as the most important fact of human existence, the necessity to choose how he or she is to live within this absurd and irrational world.

As will be seen, the existentialists do not guarantee that this *human predicament* can be solved. What they do say is that without utter honesty in confronting the assorted problems of human existence, life can only deteriorate; that without struggling doggedly with them the individual will find no meaning or value in life.

▶ S E L E C T I O N   15.1

From Friedrich Nietzsche,
THUS SPOKE ZARATHUSTRA

The Last Man

And thus spoke Zarathustra to the people: . . .

"Alas, the time is coming when man will no longer give birth to a star. Alas, the time of the most despicable man is coming, he that is no longer able to despise himself. Behold, I show you the *last man.*

"'What is love? What is creation? What is longing? What is a star?' Thus asks the last man, and he blinks.

"The earth has become small, and on it hops the last man, who makes everything small. His race is as ineradicable as the flea-beetle; the last man lives longest.

"'We have invented happiness,' say the last men, and they blink. They have left the regions where it was hard to live, for one needs warmth. One still loves his neighbor and rubs against him, for one needs warmth.

"Becoming sick and harboring suspicion are sinful to them: one proceeds carefully. A fool, whoever still stumbles over stones or human beings! A little poison now and then: that makes for agreeable dreams. And much poison in the end, for an agreeable death.

"One still works, for work is a form of entertainment. But one is careful, lest the entertainment be too harrowing. One no longer becomes poor or rich: both require too much exertion. Who still wants to rule? Who obey? Both require too much exertion.

"No shepherd and one herd! Everybody wants the same, everybody is the same: whoever feels different goes voluntarily to a madhouse.

"'Formerly all the world was mad,' say the most refined, and they blink.

"One is clever and knows everything that has ever happened: so there is no end of derision. One still quarrels, but one is soon reconciled—else it might spoil the digestion.

"One has one's little pleasure for the day, and one's little pleasure for the night: but one has regard for health.

"'We have invented happiness,' say the last men, and they blink."

Two Existentialists

Existentialism as a philosophical movement was something of a direct reaction to perceived social ills and was created by artists and writers as much as by philosophers per se. So it isn't remarkable that two of the greatest existentialist philosophers, **Albert Camus** and **Jean-Paul Sartre**, wrote drama, novels, and political tracts as well as philosophical works. Both also thought it important to disseminate their ideas into society as a whole in the hope of having some direct influence. Both were involved in the French Resistance during World War II against the terror of German fascism. Both thought—despite their belief in the absurdity of life—that responsible social action is as necessary as is an understanding of the sociopolitical forces at work in the world.

Camus and Sartre are by no means the only existentialist philosophers. Other famous existentialists include Gabriel Marcel and Simone de Beauvoir in France, Karl Jaspers in Switzerland, Martin Heidegger in Germany, Miguel de Unamuno and José Ortega y Gasset in Spain, and Nicola Abbagnano in Italy. But Camus and Sartre are especially representative of the movement, and we will focus on them. Camus, we might note, was reluctant to be classified as an existentialist because that lumped him together with Sartre, with whom Camus quarreled.

Albert Camus

Camus (1913–1960) grew up in poverty in Algeria and fought in the French Resistance against the Nazis. He saw much suffering, waste, and death even before the war; and, perhaps not surprisingly, the principal philosophical question, for him, was: *Is there any reason not to commit suicide?* Camus believed that this question arises when a person stops deceiving himself and begins seeing the world without pre-given illusions.

Many people, Camus believed, live their whole lives and die without ever seeing things as they really are. More specifically, instead of see-

Life Is Absurd

One of Camus's principal theses is that life as we find it is absurd. The notion of absurdity implies that there is no ultimate reason that things are the way they are. It also implies that life is unjust and frustrates human needs. Most important, perhaps, that the world is absurd seems to mean, for Camus, that it provides no absolute or necessary basis of value.

That we must make choices and decide how to act in a valueless and absurd world is often called the "existential predicament."

ing the "tragic nature of life," they waste their lives in "stupid self-confidence." That is, although they in fact spend their lives in or near despair in an absurd world that continually frustrates true human needs, they mask the fact with a forced optimism. And the more "profitable" such false optimism is, the more entrenched it becomes. In Camus's view, for many of us self-deception has become a dominant mode of being. This implies as well that often we are strangers to ourselves and to our own inability to meet our fundamental needs.

What are these basic needs? According to Camus, there are two: the need for clarity or understanding, and the need for social warmth and contact. Unfortunately, however, we live in an absurd world, a world in which these basic human needs are unmet. On one hand, the need for clear understanding of the world founders on the "opaqueness and density of the world"; indeed, it founders on the very fact that the world is absurd and consequently provides no sufficient reason for why things happen one way and not another.

The second essential need, the need for human warmth and contact, also remains unfulfilled, Camus thought. Humans in this violent age tend to remain strangers to one another (as well as to themselves); they live solitary existences in which relationships are matters of convention rather than of mutual sharing and understanding. The absurdity of life in frustrating essential human needs means that hoped-for happiness often turns to misery and despair—even though many hide this tragedy from themselves behind a façade of baseless hopes.

Camus likened life to the fate of Sisyphus in the myth of the same name. Sisyphus had provoked the wrath of the gods and was condemned to roll a huge stone up a hill, only to see it roll back down again. This repeated itself forever. Human beings, according to Camus, are similarly condemned to lives of "futile and hopeless labor," without reasonable hope of fulfilling their true needs. No matter how hard we try to live a just and meaningful existence, it is unlikely that our efforts will lead to lasting results.

In this context it may easily be understood why Camus considered

Camus on Life

Men die and they are not happy.

It is from the clash between our desire for complete explanation and the essential opacity of the world that the absurd is born.

[The Gods] had thought with some reason that there is no more dreadful punishment than futile and hopeless labor.

I draw from the absurd three consequences, which are my revolt, my freedom, and my passion . . . I transform into a rule of life what was an invitation to death—and I refuse suicide.

He who despairs of events is a coward, but he who hopes for the human lot is a fool.

Truth is mysterious, elusive, always to be conquered. Liberty is dangerous, as hard to live with, as it is elating. We must march towards these goals painfully but resolutely, certain in advance of our feelings on so long a road.

We are still waiting, and I am waiting, for a group of all those who refuse to be dogs and are resolved to pay the price that must be paid so that man can be something more than a dog.

The true rebel chooses the present over the future, the fate of humanity for the delusion of power. He gives us an example of the only original rule of life today, "to learn to live and to die, and, in order to be a man, to refuse to be a god."

In all circumstances of his life, the writer can recapture the feelings of a living community that will justify him. But only if he accepts as completely as possible the two truths that constitute the nobility of his calling: the service of truth and the service of freedom.

---

the question of suicide to be a primary philosophical issue. Why indeed should one wish to continue living under such circumstances as Camus has depicted? Nevertheless, Camus regarded suicide as unacceptable. Suicide, he thought, is a kind of weak-minded acquiescence to an unjust destiny. Camus believed, perhaps paradoxically, that by struggling against the Sisyphusian fate to the end, by rebelling against the absurdity and tragedy of life, it is possible to give life meaning and value. His position indeed is that only through this struggle with an absurd world can the individual achieve fulfillment, solidarity with others, and "a brief love of this earth."

Increasingly Camus focused his concern on the grotesque inhumanity and hideous cruelty of a world torn asunder by war and Nazism. Civilization, he thought, certainly with some justification, is suffering from a "plague" of epidemic proportions, a plague that kills many and sickens all. In such an unjust world one finds oneself committing violent acts merely to survive. Camus viewed the world as, in effect, sponsoring an ongoing competition in murder, as a place in which it is difficult to raise a finger without killing somebody. Capital punishment, he thought, is just one example of how the "decent citizen" is reduced to the level of a murderer. And in outright warfare the morality of violence exceeds control and comes into the open.

Camus wrote that "one cannot always live on murders and violence." By living out the values of the lowest animals, the individual is delivered up to the merciless power of despair and cynicism. Camus loathed the "absolute cynicism" of modern society that, he implied, drove humans to desperation and prevented them "from taking responsibility for their own life."

Thus, Camus came increasingly to insist that each individual must spend life fighting the plague—that is, the degeneracy of the world. Each must resist the temptations offered by cunning and violence; what is called for, he thought, is a "revolt" against the existing "order." Perhaps as a way of fighting the plague, Camus's thinking after the war became increasingly concerned with social and political issues. This represents a shift from his early works, which are focused much more strictly on the concerns of the individual.

But Camus thought that the revolt against a revolting world must be "measured" and limited. What Camus means is made clearer in his play *Caligula* (1944), in which the Roman emperor Caligula is presented as an example of a man who discovers the implicit cruelty and viciousness of human existence. In order not to fall victim to this evil, Caligula revolts against it in an unmeasured way, through his own acts of cruelty and viciousness. Such an unmeasured reaction was unacceptable to Camus; it meant becoming more bestial than the other beasts. In short, for Camus, the violence of the world does not excuse or justify violence in response.

Thus, the best that is possible for the individual, Camus implied, is a measured revolt wherein he or she spends life resisting violence and injustice. The effort, he maintained, must be predicated on the assumption that "any mutilation of mankind is irrevocable." The individual must fight for justice and liberty and against all forms of tyranny: "Let us die resisting," he wrote. Yet we must have no illusions or false optimism about the possible results of our action. For it may well be that nothing will improve: in an absurd world nothing is guaranteed.

Selection 15.2 is from Camus's 1955 essay, "The Myth of Sisyphus."

▶ S E L E C T I O N 15.2

From Albert Camus, "THE MYTH OF SISYPHUS"

Absurdity and Suicide

There is but one truly serious philosophical problem and that is suicide. Judging whether life is or is not worth living amounts to answering the fundamental question of philosophy. All the rest—whether or not the world has three dimensions, whether the mind has nine or twelve categories—comes afterwards. These are games; one must first answer. And if it is true, as Nietzsche claims, that a philosopher, to deserve our respect, must preach by example, you can appreciate the importance of that reply, for it will precede the definitive act. These are facts the heart can feel; yet they call for careful study before they become clear to the intellect.

If I ask myself how to judge that this question is more urgent than that, I reply that one judges by the actions it entails. I have never seen anyone die for the ontological argument. Galileo, who held a scientific truth of great importance, abjured it with the greatest ease as soon as it endangered his life. In a certain sense, he did right.[1] That truth was not worth the stake. Whether the earth or the sun revolves around the other is a matter of profound indifference. To tell the truth, it is a futile question. On the other hand, I see many people die because they judge that life is not worth living. I see others paradoxically getting killed for the ideas or illusions that give them a reason for living (what is called a reason for living is also an excellent reason for dying). I therefore conclude that the meaning of life is the most urgent of questions. How to answer it? On all essential problems (I mean thereby those that run the risk of leading to death or those that intensify the passion of living) there are probably but two methods of thought: the method of La Palisse and the method of Don Quixote. Solely the balance between evidence and lyricism can allow us to achieve simultaneously emotion and lucidity. In a subject at once so humble and so heavy with emotion, the learned and classical dialectic must yield, one can see, to a more modest attitude of mind deriving at one and the same time from common sense and understanding.

Suicide has never been dealt with except as a social phenomenon. On the contrary, we are concerned here, at the outset, with the relationship between individual thought and suicide. An act like this is prepared within the silence of the heart, as is a great work of art. The man himself is ignorant of it. One evening he pulls the trigger or jumps.

Of an apartment-building manager who had killed himself I was told that he had lost his daughter five years before, that he had changed greatly since, and that that experience had "undermined" him. A more exact word cannot be imagined. Beginning to think is beginning to be undermined. Society has but little connection with such beginnings. The worm is in man's heart. That is where it must be sought. One must follow and understand this fatal game that leads from lucidity in the face of existence to fight from light.

There are many causes for a suicide, and generally the most obvious ones were not the most powerful. Rarely is suicide committed (yet the hypothesis is not excluded) through reflection. What sets off the crisis is almost always unverifiable. Newspapers often speak of "personal sorrows" or of "incurable illness." These explanations are plausible. But one would have to know whether a friend of the desperate man had not that very day addressed him indifferently. He is the guilty one. For that is enough to precipitate all the rancors and all the boredom still in suspension.[2]

But if it is hard to fix the precise instant, the subtle step when the mind opted for death, it is easier to deduce from the act itself the consequences it implies. In a sense, and as in melodrama, killing yourself amounts to confessing. It is confessing that life is too much for you or that you do not understand it. Let's not go too far in such analogies, however, but rather return to everyday words. It is merely confessing that that "is not worth the trouble." Living, naturally, is never easy. You continue making the gestures commanded by existence for many reasons, the first of which is habit. Dying voluntarily implies that you have recognized, even instinctively, the ridiculous character of that habit, the absence of any profound reason for living, the insane character of that daily agitation, and the uselessness of suffering.

What, then, is that incalculable feeling that deprives the mind of the sleep necessary to life? A world that can be explained even with bad reasons is a familiar world. But, on the other hand, in a universe suddenly divested of illusions and lights, man feels an alien, a stranger. His exile is without remedy since he is deprived of the memory of a lost home or the hope of a promised land. This divorce between man and his life, the actor and his setting, is properly the feeling of absurdity. All healthy men having thought of their own suicide, it can be seen, without further explanation, that there is a direct connection between this feeling and the longing for death.

The subject of this essay is precisely this relationship between the absurd and suicide, the exact degree to which suicide is a solution to the absurd. The principle can be established that for a man who does not cheat, what he believes to be true must determine his action. Belief in the absurdity of existence must then dictate his conduct. It is legitimate to wonder, clearly and without false pathos, whether a conclusion of this importance requires forsaking as rapidly as possible an incomprehensible condition. I am speaking, of course, of men inclined to be in harmony with themselves.

Stated clearly, this problem may seem both simple and insoluble. But it is wrongly assumed that simple questions involve answers that are no less simple and that evidence implies evidence. *A priori* and reversing the terms of the problem just as one does or does not kill oneself, it seems that there are but two philosophical solutions, either yes or no. This would be too easy. But allowance must be made for those who, without concluding, continue questioning. Here I am only slightly indulging in irony: this is the majority. I notice also that those who answer "no" act as if they thought "yes." As a matter of fact, if I accept the Nietzschean criterion, they think "yes" in one way or another. On the other hand, it often happens that those who commit suicide were assured of the meaning of life. These contradictions are constant. It may even be said that they have never been so keen as on this point where, on the contrary, logic seems so desirable. It is a commonplace to compare philosophical theories and the behavior of those who profess them. But it must be said that of the thinkers who refused a meaning to life none except Kirilov who belongs to literature, Peregrinos who is born of legend,[3] and Jules Lequier who belongs to hypothesis, admitted his logic to the point of refusing that life. Schopenhauer is often cited, as a fit subject for laughter, because he praised suicide while seated at a well-set table. This is no subject for joking. That way of not taking the tragic seriously is not so grievous, but it helps to judge a man.

In the face of such contradictions and obscurities must we conclude that there is no relationship between the opinion one has about life and the act one commits to leave it? Let us not exaggerate in this direction. In a man's attachment to life there is something stronger than all the ills in the world. The body's judgment is as good as the mind's, and the body shrinks from annihilation. We get into the habit of living before acquiring the habit of thinking. In that race which daily hastens us toward death, the body maintains its irreparable lead. In short, the essence of that contradiction lies in what I shall call the act of eluding because it is both less and more than diversion in the Pascalian sense. Eluding is the invariable game. The typical act of eluding the fatal evasion that constitutes the third theme of this essay is hope. Hope of another life one must "deserve" or trickery of those who live not for life itself but for some great idea that will transcend it, refine it, give it a meaning, and betray it.

Thus everything contributes to spreading confusion. Hitherto, and it has not been wasted effort, people have played on words and pretended to believe that refusing to grant a meaning to life necessarily leads to declaring that it is not worth living. In truth, there is no necessary common measure between these two judgments. One merely has to refuse to be misled by the confusions, divorces, and inconsistencies previously pointed out. One must brush everything aside and go straight to the real problem. One kills oneself because life is not worth living, that is certainly a truth—yet an unfruitful one because it is a truism. But does that insult to existence, that flat denial in which it is plunged come from the fact that it has no meaning? Does its absurdity require one to escape it through hope or suicide—this is what must be clarified, hunted down, and elucidated while brushing aside all the rest. Does the Absurd dictate death? This problem must be given priority over others, outside all methods of thought and all exercises of the disinterested mind. Shades of meaning, contradictions, the psychology that an "objective" mind can always introduce into all problems have no place in this pursuit and this passion. It calls simply for an unjust—in other words, logical—thought. That is not easy. It is always easy to be logical. It is almost impossible to be logical to the bitter end. Men who die by their own hand consequently follow to its conclusion their emotional inclination. Reflection on suicide gives me an opportunity to raise the only problem to interest me: is there a logic to the point of death? I cannot know unless I pursue, without reckless passion, in the sole light of evidence, the reasoning of which I am here suggesting the source. This is what I call an absurd reasoning. Many have begun it. I do not yet know whether or not they kept to it.

When Karl Jaspers, revealing the impossibility of constituting the world as a unity, exclaims: "This limitation leads me to myself, where I can no longer withdraw behind an objective point of view that I am merely representing, where neither I myself nor the existence of others can any longer become an object for me," he is evoking after many others those waterless deserts where thought reaches its confines. After many others, yes indeed, but how eager they were to get out of them! At that last crossroad where thought hesitates, many men have arrived and even some of the humblest. They then abdicated what was most precious to them, their life. Others, princes of the mind, abdicated likewise, but they initiated the suicide of their thought in its purest revolt. The real effort is to stay there, rather, in so far as that is possible, and to examine closely the odd vegetation of those distant regions. Tenacity and acumen are privileged spectators of this inhuman show in which absurdity, hope, and death carry on their dialogue. The mind can then analyze the figures of that elementary yet subtle dance before illustrating them and reliving them itself.

---

[1] From the point of view of the relative value of truth. On the other hand, from the point of view of virile behavior, this scholar's fragility may well make us smile.

[2] Let us not miss this opportunity to point out the relative character of this essay. Suicide may indeed be related to much more honorable considerations—for example, the political suicides of protest, as they were called, during the Chinese revolution.

[3] I have heard of an emulator of Peregrinos, a post-war writer who, after having finished his first book, committed suicide to attract attention to his work. Attention was in fact attracted, but the book was judged no good.

Jean-Paul Sartre

Albert Camus was agnostic, maintaining that he did not know whether or not there is a God. Sartre (1905–1980) was atheistic. Man, Sartre said, is *abandoned,* by which "we mean that God does not exist." And according to Sartre, the abandonment of man—that is, the nonexistence of God—has drastic philosophical implications. Basically, there are four.

First, because there is no God, there is no maker of man and no such thing as a divine conception of man in accordance with which man was created. This means, Sartre thought, that there is no such thing as a human nature that is common to all humans; no such thing as a specific essence that defines what it is to be human. Past philosophers had maintained that each thing in existence has a definite, specific essence; Aristotle, for example, believed that the essence of being human was being rational. But for Sartre, the person must produce his or her own essence, because no God created human beings in accordance with a divine concept. Thus, in the case of man, Sartre wrote, "existence precedes essence," by which he meant very simply that you are what you make of yourself. You are what *you* make of yourself.

The second implication of the nonexistence of God is this. Because there is no God, there is no ultimate reason why anything has happened or why things are the way they are and not some other way. This means that the individual in effect has been *thrown* into existence without any real reason for being. But this does not mean that the individual is like a rock or a flea, which also (because there is no God) have no ultimate reason or explanation. Rocks and fleas, Sartre would say, only have what he calls "being-in-itself" (in French, *être-en-soi*), or mere existence. But a *human being,* according to Sartre, not only exists, that is, has being-in-

Is Sartre Only for Atheists?

If God does exist, then technically speaking we are not "abandoned." But some of the main problems that arise from abandonment seem also to arise merely if we cannot *know* whether God exists. For if we do not know whether God exists, then we do not know whether there is any ultimate reason why things happened the way they did, and we do not know whether those values we believe are grounded in God really do have objective validity.

In fact, even if we do know that God exists and also know that values are grounded in God,

we still may not know *which* values are grounded in God: we may still not know what the absolute criteria and standards of right and wrong are. And even if we know what the standards and criteria are, just what they *mean* will still be a matter for subjective interpretation. And so the human dilemma that results may be very much the same as if there were no God.

Nonatheists should not dismiss Sartre too hastily.

Profile: Jean-Paul Sartre (1905–1980) and Simone de Beauvoir (1908–1987)

Jean Paul Sartre studied philosophy at the Sorbonne. He also studied the philosophies of Husserl and Heidegger, and spent one year in Berlin. While still a graduate student he met **Simone de Beauvoir,** who later played a key role in the early phases of the women's liberation movement, especially with her famous book, *The Second Sex* (1948). Their friendship and mutual support lasted until Sartre's death, though in the opinion of historian Paul Johnson, "in the annals of literature, there are few worse cases of a man exploiting a woman." (Sartre never wrote anything about their relationship.)

During World War II, Sartre served in the French army, became a German prisoner of war, escaped, and worked in the Resistance movement. Throughout his life he supported political causes and movements, including the French Communist party. In 1951, he tried unsuccessfully to found a new political party, radically leftist but non-Communist in orientation.

In 1964, Sartre declined the Nobel Prize in Literature, believing that such awards could make a writer too influential.

When Sartre died, 18,000 people marched behind his coffin through the streets of Paris.

itself, but also has "being-for-itself" (*être-pour-soi*), which means that a human being, unlike an inanimate object or vegetable, is a self-aware or conscious subject that creates its own future. We will return to this point momentarily.

Third, because there is no God and hence no divine plan that determines what must happen, "there is no determinism." Thus, "man is free," Sartre wrote; "man is freedom"; in fact, he is *condemned* to be free. Nothing forces us to do what we do. Thus, he said, "we are alone, without excuses," by which he means simply that we cannot excuse our actions by saying that we were forced by circumstances or moved by passion or otherwise determined to do what we did.

Fourth, because there is no God, there is no objective standard of values: "It is very troubling that God does not exist," Sartre wrote, "for with him disappears every possibility of finding values . . . there can no longer be any good a priori." Consequently, because a Godless world has no objective values, we must establish or invent our own values.

Consider briefly what these various consequences of our "abandonment" entail. That we find ourselves in this world without a God-given "human nature" or "essence"; that we are active, conscious, and self-aware subjects; that we are totally free and unconstrained (and unexcused) by any form of determinism; and that we must create our own

Sartre and Kant on Ethics

"I choose myself perpetually," Sartre wrote. By this he meant that we each are in a continual process of constructing ourselves and our values or ethics. And, as discussed in the text, Sartre believed that when a person determines something to be right for him or herself, he or she is also determining it to be good for all.

This universalization of individual choices is reminiscent of Immanuel Kant's supreme precept of morality, the categorical imperative, according to which you must only act in such a way that the principle on which you act could be a universal law. Kant, however, as we saw in Part 3, grounded the categorical imperative and hence all morality in reason, which he thought determines *a priori* what is right and wrong. Sartre, however, maintains that there is no *a priori* moral law and that Kant's formal law is inadequate as a guide for concrete action in everyday life. It is rather what a person does that in fact determines his morality. "In choosing myself, I choose man," Sartre said.

It is perhaps arguable, however, that *this* principle ("in choosing myself, I choose man") is for Sartre a universal principle underlying morality.

values—these facts mean that each individual has an awesome responsibility, according to Sartre:

First of all, we are responsible for what we are. "Abandonment implies that we ourselves choose our being," he wrote. Second, we must *invent* our own values. And third and finally, because, according to Sartre, "nothing can be good for us without [also] being [good] for all," in inventing our own values we also function as *universal legislators* of right and wrong, good and evil. In choosing for ourselves, we choose for all. "Thus," he wrote, "our responsibility is much greater than we had supposed it, for it involves all mankind."

This responsibility for oneself and thus for all humankind, Sartre thought, we experience as anguish, and it is clear why he maintained that this is so: our responsibility is total and profound, and *absolutely inescapable.* You might perhaps object that many people, perhaps even most, certainly do not seem to be particularly anxious, let alone anguished. It is true, Sartre admitted, that many people are not consciously or visibly anxious. But this merely is because they are hiding or fleeing from their responsibility: they act and live in self-deception, inauthenticity, and **"bad faith."** Further, he said, they are ill at ease with their conscience, for "even when it conceals itself, anguish appears."

It is not difficult to understand why one might seek to avoid shouldering one's responsibility to oneself and thus to others, for as Sartre depicted it, this responsibility is overwhelming. But in Sartre's view something else also contributes to the difficulty of this task: one does not know *what* to choose because the world is experienced as absurd. It is experienced as absurd, Sartre maintains, because, since God does not exist, it lacks necessity—it lacks an ultimate rhyme or reason for being this way and not that way. It (the world) therefore is experienced as fun-

Sartre on Life

Human life begins on the other side of despair.

Man's freedom is to say no, and this means that he is the being by whom nothingness comes into being.

Thus, there is no human nature, because there is no God to have a conception of it. Man simply is. . . . Man is nothing else but that which he makes of himself. That is the first principle of existentialism.

Nothing will be changed if God does not exist; we will rediscover the same norms of honesty, progress, and humanity.

To live "authentically" we must be conscious of our freedom to choose and be concerned with the effect our choice will have on all men.

The existentialist does not believe in the power of passion. He will never think that a noble passion is a devastating torrent which leads man to [do] certain actions, and which, consequently, is an excuse. He thinks that man is responsible for his passion.

damentally senseless, unreasonable, illogical, and, therefore, nauseating. It calls forth both revulsion and boredom. It is "perfectly gratuitous" (*gratuité parfaite*) and often just simply too much (*de trop*).

Nevertheless, according to Sartre, it is only through acceptance of our responsibility that we may live in **authenticity.** To be responsible, to live authentically, means intentionally to make choices about one's life and one's future. These choices are made most efficaciously, Sartre maintained, by becoming "engaged" in the world and by selecting a *fundamental project*. A life gains wholeness and purpose through adoption of such a fundamental project, for this project can mobilize and direct all one's life energies and permit one to make spontaneous choices. Through this project, in short, the individual creates a world that does not yet exist and thus gives meaning to his or her life.

So Sartre's metaphysics (or anti-metaphysics), which stood opposed to the belief in God, determinism, necessity, and the objectivity of values, in effect leaves the human individual in what may plausibly be called an absurd situation. There is nothing that one must do; there is nothing that must be done. To find meaning in life, the individual must create his or her world and its values by making authentic choices. These choices first take the form of intentions directed toward future events. Then they become actions of an engaged being in a world of people, a political (and politically troubled) world. The choices that we make are made by us for all humankind and are, therefore, in this limited sense "absolute" ethical principles. Although we initially find ourselves in an absurd world not of our choosing, we can remake that world through our choices and actions, and we must do so, as difficult as that may be.

Sartre and Heidegger

In the early 1930s, Sartre studied for a short time in Germany and was deeply influenced by Martin Heidegger. Sartre attributed the concept of abandonment (treated in the text) to Heidegger, and, like Heidegger, Sartre was concerned with the concepts of bad faith, authenticity, a life's project, and others.

Still, in decisive ways, Sartrian and Heideggerian philosophies are dissimilar. Heidegger, on one hand, never did abandon his belief in Being as the basic principle of philosophy, whereas for Sartre individual existence was of paramount importance. Sartre believed that, as a consequence of the nonexistence of God, nothing about Being is necessary; Heidegger, on the other hand, believed that Being is absolutely necessary. Politically, Sartre considered himself a Marxist and accepted much of the Marxist view of historical events; Heidegger, in comparison, was not in any sense sympathetic to the Marxist world view.

On balance, the philosophies of Sartre and Heidegger are quite different, despite the superficial resemblances.

This exposition of Sartre's thought focuses on his understanding of what might be called the existential predicament. His thinking evolved over time and he became increasingly concerned—like Camus—with social and political issues. These interests and his fascination with Marxist philosophy led to a modification of his existentialist stance, but we can do no more in this book than mention this. We have also not dealt with his epistemology, his aesthetics, or his views on psychoanalysis.

You Are What You Do

According to Sartre, you create yourself through your choices, as we have explained in the text. But be aware that for Sartre these self-creating choices are not found in mere "philosophical" abstractions or speculations. The choices that count, for Sartre, are those that issue forth in actions. "There is reality only in action," he wrote—"man is nothing other than the whole of his actions."

This means that, according to Sartre, no hidden self or true you lies behind your deeds. If, for example, in your actions you are impatient and unforgiving, it is a fiction for you to think, "Well, if others could see into my heart they would know that in reality I am patient and understanding." If you are cowardly in your deeds, you deceive yourself if you believe that "in truth" or "deep, down inside" you are courageous. If you have not written great poetry, then it is an illusion for you to believe that you nevertheless have the soul of a great poet.

It is easy to see why Sartre believed that his doctrine horrified many people. Many people think of their behavior as but poorly reflecting their true character, which they believe is in some way superior to the character that displays itself in their actions. Those who think this deceive themselves, according to Sartre.

▶ S E L E C T I O N   15.3

From Jean-Paul Sartre,
EXISTENTIALISM AND HUMANISM

What is this that we call existentialism? . . . Actually it is the least
shocking doctrine, and the most austere; it is intended strictly for tech-
nicians, and philosophers. However, it can easily be defined. What
makes the matter complicated is that there are two kinds of existentialists: the first who are Christian, and among whom I will include
Jaspers and Gabriel Marcel, of the Catholic faith; and also, the atheistic
existentialists among whom we must include Heidegger, and also the
French existentialists, and myself. What they have in common is simply the fact that they think that existence precedes essence, or, if you
wish, that we must start from subjectivity. . . .

. . . What does it mean here that existence precedes essence? It
means that man exists first, experiences himself, springs up in the
world, and that he defines himself afterwards. If man, as the existentialist conceives him, is not definable, it is because he is nothing at
first. He will only be [something] afterwards, and he will be as he will
have made himself. So, there is no human nature, since there is no
God to think it. Man simply is, not only as he conceives himself, but
as he determines himself, and as he conceives himself after existing,
as he determines himself after this impulse toward existence; man is
nothing other than what he makes himself. This is the first principle
of existentialism. It is also what we call subjectivity. . . . Man is at first
a project which lives subjectively, instead of being a moss, a decaying
thing, or a cauliflower; nothing exists prior to this project; nothing is
intelligible in the heavens, and man will at first be what he has planned
to be. Not what he may wish to be. . . . If existence really precedes
essence, man is responsible for what he is. Thus, the first step of existentialism is to show every man [to be] in control of what he is and to
make him assume total responsibility for his existence. And, when we
say that man is responsible for himself, we do not [only] mean that
man is responsible for his precise individuality, but that he is responsible for all men. . . . When we say that man determines himself, we
understand that each of us chooses himself, but by that we mean also
that in choosing himself he chooses all men. Indeed, there is not one
of our actions which, in creating the man we wish to be, does not [also]
create at the same time an image of the man we think we ought to be.
To choose to be this or that, is to affirm at the same time the value of
what we choose, for we can never choose evil; what we choose is
always the good, and nothing can be good for us without [also] being
[good] for all. . . .

This enables us to understand what some rather lofty words, like
anguish, abandonment, despair mean. As you will see, it is quite simple. First, what do we mean by anguish? The existentialist readily

declares that man is [in] anguish. That means this: the man who commits himself and who realizes that it is not only himself that he chooses, but [that] he is also a lawgiver choosing at the same time [for] all mankind, would not know how to escape the feeling of his total and profound responsibility. Certainly, many men are not anxious; but we claim that they are hiding their anguish, that they are fleeing from it; certainly, many men believe [that] in acting [they] commit only themselves, and when one says to them: "what if everyone acted like that?" they shrug their shoulders and reply: "everyone does not act like that." But really, one should always ask himself: "what would happen if everyone did the same?" and we cannot escape this troubling thought except by a kind of bad faith. The man who lies and who excuses himself by declaring: "everyone does not act like that," is someone who is ill at ease with his conscience, because the act of lying implies a universal value attributed to the lie. Even when it conceals itself, anguish appears. . . .

And when we speak of abandonment, an expression dear to Heidegger, we mean only that God does not exist, and that we must draw out the consequences of this to the very end. . . . The existentialist, on the contrary, thinks that it is very troubling that God does not exist, for with him disappears every possibility of finding values in an intelligible heaven; there can no longer be any good a priori, since there is no infinite and perfect consciousness to think it; it is not written anywhere that the good exists, that we must be honest, that we must not lie, since precisely we exist in a context where there are only men. Dostoyevsky has written, "If God did not exist, everything would be allowed." This is the point of departure for existentialism. Indeed, everything is allowed if God does not exist, and consequently man is abandoned, because neither in himself nor beyond himself does he find any possibility of clinging on [to something]. At the start, he finds no excuses. If, indeed, existence precedes essence, we will never be able to give an explanation by reference to a human nature [which is] given and fixed; in other words, there is no determinism, man is free, man is freedom. Moreover, if God does not exist, we do not find before us any values or orders which will justify our conduct. So, we have neither behind us nor before us, in the luminous realm of values, any justifications or excuses. We are alone, without excuses. It is what I will express by saying that man is condemned to be free. Condemned, because he has not created himself, and nevertheless, in other respects [he is] free, because once [he is] cast into the world, he is responsible for everything that he does. . . .

Abandonment implies that we ourselves choose our being. Abandonment goes with anguish. As for despair, this expression has a very simple meaning. It means that we will restrict ourselves to a reliance upon that which depends on our will, or on the set of the probabilities which make our action possible. . . . From the moment when the possibilities that I am considering are not strictly involved by my action,

I must take no further interest in them, because no God, no design can adjust the world and its possibilities to my will. . . . Quietism is the attitude of men who say: "others can do what I cannot do." The doctrine that I am presenting to you is exactly opposite to quietism, since it claims: "there is reality only in action." It goes further [than this] besides, since it adds: "man is nothing other than his project, he exists only in so far as he realizes himself, thus he is nothing other than the whole of his actions, nothing other than his life." According to this, we can understand why our doctrine horrifies a good many men. Because often they have only one way of enduring their misery. It is to think: "circumstances have been against me, I was worth much more than what I have been; to be sure, I have not had a great love, or a great friendship, but it is because I have not met a man or a woman who was worthy of it. I have not written very good books because I have not had the leisure to do it. I have not had children to whom to devote myself because I did not find a person with whom I could have made my life. [There] remains, then, in me, unused and wholly feasible a multitude of dispositions, inclinations, possibilities which give me a worth that the simple set of my actions does not allow [one] to infer." Now, in reality, for the existentialist there is no love other than that which is made, there is no possibility of love other than that which manifests itself in a love; there is no genius other than that which expresses itself in works of art. The genius of Proust is the totality of Proust's works; the genius of Racine is the set of his tragedies, beyond that there is nothing. Why [should we] attribute to Racine the possibility of writing a new tragedy, since precisely he did not write it? In his life a man commits himself, draws his own figure, and beyond this figure there is nothing. Obviously, this thought may seem harsh to someone who has not had a successful life. But, on the other hand, it prepares men to understand that only reality counts, that the dreams, the expectations, the hopes allow [us] only to define a man as [a] disappointed dream, as miscarried hopes, as useless expectations; that is to say that that defines them negatively and not positively. However, when we say "you are nothing other than your life," that does not imply that the artist will be judged only by his art-works, for a thousand other things also contribute to define him. What we mean is that man is nothing other than a set of undertakings, that he is the sum, the organization, the whole of the relations which make up these undertakings.

Phenomenology

Phenomenology, much more than existentialism, has been a product of philosophers rather than of artists and writers. But like existentialism, phenomenology has had enormous impact outside philosophical circles. It has been especially influential in theology, the social and political

One of the initiators of the phenomenological movement was **Franz Brentano** (1838–1917), whose thesis of *intentionality* was discussed in the last chapter. Brentano was a teacher of Edmund Husserl, treated in the text.

The idea of Brentano's that became a starting point for Husserl's phenomenology is intentionality: that an object is always "intended" in consciousness, which just means that consciousness is always consciousness *of something.* To put it somewhat differently, consciousness is nothing apart from the objects it considers or "intends." On the basis of Brentano's insight, Edmund Husserl in effect reformulated and drastically expanded Descartes's *cogito* into a science of consciousness-with-its-objects—that is, into a science of phenomena.

sciences, and psychology and psychoanalysis. Also, like existentialism (and analytic philosophy), phenomenology is a movement of thinkers who have a variety of interests and points of view. We will limit our discussion, however, to two philosophers from this tradition, Edmund Husserl and Martin Heidegger.

The obvious antecedents of phenomenology go back at least as far as Hegel's *Phenomenology of Mind*, in which beings are treated as phenomena or objects for a consciousness (though the movement regarded itself as anything but Hegelian). But even more important for phenomenology was Kant's *Critique of Pure Reason*, in which Kant argued that all objective knowledge is based on **phenomena,** the data received in sensory experience.

These phenomena, as you may recall from Part 2, are, according to Kant, immediately organized by the understanding through *a priori* certain categories and the intuited forms of space and time. All knowing, Kant said, is limited to phenomena and does not extend to things in themselves. Many Kantian ideas recur in the phenomenological movement, as will shortly become clear. The influence of Descartes and Plato on phenomenology will also be evident.

Edmund Husserl

The first great phenomenologist was **Edmund Husserl** (1859–1938). Husserl had a background in the sciences and in mathematics. Perhaps as a consequence, he had a strong need for "clarity." He said, "I must win clarity, else I cannot live; I cannot bear life unless I can believe that I shall achieve it." This commitment to clarity explains his admiration for Greek philosophy, and especially for Plato.

Husserl shared the existentialist belief that Europe was sick and in crisis, but his diagnosis of the cause of the crisis was rather the opposite of that offered by Schopenhauer, Nietzsche, Kierkegaard, and the existentialists. For these thinkers, a principal cause of the malaise was the excessive optimism and abstraction of rationalism and idealistic metaphysics. Husserl, in contrast, thought the crisis was the consequence of Europeans' declining faith in rationality and in the possibility of rational certainty. He believed that one result of this antirationalism was a devolution of scientific and philosophical thinking to relativistic and pragmatic standards and methods. Psychologism, historicism, and simplistic sensualism were the baneful results, he thought, of such antirationalist sentiment.

What was needed, according to Husserl, was a return to the clarity and certainty of earlier philosophy. To achieve these ends, Husserl proposed to establish a new scientific foundation for human knowing. He sought to redefine philosophy as a *universal phenomenology of consciousness*, a phenomenology that is the same for every consciousness and can be made as well into an absolutely certain science.

What does it mean, this talk of a universal phenomenology of consciousness?

Husserl considered the natural sciences to be uncritical and naive. They rest, he thought, on the dualist assumption that there exist both a physical or objective world, and, separate from it, a subject or independent mind that can only be studied following the naturalistic methods of the sciences. (This assumption, it seems clear, is pretty widely held.) From this naturalistic-dualistic point of view, Husserl said, "there can be no pure self-contained search for an explanation of the spiritual"; there can be no understanding of the self that is independent of supposed knowledge of the physical world. Husserl rejected this dualistic assumption and what it entailed about knowledge of the self.

Accordingly, Husserl developed transcendental phenomenology, whose purpose it was to investigate phenomena (see box) without making *any* assumptions, presuppositions, inferences, or judgments about the world. To investigate phenomena in this way is to "parenthesize" or "bracket" presuppositions, or, what means the same, to *perform the phenomenological reduction*. To **parenthesize** is simply to examine phenomena while suspending beliefs and opinions about the existence or nature of an "external" or "physical" or "objective" world. It is to consider phenomena *just as they come*, without making any judgments that in any way go beyond them. "We must not make assertions about that which we do not ourselves *see*," Husserl said. To consider phenomena in this way, totally detached from any particular bias, perspective, or philosophy, to consider them in "disregard [of] all our present knowledge," may, Husserl thought, allow us to discover what is absolutely certain in consciousness.

Now Husserl accepted Brentano's idea—discussed in Part 6 on analytic philosophy—that consciousness is always consciousness *of something*. Consciousness is *intentional*, which is a technical way of saying that the conscious ego is always cognizant of an "intended" object toward which its attention is directed. Thus, the ego "contains" its objects, so to

Phenomena

It is difficult to convey precisely what is meant by **phenomena.** It may help, however, to consider the age-old distinction between the way something appears and the way it is. A penny as it appears to you, for instance, is thought to be distinct from the way "it really is." (For example, it may appear elliptical, even though "it really is" round.) Now, from Husserl's point of view, this distinction (between "appearance" and "reality") is the scientific/dualistic distinction between the subjective (the way the penny appears) and the objective (the way it really is). Science, of course, is supposedly concerned with the way things "really are," that is, with the "objective penny." Husserl wished to concern himself with the subjective penny, that is, with the penny-as-appearance or penny-as-experience. It is this "apparent" or "subjective" penny that is an example of a "phenomenon."

However, it is somewhat misleading to refer to this phenomenal object, the subjective penny, as an *appearance*. To refer to it in this way is to presuppose that it is the appearance *of* something (the "real" penny) and thus is to assume that there are things out there "in the objective world" beyond the appearances. In short, to refer to the subjective penny as an "appearance" is to assume the scientific/dualistic perspective, which we must not do if we are to perform the phenomenological reduction. We must concentrate on phenomena themselves and not think of them as appearances or representations of a world beyond them. It is the stream of conscious experience—the phenomena—that Husserl is interested in.

speak. But *these* objects, these phenomenal or intentional objects, are not the objects that scientists think of themselves as investigating, and the ego or self that contains them likewise is not the "empirical" ego or self that is studied by the scientist or psychologist. When we perform the phenomenological reduction (i.e., when we parenthesize or suspend judgment about the existence of objects outside of consciousness), we discover a "transcendental ego" and its realm of "intended" objects, a realm of being that is the foundation for a new kind of knowing or completely indubitable science: **phenomenology.** This, at any rate, was Husserl's theory.

According to Husserl, phenomenology must honor Descartes as its genuine founder. Now, it is plain why Husserl held this. Descartes discovered absolute certainty in his own conscious existence, in his thinking. Likewise, Husserl discovers absolute certainty in his own consciousness. But there is a major difference between the two thinkers. Husserl, unlike Descartes, is explicitly aware of the intentionality of consciousness. Husserl understood that there is never bare thinking, perceiving, doubting, and so forth, for one always thinks of *something*, and perceives and doubts *something*, namely, the intended object. Thus Husserl reformulated Descartes's "I think" (*ego cogito*) to become "I think something" or "I think what is thought" (*ego cogito cogitatum*).

Further, whereas Descartes tried to establish the indubitability of the existence of an objective realm, a realm of "extended substance" (i.e.,

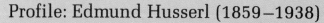

matter) that he thought lay beyond human consciousness, Husserl, in contrast, parenthesizes or puts aside all consideration of this "external" realm and focuses on the realm of his conscious self and its "intended" objects. From Husserl's focus, what we would call the objects of imagination can receive as much attention and consideration as what we would call "perceptions of the physical world."

Husserl declared that philosophy should return "to the things themselves" (*zu den Sachen selbst*). These things, of course, are phenomena, the contents of consciousness; they are the objects disclosed in conscious experience by phenomenological analysis and are not merely the objects of scientific scrutiny or dualism-infected common sense.

Moreover, (according to Husserl) in phenomenological analysis the *essences* or innermost nature of these things is revealed, as well as the laws that rule and regulate the interrelatedness of all these essences. Conscious experience—the stream of phenomena—is a life-world (*Lebenswelt*) in which all things are interconnected and interrelated in specific and definite ways, and which emerges as a new realm of being for examination and description.

Husserl's philosophy thus opens up for scrutiny and consideration a realm of being that escapes the uncertainty, relativity, and conditional status of the empirical world. This opening is made possible by a more original kind of knowing that is rooted in the "pure" intentional life of consciousness. "The pre-eminent mode of consciousness . . . consists in the self-exhibiting . . . of a state of affairs . . . a universality, a value or other objectivity in an immediate intuition." It is only through phenomenological analysis that the realm of true being can be known with absolute certainty, Husserl thought.

Is This Idealism?

Husserl's phenomenological realm is somewhat reminiscent of Plato's realm of Ideas, and some critics thought Husserl's philosophy represented a falling back into traditional idealistic metaphysics, in which, in effect, being is reduced to thought.

Can phenomenology escape the charge that it reduces being to thought? This is the question that

Husserl's student, Martin Heidegger, answered negatively. Thus Heidegger, as shall be seen, sought to reestablish the primacy of being over thought. For Heidegger, thought does not create being, as he interpreted Husserl as implying; rather, being makes thought possible.

Selection 15.4 is from Husserl's *Ideas*, one of his most important works. In the first part of the selection, Husserl describes the "natural standpoint," the dualistic perspective assumed by natural science (and common sense). In the second part he explains the concept of parenthesizing (also translated as "bracketing").

▶ S E L E C T I O N 15.4

From Edmund Husserl,
"THE POSITING WHICH BELONGS TO THE
*NATURAL ATTITUDE AND ITS EXCLUSION"**

We begin our considerations as human beings who are living naturally, objectivating, judging, feeling, willing *"in the natural attitude."* What that signifies we shall make clear in simple meditations which can best be carried out in the first person singular.

I am conscious of a world endlessly spread out in space, endlessly becoming and having endlessly become in time. I am conscious of it: that signifies, above all, that intuitively I find it immediately, that I experience it. By my seeing, touching, hearing, and so forth, and in the different modes of sensuous perception, corporeal physical things with some spatial distribution or other are *simply there for me, "on hand"* in the literal or the figurative sense, whether or not I am particularly heedful of them and busied with them in my considering, thinking, feeling, or willing. Animate beings too—human beings, let us say—are immediately there for me: I look up; I see them; I hear their approach; I grasp their hands; talking with them I understand immediately what they objectivate and think, what feelings stir within them, what they wish or will. They are also present as actualities in my field of intuition even when I do not heed them. But it is not necessary that they, and likewise that other objects, be found directly in my *field of perception*. Along with the ones now perceived, other actual objects are there for me as determinate, as more or less well known, without being themselves perceived or, indeed, present in any other mode of intuition. I can let my attention wander away from the writing table which was just now seen and noticed, out through the unseen parts of the room which are behind my back, to the verandah, into the garden, to the children in the arbor, etc., to all the Objects I directly "know of" as being there and here in the surroundings of which there is also consciousness—a "knowing of them" which involves no conceptual thinking and which changes into a clear intuiting only with the advertence of attention, and even then only partially and for the most part very imperfectly. . . .

In my waking consciousness I find myself in this manner at all times, and without ever being able to alter the fact, in relation to the world which remains one and the same, though changing with respect to the composition of its contents. It is continually "on hand" for me and I myself am a member of it. Moreover, this world is there for me not only as a world of mere things, but also with the same immediacy as a *world of objects with values, a world of goods, a practical world.* I simply find the physical things in front of me furnished not only with merely material determinations but also with value-characteristics, as beautiful and ugly, pleasant and unpleasant, agreeable and disagreeable, and the like. Immediately, physical things stand there as Objects of use, the "table" with its "books," the "drinking glass," the "vase," the "piano," etc. These value-characteristics and practical characteristics also belong *constitutively to the Objects "on hand" as Objects,* regardless of whether or not I turn to such characteristics and the Objects. . . .

The world of numbers is likewise there for me precisely as the Object-field of arithmetical busiedness; during such busiedness single numbers of numerical formations will be at the focus of my regard, surrounded by a partly determinate, partly indeterminate arithmetical horizon; but obviously this factual being-there-for-me, like the factually existent itself, is of a different sort. *The arithmetical world is there for me only if, and as long as, I am in the arithmetical attitude.* The *natural* world, however, the world in the usual sense of the word is, and has been, *there for me continuously* as long as I go on living naturally. As long as this is the case, I am *"in the natural attitude,"* indeed both signify precisely the same thing. . . .

All that which holds for me myself holds, as I know, for all other human beings whom I find present in my surrounding world. Experiencing them as human beings, I understand and accept each of them as an Ego-subject just as I myself am one, and as related to his natural surrounding world. But I do this in such a way that I take their surrounding world and mine Objectively as one and the same world of which we are all conscious, only in different modes. Each has his place from which he sees the physical things present; and, accordingly, each has different physical-thing appearances. Also, for each the fields of actual perception, actual memory, etc., are different, leaving aside the fact that intersubjectively common objects of consciousness in those fields are intended to as having different modes, different manners of apprehension, different degrees of clarity, and so forth. For all that, we come to an understanding with our fellow human beings and in common with them posit an Objective spatiotemporal actuality as our *factually existent surrounding world to which we ourselves nonetheless belong.* . . .

Once more, in the following propositions we single out something most important: As what confronts me, I continually find the one spatiotemporal actuality to which I belong like all other human beings who are to be found in it and who are related to it as I am. I find the "actuality," the word already says it, as a *factually existent actuality and also accept it as it presents itself to me as factually existing.* No doubt about or rejection of data belonging to the natural world alters in any respect the *general positing which characterizes the natural attitude.* "The" world is always there as an actuality; here and there it is at most "otherwise" than I supposed; this or that is, so to speak, to be struck *out of it* and given such titles as "illusion" and "hallucination," and the like; [it is to be struck out of "the" world] which—according to the general positing—is always factually existent. To cognize "the" world more comprehensively, more reliably, more perfectly in every respect than naive experiential cognizance can, to solve all the problems of scientific cognition which offer themselves within the realm of the world, that is the aim of the *sciences belonging to the natural attitude.* . . . *Instead of remaining in this attitude, we propose to alter it radically.* What we now must do is to convince ourselves of the essential possibility of the alteration in question.

The general positing, by virtue of which there is not just any continual apprehensional consciousness of the real surrounding world, but a consciousness of it as a *factually existing* "actuality," naturally does *not consist of a particular act,* perchance an articulated judgment *about* existence. It is, after all, something that lasts continuously throughout the whole duration of the attitude, i.e., throughout natural waking life. That which at any time is perceived, is clearly or obscurely presentiated—in short, everything which is, before any thinking, an object of experiential consciousness issuing, from the natural world—bears, in its total unity and with respect to all articulated saliencies in it, the characteristic "there," "on hand"; and it is essentially possible to base on this characteristic an explicit (predicative) judgment of existence agreeing with it. If we state such a judgment, we nevertheless know that in it we have only made thematic and conceived as a predicate what already was somehow inherent, as unthematic, unthought, unpredicated, in the original experiencing or, correlatively, in the experienced, as the characteristic of something "on hand."

We can now proceed with the potential and inexplicit positing precisely as we can with the explicit judgment-positing. One procedure, possible at any time, is the *attempt to doubt universally* which *Descartes* carried out for an entirely different purpose with a view toward bringing out a sphere of absolutely indubitable being. We start from here, but at the same time emphasize that the attempt to doubt universally shall serve us only as a *methodic expedient* for picking out certain points which, as included in its essence, can be brought to light and made evident by means of it. . . .

We do not give up the positing we effected, we do not in any respect alter our conviction which remains in itself as it is as long as we do not introduce new judgment-motives: precisely this is what we do not do. Nevertheless the positing undergoes a modification: while it in itself remains what it is, we, so to speak, "put it out of action," we "exclude it," we "parenthesize it." It is still there, like the parenthesized in the parentheses, like the excluded outside the context of inclusion. We can also say: The positing is a mental process, *but we make "no use" of it*, and this is not understood, naturally, as implying that we are deprived of it (as it would if we said of someone who was not conscious, that he made no use of a positing); rather, in the case of this expression and all parallel expressions it is a matter of indicative designations of a definite, *specifically peculiar mode of consciousness* which is added to the original positing simpliciter (whether this is or not an actional and even a predicative *positing* of existence) and, likewise in a specifically peculiar manner, changes its value. *This changing of value is a matter in which we are perfectly free, and it stands over against all cogitative position-takings* coordinate with the positing and incompatible with the positing in the unity of the "simultaneous," as well as over against all position-takings in the proper sense of the term. . . .

[O]ur purpose is to discover a new scientific domain, one that is to be gained *by the method of parenthesizing* which, therefore, must be a definitely restricted one.

The restriction can be designated in a word.

We put out of action the general positing which belongs to the essence of the natural attitude; we parenthesize everything which that positing encompasses with respect to being: thus the whole natural world which is continually "there for us," "on hand," and which will always remain there according to consciousness as an "actuality" even if we choose to parenthesize it.

Thus I exclude all sciences relating to this natural world no matter how firmly they stand there for me, no matter how much I admire them, no matter how little I think of making even the least objection to them; I make *absolutely no use of the things posited in them*. Nor *do I make my own a single one of the propositions belonging to [those sciences]*, even though it be perfectly evident none is accepted by me; *none gives me a foundation*—let this be well noted: as long as it is understood as it is presented in one of those sciences as a truth *about actualities* of this world. *I must not accept such a proposition until after I have put parentheses around it.* That signifies that I may accept such a proposition only in the modified consciousness, the consciousness of judgment-excluding, and therefore *not as it is in science, a proposition which claims validity and the validity of which I accept and use.* . . . The whole prediscovered world posited in the natural attitude, actually found in experience and taken with perfect "freedom from theories" as it is actually experienced, as it clearly shows itself in the concatenations of experience, is now without validity for us; without being tested and also without being contested, it shall be parenthesized. In like manner all theories and sciences which relate to this world, no matter how well they may be grounded positivistically or otherwise, shall meet the same fate.

---

*Editor's footnotes have been omitted.

Martin Heidegger

Heidegger (1889–1976) was stimulated by Husserl's *Logical Investigations* (1900) and especially by Husserl's call to return to the things themselves. He, too, was convinced that it is necessary to look at things with fresh eyes, unshrouded by the prejudices of the present and the past. He, too, wanted rigorously to ground the truth of things in a deeper source. But for Heidegger, this source is not phenomena, as it was for Husserl, or anything subjective at all. On the contrary, for Heidegger the ultimate source is *Being itself*.

Profile: Martin Heidegger (1889–1976)

Heidegger was born in the small town of Messkirch near the Black Forest of Germany. Originally he went to the University of Freiburg to study theology, but he soon after began studying philosophy. Heidegger studied Husserl's philosophy closely and became personally acquainted with Husserl after the latter took a chair in Freiburg in 1916.

Almost from the beginning Heidegger stood out—not merely because of his countrified mode of dress, but also because of his profound thought. Over the years Heidegger grew increasingly critical of Husserl's philosophy, and, though he was named to Husserl's chair in philosophy at Freiburg in 1928, their friendship came to an end.

Although Heidegger did not teach formally after World War II, he remained in Freiburg until his death. His works are in the process of being published—in eighty volumes.

Heidegger and the Nazis

Initially Heidegger was quite taken with the National Socialist (Nazi) party in post–World War I Germany and apparently remained a party member until the end of the war. This was rather a prestigious gain for the Nazis, especially when Heidegger was made rector of the University of Freiburg.

During Heidegger's brief term as rector, he made speeches and was otherwise active in support of Hitler and his movement. He withdrew as rector after ten months. Later, he called his support of the Nazis his greatest blunder. He did, however, remain a member of the party until the end of the war. His silence on these matters after the war has led to a questioning of his actual repentance.

Although Being is continuously manifesting itself in things, according to Heidegger, Being itself has been forgotten. Humans have been caught up in their own ideas. Being has been reduced to a world of "objects" that are manipulated and dominated by human "subjects" through a series of man-made logics. Logic is equated with truth when in fact, according to Heidegger, it is only a means to control and use things after human designs; that is, logic is logistics.

Heidegger believed that it is both arrogant and destructive to assume that humans are the masters of nature, or to follow Protagoras's dictum that man is the measure of all things. This assumption of the absolute power of humanity was for Heidegger the real cause of the cultural destitution and social dissolution within the twentieth century. Heidegger thought that we live in an intellectually impoverished (*dürftig*) time, and that it is likely to become worse until we abandon our presumptuousness and return to the wisdom inherent in Being itself. The return must involve *listening* to Being instead of toying with things arbitrarily.

According to Heidegger, we are basically ignorant about the thing that matters most: the true nature of Being. Our lives are a kind of Socratic search for this lost and unknown source of all things. Consciousness of the priority of Being would mean a new beginning for philosophy as well as for Western civilization, he held.

Heidegger, therefore, initially sought to establish a fundamental ontology or a scientific study of Being as the root of all meaning and necessity in things. This effort broadened out later and became a quest for an even more direct approach to Being itself. Early on—as, for example, in his first major work, *Being and Time* (1927)—his ideas still contained much that is Husserlian and Kantian in approach. He still sought true knowledge in *a priori* structures found in the human mind. It is only in his later thinking—after he had what he called a fundamental "turning about"—that he sought to uncover Being directly, beyond the *a priori* categories or structures of human perception and thought. He did so without assurance that any absolute certainty about Being itself is even possible.

It is usually with reference to his earlier work that Heidegger is sometimes called an existentialist. Heidegger himself resisted this appellation. Yet he was very much influenced by Kierkegaard and Nietzsche, and the concern expressed in his early works with such existentialist themes as fear, dread, meaninglessness, inauthenticity, and death is very evident.

At the heart of *Being and Time*, for example, is the notion of *Sinn* (sense, meaning), the absence of which in life is said to be the problem of human existence. For Heidegger, the human being is "*thrown into the world*" and soon experiences both fear and dread when confronted with forces beyond his understanding. The better part of human life, he maintains, needs be used in "*headbreaking,*" that is, in attempting to discover what the appearances mean—what they suggest and hide.

Further, humans are "*beings-in-the-world,*" which means that they can be open only to what is within the horizons of their world. They exist and are conscious within a world with other beings, but the meaning of human relationships are at first but dimly perceived and poorly understood. As a consequence of their lack of insight and understanding, many humans live ungenuine and inauthentic lives. They do not make adequate or appropriate choices for themselves because they do not understand who they are or what they are confronting. And although they may experience unease living in a world beyond their comprehension, they make too little effort to extend their comprehension. They suffer from a kind of "primitive" being which Heidegger refers to as *everydayness*. They fail to fulfill their real potential. Thus Heidegger invoked the concept of everydayness to explain why human beings continue to lead unthinking lives.

Another typical existential theme connected by Heidegger with an everyday existence is an inauthentic mode of communication, namely, *chatter*. Speech is reduced to a meaningless flood of words that camouflages fear, prevents understanding, and precludes any meaningful communication. Nothing truly meaningful is ever said or allowed to be said.

An authentic existence can only be found, according to Heidegger, if one can understand oneself as a totality. And seeing oneself as a whole can only happen by facing the hard fact that one is mortal. We are, Heidegger said, "*beings-unto-death.*" By facing death, we can see and delineate the limits of our being. We begin to see the limited amount of time yet available and begin to realize it must not be wasted.

The innermost nature of the human being, according to Heidegger, is caring—a concern for beings in the world. This caring takes place over time. And thinking must be timely as well. Thus, for Heidegger, we are essentially *temporal* beings.

According to Heidegger, the temporality of human thinking is "*ecstatic,*" that is, it is intentionally directed toward the future, which means simply that humans think and act toward an anticipated future. The most effective way of embracing one's future, he thought, is by throwing oneself open into Being. This project (*Entwurf*) opens the person to the fundamental truth of Being that has been forgotten. Therefore, the individual who has been thrown into the world finds his or her ground and truth in the openness and lighting of the truth of Being itself.

As noted earlier, Heidegger thought that the cultural and intellectual poverty of the twentieth century is a direct result of the pervasive assumption that the value of things is solely determined by human intelligence and human will (the assumption that man is the measure of all things). This assumption or metaphysical stance, he thought, has led not merely to individual loneliness, alienation, and unfulfillment, but to social destructiveness as well. For Heidegger, this metaphysical point of view, which he perceived as entrenched in Western civilization since Plato, assumed the superiority of Ideas over any physical reality existing "outside" the mind. In Heidegger's opinion, Nietzsche's "will-to-power," where the will becomes the absolute determiner of the value of things and of oneself, represented the philosophical culmination of this Platonic metaphysics.

Poetry   According to the later Heidegger, instead of imposing our thought on things, we must be *gelassen. Gelassenheit,* for Heidegger, means thinking in a quiet, nonimpositional way so that one can *catch a glimpse* of Being as it shows itself. Thought, he believed (in contrast with phenomenologists), cannot impose itself on Being because Being makes thought possible. What is required, therefore, he said (in contrast with the existentialists), is a new kind of thinking in which humans look to Being itself for enlightenment and not merely to themselves. This kind of thinking occurs, according to Heidegger, in the best *poetry.* And some poets, such as Hölderlin, can serve as examples of this kind of thinking. Poetic thinking can uncover the as yet unseen, unthought, and unspoken. Therefore, he said, systematic philosophy with its grandiose and willful schemes, with its mind-body and other dualist splits, with its metaphysics and metaphysical traditions, must give way to this more original kind of thinking. Through this deeper way of thinking, he said, we may at long last rediscover the depth of what has been forgotten—Being itself.

Poetry and Philosophy

In his later years Heidegger not only avoided the word "metaphysics" to describe the philosophy of Being but even tended not to use the word "philosophy." He thought a new kind of "thinking" was needed, one that might focus again on the light of Being. One kind of thinking, in his view, was particularly apt for this task, namely, poetic thinking. Poetry, according to Heidegger, has a unique access to what has not yet been spoken and has not yet even been thought. Poetry can bring humans back into an awareness of their source, namely, Being itself.

Heidegger wrote tracts on many poets, including Hölderlin, Rilke, Trakl, and others. But he also wrote poems that suggest how the poet might bring a glimmer of light to the darkness within existence. For example:

When the early morning light quietly
    grows above the mountains . . . .
The world's darkening never reaches
    to the light of Being.

We are too late for the gods and too
    early for Being. Being's poem,
    just begun, is man.
To head toward a star—this only.
To think is to confine yourself to a
    single thought that one day stands
    still like a star in the world's sky.

But to enter into the abyss of Being, for Heidegger, is a difficult, long, and solitary undertaking. It requires patience and large-mindedness, and courage, too. He wrote:

All our heart's courage is the
    echoing response to the
    first call of Being which
    gathers our thinking into the
    play of the world.

It is the poet, for Heidegger, who ventures out into the unknown, in order to find the "unique thought" that will bring the necessary light for the coming time.

In Selection 15.5, Heidegger illustrates this deeper understanding of Being through poetry. After you have read the next chapter, on Eastern philosophy, you may wish to reread this selection, for the influence of Eastern thought on Heidegger is very marked.

Heidegger and Lao Tzu

Especially later in his life, Heidegger grew interested in Eastern philosophy and especially the philosophy of Lao Tzu (see Chapter 16). Perhaps Heidegger's new way of thinking—listening to Being—represents a coming together of Eastern and Western philosophizing. Certainly there are common currents and themes. Both believed that "nature is not human-hearted" (Lao Tzu) and that what is called human "knowledge" is mostly ignorance. Both felt that "those who care will be cared for" (Lao Tzu). What is necessary, according to both, is to take nature [Being] as a "guide." And it is as Lao Tzu suggests: "In the clarity of a still and open mind, the truth will be revealed."

▶ S E L E C T I O N   15.5

From Martin Heidegger,
"THE THINKER AS POET"

When the little windwheel outside
the cabin window sings in the
gathering thunderstorm . . . .

> When thought's courage stems from
> the bidding of Being, then
> destiny's language thrives.

> As soon as we have the thing before
> our eyes, and in our hearts an ear
> for the word, thinking prospers.

> Few are experienced enough in the
> difference between an object of
> scholarship and a matter thought.

> If in thinking there were already
> adversaries and not mere
> opponents, then thinking's case
> would be more auspicious.

When through a rent in the rain-clouded
sky a ray of the sun suddenly glides
over the gloom of the meadows . . . .

> We never come to thoughts. They come
> to us.

> That is the proper hour of discourse.

> Discourse cheers us to companionable
> reflection. Such reflection neither
> parades polemical opinions nor does it
> tolerate complaisant agreement. The sail
> of thinking keeps trimmed hard to the
> wind of the matter.

> From such companionship a few perhaps
> may rise to be journeymen in the
> craft of thinking. So that one of them,
> unforeseen, may become a master.

———

When in early summer lonely narcissi
bloom hidden in the meadow and the
rock-rose gleams under the maple . . . .

The splendor of the simple.

Only image formed keeps the vision.
Yet image formed rests in the poem.

How could cheerfulness stream
through us if we wanted to shun
sadness?

Pain gives of its healing power
where we least expect it.

When the wind, shifting quickly, grumbles
in the rafters of the cabin, and the
weather threatens to become nasty . . . .

Three dangers threaten thinking.

The good and thus wholesome
danger is the nighness of the singing
poet.

The evil and thus keenest danger is
thinking itself. It must think
against itself, which it can only
seldom do.

The bad and thus muddled danger
is philosophizing.

———

When on a summer's day the butterfly
settles on the flower and, wings
closed, sways with it in the
meadow-breeze . . . .

All our heart's courage is the
echoing response to the
first call of Being which
gathers our thinking into the
play of the world.

In thinking all things
become solitary and slow.

Patience nurtures magnanimity.

He who thinks greatly must
err greatly.

From "Aus der Erfahrung des Denkens, in *Poetry, Language, Thought*, translated by
Albert Hofstadter. New York: Harper & Row, 1975.

Checklist

To help you review, here is a checklist of the key philosophers and concepts of this chapter. The brief descriptive sentences that appear with each philosopher summarize one of his leading ideas. Keep in mind that some of these summary statements represent terrific oversimplifications of complex positions.

Philosophers

- **Arthur Schopenhauer** Emphasized the irrationality of the universe and the people within it; regarded Hegelian metaphysics as deluded and beneath contempt.
- **Friedrich Nietzsche** Also reacted strongly against Hegelian idealism; anticipated important themes of existentialism.
- **Søren Kierkegaard** Another nineteenth-century philosopher who rejected the Hegelian idea of a rational universe and anticipated some of the themes of existentialism.
- **Fyodor Dostoyevsky, Leo Tolstoy, Franz Kafka, Eugene Ionesco, and Samuel Beckett** Nineteenth- and twentieth-century writers who depicted the emptiness, meaninglessness, triviality, and loneliness of existence, the self-doubt and anxiety of the individual, as well as the inability of humans to communicate with one another and their profound need to choose how to live within an irrational world.
- **Albert Camus** French existentialist writer; emphasized the absurdity of the world and the inability of the individual to meet genuine human needs within it.
- **Jean-Paul Sartre** French existentialist writer; emphasized the significance of abandonment and its implications.
- **Simone de Beauvoir** French existentialist writer who occupied an important place in feminist philosophy.
- **Franz Brentano** Emphasized the intentionality of consciousness.
- **Edmund Husserl** First great phenomenologist.
- **Martin Heidegger** Emphasized the importance of returning to Being itself independent of the mental categories we assign to it.

Concepts

Continental philosophy

existentialism

existentialist predicament

abandonment

"existence precedes essence"

bad faith

"condemned to be free"

authenticity

fundamental project

"I choose myself perpetually"

"in choosing myself, I choose man"

phenomenology

universal phenomenology of consciousness

intentionality

parenthesizing

phenomenological reduction

Sinn

"thrown into the world"

everydayness

chatter

being-unto-death

Gelassenheit

**Questions for
Discussion
and Review**

1. Discuss the extent to which we are responsible for the situations in which we find ourselves. Does responsibility begin at birth or at what other time?

2. Discuss the extent to which we are responsible for the situations in which others find themselves. If we cannot hold others to blame for our troubles, does it make sense for us to hold ourselves to blame for theirs?

3. Can humans communicate with one another? (Do not assume that communicating is the same as talking.) Are people ever really *not* strangers? Explain.

4. If there is no objective right and wrong, good and bad, then how should we determine how to live?

5. Suppose you set a goal for yourself and then achieve it. What do you do then—set other goals and achieve them? Why?

6. Are any goals inherently better than others? Why?

7. What is "bad faith," and how do we recognize whether or not we have it?

8. Discuss in what sense suicide is the "principal philosophical question."

9. What does it mean to say that we live in an absurd world? *Do* we live in an absurd world?

10. Explain the myth of Sisyphus. Discuss the extent to which this situation is an accurate depiction of life.

11. What does it mean to say that we are abandoned?

12. What does it mean to say that existence precedes essence?

13. Does a belief in God rescue us from the existentialist predicament?

14. What does Sartre mean by saying that we are condemned to be free? What does he mean by saying, "I choose myself perpetually"? And what does he mean by saying, "In choosing myself, I choose man"?

15. Is consciousness anything apart from the objects it "intends"?

16. Explain "parenthesizing."

17. Was Heidegger an idealist? Explain.

18. Do you think it is true that most humans live inauthentic lives?

19. Is most human conversation really "chatter"? Is most of *your* conversation really chatter?
20. Can having a "fundamental project" save us from a "lost life"? Explain.

Suggested Further Readings

Samuel Beckett, *Waiting for Godot* (New York: Grove, 1954). In its way, this play is the ultimate expression of the predicaments faced by human beings in an absurd world.

Albert Camus, *Myth of Sisyphus and Other Essays* (New York: Random House, 1959). Camus's thematic rendering of the absurdity of the world and possible reactions to it.

Fyodor Dostoyevsky, *Notes from the Underground* with *The Grand Inquisitor* (New York: E. P. Dutton, 1960). A presentation of life's suffering, irrationality, and absurdity, themes that were to become hallmarks of existentialism in the next century.

Martin Heidegger, *Basic Writings* (New York: Harper & Row, 1977). A sampling of Heidegger's writings from his earlier and later periods of thought, covering his most important themes.

Edmund Husserl, *Ideas Pertaining to a Pure Phenomenology and to a Phenomenological Philosophy*, in Edmund Husserl, *Collected Works*, F. Kersten, trans. (The Hague: Martinus Nijoff Publishers, 1982). An introduction to Husserl's transcendental phenomenology.

Franz Kafka, *The Metamorphosis, The Penal Colony, and Other Stories* (New York: Schocken, 1988). A good collection of Kafka's stories.

Søren Kierkegaard, *Fear and Trembling* (New York: Penguin, 1986). An excellent introduction to some of the themes developed later by the existentialists.

Friedrich Nietzsche, *A Nietzsche Reader*, R. J. Hollingdale, trans. (New York: Penguin, 1978). A good contemporary translation of selections that provide a broad overview of Nietzsche's concerns.

Jean-Paul Sartre, *Existentialism and Humanism* (London: Methuen, 1987). A clear, nontechnical depiction of some of the principal concepts of existentialism, including essence, existence, freedom, and responsibility.

Arthur Schopenhauer, *Essays and Aphorisms*, R. J. Hollingdale, trans. (New York: Penguin, 1973). A nice introduction to the psychological insights of Schopenhauer.

Continental Philosophy

SUMMARY AND CONCLUSION

We've seen that many themes of existentialism and phenomenology were introduced in the nineteenth century and before. Both movements originated in part in response, as did analytic philosophy, to the rationalistic idealistic metaphysics of that century. In addition, existentialism and phenomenology both arose in reaction to a perceived crisis in nineteenth- and twentieth-century European society, a crisis whose manifestations ranged from individual despair and disorientation to widespread catastrophic social violence and inhumanity. But whereas existentialists saw this crisis as in part the result of an excessive belief in the rationality of the world, transcendental phenomenologists like Husserl attributed it to undue antirationalism and a forgetting of ancient thinkers like Plato.

Existentialists like Camus and Sartre, we have seen, were concerned, primarily, with the problems of coping in an absurd world; phenomenologists like Husserl, in contrast, sought certainty in the vast realm of human subjectivity. Heidegger, who in his early work subjected human existence to phenomenological analysis, treated such existentialist themes as the temporality of humans and our relationship to death and concerned himself especially with the inauthenticity of much of modern existence. But Heidegger had a grander project—to reopen the quest for Being. It is only by regaining an understanding of Being that humans may recover an authentic mode of existence, he believed. Heidegger thought that if human thinking can be refocused on Being, the consequence will be a new starting point for Western civilization as well as for philosophy.

PART 8

Eastern Philosophy

CHAPTER 16

The Wisdom of the East

*The tree that brushes the heavens
grew from the tiniest sprout.
The most elegant pagoda, nine stories high,
rose from a small pile of earth.
The journey of a thousand miles
began with but a single step.*

—LAO TZU

Is there really a point in studying Eastern thinkers, some of whom lived more than two thousand years ago? Can they possibly have anything to say to us?

The answer is yes, for the foreign enlightens the domestic in more than wine and cheeses. As the German poet Hölderlin suggested, we can never understand our home until we have left it. The philosophy of another civilization provides a new vantage point from which to view our own thought; it offers us a different perspective, one from which we may reconsider and reevaluate what is important to us in our own philosophy. Besides, it is a potential source of fresh ideas and new concepts.

The study of ancient Eastern philosophers is, of course, more than a journey in distance. It is a travel back in time to periods in the history of thought that have left messages of perhaps telling importance to us today. For many of the Westerners who have studied it, the philosophy of ancient Eastern thinkers has offered secure guidance to the full and contented life.

In this chapter we will consider the three main philosophies of China: **Confucianism, Taoism,** and **Buddhism.** Buddhism, as will be seen, originated in India. In addition, we will discuss Hinduism, Japanese Zen Buddhism, and the philosophy of the samurai, another traditional Japanese way of thought. No effort will be made to present the history of these important traditions or to trace their evolution over the centuries. Our

intent is merely to introduce the philosophy of their original or most
important thinkers.

Confucianism

Three great systems of thought dominate Chinese civilization: Confucianism, Taoism, and Buddhism. The most dominant is the one founded
by **Confucius** (551–479 B.C.).

Confucius

Confucius loved learning, and by age fifteen he had committed his life
to a diligent study of the ancient wise men. In addition, he sought a better
way and order of doing things. Learning and knowledge, Confucius
believed, must be practical. They must transform life for the better. The
result of his own learning was a system of moral, political, and social
precepts bound together by what is best called a philosophy of nature
and by a faith in the perfectibility of the human character.

That the human person is perfectible was a central tenet of Confucius's thinking. The human person, Confucius believed, is not always
good but can become better. Betterment, he thought, comes through learning and service to others. No one begins with wisdom, but with diligence
and determined study wisdom can be acquired; and once acquired, wisdom becomes an instrument for perfecting oneself, the family, and society. Even nature itself, Confucius believed, cannot resist the power of
wisdom: "It is man that can make the Way great," he said, "and not the
Way that can make man great."

The Way, as here mentioned by Confucius, is a key concept in his
philosophy. For Confucius as for the Taoists, whom we discuss later, **the
Way** or **Tao** (*tao* means "path" or "way" in English) is basically the path
taken by natural events. Confucius uses the word "Way" or "Tao" often
and in different senses. There is a way of the good man, a way of music,
a way of proper government, and a cosmological way. Confucius even
speaks of "my *tao*." Although interpreters are not in total agreement about
this, it would seem that the Tao, for Confucius, is not a fixed and eternal
transcendental principle that stands outside and above events and determines them. Rather, it is affected in no small part by human thought and
human action. "It is man that can make the Way great." One can study
the practices of the wise ancients to learn how to make the Way great in
one's own time. Essentially, this means knowing how best to regulate
your life. Confucius set forth ideals of human behavior based on his
understanding of the Way. He believed that once you have achieved a
knowledge of the Tao or Way of things, you cannot die in vain.

For Confucius, everything "thrives according to its nature." One way
in which heaven works, he thought, is through the principle of the *Mean,*

Profile: Confucius (551–479 B.C.)

Confucius, or, in Chinese, K'ung Fu Tzu (K'ung the Great Master), was born "without rank in humble circumstances" in the small Chinese kingdom of Lu. Information about his life is scanty and is derived chiefly from the *Analects*, a collection of his sayings assembled by his disciples. Because of his father's death, he had to work at an early age to help support his mother. He was largely self-taught and his hunger for learning was insatiable. With the exception of a brief period in which he served as prime minister of Lu, he did not have many opportunities to put his principles about statecraft into practice.

Confucius's ideas have influenced Chinese and Asian ways of life like those of no other philosopher, although their impact varied from period to period. From the third to the seventh century, Confucianism was eclipsed by other philosophies, but under the T'ang dynasty (618–907) it became the state religion. Neoconfucianism (which incorporated both a more developed metaphysics and Taoist and Buddhist principles) emerged during the Sung dynasty (960–1279) and was the predominant stream of Chinese philosophy until its decline in the twentieth century, which was especially rapid after the Communist revolution in 1949. This was, in part, a consequence of the difference between Chinese communism and the more traditional world views. But it was also a side effect of the change in the system of state civil service examinations, which had formerly been based on the Chinese classic texts, including Confucius.

which provides a standard of measure for all things. Human behavior should avoid extremes and seek moderation. In the philosophy of Confucius, when things function in accordance with this principle of the Mean, they stand in a relationship of mutual dependence. In other words, the principle essentially requires reciprocal cooperation among things—between people and between people and nature. And when the principle is followed, things flourish and nourish one another without conflict or injury.

Confucius formulated this principle of reciprocity in a general way as it applied to human affairs by saying, "Do not do to others what you would not want them to do to you." Thus likewise, according to Confucius, "A virtuous man wishing to establish himself seeks also to establish others, and wishing to enlighten himself, seeks also to enlighten others." Just as nature is built on a principle of reciprocal cooperation rather than strife, so reciprocal cooperation must reign in human affairs, he believed.

Another key concept in Confucius's thought is that of the *sage* or *superior man*. The sage represents, in effect, an ethical ideal to which humans should aspire. To achieve the status of sage, Confucius believed, requires having intimate knowledge both of change and of the order of

Confucius's Humanism

The switch in Chinese thought from concern for the deity to the concern for human effort and excellence began hundreds of years before Confucius was born. Nonetheless, it was Confucius who made humanity (*jen*) a cornerstone of Chinese philosophy. "The measure of man," he said, "is man." The nature and duties of the human being must be studied diligently and cultivated, he insisted, and humanity is to be loved.

To help others, Confucius said, one must first establish one's own humane character, which is done by imitating models of superior men from the past. Once the individual has a character that contains nothing contrary to humanity, he can rely on his humanity in all his actions. Through humanistic thinking and acting, according to Confucius, the superior man makes the Way (Tao) great.

things; it requires, more specifically, having a correct understanding both of human relationships and the workings of nature. A correct understanding, according to Confucius, involves, among other things, setting right in thought or *rectifying* what is distorted or confused, and especially involves the correct use or *rectification* of names. (This meant knowing, for example, when it is legitimate to accord someone a title or rank.) The sage or superior person, according to Confucius, puts this correct understanding into action and seeks the mutual cooperation that enables others to fulfill their own destiny.

According to Confucius, the sage's actions are superior to those of other men because his model of behavior is superior. Specifically, he patterns his behavior on the great men of the past. In addition, he constantly learns from his own personal experience. (Confucius said that if he were able to study change for fifty years, he would finally be free of mistakes.) Wisdom requires constant learning, and constant learning allows the superior man better to know the measure of things and to perform his duty accordingly.

Thus, the sage, in the philosophy of Confucius, not only thinks correctly, but also lives correctly. Indeed, according to Confucius, for the sage no discrepancy exists between thought (or speech) and action. The sage does not think (or say) one thing and do a different thing: he matches word with deed.

Further, according to Confucius, the superior man is an altruist who provides impartial and equitable service to others. He is kind and benevolent; he does not repay evil with evil but rather with uprightness. His concern is with reform, not revenge. And his virtuous behavior is a matter of habit that holds even in the direst crisis. For this reason, Confucius believed, the sage can be counted on at all times. His fairness makes him a figure of trust to all, including the rulers of state.

Now the rulers of the Chinese states of Confucius's time did not entrust their affairs to superior men; nor did the rulers themselves merit

Confucius: Insights on Life

At fifteen, I began to be seriously interested in study; at thirty, I had formed my character; at forty, doubts ceased; at fifty, I understood the laws of Heaven; at sixty, nothing that I heard disturbed me; at seventy, I could do as my heart desired without breaking the moral law.

I never take a walk in the company of three persons without finding that one of them has something to teach me.

The superior man is distressed by his want of ability; he is not distressed by men's not knowing him.

The superior man prizes three things. The first is gentleness, the second is frugality, the third is humility. By being gentle he can be bold; by being frugal he can be liberal; and by being humble he becomes a leader among men.

A man who is strong, resolute, simple, and slow to speak is near to humanity.

The way of the superior man is threefold, but I have not been able to attain it. The man of wisdom has no perplexities; the man of humanity has no worry; the man of courage has no fear.

---

this title. Instead, these states were dominated by military regimes that ruled by force and were constantly at war with one another, and whose subjects lived in a state of dread. In the opinion of Confucius, the ignoble policies of such inferior rulers were based on four root evils: greed, aggressiveness, pride, and resentment, which singly or together cause a ruler to rationalize and to excuse the most odious behavior on his part. Further, according to Confucius, a ruler is invariably the model for the behavior of his subjects, and as a consequence societies ruled by vicious men are themselves vicious societies.

By contrast, a state so fortunate as to be ruled by a superior man, Confucius believed, would be peaceful, secure, and prosperous. Because the superior man is governed by the principle of the Mean, as a ruler he will be unswervingly just and impartial and will seek to establish a fair distribution of wealth, which in turn will promote security and peace. And because his behavior will be emulated by his subjects, he will rule through virtuous example rather than by force of arms. Further, because he is conscientious in his service to all, he will act without fear or sadness.

Confucius's philosophy touched not only on the state and individual, but also on the family. In fact, for Confucius, the well-ordered family is a model for the well-ordered state and ultimately the world as a whole. The family, Confucius believed, should, like the state, be patriarchal and authoritarian.

Thus, the proper functioning of the family depends on the obedience of the subordinate members and the responsible governance of the par-

Confucius on Virtue

Confucius's moral viewpoint and his actual life were in no way separate; his desire to learn was a desire to cultivate the best in himself. He believed that only a virtuous man could be of benefit to others.

What I do not want others to do to me, I do not want to do to them.

Man is born with uprightness. If one loses it he will be lucky if he escapes with his life.

The superior man understands righteousness; the inferior man understands profit.

The man who, in view of gain, thinks of righteousness; who, in the view of danger, is prepared to give up his life; and who does not forget an old agreement, however far back it extends—such a man may be reckoned a complete man.

To see what is right and not to do it is want of courage.

If the superior man abandons virtue, how can he fulfill the requirements of that name?

The superior man loves his soul: the inferior man loves his property. The superior man always remembers how he was punished for his mistakes; the inferior man always remembers what presents he got.

ents (and ultimately the father) in accordance with the principle of the Mean; and on the fundamental virtues of filial piety and brotherly respect. Together, these two virtues, according to Confucius, allow an optimal functioning of the five primary human relationships generally: those between ruler and subject, between parent and child, between elder and younger brother, between husband and wife, and between one friend and another. In the well-ordered family, because relationships are clearly

Confucius's Worldliness

Confucius limited his investigation and concern to this changing world: his philosophy was this-worldly and not other-worldly. When he was asked by Ke Loo about serving the spirits of the dead, he answered: "While you are not able to serve men, how can you serve their spirits?" And he said: "We don't know about life; how can we know about death?" It is in this world that the human being must live and with other people that he must associate, Confucius emphasized.

Nevertheless, Confucius understood the importance of religious ritual for the state and was fastidious in carrying out its mandates. To achieve a proper balance in this regard is the mark of a superior man, he said: "Devote yourself earnestly to the duties due to men, and respect spiritual beings but keep them at a distance. This may be called wisdom."

Confucius on Government

To govern means to make right. If you lead the people uprightly, who will dare not to be upright? Employ the upright and put aside all the crooked; in this way the crooked can be made to be upright. Go before the people with your example, and spare yourself not in their affairs. He who exercises government by means of his virtue may be compared with the polar star, which keeps its place, and all the stars turn toward it.

According to the nature of man, government is the greatest thing for him. There is good government when those who are near are made happy and when those who are afar are attracted.

Remember this, my children: oppressive government is more terrible than tigers.

A ruler has only to be careful of what he likes and dislikes. What the ruler likes, his ministers will practice; and what superiors do, their inferiors will follow.

Guide the people with government measures and control or regulate them by the threat of punishment, and the people will try to keep out of jail but will have no sense of honor or shame.

Guide the people by virtue and control and regulate them by respect, and the people will have a sense of honor and respect.

Do not enter a tottering state nor stay in a chaotic one. When the Way prevails in the empire, then show yourself; when it does not prevail, then hide.

Tzu-kung asked about government. Confucius said, "Sufficient food, sufficient armament, and sufficient confidence of the people." Tzu-kung said, "Forced to give up one of these, which would you abandon first?" Confucius said, "I would abandon armament." Tzu-kung said, "Forced to give up one of the remaining two, which would you abandon first?" Confucius said, "I would abandon food. There have been deaths from time immemorial, but no state can exist without the confidence of the people."

---

defined, life will be stable and will provide the means for all members of the family to develop their capacities to the fullest extent.

Confucius's ideal of the superior man, who is wise, humane, honest, and just and whose actions spring from morality and not greed or pride; his urging of a society built not on force or military power but on justice and fairness; his belief in the inherent worth, perfectibility, and goodness of humankind; and his overall concern for humanity and human relationships all represented a strong and influential new vision in Chinese thought.

Mencius

The work of the great Confucian philosopher **Mencius** (371–289 B.C.) is regarded as second only to that of Confucius himself. Mencius, like Con-

Mencius

Mencius, or more precisely, Meng-tzu, was born in what is today the Shantung province of China. He purportedly was taught by Confucius's grandson. Like Confucius, he lived in a time of political turmoil and he spent forty years traveling and teaching. His works eventually became part of the "Four Classics" of ancient China and are based on his belief in the original goodness of human nature. The following quotations reveal some of his insights on life.

The great end of learning is nothing else but to seek for the lost mind.

To preserve one's mental and physical constitution and *nourish one's nature* is the way to serve Heaven.

If you let people follow their feelings (original nature), they will be able to do good. This is what is meant by saying that human nature is good. If man does evil, it is not the fault of his natural endowment.

Humanity, righteousness, propriety, and wisdom are not drilled into us from outside. We originally have them with us. Only we do not think [to find them]. Therefore, it is said, "Seek and you will find it, neglect and you will lose it."

With proper nourishment and care, everything grows, whereas without proper nourishment and care, everything decays.

Those who follow the greater qualities in their nature become great men and those who follow the smaller qualities in their nature become small men.

That whereby man differs from the lower animals is small. The mass of the people cast it away, while the superior men preserve it.

The disease of men is this—that they neglect their own fields and go weed the fields of others.

Thus it may be said that what they require from others is great, while what they lay upon themselves is light.

fucius, was very saddened by the quality of life during his time. He spoke of princes who were deaf and blind to the terrible events about them that "boom like thunder and flash like lightning." Nevertheless, a central tenet of his thought, as with Confucius, was that human beings are basically good.

According to Mencius, the natural goodness of humans had become perverted by circumstances. Still, he said, each person has the potential for becoming perfect: doing so is a matter of recovering his lost mind and forgotten heart; it is a matter of thinking and feeling *naturally*, a matter of following intuition and conscience.

Mencius never lost his optimism about the possibility of human betterment. For him, if anything is tended properly it will grow and thrive. Therefore, human beings should nourish the noble or superior part of themselves, so that it will come to predominate. Each person,

Mencius on Virtuous Activity

It is said that the superior man has two things in which he delights, and to be ruler over the empire is not one of them.

That the father and mother are both alive and that the condition of his brothers affords no cause for anxiety, this is one delight.

That when looking up he has no occasion for shame before Heaven, and below he has no occasion to blush before men—this is the second delight.

In the view of a superior man as to the ways by which men seek for riches, honors, gain, and advancement, there are few of their wives who would not be ashamed and weep together on account of them.

Men must be decided on what they will not do, and then they are able to act with vigor on what they ought.

If on self-examination I find that I am not upright, shall I not be in fear even of a poor man in loose garments of hair cloth?

If on self-examination I find that I am upright, neither thousands nor tens of thousands will stand in my path.

I have not heard of one's principles being dependent for their manifestation on other men.

Benevolence is man's mind and righteousness is man's path.

How lamentable it is to neglect the path and not pursue it, to lose the mind and not know to seek it again.

Benevolence subdues its opposite just as water subdues fire.

Those, however, who nowadays practice benevolence do it as if with one cup of water they could save a whole wagon load of fuel which was on fire, and, when the flames were not extinguished, were to say that water cannot subdue fire. This conduct greatly encourages those who are not benevolent.

however, will decide for himself whether or not he will transform his life for the better.

For the individual who has chosen to seek it, the way to self-betterment, the way to a noble existence and the upright life, according to Mencius, can be found only within himself, within his own conscience. Conscience, for Mencius, is "the mind that cannot bear suffering [on the part of others]." The pathway to the upright life, however, must include *self*-suffering and difficulty, he said. "When Heaven is about to confer a great office on any man," he said, "it first exercises his mind with suffering, and his sinews and bones with toil. It exposes his body to hunger and subjects him to extreme poverty. It confounds his undertakings. By all these methods, it stimulates his mind, hardens his nature, and supplies his incompetencies."

Difficulty and suffering, according to Mencius, are to be considered privileges and opportunities to develop independence, excellence, mental alertness, freedom from fear, and quietude of spirit. He goes so far as

Mencius and Thomas Hobbes on Human Nature

Mencius was quite aware that, by and large, people in his time were violent, self-serving, inclined to stop short of the mark in everything they attempted, and successful only in bringing premature death on themselves. But for Mencius, this evil came on people because circumstances had not allowed them to cultivate their inherent nobility and to search out within themselves love, wisdom, virtue, a sense of duty, and self-perfection. Human nature, according to Mencius, is inherently good, and this goodness can be actualized if people would develop their potentiality—as would happen under a just and humane regime.

Among the many Western philosophers who have also viewed people as selfish and violent, Thomas Hobbes (1588–1679) is probably the most famous. In the state of nature, Hobbes wrote, the life of man is "solitary, poor, nasty, brutish, and short." But Hobbes, unlike Mencius, attributed the ugly ways of humankind to human nature. So Hobbes believed that only through force wielded by an absolute sovereign can humans be prevented from devouring one another: *Homo lupus homini,* said Hobbes, quoting the Roman poet Plautus (c. 254–184 B.C.): *Man is the wolf of man.* Mencius, in contrast, believed that a wise ruler will successfully call forth the goodness inherent in human nature through mild and benevolent leadership.

Whether their malevolent actions mean that human beings, while essentially good by nature, exist in a fallen state; or whether they indicate that human nature is essentially bad, is a question that has not been resolved. Perhaps it is not resolvable.

to imply that prudence and the other virtues are hardly possible for those who have not suffered deeply.

In the process of perfecting one's own life, Mencius said, one is put in a position of benefiting one's family and, through teaching and leadership, society as a whole. Indeed, true happiness, he said, does not consist in ruling an empire merely for the sake of power, the desire for which is the driving ambition of the inferior mind, the mind that, like that of an animal, contains no notion of what is great or honorable. True happiness consists in seeing one's parents and family alive and free from anxiety and in helping one's society. Further, he maintained, whoever is happy in this way also is happy in another way, for he need never feel shame for his actions.

Thus it may be seen that Mencius, too, like Confucius, was concerned not only with the individual but also with the state. Disorder in a state, he believed, is often caused by a ruler who takes no notice of conditions within his own state, a ruler who—again like an animal—is indifferent to all but his own selfish interests and petty ambitions. This indifference and selfishness is a form of blindness, maintained Mencius, and a state governed without vision, he said, inevitably falls into ruin and death.

Further, according to Mencius, the subjects of the state ruled by the inferior person follow the example of their leader and also become like beasts set to devour each other. In this thought Mencius echoed Confu-

Mencius on Government

If a man should love others and the emotion is not returned, let him turn inward and examine his own benevolence.

If a man is trying to rule others, and his government is unsuccessful, let him turn inward and examine his wisdom.

If he treats others politely and they do not return the politeness, let him turn inward and examine his own feelings of respect.

Only the benevolent ought to be in high stations. When a man destitute of benevolence is in a high station, he thereby disseminates his wickedness among all below him.

King Wan looked on his people as he would on a man who was wounded, and he looked toward the right path as if he could not see it.

Virtue alone is not sufficient for the exercise of government; laws alone cannot carry themselves into practice.

[In a state] the people are the most important; the spirits of the land (guardians of territory) are the next; the ruler is of slight importance. Therefore to gain [the hearts of] the peasantry is the way to become emperor.

Killing a bad monarch is not murder.

If a ruler regards his ministers as hands and feet, then his ministers will regard him as their heart and mind. If the ruler regards his ministers as dogs and horses, his ministers will regard him as any other man. If a ruler regards his ministers as dirt and grass, his ministers will regard him as a bandit and an enemy.

To say that one cannot abide by humanity and follow righteousness is to throw oneself away. Humanity is the peaceful abode of men and righteousness is his straight path.

All men have the mind which cannot bear [to see the suffering of] others. . . . When a government that cannot bear to see the suffering of the people is conducted from a mind that cannot bear to see the suffering of others, the government of the empire will be as easy as making something go round in the palm.

Humanity, righteousness, loyalty, faithfulness, and the love of the good without getting tired of it constitute the nobility of Heaven, and to be a grand official, a great official, and a high official—this constitutes the nobility of man.

cius. But, unlike Confucius, Mencius held that killing such a monarch is not murder, for the establishment of a humane government is not possible under such an individual.

The good ruler, Mencius maintained, is benevolent toward his subjects as a father is toward his children and will seek to establish a good order and a just regime. He displays, in addition to benevolence, three other primary virtues or attributes: righteousness, propriety, and knowledge. Further, the good ruler is mild in manner and governs with mind and heart rather than with the strong arm. Because of his mild manner, he encounters no enemies; and because he is humane and his subjects accordingly have confidence in his goodness, he will have only little opposition.

In short, this superior ruler, who has himself suffered on the path to betterment, acquires the mind that cannot bear the suffering of others, and, because it is humane and just, his governance is the foundation of all present and future good within the state.

Thus Mencius's philosophy exhibits the humanistic concerns and faith in human goodness and perfectibility that characterize Confucian philosophy in general. Both Mencius and Confucius were aware, however, that in practice humans are often self-seeking and that their potential for goodness must be cultivated or nurtured. As may be seen in the inserts, Mencius offers much advice and sets forth many telling maxims that, in effect, constitute a method for cultivating the better part of human nature.

Taoism

Taoism, another great system of Chinese thought, derives chiefly from **Lao Tzu** (c. seventh–sixth century B.C.) and his chief follower, **Chuang Tzu** (c. fourth century B.C.). We will look at these two in turn.

Lao Tzu

In an oft-reported meeting between Confucius and Lao Tzu, Confucius expressed his admiration for the depth of Lao Tzu's thought. Lao Tzu, in turn, is said to have expressed doubts about the heroes of the past whom Confucius had chosen as models of behavior. Lao Tzu also tried to convince Confucius of the hopelessness of the latter's attempts to improve society by direct action.

This little story nicely indicates an essential difference between Confucius and Lao Tzu and between Confucianism and Taoism. Confucius sought to become an adviser to a ruler and directly to change society for the better, using heroes of the past as models. Lao Tzu's vision of things and strategy for change are very different, as will be seen. And within the Taoist tradition, one strain of thought even uses Lao Tzu's ideas as a means cunningly to obtain and retain power (the military and political strategies of Sun Tzu—see box on the martial arts—might be mentioned as an example). Our way of looking at Lao Tzu's ideas is thus not the only possible one, and there are also a variety of different ways of interpreting his thought within the long Taoist tradition.

Lao Tzu's view of humankind is in at least one respect like that of the Greek philosopher, Socrates. Both thought that even the wisest of humans is still quite ignorant. And to act on that ignorance under the pretense that it is knowledge, both held, is folly that leads not to progress and betterment within the individual and society but to the opposite

Lao Tzu

Almost nothing is known of Lao Tzu's life because he spent it trying to remain unknown and nameless. He is thought to have been born in the late seventh or early sixth century B.C. and to have worked in the archives at Loyang (present-day Hunan province). Confucius is thought to have visited the older man during one of his journeys, as noted in the text. These quotations reveal some of Lao Tzu's insights on the Tao or Way.

> The Tao that can be told of is not the eternal Tao;
> The name that can be named is not the eternal name.
> The Nameless is the origin of Heaven and Earth.

> Can you understand all and penetrate all without taking any action?
> To produce and to rear them,
> To produce, but not to take possession of them,
> To act, but not to rely on one's own ability,
> To lead them, but not to master them—
> This is called profound and secret virtue.

> Reversion is the action of Tao.
> Weakness is the function of Tao.
> All things in the world come from being.
> And being comes from non-being.

> Tao produced the One.
> The One produced the two.
> The two produced the three.
> And the three produced the ten thousand things.

> To know that you do not know is the best.
> To pretend to know when you do not know is a disease.

> The sage desires to have no desire . . . and returns to what the multitude has missed (Tao).
> Thus he supports all things in their natural state, but does not take any action.

> A good traveler leaves no track or trace.

effect. It is especially here that Taoists like Lao Tzu and Chuang Tzu found Confucius wanting. They thought that he sought to impose solutions without knowledge or understanding.

According to Lao Tzu, what is needed is not interference with the world but humble understanding of the way it functions, namely, understanding of the Tao. Humans cannot force "change" on the world without injuring themselves. All arbitrary interventions using "models" of the past simply lead to further disorder. The sage, he maintained, is the one who knows enough to do nothing: instead of intervening, he simply follows the patterns of the universe, of the ineffable Tao that gives order and substance to all things.

Now the Tao, for Lao Tzu, is one, natural, and eternal. It gives rise to the expansive forces (*yang*) in the universe, and it gives rise to the contractive forces (*yin*). The Tao is like an empty bowl that holds and yields the vital energy (*ch'i*) in all things. It is also the *means* by which

The Tao, Logos, and God

Ancient Chinese and Western philosophy show a striking similarity in their identification of the first principle (beginning) of all being and truth. In ancient Chinese philosophy this first principle is the eternal Tao, the source of all necessity, meaning, order, and existence, the Way the universe functions. Yet the Tao itself, according to Taoism, remains hidden, its nature ineffable. Any attempt to define the Tao or even to describe it in words must fail. According to Lao Tzu, it is the sign of the truly wise man that he will not even try to name it. He only seeks to submit to it and follow it humbly.

In ancient Greek philosophy a like notion was posited as the root of all things. Heraclitus (c. 535–c. 475 B.C.) named it *logos* and regarded it as the source of all order, lawfulness, and justice. There is no consensus on how *logos* should be translated into English, and dictionaries provide many different meanings for the term, including "reason," "proportion," "word," and others.

Logos, as Heraclitus sees it, is almost entirely unknown by earthly mortals—in part, because nature loves to hide. Humans, Heraclitus thought, see the world in terms of opposites and as full of strife. But the deeper reality is the logos, the unity of opposites in which all is one. Seeing this deeper reality is reserved only for the gods and for those few humans who can escape conventional modes of understanding, according to Heraclitus.

The concept of God as it evolved in traditional Christian philosophy is a variation of Heraclitus's notion of logos as developed by Plato and Aristotle and reinterpreted by St. Augustine, St. Thomas Aquinas, and others. In fact, the "Word" that was "in the beginning" in *Genesis* was *logos* in the Greek text. (*Genesis* may not have been originally composed in Greek, of course.)

things come to be, take shape, and reach fulfillment. In contrast to Confucius, who believed that the Tao can be improved on (remember Confucius's remark that "it is man that can make the Way great") Lao Tzu believed that the Tao cannot be improved on, for it *is* the natural order of things.

According to Lao Tzu, the wise person, the sage, cultivates tranquility and equilibrium in his life in order to recognize the Tao. He comes to recognize that the enduring foundation of life is peace, not strife. The harshest storm, the sage understands, can only last a short while. He frees himself of selfish desires and turns his attention to the deep-rooted Tao, where all is one; and by doing so he acquires the secrets both of the quiet and the long-lasting life.

By following the Tao, Lao Tzu held, the behavior of the sage is natural and free, for he harbors no unfit desires and no unnatural expectations. He simply does what is appropriate in the present circumstances. Like water, he accepts the lowest places with contentment and without resistance. He deems valuable what others consider worthless and have discarded. And, because he is selfless, he seeks to care for all things and to benefit them rather than use them for his own ends.

The sage's way, maintained Lao Tzu, is modest, slow, and cautious. Again like water, the sage is soft rather than hard, and (like water), while

Lao Tzu on Virtuous Activity

Good words shall gain you honor in the marketplace, but good deeds shall gain you friends among men.

There is no guilt greater than to sanction unbridled ambition.
No calamity greater than to be dissatisfied with one's own lot.
No fault greater than to wish continually of receiving.

With the faithful I would keep faith; with the unfaithful I would also keep faith, in order that they may become faithful.

The ability to perceive the significance of the small things of the world is the secret of clear-sightedness; the guarding of what is soft and vulnerable is the secret of strength.

The superior man hoards nothing. The more he uses for the benefit of others, the more he possesses himself. The more he gives to his fellow men, the more he has of his own.

The superior man is skillful in dealing with men, and so does not cast away anyone from his doorway.

The superior man prizes three things. The first is gentleness, the second is frugality, the third is humility. By being gentle he can be bold; by being frugal he can be liberal, and by being humble he becomes a leader among men.

The superior man anticipates tasks that are difficult while they are still easy, and does things that would become great while they are small. Therefore, the superior man, while he never does what is great, is able on that account to accomplish the greatest of things.

The superior man diminishes his actions and diminishes them again until he arrives at doing nothing on purpose.
Having arrived at this point of non-action, there is nothing that he does not do.

He who keeps his mouth open and spends his breath in the continual promotion of his affairs will never, in all his life, experience safety.

appearing to do nothing, he achieves lasting effects. To others, the results seem mysteriously produced, for they are produced without apparent effort. The sage is merely following the flow and letting events unfold themselves at their proper time and in their own way. Further, in doing so, he seeks to remain hidden and he takes no credit for what is achieved, for, as said before, he seeks neither possession nor domination. This absence of selfish desire is his secret virtue.

Lao Tzu believed that all enduring change is brought about by weakness, not by strength; by submission, not by intervention. Like an infant, the sage conserves his vital force and progresses gradually day by day. His strength lies in his softness and flexibility. As he lives in accord with the Tao, he is preserved from harm.

Lao Tzu and the Martial Arts

As mentioned in the text, Lao Tzu was against the use of force unless absolutely necessary. His secret for living was to *yield* whenever possible. Far more could be achieved by withdrawing than by attacking or competing. He wrote:

> The strategists have a saying . . .
> I dare not be a host,
> but rather a guest;
> I dare not advance an inch,
> But rather retreat a foot.

Taoist philosophy was extended to military and political strategy by, among others, the sixth-century-B.C. general Sun Tzu, whose *The Art of War*, a treatise on tactics, logistics, and espionage, strongly influenced many Chinese leaders to the present day (including Mao Tse Tung). Taoism is also the essential philosophy of the most sophisticated of the martial arts, for example, tai chi ch'uan. For Lao Tzu, the soft and supple always conquers the hard and rigid.

Lao Tzu extended his philosophy of nonstriving to the political sphere. He recognized the disadvantages of coercion: the use of force brings retaliation, and mutual hostility quickly escalates to the detriment of both sides. As coercion and the use of force arise from greed, he advocated a political strategy of nonacquisitiveness in which weapons are regarded as instruments of destruction and wars are to be fought only when absolutely necessary and then only with regret.

The wise ruler, Lao Tzu believed, understands that violence is a last resort and knows that it can often be avoided by anticipation, by reconciling potential enemies and resolving difficulties when they first arise. It is because such a ruler sidesteps problems by anticipation that his success is unfathomable to others. And because he recognizes that there is no safety in the use of force, he remains calm and unhurried in dealing with any problems that cannot be avoided. His preference is to yield rather than to attack. Gentleness brings him eventual victory with apparently no effort. His strategy is "not to advance an inch but rather to retreat a foot." Slowly he wins over the enemy without the use of weapons. And the gain is lasting because it is achieved without the destructiveness of war and therefore without the long memories of resentment.

To achieve peace and stability, the sage ruler has no wish to dominate or exploit others, Lao Tzu believed. Rather, the wise ruler encourages openness and broadmindedness. Cognizant of the sometime violent ways of the world, he is cautious and reserved. The very essence of his method lies in not requiting injury with injury, a practice that leads only into the endless cycle of revenge. He responds to injury with kindness. He remains faithful even to the unfaithful. In this way, he gradually and effortlessly turns people from that lower nature that tends to dominate in times of war and strife, away from aggressive ambition to thoughtfulness and the search for modest goals.

Lao Tzu on Government

It is the way of Heaven to take from those who have too much and give to those who have too little. But the way of man is not so. He takes away from those who have too little, to add to his own superabundance.

He who assists the ruler with Tao does not dominate the world with force.
The use of force usually brings requital.
Wherever armies are stationed, briers and thorns grow . . .
Whatever is contrary to Tao will soon perish.

Weapons are the instruments of evil, not the instruments of a good ruler.
When he uses them unavoidably, he regards calm restraint as the best principle. Even when he is victorious, he does not regard it as praiseworthy.
For to praise victory is to delight in the slaughter of men.

Tao invariably takes no action, and yet there is nothing left undone.

If kings and barons can keep it, all things will transform spontaneously.
If, after transformation, they should desire to be active,
I would restrain them with simplicity, which has no name.
Simplicity, which has no name, is free of desires.
Being free of desires, it is tranquil.
And the world will be at peace of its own accord.

Violent and fierce people do not die a natural death.
I shall make this the father [basis or starting point] of my teaching.

Govern the state with correctness.
Operate the army with surprise tactics.
Administer the empire by engaging in no activity.

A kingdom, according to Lao Tzu, cannot be preserved by force or cunning. Further, he said, too much government only means confusion. Too many laws create disorder rather than preventing it. Too much activity upsets the balance within a state, just as it does in the life of the individual. The wise ruler does only what is absolutely necessary; because his heart is calm and nonacquisitive, his subjects are not excited to hysteria either by fear or avarice. The state achieves a stability in which all things come to completion in accordance with the Way.

In sum, according to Lao Tzu the way of life recommended by the Tao is one of simplicity, tranquility, weakness, unselfishness, patience and, above all, nonstriving or nonaction—allowing the world to follow its natural course. This way of life is its own reward, for Lao Tzu. Thus he, like Confucius, was concerned with this world, the world of living people; he, like Confucius, was concerned with the human condition and not with otherworldly or supernatural subjects. Unlike Confucius, he did not believe that the Way can be improved on; and therefore, unlike Confucius, he did not think the wise ruler would seek to impose his way of thinking on the state.

Today's reader may well think Lao Tzu's philosophy naive or idealistic. But Lao Tzu was only too aware that a path of quiet nonstriving was one that few, if any, had chosen or would choose to tread. He made it quite clear that he did not expect rule by force to die out soon or quickly to be replaced by a policy of noninterference. He only drew up what he thought would be a superior way of living for any who might wish to consider his opinion in the matter.

Chuang Tzu

Chuang Tzu (c. fourth century B.C.), the most important Taoist next to Lao Tzu, was a contemporary of Mencius—though he and Mencius were not familiar with one another's philosophy. As might be expected, Chuang Tzu's philosophy is quite similar to Lao Tzu's, as you will see.

Chuang Tzu perceived that many people live their lives as "slaves of power and riches." Chained by ambition and greed, they are unable to rest and are in constant friction with the world around them. They often feel trapped and do not know how to change their situation. They seem blind to what is happening and why it is happening. Their lives are driven and hectic, and they are in constant warfare with an indifferent world, a world that does not acquiesce to their desires.

But the world has its own wisdom, Chuang Tzu believed, as did Lao Tzu before him, and things come to fruition only at their proper time. Nature cannot be forced or hurried, because nature, Chuang Tzu believed, unfolds according to the Tao: a tree's fruit must be picked only when it is ripe, not before and not after. If people choose to impose their will on the world, the result is strife, disquietude, and disruption.

Chuang Tzu also believed, as did Lao Tzu, that there is no need for people to force things for the sake of ambition or in the pursuit of profit, or, indeed, for any other objective. Because it is the Tao, and not the person, that determines what is possible and what will happen, the wise individual accepts the course of events as it unfolds, with neither hope nor regret, for the Tao brings all things to fulfillment in due time. Thus for Chuang Tzu, as for Lao Tzu, the secret of the sage—the key to freedom from fear and stress—is simply to follow the Way of things, responding to them appropriately, and dwelling in nonaction. The sage is a mirror: he seeks to be utterly clear about what is before him, but he has no wish to change things.

As was true for Lao Tzu, Chuang Tzu applied his principles to statecraft, though he placed somewhat less emphasis on political affairs than did Lao Tzu. The sage ruler, Chuang Tzu believed, first gains knowledge of himself and of his subjects—gains knowledge of his and their nature and destiny—then effortlessly "goes along with what is right for things." He permits nothing to disturb either his own inner harmony or the har-

Chuang Tzu

Chuang Tzu was born in the fourth century B.C. in the kingdom of Meng, which borders the present-day Shantung. He had a wife and was poor and worked for an office connected with the city of Tsi Yuan. Little else is known about him except that he enjoyed differing with the followers of Confucius. He was not interested in holding public office because doing so, he feared, might disturb his peace of mind. A few of his insights on life in general emerge in the following quotations:

> The mind of a perfect man is like a mirror. It grasps nothing. It expects nothing. It reflects but does not hold. Therefore, the perfect man can act without effort.

> Proof that a man is holding fast to the beginning lies in the fact of his fearlessness.

> The still mind discovers the beautiful patterns in the universe.

> Flow with whatever may happen and let your mind be free: Stay centered by accepting whatever you are doing. This is the ultimate.

> Only the intelligent know how to identify all things as one. Therefore he does not use [his own judgment] but abides in the common [principle]. The common means the useful and the useful means identification. Identification means being at ease with oneself. When one is at ease with himself, one is near Tao. This is to let [nature] take its own course.

> Heaven and earth are one attribute; the ten thousand things [infinite things] are one horse.

> When "this" or "that" have no opposites, there is the very axis of Tao.

> He who knows the activities of Nature lives according to Nature. . . . How do we know that what I call Nature is not really man and what I call man is not really Nature?

> Your master happened to come because it was his time, and he happened to leave because things follow along. If you are content with the time and willing to follow along, then grief and joy have no way to enter in.

mony within the state. Like a tiger trainer, who anticipates the wildness of his charges, he knows how to deal with the violence of others before it arises, thus minimizing the need for force. In his fearless adherence to the Way, he remains free from selfish designs and preset goals. Because he puts forth no special effort, his success is unfathomable to others. This philosophy is, of course, quite similar to that espoused by Lao Tzu. (And Chuang Tzu, like Lao Tzu before him, was quite aware that rulership in accordance with these principles would be a rare occurrence.)

Chuang Tzu, it is perhaps well to add, is famous for his principle of the "equality of things," according to which opposites—life and death, beauty and ugliness, and all the rest—are in fact equal as a single entity within the Tao. Thus, he reasoned, the wise individual, the sage, does not distinguish between himself and the world, and thus finds oneness with Tao.

Cook Ting

Cook Ting was cutting up an ox for Lord Wen-hui. At every touch of his hand, every heave of his shoulder, every move of his feet, every thrust of his knee—zip! zoop! He slithered the knife along with a zing, and all was in perfect rhythm, as though he were performing the dance of the Mulberry Grove or keeping time to the Ching-shou music.

"Ah, this is marvelous!" said Lord Wen-hui. "Imagine skill reaching such heights!"

Cook Ting laid down his knife and replied, "What I care about is the Way, which goes beyond skill. When I first began cutting up oxen, all I could see was the ox itself. After three years I no longer saw the whole ox. And now—now I go at it by spirit and don't look with my eyes. Perception and understanding have come to a stop and spirit moves where it wants. I go along with the natural makeup, strike in the big hollows, guide the knife through the big openings, and follow things as they are. So I never touch the smallest ligament or tendon, much less a main joint.

"A good cook changes his knife once a year—because he cuts. A mediocre cook changes his knife once a month—because he hacks. I've had this knife of mine for nineteen years and I've cut up thousands of oxen with it, and yet the blade is as good as though it had just come from the grindstone. There are spaces between the joints, and the blade of the knife has really no thickness. If you insert what has no thickness into such spaces, then there's plenty of room—more than enough for the blade to play about it. That's why after nineteen years the blade of my knife is still as good as when it first came from the grindstone.

"However, whenever I come to a complicated place, I size up the difficulties, tell myself to watch out and be careful, keep my eyes on what I'm doing, work very slowly, and move the knife with the greatest subtlety, until—flop! the whole thing comes apart like a clod of earth crumbling to the ground. I stand there holding the knife and look all around me, completely satisfied and reluctant to move on, and then I wipe off the knife and put it away."

"Excellent!" said Lord Wen-hui. "I have heard the words of Cook Ting and learned how to care for life!"
—Chuang Tzu

Cook Ting does not wear himself out by trying to force things. This would mean unnecessary friction. Like water, he seeks the empty places. When things become knotted, he only slows down and proceeds carefully. Even then, there is no need for friction or confrontation. Cook Ting's task is done by following rather than disturbing the order of things. By anticipating problems, he solves them before they become major. Total satisfaction is his reward.

Chuang Tzu gave the story of Cook Ting as an illustration of the secret of the sage—to follow the Way of things, responding to them appropriately and never with force.

Chuang Tzu's philosophy is also distinctive for the emphasis he placed on the danger of usefulness. Useful trees, like fruit and nut trees, he explained, are constantly cut back, kept small, and soon stripped of their fruit. Only "useless" trees live out their full term of life unhindered and unsavaged—but then it is only these useless trees that are able to provide shade and beauty. Likewise, Chuang Tzu reasoned, the sage avoids becoming too useful, if he is to fulfill his destiny. These and other nuggets of Chuang Tzu's philosophy are set forth in the nearby boxes.

Chuang Tzu on Virtuous Activity

Chuang Tzu was fishing in the river Phu when the king of Khu sent two high officers to him with the message, "I wish to trouble you with the charge of all within my territories."

Chuang Tzu kept holding his rod without looking around and said, "I have heard that in Khu there is a magnificent tortoise shell, the wearer of which died three thousand years ago, and which the king keeps in his ancestral temple. Was it better for the tortoise to die, and leave its shell to be thus honored? Or would it have been better for it to live, and drag its tail after it over the mud?"

The two officers replied, "It would have been better for it to live and drag its tail through the mud."

"Go your way," said Chuang Tzu. "I will keep on dragging my tail after me through the mud."

Public spirited, and with nothing of the partisan; easy and compliant, without any selfish tendencies; following in the wake of others, without a double mind; not easily distracted because of any anxious thoughts; not scheming in the exercise of one's wisdom; not choosing between parties, but going along with all—all such courses are the path to true enlightenment.

Vacuity, tranquility, mellowness, quietness, and taking no action are the roots of all things. . . . These are the virtue of rulers and emperors when they manage things above.

If one assumes office with them [scholars] to pacify the world, his achievements will be great . . . and the empire will become unified. In tranquility he becomes a sage, and in activity he becomes a king. He takes no action and is honored. He is simple and plain and none in the world can compete with him in excellence. For such a one understands this virtue of Heaven and Earth. He is called the great foundation and the great source of all being and is in harmony with nature. One who is in accord with the world is in harmony with men. To be in harmony with men means human happiness, and to be in harmony with Nature means the happiness of Nature.

Buddhism

The third great traditional movement in Chinese philosophy is Buddhism, which arose in India in the person of a prince, Siddhartha Gautama, later known as **Buddha** (563–483 B.C.). As may be inferred from the date and place of its beginning, Buddhism was originally free from any influence from Confucian or Taoist thought. This eventually changed, as will be seen, when Buddhism was exported to China. Originally, Buddhism essentially was a philosophical response to what might be called the problem of suffering—and suffering is here to be understood in the broad sense as including not merely outright pain and misery but also sorrow, disappointment, frustration, discontent, disaffection, pessimism, and the sense of unfulfillment that so often grows with the passing of the years.

Buddha

When he was twenty-nine, Buddha, tortured by the suffering he saw around him, abandoned a life of luxury as well as a wife and son, to discover why it is that suffering exists and what its cure must be. After six years of wandering and meditation, he found enlightenment.

Buddha's answer to the problem of suffering was contained in his doctrine of the **Four Noble Truths:** (1) There is suffering; (2) suffering has specific and identifiable causes; (3) suffering can be ended; (4) the way to end suffering is through enlightened living, as expressed in the **Eightfold Path** (coming up right away).

Suffering is in part the result, according to Buddha, of the transience and hence uncertainty of the world: indeed, all human problems are rooted in the fact of change and the uncertainty, anxiety, and fear that it causes. Suffering is also in part the result of karma. *Karma* is the doctrine that one's point of departure in this life is determined by one's decisions and deeds in past lives, and that decisions and deeds in this life determine one's beginning points in future incarnations.

But the most immediate causes of human suffering, according to Buddha, are ignorance, which closes the door to enlightenment, and selfish craving, which enslaves an individual to his desires and passions. The individual who is ruled by his desires cannot possibly be happy in an ever-changing, uncertain world, especially because what happens is so much beyond one's control. For even when life goes as is hoped for, there is no guarantee that it will continue that way, and inevitably anxiety and fear overwhelm temporary satisfaction.

According to Buddha, through meditation and self-abnegation selfish craving can be stilled and ignorance overcome. The result of doing so is a cessation of suffering in **nirvana,** a permanent state of supreme enlightenment and serenity that brings the continuing cycle of reincarnation to an end for the individual.

But Buddha held that attainment of nirvana requires more than merely repressing selfish desires. It requires understanding that what is ordinarily thought of as one's body and one's consciousness are not real, are not the true Self. This understanding, this totally nonegoistic perspective, is itself freedom from egoistic thoughts and desires and brings with it as well freedom from all fear and anxiety. By rejecting the fetters of egoistic craving, the individual overcomes the false self and releases himself into "the unsurpassed state of security . . . and utter peace" that is nirvana.

The way to the cessation of suffering is the Eightfold Path. In effect, the Eightfold Path sets forth the means of proper living:

1. *Right View,* which implies having adequate knowledge about those things that make human life sick and unwholesome—ignorance, selfish craving and grasping, and so on.

Profile: Siddhartha Gautama Buddha
(c. 560−480 B.C.)

Siddhartha Gautama, the Buddha, was born in northeastern India. His father was a wealthy king or clan chieftain, Shuddhodana by name; through his mother, Maya, he was related to the Shakya tribe of Nepal. The family enjoyed a luxurious lifestyle and the father sought to keep Siddhartha sheltered from the dust and trouble of the outside world. The young Siddhartha was athletic, handsome, and highly intelligent. He was married at the age of sixteen to Yasodhara, who eventually gave birth to a son, Rahula.

One day on a visit to the city of Kapilavastu, Siddhartha became deeply disturbed by the sight of suffering in its various guises. First, he encountered an old man whose body showed the ravages of the years. Next he saw a man in the throes of a virulent disease. Finally, he passed a funeral with its corpse and attendant mourners, meeting the problem of death on one hand and anguish on the other. His last experience of that eventful day was to behold a monk deep in meditation. All these sights had a profound effect on Siddhartha, and the problem of suffering became the central focus of his thoughts. At the age of twenty-nine, he slipped away from his family during the night and entered the forest to seek a solution to the conundrum of suffering, shaving his head and taking on the raiments of poverty.

Early on in his quest, Siddhartha studied under at least two Hindu ascetics. From them he learned a form of yoga as well as the arts of breathing and motionless meditation. Later Siddhartha joined a small band of ascetics who begged for a living. Like them, Siddhartha performed many acts of self-abnegation and self-renunciation. He grew extremely thin from excessive fasting and one day fell unconscious from his attempts to control his senses. When he awoke, he was fed milk and gruel. From that moment, it was clear to Siddhartha that ascetic practices, in and of themselves, do not lead to enlightenment.

Siddhartha dwelt in the forest for about six years. Thereafter he is thought to have sought a *middle way* between sensual indulgence and ascetic self-denial, striving for enlightenment through concentrating his mind in deep meditation. Siddhartha achieved enlightenment one day while meditating under a fig tree near the present-day town of Gaya in northeastern India. He continued to meditate for seven days. Henceforth this tree was known as the Bodhi tree—the tree of enlightenment.

For almost fifty years, Siddhartha, now the Buddha or Enlightened One, went about teaching the way of dealing with suffering. He founded a group or order, to which his wife and son ultimately belonged. Before he died (in about 480 B.C.), his philosophy had already found a large following. For Western readers, perhaps the most affecting account of the life of Buddha is presented by Hermann Hesse in his novel *Siddhartha*.

Buddhism and the West

The parallel concern of Buddhists and Stoics (see Part 3) with the problem of suffering is intriguing, but it is difficult to say whether any reciprocal influence took place between Buddhism and the philosophies of ancient Greece and Rome. The first major modern Western philosopher to be influenced in a significant way by Buddhist thought was Arthur Schopenhauer (1788–1860). Schopenhauer believed that human life is basically not rational and that humans are driven by blind and insatiable will. Only by overcoming one's ego and desires can a state of calm bliss be achieved, according to Schopenhauer.

After Schopenhauer, Buddhist and other Asian ideas have increasingly come to the West, mostly via Indian and Japanese gurus, monks, and martial artists. Many of these ideas are now entering the mainstream of popular culture.

2. *Right Aim,* which requires overcoming selfish passions and desires by an effort of will and thus having no resentment, envy, or reason to harm another person.

3. *Right Speech,* which means refraining from lies, deceptions, harmful gossip, idle chatter or speculation about others, and so on.

4. *Right Action,* which means not responding to improper desires and cravings, including those that are sexual; and above all means not taking a human life. Right Action also includes doing good deeds (described by Buddha as the "treasure" of the wise).

5. *Right Living,* which requires obtaining one's livelihood through proper means and living one's life free from selfish cravings and graspings.

6. *Right Effort,* which means struggling against immoral and corrupt conditions.

Eastern Philosophy and Eastern Religion

Eastern philosophy and Eastern religions are closely intertwined. Both Confucianism and Taoism took on the trappings of religion, with priests, rituals, and moral codes. Some forms of Taoism also were influenced by Chinese popular religions and superstitions. Today in Taiwan, for example, there are six levels of Taoism, including two kinds of Taoist priests, the red and the black. Only the highest level reflects the Taoist philosophy in its purest form, free from religious and superstitious add-ons.

Buddhism in China was influenced not only by Confucianism and Taoism, but by popular religions as well. In India, a similar interaction took place among the ancient Buddhist writings and various religious belief systems and practices.

7. *Right Mindfulness,* which is the source of Right Effort. Right Mindfulness implies having a duty to attain enlightenment and to understand the nature and effects of selfish craving. The right-minded person, according to Buddha, has no sense of attachment toward body, feelings, perceptions, activities, and thought, and naturally controls all covetous longings and desires.

8. *Right Contemplation,* which means rejecting sensual lures and suppressing sensual appetites, and especially rejecting the desire for pleasure and avoidance of pain.

As can be seen, the first two stages on the Eightfold Path have to do with the initial mental outlook of the individual; the next four specify appropriate behavior; and the last two pertain to the higher mental and spiritual qualities involved in a total disattachment from self.

Two additional concepts traditionally believed to have been introduced by Gautama Buddha became important for the later Buddhism. The first Gautama Buddha identifies in his *Sayings* as "clinging to existence" (*upadana*). This clinging is an extreme form of egoistic craving or desire and must be "destroyed" if the human being is ever to reach a state of peace and imperturbability. This clinging can take different forms—a clinging to the body and its worldly pleasure (*kāmûpādāna*), a clinging to views (*ditthûpādāna*), a clinging to rules and rituals (*sīlabbatûpadāna*), and a clinging to ego beliefs (*attavādûpadāna*). It is necessary to cultivate nonclinging or nonattachment, but in such a way that there is not clinging to nonclinging.

The other important concept is silence (*moneyya*). Gautama Buddha sat and meditated under the bodhi tree to reach enlightenment. Such enlightenment requires going beyond the verbiage and logics of discursive reasoning. In the *Sayings,* Gautama Buddha is thought to have spoken of three kinds of silence: the silence of body, the silence of mind, and the silence of word. Only the person who is silent in all three ways can be said to be free of taint. It is not surprising, then, that silent meditation becomes a critical way to enlightenment in later developments of Buddhism.

Buddha believed that he had found the cause of suffering in the world and a way of escaping it as well. He set forth a strategy for eliminating unnecessary fear and specified a way of living that is calming for the person but that also allows the person to be of service to others. Buddha did not believe in a divine creator or in divine salvation; thus, in his thinking, the problem of suffering is one that humans must cope with themselves.

Buddhism was purportedly brought to China by the Indian monk Bodhidharma about A.D. 520. There it gradually mixed with Taoism, Confucianism, and other influences and underwent a rather marked transformation. This change is quite noticeable in what is now called Ch'an or Chinese Zen Buddhism, to which we next turn.

Zen Buddhism

The growth of Ch'an Buddhism (Chinese Zen Buddhism) was slow at first. But over the centuries this sect spread throughout China and into neighboring countries like Japan and Korea. In our century it has taken root in the United States and Europe. Its current spread in the West seems to indicate that Ch'an Buddhism responds to a need in a highly complex, technological world.

Buddhism in China and Japan has a long and rich history. Here it will only be possible to look briefly at two of its most original and profound thinkers, the sixth patriarch of Chinese Zen, **Hui Neng** (638–713), and **Dogen Zenji** (1200–1253) of the Japanese Soto tradition. The philosophies of these two thinkers complement each other and give an overall perspective on basic elements in the Zen Buddhist tradition.

Hui Neng

Hui Neng (638–713) lost his father in childhood and had to sell firewood to keep his mother and himself alive. He was illiterate.

One day, while delivering firewood to a shop, Hui Neng heard the chanting of the Buddhist *Diamond Sutra* (perhaps the most important scripture of Chinese Buddhism, in which Buddha strips his student Sub-huti of his coarse views and allows him to see the fundamental oneness of all things and the immutability of perceived phenomena). Hui Neng immediately grasped the deep truth latent in its words. But not until some time later did a gift of money enable him to confirm his perception of truth by seeking out Master Hung-jen, the fifth Chinese patriarch of Ch'an Buddhism, at Huang-mei Mountain in Hupei.

During the first meeting with the fifth patriarch, Hui Neng did not hesitate to manifest the unshakable strength of his vision, and he was accordingly accepted in the Huang-mei monastery. For eight months, however, he worked in the kitchen without even entering the main temple.

Zen and Ch'an

Zen Buddhism, as the text explains, is one of the Buddhist sects of Japan and China. (Buddhism, it may be recalled, originated in India.) *Zen* is Japanese and *Ch'an* is Chinese, and both words derive from the Sanskrit word for meditation, *dhyana*. When Buddhism first came to China, it emphasized the importance of meditation, rather than any particular scripture or doctrine, as the key to ultimate reality.

Although the heading for this section is "Zen Buddhism," we discuss both the Chinese and Japanese traditions, Zen and Ch'an. It should be noted that other forms of Buddhism developed as well, but the Zen tradition is the one that has awakened the most philosophical interest in the West.

At this time, the fifth patriarch was seeking a successor and asked the monks to write a poem showing the depth of their insight into truth. Only the person who has a direct intuition into the truth achieves peace of mind, the Ch'an Buddhists believed, and they also thought that each person must discover this truth for himself. That all is ultimately one was a basic precept of the fifth patriarch. This one reality was thought to be our true self-nature and was held to be immanent within human beings from the beginning. To see this ever-present truth exactly as it is would require going beyond the usual way of thinking, which breaks down ultimate being into distinct entities and classifies and relates them, so that they are understood only in terms of the categories to which they belong and their relationships to one another. Hence poetry rather than a normal form of discourse would be required to express insight into this truth, for normal forms of thought and language can express neither the uniqueness of the individual entity nor the underlying oneness of all things. Perhaps you are reminded here of Heidegger, discussed in the previous chapter.

Shen-hsui, the senior monk at the monastery, was the only one who dared to write the requested poem, and the other monks doubted their ability to surpass him in depth of understanding. His contribution, however, according to tradition, only showed that he had not seen the ultimate truth and had not escaped the confines of normal thought. Hui Neng, though illiterate, is said immediately to have sensed the inadequacy of the vision conveyed by this poem when he overheard it being recited by another monk and to have composed a reply to the poem on the spot. Hui Neng's response, recorded by another monk, may be found in a nearby box.

The monks, it is said, were astounded by the words of this twenty-three-year-old illiterate who had not yet even been admitted into the meditation hall. The fifth patriarch was moved as well and immediately recognized in Hui Neng his successor. Perceiving the possibility of jeal-

Hui Neng's Poem of Enlightenment

Hui Neng's spontaneous poem in answer to the request by the fifth patriarch of Ch'an Buddhism revealed immediately that he saw the fundamental nature of truth:

Hui Neng intimates here that the ultimate reality or truth is beyond all conceptualization, as explained in the text.

> Fundamentally no bodhi-tree exists
> Nor the frame of a mirror bright.
> Since all is voidness from the beginning
> Where can the dust alight?

Hui Neng

As mentioned in the text, Hui Neng sought out the fifth patriarch of Ch'an Buddhism, Master Hung-jen, who eventually confirmed Hui Neng's insight into the truth and appointed him his successor. On meeting the fifth patriarch, Hui Neng is said to have said: "I confess to Your Reverence that I feel wisdom constantly springing from my own heart and mind. So long as I do not stray from my nature, I carry within me the field of bliss."

Other interesting quotations of Hui Neng as to life and truth are as follows:

How could I expect that the self-nature is in and of itself so pure and quiet! How could I expect that the self-nature is in and of itself unborn and undying! How could I expect that the self-nature is in and of itself self-sufficient, with nothing lacking in it! How could I expect that the self-nature is in and of itself immutable and imperturbable! How could I expect that the self-nature is capable of giving birth to all dharmas [laws]!

The *Bodhi* or Wisdom, which constitutes our self-nature, is pure from the beginning. We need only use our mind to perceive it directly to attain Buddhahood.

One Reality is all Reality.

Our original nature is Buddha, and apart from this nature there is no other Buddha.

Within, keep the mind in perfect harmony with the self-nature; without, respect all other men. This is surrender to and reliance on one's self.

Light and darkness are two different things in the eyes of the ordinary people. But the wise and understanding ones possess as penetrating insight that there can be no duality in the self-nature. The Non-dual nature is the Real Nature ... both its [the Real Nature's] essence and its manifestations are in the absolute state of suchness. Eternal and unchanging, we call it the Tao.

ousy and anger among the monks, he is said to have had Hui Neng come to him in the middle of the night to receive the robe and bowl symbolic of his new status as sixth patriarch and to learn the wisdom of the *Diamond Sutra*. According to tradition, Hung-jen, the fifth patriarch, convinced that the truth of the *Buddha-Dharma* (ultimate reality) would ultimately prevail through Hui Neng, instructed Hui Neng to leave the monastery immediately and to remain in hiding until he was ready to teach.

What is the ultimate Dharma (reality/truth/law)? Hui Neng gave it a number of different titles: the Self-Nature, the Buddha-Dharma, the Real Nature, and the eternal and unchanging Tao (note the Taoist influence implicit in the last name). All things, he said, are in reality one: there are no "things." Human thought and understanding, to make sense of a totality that cannot be grasped at once, impose categories, contrasts, and distinctions on reality (including thirty-six basic pairs of contrasts or opposites such as light and darkness, *yin* and *yang*, birth and death, good and bad, and so on). But in truth there is only one thing, the Real Nature, and, as it is in itself, it exists prior to any distinctions or categorizations; it is (so to speak) beyond good and evil, permanence and impermanence, content and form. It is an absolute state of "suchness" that neither comes nor goes, neither increases nor decreases, neither is born nor dies. It is exactly as it is: it is reality and truth.

According to Hui Neng, though this ultimate reality or truth is in principle accessible to all, it remains hidden to many of us because we are focused on false attachments and selfish interests: in short, we lack a balanced, objective outlook. And, as a result of this imbalance in our perspective, our efforts too are one sided in pursuit of our goals. Hui Neng made it his purpose to free humans from selfish, one-sided visions of reality. His recommendation was for a state of "no-thought" or "mindlessness," in which the mind does not impose itself on the truth but remains open and spontaneous—a mirror reflecting the wisdom inherent in reality, one that reflects but does not impede the flow of events.

To deepen one's spirit, he said, is to live in harmony with the true or "self-nature" of all things. When the mind is right, it thinks without bias or partiality and is thus considerate of the needs of each and every thing.

The blend of Taoist, Confucian, and Buddhist precepts are thus very much in evidence in Hui Neng's thought.

Dogen

At this point we depart from China for Japan, where Zen was introduced from China in the twelfth and thirteenth centuries. As we have seen, under Hui Neng Zen emerged as a distinct and separate Buddhist sect that combined elements of Indian Buddhist and Chinese thought. When it traveled to Japan, the sect was influenced by Japanese culture as well.

Ultimately two main divisions emerged within Japanese Zen Buddhism, the *Rinzai* and the *Soto*. The latter tradition, on which we shall concentrate here, began with **Dogen Zenji** (1200–1253).

By age fourteen, Dogen was already a monk. He eventually became dissatisfied with the decadent state of Tendai Buddhism, which, being egalitarian and anti-elitist in nature, adopted many popular rituals like chanting the name of Amitabba Buddha. Dogen therefore sought out a Tendai monk, Eisei, who had twice traveled to China to study Ch'an Buddhism. Eisei died soon after the encounter with Dogen, but Dogen continued his studies for nine years under Eisei's successor, Myozen. Afterward, Dogen went to China himself to deepen his studies, and eventually he came under the tutelage of Ju-Ching, at T'ien T'ung Shan monastery. After five years, he returned to Japan in 1227.

Dogen continued to teach and write in monasteries in and around the old capital city of Kyoto until 1243. During this time, he came increasingly in conflict with the predominant Tendai tradition and eventually

Zen Buddhism in Japan

There are two major forms of Zen Buddhism in contemporary Japan: Rinzai Zen and Soto Zen. Over the centuries, each has mutually influenced the other. The difference between the two has more to do with method than with doctrine. Both seek enlightenment apart from the scriptures.

Rinzai Zen, named after the famous Zen monk **Rinzai** (785–867) seeks sudden enlightenment, as preached by Hui Neng. To achieve the *satori* or enlightenment experience, *koans* are often used in addition to sitting in meditation (*zazen*). *Koans* are illogical, even nonsensical, puzzles that are designed to break the stranglehold of conceptual thought so that the absolute, indivisible truth or reality may be suddenly and utterly seen or intuited. Among the most famous of all *koans* is, "What is the sound of one hand clapping?"

The Soto Zen tradition places less emphasis on sudden enlightenment and tends not to use *koans*. As exemplified by Dogen, enlightenment is to be found slowly through *zazen* (meditation) and also by performing all daily duties in the same state of awareness as when sitting in *zazen*. This tradition recognizes no single moment of *satori*, for enlightenment is believed to be possible in all moments.

withdrew into the mountains to establish the Eikei monastery. To this day, Eikeiji is the principal monastery of the Soto branch of Japanese Zen Buddhism.

Many of life's numerous problems, Dogen realized, are not easily solvable. There is, for example, the problem of the impermanence of life. Life passes like the rush of a spring stream, flowing on, day after day, and then it is gone. Dogen, therefore, urges humans not to waste a single second. Time must be utilized in a worthy pursuit, a single objective that merits an all-out effort. The life goal must be nothing small, selfish, or narrow minded. It must be chosen from a broad perspective and with an eye to benefit others as well as oneself. Dogen's philosophy is, in essence, a prescription for an unwasted or noble life, a life of happiness here and now.

It is difficult, of course, Dogen realized, to choose how to live, and equally difficult, if not more so, to carry out that choice. One lives in an uncertain and hurried world, and "our minds go racing about like horses running wild in the fields, while our emotions remain unmanageable like monkeys swinging in the trees." The rapidity of life and the uncertainty of its course makes people's lives full of torment and confusion. They do not understand its nature, or how best to manage themselves.

Moreover, according to Dogen, the mind overwhelmed by a world not understood seeks safety in selfish and self-protective acts. Life is perceived as a succession of real and suspected dangers, and it is viewed in stark contrasts of good and bad, right and wrong, black and white. This perception of the world is what Dogen calls the "Lesser Vehicle," and it arises out of ignorance and fear. The ignorant, fearful mind constructs a list of things deemed bad and to be avoided, and anger and

Dogen

Dogen, a Zen monk since early youth who traveled to China for further studies, gained a reputation as a strict teacher. His writings have had a profound influence up to the present day. Many of his works have been translated into English and have played an important part in the growth of Zen Buddhism. The following are his prescriptions for virtuous activity.

> To plow deep but plant shallow is the way to a natural disaster. When you help yourself and harm others, how could there be no consequences?

> Everyone has the nature of Buddha; do not foolishly demean yourself.

> Even worldly people, rather than study many things at once without really becoming accomplished in any of them, should just do one thing well and study enough to be able to do it even in the presence of others.

> While simply having the appearance of an ordinary person of the world, one who goes on harmonizing the inner mind is a genuine aspirant to the Way. Therefore as an Ancient said, "Inside empty, outside accords." What this means is to have no selfish thought in the inner mind, while the outer appearance goes along with others.

> Emperor Wen of Sui said, "Secretly cultivate virtue, await fulfillment." . . . If one just cultivates the work of the Way, the virtues of the Way will appear outwardly of their own accord.

> To practice the appropriate activity and maintain bearing means to abandon selfish clinging. . . . The essential meaning of this is to have no greed or desire.

> Students of the Way, do not think of waiting for a later day to practice the Way. Without letting this day and this moment pass by, just work from day to day, moment to moment.

> It is written (in the *Vinaya*), "What is praised as pure in character is called good; what is scorned as impure in character is called bad." It is also said, "That which would incur pain is called bad; that which should bring about happiness is called good."
> In this way should one carefully discriminate; seeing real good, one should practice it, and seeing real evil, one should shun it.

> Jade becomes a vessel by carving and polishing. A man becomes humane by cultivation and polish. What gem has highlights to begin with? What person is clever at the outset? You must carve and polish, train and cultivate them. Humble yourselves and do not relax your study of the Way.

> There is a saying of Confucius: "You can't be apart from the Way for even a second. If you think you are apart from it, that's not the Way." He also said, "As the sages have no self, everything is themselves."

resentment are felt toward perceived sources of danger. The individual caught in a dark and threatening world he does not understand finds little rest or peace, and doing violence to himself or others is a frequent consequence of his entrapment.

This state of malcontent, according to Dogen, in which the world is perceived in terms of stark and fearful divisions, remains with the individual until he or she achieves clarification about the true nature of things. But everyone, Dogen said, has the nature of Buddha. Everyone can see the truth and live calmly and peacefully in its presence. It is simply necessary to abandon the selfish and narrow perspective in favor of the broad and unbiased view, in which the mind is expanded beyond the limitations of divisive categories like good/bad and desirable/undesirable; in which greed gives way to generosity, self-serving to other-serving. It is necessary to see things as the ancient sages did, from the perspective of the universe or "Buddha-Dharma" or "universal Self." To do this is to practice the Great Way.

Understanding from this broad perspective, Dogen thought, also involves acceptance—going along with things, following the Way. This, he said, is the wisdom of emptiness—allowing things to be without exercising any preference or desire whatsoever. The similarity to the philosophy of Chuang Tzu is evident.

How does one acquire this perspective of the universal Self? For Dogen, the answer is practice—seeking to help others without reward or praise, caring for others as a parent would. If one makes a continuous effort to do all things with a parental mind and without seeking profit or praise, then one's life will be suffused with the attitude of a "Joyful Mind," in which life takes on a buoyancy and lightness that cannot be diminished by any external event.

Thus Dogen endeavored to set forth a way to achieve permanent joy in *this* life, a way of living that enables the human to achieve a majestic dignity, uncompromisable nobility of character, and peace. "No one or anything could ever make merit decay in any way," he said. In his precepts, Dogen continued the tradition begun by Chuang Tzu, Lao Tzu, and Hui Neng. Life does involve suffering, pain, and transience. But despite the presence of these and of evil, too, life, if lived according to the Tao, should be a joyful and fulfilling event. Dogen urged, "Rejoice in your birth in the world." If one does not escape the fears and insecurities of the small self, life is a torment. But if one lives as would the Magnanimous Mind, then one is living out the truth of the Way itself—the Way of the Buddha-Dharma.

Hinduism

No chapter on Eastern philosophy would be complete without at least a brief look at Hinduism. **Hinduism,** from the Urdu word for India, *Hind,* is the Western term for the religious beliefs and practices of the majority of the Indian people.

The origins of Hinduism stretch back into the unknown past. Unlike other religions, it had no founder, and there is no single religious body to judge orthodoxy. In fact, Hinduism does not even contain a unified set of doctrines—or, to the extent it does, they are given diversified interpretations. All this makes it difficult to talk about Hinduism in a limited space. Speaking of Hinduism as a single belief system is something like speaking of philosophy in the same way. It is best to view it as a spiritual attitude that gives rise to a wide range of religious and philosophical beliefs and practices. These range from the worship of village and forest deities, which often take zoomorphic forms, to sophisticated metaphysical theories.

Common to all forms of Hinduism, however, is acceptance of the authority of the Vedic scriptures as the basis for understanding the true hidden nature of things. The *Vedas* are the most ancient religious texts of Hinduism—indeed, they are the oldest religious texts in an Indo-European language. The *Veda* was the literature of the Aryans, who invaded northwest India around 1500 B.C. Many, if not most, Hindu writings are commentaries on the Vedic scriptures.

In terms of popular religion, three contemporary movements might be mentioned. *Saivism* worships Siva as the supreme being and source of the universe; *Saktism* worships Sakti, the female part of the universe, and wife of Siva. *Vaisnavism* worships the personal god Vishnu. Buddha, according to orthodox Hindus, was an incarnation (*avatar*) of Vishnu.

The basis of Hindu *philosophy* is the belief that reality is absolutely one, that there is only one ultimate reality-being-consciousness. Six classical philosophical schools or traditions, however, interpret this reality variously: these six "insights," as they are called, are *Nyāya*, *Vaiśesika*, *Sāmkhya*, *Yoga*, *Mīmāmsā*, and *Vedānta*. All are designed to lead the searcher to a knowledge of the Absolute and the liberation of the soul. Vedanta is the best known in the West (*Vedanta* means "the end of the Veda").

Philosophically, the most important Vedic scripture is the last book, the *Upanishads*. The *Upanishads*, which date from about the eighth to the fifth centuries B.C., are the inspiration for the six systems of philosophy just mentioned. The *Upanishads* are best known for the theories of *brahman* (the ultimate cosmic principle or reality) and *atman* (the inner self), and the identification of *brahman* with *atman*. There are four great sayings (*mahavakya*) of the *Upanishads*, which are all ways of saying that *brahman* and *atman* are one:

1. Consciousness is *brahman*.
2. That art thou.
3. The self is *brahman*.
4. I am *brahman*.

Now, *brahman* is considered the ultimate reality or principle and the source and sustainer of all things, including people and gods. It is absolute and eternal spirit—the supreme consciousness, the One, the One-and-only-One. A lower manifestation of *brahman*—namely, *brahma*—may be thought of as an individual deity or personal god, but *brahman* itself is without attributes or qualities. This absolute remains the hidden, unknown, ultimate mystery.

Ommmmm

During the 1960s Indian philosophy, or what passed for it, became popular in the American youth culture, thanks in part to the Beatles' interest in it and in the music of the Indian sitar master, Ravi Shankar. In San Francisco and New York and Madison, Wisconsin, it was common to see hippies chanting, "ommmm," "ommmm," "ommmm" in an effort to induce a mystical state of higher consciousness.

What is "ommm"? It's the sound of the letters *A*, *U*, and *M*, which are the symbols in Hindu writings for the three ordinary states of consciousness: waking experience, dreaming sleep, and deep sleep. There is in addition, according to Hinduism, a fourth state (in Vedanta philosophy, *moksa*), one of higher awareness, which is described in the *Mandukya Upanishad* as "the coming to peaceful rest of all differentiated existence." *Yoga* is the general term for the spiritual disciplines in Hinduism and Buddhism that aim at the attainment of this higher state. It is also the name of one of the six orthodox systems of Hindu philosophy (see text).

Atman, on the other hand, is the self, the soul, the principle of individual life. Ultimately, however, the individual must come to a realization, through meditation and contemplation, that *brahman* and *atman* are the same thing—*brahman-atman*. With the realization of this absolute oneness of all things comes recognition of the relative nonreality of the world and of the individual ego. The identification of *brahman* and *atman* is sometimes spoken of by commentators as a pantheism, but it goes beyond the claim that all things are God. In Hinduism, the gods are parts or symbolic personifications of the absolute principle, *brahman*.

Further, the identification of *brahman* and *atman* has been subject to various interpretations over the centuries. It has been looked on both as transcendent and as an immanent. Samkara, who is thought to have lived between A.D. 788 and 820 (though these dates are controversial) and who gave the most rigorous interpretation of the *Upanishads,* was a pure monist who thought that all things are one—only the ultimate principle exists and all else is an illusion. But another way of looking at the ultimate principle or reality was introduced by Rāmānuja (b. A.D. 1027). He believed in the ultimate principle, but he also believed that souls are real and that the world is not merely an illusion. For a time, at least, the souls and the world must be separate from the ultimate principle in order to be of service to it, he held.

Yet a third way of interpreting the underlying ultimate reality is represented by the outright dualism of Madhva (1199–1278), who believed that, although the ultimate principle is the cause of the world, the soul still has a separate and independent existence of its own. You can see that Hindu philosophy in fact admits a variety of viewpoints.

Much of the wisdom of Hinduism in all times lies in its sages. This certainly holds true for this century, whose wise men include

Rabīndranāth Tagore (1861–1941), Aurobindo Ghose (1872–1950), and Mohandas K. Gandhi (1869–1948). Tagore won the Nobel Prize in 1913 for his poetry, in which he expressed the human quest for freedom and the divine. Aurobindo, who was educated in the West, sought political freedom for India. After being accused of terrorism and violence, he withdrew from political life altogether and developed a theory of spiritual evolution according to which the individual through self-effort can rise to ever higher states of spiritual consciousness.

Gandhi, of course, is known everywhere for his use of nonviolence to help attain political freedom for India and for striving to instill a sense of self-respect in all human beings (he called the lowest caste, the "untouchables," the children of God). Through the example of his simple life and teachings, Gandhi tried to make the traditional values of Hinduism available to all.

The Philosophy of the Samurai (c. 1100–1900)

Japan's warrior class, the samurai, were also the ruling class for long periods of time. Their wisdom was transmitted in the form of martial precepts, the earliest dating to the twelfth century or earlier. These precepts were handed down the generations within the class and they were often used to train the samurai and to teach them the art of **bushido,** that is, the art of being a samurai warrior.

The literature of the samurai tradition has influenced all areas of Japanese thought and behavior. Westerners who have wished to understand the basis of the Japanese economic "miracle" since World War II have looked to such samurai classics as Miyamoto Musashi's *A Book of Five Rings* and Yamamoto Tsunetomo's *Hagakure.* Also influential in determining the Samurai world view were the Chinese classical views, including the writings of Confucius, Lao Tzu, and Sun Tzu as well as the *I Ching* or *Book of Changes.* Musashi (1584–1645) was one of Japan's greatest swordsmen and military strategists. His ideas teach martial strategy, but they seem to lend themselves equally well to business methods and to life generally. Yamamoto Tsunetomo (1659–1719) served only a short time as a retainer before his master died. Thereafter, he withdrew from the world and lived as a recluse studying Zen Buddhism. During the final years of his life, his thoughts on the essence of the samurai way of life were written down and preserved. The ideals of the samurai tradition have endured and still determine to no small extent the life and thought of modern-day Japan.

The world view expressed in Tsunetomo's *Hagakure* will be familiar to readers of the material on Dogen. Human life at best he sees as "a short affair." No time may be squandered without regret and loss. Yet brevity is not what makes life so difficult and painful; this effect comes rather from life's uncertainty. Humans exist in a world of constant and unpredictable change.

The Ancient Philosophies Today

Early in its history, Taoism had a relatively strong influence on rulers in China. But as Confucianism replaced it as the dominant value system within society, beginning with the T'ang dynasty (618–906) it increasingly focused on religious functions, an area in which it eventually had to compete with Buddhism. More and more, Taoism came to encompass magic, soothsaying, and incantations for healing and for warding off evil spirits. To this day, Taoist priests perform ceremonies at funerals and on other important occasions. Reportedly Taoist hermits are still living out the highest forms of Taoist practice in the mountains of China.

As Confucianism established itself as the dominant moral and political philosophy, the Confucian classics became the basis of civil service examination, and in this way Confucianism became even further embedded into Chinese thinking. Between the eleventh and eighteenth centuries there was a significant Neoconfucian movement, one of whose major figures was Wang Yang-ming (1472–1529).

Confucianism received a severe blow from the Communist revolution in 1949, and Mao Tse-Tung made it a repeated target for ridicule. This does not mean that Mao was not himself influenced by Confucius both in his style of writing and of ruling, nor does it mean that Mao was loathe to use Confucianism to his own ends—for example, in transferring the individual's family allegiance to state allegiance. In any case, with the current liberalization in China Confucian thought is again making itself apparent.

Chinese Buddhism developed a number of different schools from the fourth to the ninth centuries. Ch'an Buddhism was especially powerful and innovative during the seventh to ninth centuries. Chinese Buddhist temples have provided religious services for the people from that time even until the present day. Further, the influence of Ch'an Buddhism spread to Japan, where Zen Buddhism and other forms of Buddhism have endured until the present. Currently Zen Buddhism especially enjoys growing popularity in the United States and the West generally.

When these changes are not anticipated, the result is often disastrous. Therefore, a samurai must train himself to be ready at all times for anything that may happen. He must train to anticipate all eventualities and deal with them before they become a problem. A samurai precept is, "Win beforehand."

According to Tsunetomo, not only the uncertainty of events is problematic. Human beings themselves are often flawed, ignorant, selfish, and unreasonable. Accordingly, the samurai must learn to be self-reliant. He cannot and does not depend on others acting properly. He knows that humans beings will not always act either reasonably or justly. He is prepared for treachery and cowardice and awaits their arrival. Only by practicing alertness and bravery can a samurai avoid wasting his life.

Because of the uncertainty of the world and the unreliability of the human character, the samurai must learn the arts of war as well as the arts of peace. Human beings, like states, must be able to defend themselves. Kuroda Nagamasa (1568–1623), known as a great military strat-

Courage and Poetry

Samurai warriors often sought to discipline their spirit and free themselves from fear by training with Buddhist masters. At various times, samurai and Zen monks both used poetry, especially short forms of poetry like *haiku*, to test the strength and validity of their insight into truth. At a critical moment, just before death, for example, a trainee was expected spontaneously to write a poem that revealed his perfect freedom under all circumstances as well as the depth of his insight. He was expected to remain calm, clear-headed, and imperturbable even at the point of a sword. There are stories of captured warriors being spared death if they were sufficiently intrepid and their poem manifested deep wisdom.

The greatest of all the Japanese *haiku* writers was **Basho** (1644–1694). He was deeply involved with Zen, and his death poem is regarded as profound:

> Stick on a journey,
> Yet over withered fields
> Dreams wander on.

Dogen also gives an example of the genre:

> Scarecrow in the hillock
> Paddyfield
> How unaware! How useful!

Here are two more poems considered to reveal the deep insight and spontaneous expression of the truly free individual:

> Coming and going, life and death:
> A thousand hamlets, a million houses.
> Don't you get the point?
> Moon in the water, blossom in the sky.
> —Gizan (1802–1878)

> Fifty-four years I've entered [taught]
> Horses, donkeys, saving limitless beings.
> Now farewell, farewell!
> And don't forget—apply yourselves.
> —Jisso, 1851–1904

egist, wrote: "The arts of peace and the arts of war are like the wheels of a cart which, lacking one, will have difficulty in standing."

The samurai strives to realize Confucius's notion of the complete man, who is both scholar and warrior. Life requires constant training and learning. Without learning, a person would be ignorant of what is necessary; without hard training, he would be unable to carry the necessary actions into effect quickly and efficiently. The samurai works hard to know where his duty lies and to carry it out "unflinchingly." To do this, he hardens himself to suffering. He welcomes death if it comes in pursuit of duty. He learns to abhor luxury and considerations of money in order not to be attached to them or to life generally.

An important part of the samurai's study is past traditions, particularly the Confucian and other classical Chinese philosophies, and Zen Buddhism. These determine and shape *bushi* (see the nearby box) and are in turn unified and synthesized by *bushi* into a single, effective way of life.

The Influence of Confucius

As mentioned, the model of the perfect samurai closely shadows the Confucian idea of the complete man. He is a scholar warrior, literate yet deeply knowledgeable about practical affairs. He knows that life involves change and that survival depends on understanding the inner workings of change. Though a few samurai teachers emphasized the art of war and the ways of increasing courage, more usual is the view of the *Hagakure*. Here the samurai is called on to develop his knowledge of whatever might be useful, "querying every item night and day." Above all, he must understand the Confucian principle of the Mean: more than merely the middle way between two extremes, the Mean is the universal standard that determines what is right and appropriate. The wise samurai reads the sayings of the ancients as the best way to find out what the Mean recommends and how best to follow it.

For Confucius, the three basic and interrelated qualities to be pursued are humanity, wisdom, and courage. According to the samurai tradition, these virtues allow those who have them to enjoy a useful life of service as well as a life free from anxiety and fear.

As Confucius also prescribed, the samurai should be filial, making every effort to respect and honor his parents; he should be polite, discreet in manners and conduct, proper in dress and speech, and upright and sincere. He must not lie. There is the story, for example, of the samurai who refused to take an oath because the word of the samurai is more certain than any oath.

In historical Japan, those who possessed these qualities exhibited enormous dignity. The samurai's dignity displayed itself in every action and in every word. His solemn behavior and resoluteness frequently struck fear in the ordinary observer. The samurai code sought to create a character that was flawless in behavior and taut in spirit.

The Magnificent Seven

One of the most popular Hollywood movies of all time was the 1960 John Sturges Western, *The Magnificent Seven*, a story about seven gunslingers hired by a Mexican village as protection against a band of cutthroat bandits who preyed on the helpless villagers. Unknown to many American audiences at the time, the film was a remake of Akira Kurosawa's *The Seven Samurai* (1954), which at one point had been titled "The Magnificent Seven" for release in the United States. Kurosawa's story about a sixteenth-century Japanese village that hires professional warriors to protect them depicts the martial skill, humaneness, and strict sense of justice and honor of the samurai, whose virtues enable them to confront adversity unflinchingly and victoriously. Sturges's movie helped focus attention in America on Kurosawa's film, which in turn led to much interest in the United States in the samurai tradition.

Another samurai virtue had its roots in the philosophy of Confucius: the samurai was to be economical, and, as noted, avoid luxury. He was to save what he could, but only with an eye to using it on campaign when it was needed.

Because of his virtues, the samurai could be expected to establish and maintain an ordered state in the midst of the most chaotic times. His own steady and unshakable behavior would then serve as a model to be trusted and followed by all others. This, of course, is a Confucian theme.

The Influence of Zen Buddhism

It is slightly ironic that members of the warrior class in Japan went to Zen monks for training, for Zen monks dedicated their lives to saving all living beings. Kamakura, a Zen center, which dates back as far as the thirteenth century, was especially noted for training samurai warriors. Perhaps the most famous instance of this relationship was the influence of the Zen monk Takuan (1573–1645) on two of Japan's greatest swordsmen and strategists, Miyamoto Musashi (1584–1645) and Yagyu Munenori (1571–1646). All three men produced classic works that were used in the training of samurai.

The samurai, recall, were warriors who trained themselves to be ready at any moment to fight to the death. The ability to fight, of course, is frequently hampered by fear; for fear, if it does not paralyze a fighter completely, may well prevent the lightning-fast response that may be the difference between winning or losing. Though samurai engaged in ceaseless martial arts training, a state of fearlessness sometimes escaped even the best of them. Some samurai, therefore, sought out Zen masters in order to free themselves of their own fear.

Fear, according to the Zen Buddhist, arises from an excessive attachment or clinging to things and to life generally, a perspective of possessiveness from which anything and everything is viewed as a threat. The remedy to fear—the samurai learned from the Zen masters—is to free

Governance by the Warrior

According to William Scott Wilson's *Ideals of the Samurai*, the word *bushi* (samurai warrior) is first recorded in an early history of Japan, one dated A.D. 797. These educated warriors served at the time in close attendance to the nobility. The weakness of civil government, however, led to the practice of clans and private estates developing their own armies and to increasing involvement by samurai in government. The warrior class eventually replaced the court aristocracy, and the late twelfth century marked the beginning of warrior-class rule, which lasted 700 years.

Samurai Insights (from Yamamoto Tsunetomo, *The Hagakure*)

Everything in this world is a marionette show.

[The samurai] remains undistracted twenty-four hours a day.

A samurai's word is harder than metal.

The Way of the samurai is in desperateness. Ten or more men cannot kill such a man.

With an intense, fresh, and undelaying spirit, one will make his judgment within the space of seven breaths. It is a matter of being determined and having the spirit to break right through to the other side.

If one will do things for the benefit of others and meet even those whom he has met often before in a first-time manner, he will have no bad relationships.

A samurai's obstinacy should be excessive.

It is natural that one cannot understand deep and hidden things. Those things that are easily understood are rather shallow.

Courage is gritting one's teeth . . . and pushing ahead, paying no attention to the circumstances.

There is nothing other than the single purpose of the present moment.

I never knew about winning . . . but only about not being behind in a situation.

There is nothing that one should suppose cannot be done.

One must be resolved in advance.

Human life is a short affair. It is better to live doing the things that you like.

If one will rectify his mistakes, their traces will soon disappear.

At a glance, every individual's own measure of dignity is manifested just as it is.

One cannot accomplish things simply with cleverness.

By being impatient, matters are damaged and great works cannot be done. If one considers something not to be a matter of time, it will be done surprisingly quickly.

A man's life should be as toilsome as possible.

People become imbued with the idea that the world has come to an end and no longer put forth any effort. This is a shame. There is no fault in the times.

When I face the enemy, of course it is like being in the dark. But if at that time I tranquilize my mind, it becomes like a night lit by a pale moon. If I begin my attack from that point, I feel as though I will not be wounded.

It is the highest sort of victory to teach your opponent something that will be to his benefit.

Win first, fight later.

There is nothing so painful as regret.

Money is a thing that will be there when asked for. A good man is not so easily found.

Meditation on inevitable death should be performed daily. . . . It is to consider oneself as dead beforehand.

oneself from attachments and personal preferences, to rid oneself of the desire to possess anything, including life itself. The samurai was taught to overcome himself, so to speak—to free himself from all thoughts of gain or loss. He was taught to accept what happens without joy or sadness, without complaint, and even without resignation. This hard lesson was thought to require constant meditation on death so that the warrior was ready to "die completely without hesitation or regret."

In this way Zen training sought to rid the samurai of the self-imposed paralysis of fear. Both the Zen and the samurai traditions shared the same ideal: to attain *an unobstructed state of instant, untainted response.* For the samurai this state of mind was the key to total preparedness.

The samurai tradition therefore emphasized that through a vigorous training of the body and the mind the individual can perfect his character to respond immediately to any situation. Such training can create a resolute single-mindedness, in which the present moment is all there is and the present action alone is real, that is both efficient and powerful.

The ultimate goal of both Zen Buddhist and samurai training is the state of *mushin,* that is, the state of no mind, no thought. This is a state of awareness beyond calculation in which one moves "no-mindedly" in the here and now, doing exactly what is appropriate without any hesitation. This mind is the "secret" of the great swordsmen like Musashi and Yagyu Munenori.

The samurai tradition, together with Confucianism and Zen Buddhism, provided the Japanese with a noble ideal of character, a context in which the efficiency of Japanese society, and much of what is good and successful in Japan, may perhaps be understood. Certainly the vision of the noble person who trains all his life to be of benefit to others seems a fulfillment of the ideal of humanity put forward by Confucius, Zen, and the samurai. On the other hand, the chauvinist nationalism of the Japanese in World War II, the unquestioning obedience to authority, and the glorification of death may also perhaps be explained by reference to these same influences. It is interesting to speculate what these traditions might have yielded, what their effect on Japanese society might have been, if they had been stripped of their authoritarian and excessively militaristic qualities.

To help you review, here is a checklist of the key philosophers and concepts of this chapter. The brief descriptive sentences that appear with each philosopher summarize one of his leading ideas. Keep in mind that some of these summary statements represent terrific oversimplifications of complex positions.

Checklist

Philosophers

- **Confucius** Founder of the most dominant system of Chinese thought; emphasized the perfectibility of people as well as their ability to affect things for the better.

- **Mencius**   Confucian thinker second in importance to Confucius.
- **Lao Tzu**   Founder of Taoism; held that the Tao is ineffable and beyond our ability to alter; emphasized the importance of effortless nonstriving.
- **Chuang Tzu**   Most important Taoist after Lao Tzu; stressed the equality of opposites and the danger of usefulness.
- **Sun Tzu**   Sixth-century B.C. Taoist philosopher and general; applied Taoist philosophy to military strategy.
- **Siddhartha Gautama Buddha**   Indian prince, founder of Buddhism. Sought the causes of and cures for human suffering.
- **Hui Neng**   Sixth patriarch of Chinese Zen; emphasized the oneness of all things.
- **Dogen Zenji**   Zen monk; stressed the importance of acquiring the perspective of the universal Self, given the impermanence of life.
- **Miyamoto Musashi, Yamamoto Tsunetomo, Yagyu Munenori**   Samurai writers who helped record and preserve samurai ideals of preparedness; indifference to pain, death, and material possessions; wisdom; and courage.
- **Basho**   Greatest Japanese haiku writer.

Concepts

Analects

Way/Tao

Mean

sage

rectification

jen

Confucianism

Taoism

yin/yang

soft and supple

Buddhism

Four Noble Truths

Eightfold Path

karma

nirvana

Ch'an Buddhism

Zen Buddhism

dhyana

dharma

Rinzai Zen

Soto Zen

satori

koan

zazen

Hinduism

Veda

Upanishads

Vishnu

brahman

atman

samurai

haiku

bushido

mushin

"win beforehand"

---

1. Do you agree with Confucius's belief in the goodness and perfectibility of humans? Give reasons.

2. What is the Tao?

3. Compare and contrast the philosophies of Confucius and Lao Tzu. Take sides and determine whose prescriptions are soundest, and why.

4. Evaluate Mencius's idea that difficulty and suffering are opportunities to develop independence and peace of mind.

5. Do the subjects of the state adopt the ethical standards of their leaders? Or is it the other way around?

6. "Benevolence subdues its opposite just as water subdues fire." Evaluate this claim.

7. Are Lao Tzu's prescriptions for behavior realistic and practical? Explain.

8. Are power and riches chains, or are they the keys to freedom and happiness?

9. Do you believe in reincarnation? Why?

10. What is the sound of one hand clapping? Is this an intelligible question?

11. Comment on Hui Neng's power of enlightenment (see box).

12. How important is it to have a life goal?

13. Is it possible for a person completely to abandon selfish desires?

14. How important is it to be self-reliant? Is total self-reliance possible?

15. Should the complete person be both wise and brave? If you wished to improve your wisdom or free yourself from fear, what would you do? How would you know if you succeeded?

Questions for Discussion and Review

Suggested Further Readings

John Blofield, *The Secret and Sublime* (New York: E. P. Dutton, 1973). A very readable presentation of the philosophy of Taoism, popular Taoism, Taoist mysticism, and the relationship of Taoism and yogic practices.

Confucius, *The Analects*, D. C. Lau, trans. (New York: Penguin, 1979). A good, inexpensive, and readily available collection of Confucius's philosophical insights.

Dogen and Kosho Uchiyama, *Refining Your Life*, Thomas Wright, trans. (New York: Weatherhill, 1983). Dogen in this short treatise on Zen cooking provides an extraordinary method of performing any activity well and of living life as a whole.

Aislee T. Embree, ed., *The Hindu Tradition* (New York: Vintage Books, 1972). Readings that review the development of Hindu thought from the beginnings to the present.

D. C. Lau, trans., *Mencius* (Hammondsworth, England: Penguin, 1970). A highly readable translation of Mencius's writings.

Trevor Leggett, *Zen and the Ways* (Rutland, Vt.: Charles E. Tuttle, 1987). Shows how the meditative calmness taught in Zen can be applied to the ways of the martial arts and of life generally.

Miyamoto Musashi, *A Book of Five Rings*, Victor Harris, trans. (New York: Bantam, 1982). Written by the most famous swordsman and samurai, this is the great book of Japanese strategy. It is a guide for making decisions and acting decisively in even the worst of times.

Sarvepalli Radhakrishnan and Charles A. Moore, *A Source Book in Indian Philosophy* (Princeton: Princeton University Press, 1957). A splendid historical selection of philosophical writings with background information.

D. Howard Smith, *Confucius and Confucianism* (London: Paladin, 1973). Places the teachings of Confucius in historical context and treats the interaction of Confucianism with Taoism and Buddhism.

Yamamoto Tsunetomo, *Hagakure* (Tokyo: Kodansha International, 1979). The seventeenth-century classic that encapsulates the ethics, strategies, and world view of the samurai class. Enlightening in itself, the *Hagakure* can also be used to understand contemporary Japanese ways of thinking.

Chuang Tzu, *The Complete Works*, Burton Watson, trans. (New York: Columbia University Press, 1968). A highly regarded translation of Chuang Tzu that is said to retain the wit of the philosopher himself.

Lao Tzu, *Tao Te Ching* (New York: Penguin, 1973). A good and inexpensive translation of a classic.

Wing-tsit Chan, *A Source Book in Chinese Philosophy* (Princeton: Princeton University Press, 1963). First-rate anthology of Chinese philosophical writings placed in historical and philosophical context.

Eastern
Philosophy

SUMMARY AND CONCLUSION

The three principal systems of Chinese philosophical thought are Confucianism, Taoism, and Buddhism.

Confucius and Mencius, the two most important Confucian thinkers, were practical, socially minded philosophers, who placed great emphasis on the perfectibility and innate goodness of human beings and on human ability to affect the Tao, or Way of things, for the better.

Lao Tzu and Chuang Tzu, the principal Taoists, regarded the Tao as ineffable and beyond man's ability to alter and believed that the superior person reveals wisdom through understanding and effortless nonstriving.

Buddhism, which originated in India, set forth an Eightfold Path for coping with suffering; and, in China, where it is known as Ch'an, it was modified with Taoist and Confucian elements and emphasized the oneness and indivisibility of ultimate being. Zen, or Japanese Buddhism, evolved from Chinese Ch'an Buddhism; Dogen, of the Soto branch of Zen, stressed the importance of acquiring the perspective of the universal Self as a means of attaining enlightenment and enduring joy.

The samurai philosophy exhibited marked Confucian and Zen Buddhist influences; it was Confucian especially in the importance it attached to practical wisdom as a counterbalance to proficiency as a warrior, and it showed the influence of Zen in the emphasis it placed on a universal perspective and the containment of selfishness as the antidote to fear.

Hinduism is the term that embraces the religious beliefs and practices of the majority of the Indian people. Common to all forms of Hinduism is acceptance of the authority of the Vedic scriptures. The last of these scriptures, the *Upanishads,* are the most important philosophically and are best known for identifying *atman* with *brahman,* though this identification is subject to various interpretations.

Logic

There is only one way to prove a proposition, and that is by means of an **argument.**

Example of an argument:

1. Pain and suffering are real.
2. If pain and suffering are real, then God does not exist.
3. Therefore, God does not exist.

In this argument, propositions (1) and (2) are used in an effort to prove (3). They—propositions (1) and (2)—provide the reasons for accepting (3) and are known as the *premises* of the argument. Proposition (3) is the *conclusion* of the argument.

Outside logic texts, arguments are not usually stated so "formally." What you are more likely to encounter is something like this, which is exactly the same argument stated more casually.

Pain and suffering are real, so there is no God.

When the argument is stated this way, the arguer thinks premise (2) is so obvious that he or she is not even bothering to state it. This is still the same argument as given earlier, however.

Logic is concerned with arguments: their types and structures; the relationships among the propositions within them; the basic assumptions and principles governing these relationships; the extent to which mathematics, science, and ordinary thought exemplify these relationships; and other related matters. Most especially, logic is concerned with whether the premises of a given argument warrant acceptance of the conclusion.

Twentieth-century logic is a vast and technical discipline and we are going to beg your forgiveness for not going into it in this book. What we want to do here is simply give you a useful introduction to the subject, one that focuses on some of the types of arguments you will encounter in this book and in real life.

Deductive and Inductive Arguments

It is *impossible* for the conclusions of some arguments to be false if their premises are true. If your argument is *supposed* to be like that, it is a **deductive argument.** And if indeed it *is* impossible for your conclusion to be false if the premises are true, then your argument is a *valid* deductive argument. And finally, if the premises of your valid deductive argument *really* are true, then your argument is

598

sound. The example above is a valid deductive argument. Whether or not it is sound (i.e., whether or not the premises are in fact true) we will leave up to you.

If, on the other hand, your argument is only supposed to show that it is *improbable* that the conclusion is false if the premises are true, then it is an **inductive argument.** Inductive arguments are neither valid nor invalid nor sound; they are just *strong* or *weak*, depending on just how probable the conclusion is, given the premises.

Example of an inductive argument:

Sixty percent of those surveyed in the Gallup Poll believe in God, so sixty percent of all Americans believe in God.

In this example, the premise (the proposition about the Gallup Poll) is intended to show that the conclusion is probable, not that it could not possibly be false.

Common Types of Deductive Arguments

Here are the two most common valid types or "patterns" of deductive arguments.

Valid deductive pattern 1: (p and q stand for propositions)

If p then q.

p.

Therefore q.

Example:

If pain and suffering are rare, then God is good. Therefore, because they are rare, God is good.

Valid deductive pattern 2:

If p then q.

Not-q.

Therefore, not-p.

Example:

If God is all-good, then pain and suffering are rare. So, because they aren't, God is not all-good.

Now here are two invalid patterns of deductive arguments that are sometimes mistakenly viewed as valid.

Invalid deductive pattern 1:

If p then q.

q.

Therefore, p.

Example:

If God is all-good, then pain and suffering are rare. That proves that God is good, because pain and suffering *are* rare.

Invalid deductive pattern 2:

If *p* then *q*.

p isn't true.

Therefore *q* isn't true.

Example:

If pain and suffering are rare, then God exists. That shows that God doesn't exist, because pain and suffering are not rare.

The four patterns just given are the most frequently used patterns of deductive argument. Two other patterns of deductive argument are common, however.

One is called **reductio ad absurdum,** or, sometimes, just the **reductio proof** (see Chapter 11 for one example). The principle here is that if some proposition *p* "reduces to" or entails some other proposition that is absurd, nonsensical, or just patently false, then *not-p* must hold true. Here are two examples:

Examples of reductio proof:

1. God is not self-caused, because if He were, then He would have to exist before Himself, which is absurd.

2. If there truly is a good and all-powerful God, then pain and suffering must serve His purpose, and that means they actually are good things. But that's ridiculous, because it means that it's a good thing that Uncle Charlie's terminal cancer is causing him so much agony. So I don't agree that there is a good and all-powerful God.

Schematically, these two *reductio* proofs look like this:

1. *p*, because if *not-p*, then *q*, and *q* is absurd.

2. *p*.

If *p* holds, then so does absurd result *q*.

Therefore *not-p*.

As you can see, *reductio* proofs are closely related to valid pattern 2, noted earlier. As you can also see, the *reductio* pattern of argument is persuasive only if the result touted as absurd truly is absurd. Actually, a *reductio* proof is valid in the technical sense defined only if the allegedly absurd result cannot possibly be true.

And finally, the other commonly encountered valid pattern is **"begging the question."** But watch out for this pattern! Begging the question is what you get if your premises assume the very conclusion they are supposed to prove. So even though begging the question is technically valid, it is worthless as proof. Anyone who disputes your conclusion won't accept your premises, if your premises assume the very point at issue.

Here's the standard example:

Example of begging the question:

It says in the Bible that God exists. Because the Bible is the revealed word of God, what it says is true. Therefore God exists.

> God is unlimited. This follows immediately from the fact that God has no limits.

Schematically, question-begging arguments ultimately amount to this:

p.

Therefore, p.

The vast majority of deductive arguments you encounter in this book, and in philosophy outside this book, are instances of one or another of these six patterns.

Common Types of Inductive Arguments

The two most common types of inductive arguments are inductive generalizations and analogical arguments.

In the premises of an **inductive generalization,** something is said to be characteristic of a *sample* of a class of things and the conclusion is that the same thing is characteristic of *all* (or most) of the class. Schematically, it looks like this:

> A certain percentage or portion of a sample of class C has characteristic F.
>
> Therefore, about the same percentage or portion of the entire class C has characteristic F.

Examples of inductive generalizations:

1. Thirty percent of a sample of seniors at Hollow University are atheists, so about thirty percent of all the seniors at Hollow University are atheists.

2. A majority of Americans surveyed by ABC believe God answers their prayers, so it is clear that a majority of Americans are not atheists.

3. All events so far experienced have been caused; therefore all events, period, are caused.

Again, inductive generalizations are not just simply "valid" or "invalid." Instead, they are to varying degrees strong or weak, depending on just how probable the conclusion is, given the premise or premises. And how probable the conclusion is, given the premise or premises, depends mainly on the extent to which the sample of class C is truly *representative* of the entire class C.

In an **analogical argument,** the fact that two or more things are alike in certain respects is given as reason for believing that they are alike in further respects.

Example of an analogical argument:

> The human eye in certain obvious ways resembles an autofocus camera. Therefore, because an autofocus camera is the product of intelligent design, the human eye is the product of intelligent design, i.e., God.

Analogical arguments are also strong or weak in varying degrees, depending on how alike the items in the analogy are.

These, then, are the most common basic types of argument.

Truth

About any belief (statement, assertion, proposition, claim, etc.) we may ask two different questions:

　　1. What is it for this belief to be true, assuming that it is?

　　2. What are the standards or criteria by means of which it may be determined whether or not this belief is true?

　　Yes, other questions might be asked of the belief, but it is in answer to these questions that so-called philosophical theories of truth have been proposed.

　　Recent practice is to regard question (2) as a request for a theory of *justification*. Only the first question is a query about the *nature* of truth.

Principal Philosophical Theories of Truth

In this appendix, then, we will discuss answers to the question: What is it for a belief to be true? Further, we'll limit the discussion to empirical beliefs—those known to be true or false only by observation.

　　Here, then, are the leading "theories of truth."

Correspondence Theory

According to the **correspondence theory of truth,** a belief is true if and only if it corresponds to its object—that is, to what it is a belief about.

　　If this theory strikes you as correct, then you should be aware of the notorious difficulties it encounters.

　　First, what *is* a belief about? To what, exactly, does a true belief correspond? I believe my stapler is on my desk. Does my belief correspond only to the stapler and to the desk, or does it correspond to the *fact* that my stapler is on my desk? Surely the latter, you say? But then, what is a fact? Do facts exist on the side of the objects—that is, along with the stapler and desk—or are they a contribution to reality made by the mind—that is, do they exist on the side of the belief? To date, there is no generally accepted account of the nature of facts or of what true beliefs correspond to.

　　A second difficulty: To what do negative beliefs, and general beliefs, and compound beliefs, and beliefs about future and past events, and about mythical entities, and about probabilities correspond, if they are true? To what do beliefs expressed as subjunctive conditional propositions ("If such-and-such were the case, then . . .") correspond, if they are true?

　　And what about false beliefs? Well, we might say that they *fail* to correspond. But there are many different false beliefs. Does one failure of correspondence differ from another failure of correspondence?

A third difficulty in the correspondence theory: What, exactly, is *correspondence*? In one sense of the term *correspond*, to say that a belief corresponds to reality just is to say that it is true (it's because the word carries this sense that the correspondence theory seems so intuitively plausible). But in that sense of *correspond*, we do not clarify or elucidate the concept of truth by saying that a true belief corresponds to reality: we do not make clear in what way or just how a true belief hooks on to reality. After all, a belief is not very much like a fact, if that's what a true belief corresponds to. So just *how* does a true belief correspond to a fact? By picturing it? By mirroring it? By copying it? Or what?

And here is one more problem: The correspondence theory seems to presuppose the existence of a reality external to one's mind, a realm to which one's beliefs may or may not correspond. Common sense may have no difficulty with this presupposition, but philosophy does. Its validity has been debated throughout the history of philosophy and has been subject to recent vigorous attack.

Coherence Theory

According to the **coherence theory of truth,** an empirical belief is true if and only if it *coheres* with a system of other beliefs, which together form a comprehensive account of reality.

What is meant by "coheres"? Well, that's one of the big problems in the theory: Just what is it for a system of beliefs to cohere?

Although it may not be possible to clarify fully this idea of coherence, we think you can get some idea of the thinking behind the coherence theory if you consider a false arithmetical proposition, such as "$2 + 3 + 3 = 57\frac{1}{4}$."

What makes this proposition false? Well, it just doesn't cohere with the rest of arithmetic. It doesn't fit into the system.

According to the coherence theory, the truth of even empirical propositions, propositions about the world, must be analyzed along similar lines.

Still, this analogy does not help very much. Coherent beliefs must, of course, be logically consistent, and beyond this they must be connected by some sort of relationships of mutual entailment. But what sort is not very clear.

Nevertheless, before you reject the coherence theory, consider this: With the coherence theory we have only two things to explain, beliefs and coherence. With the correspondence theory we have three things to explain: beliefs, correspondence, and facts.

There are other problems associated with the coherence theory, however. To run through the most notorious:

1. Might there not be more than one internally coherent system of beliefs? (Indeed, might not virtually every belief belong to some system or other?) How does one select from among alternative systems?

2. What's to guarantee the truth of the *whole system* of beliefs?

3. Because, according to the coherence theory, the internal coherence of the system of beliefs constitutes the truth of the system and its member beliefs, it must be asked: What connects the entire system of beliefs, or any belief within it, to external reality, if indeed there is an external reality?

4. Doesn't the theory require that we know *everything* that is true before we can know *anything* that is true?

Other Theories

Sometimes a third major theory of truth is mentioned in philosophical discussions, the so-called **pragmatic theory of truth,** worked out in various forms by the American pragmatists C. S. Peirce (1839–1914), William James (1842–1910), and John Dewey (1859–1952).

However, Peirce's theory of truth ("The opinion which is fated to be ultimately agreed to by all who investigate, is what we mean by the truth") really seems to be a type of coherence theory, and James and Dewey, though having their differences about truth, seemed both to offer theories of *justification*, that is, theories concerning when it is appropriate or justified to assert a claim as true. In scientific affairs, James maintained, the truth of a belief is established by experimental verification; metaphysical and theological beliefs, in contrast, are to be deemed true if they provide the individual with "vital benefits." For Dewey, a belief is something like a map: when you have determined that it helps you find your way out of the woods and safely to home, you may regard your belief map as true.

Still other theories of truth have been defended, most importantly the so-called **performative theory of truth,** associated with Oxford philosopher P. F. Strawson (1919–). According to this theory, to assert that a proposition is true is really to emphasize or endorse or concede or confirm the proposition itself rather than to attribute a property to it. Because the word *true* is a linguistic device used to emphasize or agree with a claim, there is no point in searching for the nature of truth, proponents of this theory hold.

The concept of truth is basic, and the question, What is it for a belief to be true? seems straightforward enough. Nevertheless, no theory of truth has been universally accepted by philosophers.

Knowledge

Epistemology, as we stated in Part 2, is concerned primarily with two questions: What is knowledge? and Is knowledge possible? Part 2 was devoted mainly to the second issue.

So a word here about the first question.

What, then, *is* knowledge?

There is evidently a difference between knowing *how to do something*—knowing how to tune up a car, for example, or how to speak German—and knowing *that something is true*—knowing that it is time for a tune-up, say, or that the German word for "window" is *Fenster.* Epistemologists usually are concerned with understanding "knowing that." They wish to determine what it is to know that something is true.

What is it to know that something is true? What is it to know, for instance, that you are alive right now and that you are reading this book? Is it merely to believe these things? Or is knowledge something beyond or different from belief? Does knowledge differ from mere information, from the data stored in computers or books, for example? Does it include what is remembered—that, for example, you had toast and jelly, or whatever, for breakfast?

Plato was the first philosopher to consider carefully the question: What is knowledge? His most extensive treatment of the matter is found in the *Theaetetus,* a dialogue devoted almost entirely to the question.

In this dialogue it first is suggested that knowledge may be equated with sense perception. This idea sounds plausible. After all, to see a candle burning would be to know a candle is burning; to hear Socrates talking would be to know that he is talking; to feel pain would be to know you are in pain; and so forth. In addition, sensory experience seems quite beyond doubt, just as knowledge apparently is.

Nevertheless, Plato rejects the suggestion. If you come to know that something is true, he argued, you can retain your knowledge even after you are no longer in sensory contact with the thing about which you have knowledge. And besides, he pointed out, whereas sense perception only provides information within this or that sensory channel, knowledge reaches across sensory channels. When I eat a strawberry, my taste informs me of its sweetness, and my eyes inform me of its redness, but my knowledge brings together the redness and the sweetness. So knowledge seems to involve some sort of integrative activity on the part of the mind that goes beyond sense perception.

Plato then considers the idea that knowledge is correct thinking or true belief. But he rejects this idea because true belief may be based on hearsay evidence or just a lucky guess.

He then concludes that knowledge consists of "correct belief together with an account." Unfortunately, he was unable to clarify this concept of an "account," either to his own or to anyone else's satisfaction.

Most philosophers who considered the matter after Plato thought that he was on the right track in the *Theaetetus* to maintain that knowledge is true belief together with an account. Most contemporary philosophers, however, would not put things just that way. Instead, they would say this: For you to know that something is true—say, that Socrates is dead—means that three conditions must hold, namely:

1. You must believe that Socrates is dead.
2. Your belief that Socrates is dead must be true.
3. Your belief that Socrates is dead must be *justified*: it must be based on evidence, grounds or reasons that warrant that belief.

As can be seen, "justification" is just the modern word for what Plato called an "account."

Unfortunately, there is a big difficulty in this justified-true-belief (JTB) analysis of knowledge. For it seems possible to imagine situations in which a person meets the three conditions stated and yet does not have knowledge. For instance, suppose that you believe that your car won't start. Suppose further that you believe this for the excellent reason that you removed the battery. Suppose finally that your car indeed won't start. This is a case of justified true belief. Is it a case of knowledge?

Ordinarily, perhaps it is. But imagine that while your back was turned, two things happened. First, unknown to you, someone put a brand new battery in the car. And second, when she did it, she accidentally severed the connection between the battery and the starter. The result? Your justified true belief that the car won't start doesn't qualify as knowledge. So the JTB analysis of knowledge seems defective.

Around twenty-five years ago, examples of this sort to the justified-true-belief analysis of knowledge were noted by Edmund Gettier, who presently teaches at the University of Massachusetts, and soon philosophy journals were flooded with articles proposing modifications to the JTB theory in the light of Gettier-type counterexamples. According to one modification, for example, proposed by Alvin I. Goldman, a belief is justified to the extent required for knowledge if and only if it is *caused* by the facts that make it true.

Thus, for instance, in the example just given, I am not justified in believing that the car won't start because the facts that caused my belief are not the facts that made that belief true.

Unfortunately, there are counterexamples that defeat that modification, and similar stories can be told for other modifications that have been proposed.

Perhaps the underlying problem is this: Possibly, for a belief to be justified to the extent required for knowledge, it must be inferred from other beliefs that are themselves known to be true. Thus, to use the example, we might say that you weren't justified in believing that the car wouldn't start. You weren't justified, because you inferred that belief from the proposition that the car didn't have a battery and you didn't really know that proposition was true.

But if everything that is known must be inferred from something else that is known, then how could knowledge ever have gotten started? This requirement for justification seems to lead to skepticism.

Perhaps, then, we should maintain that some beliefs, to be justified, don't have to be *inferred* from other beliefs; in other words, perhaps some beliefs are just plain *self-justifying*.

Unfortunately, independent epistemological inquiry raises difficulties with the idea that any beliefs are self-justifying, as we saw in Part 2.

Another alternative might be to say that some beliefs, to be justified, don't have to be inferred from beliefs *known* to be true. But if that is so, then we can know something on the basis of something else that is not known, and that seems curious.

So there are problems with all three alternatives.

The real problem, of course, is that the concept of justification is really not very clear. In fact, it isn't much clearer than Plato's concept of an account. Knowledge seems to be justified true belief, but it isn't very clear what the justification part involves. Current epistemological inquiry into the nature of knowledge is focused on this problem.

Glossary

Absolute, the That which is unconditioned and uncaused by anything else. It is frequently thought of as God, perfect and solitary, self-caused eternal being that is the source or essence of all that exists but that is itself beyond the possibility of conceptualization or definition.

Absolute Idealism The early nineteenth-century school of philosophy that maintained that being is the transcendental unfolding or expression of thought or reason.

aesthetics The philosophical study of art and of value judgments about art and of beauty in general.

analogical argument An argument that attributes to one thing a characteristic found in a similar thing or things.

analysis Resolving a complex proposition or concept into simpler ones in order to gain better understanding of the original proposition or concept. *Analysis* comes from a Greek word meaning to "unloosen" or "untie."

analytic philosophy The predominant twentieth-century philosophical tradition in English-speaking countries. Analytic philosophy has its roots in British empiricism and holds that analysis is the proper method of philosophy.

anarchism A utopian political theory that seeks to eliminate all authority and state rule in favor of a society based on voluntary cooperation and free association of individuals and groups.

***a priori* principle** A proposition whose truth we do not need to know through sensory experience and that no conceivable experience could serve to refute.

argument A series of propositions one of which is supposedly supported by the others.

argument from design A proof for the existence of God based on the idea that the universe and its parts give evidence of purpose or design and therefore require a divine designer.

ataraxia The goal of imperturbability and tranquility of mind that was considered the highest good by ancient thinkers such as the Skeptics.

Atomism The ancient Greek philosophy that holds that all things are composed of simple, indivisible minute particles.

bad faith In the philosophy of Jean-Paul Sartre, essentially self-deception or lying to oneself, especially when this takes the form of blaming circumstances for one's fate and not seizing the freedom to realize oneself in action.

begging the question An argument begs the question if its premises assume the point at issue as a preexisting given.

behaviorism The methodological principle in psychology according to which meaningful psychological inquiry confines itself to psychological phenomena that can be behaviorally defined; also the theory in philosophy that when we talk about a person's mental states we are referring in fact to the person's disposition to behave in certain ways.

bracketing *See* **parenthesizing.**

Buddhism A philosophical tradition founded by Gautama Siddhartha Buddha in the fifth century B.C. that took on various forms as a religion and spread throughout Asia. Buddhism attempts to help the individual conquer the suffering and mutability of human existence through the elimination of desire and ego and attainment of the state of *nirvana.*

bushido The way or ethic of the samurai warrior, based on service and demanding rigorous training, usually both in the military and literary arts.

capitalism An economic system in which ownership of the means of production and distribution is maintained mostly by private individuals and corporations.

categorical imperative Immanuel Kant's formulation of a moral law that holds unconditionally, i.e., categorically. In its most common formulation, states that you are to act only in such a way that you could desire your action to be a universal law.

causal explanation An explanation of the cause or causes of an event.

"clear and distinct" criterion René Descartes's criterion of truth, according to which that, and only that, which is perceived as clearly and distinctly as the fact of one's own existence is certain.

cogito, ergo sum "I think, therefore I am." The single indubitable truth on which Descartes's epistemology is based.

cognitivist One who believes that knowledge is possible.

coherence theory of truth The theory that an empirical belief is true if and only if it "coheres" with a body of propositions that collectively forms a comprehensive account of reality.

communism An economic system in which goods are owned in common and are available to all as needed.

Communism The ideology of the Communist Party.

conceptualism The theory that universals are concepts and exist only in the mind.

Confucianism A philosophical tradition that began with Confucius in the sixth century B.C. and continues to the present day. Confucianism is a practical philosophy that hopes to establish a better world order by means of the moral perfection of the individual.

conservatism A political philosophy based on respect for established institutions and traditions and that favors preservation of the status quo over social experimentation.

Continental philosophy The philosophical traditions of Europe excluding British and Irish philosophy; includes phenomenology and existentialism.

contractarian theory The political theory according to which a legitimate state exists only by virtue of an agreement or "contract" among the subjects of the state.

"Copernican revolution in philosophy"   A new perspective in epistemology, introduced by Immanuel Kant, according to which the objects of experience must conform in certain respects to our knowledge of them.

correspondence theory of truth   The theory that a belief is true if and only if it corresponds to its object.

cosmological argument   An argument for the existence of God according to which the universe and its parts can be neither accidental nor self-caused and must ultimately have been brought into existence by God.

cultural relativism   The doctrine that each culture has its own set of standards and values, which may or may not be identical with those of other cultures.

Cynicism   A school of philosophy founded around the fifth century B.C., probably by Antisthenes or Diogenes. The Cynics sought to lead lives of total simplicity and naturalness by rejecting all comforts and conveniences of society.

deductive argument   An argument whose premises are intended to provide absolutely conclusive reasons for accepting the conclusion.

descriptive egoism   The doctrine that maintains that in conscious action a person always seeks self-interest above all else.

descriptivism   A philosophy that seeks to describe the moral principles that people accept rather than prescribing the principles they should accept; alternatively, the philosophy that seeks to determine what people ought to do if they wish to achieve a certain end.

determinism   The doctrine that a person could not have acted otherwise than as she or he did act.

Ding-an-sich   German for "thing-in-itself": a thing as it is independent of any consciousness of it.

divine law   In the philosophy of Thomas Aquinas, God's gift to humankind, apprehended through revelation, that directs us to our supernatural goal, eternal happiness.

dream conjecture   The conjecture used by Descartes that all experience may be dream experience.

dualism   Two-ism; the doctrine that existing things belong to one or another but not both of two distinct categories of things, usually deemed to be physical and nonphysical or spiritual.

efficient cause   One of Aristotle's four kinds of causes, specifically the agency that initiates a change, the "doer" of an action.

egoism   The doctrine that in conscious action one seeks (or ought to seek) self-interest above all else.

egoistic ethical hedonism   The theory that one ought to seek one's own pleasure above all else.

Eightfold Path   The way or practice recommended in Buddhism that includes: Right View, Right Aim, Right Speech, Right Action, Right Living, Right Effort, Right Mindfulness, and Right Contemplation.

emotivism   The theory that moral (and other) value judgments are expressions of emotions, attitudes, and feelings.

empiricism   The philosophy that all knowledge originates in sensory experience.

Epicureanism The philosophy of followers of Epicurus, who believed that personal pleasure is the highest good but advocated renouncing momentary pleasures in favor of more lasting ones.

epicureanism The practices of an epicure, one who has sensitive and discriminating tastes in food or wine.

epistemological detour The attempt to utilize epistemological inquiry to arrive at metaphysical truths.

epoché The suspension of judgment concerning the truth or falsity of a proposition. Edmund Husserl's *epoché* is the suspension of judgment regarding the being or nonbeing of the physical world and its objects, which he thought would open the way to a sighting of pure consciousness itself.

Esse est percipi Latin for "to be is to be perceived," a doctrine that George Berkeley made the basis of his philosophy: Only that which is perceived exists. Berkeley held, however, that the minds that do the perceiving also exist.

eternal law In the philosophy of Thomas Aquinas, the divine reason of God that rules over all things at all times.

ethical hedonism The doctrine that you ought to seek pleasure over all else.

ethical naturalism The belief that moral value judgments are really judgments of fact about the natural world.

ethical relativism The theory that there are no absolute and universally valid moral standards and values and that therefore the moral standards and values that apply to you are merely those that are accepted by your society.

ethics The branch of philosophy that considers the nature, criteria, sources, logic, and validity of moral value judgments.

evil demon conjecture The conjecture used by Descartes that states: For all I know, an all-powerful "god" or demon has manipulated me so that all I take as true is in fact false.

existentialism A tradition of twentieth-century philosophy having its roots in the nineteenth century but coming to flower in Europe after World War II. Of central concern is the question of how the individual is to find an authentic existence in this world, in which there is no ultimate reason why things happen one way and not another.

ex nihilo Latin for "out of nothing."

external relations To believe that relations are external is to believe that a thing's relations to other things are not a part of the essence or nature of the related things.

Fascism The totalitarian political philosophy of the Mussolini government in Italy that stressed the primacy of the state and leadership by an elite who embody the will and intelligence of the people. The term is sometimes more generally used for any totalitarian movement.

final cause One of Aristotle's four kinds of causes, specifically the ultimate purpose for which something happens.

first-order thinking Thinking about a subject directly; contrasted with second-order thinking, which is thinking about discourse on the subject.

Form In Plato's philosophy, that which is denoted by a general word, a word (such as "chair") that applies to more than a single thing.

foundationalism The doctrine that a belief qualifies as knowledge only if it logically follows from propositions that are incorrigible (incapable of being false if you believe that they are true).

Four Noble Truths Buddha's answer to the central problem of life: (1) There is suffering; (2) suffering has specific and identifiable causes; (3) suffering can be ended; (4) the way to end suffering is through enlightened living, as expressed in the Eightfold Path.

free market economy An economic system built around the belief that supply and demand, competition, and a free play of market forces best serve the interests of society and the common good.

functionalism The doctrine that what a thing is must be understood and analyzed not by what it is made of but by its function. For example, anything that functions as a mousetrap is a mousetrap, regardless of what it is made of or how it looks or is assembled.

general will In the philosophy of Jean-Jacques Rousseau, the will of a politically united people, the will of a state.

hedonism The pursuit of pleasure.

Hellenistic Age The period of Macedonian domination of the Greek-speaking world, from around 335 B.C. to about 30 B.C.

Hinduism The Western word for the religious beliefs and practices of the majority of the people of India.

human law In the philosophy of Thomas Aquinas, the laws and statutes of society that are derived from our understanding of natural law.

hypothetical imperative An imperative that states what you ought to do if a certain end is desired.

Idea *See* **Form.**

idealism The doctrine that only what is mental (thought, consciousness, perception) exists and that so-called physical things are manifestations of mind or thought.

identity theory The theory that mental states and events are brain states and events.

incorrigibility The property of a proposition that cannot be false if you believe it is true.

inductive argument An argument whose premises are intended to provide reasons for accepting the conclusion as probable.

inductive generalization An argument that attributes a characteristic of a sample of a group to all or most members of the group.

instrumentalism A theory held by John Dewey, among others, that ideas, judgments, and propositions are not merely true or false; rather, they are tools to understand experience and solve problems.

intentionality The characteristic of consciousness that defines it as consciousness *of* something: it always points to or contains an object beyond itself.

interactionist dualism The theory that the physical body and the nonphysical mind interact with each other.

internal relations To believe that relations are internal is to believe that a thing's relations to other things are a part of the essence or nature of the related things.

inverted spectrum hypothesis   Paul Churchland's name for the supposition that, although two people may agree that they are looking at the same color, the sensations they experience may be different.

invisible hand explanation   An explanation of a phenomenon as an unforeseen indirect consequence of action taken for some other purpose.

liberalism   A political philosophy whose basic tenet is that each individual should have the maximum freedom consistent with the freedom of others.

Leviathan   The coiled snake or dragon in the Book of Job in the Bible. In the philosophy of Thomas Hobbes, "that mortal God, to which we owe our peace and defense"; that is, the state created by social contract (or its sovereign).

libertarian   Someone who believes in free will; alternatively, someone who upholds the principles of liberty of thought and action.

logic   The study of the methods, principles, and criteria of correct reasoning.

logical atomism   The metaphysical theory that the world does not consist of things but of facts, that is, things having certain properties and standing in certain relationships to one another. The ultimate facts are atomic in that they are logically independent of one another and are unresolvable into simpler facts; likewise, an empirically correct description of the world will consist ultimately of logically independent and unanalyzable atomic propositions that correspond to the atomic facts.

logical construction   Xs are logical constructions out of Ys if statements about Xs could be replaced without loss of meaning by statements about Ys. For example, you could (theoretically) replace statements about the "average taxpayer" with statements about real-life, flesh-and-blood taxpayers; therefore, the average taxpayer is a logical construction out of real-life taxpayers.

logical positivism   The philosophy of the Vienna Circle, according to which any purported statement of fact, if not a verbal truism, is meaningless unless certain conceivable observations would serve to confirm or deny it.

Marxism   The socialist philosophy of Karl Marx, Friedrich Engels, and their followers that postulates the labor theory of value, the dialectical interplay of social institutions, class struggle, and dictatorship of the proletariat leading to a classless society.

materialism   The theory that only physical entities exist, and that so-called mental things are manifestations of an underlying physical reality.

means (forces) of production   In Marxism, the means of producing the satisfaction of needs.

metaethics   The philosophical investigation of the sources, criteria, meaning, verification, validation, and logical interrelationships of moral value judgments.

metaphysics   The branch of philosophy that studies the nature and fundamental features of being.

monad   From the Greek word meaning "unit." Pythagoras used the word to denote the first number of a series, and Gottfried Wilhelm von Leibniz used it to denote the unextended, simple, soullike basic elements of the universe.

monism   One-ism; the philosophy that there is only one ultimate substance or type of thing. Materialism and idealism are both monistic theories.

moral argument for the existence of God The argument that maintains that morality, to be more than merely relative and contingent, must come from and be guaranteed by a supreme being, God.

naturalism The doctrine that the universe is all there is and that physical laws are adequate to explain all its features.

naturalized epistemology The view that the important epistemological problems are those that can be resolved by psychological investigation of the processes involved in acquiring and revising beliefs.

natural law In the Stoic philosophy, a principle of rationality that infuses the universe, to which human behavior ought to conform; in the philosophy of Thomas Aquinas, God's eternal law as it applies to humans on earth and dictates the fundamental principles of morality; in ordinary English, a law of physical science.

natural right A right thought to belong by nature to all human beings at all times and in all circumstances.

necessary being A being whose nonexistence is impossible.

negative skeptic Oliver Johnson's name for the total skeptic who challenges the cognitivist to prove, without begging any questions, that knowledge is possible.

Neoplatonism A further development of Platonic philosophy under the influence of Aristotelean and Pythagorean philosophy and Christian mysticism; it flourished between the third and sixth centuries. Neoplatonism stressed a mystical intuition of the highest One or God, a transcendent source of all being.

neutralism The theory that existing things are neither mental nor physical; alternatively, the theory that each existing thing is both mental and physical.

neutral monism The theory that mind and matter are reducible to or are manifestations of the same kind of thing, which itself is neither mental nor material.

nihil in intellectu quod prius non fuerit in sensu Nothing is in the intellect that was not first in the senses; an epistemological principle formulated by Thomas Aquinas as an extrapolation of Aristotle's thinking.

nihilism The rejection of traditional values and beliefs.

nirvana In Buddhism, the highest good; the extinction of will and of the accompanying ego, greed, anger, delusion, and clinging to existence. Achievement of *nirvana* means being freed from all future rebirths.

normative Of, relating to, or prescribing norms or standards.

noumena In the philosophy of Immanuel Kant, things as they are in themselves independently of all possible experience of them.

nous A Greek word variously translated as "thinking," "mind," "reason," "spirit," and "intellect."

objective reality The reality possessed by anything whose existence or characteristics do not depend on our consciousness of them.

objectivism The theory that the universe and the things in it do not depend on our consciousness of them for their existence or characteristics.

ontological argument The argument that God's existence is entailed by the definition or concept of God.

original position John Rawls's name for a hypothetical condition in which rational and unbiased individuals select the principles of social justice that govern a well-ordered society.

paradox of analysis   The problem that an analysis of a proposition must apparently either be incorrect or trivial.

paradox of hedonism   Henry Sidgwick's term for the fact that the desire for pleasure, if it is too strong, defeats its own aim.

parallelism   The doctrine that there are two parallel and coordinated series of events, one mental and the other physical, and that apparent causal interaction between the mind and the body is to be explained as a manifestation of the correlation between the two series.

parenthesizing   In Husserl's philosophy, the act of considering phenomena as they are in themselves, without making any assumptions about the existence or nature of an objective world or their relationship to it.

performative theory of truth   In the philosophy of P. F. Strawson, the theory that to assert a proposition is true is to endorse it rather than to attribute a property to it.

phenomena   Things as they appear to us or, alternatively, the appearances themselves; in the philosophy of Immanuel Kant, objects as experienced and hence as organized and unified by the categories of the understanding and the forms of space and time.

phenomenalism   The theory that we only know phenomena; in analytic philosophy, the theory that propositions referring to physical objects can, in principle, be expressed in propositions referring only to sense-data.

phenomenology   A tradition of twentieth-century Continental philosophy based on the phenomenological method, which seeks rigorous knowledge not of things-in-themselves but rather of the structures of consciousness and of things as they appear to consciousness.

philosophical behaviorism   *See* **behaviorism.**

philosophy of mind   That area of analytic philosophy concerned with the nature of consciousness, mental states, the mind, and the proper analysis of everyday psychological vocabulary.

physicalism   Materialism.

pragmatic theory of truth   In the philosophy of C. S. Peirce, a species of correspondence theory; in the philosophies of John Dewey and William James, a theory of justification, according to which (roughly) a belief may be accepted as true if it "works."

prescriptive egoism   The doctrine that in all conscious action you ought to seek your self-interest above all else.

***prima facie* duty**   In the philosophy of W. D. Ross, something it is your moral duty to do unless it is overridden by a higher moral duty.

private language   In the philosophy of Ludwig Wittgenstein, a language that can only be understood by a single individual.

principle of reason   An *a priori* principle.

principle of sufficient reason   The principle that there is a sufficient reason for why things are as they are and are not otherwise.

productive relations   In Marxism, social institutions and practices.

psychological hedonism   The theory that pleasure is the object of a person's desire.

Pyrrhonism   A school of philosophical skepticism initiated by Pyrrho of Elis (c. 360–270 B.C.) whose members advocated suspending judgment on all issues.

rationalism   The epistemological theory that reason is either the sole or primary source of knowledge; in practice, most rationalists maintain merely that at least some truths are not known solely on the basis of sensory experience.

realism   The theory that universals exist outside the mind.

reduction   Another word for analysis.

reductio **proof**   Proving a proposition by showing that its nonacceptance would involve an absurdity.

representative realism   The theory that we perceive objects indirectly by means of representations (ideas, perceptions) of them.

second-order thinking   *See* **first-order thinking.**

sense-data   That which you are immediately aware of in sensory experience; the contents of awareness.

skepticism   The doctrine that true knowledge is uncertain or impossible.

social contract   An agreement among individuals forming an organized society or between the community and the ruler that defines the rights and duties of each.

socialism   The theory that communal ownership of land, capital, and the means of production is the best way of serving the common good.

Stoicism   The ethical philosophy of the ancient Greek Stoics, who emphasized the serene or untroubled life as the highest good and thought it best reached through acceptance of the natural order of things.

stoicism   The practice of a stoic, one who is indifferent to pleasure and pain.

straightforward reductivist physicalism   The theory that all true propositions can, in principle, be expressed in the language of physics.

subjectivism   In ethics, the doctrine that what is right is determined by what people believe is right; elsewhere, the theory that limits knowledge to conscious states.

tabula rasa   Latin for "blank tablet"; also, John Locke's metaphor for the condition of the mind prior to the imprint of sensory experience.

tacit consent   An implied rather than explicit consent, as, for example, when you consent to the laws of your state by continuing to live in it.

Taoism   One of the great philosophical traditions in China according to which the individual will find peace and tranquility through quietly following the Tao.

Tao   In Chinese philosophy, the Way: the ultimate and eternal principle of unity, meaning, and harmony in the universe.

teleological argument   *See* **argument from design.**

teleological explanation   An explanation of a thing in terms of its ends, goals, purposes, or functions.

thing-in-itself   English for *Ding-an-sich*: a thing as it is independent of any consciousness of it.

universal   That which is denoted by a general word, a word (such as "chair") that applies to more than a single thing.

universalistic ethical hedonism   The doctrine that one ought to seek, over everything else, the greatest pleasure for the greatest number of people.

utilitarianism   The doctrine that the rightness of an action is identical with the happiness it produces as its consequence.

value judgment   A proposition that explicitly or implicitly assigns a value to something.

veil of ignorance   In Indian philosophy, the perspective from which the world is viewed as a multiplicity of things; also, John Rawls's metaphor for the conditions under which rational individuals are to select the principles of justice that govern the well-ordered society.

verifiability principle   See **verifiability criterion of meaning.**

verifiability criterion (theory) of meaning   The dictum that any putative statement of fact, unless it is a verbal truism, is meaningless if no conceivable observations could serve to confirm or deny it.

Vienna Circle   A group of philosophers and scientists centered at the University of Vienna in the 1920s and 1930s who espoused logical positivism.

Way, the   See *Tao.*

Zen Buddhism   A form of Buddhism that reached its zenith in China and later developed in Japan, Korea, and the West. Its name (Chinese *Ch'an*, Japanese *Zen*) derives from the Sanskrit *dhyana* (meditation). In early China, the central tenet of Zen Buddhism was meditation rather than adherence to a particular scripture.

Credits

Photos and Illustrations

After Image, page 282, © Hiroyuki Matsumoto/After Image, 1989

Alinari/Art Resource, New York, page 190, Masaccio, *Expulsion from the Garden*, Firenze, Chiesa del Carmine

Amon Carter Museum, page 374, © 1981 Laura Gilpin Collection, Amon Carter Museum, Fort Worth, Texas

The Bettmann Archive, pages 39, 45, 52, 70, 80, 85, 91, 99, 101, 156, 164, 170, 244, 300, 306, 313, 327, 383, 422, 509, 511, 524, 534, 539, 555, 575

Cambridge University Library, page 460, by permission of the Syndics of Cambridge University Library

Cordon Art, page 124, © 1989 M. C. Escher Heirs/Cordon Art—Baarn—Holland

Burt Glinn/Magnum Photos, page 550

Life Picture Service, page 452, Ralph Morse, Life Magazine, © Time, Inc.

Kevin Opstedal, pages 17, 68, 132, 141, 144, 155, 178, 245, 247, 251, 298, 308, 315, 404, 411, 438, 475

The Royal Photographic Society, Bath, England, page 22

Jerry Uelsmann/Witkin Gallery, page 504

Text Credits

Page 41 From Plato, *Parmenides,* in *The Collected Dialogues of Plato,* Edith Hamilton and Huntington Caerns, ed., trans. by F. M. Cornford. Reprinted by permission of Routledge.

Page 47 From *Metaphysics,* trans. R. D. Ross from *The Oxford Translation of Aristotle,* ed. W. D. Ross, Vol. 8 (2nd ed. 1928). Reprinted by permission of Oxford University Press.

Page 54 From Augustine, *An Augustine Synthesis,* arranged by Erich Przywara. New York: Harper & Brothers, 1958.

Pages 61, 386 From Thomas Aquinas, "Whether the Soul Is Man," *Summa Theologica,* in Anton C. Pegis, ed., *Basic Writings of St. Thomas Aquinas.* Reprinted by permission.

Pages 73, 139, 391 Excerpts from René Descartes, *The Philosophical Works of Descartes,* E. S. Haldane and G.R.T. Ross, trans. Copyright 1968 Cambridge University Press. Reprinted with the permission of Cambridge University Press.

Page 93 Reprinted by permission of Collier Books from *The Philosophy of History,* by Georg Hegel, translated by J. Silbree. Copyright 1944 P. F. Collier.

Pages 105, 172 Extracts from *Our Knowledge of the External World,* by Bertrand Russell, reproduced by kind permission of Unwin Hyman Ltd. Copyright 1956 George Allen & Unwin, Ltd.

Pages 108, 261 Reprinted from *Language, Truth and Logic,* by A. J. Ayer, Dover Publications. Reprinted by permission.

Page 116 Excerpts from "Letter on Humanism" from *Basic Writings,* by Martin Heidegger. Copyright © by Harper & Row and David Farrell Krell. Reprinted by permission of Harper & Row, Publishers, Inc.

Page 134 Reprinted by permission of the publishers and the Loeb Classical Library from Sextus Empiricus: *Outlines of Pyrrhonism,* Vol. I, translated by R. G. Bury, Cambridge, Mass.: Harvard University Press, 1933.

Page 167 Copyright © 1969 by St. Martin's Press, Inc. From *Immanuel Kant's Critique of Pure Reason,* trans-

lated by Norman Kemp Smith. Reprinted by permission of St. Martin's Press, Incorporated.

Page 176 From C. H. Whiteley, *An Introduction to Metaphysics,* Methuen & Co., Ltd., London, 1950. Reprinted by permission of Methuen & Co. Ltd.

Page 183 From Oliver Johnson, *Skepticism and Cognitivism: A Study in the Foundations of Knowledge,* published by University of California Press. Copyright © 1979 The Regents of the University of California.

Page 199 *The Republic of Plato,* trans. F. M. Cornford (1941). Reprinted by permission of Oxford University Press.

Page 211 *Epicurus: The Extant Remains,* trans. Cyril Bailey (1926). Reprinted by permission of Oxford University Press.

Page 213 Reprinted by permission of the publishers and the Loeb Classical Library from Epictetus: *The Discourses,* Vol. II, translated by W. A. Oldfather, Cambridge, Mass.: Harvard University Press, 1925.

Page 217 From Augustine, *The Works of Aurelius Augustine,* ed. M. Dods, by permission of T. & T. Clark Ltd., Edinburgh.

Page 219 From Aquinas's *Summa Contra Gentiles,* published by Benziger Publishing Company, 1928.

Page 241 From Immanuel Kant, *Foundations of the Metaphysics of Morals,* trans. Lewis White Beck, The Liberal Arts Press, published by Bobbs-Merrill.

Page 255 From George E. Moore's *Principia Ethica.* Copyright Cambridge University Press. Reprinted with the permission of Cambridge University Press.

Page 257 From *The Right and the Good,* by W. D. Ross (1930). Reprinted

619

Index

Metaphysics

— St. Thomas Aquinas (1225–1274)

Ren

Ren

Epistemology

Ren

Ren

Ethics

— St. Thomas Aquinas (1225–1274)

**Political
Philosophy**

— St. Thomas Aquinas (1225–1274)

Niccolò Machiavelli (1469–1527)

**Philosophy
of Religion**

— St. Anselm (c. 1033–1109)
— St. Thomas Aquinas (1225–1274)

René

**Analytic
Philosophy**

René

**Continental
Philosophy**

**Eastern
Philosophy**

— Dogen Zenji (1200–1253)

Miyamoto

Yagyu Mu

— Hui Neng (638–713)